COMPONENTS OF
DEFENSE POLICY

COMPONENTS OF DEFENSE POLICY

Edited by

Davis B. Bobrow

Princeton University

RAND McNALLY & COMPANY · CHICAGO

ACKNOWLEDGEMENTS

ANY EDITOR'S greatest debt is to his contributors. I thank them for their permission to reprint their work and Morton Gorden for his original essay. To the late Morton Grodzins, I owe the opportunity to edit this reader. I believe its contents are in accord with his belief that personal convictions about public policy and rigorous analysis are not incompatible. Sue Bobrow encouraged me throughout the tasks of assembling the reader and, more importantly, strongly argued that undergraduates have the ability to gain command of outstanding professional work.

In the order in which the essays appear, I would like to credit their original publishers and thank them for the cooperation which made this reader possible.

To Prentice-Hall, Inc., and to The RAND Corporation for permission to reprint from "U.S. Editor's Analytic Introduction," pp. 7–27, 30–34, by Herbert S. Dinerstein, Leon Gouré, and Thomas W. Wolfe from the book *Soviet Military Strategy*, ed. by Marshal V. D. Sokolovskii. © Copyright 1963 by The RAND Corporation. Published by Prentice-Hall, Inc. Englewood Cliffs, New Jersey.

To *World Politics* for permission to reprint "Peking's Military Calculus," by Davis B. Bobrow from Vol. XVI (January, 1964), pp. 287–301.

To *Australian Outlook* for permission to reprint "Non-Alignment and the Power Balance," by Coral Bell from Vol. 17 (August, 1963), pp. 117–129.

To *Foreign Affairs* for permission to reprint "Strategic Planning and the Political Process," by Samuel P. Huntington from Vol. 38 (January, 1960), pp. 285–299. Copyright by the Council on Foreign Relations Inc., New York.

To the American Political Science Association for permission to reprint "The New Civil-Military Relations," by Gene M. Lyons which appeared in the *American Political Science Review*, Vol. LV (March, 1961), pp. 53–63.

To *Foreign Affairs* for permission to reprint "The Challenge to Military Professionalism," by Col. Robert N. Ginsburgh, Vol. 42 (January, 1964), pp. 255–268. Copyright by the Council on Foreign Relations Inc., New York.

To the American Political Science Association for permission to reprint "Scientists, Foreign Policy, and Politics," by Warner R. Schilling which appeared in the *American Political Science Review*, Vol. LVI (June, 1962), pp. 287–300.

To the Survey Research Center of the University of Michigan for permission to reprint from *The U.S. and the U.S.S.R.: a Report of the Public's Perspectives on United States-Soviet Relations in Late 1961*, by Stephen B. Withey (March, 1962), pp. 1–19.

To the *Western Political Quarterly* for permission to reprint "Defense Spending: Key to California's Growth," by James L. Clayton from Vol. XV (June, 1962), pp. 280–293.

To the Center of International Studies, Princeton University, for permission to reprint *Deterrence by Denial and Punishment*, by Glenn H. Snyder (Center of International Studies Research Monograph No. 1).

To the Academy of Political Science, Columbia University, for permission to reprint "The Limiting Process in the Korean War," by Morton H. Halperin, which appeared in *The Political Science Quarterly*, Vol. 78 (March, 1963), pp. 13–39.

To the *Marine Corps Gazette* for permission to reprint "Guerrilla Warfare and U.S. Military Policy: A Study," by Peter Paret and John Shy, Vol. 46 (January, 1962), pp. 25–32. Reprinted by permission of the copyright holder, the Marine Corps Association, publishers of the Marine Corps Gazette, professional journal for Marine officers. Copyright © 1962 by Marine Corps Association.

To the United States Government Printing Office for permission to reprint the statements by Herman Kahn and by SANE from *Civil Defense-1961*, Hearings Before a Subcommittee of the Committee on Government Operations, House of Representatives, 87th Congress, First Session, pp. 168–183, 544–549.

To the *Journal of Conflict Resolution* for permission to reprint "Disarmament as a Strategy," by Clark C. Abt, Vol. VII (September, 1963), pp. 293–308.

To *Foreign Affairs* for permission to reprint "The Role of Deterrence in Total Disarmament," by Thomas C. Schelling, Vol. 40 (April, 1962), pp. 392–406. Copyright by the Council on Foreign Relations Inc., New York.

To *World Politics* for permission to reprint portions from "Intelligence and Policy-Making in Foreign Affairs," by Roger Hilsman, Jr., Vol. V (October, 1952), pp. 1–25.

To *World Politics* for permission to reprint portions from "Assumptions of Rationality and Non-Rationality in Models of the International System," by Sidney Verba, Vol. XIV (October, 1961), pp. 93–95, 106–113.

To the *Journal of Conflict Resolution* for permission to reprint "The Belief System and National Images: a Case Study," by Ole R. Holsti, Vol. VI (September, 1962), pp. 244–252.

To the Academy of Political Science, Columbia University, for permission to reprint "The H-Bomb Decision: How to Decide Without Actually Choosing," by Warner R. Schilling which appeared in the *Political Science Quarterly*, Vol. 76 (March, 1961), pp. 24–46.

To *The Reporter* for permission to reprint "The Policymaker and the Intellectual," by Henry A. Kissinger, Vol. 20 (March 5, 1959), pp. 30–35. Copyright 1959 by The Reporter Magazine Company.

To The RAND Corporation for permission to reprint from *Military Systems Analysis*, by E. S. Quade, RM-3452-PR (January, 1963), pp. 1–26.

D. B. B.

TABLE OF CONTENTS

[vii]

Part Four: Quality Control

COMPONENTS OF DEFENSE POLICY

Davis B. Bobrow

IN RESPONSE TO the prolonged stress of the cold war, a field of inquiry has evolved known as defense policy analysis. The more visible elements of this development are nonprofit research organizations linked to particular parts of the Department of Defense, defense policy courses in major universities, and a flood of literature on problems of war and peace. In the less than twenty years since the end of World War II, a significant group of specialists in defense analysis has emerged, and their subject has become recognized as a legitimate focus for serious, sophisticated inquiry.

Given its extremely rapid growth, it is not surprising that few efforts have been made to clarify the meaning of defense policy analysis as a field of inquiry. Understandably, the pressures to use the skills of its practitioners to ameliorate policy problems have postponed this task. American commitments around the world and the dilemma of the balance of terror initially justified this postponement. Also, rapid advances in the technology of war, symbolized by the intercontinental missile, have operated to relegate the social science parts of defense policy analysis to second place.

The purpose of this essay is to set forth proper boundaries and to catalogue the problems within those boundaries which comprise the social science sector of defense policy analysis. To the extent that it succeeds, four advantages will result. First, we will have an agenda of the questions of defense policy which social scientists should try to answer. Second, we will locate present gaps in our knowledge and the significance of those gaps for existing answers. Third, we will have provided channels to link completed specific studies. Fourth, we will have formulated questions on a high enough level of generality to perceive the relevance of existing social science knowledge previously unapplied to defense policy analysis. In sum, this essay provides a map in the sense of a comprehensive set of related questions to guide and unify social science inputs to defense policy analysis.

The domain of social science in defense policy analysis (from this point on, I shall assume that the social science qualification is understood) consists of the necessary intellectual tasks for us to know:

1. the content and determinants of the set of war and peace alternatives open to national elites;
2. the content and operations of the factors determining which of these alternatives are chosen;

3. the content and determinants of the consequences of the alternatives open to national elites.

These boundaries are meant to communicate that defense policy analysis may have to concern itself with problems of method as well as of substance, i.e., how to discover answers to questions as well as what are the answers. Also, these boundaries include decisions not to fight as well as those to fight; there is no pro-war bias inherent in the field.

I. THE APPROACH

The purpose of defense policy analysis, as of all science, is to generate accurate *predictions,* i.e., estimates of what will happen in the future based on characteristics of the present and the past. The defense policy of governments and the defense policy preferences of individuals are based on explicit or implicit expectations, i.e., predictions. For example, in the Cuban missile crisis, both the American and Soviet governments chose their moves in the light of how their experts predicted the other government would react. Of course, prediction is at present a tricky and imperfect business for social scientists, and our predictive ability is meager. However, these limitations can be relaxed. To the extent that they are weakened, defense policy analysis can augment the intuitive understanding of military professionals and earn its practitioners the title of "scientific strategists." Obviously, predictions increase in value as they accurately forecast a *chain* of developments. The defense policy game has many innings.

If defense policy analysts are to recommend war and peace alternatives in addition to predicting their consequences, they must have a set of explicit and precisely ranked policy objectives. An analytic judgment of the merits of a defense policy alternative cannot be made separate from a desired end-product. For example, the merits of an intense American effort to maximize nuclear superiority over the Soviet Union differ according to whether the American objective is to frighten or to secure the trust of the Soviet regime.

The goal of prediction means that the defense policy analyst attempts to answer "what will happen if . . . " questions as contrasted with "what ought to happen . . . " questions. This means that he is trying to predict *behavior,* and not to decree morality. Specifically, he tries to predict what people will and will not do with regard to instruments of war. Consequently, we can discard the weary controversy over the relative importance of capabilities and intentions, e.g., over the relative importance of the damage that a nuclear warhead can wreak versus the probability that the warhead will be launched. At any given point in time, capabilities determine the range of choices which can be available to decision-makers. However, intentions determine which item in the range they choose. Both are essential to the defense policy behavior of the elites of all countries.

Because the subject for prediction is behavior, the analyst orients his research in terms of effects on behavior. Accordingly, he does not study legal and moral systems or tables of organization to learn about them, but to learn about their effects on the defense policy actors who subscribe to the systems or work in the organizations.

The method best suited to the prediction of defense policy behavior is that of *systems analysis*. Crudely, in this method the analyst, first, forms a model of all the factors pertinent to his problem and their relationships, and, second, inserts the appropriate data into the model to project the outcome. Of course, this does not mean that every defense policy analyst must consider every factor pertinent to defense policy in his particular project. However, he should be aware of the need for the input of other components of defense policy to his restricted analysis and design it so that these can be made by others. The goal of prediction requires this systems approach. Predictions are, after all, statements about the product of the interaction of all the factors involved in the problem under study. Should some factors be excluded, or their relationships distorted, the analyst can unknowingly miscalculate the outcome. The map developed in this essay tries to provide a set of directions to the factors and relationships which comprise the total system confronting defense policy analysts.

II. RULES OF THE GAME

The basic outlines of our map of defense policy follow from two brief sets of assumptions or rules of the game. I believe that, on the level at which they are stated, these rules operate in the overwhelming majority of instances of defense policy behavior. Of course, the specifics of their operation differ according to differences in the situation, e.g., a guerrilla war in South Vietnam as compared with the great power confrontation in World War II. They merit explicit statement because otherwise analysis may overlook them and suffer severely.

The first set of rules incorporates the political setting and process inherent in defense policy.

1.1 War and peace alternatives are means to political ends, i.e., to make the distribution of power, prestige, and wealth different from the result if another alternative had been chosen. Accordingly, combat techniques should be adjusted to their political purpose. If national leadership does not enforce this consistency, victory on the battlefield can be actively inimical to the war objectives.

1.2 Political intercourse can continue throughout war in the sense that the conflict can serve as a bloody bargaining table for the contradictory claims of the participants. If this bargaining function of war goes unrecognized, the duration and intensity of the conflict can easily undershoot or overshoot the mark. If one grants an efficiency assumption, that the point is to gain one's ends at minimum costs, combat measures are chosen for their bargaining potential and bargaining channels are kept open.

1.3 No two actors or groups of actors in a defense policy situation have identical sets of interests. This applies whether they are individuals within the same government department or leaders of different nations, whether they are elites of allies of the Soviet Union or of the United States. Consequently, they try to induce each other to give in on an item of value through some combination of persuasion and coercion. It follows that for agreements to be reached, either within governments or between governments, one or both parties will have to make a sacrifice. Equality of power can produce lowest common denominator agreements which can leave all parties dissatisfied and the defense problem unscratched. Inequality of power can produce grudging concessions and correspondingly unstable agreements.

1.4 Domestic politics unavoidably affect the defense policy behavior of national leaders, and almost all national leaders believe that they are involved in a competition for authority at home. As a result, their defense policy choices are influenced by the pressures at home and the effect which the expected outcome will probably have on the leader's domestic position. The probability is slim that leaders will opt for a defense policy choice which they expect will greatly strengthen their domestic opponents.

The second set of rules deals with basic psychological tendencies which affect defense policy behavior.

2.1 Men act on the basis of the reality which they themselves perceive, not on that perceived by others. Accordingly, defense policy prediction must take account of the frameworks through which domestic and foreign actors see the world. For example, one cannot predict the North Vietnamese response to the dispatch of American troops to Thailand unless one discerns what significance the leaders in Hanoi attach to this action.

2.2 Men tend to employ at least two sets of interpretive standards: one for themselves and one for others. For example, Americans tend to see the United States capability to destroy Soviet cities not as a threat of aggression but as a guarantee of peace. On the other hand, we tend to perceive the corresponding Soviet capability not as a guarantee of peace, but as a threat of aggression. Because we rarely accept the pervasiveness of this double standard, we tend to misinterpret the behavior of others and incorrectly predict their response to our actions.

2.3 Men tend to raise the probability of the outcome which they desire and lower that of the outcome which they find "unthinkable." This temptation of the agreeable is associated with no particular defense policy preference. Unilateral disarmers want to believe in the basic goodwill of the Soviet regime. Preventive warriors want to believe that America can acquire the weapons to overwhelm Russia without retaliation. Designers of a complex radar network want to believe that enemy vehicles will operate in the scanning range of their device. Obvious possibilities for error follow from this tendency.

2.4 Men feel secure in relation to their fear of attack rather than in relation to actual threats of attack. Partly for this reason, fear of attack is not predictably proportionate to the relative power position of a nation. If one assumes that a high degree of fear must be present for people to pay the costs of a great-power military establishment, military strength may well have a positive correlation with feelings of fear rather than of security.

These rules have important implications for the nature of our map, which is to say that they speak to the content of systems analyses of defense problems. The need to include political and psychological factors if one wants to predict defense policy behavior means that the systems analysis method must be applied to them. Admittedly, the method can be more easily used on "objective" and already quantified factors. However, predictions based solely on the manipulation of such factors rest on the unfounded hope that more subjective and elusive considerations either have insignificant effects or balance each other off. For defense policy choices of major significance, they probably matter and do not completely counteract each other. For example, American systems analyses of economic and technological factors indicate that De Gaulle is inane to develop an independent nuclear force. De Gaulle, operating in terms of political considerations excluded from these analyses, arrives at the opposite conclusion and behaves accordingly. As this same contemporary example indicates, when political and psychological factors are not recognized, emotional reactions may result from unexpected frustrations.

III. A MAP OF THE FIELD

The major questions of defense policy analysis can be divided into four categories: the strategic context; defense policy-making; strategic alternatives; and quality control. Viewed from the vantage point of any one nation, the "strategic context" includes the relevant traits of other states. "Defense policy-making" includes the domestic factors which affect the choice and implementation of defense policy by that nation. "Strategic alternatives" includes the war and peace alternatives and the factors which determine the feasibility and usefulness of the alternatives. (Usefulness is measured in terms of official defense policy objectives.) Finally, "quality control" includes four variables whose operations determine the extent to which a nation makes the best possible use of its defense capabilities. According to this categorization, the policy-making process of foreign states falls into the strategic context, while military measures to deal with foreign states come under strategic alternatives.

The Strategic Context

On a general level, the external actors who make up the strategic context can be classified as allies, enemies and non-aligned. Four questions apply to all members of the strategic context, whichever subdivision they occupy. What is their defense policy in terms of goals, preferred means, and roles assigned to others? What perceptions do they have of the nation in relation to which they are all external actors? What constraints in defense policy does their domestic environment impose and what capabilities does it provide? What predispositions does their perception of historical experience bring to bear on their evaluation of defense policy choices? Answers to the first question will demarcate areas of consensus and conflict between that nation and external actors, i.e., the issues on which opposition and assistance can be expected. Answers to the second suggest how others perceive the defense policy behavior of the nation from which the analyst looks out. Information on their internal situation indicates what defense policy alternatives they find compatible and incompatible with their domestic situation. The perceived historical experience assists the analyst to estimate which defense options the external actors believe likely to succeed and to fail.

Beyond this point, the defense policy analyst needs to ask different questions for each group of external actors. To know what allies intend to do and to assist their associates to do, the analyst must discover the payoffs which they expect from membership in the alliance. These can include: military strength to make an attack on or resist an attack by a common enemy; military strength and political prestige to apply to states other than the common enemy(ies); promises of allied support to maintain the regime which agreed to the alliance; and the release of funds which would otherwise have to be committed to the indigenous military establishment. Obviously, the mixture of payoffs desired may vary from ally to ally with the consequence of disagreement on joint action and on alliance performance.

To determine the extent to which the interests of allies are complementary, and the coalition has value to all its members, the analyst should examine: (1) the attitudes of influential groups in the member states, particularly their degree of confidence in and identification with the leaders of their allies, and the content of their fears for national security; (2) the degrees of complementarity and similarity in national characteristics such as location, military posture, political stability, and foreign trade; and (3) the extent to which the perceived interests of leaders of all member states overlap and are ranked and weighted similarly.

Together, these factors determine the value and stability of an alliance. However, just as with the other components of defense policy, the analyst would be wrong to assume a simple cumulative relationship. Instead, he must be alert for correlations between positions on particular factors and the nature of the influence which the factors tend to exert on each other. Two examples dealing with alliances will illustrate these points. There appears to be a positive correlation between the military strength of an ally and its independence within the alliance. Accordingly, a militarily weak ally tends to be relatively more reliable but less helpful in a showdown than a militarily strong ally. It also seems that alliance cohesion declines when the enemy threat appears to be overwhelming and when it appears to be insignificant. Accordingly, a government which gives top priority to a cohesive alliance should try to make a powerful enemy seem neither committed to large-scale aggression nor reliably pacific.

Those external actors which occupy the enemy category pose a somewhat different problem for the defense policy analyst. He wants to know how they can, at best, be altered to fit into another category, and, at least, how their hostile intentions can be frustrated. Before he can estimate the probability of alteration, he must locate the sources of hostility. His inquiries should include the contribution to a hostile posture of: the personality of enemy leaders; the rules of behavior contained in their official ideology; pressures in the enemy camp which its leaders can damp by means of a hostile defense policy; their ties with other enemies; and their historic fears of the country to which they are hostile.

To evaluate means to frustrate hostile intentions, the analyst tries to discover the cost-gains calculus of the enemy leadership. This knowledge indicates what combination of punishments and rewards can induce the enemy to accept denial. If the enemy is a thermonuclear power, the analyst should give priority to finding the threshold of denial above which the enemy will use his nuclears. Finally, the analyst should assess the compatibility of the most promising methods for denial with those for alteration. These may be incompatible. For example, the creation of the West German army by the United States served a denial function; it also has operated to support Soviet enmity toward the United States.

In spite of the great diversity among external actors in the non-aligned category, two questions should be asked of them all. First, what distribution of power between coalitions in the international arena do they prefer? The answer suggests the extent to which the non-alignment of a particular external actor implies neutrality or partiality. Second, what level of tension between the coalitions do they prefer? This answer suggests the extent to which the non-aligned actor seeks to play off the coalitions against each other and his willingness to play a mediating role between them.

If the analyst has under examination the group of currently non-aligned states in Asia, the Middle East and Africa, he should try to project the probabilities and the consequences of three situations. First, numerous small, militarily weak and internally disunited and unstable states continue to exist. Second, the same situation persists with one major difference: the state becomes internally unified and stable. Third, these states coalesce into a relatively small number of militarily strong and domestically cohesive and stable nations. The first situation promises major opportunities for manipulation by the great powers and the chance to continue their competition by support of local factions in frequent internal wars: such states do not become significant rivals to the great powers in their region and do not pull their allies away. The second situation offers diminished opportunities for great power manipulation and for conflict by proxy. Although such states do not compete with great powers directly, they offer an appealing alternative to their dissatisfied small allies. Finally, in the third situation, the influence of the great powers declines further, and they may face a significant competitor who gradually builds a coalition around himself.

Should he be advisor to the great power in an existing coalition, the analyst needs to know the following to assess the desirability of each situation: (1) the probability that presently weak, disunited and unstable nonaligned states will fall under the influence of his client or that of his client's enemies; (2) the probability that intervention by his client will result in an undesired war with these enemies; (3) the probability of direct enemy attack should the states become sufficiently stable to curtail other forms of intervention; (4) the extent to which continued non-alignment by the states in question adequately serves his client's interests; and (5) the extent to which an emergent power would pursue policies which would hinder asymmetrically the objectives of his client relative to those of his client's enemies.

Defense Policy-Making

The second section of the map includes the internal characteristics of a state which affect the choice and implementation of its defense policy. To fall within these boundaries, the characteristic must affect the behavior of public officials charged with defense policy responsibilities. Accordingly, this section deals with internal actors in the politics of a nation and involves other domestic factors only as they determine the behavior of the participants in the domestic politics of defense. In general, the actors in the domestic politics of defense fall into four categories: defense professionals; members of the government whose areas of responsibility overlap those of defense professionals; advisors whose professional expertise has relevance to particular defense problems; and those members of the public whose acceptance must be secured before defense policies can be implemented.

The defense professional category contains: military personnel; civilians in military and intelligence ministries; private citizens who make a career of defense policy research and development; and businessmen and managers whose organizations primarily work on projects for use by defense professionals. The second category includes: heads of state; members of the government departments responsible for finance, foreign policy, and the peaceful uses of devices with military applications; and members of the legislature. The advisor category includes persons whose professional expertise, while not in defense policy, is exploited by defense professionals to illuminate particular problems. For example, these can be experts on enemy countries or on underwater acoustics. Finally, the general public category includes those citizens who actors in our first two categories believe must accept official defense policy for it to work and must tolerate an actor's performance in defense matters for his career in public office to continue.

Two sets of questions can be asked of all the internal actors, whichever subdivision they occupy. The first set concerns what the internal actors want the national defense policy to be. What challenges do they believe external actors pose? What do they believe the national defense posture should be? What implications do they believe different strategic alternatives have for their career and the status of their immediate organization? What priority do they attach to defense policy relative to other sectors of public policy? The first two questions deal with what problems they perceive for defense policy and which means seem best suited to resolve those problems. Answers to the third question introduce the biases which can result from self-interest and institutional loyalty. Data from the last question indicate the extent to which the actors prefer to subordinate their defense policy preferences to other national needs.

Obviously, consensus on the answers to these questions is most unlikely. Accordingly, the analyst should employ a second set of questions to determine the probability that the conclusions of one actor or group of actors shape national defense policy more than those of another. What do actors believe to be their area of responsibility and degree of competence in defense policy matters? What image do actors have of each other's area of responsibility and degree of competence? To what extent can actors use their behavior on other defense and non-defense matters as a bargaining counter for concessions on the defense issue at hand? What resources does the actor command which he can employ to secure his preferences?

The first question tries to clarify what each actor believes it appropriate for him to do on defense policy matters. The second question tries to clarify what each believes it appropriate for other actors to do on defense policy matters. The paired answers should tell the analyst the extent to which one actor will, without bargaining, defer to another. For example, if defense professionals believe that they alone have the responsibility and the competence to select strategic alternatives, they will try to do so. If congressmen agree with the self-image of the defense professionals, they grant them that prerogative. The third question is directed to the role of simultaneous and future bargaining situations on the actors. Obviously, the Air Force is more likely to refrain from conflict with the Secretary of Defense over alternative designs for a new fighter if it believes that he can and will get even by curtailing its jurisdiction over space programs. Answers to the last question indicate the relative access of the actors to men and money, and suggest differences in their ability to mobilize support for their preferences and opposition to alternatives with which they disagree.

The analyst will want to supplement these common sets of questions with others to be asked of actors in one or another of our four categories. For the defense professionals, the analyst investigates: the extent and nature of friction along civilian-military lines and along inter-service and inter-branch lines; the extent to which defense professionals maintain a façade of agreement; the extent to which they have formed alliances with public figures in our second category. The first two inquiries explore the extent of tension with the career officers, the probabilities that the defense professionals act as a bloc and the distribution of advocates according to institutional loyalty on issues brought into the open. The last inquiry helps the analyst to estimate the interests of different defense professionals in widening participation in a controversy. For example, if the Strategic Air Command has powerful friends in Congress and the Tactical Air Command does not, the latter has little to gain by pressing a conflict to the point where SAC involves its congressional supporters.

For public officials in an overlapping relationship to defense policy, the analyst investigates the correspondence of different defense policy choices with their main programs and objectives. Two examples will illustrate. If the Secretary of the Treasury has dedicated himself to the goal of a balanced budget, he tends to favor defense policy choices which make minimal budgetary demands. If a congressman feels dependent on the votes of Jewish voters for re-election, he tends to oppose a defense policy choice which strengthens Egypt.

For expert advisors, the analyst examines the extent to which: they allow themselves to be used as a prestige "halo" for defense professionals; they consciously or unconsciously deliver opinions on defense policy matters beyond their expertise. This information will assist the analyst to predict the extent to which the advisors will attempt to sway their clients toward the defense policies which they prefer.

For the fourth category, the general public, the analyst directs his efforts toward determining the extent to which: they notice defense policy actions by public figures; they form judgments about the defense policy behavior of public officials on the basis of concrete actions or vague images. This information suggests the nature of the constraints which the general public imposes on the defense policy behavior of its leaders.

Strategic Alternatives

The strategic alternatives section of the map contains the war and peace options from which statesmen can choose. At this time, governments of the great powers can choose from eight basic, and for the most part *non-exclu-*

sive, alternatives: C/B/R (chemical, bacteriological, radiological) warfare; nuclear deterrence; strategic nuclear war; limited war (using conventional and tactical nuclear weapons); sub-limited war (guerrilla and counter-guerrilla warfare and special operations); military assistance; civil defense; and arms control and disarmament. Although the choices open to governments vary greatly, the same basic list of questions can clarify their usefulness, i.e., contribution to recognized defense policy objectives, and feasibility, i.e., whether they can be put into practice.

An earlier section emphasized the effect of perceptions on behavior. Applied to the choice of strategies, this principle directs us to two sets of perceptions which their holders use to estimate usefulness and feasibility. The first is function, the need or job which actors feel they must find a strategy to fill in order to attain defense policy objectives. Actors judge strategies to be useful to the extent that they promise to perform a recognized function. The second is capability, the resources to pay the costs required to implement the strategy. Actors judge strategies to be feasible to the extent that they feel able to pay their expected costs. Perceptions of functional needs reflect estimates of the strategic context. Those of capability resources reflect conclusions about the area we call defense policy-making.

Functions, particularly in the nuclear era, can usefully be distinguished as primarily deterrent and primarily defensive. Crudely, the deterrent function is to prevent the behavior which initiates war; the defensive, to carry war to a successful conclusion. Of course, the same strategic option can serve both functions. For example, if a great power wages prolonged war against guerrillas in a small nation, that action may demonstrate its will to use nuclear weapons if provoked (deterrent), and to prevent the piecemeal loss of small allies (defensive).

Capabilities can usefully be classified as political or technical-economic. The political element consists of the means which the advocates of a strategy must employ to overcome and/or win over the opponents. The technical-economic element consists of the human and material resources necessary to implement strategy. Often the absence of sufficient technical-economic resources follows from inadequate political capabilities.

Gross function and capability questions can narrow the field of appropriate strategies, but leave several possibilities. The task of the analyst becomes to determine which possible strategy will perform the function with the least drain on capabilities. To determine this, the analyst must specify the functional and capability aspects of each strategy and the factors which determine each.

To illustrate the questions that arise on the function side of the calculation, we can use the example of nuclear deterrence. This strategy fails unless the user, e.g., the United States, successfully communicates to the enemy, e.g., the U.S.S.R., that it will inflict overwhelming damage on him if and only if he takes certain actions. Accordingly, if a deterrent function is to be filled, the analyst must determine what American strategic options make this communication most understandable and believable to the Soviets. To use the same strategy to illustrate, nuclear deterrence assumes that the major strategies open to the enemy do not include small guerrilla wars fought by proxies. If that is the preferred option of the enemy, nuclear deterrence only partially fulfills its function. Strategic options are designed to obstruct one or several enemy courses of action. Accordingly, the analyst must weigh the probability that the enemy can simply turn to some unobstructed course of action.

The more specific the functional requirement in question, the more important it becomes for the analyst to examine his conclusion in terms of other functions of the national defense posture. A strategic option may be appropriate for one functional requirement and actively inimical to others. The analyst should consider the effects of the strategy on allies and non-aligned states as well as on the enemy. For example, to evaluate the usefulness of an American strategy to use tactical nuclear weapons against any Soviet invasion of Western Europe, one must weigh the response of Europeans to the prospect of nuclear war on their soil. The analyst should also consider the effect use of a particular strategy has on subsequent behavior. A strategic option can fulfill its function in the immediate future and still hinder more long-range objectives. For example, American air strikes against guerrilla-infested villages in South Vietnam can kill guerrillas. They also can kill civilians in the villages and obstruct efforts to win the popular support required for victory.

The capability requirements of the strategy or strategies under examination must also be specified. To determine what political capabilities are required and available, the analyst investigates: the relative power of the defense policy-makers whose status rises and declines if a particular strategy becomes policy; the availability of substitute rewards; the time interval before the strategy will produce visible rewards; the visible losses and sacrifices which precede and accompany the payoff. An example will clarify each point. If the President makes a defense policy choice which strengthens the Space Agency at the expense of the Department of Defense, he must be able and ready to pay the cost of backlash from Defense. Should a strategy deprive the Navy of new carriers, the funding of additional Polaris submarines will lessen the volume of Navy protests. Pressures to cut off research and development funds for a weapons system mount as years pass without an operational prototype. If the casualties in an American-sponsored limited war are Americans, political pressures in this country to resolve the conflict exceed those when the casualties are foreigners.

To determine what technical-economic capabilities are required and available, the analyst investigates: the state of the relevant technology; absolute costs (resources consumed); multiplier side-effects of that consumption on technical-economic capabilities; negative multiplier side-effects on technical-economic capabilities. Again, examples may be helpful. Repetition of techniques already well mastered provides less of a capability problem than attempts at major innovation. A nation with 10,000 electrical engineers obviously can provide more competent personnel for work on electronic instruments of war than can a nation with 1,000 electrical engineers.

Even this crude analysis indicates that the evaluation of strategic alternatives requires skills from many of the social and natural sciences. To combine the many relevant considerations into a meaningful policy conclusion, the analyst must have integrative skills of a high order. Of course, he must weigh the factors and relate them. However, to enable the policy-maker to compare strategies adequately, the analyst should also calculate the rewards if the strategy succeeds, modified by the probabilities of success, and the losses if the strategy fails, modified by the probability of failure. After all, it is often unrealistic to expect policy-makers to choose a strategy whose failure would deprive them of the opportunity ever to make choices again.

Quality Control

We borrow the term quality control from the sphere of production because it suggests a cluster of factors which, in spite of their absence from the visible process of production, significantly affect the ultimate product. Quality control in a business indicates the desire of its manager to check the workings of his men and machines, and the assumption on his part that mistakes can be minimized through careful observation and analysis. To pay for quality control, the manager must accept in principle the need to adapt to its findings. He also must be dissatisfied with present methods, and willing to try to improve. In sum, quality control has denotations of accurate *information, rationality* in decisions, *flexibility* and *innovation*. Behavior associated with different points of these variables affects the production of defense policy just as it does the production of color TV sets. Namely, it affects reputation and position *vis-à-vis* competitors.

The information component of defense policy quality control includes the content of and degree of similarity between two descriptions of reality. The first contains what gets through the mental screen of a particular defense policy actor or group of actors; the second, what is perceived by the less involved analyst. To predict the behavior of defense policy actors, the analyst must know what they think reality to be, i.e., what they believe to be true about the components included in the strategic context, defense policy-making, and strategic alternatives sections of our map. To predict the correspondence between what each actor expects a defense policy choice to accomplish and what an accurately informed, impartial observer would predict, the analyst must measure the unreality of the actor's "perceived reality."

To predict the content of "perceived reality," and thus behavior, and to predict the extent of false expectations, the analyst should investigate two sets of factors. The first set deals with the boundaries of the data which defense policy institutions, particularly intelligence organs, gather and their reliability. For example, he asks whether data on politically unstable societies cover counter-elites as well as the current rulers. He will also want to know whether different data sources receive credit ratings based on past accuracy. The analyst seeks to learn where there is a dearth as well as where there is an abundance of data. The second set of factors deals with the use of collected data. The analyst must discover what criteria are used to decide which bits of data are facts, and what facts are significant. He will want to know what relationships between the data receive attention. For example, has the timing of appeals for arms control and disarmament by a hostile government been plotted against peaks of pressure from that government's constituents for more consumer goods? After these two sets of factors have been examined, the results can be compared with what our map of defense policy analysis implies to be desirable. The gaps indicate the distortions built into a defense policy actor's information.

The rationality component of defense policy quality control concerns the extent to which a defense policy actor selects means best suited to his ends. Within the limits of his information, does he select what for him is the most efficient available course of action? The reader should note that, according to this definition, someone can be both rational and totally unrealistic. The rational defense policy actor is simply consistent and calculating within the boundaries of his perceptions. The reader should also note that rationality by this standard makes the actions of a defense policy actor predictable. If the analyst knows how the actor perceives the other components of the defense policy map, and if he knows the goals to which the actor has committed himself, he can infer what means the actor will choose.

To investigate for the presence of such "subjective" rationality, the analyst asks to what extent the individuals or groups in question: (1) hold a conscious set of goals with clearly defined priorities; (2) try to insure that all feasible means have been considered and their consequences calculated; and (3) examine the projected affects of alternative means for a number of years and for impact on the whole set of goals.

Flexibility, the third component of defense policy quality control, includes the factors which determine the extent to which defense policy actors are willing and able to modify their present and future behavior. Obviously, actors can get locked into a policy because of rigid selection of information or a low degree of rationality. For example, they may block all data which make present policies seem unsuccessful. They may attach a sufficiently high priority to one of their goals to pursue it even if the available means have a low probability of success and are extremely costly. To this extent, flexibility reflects the first two quality control components.

However, other factors determine ability to maneuver in the present, and the use of that leeway affects the ability to maneuver in the future. This can be seen if we investigate the requirements for and consquences of three uses of flexibility. These are the leeway to: (1) make a doctrinal commitment which lays down guidelines for the specifics of defense policy for more than several years; (2) adopt a specific measure, which claims not to impinge on other defense policy choices, for no more than several years; and (3) avoid the choice of measures to deal with a defense policy problem. The probable ability of defense actors to opt for any one of these courses depends on the perceived scope and urgency of the problem, and the distribution of influence in support of alternative solutions. Desire for a major commitment correlates positively with the perceived scope and urgency of the problem. Tolerance of "decisions not to decide" correlates inversely with the perceived scope and urgency of the problem. If influence is scattered in support of a number of alternatives, more leeway exists to avoid a decision than if it is concentrated behind one solution.

The consequences of each course of action for flexibility in the future are determined by the accuracy of predictions about the development of the problem and about the domestic politics of defense. Because a doctrinal commitment rests on the assumption that the future development of the problem is clear, and because it determines numerous specifics of defense policy, unforeseen developments can leave a government without ready modifications. For example, the doctrine may assume a nuclear monopoly and de-emphasize conventional war forces, but a hostile country acquires a nuclear capability. The specific commitment alternative assumes that the problem does not explode in significance. However, external actors can undercut that assumption. For example, a hostile government can dramatize great power aid to a small ally engaged in guerrilla war and make the small commitment into a major prestige stake. Decisions not to decide assume that alternatives will not become less promising; however, they may. To illustrate, the United States may temporize about increasing or curtailing military assistance to a government confronted by a radical revolutionary movement. Within several years, the revolutionaries may have formed ties with China or the Soviet Union, and the government may have disintegrated to the point where it cannot be saved by an increase in United States military aid. The flexibility consequences of doctrinal commitment and of no commitment are especially dependent on developments in the domestic politics of defense. Doctrinal commitments may strengthen particular parts of the government and industrial groups to the point where they can postpone or block reassessment of the merits of the doctrine. Should a deteriorating strategic situation follow decisions not to decide, a political climate of frustration and fear may result which deprives the government of the political capability to adopt mixed and subtle strategic alternatives.

Innovation, the final component of defense policy quality control, includes the factors which determine the willingness of a government to support breakthroughs in the social and natural sciences and the consequences of such support. To predict willingness to innovate, the analyst should investigate: (1) the strength of general beliefs that innovation can solve policy problems; (2) the perceived inadequacies of present technological and social science devices; (3) the perceived pattern of support for defense-related innovation by hostile governments; (4) the political influence of intellectual and economic groups who desire government support for research and development; and (5) the time interval policy-makers believe will precede a decisive military conflict.

To predict the consequences of support for defense-related innovation, the analysts must assess the accuracy of four predictions. The first concerns the devices needed at the time that the innovation becomes operational. Given the long lead-time necessary to achieve and implement major innovations, a projection of five to ten years is usually required. The second concerns the feasibility of the proposed innovation. The problem is neither to underestimate nor to overestimate the obstacles to currently nonexistent technical capabilities. The third prediction concerns the gain from the funded research effort relative to the loss of innovations which might otherwise have been realized. The final prediction estimates the reaction of enemy leaders to a government's sponsorship of a program of defense innovation. Obviously, if the enemy enters into an "innovation race" the gains from innovation tend to diminish.

*   *   *

The preceding map may seem to present a bewildering array of questions. In fact, the array is large, and we badly need conceptual frameworks to help us cope with the complexity of defense policy issues. If the reader has been stimulated to reflect on his implicit framework and to formulate a more adequate explicit framework than the one suggested here, this article has achieved its purpose.

PART ONE:

The Strategic Context

SOVIET MILITARY STRATEGY[1]

Herbert S. Dinerstein
Leon Gouré
Thomas W. Wolfe

THE QUEST for a unified military doctrine that would reflect the general political line of the Soviet state was, in fact, one of the major questions that first engaged Soviet military theorists in the early twenties. During the long period of Stalin's ascendancy, this question tended to drop out of sight, for the framing of basic military doctrine was largely taken out of the hands of the theoreticians by Stalin himself. However, with the advent of nuclear weapons and Stalin's departure from the scene, the search for a unified military doctrine responsive to the revolution in military technology took on new importance, and again became a dominant object of military-theoretical discussion. A contemporary expression of the great value placed on development of Soviet military doctrine was given recently in the following words by Marshal R. Ia. Malinovskii, the Soviet Minister of Defense:

> Under conditions where the development of weapons goes on at a singularly tempestuous pace, great significance attaches to military-theoretical work . . . in recent years our military-technical thought has made great progress . . . we now have a deep theoretical foundation, which flows from the political nature of our state military doctrine. Soviet military doctrine—based on the policy of our party and resting its leading recommendations on the conclusions of military science—helps us to penetrate deeply into the nature of modern war and its initial period, helps us to determine the most suitable modes of operation in it, and points out the path for development and preparation of our armed forces.[2]

Despite this reverence toward a unified military doctrine and the assumption that it will unlock the mysteries of war and smooth the path of the policy-makers, there also has been abundant evidence that matters have turned out somewhat less satisfactorily than the design would call for.

Several areas of difficulty can be identified. One of these grows out of the quite human circumstance that even in a supposedly monolithic society men

---

[1] The title is mine. [Ed.]

[2] Speech by Minister of Defense of the USSR, Marshal of the Soviet Union R. Ia. Malinovskii to the All Army Conference on Ideological Questions, *Red Star*, October 25, 1962.

sometimes find it difficult to agree with each other. The editor of a Soviet professional military journal gave voice to this particular difficulty some time ago in the pages of his publication while making a plea for a unified military doctrine. The editor, Major General P. Zhilin, wrote in 1961 that in view of all the military and political changes taking place in the world, "now, as never before, it is necessary to have a unity of views on all the most important problems of military art and employment of troops." After noting that many discussions of this question had been going on "in the pages of the military press and within the walls of the General Staff academy," General Zhilin added, "unfortunately, in these discussions, no unity of views has been achieved." [3]

Another area of difficulty arises from the perplexing way in which the domain of "military-technical" thought shades into Marxist-Leninist political territory. Because the boundary line is indistinct, it has never proved easy to develop a body of military theory that does not err in the direction of being either too narrow or too diffused to provide appropriate working precepts for military strategy and policy.

The writers of Soviet military texts have customarily sought a middle road between a "narrow technical" approach to military theory, which would be vulnerable to criticism as un-Marxist, and a very broad approach to the study of war as a "social-historical phenomenon," which would, as one group of writers has put it, "dissolve" military science in a sea of social and political considerations and rob it of military specificity. [4]

In a sense, the problem is one of compressing the definition of war so that military-technical aspects of doctrine and strategy can be appropriately dealt with by professional military men and technicians while other aspects are left in political hands. In the view of Major General Zhilin, in the same article mentioned above, it could be said as of May 1961 that "the political side of Soviet military doctrine is laid out with exhaustive clarity in a series of official documents of the Party and Government," but: "in the military-technical parts of doctrine . . . there are still not a few disputable and vague propositions." [5] As the reader of the present volume will see for himself, some propositions of a military-technical character still remain in this state.

Another species of problems in the framing of Soviet military doctrine arises in the area where ritual and reality get in each other's way. The difficulties here face both the Soviet military theorist and those who seek instruction from his work. Sometimes it is a question of using old terminology and formulas to ease the transition to new military thought, or some-

---

[3] Major General P. Zhilin, "Discussion about a Unified Military Doctrine," *Voenno-istoricheskii zhurnal* (*Journal of Military History*), No. 5, May 1961, p. 73.

[4] A characteristic discussion of this problem can be found in a text written jointly in 1960 by Major General M. V. Smirnov and several other military theorists. *O sovetskoi voennoi nauke* (*On Soviet Military Science*), Voenizdat Ministerstva Oborony Soiuza SSR, Moscow, 1960, p. 68.

[5] Zhilin, *op. cit.*, p. 73.

times the opposite—giving lip service to new ideas but clinging in substance to old conceptions. In either case, the real message may have to be disentangled from the ritual form in which it is wrapped. There are other aspects of the ritual-reality question that may present more serious and subtle problems of understanding; it is not feasible to explore the range of these problems here, but an example may be worth noting.

It is a preachment of Marxist-Leninist doctrine, for instance, that the morale of capitalist armies is poor and that they have no stomach for fighting to preserve a rotten system in which they feel they have no stake. Is Soviet military theory significantly influenced by this notion in assessing Western military power, or does it merely make a ritual bow in the proper direction and go on to a sober appraisal of the problem in nondoctrinal terms? The answer may never be altogether clear, but as the present book seems to testify, the Soviets presumably have a high respect for Western capabilities and seem prepared to lay aside at least some ritual beliefs when appraising the prospective opponent.

At the same time, one needs to avoid the mistake of confusing ritual beliefs with theoretical tenets that are strongly held by the Soviets, or of supposing that doctrine in general has only a negligible influence on Soviet military thought and behavior. Many doctrinal tenets do, in fact, appear to carry important weight.

One example is the significance attached to correct selection of the "main link," "the main task," or the "main blow." Whether the field of activity be military or political, this notion—an important element in Bolshevik doctrine—has continued to exert strong influence on Soviet analysis and behavior. When a particular problem therefore is defined as "the main task," such as the statement in the present volume that "working out methods for reliably repelling a surprise nuclear attack by an aggressor is the main task of Soviet military strategy," the reader is justified in assuming that a high priority lies behind the rhetoric.

Similarly, the idea that correct calculation of the "relation of forces" underlies sound strategic planning and decisionmaking is another doctrinal tenet that operates with special conviction in the Soviet case. Although this idea is hardly a distinctive Soviet discovery, the emphasis given it in Soviet thought suggests that any work outlining a military strategy for the Soviet Union will tend to be particularly sensitive to the relative strength of the major antagonists, as well as to beliefs held in the world about the military power balance.

Another problem area in the search for a unified set of military-theoretical views relates to the inherent difficulty of keeping any body of military doctrine abreast of weaponry in a fast-moving technological age. As the reader will note, the authors of *Soviet Military Strategy* themselves acknowledge quite frankly the difficulties they have faced in connection with the weaponry-doctrine problem. For example, after noting that modern technology has within a very short period of time made available enormously powerful new weapons, they go on to say (p. 331) :

> However, the search for new combat methods, new forms of troop organization and new avenues of development of armed forces appropriate for these powerful weapons has proven to be a difficult problem over whose solution theoreticians and practitioners of the military art both here and abroad are laboring persistently.

This problem, indeed, with its far-ranging implications for political and economic decisions as well as military planning, tends to dominate the scene. More than any of the other difficulties mentioned above, it helps to explain why military doctrine, like strategy and policy in general, turns out in Soviet experience to be shaped by pragmatic considerations no less than by theoretical ones.

If one were to attempt to reduce the Soviet strategic policymaking process to a simplified model, drawing on Soviet descriptions of the way it is supposed to work in theory, the result would come out somewhat along the following lines.

In the model image, political commandments flow from the top leadership of Party and government to those who develop Soviet military doctrine. A unified body of military doctrine is generated in turn, bringing together the best conclusions of military-technical thought, integrated with Marxist-Leninist political wisdom. Based on this unified body of military doctrine, appropriate policies and decisions are adopted concerning strategy, force structure, training, and the like. In the process of settling on the most suitable military strategy and policies, the parameters set by economic, technical, political-morale, and other factors come into play. Finally, the circle is closed, as a military posture responsive to the political commandments of the top leadership emerges for support of over-all state policy in peace or war.

This image of the strategic policy process implies a more or less monolithic bureaucratic apparatus, permitting some measure of internal debate on doctrinal and policy issues, but so endowed that when a decision is made, all elements of the bureaucracy fall into line and any policy opposition ceases. In theory, therefore, the strategic policy process unfolds in a purposeful, planned way—yielding a military strategy, posture, and force structure meshed neatly with and answering closely to aims set by the top political leadership.

In practice, however, a somewhat different picture appears to prevail. The bureaucratic decisionmaking process is by no means so smoothly monolithic, but is rather exposed to the play of competing interests among various segments of Party, government, and military bureaucracies. In this more complicated world, the theoretical image of the strategic policy process begins to break down. Doctrine, strategy, forces, technical and economic realities react on each other, and various pragmatic considerations intrude. The result more often than not seems to be the less-than-perfect answer, the necessity to live with a series of adjustments and compromise solutions.

* * *

CHARACTER OF THE SOVIET STRATEGIC DEBATE

During the decade since Stalin's death, Soviet military doctrine and strategy have been subjected more or less continuously to debate and modification. One can distinguish at least three perceptible phases in this process. The first phase may be said to have run from about 1953 to 1957, coinciding roughly with the period of Khrushchev's rise to undisputed power. During these years, Soviet military thinking—freed from the restrictive hold of "'Stalinist" military science—underwent a series of adjustments to the revolution in military affairs brought about by the nuclear weapon and the jet aircraft. The strategic issues of this period, closely interwoven with foreign policy and internal political-economic considerations, have been examined in detail elsewhere and need not be reviewed here.[6] It was only toward the end of this period that the Soviet Union acquired advanced weapons in sufficient numbers to make the development of a doctrine for their employment an urgent question. At first, therefore, the main emphasis of debate was on how to adapt the new weapons to traditional Soviet concepts, and only later did it become necessary to recast Soviet doctrine.

The second phase of the strategic dialogue opened after the influence of ballistic missile technology had begun to make itself felt about the end of 1957, and at a time when Khrushchev found himself fully in political command. The process of digesting the weapons revolution of the nuclear-missile age grew increasingly painful in this period for at least the traditionally oriented elements of the Soviet military bureaucracy, now faced with Khrushchev's apparent conviction that the new missile technology offered a way to buttress Soviet security while, at the same time, paring down the oversized conventional portion of the military establishment. One can regard this phase as coming to a close in January 1960 with Khrushchev's "new strategy" speech, which may have been intended as *the* definitive revision of Soviet strategic concepts and force structure in keeping with the requirements of the nuclear-missile age—as Khrushchev saw the situation.

As matters turned out, however, the strategic dialogue did not subside

---

[6] The reader will find an extensive analysis of the post-Stalin military debate of this period in Herbert S. Dinerstein, *War and the Soviet Union*, Frederick A. Praeger, Inc., New York, 1959. Another account covering the same period may be found in Raymond L. Garthoff, *Soviet Strategy in the Nuclear Age*, Frederick A. Praeger, Inc., New York, 1958. See also J. M. MacMintosh, *Strategy and Tactics of Soviet Foreign Policy*, The Macmillan Co., London, 1962, particularly pp. 88–105.

with Khrushchev's new strategy presentation, which, on the contrary, only served to open a new phase in the continuing debate. It is this latter phase, to which publication of the present volume in the Soviet Union in 1962 is immediately related, upon which attention will be focused here. Broadly speaking, the strategic dialogue of these past three years seems to have followed three separate but interrelated tracks:

1. A continuing polemic between Khrushchev and the professional military as a whole.

2. A subsidiary debate between what might be called "radical" and "traditionalist" outlooks within the Soviet military itself.

3. An external dialogue over the strategic power balance in which Soviet and U.S. leadership spokesmen have been the prime participants.

It would be wrong to give the impression that the internal aspects of the continuing Soviet debate on military policy and strategy reveal nothing but contention. There is also a broad consensus on many matters. One should also bear in mind that policy discussion and debate have become somewhat more common in Soviet public life in the past few years than was formerly the case. This applies not only to military policy, but also to other policy areas. Hence, the airing of differences does not necessarily indicate an internal struggle of the kind that can end only with one faction or another losing power.

With regard to the dialogue over military questions, lines in the debate have not by any means always been sharply drawn. On some issues, participants have shifted ground, and proponents of a particular school of thought at one stage of the debate may sometimes be found siding with a contending school at a later stage.[7] To some extent, particularly in such publicly available professional military journals as *Communist of the Armed Forces* and the *Journal of Military History,* there seems to have been a definite attempt to encourage discussion of various controversial doctrinal questions.[8]

Nevertheless, after allowance is made for a certain amount of officially

---

[7] This is particularly true with regard to military men who first took up the military doctrinal discussion in the period shortly after Stalin's death. Some of those who were standard bearers of a progressive approach at the time of breaking away from Stalinist military doctrine, such as Marshal Rotmistrov and Lieutenant General Krasil'nikov, later have come to find themselves in traditionalist company, in the context of the dialogue of the early sixties. In a way, this may reflect a shift in the grounds of the dialogue itself as much as a change in the views of the participants.

[8] The editors of these journals have, for example, invited presentation of various viewpoints on such questions as the importance of the initial period of a war, the relative influence of "subjective" leadership judgments and "objective" strength factors on success in war, the adequacy of Soviet military doctrine, and so on. In general, there has been a tendency for each of these professional journals to favor a particular school of thought; thus, the traditionalist outlook is reflected most often by the *Voennoistoricheskii zhurnal* (*Journal of Military History*), while the modernist or radical outlook is more likely to appear in *Kommunist vooruzhennykh sil* (*Communist of the Armed Forces*).

sanctioned debate and competition of views within the context of professional military inquiry, it is fairly clear that the strategic dialogue has spilled over into areas of basic disagreement, with practical implications for defense policy and strategy. The polemic involving Khrushchev and the military following his January 1960 speech to the Supreme Soviet is a case in point.

Dialogue Between Khrushchev and the Military

Khrushchev's January 1960 report to the Supreme Soviet dealt both with Soviet disarmament proposals and with a new military policy.[9] The report apparently was drawn up after consideration of these questions in the Central Committee in December 1959. In this speech, Khrushchev stressed the notion that missiles, for which he claimed a Soviet lead, would be the dominant element in any future war and that conventional armaments, including surface navies and air forces along with large standing armies, were rapidly becoming obsolete. Although maintaining that strategic nuclear blows at the outset of a war would bring unprecedented destruction and might tempt the capitalist adversary to toy with the idea of a surprise attack, Khrushchev argued at the same time that surprise atack was not a feasible policy because any "sufficiently large" state (by which he clearly had in mind the Soviet Union) would always retain enough residual strategic capability to strike back. On these grounds he also maintained that Soviet retaliatory capability deterred the West from starting a war, except possibly in the case of a "madman." Furthermore, Khrushchev took this occasion to boast that not only did the Soviet Union now possess "formidable" weapons, but that "those which are, so to speak, about to appear, are even more perfected, even more formidable."

This generally reassuring picture of the Soviet military posture was accompanied by the announced intention to reduce Soviet manpower under arms by one-third—an economically attractive move warranted, according to Khrushchev, by the increased firepower that nuclear weapons now gave the Soviet armed forces.[10] "In our time," Khrushchev said:

> . . . the defense potential of the country is not determined by the number of our soldiers under arms, by the number of persons in uniform . . . the defense capability of the country depends, to a decisive extent, on the total firepower and the means of delivery available. . . . The proposed reduction will in no way weaken the firepower of our armed forces, and this is the main point.

[9] "Disarmament: The Way To Strengthen Peace and Assure Friendship among People," Report by Comrade N. S. Khrushchev to a Session of the Supreme Soviet of the USSR, *Pravda,* January 15, 1960.

[10] Khrushchev announced a reduction of 1,200,000 from a total of 3,623,000 men in the Soviet armed forces. It should be noted that in this speech Khrushchev's position on manpower reduction was partly qualified by the admission that in the event of imminent war a significant increase in the armed forces might be appropriate.

In the months following this Supreme Soviet speech, it became apparent that there was considerable resistance among the Soviet military to Khrushchev's thinking and its practical implications for security policy.[11] Without daring to oppose Khrushchev openly, various military spokesmen began to back and fill in an apparent effort to protect vested military interests and to modify portions of the Khrushchev doctrine at variance with their professional notions of sound military strategy, suitable force structure, and so on.

The bulk of Soviet comment on Khrushchev's January statement naturally applauded it as a significant contribution to Soviet military science and occasionally his position received specific intellectual support in the military press, such as an endorsement of the troop reduction program by Major General G. Pokrovskii, a prominent Soviet military theoretician, who argued that the doctrine of substituting firepower for large numbers of troops was consistent with the general trend of modern warfare.[12] However, reservations toward Khrushchev's thinking from the military side of the house became increasingly evident in 1960 and early 1961.[13] In retrospect, these reservations were brought most clearly into focus in an important speech by Marshal R. Ia. Malinovskii, the Soviet Defense Minister, at the XXIInd Party Congress in October 1961.[14] Although the context of the situation in which Malinovskii spoke had been altered by the passage of events, as will be pointed out presently, his speech nevertheless serves as one of the major landmarks in the dialogue between Khrushchev and the military.

In his speech at the Party Congress, Malinovskii took pains not to set his views off in open opposition to Khrushchev, to whom he even applied the seldom-used but flattering term, "our Supreme High Commander." At the same time, the Soviet Defense Minister advanced a set of "theses" of "Soviet military doctrine" that did in fact differ in a number of notable respects from Khrushchev's formulation of January 1960.

To begin with, Malinovskii's statement gave a considerably less optimistic picture of the Soviet defense outlook than that projected earlier by Khrushchev. For example, Khrushchev had deprecated the feasibility of surprise attack on the Soviet Union and expressed full confidence in the credibility

---

[11] In fact, the first hint of some divergence of views came immediately after Khrushchev's report. In a speech following the report, Marshal Malinovskii supported Khrushchev's position, including the proposed troop cut, but at the same time he cautioned against over-reliance on missile forces and voiced a reminder that military success would depend on combined use of all types of forces. *Pravda,* January 15, 1960.

[12] G. Pokrovskii, "Firepower of the Armed Forces and a Country's Defense Capability," *Sovetskii flot (Soviet Fleet),* March 9, 1960.

[13] An example was a special article in *Red Star,* April 5, 1961, under the heading "New Technology and Mass Armies." The editors' foreword used the familiar device of saying that a number of readers had asked how modern technology and warfare had influenced the size of armies. The responding article, written by Colonel A. M. Iovlev, made clear the military view that modern weapons and the general international situation had not reduced the requirement for mass armies.

[14] Speech by Marshal R. Ia. Malinovskii to the XXIInd Congress of the CPSU, *Pravda,* October 25, 1961.

of the Soviet deterrent. Whereas Khrushchev suggested that the West would not dare to attack the Soviet Union, except as the irrational act of a Western "madman," Malinovskii now stressed that "in realistically appraising the situation," one must hold that the West was making serious preparations for a surprise nuclear attack. By emphasizing that the most important task of the Soviet armed forces was to be "in constant readiness to repel reliably a surprise attack by the enemy," Malinovskii seemed to be advancing a view at variance with Khrushchev's earlier judgment on the likelihood and feasibility of such a threat to Soviet security. In stressing the danger of surprise attack, Malinovskii also dwelt on the need to improve the posture of the Soviet armed forces for "breaking up the aggressive designs [of the enemy] by dealing him a crushing blow in time." This carefully phrased formula gave new cognizance to the idea of pre-emptive attack, which had not appeared in Khrushchev's January 1960 speech.[15]

Revival of the pre-emption theme on this occasion may well have been calculated for its political effect on the United States in connection with the Berlin situation. In this light, it did not, of course, betoken any immediate difference of view between Khrushchev and the military. However, one might note that a doctrine of pre-emption did pose issues of a troubling nature for Soviet military policy, which could become a source of contention, both between Khrushchev and the military, and among the military themselves. For example, it would tend to focus attention on the question of which branches of the armed forces should be strengthened and kept ready to assure a pre-emptive capability, and therefore, which claims on resources should come first. Since maintenance of a high state of readiness tends to be very expensive, this too could complicate decisions facing the Soviet leadership—as between expenditure for building up additional forces on the one hand, or for keeping forces-in-being at a high state of alert on the other.

The image of a future war in Malinovskii's exposition differed in a significant way from that drawn by Khrushchev. While both shared the view that a future war would "inevitably" be a missile-nuclear war, and that the use of such weapons in the initial period would have decisive influence on the

---

[15] Initial advocacy of the need for a pre-emptive capability was advanced in an earlier phase of the strategic dialogue in 1955 by Marshal Pavel Rotmistrov, one of the first open critics of Stalinist military doctrine. The subject subsequently dropped out of public discussion for several years, coming back into view in 1960–1961 in the professional military press. For example, in the *Voenno-istoricheskii zhurnal* (*Journal of Military History*), No. 4, April 1960, p. 119, Major General I. N. Rukhle argued that one of the first problems for military theory was to study how to "guarantee for oneself the advantages of successful delivery of a surprise first blow or the prevention of such a blow on the part of a probable enemy." In the same journal ("Questions of Soviet Military Science in the Works of V. I. Lenin," No. 3, March 1961, p. 10), the need to beat one's opponent to the draw in the event of war was discussed by General V. Kurasov, who cited Lenin as the authority for his views. However, Malinovskii's statement on pre-emption at the XXIInd Party Congress gave the subject an official cognizance that was absent in the earlier professional discussion. Further attention will be given later to the treatment of pre-emption.

war's outcome, Malinovskii brought in a traditional notion conspicuously glossed over by Khrushchev, namely, that final victory could be assured only by "combined action of all arms and services." Malinovskii also affirmed that a future world war would be carried out by "mass, multi-million-man armed forces," which seemed to imply that it might turn out to be a protracted war rather than a short, decisive one. This important hedge by Malinovskii exposed a central issue that had been raised by Khrushchev's 1960 Supreme Soviet speech. If the Soviet Union could not rely on missiles and nuclear weapons alone to bring quick victory in a short war, but rather required large and diversified forces to wage nuclear war successfully, then Khrushchev's theorizing on the obsolescence of conventional arms and massive armies and his espousal of practical measures to reduce Soviet forces by one-third were inconsonant with Soviet security—as Malinovskii and presumably other key military leaders viewed it.

It should, of course, be noted that Khrushchev accepted the idea that larger forces might be needed in the event of war. In a sense, therefore, the central point at issue between Khrushchev and the military was over requirements for peacetime forces-in-being, which, in turn, implied a conflicting estimate of the effectiveness of Soviet deterrence of their opponents or, if deterrence failed, the likelihood of timely warnings. Khrushchev was saying, in effect, that even though Soviet forces might be less than adequate to fight a war, they were adequate to assure deterrence. The military leaders, on the other hand, were saying that deterrence might fail and therefore they must be in better shape to fight a war if one should occur—an attitude not unlike that which military men anywhere might hold.[16] The military apparently did not altogether agree among themselves, however, on what kind of a war they might have to fight and what forces would be needed for it.

Although Malinovskii's "theses" on military doctrine in October 1961 served to illustrate the theoretical gap between Khrushchev's January 1960 views and those of the military, the gap had actually been narrowed appreciably under the pressure of intervening events by the time Malinovskii spoke at the XXIInd Party Congress.[17] In the summer of 1961, the troop-reduc-

---

[16] The difference in point of view between Khrushchev and the military might be described another way, with Khrushchev arguing essentially on the basis of his estimate of enemy intentions and the military on the basis of enemy capability. However, when seeking a rationale for strengthening the Soviet defense posture, the military also were obliged to go beyond the capabilities argument and to use the alleged intention of the West to start a preventive war to justify a claim on more resources, a higher state of readiness, larger forces, more attention to civil defense, and so on.

[17] In fact, Malinovskii's presentation to the Party Congress seemed to be meant to get the point across in public that the political and military leadership were now in accord on matters that had been under contention since the 1960 "new strategy" speech. This was especially suggested by the pains Malinovskii took to allude to the joint sanction of the Party Presidium and the government for the military establishment's obligation to "devote special attention to the initial period of a possible war." (For the full statement made by Malinovskii on this point see Note A to Chapter 1, pp. 96–98).

tion program had been halted and the explicit military budget had been increased by one-third, while on the eve of the Party Congress itself, a resumption of nuclear testing—to include weapons of supermegaton yield—was announced. Although Khrushchev may have felt these moves were necessary mainly for their political-military effect during the Berlin crisis, they were, of course, favored by the military leadership. These concrete steps in a direction congenial to the military viewpoint had also been accompanied by Khrushchev's public retreat from some of the more extreme notions he had aired earlier, notably his views on the obsolescence of aircraft, ground forces, and the like.

The nexus of developments that led to a reframing of Soviet defense policies and a narrowing of the gap between Khrushchev's strategic formulations and the prevailing outlook of the military cannot be examined at length here. However, one might mention briefly such factors as the following:

The U-2 episode in May 1960, which raised questions as to how seriously Soviet military security may have been compromised by loss of secrecy.

General deterioration of the international situation following the abortive summit meeting in Paris in May 1960, which probably strengthened the hand of elements in the Soviet bureaucracy favoring sterner economic and defense policies than those with which Khrushchev had identified himself.

Resentment and morale problems within the armed forces, notably in the officer corps, which accompanied initiation of the troop-cut policy in 1960.

Status of the Soviet ICBM program, which in light of both technical and operational difficulties often associated with early generation systems may have raised doubts about over-reliance on such weapons and helped undermine Khrushchev's one-sided emphasis on them.

Technological developments leading to new evaluation of manned aircraft systems, such as Soviet development of a "stand-off capability" to deliver missiles from aircraft, and of very large-yield weapons, which in their early configuration might require delivery by aircraft.

U.S. reaction to revival of the Berlin crisis, taking the form in 1961 of U.S. defense budget increases, expansion of Polaris and Minuteman programs, measures to improve survivability and control of strategic forces, strengthening of conventional forces, etc.—all of which provided further pressure on the Soviet leaders for reappraisal of their military posture.

Concern within elements of the Soviet bureaucracy lest resource reallocation to improve consumer welfare and relieve such problems as the agricultural crisis be accomplished at the expense of defense requirements, with consequent pressure on Khrushchev to shift his policies.

In addition to the above factors, Soviet military policy considerations in the 1960–1961 period were probably affected to some extent by the Sino-Soviet dialogue, which became increasingly sharp from the fall of 1960 onward. While this dialogue did not immediately involve military doctrine in a narrow sense, it did bear on broad questions of the risk of war, the consequences of nuclear warfare, and the like. In general, the effect of the dispute with Peking may have been to bring Soviet military opinion and Khrushchev's thinking closer together to avoid leaving openings in the Soviet position that the Chinese could seek to exploit.

Dialogue Within the Military

Concurrent with the unfolding of events that helped alter the dialogue between Khrushchev and the military in the period leading up to and following the presentation of Malinovskii's "theses" to the XXIInd Party Congress, a secondary debate ran on within the military itself. This debate has involved two identifiable schools of military thought, although the lines between them have often tended to be somewhat blurred. In general, one school might be said to represent "modernists" and "radical innovators," the other, "traditionalists" and those of more or less conservative bent. Neither school, however, professes any interest in a return to the doctrinal environment of the Stalinist period.

The central theme of the modernist school has been the need to discard old doctrinal views and to develop new concepts to exploit modern technologies of war. The more extreme adherents of this school argue that the technology of the nuclear-missile age has "cancelled out all previous concepts of the character of war." [18] They therefore hold that military-theoretical thought must lose no time in working out new concepts and methods to utilize modern weaponry. Radical innovation based on "scientific prediction" of the character of future war is favored by this school rather than relying too much on the "generalized experience of past wars."[19]

The traditionalist school, on the other hand, has tended to caution against extremes and to argue for a more moderate course of military innovation. While not denying the powerful influence of new weaponry on military doctrine and forces, and the need for change, adherents of this school hold that time-tested concepts and practices should not be lightly thrown overboard for the mere sake of embracing something new. As one traditionalist has put it: "Some of our comrades, under the influence of great technical advances, show a tendency to underestimate and even ignore the experience

---

[18] Colonel P. Sidorov, "To Tirelessly Strengthen the Country's Defense Capability," *Kommunist vooruzhennykh sil (Communist of the Armed Forces)*, No.12, June 1961, pp. 63, 65.

[19] Colonel N. Sushko, *et al.*, "The Development of Marxist-Leninist Teaching on War under Modern Conditions," *Kommunist vooruzhennykh sil (Communist of the Armed Forces)*, No. 18, September 1961, pp. 27–28.

of past wars."[20] Theorists of this school in general favor an historical approach to working out a theory of future war, and they urge that development of new concepts should be combined with careful study of the past, especially of relevant lessons from World War II.[21]

In general, the modernist school, particularly the more extreme radical innovators among its adherents, might be said to represent a minority military outlook more sympathetic to Khrushchev's thinking than the majority viewpoint reflected by the traditionalist school. In fact, some of the radicals may be the conscious spokesmen of Khrushchev within the military. One military theorist who may belong in this category is Major General N. Talenskii, well known for his contributions to the doctrinal dialogue since the early post-Stalin period. It was Talenskii who in September 1953 took the first major step toward a revision of the Soviet view of warfare in the nuclear age with a ground-breaking article in the journal *Military Thought* entitled "On the Question of the Laws of Military Science." [22] He has since written periodically for both Soviet and international audiences, propagating through widely noted articles in 1960 and 1962 views on the character of nuclear warfare and its implications for international politics, which closely resemble those favored by Khrushchev.[23]

Among military men identifiable from their published views with one outlook or the other, the radical innovators as a rule appear to be less senior in rank than the traditionalists. However, a number of top-ranking officers in responsible posts, including Marshal Malinovskii, seem to have taken care not to become publicly identified too closely with extreme elements of either side, perhaps to preserve their freedom of action between political leaders like Khrushchev on the one hand, and their more conservative-minded military colleagues on the other.

As in the case of the dialogue between Khrushchev and the military, broad underlying pressures on Soviet strategy have been critical to the radical-traditionalist debate, even though the discussion has been carried on in the narrower idiom of military theory. One might say that these pressures come from three directions: economic, technological, and what the United States does or in future may do. The radical and traditionalist wings have, in general, expressed differing views in all three of these areas.

In the economic area, the traditionalists have tended to emphasize prefer-

---

[20] General P. Kurochkin, "On Study of the History of Military Art under Contemporary Conditions," *Voenno-istoricheskii zhurnal (Journal of Military History)*, No. 8, August 1961, p. 4.

[21] Marshal A.A. Grechko, "Military History and the Contemporary Scene," *Voenno-istoricheskii zhurnal (Journal of Military History)*, No. 2, February 1961, pp. 5–7.

[22] See Dinerstein, *op cit.*, pp. 36–49.

[23] Two of the widely circulated Talenskii articles were "Modern War: Its Character and Consequences," *International Affairs*, No. 10, October 1960; and "The 'Absolute Weapon' and the Problem of Security," *International Affairs*, No. 4, April 1962.

ential heavy industry-defense policies, placing themselves in the van of general military opposition to Khrushchev's efforts in 1960 and early 1961 to free a larger share of resources for other sectors of the economy. The radicals, on the other hand, seem to have felt that modern technology, even though expensive, offered the possibility of savings through reduction of large, traditionally oriented forces. Their position thus has tended to be more compatible with the economic development promises of the new Party Program announced in the summer of 1961 than that of the traditionalists. Within the sphere of military theory, these differences of outlook were reflected in 1960–1961 in a series of articles in the military press centering on such questions as the role of the economic factor in modern war and the problems of mobilization under nuclear conditions. In general, the prevailing line in this portion of the dialogue seemed to favor the traditionalist outlook. It was argued, for example, that modern military technology does not reduce the requirements for priority development of heavy industry and that economic preparation must be based on the expectation of supplying the country's military needs in a long war, rather than depending on strategic reserves prepared ahead of time.[24]

In the area of technology, the radical view has stressed the importance of not hobbling technological possibilities by waiting until technical advances become available in mass quantities before conceiving new ideas for their use. This has seemed to imply a radical leaning toward the notion that large investment of resources and scientific effort in research and development today will pay off handsomely in the future, and help compensate for the margin of U.S. industrial superiority. The traditionalist preference for maintaining large forces-in-being, by contrast, would imply a priority claim on presently available resources for this purpose.

With respect to the United States, both radical and traditionalist viewpoints have seemed to converge in cultivating an image of an enemy from whom only the worst can be expected, and hence, which allows no slackening of Soviet defense efforts. However, there has been some shading of view, with the radical outlook tending to reflect greater confidence in keeping the United States deterred from starting a war, or in breaking the U.S. will to resist by mass destruction attacks in case war should occur.

Down to the time when the collective authors of *Soviet Military Strategy* went to press in the spring of 1962, no clear-cut verdict had emerged for either side of the dialogue within the military between radical innovators and traditionalists. In fact, one might venture to say that as various practical decisions were taken in the defense policy area, they tended to be resolved in favor of what might best be described as a centrist viewpoint—roughly the ground occupied by Malinovskii between the radicals and traditionalists.

---

[24] Colonel General N. Lomov, "On Soviet Military Doctrine," *Kommunist vooruzhennykh sil* (*Communist of the Armed Forces*), No. 10, May 1962, p. 15.

External Strategic Dialogue Between Soviet-U.S. Leadership

Concurrent with both streams of internal dialogue that have been mentioned above, but not necessarily in precise phase with either of them, so to speak, was a third, an external dialogue on the strategic power balance between Soviet and U.S. leaders. The Soviet side of this external dialogue antedated Khrushchev's January 1960 new strategy speech somewhat, picking up momentum in the 1957–1960 period following the first Soviet ICBM test shot and Sputnik launching in the fall of 1957. In this external dialogue, the main thrust of Khrushchev's argument was that strategic superiority had shifted to the Soviet side. He supported this claim by conveying an exaggerated picture of Soviet ICBM strength, while at the same time questioning the efficacy of U.S. strategic forces, which were still obliged to rely mainly, as he put it, on "obsolete" bombers.[25]

Khrushchev's technique of exaggeration was more suggestive than explicit. He avoided documented claims of Soviet ICBM numbers, leaving the arithmetic of the so-called missile gap mainly to speculation in the Western press. However, well before the Soviet Union could count on an operational ICBM force of any meaningful size,[26] Khrushchev threatened that the USSR had the missile-nuclear capability to "wipe from the face of the earth" any countries that might dare to attack the Soviet Union or its allies.[27] This threat included the United States: "We have enough missiles for America, too," Khrushchev said.[28]

While Soviet military leaders associated themselves with the exaggerated missile claims Khrushchev was advancing down through early 1960 in the external dialogue with the West, they also may have been somewhat uneasy about these claims. One may venture to suppose that some of the military resistance to the new "Khrushchev doctrine" of January 1960 sprang from the feeling that it was stretching deterrence a bit thin.

After the U-2 episode in May 1960, there was an interesting shift in the

---

[25] Report by Comrade N. S. Khrushchev to the VIIth Session of the Supreme Soviet of the USSR, *Izvestiia,* May 8, 1957.

[26] The only specific figures that have been given for numbers of Soviet long-range missiles were interpolated in a January 19, 1963 speech by Khrushchev in East Germany. In referring to the withdrawal of Soviet medium-range missiles from Cuba, Khrushchev indicated that the United States was still covered by other missiles, by which he presumably meant ICBM's. The figure he used was "80, probably 120 missiles." Even so, his language as reported on this occasion (see *The Washington Post,* January 20, 1963) left some ambiguity as to whether he was referring to ICBM's aimed at the United States, or additional MRBM's. Incidentally, if Khrushchev's figure of 80 to 120 properly conveys the size of the Soviet ICBM force in 1963, then this further suggests that his claims of strategic superiority three years earlier were not founded on an ICBM force of appreciable size.

[27] Speech by N. S. Khrushchev at a Meeting of Soviet Journalists in the Kremlin, November 14, 1959, *Izvestiia,* November 18, 1959; N. S. Khrushchev, Report to the Supreme Soviet of the USSR, *Pravda,* January 15, 1960.

[28] Interview of N. S. Khrushchev by the Editors of the Social-Democratic Newspapers of the F. G. R., May 5, 1959, *Pravda,* May 9, 1959.

tone of Khrushchev's claims of Soviet strategic superiority. He became some-what more guarded with respect to the missile advantage claimed for the USSR, while, at the same time, asserting that the U-2 case proved that any bomber attacks against the Soviet Union were "doomed to failure." [29] He also displayed sensitivity to the implications for Soviet second-strike capa-bilities of loss of secrecy, first saying that American U-2 flights had not over-flown operational Soviet ICBM sites, and then adding that even if the location of missile sites were known, "It is impossible to put a missile base out of commission with one, two, or several blows. Missile technology now assures means for dealing a retaliatory blow in any case." [30]

In the fall of 1961, the U.S. side of the strategic dialogue underwent marked change when the United States began to express new confidence in the margin of Western strategic superiority. Several official statements by Secretaries Gilpatric, McNamara, and others explicitly confirmed the down-ward revision of U.S. estimates of Soviet missile strength. From this time on-ward, Soviet claims of strategic superiority have noticeably tended to be less extreme than those previously advanced by Khrushchev.

The main tendency of Soviet statements about the strategic balance has since been to argue for acceptance of strategic parity as the basis on which U.S.-Soviet policy should be conducted. For example, in an interview in January 1962 dealing specifically with the strategic balance, Malinovskii said: "Since our forces are equal, the American leaders should draw the correct conclusions and pursue a reasonable policy." [31] Khrushchev, in a speech in Moscow in July 1962, attacked an appraisal by McNamara three weeks earlier that the balance of forces favored the U.S.[32] However, Khrush-chev did not reaffirm Soviet superiority; rather he asserted that the mili-tary power balance could be determined only during the course of a war and ultimately by its outcome, and that therefore the United States had no justification for trying to apply a "position of strength" policy in dealing with the Soviet Union.

A particularly interesting aspect of the Soviet response to revised U.S. appraisal of the strategic balance was a renewed effort to impress on Euro-pean leaders that U.S. strategic power could not prevent their countries from being utterly destroyed in the event of war.[33] This line of response,

---

[29] Speech by N. S. Khrushchev at the Czechoslovakian Embassy in Moscow, *Pravda,* May 10, 1960.

[30] Speech of Comrade N. S. Khrushchev at the Third Congress of the Romanian Workers' Party, *Izvestiia,* June 23, 1960.

[31] Answers of Minister of Defense of the USSR Marshal R. Ia. Malinovskii to ques-tions of correspondents of *Pravda* in response to a speech by Secretary of the Defense of the United States, R. McNamara, *Pravda,* January 24, 1962.

[32] "General and Complete Disarmament: The Guarantee for Peace and Safety for All People," speech by N. S. Khrushchev to the World Congress for General Disarma-ment and Peace, July 10, 1962, *Pravda,* July 11, 1962.

[33] Cf. Alastair Buchan, "The New Soviet Strategy," *The Reporter,* November 9, 1961, p. 28.

somewhat more credible perhaps than attempting to intimidate the United States directly, indicated among other things that the concept of a "hostage Europe" was still a central element of Soviet strategic policy.[34]

Among other changes that appeared on the Soviet side of the strategic dialogue following revised U.S. estimates of Soviet ICBM numbers was a tendency to shift away from Khrushchev's "one weapon" emphasis on ICBM's and to allude more to the role and importance of other means of delivering nuclear weapons. Thus, Soviet statements began to dwell more on diversified Soviet strategic capabilities, including long-range rocket-carrying aircraft, submarine-launched missiles, and surface vessels armed with missiles, as well as ICBM's. Along with this emphasis on diversified strategic forces, there was a new attempt to establish an image of Soviet primacy in novel forms of weapons. Supermegaton bombs, "global" missiles, and anti-missile defenses fall into this category of claims. Supermegaton weapons in particular began to be treated in Soviet statements in such a way as to shift the focus of the dialogue from the relative size of U.S.-Soviet delivery forces to the greater destructive power of Soviet warheads.

On the whole, at the time the present volume was being prepared for publication, the Soviet Union was having some difficulty in holding up its side of the strategic dialogue with the United States. In a sense, the Soviet Union was laboring in the backwash of widely publicized and generally accepted assertions of Western strategic superiority, which no doubt generated further pressure on the Soviet leadership to repair the Soviet image in the world power balance.

*   *   *

What is not clear is whether the concessions on Khrushchev's part to the military point of view represent a wholehearted acceptance of that point of view, or whether the modifications in Khrushchev's point of view represent only a temporary response to an emergency situation. At the time Khrushchev had begun to alter his position and to adopt such measures in the summer of 1961 as suspension of the troop cut and an increase in the military budget, he had also, on several occasions, emphasized that these measures were "temporary" and "in the nature of a reply" to U.S. moves.[37] The implication was that Khrushchev might turn back to his previous program should an easing of tensions be achieved.

---

[34] Reporting on an interview with Khrushchev, Mr. Sulzberger of *The New York Times* wrote in 1961: "Quite blandly he asserts that these countries [Britain, France, Italy] are figuratively speaking hostages to the USSR and a guarantee against war." *Izvestiia*, September 9, 1961.

[37] For example, his speech to graduates of Soviet military academies on July 8, 1961, and his television address on August 7, 1961. *Pravda*, July 9, 1961; *Izvestiia*, August 9, 1961.

Moreover, while Khrushchev has publicly stepped away from his more extreme 1960 views on the one-sided dominance of missiles and nuclear weapons, and the obsolescence of conventional forces, he also continues on occasion to express opinions that leave some doubt as to where he stands on the role of various forces. For example, in early 1962 he said in a letter to President Kennedy that the outcome of a future war would be decisively settled by nuclear blows "before vast armies can be mobilized and thrown into battle." [38] More recently, in an interview with W. E. Knox, the head of Westinghouse International, he repeated the claim that surface navies are obsolete and said that he was spending a great deal of his time "eliminating obsolete weapons from the Soviet arsenal."[39]

Khrushchev's somewhat contradictory position on the question of the destructiveness of a nuclear war and the Soviet Union's prospects of victory if war should occur also suggests an area of continuing difference with military opinion. On the one hand, Khrushchev has gone farther than have most military spokesmen to picture the *mutually* destructive character of nuclear war. One of his more recent statements on the subject, in a speech before the VIth Congress of the East German Communist Party on January 16, 1963, put likely casualties at 700–800 million and cast strong doubt on the possibility that even a communist society could be rebuilt on the radioactive rubble of a nuclear war.[40]

On the other hand, as leader of the Soviet state, Khrushchev has found it necessary to aver that if war should occur, the Soviet Union would, despite its suffering, inevitably come out on top. This ambiguity in his position, when translated into terms of developing a Soviet military posture, seems to put Khrushchev potentially at odds with the professional military. Whereas the latter are primarily oriented toward building up the military forces and urging the civil preparations needed to make good the promise of Soviet victory in the event of war, Khrushchev's bent seems to lie in the direction of concentrating on weapons with maximum political effect and a high probability of discouraging war from starting in the first place. This situation imputes neither more nor less virtue to either party, but it does have the implication that Khrushchev's criteria for weapons selection and expenditure of resources on the Soviet defense establishment are likely to differ from the opinions of many of his professional military advisers.

Khrushchev's tendency to speak disparagingly of professional military opinion has been tempered somewhat since his widely quoted remark in late 1959 that "I do not trust the appraisal of generals on questions of strategic

---

[38] Message from the Chairman of the Council of Ministers of the USSR, N. S. Khrushchev to the President of the United States, John Kennedy, *Izvestiia,* February 24, 1962.

[39] W. E. Knox, "Close-up of Khrushchev during a Crisis," *The New York Times Magazine,* November 18, 1962, p. 129.

[40] Speech by Comrade N. S. Khrushchev to the VIth Congress of the German United Socialist Party, *Pravda,* January 17, 1963.

importance," [41] but he still continues to stress his own competence in the field of defense. For example, in an interview with Gardner Cowles in April 1962, while discussing nuclear weapons, Khrushchev said:

> As head of government I have to deal with questions of defense, and consequently, questions of modern means of warfare, and I have occasion to watch them [nuclear weapons] being tested. This is why I have a perfectly clear idea of their effects.[42]

In light of indications that Khrushchev may not always hold the opinions of his generals in high regard, it is worth noting that the present volume suggests, in a number of ways, that the same may be true in reverse. One example occurs in a section of Chapter 8, which contains a curious and somewhat fulsome exposition of the role and qualities of the top Soviet professional military leadership. On the one hand, the account has the tone of an apologia for the military leadership, painting their qualities large, stressing that in the modern age they must be soundly informed on and must apply themselves to matters extending far beyond the battlefield. This suggests that the military may be seeking to defend themselves against criticism that they are encroaching on Khrushchev's political side of the house.

On the other hand, while stressing the close link of top Soviet generals with the Party and their responsiveness to the will of the people, the account also seems to hint that some affairs are best left in the hands of experienced military leaders, which might suggest that the military feel their own domain is being encroached on by Khrushchev. A particularly interesting passage in this connection (p. 496) makes the point that history affords no examples of an army "led by inexperienced military leaders successfully waging war against an army led by an experienced military leader."

There is other internal evidences in the present volume that may reflect a delicate species of in-fighting between Khrushchev and the military. Throughout the work, for example, an ambivalent attitude can be found toward Khrushchev's individual contributions to Soviet military doctrine and strategy. While there are frequent references to him, care seems to be taken not to portray him as a uniquely endowed military genius. Indeed, in a significant passage on military doctrine that may have been written with Khrushchev partly in mind, the book emphasizes (pp. 130–131) that "military doctrine is not thought out or compiled by a single person or group of persons," but rather is the result of a "quite complex and lengthy historical process," and expresses "the general political line of the State's ruling social class" on questions of war and national defense.

---

[41] This statement was made at a Kremlin press conference on November 8, 1959, where Khrushchev remarked that "strategy is enunciated by generals" before going on to say that he did not trust their opinions. Reported in *The New York Times*, November 9, 1959, p. 4.

[42] Interview of N. S. Khrushchev by American publisher G. Cowles, April 20, 1962, *Pravda*, April 27, 1962.

This passage on military doctrine may point to a deeper unresolved issue between Khrushchev and the military than first meets the eye. To elaborate briefly, in the months following presentation of Malinovskii's theses of a new "Soviet military doctrine" in October 1961, there was a noticeable trend in the Soviet military press to expand on the military's share of credit for developing the new doctrine, and to emphasize the significance of the doctrine as a basis for state policy.[43] This appeared tantamount to arguing a case for increased military influence [on] policy-making in an area traditionally reserved to the political leadership. The present work, which was in preparation during the same period, carries this line of argument forward by seeking to equate Soviet military doctrine with the most fundamental and durable conceptions of state interest and national security, and to divorce its formulation from the competence of individual leaders. This would appear to be a challenge that Khrushchev could hardly afford to let go unheeded, for it implies that the military leadership is seeking to put itself in a position to bend policy decisions in a direction responsive to its own concept of national interests.

Even though this challenge is more implicit than explicit in the present work, the volume itself represents, in a sense, a point scored for the military side of the argument by getting the military viewpoint on the record in the form of the first comprehensive exposition of the new doctrine. Khrushchev is thus put in a position where any future efforts to substitute his own strategic conceptions for those acceptable to the prevailing military outlook would be made more difficult. At the least, he would probably find it hard to dictate on technical military matters without winning some authoritative professional military opinion over to his side, which suggests a continuation of essentially the same sort of problem he has faced up to now.

From Khrushchev's standpoint, the very fact that he cannot simply knock military heads together to get agreement with his views means that it is to his advantage to stimulate discussion and debate among the military up to some point, precisely to avoid finding himself boxed in by a unanimous military viewpoint. The radical-traditionalist dialogue within the military thus serves his ends by preventing the formation of a solid front of military opinion with which he would have to contend. To the extent, therefore, that the present volume reflects a continuation of the radical-traditionalist dialogue, Khrushchev presumably would regard it as a not unwelcome addition to the library of contemporary Soviet military thought.

*   *   *

---

[43] Among articles deserving note in this connection were: Colonel General N. Lomov, *op. cit.*, pp. 11–22; Colonel I. Sidel'nikov, "On Soviet Military Doctrine," *Red Star*, May 11, 1962; V. Siniagin, "Creation of the Material-Technical Base of Communism and Strengthening of the Defense Capacity of the USSR," *Kommunist vooruzhennykh sil* (*Communist of the Armed Forces*), No. 14, July 1962, pp. 8–16.

PEKING'S MILITARY CALCULUS[1]

Davis B. Bobrow

CHINESE COMMUNIST military policy significantly affects our preparations for war and hopes for peace. However, we have few public studies of Chinese military policy and the reasoning on which it rests.[2] This article tries to set forth the calculus or rationale which Peking employs to select military strategy and tactics. In other words, it makes no attempt to attack or defend Chinese military policy or to appraise that policy's specific strengths and weaknesses. It does try to locate the important factors that operate in the minds of Chinese decision-makers and Peking's perception of the consequences of different tactical choices. When we say that the Chinese have a calculus for military policy, we do not mean to imply that it works well or badly. We do imply that the Chinese have a military calculus which imposes a predictable pattern on their military policy. Obviously, an identical military calculus does not operate in the minds of all Chinese leaders. Accordingly, "Peking thinks" is shorthand for the "averaged" views that can be induced from the public record of Chinese words and acts.

The following analysis rests on three assumptions. First, Peking's actions and words indicate her policy at least as validly as Yugoslav, Soviet, and Western interpretations.[3] Helpfully, the Sino-Soviet dispute has led the

[1] This article was completed in January 1963. The author is indebted to Richard A. Falk, Morton Gorden, Peter Paret, Thomas P. Thornton, and Daniel Tretiak for their helpful criticism and to Andrea Herzog for research assistance.

[2] The most relevant are: A. Doak Barnett, "The Inclusion of Communist China in an Arms Control Program," *Daedalus,* Vol. 89 (Fall 1960), 831–45; Robert W. Barnett, *Quemoy: The Use and Consequence of Nuclear Deterrence* (Cambridge, Mass., 1960); Alice Langley Hsieh, *The Chinese Genie: Peking's Role in the Nuclear Test Ban Negotiations* (Santa Monica 1960), and *Communist China's Strategy in the Nuclear Era* (Englewood Cliffs 1960); Tang Tsou, "Mao's Limited War in the Taiwan Strait," *Orbis,* III (Fall 1959), 332–50; Allen S. Whiting, *China Crosses the Yalu* (New York 1960); Donald S. Zagoria, *The Sino-Soviet Conflict, 1956–1961* (Princeton 1962).

[3] This article is based on Chinese Communist mass media items. The following sources were used: For the period from January 1960 through June 1962, *Current Background* (hereafter cited as *CB*), *Survey of the China Mainland Press* (hereafter cited as *SCMP*), *Extracts from China Mainland Magazines,* later changed to *Selections from China Mainland Magazines* (hereafter cited as *ECMM* and *SCMM*). These translations are produced by the U.S. Consulate-General, Hong Kong. Also consulted for the same period were the mainland press translations of the U.S. Joint Publications Research Service of Washington (hereafter cited as *JPRS*). *Peking Review* (hereafter cited as *PR*), an English-language publication for overseas consumption, was used for

Chinese to argue openly and explictly for their interpretation of enemy behavior (that is, of the United States) and Communist foreign policy objectives (the takeover of the developing nations). Internal economic failures
have provoked a debate about the relations of economic growth and military
capability. Second, Peking's leaders are politicians practicing the art of the
possible; dogmatic and rigid ends do not require Chinese leaders to ignore
political, economic, and military realities in reaching them. In other words,
Peking's leaders resemble those of other nations to this extent: they adopt
what they believe to be the best available military policy to cope with what
they perceive to be the challenges of foreign opponents, to attain their
foreign ambitions, and to satisfy domestic political and economic needs.
Third, Peking's leaders evaluate current military policy alternatives on the
basis of what they have learned from their military successes or failures in
the past.

Accordingly, this article uses mainland sources to analyze four components
of China's military calculus: expectations regarding the United States,
foreign goals, domestic requirements, and interpretations of previous military
experience. After completing these four explorations, we should have
Peking's military "frame of reference." In other words, we should know the
dangers Peking perceives, the value and cost of the means Peking believes it
has available, and the preconceptions which operate when Chinese policy-
makers make military choices. As the reader will see, we can conclude from
each exploration that Peking integrates three methods in its military policy.
The first is political bargaining, based on the possession of a powerful military establishment and the credibility that it will be used. The second is
participation in wars that require a small investment of resources in combat
and do not risk a large-scale Western military response. The third is a conscious policy of unilateral arms control.[4]

I. THE ENEMY: AMERICA

Mao Tse-tung has stated in capsule form the Peking assessment of American objectives, policies, and capabilities. In a long-term, political sense the
Americans are "paper tigers," but in a short-term, military sense they are
"living tigers, iron tigers, real tigers which can eat people."[5] Tigers spring
on easy meals and when cornered. Until you can dispatch the tiger with

---

the period from January 1960 through November 1962. The methodology applied to
these materials is discussed in Zagoria, 24–35; and Myron Rush, "Esoteric Communication in Soviet Politics," *World Politics*, XI (July 1959), 614–20.

[4] By "arms control" I mean: "Adjustments in military postures and doctrines that
induce reciprocal adjustments by a potential opponent . . . reduce the danger of a
war that neither side wants, or contain its violence, or otherwise serve the security of
the nation."—Thomas C. Schelling and Morton H. Halperin, *Strategy and Arms
Control* (New York 1961), 143.

[5] Mao Tse-tung, *Selected Works,* IV (Peking 1961), 99.

ease yourself, you avoid becoming an easy meal and do not back the tiger into a corner; you do attempt to weaken him by setting him on unrewarding chases that sap his energy. These are the principles which explain Chinese military policy toward this country.

China assigns this goal to the United States: to "destroy the socialist camp" in order to achieve "world domination,"[6] and perceives the goal as unalterable ("a wolf is a wolf which cannot be turned into a sheep"[7]). All American elites are committed to this goal. The crucial "monopoly capital groups" require "arms expansion and war preparations."[8] As for our Arms Control and Disarmament Agency, its executives are a "pack of notorious warmongers and armaments industry bosses."[9] However, Peking sees three other American characteristics that affect the pursuit of this threatening objective of world domination. First, the American leaders and masses have little taste for the costs of war; they are "sated with bread and sleep."[10] Second, the American public's fear of "another world war" can restrain its leaders.[11] Third, the American desire to avoid costly conflict is accompanied by calculation of the costs and gains of a particular type of war at a given time and place. This calculation can induce the United States to postpone its goal; it will refrain from nuclear war if war will "not pay."[12]

In Peking's eyes, American advocacy of arms control or acts of military restraint follow from these three modifying characteristics. They in no way indicate a change in the fundamental and hostile American objective. American advocacy of arms control and disarmament, "the soft and deceptive approach," is only an attempt to secure an improved "opportunity for attack."[13] For example, the United States advocates inspection to secure more military intelligence.[14] American military restraint indicates to Peking that the United States feels the costs of nuclear war are too high. The Chinese leaders conclude that in spite of its expansionist goal, the United

---

[6] Jen Ku-ping, "The Tito Group: A Detachment of U.S. Imperialism in Its 'Grand Strategy' of Counter-Revolution," *PR*, v (October 12, 1962),13.

[7] Chou Ch'ih-p'ing, "Comrade Lin Piao in the Period of Liberation War in the Northwest," *Chung-kuo Chi'ing-nien*, No. 8 (1960), in *SCMM*, No. 217 (1960), 35.

[8] "JMJP Commentator on Kennedy's Urgent Needs," *NCNA-English* Peking (May 29, 1961), in *SCMP*, No. 8 (1962), 4.

[9] Mao Tun, "The Way to General Disarmament and World Peace," *PR*, v (July 20, 1962), 9.

[10] Mao Tse-tung, 21.

[11] "Excellent Situation for Peace Struggle Says Red Flag Article," *NCNA-English* Peking (December 31, 1959), in *SCMP*, No. 2171 (1960), 4.

[12] I Yu, "U.S. Foreign Policy Seen Through Kennedy's Messages," *Shih-chieh Chih-shih*, Nos. 3–4 (1962), in *SCMM*, No. 307 (1962), 6.

[13] Fu Chung, "The Great Victory of Mao Tse-tung's Military Dialectics," *Jen-min Jih-pao* (October 6–7, 1960), in *JPRS*, No. 4282 (1960), 3.

[14] "JMJP Censors U.S. Stand at Geneva Disarmament Conference," *NCNA-English* Peking (April 3, 1962), in *SCMP*, No. 2715 (1962), 23; "JMJP Observer on U.S. Scheme over Disarmament Talks," *NCNA-English* Peking (February 19, 1962), in *SCMP*, No. 2685 (1962), 33.

States will refrain from "escalating" local wars into "world war." [15] America has not escalated to nuclear war when faced with Communist revolution (Vietnam, Laos), counterrevolution (Hungary), or conventional war (Korea).[16] The Kennedy administration has publicly confirmed America's desire to avoid escalation. It develops conventional war capabilities in order to have a "choice" in military response.[17] Even the American turn to sub-limited war tactics is confirmation of the nation's softness; the appeal of this tactic is that American regulars will not have to be sent abroad.[18]

Peking is convinced that America can be induced not to apply her military capabilities. Since "even in the period when the U.S. imperialists had a monopoly of atomic bomb secrets, the bellicose elements dared not launch atomic war," [19] Peking concludes that there are "two possibilities, not one" with regard to world war.[20] China must present an image to the United States that promises high American costs in any attempt to attack the "socialist camp." China can communicate to the United States that it desires to avoid military action, fears nuclear war, and is willing to make non-military concessions. Such a course only lowers the American estimate of costs; it does not alter the desire of the United States for world domination. Accordingly, Washington at least will increase its demands for concessions in arms control and elsewhere; if "given an inch," it will "ask for a yard." [21] The United States will engage in more regional, conventional wars like the Korean conflict.[22] Most seriously, such a "soft" image may convince Washington that "the balance of power is in favour of imperialism";[23] the United States will then initiate a nuclear war.

Peking also rejects the opposite image—i.e., one of Communist capability and eagerness to eliminate the United States immediately. To emphasize this, it feels, will only frighten Washington into a nuclear "struggle before final doom." [24] Instead, Peking contends there is a middle ground, an image

---

[15] Mao Tun, 11.

[16] Chinese People's Institute of Foreign Affairs, ed., *Two Tactics, One Aim: An Exposure of the Peace Tricks of U.S. Imperialism* (Peking 1960), 38; "Peking Rally Backs Tokyo Conference," *PR*, v (August 31, 1962), 9.

[17] Mao Tun, 8.

[18] Yuan Lu, "Kennedy and the New Frontiers of U.S. Policy of Aggression," *Shih-chieh Chih-shih*, No. 10 (1961), in *SCMM*, No. 270 (1961), 7.

[19] "Excellent Situation for Peace Struggle," 4.

[20] Wu Chiang, "Our Age and Edvard Kardelj's Dialectics," *Hung Ch'i*, No. 5 (1962), in *SCMM*, No. 306 (1962), 25.

[21] Sung Tu, "Answers to Readers' Queries on War and Peace," *Chung-kuo Ch'ing-nien*, No. 4 (1960), in *ECMM*, No. 207 (1960), 6.

[22] Yu Chao-li, "The Great Significance of the Victory of the Cuban People's Patriotic Struggle Against U.S. Imperialism," *Hung Ch'i*, Nos. 9–10 (1961), in *SCMM*, No. 262 (1961), 7; "The Great Victory in the Struggle to Resist U.S. Aggression and Aid Korea," *Jen-min Jih-pao* (October 24, 1960), in *PR*, iii (November 1, 1960), 13.

[23] Jen Ku-ping, 15.

[24] "Hsiao Hua's Speech at National Conference of Outstanding Workers and Groups in Culture and Education," *NCNA* Peking (June 3, 1960), in *CB*, No. 622 (1960), 30.

of Chinese military preparedness and courage but also one of willingness to make partial compromises. This image will lead the United States to conclude that the time is not ripe for a military showdown, and to make concessions to postpone and terminate conflict. Washington will give way in order to settle conflicts at the conference table—e.g., as in Korea—and to reach arms control agreements.[25] This image also will strengthen the influence of the American moderates, i.e., advocates of "political scheming" rather than war, and may even lead to partial "peaceful coexistence." [26]

The challenge to the Peking policy-maker is to find the behavior pattern that best communicates this middle image. Peking recognizes that its choice is severely limited by the relative military strength of the People's Republic and the United States. Peking's military weaknesses restrict her ability to make American costs unrewarding in a nuclear or massive conventional war. The Chinese leaders recognize nuclear inferiority in their military policy of "self-dependence," [27] i.e., deterring American attack without the benefit of the Soviet nuclear shield. Peking also feels unqualified for massive conventional war with the United States. Such conflicts enable America to use her "industrial potential," to achieve economic prosperity, and to maintain Western solidarity and anti-Communist attitudes. Conversely, massive conventional conflict is the "best means to wear out the resources of Socialist countries." [28] Accordingly, China must avoid such conflicts through a two-pronged policy: (a) convince the United States that their cost is high; and (b) refrain from provoking the United States to wage such wars. Peking believes that a nuclear capability will lend credibility to its threats of a costly conflict. In the meantime, and also after China enters the nuclear club, the second part of this policy requires her to avoid direct, formal confrontation of official Chinese and official American forces. An important example is the Quemoy crisis of 1958.[29] When she acquires a nuclear capability, China may test the United States more often, but not necessarily embark on direct conflict more readily.

Peking feels that a policy of sub-limited war by proxy (the military component of "wars of national liberation") and small-scale conventional war

---

[25] "JMJP Editorial on Korea's Peaceful Unification," *NCNA-English* Peking (June 25, 1961), in *SCMP*, No. 2529 (1961), 41; "Chinese Delegate Speaks at World Peace Council Bureau Meeting," *NCNA-English* Peking (July 14, 1960), in *SCMP*, No. 2300 (1960), 26.

[26] "JMJP—A Summary of the First Six Months of the Kennedy Administration," *NCNA-English* Peking (August 2, 1961), in *SCMP*, No. 2555 (1961), 35; Mao Tun, 9.

[27] Ch'en K'e-han, "Overcoming Difficutlies, Winning Victories—On First Reading of the Fourth Volume of Selected Works of Mao Tse-tung," *Chung-kuo Ch'ing-nien*, No. 21 (1960), in *SCMM*, No. 240 (1960), 10.

[28] Hsin Ting, "Adventuresome and Weak Character of the Kennedy Administration," *Chung-kuo Ch'ing-nien*, No. 17 (1961), in *SCMM*, No. 285 (1961), 1–2.

[29] See Robert W. Barnett; Hsieh; Tang Tsou; Zagoria; and John R. Thomas, "Soviet Behavior in the Quemoy Crisis," *Orbis*, vi (Spring 1962), 38–64.

on her borders can demonstrate Chinese strength and militancy to the
United States without provoking Washington. Peking feels that China's particular strengths make the cost to America of countering such military initiatives unappealingly high. If combined with a variety of arms control measures, the United States can be induced not to escalate the conflict.

Peking perceives that sub-limited wars let her use her greater ability to
organize dedicated insurgents and render America's complex weapons and
logistical systems inapplicable. "Political force" and "subjective effort" can
produce combat victory; they can secure the "loyalty of the people" which
is decisive in guerrilla war.[30] These advantages are maximized by China's
geopolitical position in her area of prime interest, Asia. Peking believes that
America is particularly likely to attach high costs to sub-limited war in
Southeast Asia. For the United States, Southeast Asia is far away both
physically and emotionally. China doubts that "soft" Americans will support
protracted, bloody involvement at a military disadvantage in a low-priority
part of the world.

Arms control in conjunction with such military pressure is expected to
prevent American escalation. Conflicts should be kept within the boundaries
of one nation; Peking opposes Communist forces "resisting the enemy outside of the national boundaries."[31] In other words, official Chinese armed
forces should not wage war significantly beyond Peking's self-defined national boundaries. For the most part, they should not wage war in independent
states on which China makes territorial claims. Peking expects the United
States to be persuaded by this policy that the stakes in the conflict are not
valuable enough to warrant escalation. Battles and wars, though continual,
should be of limited duration; Communists should apply the "principle of
truce."[32] Such interruptions will damp American concern, and lessen attention to the conflict and thus the possibility of escalation. The scale of
weapons used should be confined to non-nuclear, ground-warfare instruments, because to take advantage of its military strengths the United States
would have to make a deliberate decision to escalate the conflict.

Recently, China has applied the techniques of time and weapons limitation to the Indian border conflict.[33] They have had the results predicted by
Peking. Washington did not escalate the conflict even to the level of air war
nor feel that India was in such danger that massive American intervention
was necessary. American media and policy-makers' statements attributed intense and unflagging militancy to the People's Republic.

---

[30] Liao Kai-lung, "Dare to Carry out Revolution, Dare to Win Victory—Some Notes
on the Study of the Fourth Volume of the Selected Works of Mao Tse-tung," *Chung-
kuo Ch'ing-nien*, No. 19 (1960), in *SCMM*, No. 235 (1960), 13; Sung Tu, 1; Fan Ke,
"The Orientation of Political Work for the Army," *Jen-min Jih-pao* (July 28, 1961),
in *SCMP*, No. 2556 (1962), 5.

[31] Fu Chung, 19.

[32] Mao is quoted in Tang Tsou, 333.

[33] Brig. Gen. W. F. K. Thompson, "When Two Empires Meet," *Survival*, v (March–
April 1963), 79–80.

To convey the desired image to the United States, Peking unilaterally initiates these arms control measures. So long as the United States refrains from escalating the conflict, Peking feels that its interests are well-served. It recognizes difficulties and limitations in dealing from a weak military hand. However, only this policy of limited aggression is seen as able to buy time to create a more effective military establishment, time to overcome the "backwardness in the technical equipment" of the People's Liberation Army.[34] America will grant sufficient time to the People's Republic only under the suasion of carefully limited military pressure.

II. FOREIGN POLICY: GOALS AND MEANS

The immediate objectives of Communist China's military policy are to remove the American military presence from her periphery and to secure dominant influence in the developing nations. Southeast Asia is the top-priority target for this second objective. Peking seeks the military policy most likely to overcome the obstacles that Washington poses to both goals, and that Moscow poses to the second. In some cases she competes with the United States and the Soviet Union for the friendship of local governments, e.g., in Burma; in others she competes with the Soviet Union for control of the local Communist or anti-Western movement.

Peking perceives Chinese and American objectives as fundamentally opposed. Washington will never consent to the "peaceful expansion of the revolution." [35] Instead, America intends to "monopolize the vast intermediate area between the U.S. and the socialist camp" as a prelude to "attacking the socialist camp." [36] Washington uses two tactics to block Peking. The "hard" tactic is the threat of military, and even nuclear, retaliation if friendly and neutralist governments are overthrown. The American "soft" tactic is the bribery of foreign aid—"sugar-coated cannonballs"—to maintain and expand Western influence. Washington hopes that this "conquer the heart" tactic will "corrode revolutionary will." [37]

Peking seeks the military policy that will prove U.S. military threats to be sheer bluff and aid offers to be completely exploitative. Additionally, the Chinese want a military policy that will block Soviet attempts to reach accommodation with Western or non-aligned governments, and/or force Moscow to appear as a selfish, *status quo* power. However, Peking's range

---

[34] Fu Chung, 31.

[35] Liao Kai-lung, in *JPRS,* No. 6743 (1961), 41.

[36] Sung Tu, 6.

[37] Tsui Ch'in, T'an Wen-jui, "Comment on the Present Foreign Policy of the United States," *Shih-chieh Chih-shih,* No. 6 (1960), in *SCMM,* No. 213 (1960), 11; Liu Chang-sheng, "On the Question of War and Peace," *PR,* III (April 26, 1960), 14. The Chinese are aware that the Soviets also offer such a cannonball in connection with their disarmament and peaceful coexistence proposals. Liu rejects the very aid to the underdeveloped nations that the Soviets propose. For the Soviet inducement, see G. Mirsky and L. Stepanov, *Asia and Africa: A New Era* (Moscow, n.d.).

of choice is limited by two constraints. First, China cannot afford to provoke the United States into a test of conventional or nuclear military capability. Second, she cannot afford to press so hard that the governments of developing nations turn to Washington for protection. When China acquires a nuclear capability, her leaders expect the United States' provocation threshold to be higher, and the confidence of other nations in American protection to be lower.

For the present, Peking feels that the military policy summarized in the preceding section respects these two constraints and best copes with the challenges of Washington and Moscow. It seems useful to review the aggressive and the restrained segments of this policy and to point out how Peking expects each to contribute to its foreign goals.

The aggressive segment contains two distinct military tactics. First, China supports indigenous Communist proxies in sub-limited wars of national liberation. Second, on rare occasions China initiates carefully limited conventional war against non-American military units on her borders. In the first case, Chinese participation is indirect; it is confined to aid in the form of small arms, training programs, and advisors. In both cases, China feels that the United States will not escalate the conflict, but will reveal the hollowness of its military threats. If Washington shuns any military response, Peking expects significantly to reduce fear of apply military pressure to non-Communist regimes. If Washington responds to the sub-limited war in kind, Peking feels this will confirm the fundamentally hostile nature of the United States. The sugar-coated aid offers will be revealed for the devious instruments they really are. The Chinese leadership also expects these two aggressive tactics to have desirable effects on the Soviet position. If a Chinese-instigated war of national liberation is launched, the Russians are confronted with a series of undesirable choices. They can oppose the insurgents or ignore the conflict, and not compete with Peking for insurgent loyalties. On the other hand, they can become the major backer of the insurgents—as they have, for example, in Laos—and undermine other foreign policy moves to lessen tension with Washington. In either event, Peking makes some gain. Direct Chinese border incursions against a non-aligned country also confront Moscow with undesirable choices. For example, in the Indian case, if Moscow supported Peking, the Kremlin's wooing of non-aligned nationalists would suffer. Even Soviet non-support of India makes Chinese friendship seem more essential to Asian governments, especially those on China's borders, than that of the Soviet Union. If the USSR instead supported India, the unity of the international Communist movement decline still further, and with it Russian influence. The CPR expects any of these Soviet choice to serve its own foreign policy goals.

Peking expects to benefit by not applying these aggressive tactics to all target societies. Target selectivity will induce the uninvolved local governments neither to support China's victim nor to invoke American protection. Accordingly, military pressure on India has been accompanied by conciliation of Pakistan, with the predicted results. To select the target for a national-liberation war, Peking looks for the "most reactionary" society available.[38] Chinese-supported attacks on this target are expected to have significant military and political advantages. Militarily, any American sub-limited military response is crucially handicapped; it is relatively easy for the Communist insurgents to secure popular support. Politically, governments in the region that are already critical of the target society are likely to be critical of American intervention in its defense. These political effects are most easily attained if the target regime is not a member of the "non-aligned club." Of course, the regimes aligned with the United States are particularly important targets for Peking. China can identify its revolutionary clients with the unexceptionable causes of nationalism and social change. She can more easily portray the United States as guided by imperialist and selfish economic motives. South Vietnam and Laos have provided such targets with the predicted results.

Peking's selection of a few of the available targets is one part of its unilateral arms control policy. It is combined with the restrictions of geography, time, and weapons discussed earlier. This ensemble of arms control measures is expected to curtail Washington's military response and the neutralists' reactions to aggression. If either type of military agression is confined to one state, other local governments will not feel sufficiently threatened to cooperate against Peking. The war is either a "domestic" conflict or a border skirmish which will be widened only if the United States interferes. If conflicts do not continue for many months, neutralist governments will not make the "painful reappraisal" necessary to cause them to ally with the United States. Peking feels it can commit and support military aggression without disturbing the cherished neutralism of uninvolved governments. These governments will not even be shaken enough to divert resources from economic development to expand their military capability. Peking's predictions and techniques have been confirmed on the Indian border. Asian and African governments have been more concerned with reestablishing peace than with India's territorial integrity.

We should note that Peking's policy—i.e., to stimulate local revolutionary forces without evoking a United States response for a pro-American policy by other third-world governments—is not served by formal, multilateral arms control agreements. Such agreements could lead potential insurgents to feel that Peking is exploiting them for its own purposes. They could lead them to question Peking's claim that America is unswervingly hostile to independent national development. Of course, Peking can negotiate with

---

[38] Mao is quoted in Tang Tsou, 333.

the United States to confirm its negative interpretation of American objectives. The failure of negotiations serves the Chinese as proof of the "evil" nature of the West.[39] In contrast, unilateral and tacit arms control behavior avoids pitfalls in foreign expansion without sapping revolutionary morale.

III. DOMESTIC REQUIREMENTS: ECONOMIC AND POLITICAL

Domestically, the Chinese Communists seek to develop an industrialized, technologically complex economy and to exact total effort and loyalty from the population. Domestic success is necessary to deter the United States and to attain China's foreign policy goals. Peking, as we have seen, believes that military action is necessary to buy time for internal development.

Peking can fulfill its domestic requirements only if it overcomes fundamental economic and political obstacles. Economically, the regime is plagued by scarcities of capital, equipment, and skilled personnel. Moscow will not significantly ease these shortages. Somehow these resources must be stretched to cover both "economic construction" and "national defense construction." Politically, the specialists and the general population must be convinced that the development programs are worth the effort. They must be convinced that the severity of the American threat demands rapid development and "national defense construction." Simultaneously, they must be convinced that the American threat is not great enough to make their efforts meaningless—that their choice is not "capitalist or dead."

China's military policy must help fill these requirements. It must be economically cheap, but deter Washington from destroying mainland economic facilities. It must communicate to the people that China is strong enough not to give in to America, but too weak to deemphasize military research, development, and production. Peking's military policy must make the United States demonstrate that it is not benign enough to leave China alone, but not ferocious enough to obliterate mainland society. For these reasons, the regime claims that Washington does not intend to make a "traditional . . . declaration of war," and forbids its propagandists to cause the people to be "uneasy and uncomfortable" about war.[40] In sum, Peking believes that its domestic requirements demand the attitudes and internal loyalty of an aggressive military posture without its risks and costs.

Peking applies these requirements to arrive at two guidelines to military policy. First, the larger the scale of the war, the more it inhibits economic

---

[39] Chang Ming-yang, "Use Two Tactics of Revolution to Oppose Two Tactics of Counter-Revolution—Notes on Study of the Selected Works of Mao Tse-tung, Vol. IV," *Shih-chieh Chih-shih*, No. 20 (1960), in *SCMM*, No. 239 (1960), 35.

[40] Huang Kang, "A Few Things of Kennedy," *Hung Ch'i*, No. 13 (1961), in *SCMM*, No. 271 (1961), 5; Ch'en Ya-ting, "A Condemnation of Bogus Socialist Literature," *Kuang-ming Jih-pao* (August 6, 1960), in *JPRS*, No. 6660 (1961), 43.

development. More resources are diverted from industrial expansion and agricultural labor; the United States is more likely to destroy existing facilities. This guideline will still apply after China detonates a nuclear device. Second, successful sub-limited wars do not interfere with economic development and help instill desirable political attitudes. They demonstrate to the Chinese people that the United States is hostile and that Peking can safely defy Washington. Economically, they are at least cheap. More positivley, sub-limited wars and small-scale border clashes may bring other nations to trade with China on favorable terms. Newly installed Communist regimes will be heavily dependent on the People's Republic; cowed non-aligned regimes will want to avoid becoming China's next target.

The military policy previously summarized conforms to these general guidelines. Once again, formal multilateral arms controls clash with Peking's goals. In contrast, unilateral and tacit arms control behavior lowers the risk of provoking the United States, but does not hinder the maintenance of a domestic climate of national crisis. Domestic requirements add to the previously summarized policy two military measures with arms control significance. The first of these measures is to limit the size of the People's Liberation Army. In order to minimize the loss of able-bodied manpower in production, only a small proportion of the available male youth is conscripted each year. This unilateral restriction seems to be observed regardless of fluctuations in the number of American military personnel. It is, of course, compatible with Peking's intent to avoid the types of war that might require a massive commitment of Chinese troops.

The second measure is the emphasis on command and control of the military establishment. Political officers, Party committees, and political indoctrination programs are used to prevent the military from "catching" the popular discontent produced by forced-draft economic development and social change. However, the Party also emphasizes that these mechanisms must be used to reduce the possibility of escalation by overzealous field commanders. Since the Party center and not the military knows best, the latter cannot evaluate the real value of local victory. Peking attempts to keep the officer corps free of "petty bourgeois intellectuals" whose "revolutionary impatience" leads them into "disastrous and clumsy" military overcommitment. Officers are allegedly cleansed of the "peasant" mentality that might prompt them to "hang on stubbornly to local matters." [41]

IV. CONFIRMING EXPERIENCE: REVOLUTIONARY LESSONS

The Chinese elite naturally tends to judge present military policy alternatives in the light of previous success and failure; it attempts to secure cadre

---

[41] Fu Chung, 25.

support by manipulating history to confirm current policy. Recent official interpretations of the "most precious historical experience" of the revolution stress three "lessons." [42] First, when the Communists failed to prepare for armed struggle, the enemy attacked. Second, when the Communists confused or overestimated military capability and political support, they suffered severe defeat. Third, when they participated in negotiations and truces, they secured the means for eventual military and political success.

When the Communists did not present a formidable military front, the enemy attacked the unready victim. During the first alliance with the Kuomintang (1924–1927), such Communist naiveté allowed Chiang Kai-shek to exterminate a large proportion of the Party. The Nationalists also interpreted Communist trust and compliance as invitations to attack. The lowered credibility of an effective Communist military response led to the massacre of much of the New Fourth Army (1941). At the present time, if Peking fails to expand its military capability and demonstrate its militancy, the United States will similarly attack.

Political support and military capability are mutually interdependent. When Communists forgot the need for both, or deluded themselves into overoptimistic estimates, they met disaster. Four variants of this fallacy are often cited. First, Party members falsely concluded that political strength negated overwhelming military disadvantage; e.g., the bloody failure of the Canton rising (1927). Second, they falsely concluded that military ventures did not require organized political support; e.g., the short-lived seizure of Nanchang (1927). Third, they deluded themselves that a relative increase in military strength warranted escalation of the armed struggle; e.g., the Li Li-san line of attack on the cities (1930). Fourth, they foolishly equated holding territory with preserving strength and thus undermined the Communist military capability; e.g., the rigid resistance to Chiang's Fifth Bandit Extermination Campaign (1933–1934). The lesson drawn stresses the virtues of patience, attention to both military and political factors, and temporary retreat. Regardless of enemy "challenges and incitements," China must "avoid a decisive battle until the objective conditions are favorable." [43] Otherwise, military defeat will be compounded by political attrition, i.e., "isolation from the masses." [44] These lessons are fully compatible with the policy of carefully controlled sub-limited war and conventional military pressure on China's borders. They also argue against a sharp change in

---

[42] The interpretation of revolutionary antecedents is drawn from Ho Kan-Chih, *A History of the Modern Chinese Revolution* (Peking 1960); Wang Shih, Wang Ch'iao, Ma Ch'i-ping, and Chang Ling, *A Brief History of the Chinese Communist Party* (Shanghai 1958), in *JPRS*, No. 8756 (1961); Hsiao Hua, "The Chinese Revolution and Armed Struggle," *Hung Ch'i*, No. 16 (1962), in *PR*, v (August 10 and 17, 1962), 6–9, 14–16.

[43] Mao is quoted in Sin-ming Chiu, "Some Basic Conceptions and Rules of Conduct of Chinese Communism," *Studies in Chinese Communism Series*, IV (January 1955), 10.

[44] Ho Kan-chih, 199.

military policy after China enters the nuclear club. Political strength will still be valuable; escalation will still not be in the Chinese interest.

The third revolutionary lesson is a tactic to use, not one to avoid. Arms control techniques, such as negotiations and truces, enabled the Communists to survive and helped create the "objective conditions" for victory. Their use against the Kuomintang after World War II produced both military and political benefits. Militarily, the Communists gained time to familiarize their army with the Japanese weapons acquired in Manchuria, and to assimilate personnel from the disbanded puppet armies. Politically, negotiations and truce privileges gave the Communists an excellent platform from which "to work for the awakening of the middle-of-the-road groups . . . to win over all the allies that could be won over." [45] This platform produced political support for Communist offers to the Nationalists; it enabled them to pin much of the responsibility for the resumption of civil war on the Nationalists. In other words, the peace-loving image acquired through arms control tactics enabled the Party to capitalize on "men's abhorrence of war" when the conflict resumed. [46]

The lesson drawn here is that it is to Peking's advantage to propose and enter into negotiations and truce agreements with the United States and local enemies. These and other Communist arms control initiatives will (a) deter the United States from using its current military superiority; (b) increase Communist popularity and political support among the people of target societies and uninvolved governments; and (c) gain time to remedy the current military inferiority of the People's Republic. Thus Indian border truce offers helped to damp the American and British response and to soothe non-aligned governments.

Peking's military policy assumes American hostility and that the admission of American military superiority or explicit concessions will only increase the military pressure exerted on China by the United States ("If we fall victim to the fear complex, they will be able to do what they like and stir up trouble" [47]). The nature of the Chinese-American competition precludes any compromise not based on the manipulation of power. "Technical" arms control agreements, e.g., nuclear force limitations, are not possible because "agreement must first be reached on matters of principle." [48] Since agreements on "matters of principle" are impossible, war is "inevitable." [49]

---

[45] Hsiao Hua, 15.

[46] Liao Kai-lung; Lin Piao, "The Victory of the Chinese People's Revolutionary War Is a Victory of the Thought of Mao Tse-tung," *Hung Ch'i,* No. 19 (1960), in *SCMM,* No. 231 (1960), 10.

[47] Kuo Mu-jo, speaking to the International Students' Union Meeting on September 15, 1958, as quoted in Robert W. Barnett, 40.

[48] Chou En-lai, as quoted by Edgar Snow in "Red China's Leaders Talk Peace, on Their Terms," *Look,* xxv (January 1961), 93.

[49] Fu Chung, 8.

Accordingly, the task of Peking military policy planners is to make the best of an "inevitable" series of military conflicts. The revolutionary experience is interpreted to prove that, in spite of its military weakness, the Party can mold and benefit from the "inevitable" armed conflicts. If her leaders are realistic and flexible, Peking expects to manipulate the "incidental" aspects of war to her advantage. The previous pages have presented Chinese preferences for the "incidental" factors of time, place, opponent, and scale of conflict ("when to fight, where to fight, with whom to fight, big war, small war").[50] Peking believes that it can force non-Communist governments to accept it choice of sub-limited, national liberation wars and small, conventional, border clashes. This is the purpose of the unilateral arms control measures: target selection and geographical, time, weapons, and manpower restrictions. Tight command and control of the People's Liberation Army are intended to ensure its obedience to conflict-limiting orders.

To Peking, American opposition to China's goals does require a "tit-for-tat" response to any American, or American-supported, military action or threat. However, China's interests are often better served by unilateral military restraint than by military action.[51]

---

[50] *Ibid.*

[51] Chang Ming-yang, 35; Liao Kai-lung, 11.

NATO AND THE
SECURITY OF POLITICS

Morton Gorden

WE MUST BEGIN with a truism, if only because truisms are subject to obsolescence in the wake of technological change. There is one truism, however, which modern technology does not change: the prime function of the military establishment is to secure the political existence of its owners. No technological advances in weaponry can change the fundamental relation between means and ends. The weapons are the means, and the political goals are the ends. Of course, means and ends affect each other. While military technology is the servant of politics, the two interact in the formulation of policy.

The function of this article is to explore the implications of the truism in an analytic survey of the political issues involved in NATO's history and prospects. We are not undertaking a history of NATO; that has been done well by others, and especially well by Robert Osgood in *NATO, The Entangling Alliance*. We are, instead, considering some components of European security policy which will be salient when, in 1969, the North Atlantic Treaty Organization is due to be formally redrawn.

While the NATO area includes North America and much of the perimeter of Europe, our focus of attention will be most often on the role of NATO as the security system for the three dominant Western European countries: Britain, Germany, and France. The security of these countries is almost totally dependent on NATO and, because they also play the dominant political role in Europe, the interaction of their security and their political goals is most salient and important for the future character of NATO. While we shall focus on these countries, their positions cannot be understood apart from global factors, and it will be necessary to connect regional European with global security arrangements. In portions of this task, we are fortunate to be able to draw upon opinion surveys of the elites of the three countries as they have been repeatedly interviewed since 1955 by Dr. Daniel Lerner of L'Institut d'Etudes Européenes and the Massachusetts Institute of Technology.[1]

---

[1] The highest-ranking politicians, civil servants, business men, and communicators in the key sectors of each profession were chosen by panels of experts and stratified sampling in each country. By 1961, many of them had been interviewed two or three times. We shall draw primarily from the 1961 survey, in which 100 elite panelists were

THE POST-WAR WORLD

World War II was born of European rivalries, but rapidly became global in scope. The failure of post-World War I diplomacy to achieve security for the European powers led to national defense by arms and the engagement of substantial forces throughout the globe. The enormous cost of World War II—in the tangible entities of lives and money and the intangibles of the sense of the-world-gone-wrong—created a profound revulsion against the use of military force to guarantee national security. The desired goal was to achieve world peace, not by national police, but by world law. The establishment of the United Nations was done in the spirit of the post-war vows that set a security policy on the base of international cooperation rather than conflict. Law would be the governor of international conflict.

This security policy was given concrete expression in a drastic unilateral disarmament program in the United States and by the affirmation in Europe, by Churchill and others, that old rivalries would be buried with the dead. Europe would be unified by institutions and controls that would never again allow differences to be settled by force. The Europeans would also submit to a law common to all Europeans. The vows were taken for regional and global security arrangements to be based on law.

The vows did not materialize. The problem was to find agreement on whose law would be supreme. The United States felt that its sense of law and world order should be the model. The Soviets too believed in world law —but on their terms. The British found it difficult to follow Churchill's suggestion if Europe were not to be unified under the laws and practices of the United Kingdom. Law without consensus on the nature of the community ended with each community proposing its own law.

The Soviets were first to assert their desire for hegemony. Exploiting the Yalta agreements, which gave the Soviet Union a favored position in Eastern Europe, the Communists set out to unify Europe under their control. By subversion and force to the east of Germany, and by international Communist parties elsewhere, the Soviet Union made it clear that the post-war world would enter a new phase.

THE COLD-WAR WORLD

Whether one chooses to mark the beginning of the West's recognition of the cold war from the Communist action in Greece, Czechoslovakia, Italy,

---

selected in each of three countries, Britain, France, and West Germany. In the present context, only parts of the surveys are used as indicators of important opinion in Europe. The results of the surveys have been reported elsewhere. For a discussion of security affairs in Europe, see especially: Daniel Lerner and Morton Gorden, "European Community and Atlantic Security in the World Arena" (M.I.T. CENIS Document C/61–38, 1961), and Daniel Lerner and Morton Gorden, "Strategic Thinking of the European Elites" (M.I.T. CENIS Document C/64–36, 1964).

France, and Berlin, or from the lesser signs which began even before the end of World War II, the cold war itself was being fought in earnest. In the decade from the late forties to the late fifties, the West evolved a global security policy to deal with its objectives. The Soviet Union wanted to assure its security by dominance, a position suited to its political outlook; but the West did not respond by trying to achieve dominance itself. Instead it sought to defend its position. The West's resistance took the form of a policy of containment. The goal was to contain Communism where it stood.

The global security position required a buildup of forces, especially in the European region. The force requirements raised a wide range of political problems to be settled in order to achieve a viable cold war policy in Europe. A short survey cannot hope to exhaust the possibilities that merit discussion. A large and important literature has developed and a few books in particular are noteworthy for their treatment of the subject in forms relevant to the present discussion: Robert Osgood in *NATO, The Entangling Alliance* and Klaus Knorr in *NATO and American Security* set out American points of view; Fred Mulley in *Politics of Western Defense,* Alastair Buchan in *NATO in the 1960's,* Alastair Buchan and Philip Windsor in *Arms and Stability in Europe,* and Pierre Gallois in *The Balance of Terror* give indications of European thinking on the magnitude and profundity of the issues raised by European security. In a limited study one can only hope to focus on a few major issues. From the outstanding issues involved, four seem to occur repeatedly in the debates over guaranteeing the security of Europe. These four are: (1) the role of America; (2) the degree of allied integration; (3) the choice of allies within the alliance; and (4) the resolution of conflict.

Because of the cost of maintaining security, and the enormous damage which modern technology may create, collective security becomes a necessary mode. Within the framework of collective security, the major issues posed for the alliance in the West reside. Whether the question at hand is the purchase of stockings for troops from a French textile manufacturer, the forward deployment of troops in Germany, the sharing of nuclear technology, or the ultimate decision to use nuclear weapons, the four major issues of collective security come to the fore.

Thus, of the many issues which can be examined in a study of European security and the interaction with political thinking, these four major issues are central: How much America? How close the ties? Who shall be the favored ally? How settle the conflict? These questions become the focus in the interaction between strategic preferences and alliance politics. The answers vary according to the strategic-political circumstances. We shall first explore them as they appeared during the cold war years under American strategic advantage. Only later shall we see how the answers have to be reviewed under the new circumstances of mutual deterrence and coexistence.

How Much America?

In 1945, with the immense disarmament program of the United States and the signing of the United Nations charter, the answer to this question seemed to be solved. Not much of America would be needed to guarantee security in a world mainly concerned with erasing the shadows cast by World War II. The beginning of the cold war, however, soon enough suggested that the security question had to be faced anew.

Even before America's involvement, the Europeans took measures on their own. The Dunkirk Treaty of March 1947, bringing Britain and France together in a mutual defense pact, marked the renewal of an old collective security arrangement in Europe. The extension of the mutual defense pact to other nations, seven in all, was made in Brussels in 1948. The admission that European security could only be guaranteed by some form of collective means was found in the signing of these two pacts.

To make collective effort viable in post-war Europe, however, America had to be added. Europe could not simultaneously reconstruct her economies, maintain her overseas commitments, and also bear the burden of costly weapons for her defense. America was willing to oblige, for her own first line of defense was generally acknowledged to be in Europe. Under the leadership of Senator Vandenberg, the Senate resolution of June 1948 heralded the beginning of an Atlantic community in which the United States would become heavily involved in the guarantee of European security. This decision reached its most formal expression in the establishment on April 4, 1949, of the North Atlantic Treaty Organization (NATO).

Thus, America's commitment to Europe became firmly established. With the pressures of the Berlin blockade and the Korean War, the scope of the American guarantee in Europe increased, and the need for a forward strategy became evident. The American commitment would have to be extended to a conventional continental defense in more than a peripheral sense. At the moment of the acceptance of the forward strategy Germany had to be brought into the NATO organization. The effect of the forward strategy was to commit the United States still further in Europe.

At this point, the American commitment and with it the answer to the question "How much America?" were settled for the next period of time. Europe would need a great deal of money and resources to hold the line against the considerable Soviet forces in Eastern Europe. The West as a whole would need forces to defend against or deter possible Russian aggression. These resources and forces came substantially from the American treasury and arsenal. Perhaps most visible of all was the American command structure superimposed to control the materiel and personnel necessary to guarantee European security. The answer to the question, "How much America?" became clear. The contribution would be substantial. America had little choice if it was to answer the Soviet challenge and keep Europe secure. For the next few years the tide appeared irreversible. America would have to continue to provide the elements to guarantee European security and to insist on its right to have dominant control over the forces in Europe. Few responsible European leaders questioned America's leadership in the cold war.

How Close the Ties?

Nations working together for collective security required cooperative policies and actions. The elite survey data for 1961 afford an opportunity to explore some of the European preferences. That some form of cooperation is essential, almost no one of the French, British, and German elite panels would deny. When asked whether the respondents approved of their country giving up sovereignty to international associations, 24 per cent of the British panel said yes "wholeheartedly"; 43 per cent of the French and 33 per cent of the German panels concurred. Of the remainder, 53 per cent of the British, 43 per cent of the Germans, and 34 per cent of the French replied "positively, with reservations." Less than one-fourth of all panels failed to endorse the principle of cooperation.

The same phenomenon occurred when the panels were asked, in relation to the control of the Polaris submarine, whether their country should give priority to collective defense or national sovereignty. Ninety-five per cent of the Germans, 84 per cent of the British, and 55 per cent of the French panels declared in favor of collective defense.

It is apparent that close ties among members of the alliance were desired by the most substantial portion of the French and British panels. This willingness to join international groups is part of a significant development in post-war Europe. The growth of European economic integration, from its beginnings in the European Coal and Steel Community to its present Common Market configuration, has been well discussed elsewhere.[2]

The implications of international cooperation for national and collective security have also been discussed, particularly in connection with the EDC.[3] The need for cooperation and its operational consequences have been well outlined in other sources.[4]

The issue on which these studies focus is: how tightly knit is the integrated defense of Europe to be? The NATO format requires relinquishment of no decisive element of sovereignty by any nation to a supranational body. The NATO Council operates with the consent of each of its member nations, and any major decisions must be taken by unanimous agreement among

---

[2] Ernst B. Haas, *Uniting of Europe: Political, Social, and Economic Forces, 1950–1957* (Stanford, 1958); V. W. Kitzinger, *The Politics and Economics of European Integration* (New York, 1963).

[3] Daniel Lerner and Raymond Aron, eds., *France Defeats the E.D.C.* (New York, 1957).

[4] F. W. Mulley, *The Politics of Western Defense* (New York, 1962); *NATO*, NATO Information Service (Paris, 1962); Robert E. Osgood, *NATO, The Entangling Alliance* (New York, 1962).

the members.[5] Thus NATO is a model of a loosely knit security system, requiring consent from all its members for any substantial action. Even this loose structure is, however, unprecedented in peacetime; and the amount of cooperation which NATO has inspired in fact goes well beyond the experience of previous alliance history. Close cooperation has been a function of common ends rather than institutional sanctions.

The NATO model, however, has not been the only option open to Europeans for their security. In October, 1950, René Pleven, the French *président du conseil,* outlined a European Defense Community draft treaty, which the French assesmbly passed by 343 to 225 votes.[6] The measure that passed the French assembly appeared to be a giant step on the road toward integration. The EDC called for a common army for member nations with a substantial degree of integration. In the present context, the story of the failure of EDC need not be reviewed, for it has already been told.

For our purposes, the essential point is that Britain did not want to become a member of the European army. This was her first official decision, which was to be repeated. Britain did not want to participate directly in the European integration movement. A second essential point is that France also decided, when the chips were down in August, 1954, *not* to join the EDC which France herself had proposed.[7]

Thus England and France were not prepared to create a European Defense Community that would require subordination of decisions affecting national security to a supranational body. The reasons for the failure go deeper than this specific issue. As several EDC supporters pointed out, there was no supranational body at the time which could direct the European army under its own political control. The outcome was that EDC, the first attempt to create an integrated European capability to guarantee European security, failed.

Immediately in its wake came a new proposal—designed to allow Germany to enter the European security system and to remove the thorny elements of supranational control from the European security plan. The Western European Union (WEU) allowed national armies to remain under national control. It invited German and Italian forces to participate in European security. With the integration of WEU into a NATO structure, the two major issues under discussion were settled. During the cold war, America would remain active—even predominant—in the affairs of European security; and it would do so in a loosely confederated alliance structure.[8]

---

[5] *NATO,* p. 43.
[6] Mulley, *op. cit.,* p. 23.
[7] Lerner and Aron, *op. cit.*
[8] Nathan Leites and Christian de la Malène, "Paris from EDC to WEU," RAND Research Memorandum, RM-1668-RC (March 1, 1956).

Who Shall Be the Favored Ally?

Another issue which has pervaded the discussion of European security has been the choice of the preferred arena for international cooperation. Within the Western alliance, where should the greatest emphasis be placed on cooperation? The answer to this question has many options. The first basic option is to deny the question; that is to say that national security can be guaranteed by the nation alone. The next major option which has presented itself has been some form of European regional integration to guarantee security. The last major option is to become more strongly tied with the United States as the leader of the Western alliance.

From the outset it appeared that the purely national choice—the denial of the need to rely upon an alliance—would be folly. The enormous expense of national defense, and the inadequacy of national defense alone, militated against this position. No post-war European nation had been able to rely entirely on itself to deter an enemy or defend itself in the event of attack. Our elite panels have already shown their preference for a system of collective security.

If the nation is no longer a viable unit of defense, the continent, or some significant portion thereof, becomes more attractive. In non-security areas, the development of European regional commitments proceeded with surprising speed and success. Examples are the Coal-Steel Community, the Common Market, and Euratom. But the failure of EDC marked the lesser readiness of Europeans to accept this form of cooperation for security issues.

Since the declaration of intent by Senator Vandenberg in 1948, the American guarantee of European security has been the most prominent option. Whatever the form of this commitment, America has been willing and able to guarantee the security of Europe. Belief in this guarantee was stressed by the elite panels: 92 per cent of the German, 89 per cent of the British, and 68 per cent of the French.

Thus, the three options for consideration of the appropriate arena for international cooperation had been reviewed. National and European means failed, and the favored ally would have to be the United States.

How Settle the Conflict?

There are many outstanding sources of conflict between Euorpe and the Soviet Union, and there are different preferences for the appropriate style to resolve conflicts. Our fourth set of issues has to do with the desire to settle conflicts by accommodation or by force. Whether one is to negotiate with the Soviet Union and try to find accommodation for the differences which exist in a peaceful manner, or whether one will stand firm against the warlike (but not real war) activities of the Soviet Union—these had become central issues of European debate. What should be the character of European policy in its conflict with the Soviet Union? The history of contact between East and West shows that one answer or the other has not always won. European debate has been continuous on the issue of disengagement from conflict or increased engagement. The elite study showed a majority of the German panel was against some form of disengagement in Central Europe. Our French panel was evenly split. The British panel, however, divided differently: one-quarter against disengagement and almost three-quarters in favor.

The choice of "style" is closely related to the belief (or disbelief) that the conflict between East and West can be resolved. How long the cold war must continue, and how fundamental are the differences between the blocs, involve major assumptions which help shape each person's source of the appropriate pattern of responses to Soviet behavior. One's conception of the European security system must be adapted to follow out the "style" that will meet the requirements for the resolution of conflict, should such resolution be deemed possible. The options of behavior are generally termed "hard" or "soft," to suggest the degree of accommodation or firmness which one takes in the face of Soviet initiatives. The options range from some sort of disarmament, with a resolution of political differences and reduction of armaments, to the other end of the spectrum—where a perpetual arms race is the only way to hold the Soviet Union to a stalemate and prevent war from occurring. The basic choices become "settlement" or "stalemate" and there is a wide range of policy options between these two extremes. The European security system must be defined to handle the directives emanating from various positions on this spectrum. Various positions have been taken at different junctures, usually following the course of Soviet tactics of threat or accommodation. As the cold war fluctuates in intensity, the style of Western behavior alters to changing, and sometimes, to change conditions.

All of these issues under discussion are *political* in nature, i.e., they have to do with the goals and the direction which each nation wants to follow. The decisions are not made on the basis of technological or economic considerations alone, but require an assessment of the values and goals of the nations involved. Such issues, therefore, become all the more complicated in debate as they become more diverse in scope. It has been suggested that the issues are not only broad in scope, but vary over time in their application to events. Amidst issues of such breadth, depth, and transience, the interaction between political and strategic considerations becomes especially complicated and intricate, and must be continually re-evaluated.

The resolution of the issues as briefly portrayed here applies to regional European security arrangements under the political-technological frame or reference of the cold war. The world was and is divided East and West. The collective security system developed to protect the West raised political questions even within the alliance. Many of the answers were based on American technological superiority over the Soviet Union. However, when the technology spread to the Soviet Union, the questions had to be asked anew. The route followed by weapons and politics is not a one-way street. The global security arrangements were significantly altered and the fact of mutual deterrence became the most salient and important fact in the reappraisal of regional European security policy and alliance politics. The world in which we now live may well be characterized as Deterred World.

THE DETERRED WORLD

Reliance on deterrence has been the most widely accepted strategy in Europe; the force structure and doctrine for its employment have been designed to implement deterrence.[9] Within the strategy of deterrence there is much flexibility for different actions. A reader on deterrence would include the three R's of the deterrence primer: *ratio, response,* and *risks;* and suggest that they can be combined in varying degrees.

Deterrence may be bought at different force levels between the two blocs. Before deterrence was mutual, one could choose a *ratio* of forces such that a counterforce superiority would give one power enough destructive potential to destroy the enemy's capability without suffering unacceptable damage himself. The superiority remaining would allow for political pressure to be brought to bear. Such a strategic capacity would make a policy of rollback of Soviet forces in Europe feasible, if it were a serious political option.

However, the invulnerability of Soviet forces and their substantial medium-range missile inventory preclude the possibility of the West achieving counterforce superiority without itself suffering great destruction. The technological advances of the Soviet Union and the decision to purchase large quantities of military goods have made the deterrent ratio more nearly a balanced one in Europe itself. Such a deterrent ratio lends itself to a policy of containment, for neither side can push the other back without the risk of bringing the conflict to a level which would render victory worthless.

Another key decision for the employment of deterrence lies in the degree of *response* available to a provocation. The spectrum of choice ranges from massive deterrence, i.e., the employment of a substantial part of the nuclear arsenal on the homeland of the enemy, to a limited local defense, i.e., the employment of just enough conventional forces in the disputed area. There are also various gradations in between these two extremes of response.

---

[9] There are also many forms of disarmament and arms control considered in the European public discussion. The notion of disarmament encompasses a large range of activities which include the rooting out of the political source of conflict between the major blocs as well as the removal of the weapons which are felt to be primarily responsible for the tension in Europe. There are a number of books which help to outline the dimensions of the disarmament movement in Europe: Alastair Buchan and Philip Windsor, *Arms and Stability in Europe* (New York, 1963); Michael Howard, *Disengagement in Europe* (Baltimore, 1958); Mulley, *op. cit.,* Chap. 12; Osgood, *op. cit.,* Chap. 10; John Strachey, *On the Prevention of War* (New York, 1963), Chaps. 9–13.

The last R, *risk,* weighs heavy in the choice of a deterrent posture. At what level of provocation is one willing to risk the use of nuclear weapons? This difficult question must be answered before the disposition of forces can be determined. The degree of risk which each nation's decision-makers are willing to take sets much of the strategic policy. There are many gradations for choice.

In fact, over the years, the NATO strategy in Europe has taken many different positions on all of the three R's. In the early years of NATO, America had a nuclear superiority of unquestioned dominance. It had sufficient counterforce capability to protect itself against losses, but it is possible that this counterforce capability did not extend itself to the Continent. The favorable ratio did not last into the sixties because Russia was able to balance the deterrent power at some time in the intervening years. The current ratio admits of no careless moves on either side. The Americans no doubt enjoy a numerical intercontinental superiority, though not complete counterforce capability without some losses; but the Soviets probably enjoy an advantage of men and machines and a minimum invulnerable nuclear deterrent, at least on the Continent. Such a ratio lends itself to a nuclear stalemate and conflict at a level lower than all-out war. Higher forms of conflict are not worth the losses; that is the fundamental reason for deterrence.

The ratio is not the only part of the deterrence posture which has changed. The response pattern has altered substantially in recent years. While America enjoyed a nuclear monopoly and in the years following, under the guidance of John Foster Dulles, the massive retaliation response was the favored policy. Any aggression in Europe would be followed by a large scale nuclear attack on the homeland of the aggressor. This policy has undergone gradual change as NATO became equipped with American tactical nuclear power to allow limited retaliation. The current American administration is attempting to provide a response capability even below the nuclear level to afford a response graduated to the level of aggression. The Americans want to provide a conventional defense to allow war to remain limited. Many Europeans, Pierre Gallois among them, have resisted the policy of graduated response because it makes the deterrent less credible in their eyes. Perhaps more important are the different points of view of what is a limited war. A conflict localized in Europe may be considered a limited tactical war for the Americans, but it must be a strategic war for the Europeans. Thus, on the question of proper response to aggression, there have been change and differing points of view on how best to guarantee European security. At the base of the disagreement is the last R, the level of acceptable risk, and this too has changed over the years.

The level of provocation which dictates a response is set by the risk which one is willing to run. A graduated response tries to avoid escalation to a higher level of conflict and is calculated to entail the minimum risk of damage. However, until recently, the risks in Europe were deliberately set high, for the NATO force structure was designed to be a shield and a sword. The size of the shield has been just enough for the Soviets to declare their intentions to invade Europe by breaking its surface. The shield has been designed to be thin and is often called a "trip wire" or "plate glass window" to symbolize that it is not a defensive shield, but only an indicator that the sword of nuclear retaliation should be employed. This has been a high risk policy, for even a small Soviet conventional attack was not able to be resisted without escalating the conflict. If we may use the elite survey as an indication, it is a risk policy which is strongly endorsed in Europe. Fully 86 per cent of the British, 84 per cent of the Germans, and 76 per cent of the French panels established their priorities to reduce the *probability* of war rather than its destructiveness.

Nonetheless, over time, the NATO shield has been moved up closer to the front and has been increased in thickness to allow some local defense for a brief period of time. With this posture, there can be a pause in the conflict to give the Soviets time to reflect on the decision to escalate. The direction which America has been urging for the Europeans is to lessen the risk of large scale atomic conflict by meeting provocations with matching responses.

As has been indicated, there are different notions of the risk in Europe and America. While avoiding escalation reduces the risk for the United States, it is the very threat of escalation which, some Europeans believe, renders limited conflict impossible. Furthermore, the risks of even a limited war in Europe are higher for the Europeans. The different points of view have been responsible for much debate over the design of the deterrent posture.

The elementary three R's of deterrence have provided the basic criteria for the guarantee of European security. The levels of force ratios, response, and risk have been set and reset throughout the history of NATO to create the deterrent design deemed most appropriate and feasible for Western security. Whatever the level set, the basic principle of deterrence has remained unchanged. Aggression must always cost more than it can gain.

The Politics of Deterrence

The new conditions of global security arrangements under mutual deterrence and coexistence force a re-evaluation of the political issues which were settled for the cold war period. When both the United States and the Soviet Union can decimate each other's societies, there is pressure on the President and the Premier to act like men of peace. Whatever global aspirations the Soviet Union may have must be dampened and the time scales for fulfillment must be enlarged. Limited involvement even becomes preferable to limited war. The cold war cannot be allowed to get too hot.

If we add the economic and political resurgence of the European region to the new strategic circumstances, then we have the essential elements which lead to a rethinking of European security arrangements. Each of the issues which we have raised in the earlier political-technological environment must be dealt with anew in the Deterred World. While the world may be deterred from war, it is not deterred from politics. A moratorium on weapons does not require a moratorium on the advancement of national goals. NATO's role has always been to secure the politics of the European region, that is, to protect the region's ability to advance its goals. Mutual deterrence and European prosperity do not change this relationship, they just create a new environment. If war has been an instrument of politics in the past, enforced peace is an instrument of politics in the present. It is a delicate instrument and statesmen are still not sure how to use it—or perhaps analysts still do not know how to evaluate the statesmen. In either case, the answers to the political questions we have raised are not yet clear. We ask again: How much America? How close the ties? Who shall be the favored ally? How settle the conflict?

How Much America?

Europeans have asked this question from two points of view. How much does America want to be involved in Europe and how much does Europe want America to be involved? Some Europeans, most notably the Gaullists, feel that America does not want to be involved as deeply as it has been. They worry that the three R's of deterrence are being set too low. They say that the gold drain from the United States treasury will force reduction of the American ratio of forces. They are convinced that the desire for a graduated response is really a withdrawal of commitment to a nuclear defense. They fear that the Americans are not willing to take the risk of losing their homeland for the defense of Europe. The critics say that America no longer wants to be involved in Europe and that she is reducing her role.

It is usually the same critics who also say that Europe does not want America to be involved—in a political sense. They point to problems and interests which are best dealt with in the European sphere of influence. They would prefer to be political masters in their own house, rather than accept the political leadership of America. This independence requires either national or European deterrent forces to handle the circumstances where the American guarantee is reputed to fail. However, the price of minimum deterrent forces is not too high for those seeking independence. Security arrangements are desired to protect political goals and independent politics require independent deterrents.

Thus far, the position outlined here has been accepted by only one government in Europe, the French government under De Gaulle. The British maintain their deterrent to keep as much political maneuverability as they can, but they have not seriously questioned the American guarantee or asserted grand designs outside the Atlantic Community. The Germans continue to rely on the American deterrent, while insisting on tangible renewals of American good faith. Nonetheless, the role of America is being questioned among Europeans. Some critics say America will become less involved but they do not lament this fact. Europeans will create their own forces and benefit from the independence. Other Europeans are concerned that America will become less involved, but they seek to find ways which will assure an important American role. This latter desire requires a re-evaluation of bonds tied during the cold war phase of the Atlantic alliance.

How Close the Ties?

The issue of ties within the alliance was settled earlier by relying on common interests to bind participants within a loosely structured NATO framework. NATO required no relinquishment of national sovereignty. However, if American interests were questioned in Europe, then some institutional link would have to be created as a demonstration of the American commitment. The institutional link would have to apply to a questionable area of commitment: the use of nuclear weapons.

The United States offered to share the costs and control of nuclear weapons in a multilateral nuclear force with the NATO nations manning a seaborne nuclear deterrent. The important limitation of the American proposal, from the point of view of doubting Europeans, was that America would retain veto power over the use of the weapon. As we reported earlier, our elite panels were in favor of collective control and were willing to give up their national sovereignty. However, America is impeded by the MacMahon Act which forbids the relinquishing of control of American weapons, and cannot agree to fulfill completely the demands of collective control. The fear of the proliferation of nuclear weapons and American nationalism combine to make potent political allies within the United States. These forces restrain America from making the ties to Europe as close as some Europeans would like.

The opportunity for close ties is also weakened by European unwillingness to be bound by American desires. American problems in Cuba and Asia are seen as American problems. In substantial areas of economic, political, and military affairs, Europeans have not agreed with American policy and do not themselves want to be tied to the American definition of the proper policy.

Thus, American and European national interests are not always seen to be compatible. While the ties may have to be closer in the Deterred World and unity of purpose and action are essential, there are strong factors limiting common action to functionally specific agreements covering areas of mutual interest among partners who have favored relations with each other.

Who Shall Be the Favored Ally?

In the absence of a politically unified Europe, the United States has conducted diplomacy through a series of bilateral ties with European nations.

The special Anglo-American connection has been the result of favorable agreements with Britain in broad questions of diplomacy and military affairs. The British have benefited from their commitment to be an Atlantic nation and have chosen to cooperate more with the United States than with their European allies. The Anglo-American Nassau Agreement in November, 1962, illustrated the British preference to continue her nuclear capabilities within an American rather than European framework—a fact which De Gaulle did not miss in his January, 1963, press conference rejecting Britain's bid for entry into the Common Market.

The French, under De Gaulle, have expressed quite another set of preferences. De Gaulle envisions a "Europe des Patries" in which sovereign nations group together to further their national interests. De Gaulle also sees the European region as the favored arena for French participation and a French leadership role. The European orientation of France and the role which De Gaulle has chosen for his country puts France and the United States in a competitive position for the leadership of Europe.

The key nation in this competition is Germany. France has bid for German favor, as has the United States. The Germans have been asked to choose and would prefer not to make a forced choice. However, Germany has thus far chosen to maintain its Atlantic tie and the security which it offers.

These nations will choose favored relations for cooperation with the nations that have the most to offer them. One of the prominent advantages each has to offer the other is the security guarantee. Political cooperation will follow where the security guarantee does not require the sacrifice of primary political goals. Britain thus far has not enunciated political goals which contrast with basic United States policy. Germany has been willing to subordinate the elusive goal of reunification to the requirements of the American security guarantee. France has either decided that its political goals cannot be sacrificed to the political strings which America puts on her guarantee or has bet that the American guarantee will be valid regardless of France's behavior. In either case France, under De Gaulle, has decided that she must be allowed political flexibility within the alliance and has chosen to act independently.

How Resolve the Conflict?

During the cold war phase of conflict between East and West, relations were characterized by alternating tension and relaxation. Postures varied from firmness to flexibility, depending on the circumstances. In the Deterred World, neither side cares to push its advantages too far. Europe is probably the only area of the world as important to the Americans and Russians as their homelands, for its loss is perceived as the last step before domination. When the stakes are this high, neither side will care to push the other to the nuclear step. Instead, the stalemate is recognized and hope for a détente is raised. Peripheral arms controls are considered to relax tensions, lessen risks, and save money. The basic political conflict is not resolved, but war is excluded as an instrument for its solution. The status of Eastern Europe and Germany is left uncertain. Conflict endures in limited forms, and neither side seeks an ultimate resolution in the short term. The major antagonists in the European region neither solve nor settle their differences, while hoping some new opportunities will present themselves.

Many Europeans see China as the new opportunity. China is viewed as a potential force to keep the Russian enemy from hostilities in Europe. Hope is raised for a long term accommodation with the Soviet Union forced by Chinese pressure from the outside and fed by the gradual growth of liberalism from within.

The resolution of conflict between East and West may have to wait for such a long term solution. The use of strategic nuclear weapons to secure either side's goals is no security at all. That is the meaning of a Deterred World.

*   *   *

The setting of defense policy in the NATO area requires an understanding of the political goals which the military capabilities are protecting. The defense policy must continually be evaluated in the light of political circumstances, and the political goals must be adjusted to what is militarily possible. Military and political factors continually interact. We have briefly examined some instances of this interaction and pointed to a few of the most important political components of defense policy.

In the Post-War World, defense policy was to be based on law and political agreements rather than military capability. In the Cold War World, the Western policy of containment required a collective security system and raised a number of political issues to be settled among the NATO members. In the Deterred World, these same issues must be re-examined and defense policy adjusted to political priorities. Political feasibilities and priorities, however, must be sensitive to the character of nuclear technology. The balancing of military and political factors will be instrumental in determining the next set of words we use to characterize our world.

NON-ALIGNMENT AND
THE POWER BALANCE

Coral Bell

"WHY SHOULD WE inherit the hatreds of others? It is bad enough that we have our own burdens." These words of Mr. Nehru's[1] convey the original emotional essence of the policy that its exponents have insisted should be called non-alignment rather than neutrality: absorption in the domestic tasks that faced the underdeveloped countries, impatience and resentment at what were seen as efforts to force them into service pulling other people's chestnuts out of the fire, and a tendency to put the two cold-war camps on the same rather squalid moral level ("the hatreds of others"). The insistence that the concept was not to be confused with neutrality of the familiar sort, and the efforts to find a sufficiently distinctive name for it ("non-alignment" or "non-commitment" or, as Marshal Tito used to say, "positive co-existence") were in themselves indicators of one main element in it, a repudiation of the traditional machinery of power-politics, in which the neutral states were of course useful and even essential cogs.

Yet despite this repudiation of power, whose antecedents lie as much with the radical-dissentient tradition in English political thought[2] as with the Gandhist doctrine of non-violence, it may be argued that the viability of non-alignment as a policy has been and is related to particular phases of the power-balance. The present moment is one not only of profound change in that balance, but of reappraisal for the concept of non-alignment. It therefore seems an appropriate time for a re-examination of the relation between them, which is of course a two-way affair. That is, one may ask not only how the position of the non-aligned powers has affected the central balance, but also how the changing central balance affects the viability of non-alignment.

Since a definition of non-alignment would certainly vary somewhat according to whether the definer was looking to Delhi or Belgrade, Cairo or Djakarta, Baghdad or Rangoon, Accra or Pnom-Penh, there seems no point in attempting to force upon it any greater precision than it has borne with those who use it. As with many political words and phrases, its very imprecision—the fact that it is susceptible of a number of interpretations—is

---

[1] Interview in *The Hindu,* 1 April 1954.
[2] Both Nehru and Menon had of course long-standing connections with this intellectual tradition.

part of its usefulness. But one can at least go so far towards a definition as to say that the driving impulse of non-alignment as a principle of foreign policy has been an effort to "opt out" of direct involvement in the central power-struggle of our time, a refusal to "stand up and be counted" for either camp. If this sounds not so unlike neutrality after all, one might rather flippantly define the difference by saying that for Mr. Nehru at least (and he has given the term its distinctive moral colouration) his relationship to the great antagonists of the power-struggle has been seen not as that of a spectator, but that of a referee, who at need would double the roles of ambulance-man, pourer of oil on troubled waters, and Greek chorus prophesying woe for the central characters and everyone else unless they (the central characters) mend their ways.

Yet the children of that complex mind show always in their lineaments not only the Kashmiri Brahmin and the devoted *New Statesman* reader, but the intellectual tradition of Harrow and Cambridge. Thus the visible influence of balance-of-power theory, despite the repudiation of power, is not surprising. In an interview just before the Colombo Powers meeting in April 1954 Mr. Nehru said "When there is substantial difference in the strength of the two opposing forces, we in Asia, with our limitations, will not be able to influence the issue. But when the two opposing forces are fairly evenly matched, then it is possible to make our weight felt in the balance." [3] He went on to say that it was essential for some nations to assume this role in the interests of world peace, since there were in the world two crusades— the Communist and the anti-Communist—either of which could involve the world in war, and that if the world became entirely divided between these blocs, war could be "very close." One might say that there was implicit in his policy a belief (though he would not have expressed it in terms so much associated with what Woodrow Wilson called "the great game now for ever discredited, of the balance of power") that the substitution of a multilateral for the bilateral or near-bilateral balance of the immediate post-war period would make for a securer peace. Certainly the existence of, and the need to woo the unaligned powers was conceived of as exercising a form of restraint on the cold-war combatants, a restraint not totally unlike that exercised by the small powers or the balancer in the traditional balance-of-power situation, even though the influence exerted on the main contestants proceeded from quite different sources. The small powers in a traditional balance system owed their influence largely to the fact that even marginal increments of military strength could be important in that context. The military strength of the uncommitted states is too slight, measured against either that of the Communist bloc or that of the NATO powers, for this to hold true of them. But the present conflict is between two theories of society, as well as two power-complexes. Both sides want to be assured they are right, as well as to know they are strong. At least for the West, which has suffered hard blows

---

[3] *Hindu,* 1 April 1954.

to its self-confidence in its dealings with Asia, the image of its own society that it sees mirrored in the eyes of the uncommitted Asians has been of importance. That is to say the ideological issue has complicated the power struggle, the uncommitted powers have been potential converts or defectors as well as potential allies, and this has meant that their susceptibilities must be much more carefully weighed than would be the case if nothing more were in question than the military strength they can contribute to either camp.

This element in the influence of the non-aligned powers, which I shall call the "floating vote" factor, has been enlarged upon a good deal by spokesmen of the countries concerned. Its significance, though real, has perhaps been exaggerated—or at least one might say that it is likely to affect the great powers only during what may be called the spells of relatively static trench-warfare in the Cold War. It is not necessarily effective at moments of crisis.

Much less adequately understood, and much less flattering for the non-aligned powers to contemplate, is an element in their position which I shall call the "ally-cost" factor, as seen by the great powers. Up to now this has been visible chiefly in American policy, especially in South Asia. It derives from the fact that the policy makers in Washington have had, in the endemic conflicts in that part of the world since 1949, to balance the prospective dangers and disadvantages of the loss of any particular area to the Communist power-sphere against the potential cost, in servicemen's lives or less valued resources, of preventing this loss.

Naturally those who had to find the actual military resources to meet new and old commitments were most conscious of this cost factor. The best exposition of the way it affected American policy is to be found in the memoirs of General Matthew Ridgway, in the account he gives of his own attitude and arguments as U.S. Army Chief of Staff in the 1954 crisis over Indo-China, in which this was a major point in debate in Washington.[4] (General Ridgway was in a much stronger arguing position vis-à-vis Dulles than Eden was, though of course British pressure reinforced the Army arguments.) Interestingly enough, it echoes the theory of Communist strategy in Asia put forward by the late M. N. Roy, the Indian historian who was head of the Eastern Secretariat of the Comintern in the twenties but later broke with the Party. Quoting Lenin as remarking that the road to Paris lay

---

[4] "To military men familiar with the map of Indo-China, the outcome of that siege [Dien Bien Phu] was a foregone conclusion . . . I also knew that none of those advocating such a step [intervention] had any accurate idea of what such an operation would cost in blood and money and national effort . . . To provide these facts I sent out to Indo-China an Army team of experts in every field . . . The idea of intervention was abandoned, and it is my belief that the analysis which the Army made and presented to higher authority played a considerable, perhaps a decisive, part in persuading our government not to embark on that tragic adventure." *Soldier: The Memoirs of Matthew B. Ridgway* (New York, Harper, 1956) pp. 275–8.

through Peking, and that London and New York would fall on the Yangtse, Roy wrote, chillingly, "Russia will not take part directly in the Thirty Years War in Asia. It will be a war between the East and the West." [5]

There were times in the period 1950–54 when this prediction seemed a plausible one enough. At the height of the Korean war it was calculated that there were over a million men engaged in fighting the battles of the West along the fringes of East Asia—Korea, Indo-China, Malaya—against what was essentially a force drawn from the Communist second-eleven, so to speak, and such success as the West did finally claim was hard-bought, and in two of these three cases inconclusive. It is one of the paradoxes of the contemporary military/political situation that though the weapons of mass-destruction grow more and more ferociously efficient, the revolutionary guerilla armed with nothing more advanced than an old rifle and a 19th century political doctrine has proved the most effective means yet devised for altering the world power-balance. One has only to reflect on the history of Ho Chi Minh in Vietnam, before 1954, or Castro's original landing in Cuba, to be disabused of any optimism about the conclusiveness of technological superiority in contemporary conflict of this sort.

However, the decisions of 1953/4 in America marked a turning-away for the succeeding six years from any line of American policy that might have produced the kind of danger apprehended by Roy, the danger of the "30 years war in Asia," with Russia sitting on the sidelines, and the West exhausting its morale and resources in a struggle in which the big battalions of Asian nationalism and Asian anti-Westernism would provide unending recruits for the other side. This is not to say that the line of analysis suggested by Roy influenced the Washington decisions: they were produced by quite other factors of which the author has given an account elsewhere. [6]

Since the accession to office of President Kennedy, and the renewed emphasis on conventional or even guerilla forces as an alternative to nuclear weapons, the possibility of this dilemma—the necessity of choosing between the potential loss of a particular area to the sphere of Soviet power, or the dangers of a campaign on disadvantageous ground that would waste the scarcest of Western resources, conventional military manpower—has arisen again. The most obvious instance was the situation in Laos, but it was also implicit in the situation in the Congo. In both these instances American policy illustrates that the non-alignment of a small power may be the "preferred choice" for it of a great power where the estimated cost of securing the small power concerned as an ally is greater than the prospective advantage of having it so. In the case of Laos this choice was made after some bitter experience, in the period 1958–61, of the difficulties of the alternative

---

[5] "The Communist Problem in East Asia—An Asian View" in *Pacific Affairs*, Sept. 1951.

[6] See *Negotiation from Strength: A Study in the Politics of Power* by Coral Bell (New York, Knopf, 1963), Chapter 5.

policy. In the case of the Congo, the decision to eschew a Cold-War contest for allies (so long as Russia could be made to do likewise) seems to have been reached at the beginning of the crisis and maintained steadily throughout it.

Until very recently the "cost" factor inhibiting Western policy in the power-competition in the "gray areas" had little parallel in Soviet policy. Admittedly costs have to be balanced against advantages as much in Moscow as in Washington, and the economic surplus out of which this competition and other expensive enterprises—the space-race and the military establishment—are financed is much smaller there. But the supply of military goods as they become quasi-obsolescent in Russia's own forces has represented an almost costless bargain in diplomatic influence, and it has never proved necessary to use actual Russian military man-power. Thus Russia was at a very considerable advantage over the West in these areas in that she had a weapon—revisionism through the revolutionary ferment—which could alter the power-map of the world to Russian advantage at very slight cost (to the Russians) and which was difficult to resist except at exorbitant cost (to the West). The non-aligned world was an arena in which Russia stood to gain a good deal (in power terms) and lose very little.

All this, however, depended on the fact that the world balance of power was essentially bipolar. A major change has come into effect with the breakdown of this bipolarity through the schism between Russia and China. (It might be maintained that the bipolar nature of the balance is also being modified at the Western end of the scale, since it appears the ambition of President de Gaulle that the "new Europe" should play for its own diplomatic hand. This may well be true, but the process is not yet sufficiently advanced for it to have an assessable impact on the field under consideration. Temporarily one may treat the balance as far as this field is concerned as triangular, even though bearing in mind that it may assume a more irregular shape.) To be of importance to the situation of the non-aligned powers it is by no means necessary that the Russo-Chinese split should become any wider than it is at present: it is only necessary that, as at present, Peking should be clearly seen to be sponsoring an alternative diplomatic strategy to that of Moscow in the contest with the non-Communist world (which has been the case since 1957) and that the rivalry should look *formidable* from the point of view of Moscow, which has perhaps been the case since 1960. These factors operate together to produce what may be regarded as a local balance of power to complicate the central contest as far as Russia is concerned, and turn revisionism-through-the-revolutionary-ferment into a decidedly two-edged weapon from the viewpoint of the Russian foreign office. The "local balance of power" is not, of course, a merely geographic one between Russia and China. It is the balance of power within the Communist world. The reason why, up to 1956 or so, Communist parties in the non-Communist world could be regarded as normally useful (though not always reliable) instruments of Russian foreign policy was the unchallenge-able prestige of Russia, for the party-faithful, as the country with a Revolu-tion not only indigenous and successful, but established and assured. By the end of 1956 there were three and a half countries, counting Northern Viet-nam, which could at least claim that their revolutions were likewise indig-enous, and another half-dozen in Eastern Europe where the revolution, if externally imposed, was nevertheless capable of developing doctrinal varia-tions of some interest. In the nature of things the faithful *in partibus infi-delium* were no longer likely to feel that there was one indisputable star to steer by. Given this fact, the Russians must be conscious not only of the ambiguity now, as regards their own interests, of revisionism-through-the-revolutionary-ferment, but also of the great natural advantages of China in the competition of the foreseeable future. For the revolutionary process maintains its dynamic only in the underdeveloped world—Africa, Asia, Latin America. Not even the most optimistic eye in the Kremlin is likely to see much sign of a prospective new revolutionary wave in Western Europe: on the contrary, what they see there is the rapidly-growing threat of an economic and political focus of attraction, the European Community, that may trouble their own security in Eastern Europe. And Communist party-membership in Western Europe has fallen to not much more than half its post-war peak. In any case, as long as the Russians remain Leninists, they can hardly deviate from the orthodox view of the underdeveloped world as the Achilles' heel of the capitalists. Yet whatever is done to step up the process of revolutionary change in the *tiers monde,* while it may tilt the over-all balance against the capitalist world, is likely also to tilt the balance with-in the Communist world in favour of China rather than Russia.

This is not simply a matter of China's presenting a more relevant model for economic and social change than Russia as far as the subsistence-farming economies of underdeveloped countries are concerned. It is also a matter of historic situation. The Russians may be Marxists, but to a non-European eye they are also members of that white-skinned, industrialized, comfortably-living segment of humanity whose base is in Europe and North America, and which has long sent its exploiting tentacles out to the non-European world. Roy has noted the importance of anti-European racialism as a main driving-force in Asian communism, especially among its middle-class leader-ship,[7] though one might expect this factor to be offset in parts of South-East Asia by anti-Chinese feeling, which has had there as extensive a history as anti-semitism in Europe, and many of the same manifestations, including the pogrom.

Moreover, it is difficult to see the rejection of Stalinism and the cultivation of quasi-liberal attitudes in Russia as a source of strength to it in the com-petition with China for the adherence of the non-European left. Quite the

---

[7] *Ibid.,* pp. 228–231.

contrary in fact, for the areas concerned might objectively be said to be, like China, in the sort of economic and social situation which favoured Stalinism in Russia itself, only much more acutely so. That is, the educated middle-class is small and weak, the great peasant base is resistant to change, and a powerful urge exists among the revolutionary leadership for a forced-march towards industrialization. Besides, these areas are even less endowed than Russia was with any kind of libertarian tradition, vestiges of which certainly remained alive in Russia even during the Stalinist freeze, and which in the more genial domestic climate permitted by Mr. Khrushchev have reasserted themselves to produce an amelioration of the Communist police-state.

However, the chief potential advantage of China in the competition with Russia is simply its diplomatic and political situation vis-à-vis the West. In essence, it resides in the fact that China had so much less to lose than Russia, and so much less reason for satisfaction with the *status quo,* and so much less cause than Russia for any ambivalence about the contest with the capitalist world, that it is inescapably endowed with strong common interests with the revolutionary-intellectual leadership in the non-European world which is the vital factor in this situation.

Even before the Cuban crisis there had been some evidence of this. At a conference of Afro-Asian writers in Cairo in March 1962 the Russians found themselves facing accusations of putting a higher priority on peaceful co-existence than on the "colonial independence struggle," and of being half-hearted about "wars of national liberation." Obviously, the denouement in Cuba has supplied illustration and substance to these charges against Russia, especially as far as the Latin American parties are concerned. No amount of Mr. Khrushchev's dilating on his claim to have saved Cuba from American invasion can disguise the degree to which he in fact pulled the rug out from under Castro's "movement of national liberation" when persistence in support of Cuba was seen to entail the risk of a nuclear showdown with America. Equivalent about-turns in Russian policy have doubtless been accepted by the party faithful in earlier years without a murmur, but that was before there was an unimpeachably orthodox Communist source to give them news of these events, as China has assiduously done in this case.

Ought one to assume any countervailing damage to China through its hostilities with India? On the present evidence, one would say clearly not, though here one must of course make a distinction between the attitude of India (including the Indian left) and the rest of the non-aligned powers. For India itself the assumptions on which policy was built appear to have been entirely undermined: the assumption that the Himalayas were an adequate protective barrier, that Russia would in any case restrain Chinese territorial ambitions in the disputed area, the assumption that the tasks of economic development would keep China too busy for such adventures for twenty-five years, the assumption that the dangers in Asia were purely economic and social, not military. Clearly all these hopeful views have been or are being re-appraised in Delhi. This does not mean that non-alignment would necessarily be discarded in favour of entry to the Western camp even if the Western powers so wished. For one thing, Mr. Nehru has indicated some remaining faith in the usefulness of Russian influence on China, and any Indian formal abandonment of non-alignment in favour of alliance with the West would diminish both Mr. Khrushchev's incentive and his ability to exert influence of this sort. If this hope regarding Russia should prove a completely broken reed (and already it has shown itself not capable of sustaining much weight) there would still remain, as counts against any complete abandonment of non-alignment, both Mr. Nehru's moral feeling about it (which should not be under-rated) and the fact that, through the whole period of India's independence, its chief diplomatic asset has been its position as "opinion-leader" and spokesman for the non-aligned states. The other states concerned may have offered conspicuously little in the way of help or even sympathy to India in its security-crisis, but a rupture with them would not visibly advance India's interests. Of course, foreign policy cannot be wholly based on a cold calculation of national advantage: popular feeling must also be taken into account, and it is possible that renewed Chinese aggression or an obvious determination to hold on to all the area of Ladakh which its army already occupies would create so much national anger in India as to force Mr. Nehru's hand. And, of course, an indication that China was interested in a serious drive into Assam (as against its present apparent policy of putting itself into a position to "negotiate from strength" concerning the Aksai Chin area) would force India to seek help from the only effective military allies it is likely to find, that is the Western powers. But short of these developments, India seems determined to wear its non-alignment with a difference, rather than abandon it altogether.

As to the rest of the non-aligned world, any assumption that the sight of India's difficulties would cause them to seek the shelter of the Western camp must be discounted. If it were normal to apply to oneself the experience of others, international politics would not present the sort of spectacle that it characteristically does. And there seems no doubt that China's diplomacy has been more successful than India's among the powers concerned, and that many of them are inclined to view the present frontier-demarcation as an illgotten Indian legacy from the British Imperialist past, and to accept with a shrug the Chinese desire to alter it, even by force. Moreover, though India's situation might be held to illustrate the dangers to a militarily-weak power of a policy of non-alignment, the situation of Cuba might equally be held to illustrate the dangers of an effort to shift from non-alignment to a place in the military camp of one of the dominant powers. (Cuba was for a time assumed by the non-alignment powers to be one of themselves: it was for instance invited to the Belgrade Conference in 1961.)

Perhaps the joint meaning of the two crises for the minor powers will eventually resolve itself into a simpler and less agreeable form still: that it is a hard world for militarily vulnerable states, and that the effective decisions remain with the dominant powers. However, the crucial point for the world at large is the effect of the new conditions of contest on the relations between the dominant powers themselves, that is between Russia and America. The central riddle of Russian policy is whether its situation vis-à-vis China in the local balance of power of the Communist world could seem, to the Russian leadership, to hold more dangers to the Russian national interest than its situation vis-à-vis America in the world balance. One can think of many reasons why Mr. Khrushchev or his successor might judge so, the chief being the possibility of "nuclear triggering." Obviously it would be a very complex equation, involving among other things the state of the military balance as regards both America and China. But for the moment we are concerned only with the way this relation affects Russian strategy in the non-aligned world.

For Russia, the non-aligned states might be regarded as in a process of change from so many stalking-horses against the West to a *glacis* against Chinese aggrandisement within the Communist world. Thus the Russian leaders have an interest in strengthening the position of the "national colonial bourgeoisie"—Messrs. Nehru and Nasser and Soekarno *et al.* The Russian line of policy with regard to India in the dispute with China offers an exemplification. There is thus clearly much to be said from the Russian viewpoint in "damping down" revolutionary social ferment in the underdeveloped world. On the other hand it is to the interest of China, as the standard-bearer of militancy within the Communist camp, to step up the struggle, not only because of potential direct accretions to her strength from wavering parties in the underdeveloped world, but because a position of orthodoxy and intransigence (so long as a total rupture is avoided) may be useful for strengthening its hand in negotiations with Russia on other issues, like economic aid.

Thus, as members of the Communist bloc the Chinese had nothing much to lose (save the support of the Indian party) by carrying their frontier-dispute with India to the point of open war. Indeed, the further their advance pushed Mr. Nehru into alliance with the West, the better their case against Mr. Khrushchev on his support of the "colonial national bourgeoisie." And of course, as Chinese, they had a good deal to win, not only in the sense of the national claim to disputed territory, and a strategic strengthening of control of Tibet, but in the demonstration of military ascendancy in Asia and even the securing, ironically, of some support from the Chinese Nationalists in Formosa. The unilateral Chinese proclamation of a cease-fire is an underlining of success, not an abandonment of it. It leaves them in a position to "negotiate from strength" in three senses. Vis-à-vis Mr. Khrushchev it has provided a demonstration of how embarrassing a position he can be pushed into if the struggle is renewed. On the territorial plane the areas of military occupancy seem designed to provide the basis for a "compromise" settlement that will endow China with a substantial area that India has long regarded as its own, the loss of which may damage Mr. Nehru and his government domestically. The cease-fire itself and the virtuous protestations of readiness for a negotiated settlement have placed on India the onus of renewing hostilities, at a time and place in which the Indian army has shown itself at a disadvantage, against the urgings of his non-aligned friends of the Colombo conference, and at the risk of having to make concessions to Pakistan which would be even less domestically palatable than any made to China. Mr. Chou En Lai's reputation as a notably astute diplomatist is well sustained: one wonders how Mr. Nehru now feels about having helped this particular djinn into his present sphere of influence in 1954.

Yet even the wiliest players of the power-political game find their techniques to some extent governed by the real distribution of the cards of power and interest. The limits of Russian acquiescence in courses deemed likely to prove dangerous to Russia itself have already been publicly indicated by Mr. Khrushchev, in his speech of 12 December 1962 pointing out that the American so-called "paper tiger" had nuclear teeth. One may also interpret the comparative nonchalance with which he accepted the outcome of events in Cuba as conveying some relief at having had it demonstrated to China how dangerous and intransigent the "American imperialists" could be when their interests were threatened. The limiting factor in Chinese ability to push its policies in the *tiers monde* to extremes is the danger of creating (or enhancing) some kind of diplomatic consensus, or sense of common interest, between America and Russia. It is not fanciful to see the faint hint of such a development in their joint settlement of the Cuba crisis.

Mr. Isaac Deutscher's analysis[8] of the nature of the understanding reached between Khrushchev and Castro during the latter's recent visit to Moscow provides an interesting illustration of the mode in which the contest between Moscow and Peking for the loyalty of the revolutionary leadership in the *tiers monde* does in fact operate to create a kind of common interest between Washington and Moscow. According to Deutscher, Castro returned home to repudiate his own and his party's "unrealistic revolutionary idealism," and to assure the Cubans that they have no real grounds to fear American aggression, because of the prevalence of sound and realistic thinking in official Washington! If this is indeed Dr. Castro's new position, one might say that Mr. Khrushchev has succeeded in converting him to a view that the Americans had been failing to persuade him of ever since 1959. Even taking all this with a handful of salt, its relevance to the growth of a minimal diplomatic consensus between America and Russia, about the management of the world balance of power, seems obvious, and has been very shrewdly and properly capitalized on by President Kennedy in his new initiative vis-à-vis Russia over the ban on nuclear tests. For the underlying issue

---

[8] *Sydney Morning Herald,* 19 June 1963.

here—the nuclear weapons oligopoly—is the other mainstay of the potential minimal diplomatic consensus between America and Russia. Together these two issues might prove strong enough to sustain a safety-net of shared power-interests under the perilous balancing-act of contemporary international politics.

This paper is being completed before the July meeting of the Russian and Chinese Communist parties, and the author is therefore conscious that what follows is itself a somewhat perilous balancing-act. Nevertheless, if one were determined to live dangerously one might hazard the view that the logical area in which to expect a further working-out of this three-cornered conflict may perhaps be Vietnam. If events were pushed towards a military crisis on the 1954 pattern in the south of the country, America would be faced with the prospect of a greater degree of intervention, and thus Russia faced with the choice of a new confrontation with American power or with selling down the river a "movement of national liberation" more genuine than some. The question is whether the local situation is ripe for such a development. It is obviously impossible through the screen of censorship for an outsider to know precisely what the military balance is, but such evidence as has leaked through, concerning for instance the operations at Ap Bac, early this year, offers some similarities to that in the north in 1953, not long before the showdown of Dien Bien Phu. In terms of the strategic theory propounded by the commanding North Vietnamese general, Vo Nguyen Giap, such conflicts pass through three stages, firstly guerilla harassment by "local" forces, secondly more ambitious mobile operations by "regional" forces and thirdly a general offensive by "regular" troops. It is said that Western successes have put the Communist drive off schedule, but one cannot overlook the possibility that the third phase may be impending. The Vietnamese Communist leadership, after some initial resistance, has apparently allowed itself to be induced into the Chinese camp and the allurements for it of a possible victory in the south to match that in the north need no underlining.

One must therefore assume that a re-enactment of the 1954 choice might in due course confront President Kennedy—that is, a choice between full-scale and overt American military involvement or a sharp deterioration in the military control exercised by the South Vietnamese government in its section of the country. Grave as would be the dangers of such a situation, there would be one element of advantage for the West in it, lacking in the 1954 parallel. The conflict between Russia and China was at that time dormant or just beginning to stir, whereas it is now so fully developed as to exert an indubitable and perhaps decisive influence on Russian choices. The two dominant powers have a major common interest: seeing that the strategic direction of world communism does not pass to China. There is a certain irony in the reflection that the underdeveloped world from which Mr. Nehru hoped to banish power-politics may prove the operative factor in a shift in power-alignments as momentous as can well be imagined.

PART TWO:

Defense Policy-Making

STRATEGIC PLANNING AND

THE POLITICAL PROCESS

Samuel P. Huntington

I

For a decade or more statesmen and scholars have been unhappy about American methods of making decisions on strategic programs—that is, decisions on the over-all size of the military effort, the scope and character of military programs (continental defense, anti-submarine warfare), the composition of the military forces (force levels), and the number and nature of their weapons. The most common criticisms have been:

1. National security policy lacks unity and coherence. Decisions are made on an ad hoc basis, unguided by an over-all purpose.

2. National security policies are stated largely in terms of compromises and generalities. The real issues are not brought to the highest level for decision.

3. Delay and slowness characterize the policy-making process.

4. The principal organs of policy-making, particularly the National Security Council, are ineffective vehicles for the development of new ideas and approaches. They tend to routinize the old rather than stimulate the new.

5. Policy-making procedures tend to magnify the obstacles and difficulties facing any proposed course of action.

6. These deficiencies are primarily the product of government by committee, especially when the committee members must represent the interests of particular departments and services.

Few persons familiar with the processes by which strategic programs are determined would challenge the general accuracy of these allegations. The persistence of the criticism since World War II, moreover, suggests that the defects are not incidental phenomena easily remedied by exhortations to high-mindedness, assertions of executive authority, or changes in personnel or Administration. Instead, it suggests the necessity of viewing the defects in the context of the political system of which they are a part, and of analyzing the functions which they serve in that system and the underlying causes which have brought them into existence.

Reprinted from *Foreign Affairs,* January, 1960.

II

In domestic legislation, it is often said, the Executive proposes and Congress disposes. Except when a presidential veto seems likely to be involved, the political processes of arousing support or opposition for bills are directed toward the Congress. In determining strategic programs, on the other hand, the effective power of decision rests not with Congress and its committees but with the President and his advisors.

Congressional incapactiy to determine force levels and strategic programs is often attributed to the lack of proper information and technical competence. This is indeed a factor, but it is only a contributory one. Congressmen often tend to consider broad questions of general military policy as technical while at the same time they do not hesitate to probe thoroughly and to render judgments about highly specialized and detailed questions of military administration. The inability of Congress to act effectively on strategic programs derives primarily not from its technical failings but from its political ones.

The initiation and elimination of programs and the apportionment of resources among them are highly political decisions involving conflicting interests and groups. They can be made only by bodies in which all the conflicting interests can be brought in focus. The principal groups concerned with the determination of strategic programs are the armed services, the Office of the Secretary of Defense, the State Department, the Treasury, the Budget Bureau, plus a few other governmental departments. The military programs have to be weighed against each other, against conflicting interpretations of the security threats and military requirements, against domestic needs and non-military foreign policy programs, and against probable tax revenues and the demands of fiscal policy. No congressional committee is competent to do this, not because it lacks the technical knowledge, but because it lacks the legal authority and political capability to bring together all these conflicting interests, balance off one against another, and arrive at some sort of compromise or decision. Congress cannot effectively determine strategic programs because the interests which are primarily concerned with those programs are not adequately represented in any single congressional body. The armed services, appropriations, finance, foreign relations, space and atomic energy committees are all, in one way or another, involved in the process. No one of them can have more than a partial view of the interests involved in the determination of any single major strategic program. Every congressional action in military affairs is to some extent *ex parte*.

Congressional bodies may become advocates of particular programs, but they lack sufficient political competence to determine an over-all program. After World War II, except when confronted by similar competing programs, Congress *never* vetoed directly a major strategic program, a force-level recommendation or a major weapons system proposed by the Administration in power. Nor did Congress ever achieve this result, with one partial exception (the Navy's second nuclear carrier), through the failure to appropriate funds recommended by the Executive. The relative inviolability of the military requests was striking when compared with those for domestic or foreign aid appropriations. Almost regularly, of course, Congress reduced the *total* military request, but it virtually never did this in a manner which seriously affected a major strategic program. Quite properly, Congressmen generally feel that they are ill-equipped to be responsible for the security of the country, and they have, by and large, recognized and accepted the decisive role of the Executive in formulating strategic programs. "God help the American people," Senator Russell once remarked, "if Congress starts legislating military strategy."

The inability and unwillingness of Congress to choose and decide does not mean that congressional groups play no role in the formulation of strategic programs. On the contrary, with respect to strategy, Congress has, like Bagehot's queen, "the right to be consulted, the right to encourage, the right to warn." The most prominent congressional role is that of prodder or goad of the Executive on behalf of specific programs or activities. With the Executive as the decision-maker, Congress has become the lobbyist. Congressional groups engage in sustained campaigns of pressure and persuasion to produce the desired strategic decisions on the part of the Executive, just as in other areas the Administration uses pressure and persuasion to move its legislation through Congress.

In lobbying with the Executive, Congress employs three major techniques. First, congressional groups may attempt, through letters, speeches, investigations and threats of retaliation in other fields, to bring continuing pressure upon the Administration to construct certain types of weapons. The Joint Committee on Atomic Energy, for instance, has been an active lobby on behalf of nuclear weapons: its members played important roles in prompting executive decisions on the hydrogen bomb, the nuclear powered submarine, the intermediate-range ballistic missiles. On the other hand, no lobby ever scores 100 percent, and the Committee was somewhat less successful with the Polaris speed-up and the nuclear-powered airplane.

Second, congressional groups may establish force-level minimums for their favored services or appropriate more money for the services than the Administration requested. In these cases, Congress attempts to use its ancient powers of authorization and appropriation for the positive purpose of establishing *floors,* whereas these powers were designed originally for the negative purpose of establishing *ceilings* to prevent a tyrannical executive from maintaining military forces without the consent of the people. Such actions undoubtedly influence the Administration in planning future force levels, and in two cases involving the National Guard and the Marine Corps, the Administration formally complied with congressional wishes. In the final analysis, however, no way has yet been evolved of compelling an Administration to maintain forces it does not wish to maintain or to spend money it does not wish to spend.

Third, Congress can bring pressure upon the Executive through investigation and debate. Although it is generally held that Congress' power to investigate rests upon its power to legislate, in actual fact Congress investigates, in the grand manner, matters which it cannot legislate. The activities of Senators McCarthy and Kefauver are obvious examples, but more reputable and worthwhile ones are furnished by the great investigations of strategy: the 1949 inquiry into "Unification and Strategy," the 1951 MacArthur investigation, the 1956 Symington airpower hearings, and the Johnson missile investigation of 1957–1958. None of these directly produced legislation but they did compel the Administration to make a public defense of its policies, enabled Congress to bring pressure to bear on the executive and helped to educate the attentive public on strategic issues.

III

Strategic programs are thus decided upon in the Executive rather than in Congress. The process of decision within the Executive, however, bears many striking resemblances to the process of decision in Congress. It retains a peculiarly legislative flavor. Legislative and executive *processes* of policy-making do not necessarily correspond to the legislative and executive *branches* of government. A policy-making process is legislative in character to the extent that (1) the units participating in the process are relatively equal in power (and consequently must bargain with each other), (2) important disagreements exist concerning the goals of policy, and (3) there are many possible alternatives. A process is executive in character to the extent that (1) the participating units differ in power (*i.e.* are hierarchically arranged), (2) fundamental goals and values are not at issue, and (3) the range of possible choice is limited.

Strategic programs, like other major policies, are not the product of expert planners rationally determining the actions necessary to achieve desired goals. Rather, they are the product of controversy, negotiation and bargaining among different groups with different interests and perspectives. The conflicts between budgeteers and security spokesmen, between the defenders of military and non-military programs, among the four services, and among the partisans of massive retaliation, continental defense and limited war, are as real and as sharp as most conflicts of group interests in Congress. The location of the groups within the executive branch makes their differences no less difficult to resolve. The variety and importance of the interests, the intensity of the conflicting claims, the significance of the values at stake, all compel recourse to the complex processes of legislation. The inability of Congress to legislate strategic programs does not eliminate the necessity to proceed through a legislative process. It simply concentrates it in the executive branch.

To be sure, the specific techniques for innovating proposals, mobilizing support, distracting and dissuading opponents, and timing decisions may differ in the executive "legislative" process from those in the congressional "legislative" process. None the less, in its broad outlines the development of a major strategic program, such as continental air defense, lacks none of the phases involved in the passage of a major piece of domestic legislation through Congress. The need for the program is recognized by an executive agency or some skill group (nuclear physicists) or consulting group close to the executive branch. The agency or group develops policy proposals to deal with the problem and arouses support for them among other executive agencies, congressional committees and, possibly, some non-governmental groups. Opposition develops. Alternative solutions to the problem are proposed. Coalitions pro and con are organized. The proposals are referred from committee to committee. Consultants and advisory groups lend their prestige to one side or another. The policies are bargained over and compromised. Eventually a decision or, more accurately, an agreement is hammered out among the interested agencies, probably through the mechanisms of the Joint Chiefs of Staff and the National Security Council, and is approved by the President. The locus of decision is executive; the process of decision is primarily legislative.

The building of a consensus for a particular strategic program is as complex and subtle as it is for either domestic policy or foreign policy. At a minimum, within the Executive, it involves complicated interlocking patterns of vertical bargaining along the executive hierarchy and horizontal bargaining through a conciliar structure. In almost no executive hierarchy is the exercise of power all in one direction: the actual authority—even the influence—of administrative superiors over their subordinates is hedged around by a variety of inhibiting considerations. Underlying the hierarchy is a set of bargaining relationships, explicit or implicit. The dispersion of power in American society and the separation of powers in government tend to reinforce this tendency. Agencies and officials in subordinate positions often are substantially independent of their administrative superiors. At best the superior may be able to persuade; at worst he may be openly defied.

Vertical bargaining is exemplified in the efforts of the Administration to secure the concurrence of the Joint Chiefs of Staff, individually and collectively, in its budgetary and force-level decisions. On the one hand, each Chief presses for what he believes is essential for his service; on the other, the Administration attempts to cut back and fit service demands into its strategic plan and budgetary goals. Each side has to balance the risks involved in alienating the other against the benefits gained in shaping the final decision. The interlarding of hierarchical and bargaining roles inevitably enhances the possibilities for ambiguity and confusion. As subordinates the Chiefs would be expected to accept but not necessarily to approve decisions made by their administrative superiors. "I'd be worried," Secretary Wilson once declared, "if Ridgway didn't believe in the good old Army." [1] On the other hand, the semi-autonomous position of the Chiefs enhances the value of their approval to their superiors. An administrative decision derives legitimacy (as well as effectiveness) in part from its acceptance and support by the subordinate officials and agencies affected by it. Consequently, great efforts are made to secure the Chiefs' concurrence. "The pressure brought on me to make my military judgment conform to the views of higher authority," General Ridgway declared, "was sometimes subtly, sometimes crudely, applied." [2] The intensity of the pressure applied was tribute to the value of the approval sought.

While vertical bargaining plays a crucial role in strategic decision-making, horizontal bargaining is probably even more widespread and important. Theoretically, of course, authority to determine strategic programs rests with the President and the Secretary of Defense. Actually, the compromising and balancing of interests tends focus about the two most important committees in the executive branch of the national government: the J.C.S. and the N.S.C. On the surface, it seems strange that two committees should play such important roles in the formulation of military policy and national security. These are areas where one might expect clear-cut lines of authority and executive decision-making. Within the executive branch, few committees of comparable stature exist in domestic areas of policy-making. The J.C.S. and the N.S.C. are significant, however, precisely because they do perform essentially legislative rather than executive functions. They have what Congress lacks: the political capability to legislate strategy. Just as agricultural policy is the product of conflict, bargaining and compromise among the interested groups represented in Congress, military strategy is the product of conflict, bargaining and compromise among the interested groups represented in the J.C.S. and the N.S.C. Hence, the same criticisms are now leveled at these committees which have long been leveled at Congress: logrolling prevails; over-all objectives get lost in the mechanism; a premium is put upon agreement rather than decision. Just as Congress often wrote tariff legislation by giving each industry the protection it wanted, the N.S.C. and the Joint Chiefs make decisions on weapons by giving each service what it desires. The individual members of these bodies suffer the classic conflict known to members of all legislatures: on the one hand, they must represent the interests of their departments or constituencies; on the other, their decisions are expected to be in the national interest.

---

[1] Duncan Norton-Taylor, "The Wilson Pentagon," *Fortune,* December 1954, p. 94.

[2] General Matthew B. Ridgway, "My Battles in War and Peace," *The Saturday Evening Post,* January 21, 1956, p. 46.

IV

In strategy, as elsewhere, effective policy requires some measure of both content and consensus. Strategic programs, like statutes or treaties, are both prescriptions for future action and ratifications of existing power relationships. A strategy which is so vague or contradictory that it provides no prescription for action is no strategy. So too, a strategy whose prescriptions are so unacceptable that they are ignored is no strategy. Consensus is a cost to each participant but a prerequisite of effective policy.

In strategy-making, as in congressional legislating, one means of avoiding disagreement is to postpone decision. The proliferation of committees serves the useful political end of facilitating and, in some cases, legitimizing the avoidance of decision. Issues can be referred from committee to committee, up and down the hierarchy. Normally the same service and departmental interests are represented on all the committees; agreement in one is just as unlikely as agreement in any other. Controversial decisions may also be removed entirely from the jurisdiction of the N.S.C. or the Joint Chiefs and devolved back upon the interested agencies; the "decision" is that each will pursue its own policy. Disagreement on major issues also may be avoided simply by devoting more time to minor ones. The J.C.S. "dips into matters it should avoid," Vannevar Bush complained in 1952, "it fails to bring well considered resolution to our most important military problems, and it fritters away its energy on minutiae." [3] The Joint Chiefs, however, were treading a classic legislative path. In almost identical terms, political scientists for years have accused Congress of refusing to grapple with major issues of public policy and of wasting time and energy on minor matters of administrative detail.

Where stringent limits are imposed from the outside, the decision-makers are especially prone to compromise. As the $14 and $13 billion ceilings firmly succeeded each other in the late 1940s, the tendency to divide the funds equally among the three services became more and more pronounced. On the other hand, if the limits permitted by superior executive authority are relatively undefined or broad, logrolling enables each agency to obtain what it considers most important. The result is "Operation Paperclip," in which Army, Navy and Air Force proposals are added together and called a joint plan. Duplication in weapons systems—Thor and Jupiter, Nike and Bomarc —is simply the price of harmony. It is hardly surprising that the J.C.S. should be referred to as "a trading post." This, after all, is the traditional legislative means of achieving agreement among conflicting interests. As one Congressman remarked to his colleagues:

---

[3] "Planning," speech at Mayo Clinic Auditorium, Rochester, Minnesota, September 26, 1952, p. 8.

If you are concerned, you politicians, with getting unanimity of action, I refer you to the Joint Chiefs of Staff. There is a classic example of unanimity of action on anything: You scratch my back and I will scratch yours. "Give me atomic carriers," says the Navy, "and you can have your B-52s in the Air Force." I do not know why General Taylor is going along, because I have never been able to find anything that the Army is getting out of the deal.[4]

The political and legislative character of the strategy-making process also casts a different light on the argument that the N.S.C. and J.C.S. have failed to initiate new policy proposals. As many observers of the domestic legislative process have pointed out, relatively few statutes actually originate within a legislative assembly. They are first developed by interest groups or executive agencies. It is therefore not surprising that relatively few strategic programs originally come to life in the committees or staffs of the N.S.C. or J.C.S. The latter necessarily serve as negotiating bodies; the responsibility for innovation lies with the participating agencies.

Just as much of the early criticism of Congress stemmed from a failure to appreciate the political roles of that body, so much of the criticism of the N.S.C. and J.C.S. stems from the application to these bodies of nonpolitical standards. At times in the past, it has been assumed that through investigation and debate all members of a legislative body should arrive at similar conclusions as to where the public interest lay. More recently, conflict within a legislature has been viewed as normal, and policy thought of as the result, not of a collective process of rational inquiry, but of a mutual process of political give and take. Congress is seldom criticized today because of conflicts and disagreements among its members. To a considerable extent, however, the J.C.S. and the N.S.C. are judged by the former theory: in them disagreement is still considered inherently evil. As one naval officer wryly commented: "How curious it is that the Congress *debates,* the Supreme Court *deliberates,* but for some reason or other the Joint Chiefs of Staff just *bicker!*" [5]

Significantly, the Joint Chiefs have also been criticized for employing precisely those mechanisms designed for reaching agreement: delay, devolution, referral, platitudinous policies, compromise, logrolling. On the one hand, the Chiefs are criticized because they cannot resolve major issues; on the other hand, they are criticized because they do resolve them through the classic means of politics.

Much criticism of strategic decision-making has failed to appreciate the tenuous and limited character of hierarchical authority in American government. Reacting against the prevalence of horizontal bargaining, the critics

---

[4] Rep. Daniel J. Flood, *Congressional Record* (85th Congress, 1st Session), May 27, 1957, p. 7733.
[5] Vice Admiral H. E. Orem, "Shall We Junk the Joint Chiefs of Staff?" *U.S. Naval Institute Proceedings,* February 1958, p. 57.

have advocated the abolition of committees and the strengthening of executive controls. In brief periods of emergency, presidential coordination may partially replace the normal bargaining processes. But no presidential laying on of hands can accomplish this on a permanent basis. Decisions on strategic programs are simply too important to be fitted into a symmetrical and immaculate model of executive decision-making. Clarifications of the chain of command and legal assertions of formal authority may reduce bargaining, but they can never eliminate it. Each of the three reorganizations of the military establishment since 1947 has purported to give the Secretary of Defense full legal authority to control his department and yet each succeeding Secretary found his control circumscribed if not frustrated. The existence of counterparts to the N.S.C. and J.C.S. in virtually every other modern state suggests that the causes which have brought them into existence may be pervasive and inherent in the problems with which they deal.

The problem of legislating strategic programs is thus the dual one of producing both content and consensus. On the one hand, little is gained by assuming that effective policy can be achieved without compromise, or that the political problems of strategy-making can be eliminated by strengthening the executive chain of command. On the other hand, it is also impossible to accept what emerges from the bargaining processes as ipso facto in the national interest. Too often, this has blatantly not been the case, and national purposes have been lost in bureaucratic feuding and compromise. The road to reform begins with recognition of the inherently complex political and legislative character of strategic decision-making. The need is for methods which will, at best, contribute both to the substance and the acceptance of policy, or, failing that, at least contribute more to the improvement of one than to the impairment of the other.

V

When the strategy-making process is viewed as essentially legislative in nature, the critical points appear to be not the prevalence of bargaining but rather the weakness of legislative leadership and the limited scope of the strategic consensus.

In the traditional legislative process, interest groups and executive agencies originate proposals, the President integrates them into a coherent legislative program, Congress debates, amends and decides. In the strategy-making process, executive agencies and related groups originate proposals, the N.S.C., the J.C.S., the President and Secretary of Defense debate, amend and decide upon them. But who plays the role of the legislative leader? Who winnows out the various ideas in the light of an over-all set of priorities or grand strategy and integrates these proposals into general programs which can then be discussed, amended and ratified? In the decade after World War II no clear concept developed as to which official or agency had the responsibility for leading the J.C.S. and the N.S.C. in their deliberations. In actual practice, leadership tended to rest with the Chairman in the J.C.S. and with the Department of State in the N.S.C. However, the case was frequently made for expanding the N.S.C. staff in the Executive Office of the President and for strengthening the Special Assistant for National Security Affairs. Similarly, it was often urged that the Secretary of Defense be provided with a mixed civilian-military policy staff which would, at least, give him an independent source of advice, and, at most, enable him to play a stronger role in making strategic decisions. Other suggestions[6] include the creation outside the executive hierarchy of a council of elder statesmen, a "supreme court" for foreign and military policy, or an "academy of political affairs" (modeled on the National Academy of Sciences) which could study national security problems, issue reports and advise the President directly.

It seems likely that either the leadership functions of the Secretary of State and the Chairman of the Joint Chiefs will become more fully recognized and clarified, or the Special Assistant and Secretary of Defense will develop the staff facilities necessary to perform these functions, or new organs of policy recommendation will come into existence. Such developments would not only facilitate consensus but also would probably improve the content of strategic decisions. The form in which issues are presented for decision often drastically affects the nature of the decision. The problem in the Executive today resides not in the presence of bargaining but rather at the point at which bargaining begins. The development of more effective leadership organs in the N.S.C. and J.C.S. would permit bargaining to be more limited and focused. The starting point would become not three separate proposals advanced by three separate departments but rather one set of proposals advanced by the legislative leader. The requirements of consensus might still cause those proposals to be torn apart tooth and limb, but, at the very least, the clear visibility of the mutilation would have certain restraining effects. It has had them in Congress.

A related and perhaps more important problem concerns the relatively limited scope of the strategic consensus. The strategy-making process goes on largely within the Executive, and the consensus arrived at, if any, is primarily an executive one. As a result, it tends to be both tenuous and tentative. Although the effective power of decision rests with the executive branch, the possibility always exists that it may be upset by forces from the outside. Consequently the activity of the Administration is largely devoted to defending a policy which has been decided upon rather than advocating a policy which has yet to be adopted.

In the traditional legislative process, an issue is debated first within the

---

[6] See Walter Millis, *The Constitution and the Common Defense.* New York: The Fund for the Republic, 1959, p. 36–46.

Executive and then publicly within and about Congress. All the debate, however, contributes directly or indirectly to shaping the final product: to pushing the legislation through without change, amending it in one direction or another, or defeating it entirely. When the President signs the bill, the policy-making process is over, and the debate stops—or at least lessens—for a while. In strategy-making, debate among the various executive agencies and related groups also contributes directly to shaping the measure. Once the decision is made, this debate subsides, but as soon as the decision becomes known to non-executive agencies and groups, the public debate begins. The likelihood of such debate may have had its effects upon the executive policy-makers before the decision was reached, but their anticipation of public reaction to policy often is, at best, an informed hunch and, at worst, a rationalization that the public will not accept policies which they do not accept themselves. Public debate of a strategic decision may also affect its implementation and may influence subsequent decisions. Coming after the initial decision, however, the debate necessarily loses much of its force and value.

It is striking that both the Truman and Eisenhower Administrations, different as they are otherwise, have been regularly criticized for not exercising "leadership" in national security policy. In each case, it is alleged, the President has failed to take the initiative in bringing strategic issues to the people, in arousing support for foreign and military policy proposals, and in educating the public to its responsibilities in the nuclear age. Such criticism assumes that the President should play the same leadership role in strategic matters that he does in domestic legislation. In the latter, the President must be the source of energy for his program, and it is normally in his interest to dramatize the issue and to broaden the public concerned with it. The concept of presidential leadership is that of Theodore Roosevelt, Wilson, F.D.R. rallying support for a legislative program which he is urging upon a recalcitrant Congress.

In the strategy process, however, the President's role is very different, and the domestic model is inapplicable. Here, the President and his Administration have little reason to desire public debate and many reasons to fear it. The decision has been made; the policy is being implemented. The extension of the public concerned with the policy can only lead to pressure to change it in one respect or another and to the exploitation of the issues by the opposition. The primary role of the Administration has to be defensive: to protect the balance of interests, the policy equilibrium which has been laboriously reached within the Executive, against the impact of profane forces and interests outside the Executive. Mr. Cutler put the matter bluntly when he declared:

There is another seamlessness in our complex world: the fabric of our national defense. Perhaps the most potent argument against public disclosure of secret projects or of short-falls (which inevitably always exist) in any one aspect of our national defense is that such disclosure builds up a Potomac propaganda war to rectify that defect or over-finance that project. But if you devote larger resources to one area of national defense, you are apt to imbalance the rest.[7]

Given the nature of the decision-making process, this concern is a natural one. The cold-war Presidents have evolved a variety of means to limit public interest in strategy, to minimize the concern of external groups with force levels and weapons, and, most particularly, to insulate and protect the executive balance from the disruption of outside interests. Hence the tendency of both Presidents and their Administrations to reassure the public, to pour on the "soothing syrup" which has so exasperated the Alsops and others, to limit the information available on American deficiencies and Soviet achievements, to discount these achievements and to minimize their significance, to preserve discipline and to suppress leaks, to discourage dissenting and disquieting testimony before congressional committees, and in general to maintain an air of calm assurance, an imperturbable façade. All these actions stem from a fear of the fragility of the executive consensus and of the irrationality and uncontrollability of the external political forces. These are the new "defensive" weapons of presidential leadership, as important to an Administration in the formulation of strategy as the old "offensive" techniques are in the promotion of domestic legislation in Congress.

A striking feature of the past dozen years has been the extent to which expressions of alarm at the decline of presidential leadership have occurred simultaneously with expressions of alarm at the growth of executive power. This apparent paradox simply reflects the fact that the increasing responsibility of the executive branch in making crucial decisions on strategic programs has undermined the ability of the President to lead. The more the President becomes, at least in theory, the judge, the less he can be the advocate. Yet, in practice, even his power to decide strategic issues is difficult to exercise. To be sure, the N.S.C. and the J.C.S. are theoretically only his advisors: no policy exists until he has approved it. But in part this is a myth to preserve the appearance of presidential decision-making. Surely the President does not over-ride united opinion among his top advisors much more often than he vetoes acts of Congress. The theory that the President makes the decisions, in short, serves as a cloak to shield the elaborate processes of executive legislation and bargaining through which the policies are actually hammered out. Consequently, the President may be less influential as a decision-maker than he is as a legislative leader. The latter function is personal to him. The former is one which he shares with a variety of other groups in the executive branch.

Whatever defects may exist in this situation cannot be removed by shifting

---

[7] "The Seamless Web," *Harvard Alumni Bulletin,* June 4, 1955, p. 665.

the point of decision away from the executive branch. The tenuous character of the decisions and the defensive role of the Administration could be modified only by broadening the scope of discussion and concern in the early stages of the policy process—*before* key decisions are made. Once adequate legislative leadership emerges in the executive branch, the debate could focus on the proposals of this leadership, provided they were made public to the fullest extent possible. Greater publicity for and public participation in strategy-making at an earlier stage would tend to restrain some of the more gross forms of "horse trading" in the Executive, and should enhance the President's actual power of decision. At present, one way in which issues are brought to the top and forced upon the President for decision is through the lobbying activities of congressional committees. Broader and earlier public discussion of strategic programs would in all probability have a similar effect, and instead of interested guesses we would be provided with concrete evidence of what "the public will support." Certainly, discussion is more useful before decisions are made than afterwards. Broadening the scope of the policy consensus could well go hand in hand with improving the quality of the policy content.

CONGRESSMEN AND THE

MAKING OF MILITARY POLICY[1]

Lewis Anthony Dexter

ROLE CONCEPTIONS OF CONGRESSMEN

This report is concerned with the way in which congressmen, especially those assigned to committees dealing with military matters, interpret their role and status, and what they assert and affirm about their exercise of influence over military policy and military men.

The conceptions held by a group of men about their role, status, responsibility, and influence presumably have some sort of relationship to what they actually do—but there is no reason for supposing that the relationship is direct and unequivocal.[2] Men may, consciously or unconsciously,[3] emphasize

---

[1] This paper was based upon 100 interviews, chiefly with members of congressional committees having military responsibility and other leading congressmen, and with a few committee staff members, administrative assistants, and legislative liaison personnel from the Department of Defense. The majority of these interviews were undertaken under contract with the Center for International Studies, Massachusetts Institute of Technology, under a Carnegie Corporation grant; others were for the Advisory Committee on Civil Defense, National Research Council. The writer had previously conducted 400 interviews with congressmen, lobbyists, and prominent constituents on foreign trade issues, often touching on "defense essentiality." This other study appears in part in R. Bauer, I. Pool, and L. Dexter, *American Business and Public Policy* (New York: Atherton Press, 1963). See also, "The Representative and His District," reprinted as Chapter I of [R. Peabody and N. Polsby, eds., *New Perspectives on the House of Representatives* (Chicago: Rand McNally, 1963)]. An emphatic disclaimer must be made of any responsibility of anyone but myself for any views or findings stated or implied herein.

[2] This point probably ought to be a perfectly obvious one, but I was delayed in interpreting the results of interviews conducted in 1955–57 because it took me five years fully to see that I was not reporting on how congressmen affect military policy but simply on *how congressmen define* their role and responsibility in regard to military policy.

Were this simply a personal error of my own, it would hardly be worth commenting upon, but I suspect that whether relying upon documents or interviews, a good many reports about politics, especially about Congress, fall into a similar error—role definition, attitude, or orientation, is interpreted as though it threw *direct* light on the substantive exercise of influence or formation of policy. An extreme, but obvious, parallel is this: a whole series of interviews with quarrelling husbands and wives could not necessarily tell us what happens when spouses disagree. What it would tell us—and an extremely important thing to know—is how husbands and wives of certain sorts interpret their roles, responsibilities, etc. But it is important to know, too, what such sources do not *by themselves* yield.

[3] I am certain that all the congressmen (not necessarily all the staff assistants or Department of Defense personnel) I interviewed were "sincere" in expressing the

or underemphasize their influence and importance; they may emphasize one aspect of their activity and underemphasize another. Tentatively, it seems reasonable to suppose that the way in which men define situations has some effect on how they behave in those situations; this point (that men's definitions tend to have real and significant consequences) presumably is just as important in studying the congressional work-roles as in studying any other social behavior.

MILITARY POLICY IS NOT CONSIDERED

Congressmen interviewed generally indicate that they have little tendency to raise or consider questions of military policy *in terms of its meaning for some national or international political objective or goal.* By military policy is meant specific decisions about interpreting or handling weapons, personnel, appropriations, missions, organization, administration. In fact, during the 1946–57 period, few examples could be found where congressional committees created any impression of seriously evaluating decisions about weapons, appropriations, personnel, missions, organization, or administration in term of national or international goals or objectives. The great difficulty in making this statement is the obvious fact that here, as elsewhere in politics, there is a rhetoric of justification which purports to explain what was decided in terms of high and serious considerations quite regardless of the relevance of these considerations to the decision-making process. I have not come across any major example where the rhetoric of justification seems to reflect much predecision policy analysis; nor have I found any other evidence during the 1946–57 period where there seems to have been much congressional concern with the over-all policy implications of military decisions.

On the other hand, instances where Congress has *appeared* to concern itself with over-all military policy seem generally to fall into one of the following categories: (1) Those where Congress feels it is able to judge between clamoring claimants—usually different military services—and give one or another of them a larger slice of the available pie. (2) Where congressmen are concerned with some local situation, usually an employment situation. Congressional support, especially support in the House of Repre-

---

definition of their stated role—of course a different situation or a different interviewing technique might have stimulated other, contradictory, but equally sincere definitions of role. There has been so little experimentation on the conscious modification of interview technique in the interviewing of elite personnel that one simply has to guess as to how "representative of the range of alternative roles which an individual may assume the particular responses in a given interview are. I would guess—partly on the basis of other interviews on other subjects with some of the same informants, partly on the basis of direct personal acquaintance with some of them and personal acquaintance with many who have worked with a number of them, and partly on "intuition"—that the responses I use are representative.

sentatives, of what Huntington has called "strategic monism," [4] consisted largely of the congressional assumption of a judicial role, tempered by the pressure of various local contractor and employment interests—all within a framework of verbal "toughness." This is stance rather than a policy.

Congressmen also occasionally wish to mollify widespread personnel complaints (*e.g.*, those emanating from the National Guard mobilization in 1961). And, of course, congressmen have personal concerns of their own (*e.g.*, personal loyalty to the Marine Corps). And, naturally, they always have straight constituent interests to defend (*e.g.*, preserving specific military installations in local areas).[5]

POLICY ANALYSIS: MILITARY VERSUS CIVILIAN

The attitudes and responses to military policy-making of members of the congressional committees concerned with military policy contrasted with

---

[4] Samuel P. Huntington, "Radicalism and Conservatism in National Defense Policy," *Journal of International Affairs,* VIII (1954), 206–33. This exceptionally brilliant analysis of the politics of national defense differs from the present report in one significant respect—it works back from the consequences of significant decisions to presumed ideologies and therefore takes seriously the justifications given in more or less formal statements for the record as to the reasons why a position has been taken. This may be a perfectly valid approach to political behavior, but in the instant case, at least, it seems to the writer that it misleads, much as the effort to categorize office-holders in terms of what they happen on some particular issue to say about "home rule" would mislead. Unfortunately, in terms of the available data and the present state of political science knowledge, there is no clear reason for choosing between Huntington's approach and others.

[5] R. H. Dawson, "Congressional Innovation and Intervention in Defense Policy: Legislative Authorization of Weapons Systems," *American Political Science Review,* LXVI (1962), 42–57 (reprinted as Chapter X of [Peabody and Polsby, *op. cit.*]), reports a congressional effort (in 1959 and following years) to assume more systematic responsibility. Unfortunately, my study and interviews were entirely confined to the pre-1959 period; however, I strongly suspect that when Dawson reports could be interpreted more precisely in terms of the role which Congress from time to time does assume as an arbiter between technologists, discussed below; in the absence of such arbitrament and of such local pressures (as to which congressmen typically do regard themselves as experts) the episode would not have occurred.

I suspect, also, that Dawson in a sense is dealing with the congressmen's public and overt picture of themselves—the kind of picture which is likely to be presented in reports and speeches—whereas I am dealing with the private picture (the covert culture) of Congress. There is nothing which of necessity makes a man's private picture of himself or a covert culture "truer" than the public picture; both must be taken into account, and, if they are different, may suggest further investigation.

However, it is possibly relevant that in 1955–56, a distinguished scholar, familiar with congressional action on military matters in recent years, initially challenged emphatically my point that Congress in fact had very little influence on military policy. He stated that he had a list of some fourteen areas in which Congress had been influential. But after he reconsidered the point, he stated he had to agree that Congress had either given a little more or a little less than the Department of Defense asked or decided between competing technoolgists, but had not, in fact, undertaken any initiative.

those of members of committees concerned with foreign economic policy. Also, members not on key committees in either field showed a similar difference between these fields. In general, the broad aspects of military policy are not considered. In the tax field, members of Ways and Means often consider the presumptive effect of particular tax legislation upon national economic policy, but military decisions are generally treated by the relevant committees as independent of broader policy decisions.

This need not be the case, for it has not always been the case. In the 1930's, available evidence suggests, Ross Collins of Mississippi, for many years a member, sometime chairman, of the Subcommittee on Military Appropriations of the House Appropriations Committee, did in fact stimulate research and development in tank warfare—and he did a great deal to keep the possibilities of tank warfare before the informed public.[6] In fact, Collins' impact in the United States may be compared with that of the military critics Fuller and Liddell-Hart in Britain and the military officer, de Gaulle, in France. (It may now be largely forgotten that de Gaulle's first claim to fame was as a theorist of mobile warfare.)

In addition, in two particular areas, the Subcommittee on Military Operations of the House Government Operations Committee during the 1950's played a similar part. For a number of years, serious thinking about *civil* defense, its mission, purpose, and meaning, has been kept alive by that subcommittee, especially by its chairman, Chet Holifield (D.-Calif.); it is probably no exaggeration to say that if it were not for the pressure of the Holifield subcommittee on the administration, the whole subject of civil defense would have lapsed into a patronage "boondoggle." Despite the word "civil," "civil defense" is in fact an item in military policy[7]—but it is quite possible that it was very psychologically important for congressional activity that civil defense was called "civil" and until 1961 had a "civil" administration. If so, this would be crucial in terms of the rest of our argument.[8] Other congressmen were probably more willing to accept Congressman Holifield's leadership here because civil defense seemed civilian; they did not think that they were infringing on military technology.[9]

[6] On Collins, see Frank C. Hanaghen, "The U.S. Army," *Harper's Magazine* (December, 1940), esp. pp. 9–13, and Ross A. Collins, "Do We Want a Mass Army?" *Reader's Digest* (June, 1941), pp. 1–9. It is greatly to be hoped that, with the present emphasis on oral history and on congressional behavior, some foundation will have the imagination and initiative, while some of the participants are still alive, to undertake interviews which would permit testing more accurately such matters as the assertions made in the text about Collins.

[7] The well-known writings of Herman Kahn make this point from one standpoint. From another—emphasis on "Defense Means Protection"—I make the same point in an article by that title, published in the *American Scholar,* XXIV (Summer, 1955), 299–308.

[8] The argument that congressmen are timid about invading the area of the military specialist; see below.

[9] Of course, this fact has been by no means an unalloyed benefit to civil defense. Some of those who advocated the action which actually took place in 1961—the

Particularly under the chairmanship of Congressman Riehlman (R.-N.Y.), but during the entire decade of the fifties, the same subcommittee has also been actively concerned with, and has probably stimulated, intelligent action about the optimal use of scientists in defense research, a matter which is at least on the fringes of military policy.

Congress has had in the past and perhaps has now some influence on military policy. But it is purely negative, probably as a consequence of dogmatic doctrines. Probably Congress made the adequate fortification of Guam by the Franklin Roosevelt Administration impossible, and perhaps that failure to fortify Guam encouraged Japanese militarists.[10]

THE ARMED SERVICES COMMITTEE
"IS PRIMARILY A REAL ESTATE COMMITTEE"

In general, it was necessary to avoid the phrase "policy" in interviews on military policy; it was too ambiguous, although it was not too ambiguous in 1953–56 interviews with congressmen on foreign economic "policy." At that time, it was rarely necessary to explain to congressmen what was meant when we came to discuss policy implications; congressional thinking about the tariff and reciprocal trade have been structured in terms of policy by a history of discussion and communications within and outside Congress.[11]

One congressman, who was probably more concerned about the apparent absence of concern with military policy in the Congress than any other member of a relevant committee with whom I talked, said:

> If I were talking to a new member of [my committee], I'd say that the main problem is to pinpoint responsibility at the White House and the boards [the various councils and committees concerned with national security] for policy determination. You can't really tell who does determine it; it moves into DOD [Department of Defense] and each of the three services, and you have a feeling [that], as relates to appropriations, there is not any unity. The capable men in each area are just

---

transfer of civil defense to the Department of Defense—supported it partly because they thought a military identification would provide it with more prestige. However, part of the objective which advocates of the transfer had in mind was not achieved when the Thomas Subcommittee of the House Appropriations Committee, the subcommittee dealing with independent offices, which was accustomed to deal very harshly with civil defense budget requests, succeeded in keeping responsibility for the civil defense budget. Supporters of civil defense had hoped that the responsibility would be transferred to the Military Appropriations Subcommittee which is inclined to be much more generous and less critical.

[10] Similarly, it is possible that the efforts of a congressman like Kastenmeier (D.-Wis.) to have the Congress, as a national policy, renounce chemical warfare, may indirectly have inhibiting effects upon support for chemical warfare.

[11] In fact, in these interviews, because I was chiefly (though not exclusively) interested in communications, I often found it necessary to steer informants away (sometimes quite sharply, as with the late Senator George of Georgia) from discussion of policy toward consideration of communications.

trying to push for more for their services which is natural, but it means they think more in terms of how to spend more and more money than they do in terms of really thinking out a strategy that would more successfully justify these great appropriations.

In our hearings, I tried for purposes of communication to do some research to determine this matter of policy. What were they thinking of? Did they anticipate [this or that] . . . ? What had they in mind to accomplish?

Then, of course, you wonder about what actually the policy of the Congress is. . . . It's never been clear to me what direction there is in the matter. . . . Policy is supposed to be wrapped up [by the Joint Chiefs] under certain restrictions, but you wonder sometimes if the chairman of the Joint Chiefs knows what is going on in the minds of other chiefs. . . .

After our lengthy hearings, I wonder to what extent members of Congress . . . bring together sufficient staff to get a real perspective. *Most questions even in what are called policy hearings are directed really towards production. This is true equally of off-the-record hearings.* People are asked questions about specific manpower requirements, et cetera, not about general policy.

It does look as though the congressional committees operate in a vacuum. It comes right back to the tragic lack of time for reflection and study on the part of members of the Congress. *So maybe they don't get clear in their minds what policy is.*

. . . I believe there should be some serious policy thinking on the ideological side. It should relate the military to State and USIA. . . .

So far as I know you are the only person in my [more than eight years of] *service in Congress, or outside, who has been making any effort to delve into these problems.* I called on several people in various government departments, DOD, the committee staff, et cetera, to try to help me to frame questions to get at these policy issues [but did not get much help]. Symington's subcommittee is concerned with program and production—not too much with big policy issues.

I can see enormous possibilities in a very careful study of the problem. Could we move into new types of weapons and a future type of defense? How can we become more potent ideologically? [The military] lack direction. We [the Congress] must assume responsibility for policy determination.

More typical was the response of a much more influential member of the House Committee on Armed Services—who, when I tried to explain that I was trying to find out what Congress did do or could do on policy said:

What the hell is the point of that? What would you do with it? I don't see that any public service could be performed by it. You can't find anything particular to say. In fact, how do we [members] know what should be considered? We mostly reflect what the military people recommend; military policy is made by the Department of Defense.

Our committee is a real estate committee.

How do we check the military recommendations? I don't know. We just ask a lot of questions—questions that are not resolved. It's most difficult to make inquiries. Take bases. DOD says we need such-and-such bases. Well, we want to know why such-and-such a size. But we don't mostly know how to evaluate the answers; we aren't equipped to do so. So 95 per cent of the legislation is what DOD recommends. It's only when you come to personnel problems, size of army, that sort of thing, that you find us doing more—and that's naturally because that affects the lives of every voter.

And perhaps the most experienced staff man on military matters on the Hill, when I told him I was studying the Armed Services Committee, repeated again and again, to be sure the idea was properly communicated, "Our committee is a real estate committee. Don't forget that. *If you study our committee, you are studying real estate transactions.*" By that, he meant that the *location of installations and related transfer, purchase, and sale of properties is the main concern of the House Armed Services Committee.*

One of the major reasons why the congressional committees involved concern themselves with accountable and avoidable waste, marginal issues in the appropriations field, personnel problems, and other such peripheral matters is the fear of lack of competence.[12]

THE TYRANNY OF INFORMATION AND IDEAS: "WHO ARE WE TO SAY 'NO'?"

Congress is today better equipped to evaluate, assay, and sometimes develop and integrate ideas than it is to invent them or stimulate their invention. But if Congress is to function smoothly, there must *somewhere* be people who invent and transmit competing ideas. That is to say, generally speaking, Congress can readily check and balance when there are within the politically alert public, sets of ideas and interests which check and balance each other, thus creating a situation within which the Congress is able to *sift, winnow, and judge.*

But if there is no check and balance *outside* the Congress, then the Congress will find it difficult to perform the legislative functions of investigation, inquiry, check, and balance. So far as congressmen are aware (or were aware in 1955–57), there is no such climate of controversy, opinion, and interest pertaining to military policy as such—outside the armed services themselves. The people for the most part certainly believe in a "strong National Defense," but beyond that, the members of Congress receive little or no articulate information on military policy from them. Most congressmen on relevant committees reported in interviews that, so far as constituent views and attitudes on military policy are concerned, there were none! This situation contrasts more or less sharply with other policy fields regarding which

---

[12] I discuss the general phenomenon of the increasing fear by the non-expert of the expert as a function of our schooling and university systems in my book, tentatively titled, "On the Sociology of Stupidity," to be published by Basic Books, 1964.

congressmen may hear a good deal from constituents; the members are well aware of the difference.

In regard to other matters of legislative concern, there are persons known to congressmen who have articulate views and to whom the congressmen can turn for ideas, suggestions, ammunition, and moral backing. The latter point is very important; few congressmen want to challenge the experts in a highly specialized field without first having their own experts to back them.[13]

In any case, members of Congress share the views which they generally attribute to their constituents: they hesitate to question the *basic* proposals of the military; that is, they regard the military as *experts,* not only on matters of organization and command, but on types of war plans, etc. Said one member of a relevant committee, better prepared by previous experience than most committee members, "The whole problem is that we are not military experts, and we have to rely upon what the military people tell us. We try to get them to cut out the window dressing, but it's hard." [14] He repeated several times in the course of our talks the rhetorical question: "Who are we to say 'no' to the military people?" Members do not feel this respect for foreign policy experts from the State Department or for tax experts from the Treasury or for economists from relevant agencies.

MILITARY SPECIALISTS EXERCISE A MONOPOLY ON THE PRESENTATION OF ALTERNATIVES

In terms of the feeling just described, most congressmen and members of the relevant committees usually, if not always, *do* follow the recommendations of the military when these are clearly and explicitly propounded. However, members of Congress do not, in fact, want to know the military's specific war plans for security reasons,[15] and in many cases, they are not at all concerned with the nature of the war plans. In general, they seemed to

---

[13] The point is not so much to be guided by the specific advice of a particular expert; it is, rather, not to stick one's neck out by finding oneself opposed to all those who are "respectable" and "informed." A few seeming experts who take a minority view are all that are sometimes needed to embolden those who latently sympathize with them.

[14] Significantly, in the course of these interviews, no member said anything (except for reference to civil defense theorists) which indicated an awareness that there is within the scientific community considerable controversy about war plans. However, I know that three or four of the members I talked with do have some knowledge of the sort of argument one would find in the *Bulletin of the Atomic Scientists,* but only one of them mentioned the matter in the framework of our interviews. In terms of the orientation of this article—*the social psychology of the occupational interfaces between* congressmen and military specialists—the omission did not need to be challenged; it would be interesting to replicate my interviews today to see if there is more spontaneous mention of the scientific discussion.

[15] That is, they are afraid they will be inhibited and restrained and embarrassed by having access to more confidential security information than they desire to know.

be assuming that there are only two possible kinds of war—either (1) a thermonuclear war, or (2) a Korean-type war. They appear to have no idea that other possibilities (of other kinds of war) are worth investigating.

The military exercises a monopoly or quasi-monopoly on presentation of alternatives, with the result that congressmen have no reason to be aware of the gamut of possibilities open to them. When the generals very largely determine the explanations they hear, and the choices they are forced to make, congressmen have little opportunity to move into an area of reflection broader than that of the generals—unless they have the time and ability to innovate.[16]

The problem of congressmen is, then, to get alternatives posed for them. The issue is not confined to the military field; it is, impressionistically speaking, probably true in all areas in which the legislative branch is faced with specialists whose occupational prestige is such that members of the legislature are apt to feel that they are sticking their necks out by contradicting them. In other words, military men often belong to a category of technological specialists who can to a considerable degree get their own way by posing the questions for the legislature; public health specialists are another such category.[17]

"How the Hell Do We Know What Should Be Considered?"

How do the members of the relevant committees reach their decisions and evaluate the proposals made by the military? The answer seems to be that usually no such evaluation is made. In answer to the question, "Aside from your common sense and whatever help the staff can supply you, is there any way to check on the military experts?" members said:

> No. The most effective way is for a congressman to have a good knowledge of the installations in his district which unfortunately I do not have.

*   *   *

> The problem as I see it is that even if we put into effect policy legislation, the executive department can circumvent it if it wants to. [This member stated that he probably attends more committee and subcom-

---

[16] In an area not one of military policy as we have defined the term, but closely related thereto, Congressman John W. McCormack (D.-Mass.) has, according to members of his staff, manifested such innovative tendencies: He has, they report, played a creative part in pressuring the Department of Defense to rationalize purchasing procedures.

[17] Of course, this is a report from the standpoint of the legislature; most military men and public health experts will probably feel that they do not get their own way; and sometimes the legislature may say "no" to them, or say more often "a little less" or "a little later," but generally the legislature does concede to them the formulation of the issues.

mittee meetings than any other member; he was referred to by several committee colleagues as "an expert."]

* * *

Lord knows we need some help; I hope you can find something which tells us what to listen to.

* * *

How the hell do we know what should be considered anyway? We mostly reflect what the military men tell us. [This was from a member widely regarded as one of the two or three ablest men on relevant committees.]

Such acceptance of the leadership of the military, so far as the House is concerned, seems to be more characteristic of the Armed Services Committee than of the Appropriations Subcommittee on Defense. Almost all members agreed with the following point:

We don't have a hell of a lot before our [Armed Services] committee. There's really much scarcity of policy legislation. . . . Maybe we have given too much authority to the Secretary of Defense and the Joint Chiefs of Staff. Congress itself has promulgated legislation which says to them "use your own judgment." . . . So policy is found in Appropriations more than anywhere else. Yes, the question of jurisdiction on these matters keeps people sore. Vinson stays at loggerheads with Cannon about it [Vinson (D.-Ga.), Chairman, Armed Services, Cannon (D.-Mo.), Chairman, Appropriations]

And, from another member of Armed Services:

Our committee accepts reports of the Department of Defense more completely than does Appropriations. We never question opinions about personnel, et cetera. [This is not absolutely correct, but more or less so.] We kid Appropriations members about this, say we aren't military experts, but they are, et cetera.

The foregoing comments apply to the House rather than the Senate. Although there are differences in the personalities of the members of the two House committees, the significant contrast seems to arise out of the functional differences between them. Armed Services is a *legislative* committee, and, as such, deals chiefly with the basic issues only once—when they are enacted into legislation. The Appropriations Committee, on the other hand, considers issues *annually,* and, as one members of Armed Services said:

Right. Appropriations *is* more important. We are over-all men and deal with the over-all things. Now, you must qualify that to this extent;

this may not be true from the standpoint of the armed services themselves. We do deal with things that might not seem very important to civilians but are tremendously important to the military—like how many general officers can there be? [A Senate committee staff member indicated that they have more personal visits on personnel matters, promotions, pensions, etc., than on any other matter.][18]

But in the conventional course of events, the Appropriations Committee is concerned mainly not so much with *legislation* as with avoiding *accountable waste*. As to getting into the *policy* field, there its members have no clear viewpoint of whether they should or should not. Thus, by and large, when Appropriations Committee members do get into a policy question, it is either by accident or because some external event has attracted attention to it, or because of the personal interest of particular members.[19]

"We Need More Interservice Squabbling"

Several fairly senior members, when asked, "What are the major characteristics of a good committee member?" replied, in effect, "Be suspicious of the military! We need guys who won't let them put anything over on us." For instance, one member said:

> Well, now, I'm sure you can supply [better] words to what I'm saying. . . . There's no way on earth to prevent military leaders from pulling the wool over our eyes. But we should keep check. . . . You have to watch their requests; many times they're made for political expedience. You've got to trust what military leaders tell you, but you can't turn them loose on things. . . . I'm not one of those who think the military are all bad, but we need a close check on them. Unfortunately you cannot have such a check unless you have well-staffed standing committees with tremendous expenditure.

Another [one of the two most impressive members of the relevant committees in 1956]:

> Congress can preserve a republican form of government and avoid a dictator by this sort of control [which Appropriations supplies]. . . . They frequently forget man is a human being; [yet] they're always talking about morale until I'm sick of the word. . . . A very important

---

[18] The parallel with school committees in cities and towns—which in some instances spend more time discussing routes and who is entitled to bus rides than considering education matters—is interesting.

[19] But the tremendous workload of the committee, plus the quite inadequate staff assistance, means that, at present, its most conscientious and penetrating members would have to make a very conscious decision to let millions of dollars of avoidable, accountable, or quasi-accountable, waste go unchecked, if they were to allow themselves the time to think through military policy problems! For anyone, and particularly for the kind of man who is likely to gravitate to the Appropriations Committee, this would be a most difficult decision.

ability [on Appropriations] is to resist the blandishments and glitter of stars and rank. I make a rule never to accept any social invitation involving a top-ranking military man. . . . [Then you have] to be thick-skinned. It's hard to say "no." The services may not attack you directly, but indirectly. . . .

But since the military is supposed to be "trying to put something over on us" [the Congress and the people], what then? Again and again, the members said, in effect: "What we need is more interservice squabbling. *When the military falls out, then and only then can the Congress find out.*"

One of the more influential staff men, a trusted advisor of one of the most influential men on the Hill, said, for example:

Looking at these things, as I must, from the big end of the funnel, it seems to me that if everything goes smoothly, nobody ever knows what's going on, neither Congress nor anybody else. But when some one of the forces gets into trouble or gets riled up, then we hear about it and learn a lot. [Of course] we don't know whether the roots are in the military services themselves or start with the DOD civilians or with the military contractors; I just don't know and I wouldn't want to be [identifiably] quoted, but I'd like to know whether Boeing has stirred things up chiefly on these B-52s. Naturally, Senator Jackson [D.-Wash.] openly says . . . he'd like to see some more jobs there.

I would say there is no secret that [in 1956] SAC has priority in people and things—*all over.* And the big squabbles arise when it [or somebody else] gets hurt. . . . But if nobody gets badly hurt, all the services will sit there as calm as can be, and Congress will hear nothing about it. . . .

This old stuff of roles and missions is the central thing in our investigations, and always there you're cutting or threatening to cut flesh, nerve, muscle; and everybody wants to be seated at the table where such a threat is made. The reason for all the sensitivity is the simple possibility of a change in roles and missions.

Fights get to Congress and lead Congress to know what's going on. . . .

If somebody comes to you and wants you to investigate such-and-such a condition, you'll learn only what they in the services want you to learn, *unless there is interservice rivalry.* Then you can find out from the Air Force or vice versa and from Strategic Air Command about Air Defense or vice versa. That is, each service, then [when there's a fight], is ready to say "those dirty dogs are doing so-and-so" and you learn something.

A staff member is quoted here because he expressed, as it happened, more articulately and systematically what many members clearly indicated or implied. Said a member who had actually campaigned on the basis of membership on a committee related to the armed services:

The thing I was least aware of before my service [here on the committee] was the interservice rivalry. Of course, my community tends towards one particular service; I'm not objecting to this [interservice rivalry]. I think a spirited competition is a very healthy thing.

This emphasis on competition and on the healthiness of it seems to imply what the staff member just quoted actually said; in a couple of instances, it came very close to the old saying, "When thieves fall out, honest men have their day." The atmosphere of not trusting the armed services was widespread in the Congress. Not that they think the military witnesses and leaders are thieves, of course, but in the words of another member:

> I suppose I'm unique among congressmen; I have a strong native bias against the military, as witness that word "garbage" which I just used as applied to what I hear from the Pentagon, but for refined intellectual reasons I'm more convinced than most that we have to have an intelligent defense policy and defend it, so I refrain from criticism except on special points. I find myself, that is, a strong supporter of an institution which I distrust profoundly.[20]

The belief that other members have a higher opinion than oneself has of the military seems fairly common, so I raised the question, "Do you really think that's unique? It seems to me to be standard."

> Oh, well, I think a lot of 'em would say "We've got to have the ————s but we hate 'em"; mine is a more refined, permanent, philosophical distrust!

"The Military Is the Real Corrupter of Congress"

Another sophisticated member, recalling the then current excitement about the efforts by oil and gas interests to bribe a senator, said:

> Relatively, if they were really to study "corruption," all that [oil business] is peanuts in my judgment; the people who are really trying to bribe and pressure Congress are from the Department of Defense. They learn you want to go somewhere, and they call you up and say, "How about travelling on one of our planes?" And it just so happens there is riding along with you a pleasant, agreeable officer from the service which gives you the ride; he does not argue with you at all, but he does call your attention to things from their standpoint.

The member then pointed out that this kind of contact is designed to give the armed services the opportunity to determine what issues the congressman thinks about. He averred that, collectively, such contacts are far more "corrupting" than oil industry efforts because they do more to shape the way Congress looks at military questions than any mere bribe. His kind of

---

[20] This member shared with several others the illusion that this was a unique point of view; in fact, it was the commonest one.

awareness, however—that all the military services *may share* a common set of assumptions or views which it would be profitable to question, or *may omit* from consideration some important point which, in terms of over-all national interest, should be taken into account—is not commonly found among members of the committees directly concerned with military issues.

In fact, congressmen frequently assume the validity of the terms in which interservice disputes are raised because they know of no other way of getting at the issues. In any event, it is a common enough human tendency to accept the framework within which an argument is conducted; but in the Congress this tendency is considerably enhanced by the feeling that the Armed Services Committee is a "*quasi-judicial* committee." [21] Perhaps the judicial role is often a desirable model for congressmen to adopt; it might in fact increase impartiality and a readiness to change one's mind on due cause being presented. On the Armed Services Committee, it leads to the notion that that committee has two chief responsibilities: (1) to listen to the requests of the various services and say "yes" or "no"; or (2) in more complex issues, to decide which of the "litigants"—Army, Navy, Air Force, Marines, or subservices—shall get the most of what is wanted in the way of missions, money, prestige, and power.[22]

But this notion appears to have the grave weakness that it assumes that through the operation of some form of invisible hand, the "litigants" will necessarily present the basic issues of public policy with which the Congress ought to be concerned. It also assumes that the interservice hostility, thus not diminished, will not interfere with genuine cooperation between the armed forces where this is desirable.

WHAT IS "TECHNICAL" AND WHAT IS "NON-TECHNICAL"?

"You Have to Gnaw and Gnaw to Get Anything Out of the Service"

Even more basic possibly, than the points already made in explaining or "justifying" congressional reluctance to tackle military policy problems is

---

[21] This notion of being engaged in a judicial process is common enough on congressional committees, naturally so in a body which contains many lawyers, some would-be judges, and some would-be members of regulatory commissions. Committee chairmen may operate on the notion that they conduct hearings with the neutrality which a judge shows in court. At the time of this investigation such chairmen as former Senator Millikin (R.-Colo., Senate Finance) or the former chairman of the House Interior Committee, now Senator Engle (D-Calif.), who had clearly-known views on controversial legislation, endeavored to portray themselves as impartially engaged in a judicial activity while conducting hearings on such legislation.

[22] Of course, on many matters, the committees could have great importance because of their latent power (the degree to which the executive branch calculates upon their acceptance or rejection of proposals may be as important as the actual approval or disapproval they articulate) rather than because of what they actually do. Hypothetically, it should be pointed out that committees would "rubber-stamp" all suggestions from a department if the department always guessed correctly what the committees would approve and submitted no other suggestions.

the little word "technical." Congressmen tend to regard as "technical" such questions for "professional" military men as the nature of war plans. But they regard as "non-technical" and fit subjects for their consideration such matters as the way in which oil is stored at overseas installations or how service credit shall be allocated for ROTC or military academy training— problems of the type which at some universities would be thankfully left as a "technical" matter for registrars to decide.[23] Similarly, Congress will evaluate or try to evaluate the efficiency of given types of rifles or waste in the procurement of military overcoats. However—with the partial exceptions of the Subcommittee on Military Operations when Riehlman (R.-N.Y.) was chairman and the Senate Foreign Relations Committee in 1959–60—they have recently shown little interest in stimulating the invention and development of newer types of weapons or innovations in "grand strategy." [24] The historic distinction between *grand* strategy—war plans involving, for instance, such matters as the desirability and feasibility of *massive* retaliation versus *measured* retaliation—and *specific* strategies is quite unfamiliar in the Congress. This explains in part why questions about military policy are often regarded as suggesting that congressmen concern themselves with *technical* military issues. In other words, many congressmen assume that there is some sort of over-all approach to military policy which need not be questioned, or which is axiomatic. In any case, questions of over-all policy are not raised by many witnesses or "litigants" (in general, it would be against the interest of *most* of the vociferous litigants who approach Congress to query prevailing assumptions). But a contrast is provided by congressmen who have recently been able and eager to consider basic policy in fields such as full employment or international trade.

A number of members made the point that the Constitution gives the President special authority over military matters because he is designated as Commander-in-Chief. This, again, seems to assume that questions about military policy must necessarily deal with specific war plans and to ignore the area of grand strategy. In any case, it might equally well be argued that the American constitutional system is supposed to operate through competition between the branches of government, that is to say, check-and-balance,

---

[23] Officers might or might not receive longevity pay credit for their years in the military academies or in the ROTC; Congress in this case has tended to support reservists against the claims to special considerations from West Pointers, etc.

[24] The Foreign Relations Committee may seem an unlikely candidate here, but the truth was well-expressed by a sophisticated and experienced staff member of another committee who said, "I think you'll find out that jurisdiction is nine-tenths assertion" among congressional committees. If several influential members of the Interior Committee desired to do so, no doubt they could study basic military policy because of their responsibilities for public lands, conservation, etc., which provide an entering wedge; the only difficulty would be that, if they did this, they would not have time to do something else which they might wish to do.

and that there is also constitutional warrant for assumption by Congress of responsibility in military matters.

One reason cited by several congressmen for hesitation about "interfering" with the executive branch on military matters is that efforts to do so during the Civil War resulted (actually or supposedly) in difficulty and trouble. Southern members, who are, of course, in senior positions when the Democratic party is in the majority, seem to be particularly influenced by this contention. Perhaps Senator Truman of Missouri, through his establishment of and leadership in a committee concerned with investigating defense mobilization, contracting difficulties, etc., and because of his own intense historical sense, called attention to or enhanced the importance of this point of view.

The question is, could Congress learn to think about military policy without getting into the war plans area? This is, of course, a standard problem of legislative-executive relationship, generalist-specialist tension, and, for that matter, top administrator-middle administrator difficulty. The president of a university, and the board of trustees under some circumstances, may properly be concerned with the curriculum but not with the content of the comprehensive examination; they may set policy within which future comprehensive examinations may be established, but they should never handle complaints about current comprehensives. Senator Truman's position (which he probably saw no reason to change when he became President) was that the Congress could not, psychologically, make the judicious sort of distinction here described, and therefore should stay out of the field altogether.[25]

Under present practice, it is probably true to say, as one active and influential congressman did, that "On these matters, you have to be a —— bulldog and gnaw and gnaw and gnaw to get any [information out] of the services." (He added, "The whole damn trouble with Congress is they let people file things.") "You've got to be a policeman and keep hounding and hounding . . . to get a job done."

POWER-SEEKING POLITICIANS VERSUS TECHNOLOGISTS?

One commonly held conception about politics is that politicians seek power actively and aggressively. Whatever other conclusions may be derived from the present report, it seems apparent that congressmen on relevant committees could readily enough strive for greater power in military affairs

---

[25] The Congress does not ordinarily get into specific administration; however, I have several times heard the assertion that under Senator McCarran's chairmanship, the Judiciary Committee did get into specifics of immigration administration. In some state legislatures, ways and means committees deal on a continuing basis with administrative matters, although of course state governments do not anticipate the same military crises the Congress must envisage.

with a reasonable chance of obtaining it. *In fact, they think that the satis-factions they obtain by not seeking power are greater than those they would get by trying to maximize it.* Among the factors which may explain such "restraint" are (1) traditions of institutional organization including "separation of powers"; and (2) the notion in Congress that professional and technical matters should be left to professional and technical men. On the basis of the present study we cannot say whether these traditions and notions are "rationalizations" of some other motivation (such as the discomfort conceivably involved in systematic thinking about the potentialities of modern war—former Civil Defense Administrator Petersen, also a politician, spoke of himself as one "who [has] been looking into hell for three years") or are independent causal factors. The writer's best guess is that they are, to a considerable extent, causal factors, the weight and significance of which are very much increased by other motivations, such as the one just mentioned, and by simple fear that a civilian who fights a technical man will be made to look ridiculous before his public.[26]

---

[26] For another discussion of self-restraint where some interpretations would predict an aggressive seeking of power, see Lewis A. Dexter, "Where the Elephant Fears to Dance Among the Chickens. Business in Politics? The Case of Dupont," *Human Organization,* XIX (1960–61), 188–94, republished with some modifications in Bauer, Pool, and Dexter, *op. cit.*

CIVILIANS AND THE MILITARY: I

THE NEW CIVIL-MILITARY RELATIONS[1]

Gene M. Lyons

HISTORICALLY the character of civil-military relations in the United States has been dominated by the concept of civilian control of the military. This has largely been a response to the fear of praetorianism. As recently as 1949, for example, the first Hoover Commission asserted that one of the major reasons for strengthening the "means of exercising civilian control" over the defense establishment was to "safeguard our democratic traditions against militarism." [2] This same warning was raised in the report of the Rockefeller Committee on defense organization in 1953. While the overriding purpose of the committee's recommendations was to provide "the Nation with maximum security at minimum cost," the report made it clear that this had to be achieved "without danger to our free institutions, based on the fundamental principle of civilian control of the Military Establishment." [3] Finally, during the debate on the reorganization proposals of 1958, senators and congressmen used the theme of a "Prussianized" military staff to attempt to slow down the trend towards centralization in the military establishment.[4]

Despite this imposing support, the concept of civilian control of the military has little significance for contemporary problems of national security in the United States. In the first place, military leaders are divided among themselves, although their differences cannot be reduced to a crass contrast between dichomatic doctrines. Air Force leaders who are gravely concerned over the need to maintain a decisive nuclear retaliatory force are by now acknowledging the need to develop a limited war capability. At the same time, Army leaders are quite frank to admit that "flexible response" requires both strategic and tactical power of sizable strength, although they are particularly committed to developing a large tactical force. If these differences appear to be only differences in emphasis, they are nonetheless crucial in a political process within which priorities must be established and choices

---

[1] This article was originally prepared for the 1960 Annual Meeting of the American Political Science Association. In the preparation and in the revision I have profited from the comments of several colleagues, at Dartmouth and elsewhere, particularly my confrere, Louis Morton.

[2] Commission on Organization of the Executive Branch of the Government, *The National Security Organization*, A Report to the Congress, February 1949, pp. 2–3.

[3] *Report of the Rockefeller Committee on Department of Defense Organization*, Committee Print, Senate Committee on Armed Services, 83d Cong., 1st sess. 1953, p. 1.

[4] See, *e.g.*, Rept. No. 1765, *Department of Defense Reorganization Act of 1958*, House Committee on Armed Services, 85th Cong., 2d session, esp. pp. 24–33.

[111]

must be made. Without firm agreement on priorities, there is little reason to expect that the military can control government policy even if civilian authorities abdicate responsibility for basic decisions. The most that can result is a compromise between different military positions. Commonly, military disagreement, if exposed, is an invitation for civilian intervention.

Secondly, the concept of civilian control of the military ignores two other factors that complicate civil-military relations. On the one hand, the military themselves accept the principle of civilian supremacy; on the other, they have been thrown into a political role in the formation of policy. The resignation of General Gavin over the budgetary restrictions of the "New Look" strategy is a case in point. The General disagreed with the judgment of his civilian superiors but, like General Ridgway before him and General Taylor after him, held his most violent fire until he was out of uniform and freed from the limits of professional restrictions.[5] His case dramatically illustrates the dilemma of the military as they move into the center of defense policy-making. Here they have to struggle between the non-partisan tenets of their creed and the requirements of effective participation in the political process. Their advice as experts is not only used by the Executive to bolster its case, but is eagerly courted by Congress and the public as a basis for testing the caliber of executive action. In one respect the political role of the military tends to dilute their own professionalism. But in another, it affords them more than one opportunity to maintain a balance between their professional code and the individual conscience. The nature of the American political system thus provides an outlet for frustration which, in other settings, has been the catalyst to set off an outburst of militarism.

In its broadest sense, the concept of civilian control of the military means military responsiveness to the policies of politically responsible government. But this too needs to be reinterpreted in the light of revolutionary changes that have greatly complicated the formation of defense policy. Preparedness is as much the product of civilian expertise in science and engineering and of civilian decisions on the allocation of national resources as it is of military planning. At the same time, it is very often the military who put defense policy to the test of political accountability by exposing the bases for decisions to congressional and public inquiry. As a result, there is a constant reversal of traditional roles, a situation that has brought civilians and military into a new set of relationships. These relationships have been reflected only in a limited way in recent organizational changes that have strengthened the central agencies of the defense establishment. To appreciate their

---

[5] The views of all three Generals have been documented in books they published shortly after they retired: James M. Gavin, *War and Peace in the Space Age* (New York, 1958), Matthew Ridgway, *Soldier* (New York, 1956); and Maxwell D. Taylor, *The Uncertain Trumpet* (New York, 1959). And see . . . Samuel P. Huntington, "Interservice Competition and the Political Roles of the Armed Services," [*American Political Science Review*, Vol. LV (March, 1961)], p. 40.

full significance, it is also necessary to understand changes in the character of both civilian and military leadership in defense affairs. Civilians are becoming "militarized" and the military "civilianized" and it is these changes that reflect more clearly than organization alone, a fundamental break with tradition in the evolution of civil-military relations.[6]

I. THE EVOLUTION OF DEFENSE ORGANIZATION

Like many institutions in American political life, a highly centralized, civilian-dominated Pentagon has developed in response to changing forces and conditions. Had the Joint Chiefs of Staff been able to function as a collegial unit rather than as a divided group of service representatives, it is possible that reorganization trends might have taken different directions. Centralization, however, was probably inevitable in one form or another. Increasing defense costs made centralized budgeting and programming a necessity. The bite of military expenditures in the total federal budget makes it impossible to ignore the impact of defense on the national economy, the government's tax program and the whole range of complex problems of resources allocation. The impact of technology has also been a centralizing factor. Indeed, work on the military applications of atomic energy had already been centralized in the Atomic Energy Commission. But work on missiles had been left in the separate services and the duplication of effort in three competitive programs brought on demands for greater coordination in propulsion programs in the late 1950's. Finally, both these areas of financial management and of research and development require skills that are "civilian," in essence, and are not yet possessed by many high ranking military officers. Thus it might be argued that "civilianization," as well as centralization, was inevitable given the nature of the problems that needed to be solved.

The growth of central civilian authority has nevertheless come in stages. The first Secretary of Defense, James Forrestal, had been opposed to the development of a large central staff even after he had come around to accept the concept of an overall defense chief. As a former Navy Secretary he was committed to the retention of strong civilian leadership in the individual services, first, to avoid a situation that might lead to the domination of a single strategic doctrine and, second, to keep civilian authority lodged at the operating levels of the military departments. He insisted that the Secretary "must be free to concentrate his efforts on the establishment of broad policy" and in so doing "must look to the secretaries of the military departments for the information and data upon which his policy is to be based and then look

---

[6] For a theoretical statement of the concept of civilian control of the military, together with references to other major analyses of the subject, see Samuel P. Huntington, "Civilian Control of the Military: a Theoretical Statement," in Eulau, Eldersveld and Janowitz (eds.), *Political Behavior* (Glencoe, Ill. 1956), pp. 380 ff.

again to them for the execution these policies." [7] Within these guidelines, he was reported to want only "a very small executive force for the single Secretary to consist of [a total of] 15 to 25 '$10,000-a-year men' and officers." [8]

The National Security Act of 1947, highly influenced by Forrestal's views, thus created a federation of military departments with little authority in the office of the Secretary of National Defense. In little more than a year, however, Forrestal himself recommended a number of statutory changes that mark the second step in the strengthening of centralized civilian authority. The critical problem he had faced was the absence of any military consensus upon which to develop strategic programs. He therefore sought to develop independent staff at the Defense Department level, including an Undersecretary of Defense, a Chairman for the Joint Chiefs of Staff and a larger Joint Staff. He also called for greatly clarified responsibility over the military departments to enable the Secretary to settle controversies over the roles and missions of the separate services and the allocation of budgetary resources.[9]

Forrestal's recommendations, largely reinforced by the report of the first Hoover Commission a year later, were the basis for the National Security Act Amendments of 1949 which created a Department of Defense where only a coordinating mechanism had hitherto existed. The Secretary, however strengthened his position became, was nonetheless still forbidden, by law, to encroach upon the "combatant functions assigned to the military services." Congress deliberately used this basic prohibition to maintain the essential identity of the individual services, a tactic that has been retained in subsequent major reorganizations in 1953 and 1958. Nevertheless, this restriction has become less limiting on the authority of the Secretary of Defense as major strategic decisions have turned on problems of weapons development and financial management rather than directly on the controversy over roles and missions.

The reorganization plan of 1953 went another step in centralizing authority in the civilian leadership by creating assistant secretaries of defense with responsibilities in functional areas, such as supply and logistics, and manpower and personnel. These posts were established with the understanding that "they should not be in the direct line of administrative authority between [the Secretary] and the three military departments, but instead should assist in developing policies, prescribing standards, and bringing to the

---

[7] See his letter to Chairman Chan Gurney of the Senate Armed Services Committee, reprinted in that Committee's Hearings, 80th Cong., 1st sess., *National Defense Establishment*, Pt. 1, p. 185. More generally, see Paul Y. Hammond, "The National Security Council as a Device for Interdepartmental Coordination," [*American Political Science Review*], Vol. 54 (Dec., 1960), pp. 899–910, and his forthcoming book, *Organizing for Defense* (Princeton University Press, 1961).

[8] Testimony of Admiral Sherman, *ibid.*, p. 155.

[9] *First Report of the Secretary of Defense,* National Defense Establishment, 1948, pp. 2–4.

Secretary of Defense information on which he may base his decisions." [10] Under these terms, the authority of the assistant secretaries was ambiguous. Administration witnesses were always cautious to assure congressional committees that the assistant secretaries of defense had no operating authority and were exclusively advisory to the Secretary. While this was theoretically so, actual practice was often to the contrary since they were frequently in a strong position to recommend that service positions be over-ruled.[11] And the authority of the Secretary of Defense to delegate powers to his assistant secretaries was confirmed under the 1958 Act, apparently clearing away the ambiguity.

The growth of centralized civilian authority has thus been related to the decline in the authority of the service secretaries. Forrestal himself had found at an early stage that the service secretaries could not administer the individual departments and still act as his deputies in the formation and execution of overall policy. As service heads they were obliged to support major positions developed by their military chiefs or risk losing the main leverage they had to be effective in their jobs. The policy process is largely a process of bargaining and persuasion. Without the confidence of the military leaders, a civilian secretary cannot hope to persuade them to alter their views. At the same time, he has little chance to gain their confidence unless he largely supports the positions they have developed. He thus plays a dual role, representing the Defense Department at the Service level and the military department at the Defense level. Under the pressures of inter-service competition for limited resources and the development of a large secretariat in the Department of Defense, the service secretary has become more and more a spokesman for his service position and less and less a positive instrument in the formation of policy by the Secretary of Defense.

But by far the greatest part of the increase of authority gained by the civilian leadership in the Defense Department has accrued because of the inability of the Joint Chiefs of Staff to come to agreed positions on the military requirements of national security. The far-reaching provisions of the 1958 Act were largely in direct response to the wide range of problems raised by service disagreement. Under the Act, the Secretary of Defense can exercise direct authority over unified commands, transfer weapons systems from one service to another and maintain centralized direction of all military research and development through the Director of Research and Engineering. The practical impact of these powers is to give the Secretary considerable influence over the roles and missions of the services which are still prescribed by law within the broad and flexible categories of land, air, and sea forces. The

---

[10] *Report of the Rockefeller Committee on Department of Defense Organization, op. cit.,* p. 11.

[11] See, for example, the dialogue between Senator Symington and the Assistant Secretary of Defense (Logistics and Supply) in Hearings, Senate Committee on Armed Services, 85th Cong., 1st sess., *Nominations,* pp. 12–14.

concept of unified commands and the sweeping authority over weapons development now enable the Secretary to bring about *de facto* unification of the armed services even within the framework of a three-departmental system.[12] But to accomplish this, he has a total civilian staff of almost 2,000—a far cry from the "15 to 25 '$10,000-a-year men' and officers" that Forrestal had wanted less than 15 years ago.[13]

II. THE "DEPOLITICALIZATION" OF THE DEFENSE DEPARTMENT

The increasing authority of civilian leadership has not been granted without misgivings. Several aspects of this trend have been viewed with concern: the turnover of civilians in the Pentagon; the inability of civilians to come to grips with problems which have no exact parallel outside the military establishment; the tendency for the Defense Department to evolve into a fourth operating agency of the military establishment; the pre-occupation of Defense officials with budgetary matters; and delays in military programs as result of the need to obtain clearances from a thickening layer of "functional" chiefs.[14] Indeed, Senator Henry Jackson has commented that " . . . at

---

[12] Almost two years after the passage of the Reorganization Act of 1958, the *Army, Navy, Air Force Journal* (May 28, 1960) summed up some of the ways Secretary of Defense Gates "is using the full powers of his office . . . to achieve increased unification within the terms of existing legislation." These included centralization of missile test ranges, centralization of toxicological research, and establishment of an All-Service Defense Communications Agency. In addition, early in 1960, Secretary Gates sent a memorandum to the Chairman of the JCS, stating: "It is requested that I be promptly informed regarding any issue on which a difference of opinion is developing within the Joint Chiefs of Staff. I intend that either the Secretary of Defense and/or the Deputy Secretary of Defense will promptly meet with the Joint Chiefs at such times as they consider the issue in question . . . " (reprinted in *Army, Navy, Air Force Journal*, January 16, 1960).

[13] This contrast has risen to plague subsequent Secretaries of Defense. Secretary McElroy facing questions on it during the reorganization hearings in 1958, offered the following: "I have heard others report to me about the expressions by Jim Forrestal about getting along with 100 people, and that kind of thing. I have also heard that after he got into the job, he found that he needed a great many more. The history is nothing that I am prepared to support because I don't know precisely what did go on there. But I honestly—while I agree with you fully that numbers are not a measure of the importance of efficiency of an organization, I mean large numbers, I wouldn't know how anybody could operate a department of this size and complexity with 100 people." Hearings, House Committee on Armed Services, 85th Cong., 2d sess., *Reorganization of the Department of Defense*, p. 6072.

[14] These misgivings are suggested by the questions raised by the staff of the Senate (Jackson) subcommittee on national policy machinery. See *Organizing for National Security*, Interim Report of the Committee on Government Operations made by its Subcommittee on National Policy Machinery, 86th Cong., 2d sess., pp. 17–19. The problem of turnover has been the subject of a proposed Senate resolution "that it is the sense of the Senate that nominees appearing before its committee shall indicate their willingness to serve so long as the President desires" (S. Res. 338), 86th Cong., 2 sess.; see also Rept. No. 1753, 86th Cong., 2d sess., *Resolution Expressing Concern of Senate over Turnover in Administrative and Policymaking Posts*.

one time we worried about a German General Staff setup in the Pentagon. I think we are at the point of a civilian general staff. . . . " Senator Jackson was not, however, critical of the establishment of new duties in the Office of the Secretary, but rather of "a failure to exercise these functions properly." [15]

The problem of "proper" performance in top defense positions is necessarily complex. Many administrators have held top positions over long periods—longer indeed than many military officers who are subject to rotation in assignment at frequent intervals. Others have had equally long tenure although they have hedge-hopped from position to position. It has, however, been difficult to attract first-rate people into high defense posts. Charles Wilson, for example, reported that, just before he took over the post of Secretary of Defense in 1953, out-going Secretary Lovett said to him: "Charlie, do not be too critical of some of these men that are here to help you do this job, because in some cases they are the thirty-third men I propositioned to come before I could get anyone." [16] In the final analysis, the caliber of leadership in high positions will depend on the President and the kind of men he wants as advisers and his willingness to use his persuasive powers to bring them into government. It will also depend, though to a lesser degree, on the pressures the Senate puts on the Executive.

When the Eisenhower Administration took office in 1953, there was an almost complete turnover in civilian leadership (and, indeed, in military leadership as well.) With the exception of the Defense Comptroller, Wilfred McNeil, all of the top Pentagon posts changed hands. This changeover was perhaps more disrupting than usual since it marked the advent of the first Republican president in twenty years. But the turnover was also very deliberate for the new Administration had almost completely divorced itself from the foreign and military policies of the Truman Administration during the presidential campaign. The new President and his chief advisers looked for a loyalty to their leadership and policies that they felt few Truman aides could muster. [17] It is nevertheless instructive to note that by the end of the second Eisenhower Administration most civilian leaders in the Pentagon had spent periods of 4 to 8 years in defense work, if not in the same post. [18] At

---

[15] Hearings, Senate Committee on Armed Services, 84th Cong., 2d sess., *Assistant Secretaries for Research and Development,* pp. 20–22.

[16] Hearings, Senate Committee on Armed Services, 83rd Cong., 1st sess., *Nomination of Charles Wilson,* Pt. 2, pp. 110–111. For a general discussion of this problem, see John A. Perkins, "Staffing Democracy's Top Side." *Public Administration Review,* Vol. 17 (Winter, 1957), pp. 1 ff.

[17] This was also true in programs outside the field of foreign and military policy, e.g., the members of the regulatory commissions and directors of TVA. For a discussion of its impact on career executives, see Herman M. Somers, "The Federal Bureaucracy and the Change of Administration," [*American Political Science Review*], Vol. 48 (March 1954), pp. 131 ff.

[18] For example: Thomas Gates, the Secretary of Defense, had served (with one short break) since October 7, 1953, as Undersecretary and Secretary of the Navy, as

the same time Thomas Gates, the last Secretary of Defense under Eisenhower, and Robert Lovett, the last Secretary under Truman, were both
urging that high defense posts be protected from partisan politics and that
both parties agree to maintain effective continuity in the civilian leadership
of national security programs.[19]

The recommendations of Secretaries Gates and Lovett are symptomatic of
the change that has slowly been developing in the character of civilian
leadership in the Pentagon in spite of the sharp setback in 1953. It is marked
by what might be called a "depoliticalization" of the Defense Department,
that is, an emphasis on standards of competence and experience in making
appointments. Appointive posts in all federal departments are, of course,
subject to both political and non-political considerations. Indeed, in the
areas of foreign and military policy, the motivation of national interest
operates to counteract the political forces of geographic distribution, party
balance and pressure groups that dominate top appointments in other departments.[20] Non-political considerations regarding background and ability
thus largely govern the selection process.

Most appointive posts in the Pentagon break down into three general

---

well as Deputy Secretary and Secretary of Defense; James Douglas, Deputy Secretary
of Defense, had served continuously since March 3, 1953, as Undersecretary and
Secretary of the Air Force, as well as Deputy Secretary; Herbert York, Director of
Defense Research and Engineering came to this post (and was the first incumbent in
1958) after long experience in defense work with the Advanced Research Projects
Agency, various scientific advisory committees, and non-profit institutions engaged in
defense activities; Charles Finucane, the Assistant Secretary of Defense for manpower
affairs, had served as Assistant Secretary and Undersecretary of the Army for almost
four years when (after a short break in service) he was brought back to the post at the
Defense level in 1958; similarly, the three service secretaries, Brucker in the Army,
Franke in the Navy, and Sharp in the Air Force had all had almost continuous
Pentagon service for at least five years.

[19] In both cases, these views were expressed in testimony before the Senate subcommittee on National Policy Machinery and were largely supported by the testimony of
other witnesses, particularly James A. Perkins, John Corson, and Roger Jones. See
Hearings, Subcommittee on National Policy Machinery, Senate Committee on Government Operations, 86th Cong., 2d sess., *Organizing for National Security*, Pts. II and
III.

[20] Patronage proved to be a vexing problem when the Eisenhower Administration
took office in 1953 after twenty years of Democratic rule. Very early in the game
Secretary Dulles was reported to have made it clear that "his department could not
be run on the basis of patronage," Robert J. Donovan, *Eisenhower, The Inside Story*
(New York, 1956), p. 98, though this did not prevent the appointment of "fat cats,"
e.g., to ambassadorial posts, or the wholesale purge of departmental personnel—referred to as "Stassenization"—in 1953, carried out in the name of a budget cut that
Dulles did not resist. By the end of the second Eisenhower term—*i.e.,* in hindsight, a
quite different vantage point—a nonpartisan policy was considered valid for the Defense Department (see reference above to testimony of Secretary of Defense Gates).
For a general discussion, see Harvey C. Mansfield, "Political Parties, Patronage, and
the Federal Government Service," in *The Federal Government Service: Its Character,
Prestige and Problems,* The American Assembly, 1954, pp. 81 ff.

groups.[21] There is, first of all, the Secretary of Defense and his immediate staff. Here the needs and thus the will of the President himself will certainly dominate, for the prime importance of the Secretary is as a top presidential adviser. His constant occupation is to serve as a deputy to the President in the performance of his constitutional duties as commander-in-chief of the armed forces. Indeed, as the problems of national security have come to absorb so much of the President's time and energy, the Secretary of Defense has come to be one of the most prominent members of both the President's cabinet and his inner circle.

But below the Secretary and his personal staff are a group of appointive posts at the Defense and military department levels, in which functional or "program" rather than constitutional or presidential, responsibility is emphasized. These include posts in the fields of financial management, manpower, and procurement and logistics. What is often as necessary as practical experience in the subject field itself, is an ability to manage complex enterprises and a deep understanding of the political and governmental processes. Thus, experience in public service is of prime importance. Men chosen for these posts might come from several sources. They might be men who possess these qualities and are also important figures in the President's party; their appointment can thus perform two functions at once—bring a professional hand to high office and meet the party's requirements for patronage. They might also be men whose identity with one of the major political parties has been incidental but whose experience with problems of public policy has made them wise selections for office regardless of party. Finally, they might be high-ranking civil servants whose records are outstanding and who are willing to give up the security of tenure for the political risks of appointive positions. Where a choice is possible, the determining factor will be the importance with which the President and his principal advisers view the balance of interests that are involved.

Finally, there are appointive posts that require a high level of specialized expertise but cannot be included within civil service categories. This is especially true in the field of research and engineering. The incumbents will often act as policy advisers and, even within the bounds of their own professional integrity, must be in basic agreement with the political dimensions of the President's defense program. At the same time, the civil service cannot

---

[21] The following discussion borrows from Wallace S. Sayre, "The Political Executive in the National Government: The Constitutional and Political Setting," prepared for the Conference on the Political Executive, Woodrow Wilson School of Public and International Affairs, Princeton University, 1956, pp. 23–24 (mimeographed). The literature on executives for government is particularly pertinent to the problems discussed here. See, for example, the report of the task force on personnel and civil service of the second Hoover Commission, dated February 1955; Paul F. David and Ross Pollock, *Executives for Government,* The Brookings Institution, 1957; and Marver H. Bernstein, *The Job of the Federal Executive,* The Brookings Institution, 1958.

provide the high degree of expertise that is required for top direction. The background and experience which the evaluation of complex weapons systems requires can rarely be gained by working in government agencies. It is more usually found in men whose prior experience has been developed in university and industrial laboratories.

Several factors can thus be identified as vital qualifications for high Pentagon posts below the Secretary of Defense himself: the benefit of government experience; the need for expertise; and the desirability of continuity. These traits have been increasingly recognizd and their recognition is operating to develop a "depoliticalization" of these posts. "Depoliticalization" nevertheless, has limits. National security issues cannot (and indeed should not) be entirely taken out of politics. Top presidential advisers must be prepared to defend the choices they make before congressional and public criticism. At the same time the President needs to have the alternative of changing his close advisers if the sense of purpose and the support that he feels is necessary to his program are missing. Capable men available for such posts, no matter how broad the recruitment sources are becoming, will, moreover, continue to be few; and many of those who agree to accept political responsibilities will be under pressure to return to private life. For that matter, some turnover in the top echelons is desirable to bring a continual freshness and critical direction to government administration. Thus, no matter how far "depoliticalization" goes, political appointees will not always be able to provide the continuity and stability in government that are the principal contributions of career professionals.

"Depoliticalization" is, however, only one of the characteristics of the larger trend towards a professionalization of civilian leadership in defense affairs. Professionalization is taking other forms as well—the influence of career executives in the development of major policy decisions, innovations in administration which have brought outside experts into government through a variety of institutional devices, and a growing interest in military affairs among civilians outside government. All of these, taken together, contribute to the changing character of civilian leadership that is, in turn, influencing the character of civil-military relations.

III. THE PROFESSIONALIZATION OF CIVILIAN LEADERSHIP

The importance of continuity and stability in government is emphasized when the nature of the policy process is clearly understood; it is likelier to be appreciated more toward the end than at the beginning of any particular Administration. Policies are usually developed with a long history of conjecture, false starts and negotiation. Very often they take shape from a series of operational responses or the byplay of a number of viewpoints rather than from a single breakthrough of brilliant analysis. Within such situations, the influence of careerists, military and civilian, is enormous. It is equally impressive in moments of crisis when only professionals have the background and experience to respond quickly. The military professionals wield their greatest influence within the military departments; a large and burgeoning staff of civilian careerists exert similar powers in the Department of Defense. They perform staff work in connection with establishing budgetary and manpower priorities, supply the background material for new programs and have usually developed a network of informal contacts that make them invaluable in inter-departmental negotiations. Indeed, General Gavin recalled (perhaps with some bitterness) that " . . . the Civil Service employees . . . in the Department of Defense . . . probably have more impact on decision-making . . . than any other individual or group of individuals, military or civilian." [22]

The hazy line that divides policy from administration and the influence of career professionals on decision-making are familiar themes in the literature of public administration.[23] In the Defense Department, professional influence has been increased by the tendency to seek solutions to problems at a technical level in order to minimize differences over vital matters of policy. In such cases, the guides for policy become efficiency and empirical verification rather than intuition and inspiration; and in any such atmosphere technicians and arbitrators play a critical role. Such tactics often reduce policy to a compromise between opposing positions, a practice that is often stultifying. In many cases it is nevertheless an inevitable consequence of policy-making within the democratic process, particularly in the field of national security. For within the goldfish bowl of American politics, there is a limit to the risks a political leader is willing to take in approving defense programs that can be argued in terms of national survival and for which there is no indisputable solution.

But like the "depoliticalization" of appointive posts, there are limits to the contribution that increased civil service influence can make to the professionalization of civilian leadership in the Pentagon. Some of these limits have already been suggested. For one thing, few civil servants possess the degree of specialized expertise that is required for technical staff work in fields such as research and engineering. Nor, for that matter, does the bureaucracy offer the environment in which careful study and reflection on basic problems, such as strategic doctrine, is encouraged and indeed rewarded. At the same time, there is little chance that the top layer of the American civil service can be transformed into an administrative class like that in Great

---

[22] Gavin, *op. c it.*, p. 166.
[23] See, for example, Paul H. Appleby, *Policy and Administration* (University of Alabama Press, 1949). For an earlier statement on this issue, see Carl J. Friedrich, "Public Policy and the Nature of Administrative Responsibility," *Public Policy* (1940, Cambridge, Harvard University Press), pp. 3 ff.

Britain; neither the social structure nor the political system to support such a class is present.[24]

Within the special context of American governmental institutions, a series of innovating techniques have therefore been developed to bring professional competence to bear on matters of public policy where neither political nor career executives can fully meet the demands. They include *ad hoc* and standing advisory committees, contractual arrangements for consultative services, the assignment of broad investigations or actual operations to outside institutions, and government-financed independent agencies set up outside the formality of the bureaucracy.[25] These administrative techniques perform a number of functions. They bring creativity to the public service in areas where it is often discouraged by the routinization of bureaucratic procedures or the dangers of interservice and political disagreement. They offer political executives (and congressional leaders) alternative sources of expert advice to the career services, civilian and military. They permit the kind of experimentation, reflection, flexibility, and deep probing that the complex problems of national security require but that the regular federal service cannot completely accommodate because of its size, its need for standardization, and its emphasis on current operations.

The strides taken in recent years to develop new modes of government administration have largely been forced by the demands of technology. The scientific programs during the second world war and the industry-based programs of the Air Force in the postwar years established precedents for government contracting in areas that now extend beyond technological projects to projects in the social and behavioral sciences. Each of the services has created a "think" organization to which it can farm out problems—the RAND Corporation of the Air Force, the Operations Research Office of the Army and the Operations Evaluation Group of the Navy. Within the Department of Defense a variety of advisory panels are available to the Secretary and his assistants—on research and development, on psychology and the social sciences and on education and manpower. In addition, the Institute [for] Defense Analys[i]s has been established "to create machinery for putting a segment of the nation's intellectual resources more effectively at the disposal of the national security effort." [26] Originally established in connection with the evaluation of competing weapons systems, the scope of the

[24] Several of the essays in J. E. McLean (ed.), *The Public Service and University Education* (Princeton, 1949) are concerned with the issue. See particularly Rowland Egger, "A Second View: An American Administrative Class?" pp. 205 ff.

[25] For a general discussion of the development of such innovations in government administration, see Don K. Price, "Creativity in the Public Service," *Public Policy,* Vol. IX (1959, Cambridge, Harvard University Press), pp. 3 ff. For a discussion of some of the aspects of Defense Department contracting for advisory and consultative services, see Hearings, Subcommittee of the House Committee on Appropriations, 86th Cong., 2d sess., *Department of Defense Appropriations for 1961,* Pt. 7, pp. 164–196.

[26] *Annual Report II,* Institute [for] Defense Analys[i]s, 1958, p. 1.

Institute now encompasses broad areas of military strategy where the support for judgments on weapons evaluation is very often to be found. Indeed the close connection with strategic issues has been the link that has extended research on military operations into the far reaches of national policy.

These innovations in administration project the professionalization of civilian leadership in defense far beyond the confines of government itself. That they extend as widely as they do is, in many ways, an indication of the response of industry, science and private scholarship to the problems of national security. Like government-sponsored research, research in industry has begun to go beyond technical subjects. General Electric, for example, publishes a *Defense Quarterly* that is devoted to the broad issues of technology and foreign and military policy. It has also established a "think" group of its own, as have other corporations such as General Dynamics, IBM and many of the large aircraft companies. While most of these "in house" divisions are set up for scientific research and development, many of them dig into military and social problems affected by technological advances. At the same time, many industrial companies contract out their research activities with institutions such as the Stanford Research Institute, a non-profit corporation which has moved into the fields of military and foreign policy in the wake of its primary interest in the frontiers of technological change.

In addition, since 1950 there has been on outpour of books and articles on national security from scholarly sources.[27] Some have actually been made possible through association with Defense Department projects or under contract with congressional groups investigating various aspects of the defense program. But a very high number of these efforts have been undertaken on private initiative, with or without foundation or university support. The subjects of these studies have ranged from the broadest issues of military strategy to more specialized problems of military organization and education. They include Kissinger's *Nuclear Weapons and Foreign Policy,* Osgood's *Limited War,* Huntington's *The Soldier and the State,* Brodie's *Strategy in the Missile Age,* the books by Walter Millis, the monographs of the Princeton Center of International Studies, the studies of the Rockefeller Brothers Fund and the volumes that have come out of the research projects conducted at the Center for International Studies at the Massachusetts Institute of Technology. In all cases, these works have plunged deep into military problems. Indeed there are indications that some military leaders are concerned that "there has been too little solid contribution from military pens to national security policy thinking for this new age . . . . "[28]

---

[27] See Laurence I. Radway, *The Study of Military Affairs,* prepared for delivery at the 1958 Annual Meeting of the American Political Science Association (mimeographed).

[28] Col. George A. Lincoln and Col. Richard G. Stilwell, "Scholars Debouch Into Strategy," *Military Review,* Vol. 40 (July 1960), p. 70. See also Captain Robert P. Beebe, "Guardians of Sea Power," United States Naval Institute *Proceedings,* Vol. 86

The practical consequence of all of these activities is that professional advice, studies and investigations on complex military issues are being made available to responsible officials from sources other than the military themselves. Civilian leaders need no longer rely entirely on the military services for the bases for policy decisions. Their own experience in service, the solid contribution of career professionals and the wide new sources of research and reflection, together with the multi-dimensional nature of defense problems, permit them to be more critical, more questioning and more constructive in their own right. Needless to say, all that has been discussed are tendencies, trends that can be perceived as we analyze the course of civil-military relations during the last ten years. Nevertheless, it seems safe to predict that these trends will continue to gain momentum—the "depoliticalization" of appointive posts, the influence of career executives, innovations in government administration and an interest in military affairs among writers, scientists and scholars. They are also bound to contribute to a growing professionalization of civilian leadership in military affairs and, in turn, this professionalization will have important repercussions on the nature of civil-military relations.

IV. THE CHANGING CHARACTER OF MILITARY LEADERSHIP

The significance of the professionalization of civilian leadership cannot be judged without some consideration of the changing character of military leadership. When General Maxwell Taylor retired in mid-1959, a veteran Washington reporter commented that this marked "the point at which the Old Army is drawing to the end of its mission—and even of its relevance." He called Taylor "the last great captain of the old hunters . . . " and his successor, General Lyman Lemnitzer, "an intellectual, a staff officer of vast experience, a kind of professor of the new kind of war." [29] The contrast is perhaps over-drawn, for it is difficult to think of the military—without its "heroic leaders," left to the impersonal calculations of the "military managers." [30] It nevertheless catches the essence of a fundamental change in the character of military leadership.

(June 1960), pp. 27 ff. The trend suggested here seems to contradict Bernard Brodie's thesis that "any real expansion of strategic thought . . . will . . . have to be developed largely within the military guild itself." (*Strategy in the Missile Age* [Princeton, 1959], p. 9. Indeed, one might say that Brodie's own pioneering work refutes his prognosis.

[29] William S. White, "The End of the Old Army," *Harper's*, June 1959, pp. 82–85. The contrast might have been more apt had Lemnitzer been compared with General Ridgway who was wholly a soldier's soldier while Taylor has certain professorial features of his own.

[30] The terms in quotations are borrowed (as is much that follows) from Morris Janowitz, *The Professional Soldier* (Glencoe, Ill., 1960).

Military leadership is changing under the impact of two forces: the revolutionary developments in weapons technology; and the close relationship between military programs and foreign and economic policies. The management of a missile program or a test range, the constabulary duties of an overseas assignment, the pseudo-diplomatic function of a military assistance advisory group, the planning involved in a Pentagon or a NATO slot—these are the tasks for which the military must prepare the officers of the future. At the same time, the threat of war, total, nuclear, limited or conventional, and the demands that open hostilities make on military leadership, are ever present. Thus the old attributes of "heroic leaders," the qualities of discipline, courage and command ability, cannot be forgotten. In this respect, the new responsibilities of military leaders have not so much altered their fundamental make-up as they have added new dimensions to their character and made them more complex human beings. This new complexity is being reflected in a number of changes in the military profession. Three of these are particularly important: the broadening base for officer recruitment; the development of higher military education; and new policies for selection and promotion to higher rank.

To a large extent, the broadening base for officer recruitment is a matter of arithmetic. In recent years the services have had to draw in more than 40,000 new officers every year, with a good percentage of these needed on a career basis. At the same time, the service academies graduate only about 1,500 new lieutenants and ensigns. As a result, the services have had to look to other sources for career officers, particularly civilian colleges and universities. This development has more than quantitative significance, however. It is also qualitative. The broadening recruitment base for young officers is bringing into the services men with new outlooks and new areas of technical competence that serve to meet the widening range of military responsibilities.[31]

The elaborate structure of higher military education is also responding to the broadening character of military responsibility. Curriculum changes in undergraduate programs at the service academies and in military programs in civilian colleges and universities are moving in two directions: first, they are incorporating new material to expose the students to the expanding technology that is making such an impact on military life; and, second, undergraduate courses are becoming less vocationalized and are taking the form of preprofessional education to lay a solid intellectual base for future career development.[32] At the post-commissioning schools—from the command and staff colleges through the service war colleges to the Industrial College of the Armed Forces and the National War College—there is an in-

---

[31] Gene M. Lyons and John W. Masland, *Education and Military Leadership* (Princeton, 1959), esp. ch. I.

[32] *Ibid.*, chs. VI and VII.

creased emphasis on the problems of international politics, the dilemmas of war and peace brought on by nuclear weapons, the impact of defense on the national economy and the complexities of life in a world of allies, international organizations and uncommitted nations. There are still weaknesses in military education: there is a tendency to be highly technical and vocational, even in dealing with social science material; service-organized programs also tend to be parochial, emphasizing the narrow views of the service itself; and the image of the world scene that is projected in military teaching is static and over-simplified. The advancements in the last fifteen years have nevertheless been striking and have taken military education far beyond the traditional emphasis on "loyalty, precedent, specific technical skill, and a gentlemanly code of conduct." [33]

Traditions, however, die hard. In the transition from one generation of military leaders to another, the qualities of the "heroic leader" continue to have primary importance and significance for those older officers who grew up in the "old Army," in the "black-shoe Navy" or even in the "propeller-driven Air Force." These are the officers, moreover, who control the machinery for selection and promotion. Here the struggle between the old and the new takes place. While assignments to the war colleges and long tours of duty in technical posts seem to be good preparation for the new roles military men are undertaking, they are not always the best routes to higher rank. Loyalty, length of service and the number of tours on sea and command duty are very often the qualifications that members of a military selection board look for. A few years ago, the Secretary of the Navy, in an attempt to break down these traditional barriers to advancement, instructed the selection board to accelerate the promotions of officers who were "head and shoulders" above their colleagues. The reverberations of these orders are still shaking the Navy's high command.[34] Accelerating promotion means advancing officers in grade because of "potential" rather than actual performance. It thus involves an exercise of judgment about human behavior, as well as future military requirements, that is, at best, difficult to make. It is more difficult during a transition period when the old consensus on military qualities is breaking down and a new concept of military leadership is evolving.

More recently, the Secretary of Defense, in December 1959, issued a directive that "all officers . . . will serve a normal tour of duty with a Joint, Combined, Allied or OSD [Office of Secretary of Defense] Staff before being

---

[33] John W. Masland and Laurence I. Radway, *Soldiers and Scholars* (Princeton, 1957), p. 5. This work is a study of the response of military education to the widening policy role of military leadership.

[34] See Vice Admiral L. S. Sabin, "Deep Selections," *United States Naval Institute Proceedings*, Vol. 86 (March 1960), pp. 46 ff; also the large number of comments on Admiral Sabin's article in the June 1960 issue of the *Proceedings* (Vol. 86, No. 6), especially Admiral Carney's letter, pp. 104–106.

considered qualified for promotion to general or flag officer rank." Significantly, the directive makes an exception of Army and Air Force officers "whose proposed advancement and qualifications for promotion are based primarily upon their scientific and technical achievement and proposed utilization in that specialty." [35] This emphasis on planning and technical experience and the deemphasis on parochial views were also underscored in the instructions of the Secretary of the Navy to the Flag Selection Board in 1960. Acknowledging the traditional concern for "a thorough sea-going background in the Line of the Navy," the Secretary brought the Board's attention to the need for "high performance on the planning level and a keen discernment of future operational requirements." He then went on, at some length, to explain that "the explosive technology of our modern weapons systems requires a high degree of concentration and knowledge in particular areas and precludes, to a great degree, the rapid rotation from job to job of many of our most outstanding officers for the purpose of qualifying them in all phases of naval warfare in the pattern of the past." [36]

Both these actions reflect the concern of civilian leaders with the new dimensions of military leadership. Nevertheless, however "civilianized" military officers may become, the profession itself will continue to be anchored in the distinct nature of its trade, the process that has so succinctly and meaningfully been called the "management of violence" by Harold Lasswell. And, in the fulfillment of their mission, the military will continue to be highly influenced by the particular tools of their craft. Indeed, without this distinction what is the meaning of the military profession as a separate group in society? And what do military leaders have to offer that physicists, engineers, diplomats and economists cannot do to meet the requirements of national security? The answer, obviously, is nothing. At the same time, within the framework of its primary and unique contribution, the military profession is dramatically changing. At the moment, it is in a state of transition from the old to the new with the dimensions of the new still unformed, still taking shape, still resembling the contours of an earlier day.

V. TOWARD A NEW CONCEPT OF CIVIL-MILITARY RELATIONS

The nature of civil-military relations is thus being changed through the strengthening of central organization in the Department of Defense, through

---

[35] Department of Defense Directive 1320.5, reprinted in *Army, Navy, Air Force Journal*, December 19, 1959. For a summary of the reaction of the services to this directive, see the article (p. 1) entitled "Pentagon Orders New Barriers to General and Flag Ranks," in the same issue.

[36] Dispatch from Secretary of the Navy William B. Franke to Admiral Herbert G. Hopwood, President of the Flag Selection Board, reprinted in the *Army, Navy, Air Force Journal*, July 16, 1960.

the professionalization of civilian leadership and through the broadening character of the military profession. These trends might also be expressed as the "militarization" of civilians and the "civilianization" of the military. When extended to their logical conclusion, they suggest new relationships between civilians and military based on a more complex division of labor than has heretofore existed. These relationships, however, are responsive to the new shape of national security in which military affairs are no longer a monopoly of the military and a clean-cut division between matters of war and peace, between foreign and military policies, is a false and misleading notion.

It is nevertheless as essential as ever that defense planning be attuned to the broader perspectives of national policy. This is a problem which can no longer be met through civilian control of the military, however. We need to be concerned with the whole complex of professional direction in defense planning and the dilemma of relating the problems of security to the goals and values of national policy. In this task there are limits to what organizational techniques can accomplish. The spectrum is too broad. There is also the danger of accepting institutional devices as a solution without pressing forward along other lines as well. These include arousing enthusiasm for public service in the leading professions in our society, developing a sense of the stakes involved in national security among the general public, encouraging the study of foreign and military policy in educational programs, strengthening the civil service, urging new recruitment and educational standards for military careers and continuing innovation in government administration. In this context the purpose of organization is not so much to control as it is to create the machinery through which to bring the full force of our intellectual resources to bear on the complex issues we have to meet.

THE CHALLENGE TO MILITARY

PROFESSIONALISM

Colonel Robert N. Ginsburgh

THE MOUNTING TENSION in civil-military relations within our Government is made up of many factors—especially, perhaps, the tightening of civilian control and the postwar changes in the nature of war and of the military profession itself. The conflicts are reported almost daily by the Pentagon press corps, and the frustrations of the military are made evident in the writings of Generals Gavin, Ridgway, Taylor, Medaris, White and Admiral Anderson. It is not that these men question the principle of civilian control. Nor is the struggle simply a contest for power. What the military are principally reacting to is the implicit challenge to their professionalism.

Undoubtedly, there exist certain elements of a power struggle for the control of defense policy. A succession of Secretaries of Defense have discovered that it is no easy job to exercise control over officers accustomed to lead and command. The very fact that Mr. McNamara has sought to exercise a greater degree of direction than has any of his predecessors is certainly one cause of the conflict. Yet this fact alone is not sufficient to explain the extent of present tensions in civil-military relationships in Washington.

Although the American military have not always been submissive to the civilian controllers, they have never seriously challenged the right or the tradition of civil control. They have recognized that the ultimate decision-maker must balance military recommendations against other considerations. It is not too difficult for a military man to accept an adverse decision based on nonmilitary considerations. It becomes extremely difficult, however, for him to reconcile himself to an adverse decision by his civilian superior based on military considerations. This strikes at the very *raison d'être* of the military man. It challenges his military professionalism.

The maintenance of a high degree of military professionalism is essential to the preservation of our nation's security without sacrifice of basic American values. The challenge to military professionalism is reflected in each of what Samuel P. Huntington calls the essential characteristics of a profession: corporateness, responsibility and—especially—expertise.

Reprinted from *Foreign Affairs*, January, 1961.

II

A sense of corporateness is especially strong in the military profession. Like other professions the military has its community of interests, common experiences and common values which bind the profession together. But two additional factors make the corporateness of the military especially strong. First, the military man can pursue his profession only within his own national military establishment. Although he may transfer some of his expertise to other areas of endeavor, he cannot continue as an active member of the military profession outside the national military establishment. Second, the sharing of common danger, inherent in the profession, provides a unifying bond—and one which grows stronger as the danger becomes more immediate.

Prior to World War II there was a third factor which contributed greatly to the military's sense of corporateness—its isolation. Geographically, politically and philosophically the military profession lived its own life in a military society set apart from American society. A fundamental challenge to military corporateness today stems from the fact that the military are no longer isolated from the mainstream of American life. There still exist isolated military bases and long tours outside the United States on ship or shore, but the military have become intermingled with civilian society both within their local communities and in the nation.

It is undoubtedly desirable that the military be closely identified with the society they have sworn to defend. But in the intermingling process, many military officers have become less willing to sacrifice personal convenience and have become more concerned with the adequacy of military pay than when they were living on military stations isolated from the impact of the more attractive wages and hours of work of the civilian community.

These two factors—personal inconvenience and pay—combined with the policy which permits early retirement have caused many military men to think of their profession as just a job rather than as a lifetime career. At an early date many military men start planning for their second careers; in fact, many dedicated military professionals have felt that they could simultaneously have greater impact on military policy and receive greater personal rewards by leaving the military profession to work for industry, the "think factories," or even for the Defense Department in a civilian capacity.

Finally, the administrative fusion of the military services in the Department of Defense has not been accompanied by a fusion of their corporate loyalties, which remain attached to the individual services. More than that, emphasis on specialization has tended to splinter the sense of corporateness within the services so that Naval officers think of themselves as black shoe or brown shoe, while Air Force officers may classify themselves as SAC types or TAC types.

III

As compared to the inter-war years, the responsibility of the military has clearly increased, but their authority has been progressively eroded. As a result of the expansion of the unified command concept, the authority of the Service Chief as an individual has been supplanted by the corporate authority of the Joint Chiefs, while the authority of the Chiefs of Staff has been reduced through the creation of the elaborate superstructure for defense policy-making in Washington. At the same time the important responsibilities of the Joint Chiefs of Staff have not lessened and exist whether or not they can agree on the actions to implement them. Their authority to act, however, depends on their reaching agreement.

A further challenge to the responsibility of the military is inherent in our form of government. Because of the separation of powers between the Executive and Congress, the individual public servant may justifiably be confused as to where his responsibility lies. This is especially true for the military. As a result of the increased importance of military affairs in our national life, questions of defense policy have been added to the political issues in the continuing power struggle between the executive and legislative branches. Congress took pains specifically to grant to the Chiefs of the military services the right to appeal to Congress—a right which President Eisenhower once described as "legalized insubordination." There remains, too, in the military profession a sense of responsibility to the people and to the Constitution which transcends the more immediate responsibility to Congress and the Administration. When beset by frustration, the military man tends to satisfy his need for a feeling of responsibility by turning to this ultimate loyalty.

Finally, the concept of responsibility is also challenged when the expertise of the military profession is put in question. When the political decision-maker asks for and accepts the opinion of an expert, he can hold him responsible for the adequacy of such advice. When he refuses to accept his advice because he challenges his qualifications, he can no longer expect to hold the expert responsible. Certainly the expert's sense of responsibility also suffers as a result.

IV

The challenge to military expertise is the most important aspect of the challenge to military professionalism, because expertise is, after all, the very basis of any profession.

Military expertise encompasses strategy, tactics and administration. Generally speaking, military expertise in tactics and administration has not been seriously challenged. The reason for this, according to Bernard Brodie, is that: "There is no doubt that tactics and administration are the areas in

which the soldier is most completely professional. The handling of battles
by land, sea or air, the manœuvring of large forces, the leadership of man
in the fact of honor and death, and the development and administration of
the organizations that affect these purposes are clearly not jobs for ama-
teurs." In the area of strategy, however, Brodie asserts as a "basic fact" that
"the soldier has been handed a problem that extends far beyond the expertise of his own profession." [1] In similar vein Joseph Kraft argues that "the
professional soldiers—not through any fault of their own, but on the contrary in consequence of their virtues—are ill-fitted for high-level strategic
thought." [2] This is indeed ironic when we consider that originally the word
"strategy," derived from the Greek *strategos*, meant simply the art of
generalship.

Even before World War I, however, wars were usually considered too
important to be left to the generals—unless the commanding general was
also chief of state. Since World War II, the political leaders have become
more concerned than ever before with the problems of war, strategy and
military affairs in general. War is no longer a question merely of victory or
defeat on the field of battle. With the advent of nuclear weapons and
strategic delivery systems, we have reached the stage where peacetime preparedness is likely to determine the outcome of a major nuclear war. Thus
not only war but also peacetime defense becomes too serious a matter to
be left to the generals.

At the same time that technology has forced political leaders to concern
themselves with military affairs, it has operated to make the military man
less of an expert. The development of new weapons has always been of
great importance in the history of warfare. In earlier times, however, the
military professional was able to assimilate the military impact over a period
of years or even generations, and if he was not necessarily the creator of the
new technology, he was almost invariably its exploiter. Today, however,
technological developments come so thick and fast it becomes difficult
to keep abreast of their existence, much less assimilate their impact on military problems. Furthermore, the professional has a much smaller role in the
creation of new weapons because their complexity requires the specialized
services of the scientist and engineer, and their magnitude generally requires
that they be produced by industry rather than government.

Thus in the continuing technological race for new and better weapons,
the scientist, the engineer and the industrialist become partners with the
military man; and he becomes dependent on them in the pursuit of his
profession. By no means silent partners, they may be in a position to insist
successfully that a particular project of great interest to the military is imprac-

---

[1] Bernard Brodie, *Strategy in the Missile Age*. Princeton: Princeton University
Press, 1959, pp. 15–16 and 9–10.
[2] Joseph Kraft, "The War Thinkers," *Esquire*, September 1962, p. 148.

tical. It may, in fact, be impractical, but it may also be that the scientist or engineer for one reason or another personally thinks it undesirable. In any ensuing dispute the military man frequently finds himself at a disadvantage. The scientist probably has more technical knowledge of the subject; and if, as is probable, the dispute involves new weapons requiring new military techniques, the military man will have little experience on which to rely. Furthermore, to the extent that warfare has advanced toward the push-button stage, there is increased emphasis on peacetime pre-planning at the expense of decision-making and military judgment during the heat of battle —the peculiar province of the military professional. Thus, the nuclear scientist can say that he knows more about nuclear physics than the military and that, after all, the military man hasn't had any actual experience in waging nuclear war, in which there isn't much need for military judgment anyway.

It is not only the natural scientists and engineers who cast doubt on the expertise of the military; it is also the political scientists and those whom David Lilienthal calls "the methodologists." [3] The military services had of course used the techniques of operations analysis during World War II, and subsequently their application was expanded within the military services to include the determination of desirable characteristics and uses of new weapons and the development of new tactical and strategic concepts. The services also created a variety of nongovernmental think factories. Thus, we find the RAND Corporation working primarily with the Air Force, the Research Analysis Corporation with the Army, the Operations Evaluation Group at M.I.T. with the Navy, and the Institute for Defense Analysis with the Joint Chiefs of Staff and Defense Department. In addition, there are some 350 other non-profit corporations, some 300 college research centers, and 1,400 industrial companies, as well as various private foundations and scientific advisory committees—all involved in some degree in the business of thinking about military problems.

Unquestionably, these think factories have performed a valuable service to the military professional in his search to adapt technology to military problems. But on occasion they have further complicated this search, and they have undoubtedly challenged his professional expertise.

Here once again, the professional military man frequently finds himself at a disadvantage in comparison with a member or "graduate" of the think factories. First, the very independence of a think factory tends to lend its findings greater prestige than if the same conclusions were reached by the government agency which employed it. This independence also gives the think factory the opportunity to approach other agencies in an attempt to persuade the government as to the correctness of its findings. Similarly, the individual "academic strategist" who has graduated from a think factory

---

[3] *The New York Times Magazine,* September 29, 1963, p. 23.

may move back and forth among other think factories, universities and government. If his ideas on military strategy and policy are not well received by one organization, he may be more successful through one of the other avenues.

The strategist in uniform, on the other hand, finds himself constrained both by the hierarchy of the strategic planning organization and the military discipline of subordination to higher authority, which make it more difficult to take issue with accepted policy. Nor can he publicize his views through magazines or books as easily as the lay strategist can. Writing for publication is an important element of the academic rather than of the military profession, and the academician is much more likely to be granted time and financial support for his research. Even when the military man combines both the opportunity and inclination to write for publication he finds himself more severely constrained by rules of military security and government policy review. These circumstances partly explain why most of the influential books and articles on military policy and strategy published since World War II have been written not by professional military men but by civilian academic strategists, many of whom have been associated with the think factories. But the cause lies also in the failure of the military colleges to "stand on the frontiers of knowledge." [4]

Thus, since the end of World War II there has gradually developed an increasing number of civilian experts on military policy. This growing body of academic or lay strategists is being used more and more to challenge the views of the professional military man. In fact, Joseph Kraft maintains that "the Academic Strategists emerge as a key factor in the maintenance of civilian control over the Armed Services. . . . Their generalizations provide civilian officials with a useful yardstick for judging rival service claims, and for keeping the whole defense establishment in line with the nation's strategic goals." On the other hand, he notes that "without the Academic Strategists, the basic decisions about how defense monies were spent would be thrust upon the professional soldiers." [5]

The growing influence of the lay strategist has been accentuated and accelerated by the so-called "Whiz Kids" who were brought to the Pentagon by the present Administration and who personify the new civilian experts. Unquestionably a brilliant and gifted group, they nevertheless—in Stewart Alsop's words—"display occasionally the intellectual arrogance that is the chief failing of the overintelligent." [6] At its extreme, this results in the assertion that there is no longer any need in nuclear warfare for military judg-

---

[4] John W. Masland and Laurence I. Radway, *Soldiers and Scholars*. Princeton: Princeton University Press, 1957, pp. 436, 509.

[5] Kraft, *op. cit.*, p. 149.

[6] Stewart Alsop, "Master of the Pentagon," *Saturday Evening Post*, August 5, 1961, p. 46.

ment because the outcome of nuclear campaigns can be predetermined by precise mathematical computations. In many ways this is reminiscent of the eighteenth-century "scientific" approach to strategy based upon a system of complicated and carefully calculated geometrical movements and angles of attack. Since the occupation of key geographical points was designed to make victory almost mechanical, it might make actual fighting unnecessary.

The proliferation of lay strategists has been accompanied by an expansion of civilian influence and a decrease in military influence in the councils of government having to do with national security policy. Thus there is no military representation on our highest military policy-making body, the National Security Council. Although the Joint Chiefs of Staff are designated as advisers to the N.S.C., they are also advisers to and subordinate to the Secretary of Defense, who is the principal adviser to the President in all matters relating to defense. And as a matter of practice the Joint Chiefs— other than the Chairman—are rarely invited to attend meetings of the National Security Council. Furthermore, between the military Service Chiefs and the civilian Secretaries, there have grown up new ranks and hosts of individuals—mostly civilian—without any corresponding decentralization of authority; in fact, taking full advantage of modern communications and computer techniques, the decision-making authority has become more centralized. As a result, the military professional faces many more roadblocks— more people who can say no and fewer who can say yes.

The invasion of the area of military strategy and policy by the lay strategist has been facilitated by the military professionals' sallies forth into nonmilitary areas—in pursuit of what Huntington calls the theory of political-military fusion. "This theory started from the undeniable fact that military policy and political policy were much more closely interrelated in the postwar world than they had been previously. It went on, however, to assert that it had become impossible to main the distinction between political and military functions at the highest level of government." [7]

One aspect of this theory was that military leaders were expected to incorporate political, economic and social factors into their thinking. This gave rise to situations in which the Joint Chiefs of Staff defended the importance of political considerations while the State Department was concerned with military arguments. The fusionist theory also gave impetus to the heavy emphasis in the senior war colleges on nonmilitary subjects. Most recently, it has stimulated professional and popular interest in problems of cold war and counterinsurgency which require successful fusion of a wide variety of military and nonmilitary techniques.

A second result of the fusionist theory was the heavy demand for military

---

[7] Samuel P. Huntington, *The Soldier and the State*. Cambridge: Harvard University Press, 1957, p. 351.

leaders to undertake nonmilitary responsibilities. Because of their wartime popularity, prestige and experience, professional military men were called upon to fill influential positions in politics, in industry and in government. Some of the governmental positions required the exercise of military as well as political functions, but others were filled by military men not because of the relevance of their experience, but because of their prestige or general executive ability and the comparative lack of experienced and available civilians immediately after World War II. Once the military professionals had breached the wall between military and nonmilitary affairs the route was widened into a two-way street, so that the military professional found himself challenged both on his own ground and on nonmilitary grounds as well. Meanwhile, the application of the fusionist theory forbade him to retire from the nonmilitary field to his former sanctuary.

In addition to political-military fusion, World War II set the stage for the fusion of the military profession itself—a fusion, however, which has not been completed. The Unification Act, born of World War II experiences pointing up the need for coordinated military actions on land, sea and air, established a coalition of the military services rather than a fusion. The military profession has not yet successfully met the challenge posed by even this much change. It requires the development of broad-gauged military professionals who can speak with authority on a full spectrum of military matters rather than a collection of individual experts in air, land and sea warfare. The more specialized expertise is still needed, but the military profession must also develop the generalists who can fuse together the particular competence of the specialists. This does not necessarily mean that the specialists themselves or their organizations must be integrated into a single service but that their individual points of view must be fused into a more broadly professional military expertise.

The singular failure of the military profession to meet this challenge has provided the lay strategist the occasion to invade the area of military affairs. In fact, the conflicts within the military profession have made it imperative for the civilian to step in to reach decisions. To avoid making purely arbitrary decisions, the informed expertise of the lay strategist has, with justification, been relied upon. In fairness to the military profession, however, we should note that the failure to develop professional generalists has been abetted by some civilians who have not wished to see the military services develop a common profession—who felt that a policy of divide-and-conquer was the surest way to maintain civilian control.

The extent of the conquest is, I think, aptly illustrated by the following commentary by Huntington on the influence of the military professional on military policy between 1945 and 1960: "It is not surprising that military leaders played a key role in implementing policy and that they seldom actually made important decisions on policy. Perhaps more striking is the relatively unimportant role which they played in proposing changes in policy.

In no case did military leaders initiate major new policies and in no case did they effectively prevent changes in old ones." [8]

V

Huntington's analysis of military professionalism leads him to conclude that "the requisite for military security is a shift in basic American values from liberalism to conservatism. Only an environment which is sympathetically conservative will permit American military leaders to combine the political power which society thrusts upon them with the military professionalism without which society cannot endure." [9] Another proposed solution is to divide the problems of national security into total war and limited war, with specialists for each. The limited war specialists would retain the traditional "heroic" characteristics of the old military profession. Huntington, in effect, would solve the fundamental problem by changing the environment which creates it. The other approach would solve the problem by dividing it in two, by ignoring the more fundamental half, and by turning the clock back to solve the other.

Either response would, of course, help to resolve the frustrations caused by the current challenge to the military profession. But the first seems to be an extreme solution unless it is the only way to preserve our nation's security; and the second does not really solve the problem.

To meet satisfactorily the challenge to its professionalism, the military must first of all become more professionally expert. Under today's conditions the military profession can meet this requirement only by developing an expertise which transcends that of the individual service. The military profession must develop strategy, tactics and techniques which can deal with the entire spectrum of organized conflict from total war to guerrilla war, in all its media—land, sea, air and space.

The development of an all-around military expertise would be aided by greater mobility of personnel among the services. This should be something more than the occasional opportunity to transfer from one service to another. More intensive use should be made of the existing exchange programs, with particular emphasis on areas of military management, especially at higher staff levels—rather than trying to make a single individual into a submariner, an infantryman, a pilot, a ship's captain and a missile expert.

The development of greater expertise will not be enough in itself, unless it can be effectively communicated to the political decision-maker. This will require a flexibility in adapting to changing political administrations and the ability to explain military concepts in the particular language of each administration. It will also require a special skill in mastering the techniques of the

---

[8] Samuel P. Huntington, *The Common Defense.* New York: Columbia University Press, 1961, p. 114.

[9] Huntington, *The Soldier and the State,* p. 464.

think factories in order to evaluate the efforts of its own thinkers and to compete successfully with the independent lay strategists.

If the desired professional military expertise is ever to be achieved, the military school system—especially the senior military colleges—will have to assume a key role. The average military man probably devotes a larger proportion of his career to formal schooling than any other professional. If the military schools are to fulfill their function adequately, the best of them must encourage original thought, research and publication comparable to that of our leading universities. In the course of study the military aspects of national strategy should be emphasized anew with the objective of developing new strategic concepts and doctrines. Politics and economics need not be ignored, but the curriculum should focus on military subjects. The courses should also develop a general knowledge of contemporary military technology and a competency in the techniques of operational research.

A prerequisite for the re-creation of military expertise is the abandonment of the fusionist theory whereby military and nonmilitary factors are so entwined that a separate expertise in the military aspects of national security is simply impossible. Obviously there is an intimate interrelationship between military and nonmilitary factors; but there is a difference, and we need to reestablish the concept that the problems of national security can, in fact, be broken into various aspects even though they interact on each other. The statesman needs sound military advice; the military professional needs firm policy guidance. Each must, of course, understand the problems of the other. The military man should be aware of the political, economic, social and other factors which affect national security, but it is not his business to evaluate them. He should limit himself to a consideration of the military aspects which are within his area of competence. The civilian authorities, both executive and legislative, should assist him in exercising self-restraint by not requiring his comments on nonmilitary matters. Similarly, the statesman who is concerned with a political problem must recognize that it may have important military implications but he should refrain from making military analyses. He should use the results of the analysis of the military expert as one of the factors bearing on his total problem.

The separation of a national security problem into its various aspects does not mean that the military man and the statesman should work independently of each other. A military analysis may well depend on the particular political, economic or psychological assumptions which are made. The establishment of these assumptions should be the task of the statesman. The military man can contribute by pointing out how various ranges of assumptions may materially affect the military estimate.

A traditionally military—and perhaps also American—response to most problems is to reorganize. While this predilection should not lead us to expect too much, it is apparent that certain organizational changes in the Department of Defense would help the military to exercise their expertise and make them more responsive and more responsible to civilian control.

First of all, the organization and procedures of the Joint Chiefs of Staff need to be streamlined so that they can act more quickly and be more responsive to the Secretary of Defense. The host of special committees, councils, assistants and groups should be realigned to report through staff directors with increased stature and authority. The Joint Staff should exercise effective direction over the various defense agencies. It would be highly desirable for the Chiefs to use the Joint Staff as their primary advisers and to give the Joint Staff officers increased stature and authority in their relations with the Service staffs. Finally, the Joint Staff should be given greater authority to act on certain operational matters within established policy. This would make it possible for the Chiefs to fulfill their responsibilities without having personally to consider and agree on all matters for which they are responsible.

A second major effort should be to improve the working relationships between the J.C.S. and the staff of the Secretary of Defense. These staffs ought to be cooperating rather than independent and completing staffs, and some realignment of functions is desirable to achieve that end. Serious consideration should be given to opening up the "closed system" of the J.C.S., whereby lateral communication is prohibited and access to its studies is only by way of the Secretary of Defense. If this system could be altered, perhaps the J.C.S. would fill the proposed position of Assistant Secretary of Defense for Plans and Operations with some of its existing functions and personnel distributed to the various existing offices of Assistant Secretaries of Defense.

A third measure would involve organizing to encourage self-criticism on the part of the military profession itself. The military professional must be able to produce new ideas and concepts if he is to compete with the lay strategist. It is perhaps too much to expect that the military, with its emphasis on discipline and the chain of command, can ever achieve the same degree of academic freedom enjoyed by the lay strategist. It should be possible, however, to encourage more original military thinking without sacrificing the traditions of obedience to higher authority. One possibility, for example, would be the creation of small groups charged with long-range planning and new conceptual thinking and made directly responsible to the military service chiefs. This system would make it possible for a new idea to be aired at the highest levels without having to follow the tortuous path of military command which tends to reject concepts not in accord with previously approved policy.

Taken together, these measures would respond to the challenges to the responsibility as well as the expertise of the military. Its sense of corporateness could also be strengthened by measures to re-create the prestige and attractiveness of a military career—without, however, trying to return the military to its prewar state of isolation. Especially effective would be the resurrection of the traditional fringe benefits of the military. Similar personnel policies within and among the individual services would also contribute. This does not require uniformity in personnel matters, ignoring differences in requirements and problems, but it does mean the elimination of conflicting policies based on historical differences which are no longer relevant.

A fundamental obstacle to achieving the various responses which have been outlined is likely to be the continuing fear of military power and the traditional anti-military bias of the liberal ethic. To the extent, however, that the suggestions made here are non-political and encourage professional expertise and responsibility, they should, in fact, lead to more effective civilian control. If civilian control seems reasonably well assured, perhaps military professionalism could be acceptable without necessarily substituting the conservative for the liberal ethic. Surely the United States is strong enough to allow Americans to choose their political philosophy—whether liberal or conservative—on grounds other than national security alone.

SCIENTISTS,
FOREIGN POLICY,
AND POLITICS

Warner R. Schilling

... we must take, so far as we can, a picture of the world into our minds. Is it not a startling circumstance for one thing that the great discoveries of science, that the quiet study of men in laboratories, that the thoughtful developments which have taken place in quiet lecture rooms, have now been turned to the destruction of civilization? ... The enemy whom we have just overcome had at its seats of learning some of the principal centres of scientific study and discovery, and used them in order to make destruction sudden and complete; and only the watchful, continuous cooperation of men can see to it that science, as well as armed men, is kept within the harness of civilization.[1]

I

These words were spoken in Paris in January, 1919 by Woodrow Wilson, addressing the second Plenary Session of the Peace Conference. Wilson believed he had found a watchdog for civilization in the League of Nations. In this he was sadly mistaken. Science and armed men have indeed been harnessed, but in order to promote and maintain the goals of conflicting polities. Whether in the pursuit of these ends the cause of civilization will yet be served remains, we may hope, an open question.

The cooperation of scientists and armed men was not a new relationship, even in Wilson's day. In the United States, for example, the president of the American Association for the Advancement of Science had declared in 1861:

... it is easy to see that there are few applications of science which do not bear on the interests of commerce and navigation, naval or mili-

---

[1] U.S. Department of State, *Papers Relating to the Foreign Relations of the United States, The Peace Conference,* 13 vols. (Washington, 1942–1947), vol. 3, p. 179.

An earlier version of this paper was prepared for discussion at the Fifth Congress of the International Political Science Association in Paris, September, 1961. The points made in it owe much to the comment and counsel of William T. R. Fox.

tary concerns, the customs, the lighthouses, the public lands, post offices or post roads, either directly or remotely. If all examination is refused . . . the Government may lose a most important advantage.[2]

As a result of the interest of a number of American scientists and government officials, the National Academy of Sciences was established in 1863 for the purpose of providing scientific advice to the United States Government. The use made of this Academy by the War Department between 1863 and 1913 bespeaks a bygone era. During those years the Department requested the Academy to constitute scientific committees on exactly five matters:

> On the Question of Tests for the Purity of Whiskey; On the Preservation of Paint on Army Knapsacks; On Galvanic Action from Association of Zinc and Iron; On the Exploration of the Yellowstone; On questions of Meteorological Science and its Applications.[3]

It would be unfair to presume from this list that the War Department was uninterested in new weapons systems. Until about the turn of the century, military technology, like industrial technology, generally developed independently of advances in basic scientific knowledge. Thus, in 1915, when Wilson's Secretary of the Navy decided to establish a "Department of Invention and Development" in the hope of securing effective weapons with which to combat that "new and terrible engine of warfare . . . the submarine," it was the inventor, Thomas Edison, who was asked to head the new organization.[4] Although the contributions of university and industrial scientists to the fighting of World War I were marked enough to have caught Wilson's imagination, it was not until a generation later, with the advent of World War II, that the mobilization of scientists brought military results which were of great and in some instances decisive importance to the course of combat.

What has transformed the relationship between science and war has been the fact that in the twentieth century the development of technology has become increasingly dependent upon advances in basic knowledge about the physical world. Moreover, in the technically advanced nations, both the rate of technological innovation and the growth of new scientific knowledge have been increasing exponentially. As crudely measured by the volume of scientific publication, scientific knowledge has been doubling every ten to fifteen years.[5] In a non-Wilsonian world, the consequences of these condi-

---

[2] Quoted in *Science and Technology Act of 1958*, Staff Study of the Senate Committee on Government Operations, 85th Cong., 2d sess., Washington, 1958, p. 110.

[3] *Ibid.*, p. 115.

[4] See Daniels' letter to Edison, in Josephus Daniels, *The Wilson Era: Years of Peace, 1910–1917* (Chapel Hill: The University of North Carolina Press, 1944), p. 491.

[5] Ellis A. Johnson, "The Crisis in Science and Technology and its Effect on Military Development," *Operations Research*, January-February 1958, pp. 14–15.

tions for national security policy have been as necessary as they are obvious. As the United States and the Soviet Union throw one weapons system after another into the effort to maintain at least a balance of terror, neither dares fall behind in either the discovery of new physical relationships or in the application of scientific knowledge to military hardware and political-military strategy. Thus, by the end of the first decade of the Cold War, about 50 per cent of the engineers in the United States and 25 per cent of the scientists were employed by the Federal government, either directly or on contract, and about 65 per cent of the scientific research in universities and 57 per cent of that in private industry was government-financed.[6]

Indicative of the new relationship between science and war, figures and graphs comparing the Great Powers in numbers of scientists and engineers have become as familiar as those in the 1930s which compared the Powers in their output of steel, coal, and oil. Nor is it only in the military field that science and technology have become vital to the course of foreign policy. Science has been harnessed to the advancement of foreign policy goals in such diverse fields as the exploration of space, birth and disease control, weather modification, economic development, and global communications.[7]

Present, prospective, and future developments in science and technology are certain to bring a host of problems and opportunities to those responsible for the conduct of foreign policy. In recognition of this fact, the governments of the major Powers have endeavored to find ways to make themselves more alert to such developments and more active in determining the course of science and technology. The United States and the Soviet Union are the most extensively engaged in this effort, but it should not be forgotten that the nations of Western and Central Europe were among the pioneers in cultivating the relationship between science and government. The three elements that have revolutionized current military technology and strategy (electronics, missiles, and nuclear weapons) had their harbingers in the World War II development of British radar, the German V-2, and the American A-bomb, and it is noteworthy that the two European developments were conceived, initiated, and directed by officials and employees of established government organizations. In contrast, the American A-bomb was the result of conceptions and initiatives that came from outside the government—and primarily from exiled Europeans at that.

As an integral part of the efforts of governments to become both more responsive to and responsible for the development of science and technology,

---

[6] See Lee A. DuBridge, "The American Scientist: 1955," *Yale Review,* Spring 1955, p. 13, and the *Bulletin of the Atomic Scientists,* March 1957, p. 82, and May-June 1961, p. 254. The figure for private industry is for the year 1959; the others are for the year 1955.

[7] For a more detailed treatment of some of the points in the preceding paragraphs and a general discussion of the effect of science on international relations, see the present writer's "Science, Technology, and Foreign Policy," *Journal of International Affairs,* Fall 1959, pp. 7–18.

scientists have been invited into the highest councils of government, and it is with some of the problems occasioned by the presence of these "new" participants in the making of national policy that the remainder of this article will be concerned. Although some illustrative material will be drawn from the experience of other governments, the paper focuses on problems associated with the participation of scientists in the American policy process.

Needless to say, the problems in policy-making that may arise will vary greatly with the kind of scientist participating (oceanographer, theoretical physicist, specialist in space medicine, industrial chemist), with the nature of the policy issue at stake (weapons development, science education, public health, the exploration of space, the allocation of funds for basic research), and with the manner in which the scientist is involved in the policy process (member of the attentive public, adviser to the President, worker in a government laboratory, official in an executive department or agency). This article will make no attempt to deal systematically with the combinations possible among these three variables (profession, issue, and involvement). The discussion will be confined to a few of the central problems that the layman and the scientist are likely to encounter in working together on national security issues; and the treatment, as will become evident, will be of a very general and suggestive order.

In their general character, the problems occasioned by the participation of scientists in the determination of high policy are not nearly so novel as is generally supposed. The scientist has been brought into the councils of government because he possesses specialized skills and information believed relevant to the identification and resolution of particular policy problems. His relationship to the policy process is therefore a familiar one, that of an expert. Just as Sputnik I precipitated the establishment of a Special Assistant to the President for Science and Technology, so the earlier problems of fighting World War II and insuring postwar employment had brought the Joint Chiefs of Staff and the Council of Economic Advisers into the Offices of the President.

The central problems in policy-making posed by the entry of scientists into the policy process are thus formally no different from those associated with any other expert involved in the determination of national security policy. In particular, four such problems can be noted. (1) Like all experts, scientists will at times disagree, and the non-scientist (be he politician, administrator, or an expert in some other field) will confront the problem of choosing a course of action in the face of conflicting scientific advice. (2) Like all experts, scientists will at times evince certain predispositions toward the resolution of the policy problems on which their advice is sought, and the non-scientist will confront the problem of identifying the policy predilections peculiar to scientists and being on his guard against them. (3) The non-scientist and scientist will comfort one problem in common, and that is how to organize themselves to maximize the contribution that science can make to the government's programs, opportunities, and choices. Finally, (4) the scientist will confront a problem common to all experts who participate in the American policy process, and that is how to engage in politics without debasing the coinage of his own expertise.

II

The difficulties the non-scientist confronts in choosing a course of action in the face of conflicting scientific advice seem inherently no more formidable than those a non-expert would face in deciding what to do in the event of conflicting advice from economists, soldiers, or specialists on Soviet foreign policy. There are at least seven procedures that the non-expert can follow in such circumstances, singly or in combination, and they appear to have about the same promise, for better or for worse, regardless of the kind of experts involved.[8]

The first step the non-scientist can take is to make certain that it is really conflicting *scientific* advice he is receiving. In the fall of 1949 President Truman asked Secretary Acheson to look into the disputes then current within the Atomic Energy Commission and elsewhere about the consequences of undertaking an intensive effort to make an H-bomb. Upon investigation the Secretary of State concluded that the scientists involved were not really very far apart except on the foreign policy issues that were his and Truman's responsibility to decide.[9]

Procedures two and three are simple: the non-scientist may be guided by quantitative or qualitative features of the division (he can side with the majority, or with that side whose past record is the more confidence-inspiring). Failing these, there is, four, the "principle of least harm" and, five, the "principle of minimal choice." In the former, one chooses that course of action which appears to involve the least cost if the technical premise on which it is based proves to be wrong. Thus in World War II, given the American belief that the Germans were hard at work on an A-bomb, it seemed more sensible to spend $2 billion on the assumption that the bomb could be made than to do little or nothing on the assumption that it could not. In the case of the "principle of minimal choice," one chooses that course of action which seems to close off the least number of future alternatives. This was the character of President Truman's first decision on the H-bomb. He decided to go ahead in the effort to explore the feasibility

---

[8] *Cf.* the implication in the following remarks of Glenn T. Seaborg, the Chairman of the Atomic Energy Commission: "Scientists don't necessarily have to make the final political decisions, but it might be easier to let a capable scientist learn political reality than to teach a politician science." Quoted in the *Bulletin of the Atomic Scientists*, February 1961, p. 79.

[9] In this and subsequent undocumented references the present writer has drawn upon personal interviews during 1956–1958 with participants in the H-bomb decision.

of an H-bomb, but nothing was decided about technical steps of a greater political or military consequence (for example, testing a device if one were fabricated, or preparing to produce the materials that would be required for weapons production in the event of a successful test).[10]

In the case of procedure six the non-scientist can make his choice among conflicting scientists on the basis of whichever technical estimate is most in accord with policy on which he was already intent. (In contrast to the first procedure, where the non-scientist endeavors to factor out of the conflict the policy preferences of the scientists, here he is factoring into the conflict his own policy preferences.) In the spring of 1942, the British scientists Henry Tizard and F. A. Lindemann (Lord Cherwell) diverged greatly in their estimates of the destruction that could be accomplished by an intensive bombing of the homes of the German working class. There was general agreement among the soldiers and politicians involved that if the lower estimate were correct there were better military uses for the resources the bombing campaign would require, but in the end the campaign was made in the expectation that the higher estimate would prove to be the more accurate (which it did not). This choice was clearly influenced by Churchill's interest in presenting the Russians with a dramatically visible contribution to the war against Germany and by the fact that British air doctrine had long presumed the efficacy of strategic bombing.[11]

In procedure seven the non-scientist is guided by his own sense for the scientific and technical problems involved. In the 1949 H-bomb debate, some of the politicians involved were little deterred by the fact that the scientists were by no means confident that they could make such a weapon and by the possibility that an all-out but failing effort might entail very high costs for the A-bomb program. These politicians were willing to press ahead in part because of their belief that the scientists were not really aware of their own potential. Similarly, when the German soldiers, scientists, and engineers engaged in the development of the V-2 divided on the question of whether it should be launched from mobile or fixed batteries, Hitler's own technical enthusiasm for large, hardened bunkers led him, unwisely as it turned out, to decide on behalf of the latter.[12]

---

[10] For the "principle of least harm," see Bernard Brodie, "Strategy as a Science," *World Politics,* July 1949, p. 479n. On the H-bomb choice, see the present writer's "The H-Bomb Decision: How To Decide Without Actually Choosing," *Political Science Quarterly,* March 1961, pp. 37–38.

[11] See C. P. Snow, *Science and Government* (Cambridge: Harvard University Press, 1961), pp. 47–51, the review of this book by P. M. S. Blackett in *Scientific American,* April 1961, pp. 192–194, and Winston S. Churchill, *The Second World War: The Hinge of Fate* (Boston: Houghton Mifflin Company, 1950), p. 281. For British air doctrine see also Herbert S. Dinerstein, "The Impact of Air Power on the International Scene, 1933–1940," *Military Affairs,* Summer 1955, pp. 67–68.

[12] Maj. Gen. Walter Dornberger, *V-2* (New York: Ballantine Books, 1954), pp. 97, 158–160, and Lt. Gen. James M. Gavin, *War and Peace in the Space Age* (New York, 1958), pp. 76–77.

In concluding this survey of the problem of conflicting advice, it should be noted that one of the more likely outcomes is that the actions of the contending scientists may prove much more influential than the procedures followed by the non-scientist. Divided experts will not always be equal in their physical or personal access to the decision-maker, in the persistence with which they state their case, or in the force and clarity of their arguments. Thus, in the H-bomb debate, there were instances where equally qualified scientists differed greatly in the time and energy they spent circulating their views of the technical (and political) prospects, and such differences were by no means without consequence for the judgments of others.[13]

III

The discussion of the policy predispositions displayed by scientists must be entered with considerable caution. The major theoretical premise involved is that all experts will evidence certain predilections with regard to policy and policy-making which are the result of the character of their expertise: their skills, knowledge, and experience. Since experts differ in the skills, knowledge, and experience they command (or in the responsibilities with which they are charged), they will differ in the biases they characteristically exhibit. Thus scientists, soldiers, and diplomats jointly concerned with a policy problem are likely to approach the question of how and in what manner it should be resolved with rather dissimilar predispositions.

These points, however, are easier stated than demonstrated. To begin with, it should be clear that, insofar as policy is concerned, "the scientific mind" is as much a chimera as "the military mind." Scientists, like soldiers and the rest of us, differ greatly in the ideas they have about the political world and the things that will (or ought to) happen in it, and their views on foreign policy matters are far more likely to be reflective of these differences than conditioned by their common professional skills and interests. Moreover, even if differences in expertise or responsibility were the only factors determining the views of policy-makers (and they certainly are not),

---

[13] Note should also be taken of the problem the policy-maker faces when all his experts are *agreed*. The present writer is unable to suggest a useful procedure here (other than variations on numbers five, six, and seven above); but that the problem is a real one can be seen in the conclusion of the German physicists that it would be infeasible for any Power to develop an atomic bomb during World War II. Some of the German scientists later stated that political considerations were partly responsible for their advice and for the fact that they made so little progress themselves on an A-bomb (*cf.* procedure one).

The German work of the A-bomb during World War II is described in Samuel A. Goudsmit, *Alsos* (New York: Henry Schuman, Inc., 1947). For various appraisals of the influence exercised by political considerations, see Robert Jungk, *Brighter than a Thousand Suns* (New York: Harcourt, Brace and Company, 1958), pp. 88–104, Hans Bethe in the *Bulletin of the Atomic Scientists,* December 1958, p. 427, and William L. Laurence, *Men and Atoms* (New York: Simon and Schuster, 1959), pp. 90–93.

one would still have to take account of the fact that scientists are as varied in their professional skills and pursuits as soldiers. The perspectives of a theoretical physicist engaged in basic research are no more to be equated with those of an organic chemist engaged in applying extant knowledge to the improvement of an industrial product than is the outlook of a staff officer in Washington drafting a war plan to be considered identical with that of a general in charge of a theatre of operations.

In addition to these difficulties, analysis must also contend with the fact that it is directed toward a moving target. The policy perspectives that a physicist may have developed as a result of two decades in a university laboratory are unlikely to endure without change after a few years on a Washington advisory committee. Many American scientists are well along the same route that transformed the policy perspectives of large numbers of the American military profession during the war and immediate postwar years. As a result of new problems and new responsibilities, these soldiers acquired new skills, knowledge, and experience. In consequence, with regard to their approach to foreign policy, some are, for all practical purposes, interchangeable between the Pentagon and the State Department, and one could wish that there were more diplomats equally well equipped to work on both sides of the Potomac.

With these reservations in mind, six policy perspectives will be presented here which seem moderately characteristic of many scientists, most of them physicists, who have participated in national security policy in recent times. Most of these predispositions were first evidenced during their work with the military during World War II, and the extent and manner in which they have been later operative in reference to larger foreign policy issues is not always easy to document, since most of the sources are still classified. Needless to say, in outlining these predispositions, one is presenting a cross between a caricature and a Weberian ideal type, not describing real people. In discussing these predispositions, the present writer does not mean to convey the impression that they are either "good" or "bad" from the point of view of policy or policy-making, or that one or another of these predispositions may not also be evidenced by groups other than scientists. The point to this discussion is that if certain orders of scientists are indeed prone to these or other policy predispositions, the non-scientist will be wise to be alert to them, even if in the event he should conclude that they are all for the good.

Naive Utopianism or Naive Belligerency

C. P. Snow has described the scientist as an impatient optimist in his approach to social wrongs; he is quick to search for something to do and inclined to expect favorable results.[14] Certainly, the scientist's profession in-

---

[14] C. P. Snow, *The Two Cultures and the Scientific Revolution* (New York: Cambridge University Press, 1959), pp. 9–11.

clines him to look at problems in terms of searching for a solution to them. When this perspective is turned to problems of international politics, however, the scientist's approach often appears open to the characterization of "naive utopianism or naive belligerency." [15] His approach to international relations appears simplistic and mechanistic. It is almost as if he conceives of policy being made primarily by forward-looking, solution-oriented, rational-thinking types like himself.

In these perspectives the scientist is likely to find little in common with the diplomat (who is inclined to believe that most of his problems have no solution, and who is in any event too busy with the crises of the day to plan for tomorrow), or with the politician (whose approach to problems is so spasmodic as to seem neither analytical nor rational, and whose policy positions are anyway soon blurred by his efforts to accommodate to the positions of others), or with the professional student of international politics (who, when the opportunity permits, lectures the scientist on the elegant complexity of the political process, but who never seems, to the scientist at least, to have any really good ideas about what to do). It is perhaps these differences in perspective that lead the scientist on occasion to seem "intellectually arrogant"; it is as if he concludes that those who have no promising solutions or are not seeking them cannot be very bright. In his predisposition toward action and solutions, the scientist comes closest to sharing the predilection of the soldier for decision, which may be one reason why their partnership has been so spectacularly successful.

The Whole Problem Approach

The first grant made by the United States Government for experimental research was in 1832 to the Franklin Institute. The scientists were asked to investigate the reasons for explosions in steamboat boilers. They reported back not only with a technical explanation but with a draft bill to provide for Federal regulation of steamboats.[16] In this they evidenced the scientist's predilection for the "whole problem approach." The reluctance of scientists to apply their expertise to mere fragments of the total problem, especially under conditions where those who prescribe the fragments do not reveal the whole of which they are a part, was evident in the work of both British and American scientists during World War II. Military officials initially approached the scientists with requests for the development of particular weapons and devices without revealing the military problems or reasoning responsible for their requests. The scientists objected to this procedure, and they were eventually able to persuade the soldiers to inform them of the general military problems involved in order that the scientists might reach their own

---

[15] I am indebted to Hans Speier for the phrasing of this point.
[16] Don K. Price, *Government and Science* (New York: New York University Press, 1954), pp. 10–11.

conclusions about the kinds of weapons and devices the military would need to meet those problems.[17]

In 1952, in connection with an Air Force project on air defense, a group of American scientists were asked to review the prospects for improving the nation's continental air defense. The scientists concluded that some new and promising systems were possible, and they submitted an estimate of what the developments might cost. They also recommended that the money be spent. The Air Force did not approve the recommendation, and as is customary in Washington the disputants on both sides began to search for allies and to leak their cases to the press. Certain Air Force officials, who feared that additional funds for air defense would come at the expense of dollars otherwise available for the Strategic Air Command and who were convinced that this would be militarily undesirable, charged that the scientists by entering into matters of military strategy and budget policy had exceeded both their assignment and their expertise. Commenting on this charge, one of the scientists involved later explained that he would have little interest in working on a study project that did not have the potential for leading into the question of whether the conclusions should be acted upon.[18]

The predisposition to want to be told and to deal with the whole problem no doubt has its base in the professional experience of scientists (and one of the central credos of science) that good ideas on a problem may come from the most unexpected quarters and that the widest possible dissemination of information about a problem will significantly enhance its chances for an early solution.[19] Still, there are problems and problems; some are open to

---

[17] This persuasion was largely accomplished through demonstrations of the military utility of the scientists' taking such an approach, although in the early history of the M.I.T. Radiation Laboratory a certain amount of polite bargaining was apparently practiced. One scientist involved, whenever told that the reason for a request was a problem for Washington, not him, to worry about, adopted the practice of working on something else until he was given a description of the problem involved. For a brief summary of the British experience, see Alexander Haddow, "The Scientist as Citizen," *Bulletin of the Atomic Scientists,* September 1956, p. 247.

[18] *Cf.* the following exchange between Gordon Gray and Jerrold Zacharias during the Oppenheimer hearing. Gray: "If you were directing a study which had to do with electronics, a pretty clearly defined field, and it started to come up with recommendations with respect to foreign policy, would you feel that an official of the Defense Department who urged that you stick to electronics was acting with impropriety?" Zacharias: "I think I would not direct a project that was as restrictive as that, sir, as to be restricted only to electronics." U. S. Atomic Energy Commission, *In the Matter of J. Robert Oppenheimer, Transcript of Hearing before Personnel Security Board,* Washington, 1954, p. 930.

For some of the issues involved in the 1952 air defense study, see *ibid.,* pp. 598–99, 749–50, 763–65, 923–24, 930–31, 935, 938, and also the account in Price, *Government and Science,* pp. 136–38.

[19] General Leslie Groves, who directed the Manhattan project, was especially sensitive to the scientists' tendency to take on the whole problem. (Some even advised him on how the garbage should be collected at Los Alamos, an act which may possibly have reflected self- rather than scientific interest.) One reason for his effort to compartmentalize the work scientists were doing was his fear that "if I brought them into the

determinate solutions, and others can be resolved only through the exercise of political power. The point about the "whole problem approach," as the air defense example illustrates, is that it not only helps propel the scientists from an advisory to a political role but it serves to make the scientist somewhat blind to the fact that he is so moving. In its most extreme form, the "whole problem approach" coupled with the "intellectual arrogance" perspective can lead to such instances as when, on one high-level advisory committee concerned with several areas of national security policy, a scientist whose formal claim to participation was a knowledge of infra-red ray phenomena was reportedly quite free with his proposals for what political policies should be adopted with regard to the United Nations.

Quantum Jumps versus Improvements

A number of scientists have advanced the proposition that the military tend to be more interested in improving existing weapons than in developing radically new ones, and they have urged that a separate civilian agency be established to undertake such development. Both scientists and soldiers have explained this difference in their approach to military research and development, "quantum jumps versus improvements," with the hypothesis that the soldier's interest in developing entirely new weapons must always be inhibited by his concern for the possibility that war may come in the near future, since in this event his interests are best served by improving existing weapons. It has also been suggested that military leaders, who must be prepared at any time to ask others to take up the weapons at hand and fight with them, cannot afford to let themselves or others become too impressed with the deficiencies of those weapons as compared with others that might have been had.[20]

An explanation less flattering to the military for this difference is the occasional assertion by scientists that theirs is a profession which stimulates original and creative thought, while that of the military tends to develop minds which accept the existing situation without too much question. As indicated in the discussion of the first predilection, this is a judgment which the scientist may extend to the diplomat and the politician as well. The structure of both the domestic and the international political process is normally such as to make "quantum jumps" in policy infeasible. Diplomats and politicians are accustomed to seeing the same old policy problems come around year after year, and they are generally intent on policies which promise only slow and modest change. Scientists, on the other hand, have been demanding and searching for quantum jumps in foreign policy ever

---

whole project, they would never do their own job. There was just too much of scientific interest, and they would just be frittering from one thing to another." *Oppenheimer Transcript*, p. 164.

[20] See, for example, Lloyd V. Berkner, "Science and National Strength," *Bulletin of the Atomic Scientists*, June 1953, pp. 155, 180.

since the end of World War II. It is symptomatic that the first proposal developed by the Advisory Committee on Science and Technology to the Democratic National Advisory Council, established in 1959, was for the creation of a new scientific agency, independent of the State and Defense Departments, whose function would be "to face all the problems of disarmament." [21]

Technology for Its Own Sweet Sake

In the summer of 1945, after the A-bomb had been tested but before the first drop on Japan, the Director of the Los Alamos Laboratory, J. Robert Oppenheimer, suggested to his superior, General Leslie Groves, that if some improvements were made in the design of the bomb it would be more effective. Groves decided against the improvements because he did not want to incur any delay in the use of the bomb, which he expected would end the war with Japan. In the summer of 1943, after the Director of the German V-2 project, General Dornberger, had finally secured a first-class priority for the use of the weapon, those responsible for producing it in quantity were increasingly handicapped by the scientists and engineers who kept improving but changing its design. Dornberger was finally obliged to issue a flat order against any further improvements.[22]

There was nothing irresponsible in these scientists' actions. Charged with the technical development of weapons, they would have been remiss in their responsibilities if they had failed to call attention to the prospects for improvement. The point to the examples is that scientists and engineers, in the pursuit of their own responsibilities and interests, may easily lose sight of those of the policy maker.

The scientists on the General Advisory Committee to the Atomic Energy Commission who recommended against the development of an H-bomb in 1949 did so in part because of their concern for the foreign-policy consequences of introducing a weapon of such destructive power into the world. Oppenheimer, the Chairman of the Committee, later stated that the thermonuclear design developed by Edward Teller in 1951 was "technically so sweet" that, if it had been available in 1949, the Committee would probably not have made the recommendation that it did. Since, with a technically more promising design at hand, one might suppose that the Committee's foreign-policy concerns would have been all the greater, some observers have concluded that in the pursuit of his technical interests the scientist can also easily lose sight of his own policy concerns.[23]

Such a judgment ignores the complexity of the Committee's position. For example, one of the reasons why the Committee thought the United States

---

[21] See the *Bulletin of the Atomic Scientists,* December 1959, p. 412.

[22] *Oppenheimer Transcript,* p. 33, and Dornberger, *V-2,* pp. 134–137.

[23] *Oppenheimer Transcript,* p. 251. For an extreme judgment, see Jungk, *Brighter Than a Thousand Suns,* p. 296.

should take the initiative in renouncing the H-bomb was precisely because the device then in view seemed likely to be both difficult to make and of dubious military value. It was thought that for this reason the Russians might be willing to follow the American example and that, if they did not, the United States would not have risked much by the delay. These were considerations which obviously would have been changed if a technically more promising design had been available in 1949.[24] Still, the comments of several scientists close to these events are not without relevance. It is their feeling that there are times when the technician does take over, that when the scientist is faced with an interesting and challenging problem his inclination is to get to work on it, and that under these circumstances he should not be the first person to be expected to keep larger policy considerations in balance.

This predisposition, "technology for its own sweet sake," appears to have its roots in two more of science's central credos: the belief in the value of pursuing knowledge for its own sake, and the belief that the best motivation for the direction of research is the strength and character of individual curiosities. But the direction and strength of scientific interests and curiosities is not necessarily coincident with the requirements of military or foreign policy. One of the most recent examples of the scientist's capacity to get caught up in a challenging problem (assigned, to be sure, by policy-makers) is afforded by the ingenious techniques scientists conceived for evading nuclear-test detection systems and for the design of new systems to meet those evasions. In the light of the later course of negotiations, an American statesman who believed there was considerable foreign-policy gain in a test-ban treaty and who believed that the Russians were at one time seriously interested in such a treaty might well conclude that the formula developed by Watson-Watt, the scientist who fathered radar, with reference to the problem of meeting wartime military requirements was not without its implications for meeting peacetime foreign policy requirements: "Give them the third best to go with; the second comes too late, the best never comes." [25] This observation is not intended as an argument that the interests of the United States would have been better served by a test-ban treaty with a "third best" detection system than by no treaty at all. The point is that the policy maker must be sensitive to the prospect that, because of the constant advance of technology, his only real choices may be of this order.

The Sense for Paradise Lost

This predisposition is likely to be more characteristic of the scientists who had their graduate training and early professional experience in the years

---

[24] See Oppenheimer's statements in *Oppenheimer Transcript*, pp. 81, 251, 897, and "The H-bomb Decision: How to Decide Without Actually Choosing," *loc. cit.*, pp. 30–36.

[25] Sir Robert Watson-Watt, *Three Steps to Victory* (London: Odhams, 1957), p. 74.

before World War II than of those who have known only war or Cold War conditions.[26] The prewar scientists took it as an article of faith that certain conditions were essential for the progress of science, in particular that scientists be free to select their research problems and that both scientists and scientific information be free to move among as well as within nations.[27] All of these conditions were violated during World War II, and as a result of the Cold War they were never fully re-established. The nuclear physicists had had perhaps the most highly developed sense of international community. They were relatively few in number, had intimate personal relationships at home and abroad, and had been experiencing an exciting exchange of discoveries since Rutherford identified the nucleus in 1911. They also lost the most, for theirs was militarily the most sensitive knowledge, and the pages of the *Bulletin of the Atomic Scientists* offer eloquent testimony to their ideological disturbance.

The result is that the senior scientists tend to be especially sensitive to possibilities which hold some promise for restoring the former order. They may usually be found on the side (or in front) of those urging freer exchange of scientific and military information with allied governments, less secrecy in the circulation of scientific (and sometimes military) information, and more extensive cultural, and especially scientific, exchanges with the Soviet Union. Similarly, the major activities of the Foreign Policy Panel of the President's Science Advisory Committee and of the Office of the Science Adviser to the Secretary of State have been in connection with the Science Attaché program, the facilitation of international scientific programs and conferences, and the exchange of scientists with the Soviet Union.[28]

Science Serves Mankind

For at least 300 years the western scientific tradition has assumed that the unrestricted generation of new knowledge about the world was a social good. Over these years science in its purest form (the discovery of the facts of nature for knowledge's sake alone) became increasingly an autonomous social institution; research scientists were largely disassociated from the practical applications of their discoveries, but they took it for granted that

---

[26] In 1955 slightly more than half of the active research physicists in the United States were under forty years of age and had received their doctorates after December 7, 1941. Lee A. DuBridge, "The American Scientist: 1955," *Yale Review*, September 1955, p. 1.

[27] These assumptions are excellently set forth in Margret Smith Stahl, "Splits and Schisms: Nuclear and Social," unpublished doctoral dissertation, University of Wisconsin, 1946, ch. 4.

[28] For the activities of the Panel and the Office, see James R. Killian, "Science and Public Policy," Address to the American Association for the Advancement of Science, December 29, 1958, as printed in *Science Program—86th Congress,* Report of the Senate Committee on Government Operations, 86th Cong., 1st sess. (1959), pp. 12–13, and *The Science Adviser of the Department of State,* Department of State Publication 7056 (Washington, 1960).

these discoveries would ultimately benefit mankind.[29] The advent of nuclear and bacteriological weapons systems which have the potential of destroying so much of mankind and his works has called this faith sharply into question. It does not take much imagination to wonder if man, in view of his apparent inability to escape from the order of conflicts which have historically resulted in war, would not be better off in a world where the knowledge that has made the new weapons possible did not exist. For some of the senior nuclear physicists this is more than a philosophical question. They are unable to avoid a sense of real personal responsibility; they reason from the premise that they were few, and if they had acted differently weapons development might not have taken the turn it did.

In the immediate postwar years, the apparent contradiction between the good of science and the evil of war was resolved by the expectation that the very destructiveness of the new weapons would lead man to renounce at last the folly of war. The course of foreign policy in later years has weakened these expectations but not destroyed them, as the recent flurry of arms-control proposals premised on the rational self-interest of both sides in avoiding mutual destruction testifies.

The need to preserve their sense of service to mankind led some American scientists to refuse to work on weapons. Similarly, there are reports that several Russian scientists were imprisoned, exiled, or placed under surveillance for refusing to participate in weapons work between 1945 and 1953, and in 1957 a number of Germany's elite physicists announced that they would have no part in nuclear weapons work.[30] Such cases are dramatic, but nowhere have they prevented the development of weapons on which governments were determined. The more consequential resolutions have been those in which scientists have simply identified the good of mankind with the strength of their nation or have endeavored to develop new weapons systems which would be as effective as the old in promoting national policy but which would result in less slaughter if used. This was part of the rationale behind the recommendation made by a group of American scientists in 1951 that the government undertake the development and production of a large number of A-bombs for tactical use in the ground defense of Western Europe. Their hope was that such an innovation would relieve the United States of the burden of having to rely solely on the threat of strategic bombing to contain the Red Army.[31]

The failure of the United States to orbit a satellite before the Soviet Union did was the result of the State Department's insensitivity to the

---

[29] See Stahl, *op. cit.*, ch. 4.

[30] See Arnold Kramish, *Atomic Energy in the Soviet Union* (Stanford: Stanford University Press, 1959), p. 105. Kramish states that it is not certain whether the objections of the Russian scientists were technical or political. For the declaration of the German physicists, see the *Bulletin of the Atomic Scientists*, June 1957, p. 228.

[31] *Oppenheimer Transcript*, pp. 584, 594–95, 891–94.

political implications of the event and the decision of the President and the Secretary of Defense not to let a satellite program interfere with military missile programs. A small part of the story, however, is to be found in the reluctance of some of the American scientists involved in the programming of the International Geophysical Year to see an American IGY satellite propelled by an operational military weapon. Their preference for the less developed but non-military Vanguard over the Army's Redstone appears to have reflected a combination of the "sense for paradise lost" and the "science serves mankind" predispositions, in this case an interest in showing the world the peaceful side of science and in demonstrating that the scientists of the world could cooperate in the interests of knowledge as well as compete in the interests of nations.[32]

IV

With regard to the two remaining problems to be discussed—how to organize relations between science and government, and how the scientist can participate in policy-making and still keep his expert standing—four points seem deserving of special emphasis: (A) the problem of organization, especially in the area of foreign policy, is still very much in the research and development stage, and so it may long remain, considering the precedent set by the problem of how to relate military experts and foreign policy; (B) in many areas of policy it will never be possible to specify what constitutes "the best" organization; the way in which policy-makers are organized is not without influence on the kind of policies they will produce, and so long as there are differences over policy there will be no agreement about organization; (C) in the American political system, at least, the science expert at the high-policy level has no real hope of keeping out of politics; his only choice is in the character of his political style; and finally, (D) it should not be forgotten that organization and policy-making are not the same as policy; successful instances of foreign policy capitalizing on or guiding developments in science and technology will not automatically follow just because scientists have been liberally injected into the policy-making process.

Organization

Current American organization in the area of science and foreign policy still reflects the emergency responses to the Russian ICBM and Sputnik I. One effect of these events was that scientists were rushed to the most important single center of power, the Office of the President, by means of the creation of the Special Assistant to the President for Science and Technology and the President's Science Advisory Committee.

---

[32] See Walter Sullivan, *Assault on the Unknown* (New York: McGraw-Hill, 1961), pp. 79–81.

The President certainly needs men around him sensitive to the areas of interaction between science and foreign policy. But a case can be made for the proposition that the center of gravity for the input of scientific advice into the policy-making process should be at a lower level than the White House. The President's political interests lie in keeping the staff about him small and generalized. Well-developed plans and programs will have a better chance of maturing in the larger and more diversified facilities that departments and agencies can provide. Secondly, as C. P. Snow concludes in his account of the differences between Tizard and Lindemann, there are risks in having a single science adviser sitting next to the center of political power. Although it should be noted that Churchill fared better with a single science adviser than Hitler did with none ("The Führer has dreamed," Dornberger was told, "that no [V-2] will ever reach England"), Snow's point has merit and it holds for institutions as well as for individuals.[33] The President will generally find his choices facilitated by the existence of multiple and independent sources of scientific advice.

This is a condition that already prevails in the case of many of the departments and agencies whose actions have significant foreign policy consequences, especially in the use of scientists by the Department of Defense, the Atomic Energy Commission, and the National Aeronautics and Space Administration. It is, however, a condition notably absent in the case of the Department of State. As it now stands, the President has more scientists to advise him on the scientific and technical aspects of various foreign policy issues, particularly in the national security field, than has the Secretary of State.

Excluding the science attachés overseas, the Department of State's Office of the Science Adviser numbers six people of whom three, including the director, are professional scientists. There are no scientists, full or part-time, in the Department's offices for policy planning, space and atomic energy, or political-military affairs. As might be inferred from these arrangements, many of the policy-makers concerned believe that their needs for scientific advice are adequately met through formal and informal communication with scientists employed in the operating agencies and departments and with the President's own Science Advisory Committee. (It should also be noted that in at least one office the need for additional political personnel is clearly more urgent than the need for scientists.) The Department's Science Adviser, who participates in the work of both the President's Committee and the Federal Council on Science and Technology, serves to facilitate such communication; otherwise both the demands placed on the Office and its own interests have limited its activity, as previously noted, to a relatively narrow range of foreign policy problems.[34]

---

[33] Snow, *Science and Government,* pp. 66–68, and Dornberger, *V-2,* p. 87.
[34] There are eighteen scientists on the President's Science Advisory Committee; its

Whether the interests of the Department of State would be better served by a larger "in-house" scientific competence is a question that an outside observer cannot easily answer. Much depends on the validity of the expectations that the Department can rely on the scientists of the operating agencies to alert it to developments and information relevant to foreign policy. Even more depends on how determined the Department is to play an active and influential part in shaping the scientific and technical programs of the government to conform to its own conception of national needs and priorities.[35] Should this determination be high, it is difficult to avoid the hypothesis that if the President has found it useful to have a relatively large science advisory body to help him monitor and direct the course of science and technology as they affect foreign and domestic policy, so too might the Secretary of State in the area of his own more limited but still extensive responsibilities.

Organization and Purpose

Since administrative organizations exist for the purpose of serving policy goals and implementing policy programs, it is to be expected that those who differ on the goals and programs of policy will differ about the proper design of administrative organizations. The desire of many scientists in 1945 to see atomic energy used for peaceful rather than military purposes was one of the reasons for their political campaign to place the postwar atomic energy program in the hands of a civilian commission instead of the War Department. Similarly, more recent differences about how to organize the government's space effort reflect, in part, policy differences about whether space will or should be an area for major military operations.

The same point can be seen in the proposal to create a Department of Science and Technology which would include the variety of "little" science programs now scattered throughout the Executive structure (for example, those of the Weather Bureau, National Bureau of Standards, the Antarctic Office) but would exclude those of the Department of Defense, the Atomic Energy Commission, and the Space Administration. The hope behind this

---

working panels also contain participants from outside the committee. In December, 1958 the Committee and the Office of the Special Assistant for Science and Technology had together some 75 scientists and engineers serving part time. See Killian, "Science and Public Policy," *loc. cit.,* p. 8. The work of the Committee and the Office are additionally described and appraised in *Science Organization and the President's Office,* Staff Study of the Subcommittee on National Policy Machinery, Senate Committee on Government Operations, 87th Cong., 1st sess. (1961).

The information presented about the Department of State is based on U. S. Department of State, *The Science Adviser of the Department of State,* and interviews with several Department officials in February 1962. Needless to say, the description and interpretation made above are entirely the present writer's responsibility.

[35] These two conditions are not unrelated. The more influence the Department exercises in determining the goals and programs of other agencies, the more confident it can be that scientists in those agencies will call the Department's attention to goals and programs which they believe to be receiving too much or too little attention.

proposal is that, combined together, the "little" programs would be able to compete more effectively in the struggle for government dollars with the "big" science programs of the military, atomic energy, and space organizations.[36]

The question of the "best" science organization is thus inescapably tied to the question of what is the "best" science policy. But who can demonstrate whether science and foreign policy would be better served by allocating dollars to a program to control weather or to a program to explore Mars? There are no determinate solutions to problems of this order. Neither, for that matter, is there any "one right amount" of the nation's scientific resources that should be allocated to basic as compared to applied research. Differences on policy questions such as these are unavoidable among scientists and non-scientists alike, and they can be resolved in but one manner: through the interplay of power and interest in a political arena.

This condition, plus the increasing dependence of scientific programs and research on government funds, plus the increasing consequences of the choices the government makes in allocating these funds, all promise to put the politicians and the scientists under increasing pressure. As the opportunities for further development in each of a thousand different scientific fields mushroom with the acceleration of scientific knowledge, whatever the government decides to support, it will be deciding *not* to support more. Indeed, it is not too difficult to see the scientists becoming practiced advocates and lobbyists for the government's support of their cherished fields and projects, or to imagine the day when the politicians start to complain about "inter-science rivalry" and begin to fancy that, if only there were a single Chief of Science, competition and duplication could be ended and the nation could have an integrated science policy.

Scientists in Politics

The American political system is not one that insulates its experts from the politics of choice.[37] The scientist involved in high-policy matters is likely to find himself propelled into the political arena, either by a push from behind or by his own interest in seeing that the "right" choices are made. Some of the incentives the scientist may have, to follow up his advice with an effort to see that it is accepted (and to take a hand in a few other matters while he is at it), were outlined and illustrated in the preceding section. It is equally important to recognize that the scientist may find himself on the political firing line, placed there by a politician interested in using the

---

[36] See Lloyd V. Berkner, "National Science Policy and the Future," Address at Johns Hopkins University, December 16, 1958, as printed in *Science Program—86th Congress,* pp. 116–18.

[37] This point, especially as it relates to science experts, is discussed in Price, *Government and Science,* pp. 61–62, and in Herman Finer, "Government and the Expert," *Bulletin of the Atomic Scientists,* November 1956, pp. 331–32.

scientist's prestige as an "expert" to disarm the critics of his (the politician's) choices.

Thus, prior to the moratorium on nuclear tests, the Eisenhower administration appeared to be using scientists and their scientific facts on fall-out as a means of justifying and defending a policy that was obviously compounded of a variety of considerations besides that of the radiological hazard. The comparison with Truman's use of the prestige of the Joint Chiefs of Staff to defend his choices in the Korean War comes easily to mind. So, too, do the statements of various Republican leaders that they had lost confidence in the Joint Chiefs and their determination, when they came to power, to get rid of the "Democratic" Chiefs and to appoint Chiefs in sympathy with Republican policies.

The scientist, in short, is not likely to orbit the centers of political power emitting upon request "beeps" of purely technical information. He will inevitably be pulled into the political arena. If his participation there is to be either productive or personally satisfying, both the scientist and the non-scientist need to be highly conscious of the character of their activity and the problems involved. The scientist (and many a non-scientist) must learn that the making of foreign policy is not a quest for the "right" answers to the problems of our time. They are only hard choices, the consequences of which will be uncertain and the making of which will often seem interminable in time and irrational in procedure.

The debate and disagreement over these choices will be heated and confused under the best of circumstances, but emotion and misunderstanding can be eased if scientists and non-scientists are both alert to the limits as well as the potential of the scientist's contribution. On the scientist's part, there is the obvious need to exercise the utmost care in making clear to himself and to others the areas where he speaks as a concerned citizen and those where he speaks as a professional expert. More difficult will be the task of learning how and to whom to address himself in each of these capacities when he is dissatisfied with the outcome of a policy decision in which he has participated. There is, as Don Price has pointed out, no clear code in Washington to govern the conduct of dissenting experts, only a "flexible" set of possible relationships with one's immediate superiors and those whose authority competes with or exceeds that of one's superiors. In contrast to the soldier, who can find some although not complete guidance in the doctrine of "civilian control," the very nature of the scientist's intellectual habits and many of his policy predispositions may make especially difficult his task in determining the limits to which he can stretch his dissent.[38]

On their part, the non-scientists need to recognize that scientists can

---

[38] See the discussion in Price, *Government and Science*, pp. 131, 133, 138–42. The point about the scientists' lacking a tradition of "civilian control" was suggested by William T. R. Fox.

hardly be expected to remain politically indifferent or inactive about the policy issues with which they are involved (especially when no one else in Washington practices such restraint). It was the naivete of this expectation that was so appalling in the conclusion of the Gray Board that Oppenheimer was a security risk because (among other reasons) "he may have departed his role as scientific adviser to exercise highly persuasive influence in matters in which his convictions were not necessarily a reflection of technical judgment, and also not necessarily related to the protection of the strongest offensive military interests of the country." [39] It is unlikely that "civil-scientist" relations will ever get any worse than this. With time and experience one can expect many of these problems to be eased, but it would be unrealistic to expect them to disappear. Military experts have participated in the making of foreign policy far longer than scientists, and the question of how they can best do so is still the subject of more than a little disagreement.

Policy Processes and Policy

In closing this discussion of scientists and the problems of their organizational and political relationships to others engaged in the determination of foreign policy, it is important to remember that the policy process can bring minds together but it cannot make them think. It is worth noting that, in the political and administrative structure of the Soviet Union, no scientist is as institutionally close to the Premier as is the Special Assistant for Science and Technology to the President of the United States and that there is no equivalent of the Science Advisory Office in the Russian Ministry of Foreign Affairs.[40] Yet one would not say that the foreign policy of the Soviet Union

---

[39] U. S. Atomic Energy Commission, *In the Matter of J. Robert Oppenheimer, Texts of Principal Documents and Letters* (Washington, 1954), pp. 19–20. Note the policy predisposition in the phrase "strongest offensive military interests."

It should not be comfortable for an American to reflect on the career of Peter Kapitsa, a Soviet physicist who was a student of Rutherford and who worked in England from 1922 to 1934 and then returned to the Soviet Union. Kapitsa was placed under house arrest in 1947 and remained there until after Stalin's death. Kapitsa has told western scientists and newsmen that his arrest was the result of his refusal to work on nuclear energy for military purposes. Kramish believes that his arrest was due to the government's dissatisfaction with his advice on certain technical approaches to weapons development. In either event, it is noteworthy that Kapitsa is believed to have recently been, on an informal basis, one of Khrushchev's main science advisers.

On the matter of his arrest, see the report by Harrison Salisbury in the *New York Times*, July 11, 1956; the *Bulletin of the Atomic Scientists*, January, 1957, p. 38; and Kramish, *Atomic Energy in the Soviet Union*, pp. 109–110. The information on his recent activity was supplied by the staff of the Subcommittee on National Policy Machinery, Senate Committee on Government Operations.

[40] On Soviet government and science organization, see *National Policy Machinery in the Soviet Union*, Report of the Subcommittee on National Policy Machinery, Senate Committee on Government Operations, 86th Cong., 2d sess. (Washington, 1949), pp. 24–35, 59–62, and Nicholas DeWitt, "Reorganization of Science and Research in the U.S.S.R.," *Science*, June 23, 1961, pp. 1981–91. The points made above were additionally confirmed by the staff of the Subcommittee on National Policy Machinery.

has appeared either ineffectual or insensitive in its response to developments in science and technology.

The circumstances attendant on the development of radar by the British from 1935 to 1940 provide a useful insight into both the potential and the limits of effective organization. Essential, obviously, were the scientific and technical ideas that Watson-Watt and his colleagues had in mind in 1935, ideas which in turn were the result of the earlier years of research they had been free to conduct in the facilities of a government laboratory. Certainly, it was important that there were administrative scientists in the Air Ministry who were so alert to the military problems of the Air Force that they could see on their own initiative the need to establish a special scientific committee for the study of air defense (the Tizard Committee) and who were so alert to the work of the scientific community that they made their first request for information to Watson-Watt.[41] Of consequence, too, was the fact that the personal and political relations of the members of the Tizard committee with the members of the military, administrative, and political hierarchies whose interest and cooperation were vital for the subsequent progress of the research and development program were relations characterized by mutual ease, respect, and understanding.

But these conditions would not have led from the formation of the Tizard Committee in 1935 to a chain of operational radar stations by 1940 and a Fighter Command practiced in their use if it had not been for the military ideas of members of the Royal Air Force. It was they who first thought of the formation of a committee to look specifically into the problem of detection, they who recommended more funds than those first proposed by the Tizard Committee for the development of an electromagnetic detection system, and they who were responsible for the decision to start constructing the stations and training the personnel while the equipment was still under development.[42] The explanation for this interest and support is to be found in their theories about the next World War. They believed the Germans were planning to engage in the strategic bombing of Great Britain, and they wished to be prepared for it.[43]

---

[41] The circumstances provide an interesting variation of the "whole problem approach." The Tizard Committee was initially interested in techniques for destroying aircraft or their crews, and Watson-Watt was asked in 1935 to investigate the possibility of using electromagnetic radiation for this purpose. He reported that such a use was apparently infeasible. In any event, he went on to note, the aircraft would first have to be located, and if anyone was interested electromagnetic radiation might be useful for this. Watson-Watt, *Three Steps to Victory,* pp. 81–83.

[42] For the development of radar, see *ibid.,* pp. 108–09; C. P. Snow, *Science and Government,* pp. 24–38, 60–61, 74–75; P. M. S. Blackett, "Tizard and the Science of War," *Nature,* March 5, 1960, pp. 648–49; and Basil Collier, *The Defense of the United Kingdom* (London: H.M.S.O., 1957), pp. 33, 36–39.

[43] Ironically, the British were mistaken in their theory. The German Air Force had no such strategy in mind, and in 1940 when it tried to improvise a strategic bombing campaign it had neither the equipment nor the doctrine with which to conduct the

The point is obvious but important. British scientists and science organization were in the final measure but ready tools. They were good tools, but the use to which they were put was the result of the kind of ideas the military men had about war. The same will hold in the other areas in which science may affect foreign policy. The contributions that science and technology will bring to international politics will largely turn, not so much on the particular arrangements of scientists in the policy-making process, but on the purposes of statesmen and the theories they have about the political world in which they live.

---

campaign effectively. See Herbert Dinerstein, "The Impact of Air Power on the International Scene: 1933–1940," *Military Affairs,* Summer 1955, pp. 65–71; Telford Taylor, *The March of Conquest* (New York: Simon and Schuster, 1958), pp. 24–30; and Adolf Galland, *The First and the Last* (New York: Ballantine Books, 1954), chs. 2–5.

THE U.S. AND
THE U.S.S.R.

Stephen B. Withey

THIS IS a report on one aspect of one side of the cold war. Primarily it is an attempt to find out what Americans think of the situation. Are the problems of the U.S. and the U.S.S.R. in the nature of a dispute to be settled in the minds of men by debate, negotiation and understanding? Is the cold war a contest or a race where performance is credited with victory? Is it a period of waiting, probing, mobilizing and preparing for a day of crisis? Could it be an attempt to solve with hardware a problem that is essentially social? Is it a battle for survival like Carthage and Rome, where one side is sure to win, but not both, or is it more like a fight for a Pyrrhic victory where both sides will lose? Is it ideological conflict or power struggle? How much is illusion or mirrored fear and how much is stark reality? Are there a number of strategies open or is the course of events inevitable?

The problems are so complex that the questions could be numerous. No single study could answer all the posed possibilities. No single answer should be expected. Only a sequence of studies could begin to portray the processes of reaction to events that might be regarded as components of what has been called the "cold war."

The scientifically drawn, probability sample of the adult U.S. population,[1] on which this study is based, were individually interviewed in their homes in September and October of 1961, shortly after the death of Dag Hammarskjöld, when tensions were at their peak in the Berlin crisis of that fall, and at the time of U.N. crisis over the Secretariat and that agency's policy in the Congo. There is evidence from studies done in November, 1961 and in early 1962 that tensions and apprehensions have somewhat dimin-

---

[1] The study is based on interviews with a national (48 states), probability sample (1,474 individuals) of adults (21 years or over) who are living in dwelling units that are not institutions or transient quarters such as hotels. Such a sample, in its size and more importantly in its manner of selection, is accurate in representing the national picture within a standard error of about 1.5 per cent. Twice this margin of possible error comes close to a guarantee of the range within which the true national figure would fall. For sample percentages below 20 per cent or above 80 per cent this margin of possible error is smaller. Percentages based not on the total sample but on small subclasses of people within the sample will have somewhat larger possible errors due to sampling, their size depending on the smallness of the group from which the percentages were obtained. Tables occur later in the report.

ished since the time of the survey reported here. It is possible, therefore, to regard these findings as expressing U.S. attitudes at a time of crisis, but interpretations should be tempered by the knowledge that the heat of public concern has cooled a little.

BROAD PERSPECTIVES

The cold war might be seen in the perspective of polarities—communism versus capitalism, democracy versus totalitarianism, a Russian world versus an American world—but virtually no one sees the cold war in these dimensions!

Russia is seen either as simply making a power play for extended and perhaps global control *or* she is seen as trying to spread communism. In "opposition" to this, the United States is most broadly seen as trying to keep the peace.

Only one American in five sees the United States as trying to spread democracy as a national purpose in our relations with Russia. Virtually nobody mentions capitalism. Thus the contest is most usually posed as Russian expansion versus U.S. maintaining the peace or the spread of Russian Communism versus the U.S. keeping the peace. The majority of the U.S. public, therefore, sees the cold war as a threat of force, with the threat of war as the ultimate possibility.

One-third of the U.S. public do not know how this "contest" will work out, but almost one-half think that the U.S. will do well in the long run and the U.S.S.R. will do badly. But this is more of an act of faith than anything else. A typical reply is that of a housewife who said, "But we have always won." On the other hand, almost half of the population said that they had no cues as to how we were doing in our relationships with Russia nor could they imagine any. About one in three, however, looked to Russian, or Russian proxy, successes in such trouble or crisis spots as Berlin, Laos, Cuba, the Congo, etc.

But the U.S. public does not necessarily see global war or a nuclear exchange between the great powers as the inevitable outcome. The population is about evenly split (one-third to one-third) in estimating that a big war is likely or unlikely. This balance is apparently slowly tipping toward an increase in those who think it will not happen.

There is no widespread or commonly quoted reason for thinking that war is likely. A few mention Khrushchev's policies, some refer to the arms race, a few look at trouble spots, some emphasize the breakdown in negotiations, and there is some reference to the cyclical or inevitable occurrence of war.

On the other hand, the evidence for the unlikelihood of war is not a quotation of events or trends such as, we haven't had one yet, or it didn't happen as a result of this or that crisis, but rather the bald statement that nobody wants war or it is too terrible a thing for anyone to precipitate.

But there is clear apprehension and anxiety, or at least there was in the fall of 1961. Overlooking the guessed likelihood of war, one-third of the U.S. adult population thought that, if war came, it was likely to come in two years or less. Only about half that number (15%) saw war as necessarily more than ten years away. In between assured imminence and assured distance there is a great deal of uncertainty, conditional expectations, and mixed ideas of likelihood and timing. Neither likelihood nor estimates of timing are clear indexes of threat. Only a little more than half of those who think war could come within two years also regard the likelihood as more than even chances. Eighty per cent of those who see war as more than ten years away also see the likelihood as even chances or more improbable. On the other hand, it is clear that likelihood and timing estimates are related quite strongly. The greater the guessed likelihood the more imminent the war is likely to be estimated. The lesser the likelihood the more distant the possibility.

Assume that someone with no particular authoritative or expert insight claimed that war was *more than very unlikely* (that is, there was some reasonable probability) and that with some reasonable probability it would probably occur *within the next five years.* How many people would agree with him because their own opinions agreed with such an estimate of the situation? The answer would be 42 per cent (certainly no higher, since estimates of war likelihood have dropped a little since late fall of 1961). On the other hand, the public would not be 3:2 against such a proposition. Fully one-third would feel that one cannot tell, that such estimates are impossible, and that prediction would have to depend on many things that have not yet happened.

Thus although war may be the ultimate threat, there is no majority consensus that war is inevitable, since "any reasonable probability" covers a number of possibilities or contingencies that are not firm enough to be seen as sound bases for behaving as though war were certain to come. What then does the public see as other consequences of our doing badly in the cold war? If the cold war is primarily seen as the attempt by the U.S. to contain the spread of Russian power and control short of resort to a big war, what might happen within the U.S. if the winds of fortune did not continue to blow in our favor? What would happen within the U.S. if Russian influence expanded substantially elsewhere in the world?

About 17 per cent believe that the U.S. would be defeated without war, defeat here being made equivalent to the U.S. going communist or moving to some point on the political spectrum close to that category. About the same size group (15%) believe that we would lose influence, allies, and friends and move in the direction of a second-rate power but this group does not describe further, serious domestic consequences. Only very tiny minorities—2 per cent or less, though these may represent one-half to one million people—foresee any consequences in terms of greater government spending, higher taxes, more economic aid, a political swing to the right, disruptions in the domestic economy, etc. Forty per cent see no particular consequences short of war, which tended to be seen as inevitable if *all* other measures failed.

What then should the U.S. be doing to make the chances of world war less likely? Respondents were asked that question. It would be difficult indeed to recruit majority support for any policy without convincing the one-third who know of no useful policy.

Eighteen per cent come out for deterrence and military build-up. Those not included in this category are not necessarily in favor of arms reduction by any means, but those included in this group are certainly in favor of the arms race. Fourteen per cent say that we should firmly state a position and stick with it regardless of the consequences. A high proportion of this group think that Russia is bluffing and would back down in the face of a tough stand. Many of them do not think that we need to be stronger than we are. Both of these groups advocate strength, however, and together they total about one-third of the U.S. population.

Very few would seriously propose extensive tampering with U.S. armament strength. Only 3 per cent come out for a clear policy of disarmament. Four per cent come out clearly for a strong international force, usually in a U.N. context.

On the other hand, a foreign policy that would reduce communist advantage by the wise use of economic and technical aid is supported by 17 per cent—about the same number that supported outright deterrence. Fifteen per cent, almost the same size group, feel that there is hope in negotiation and attempts at mutual understanding and agreement. A majority of this group feel that nobody wants war and that therefore the only recourse is in negotiated action.

One-third know of no useful policy and an additional 16 per cent propose miscellaneous actions that are not really national behaviors but rather individual. Thus one-half of the population are uncommitted to any policy and the remainder are divided into various schisms of opinion regarding policy. It would seem that the U.S. public, as a total group, is anxious and somewhat baffled, but it would appear to be related to the effectiveness of one policy over another rather than extensive disagreement over the objectives of policy.

Although few people volunteered a policy of disarmament, when the broad spectrum of possible policies including arms control, test bans, progressive reduction in arms, disarmament, etc., was raised, over half of the population thought that such steps should certainly be tried and continued. Between a quarter and a third thought that such steps would be worthwhile, and a quarter, although skeptical over their worth, still thought that the U.S. should continue a strong policy of interest in these measures.

There was a fairly high degree of satisfaction with the current Administration reported during the interviews, though this does not, of course, imply the absence of criticism. On the broad perspectives, so far reported, there seemed to be little to distinguish those who called themselves Republicans from those who called themselves Democrats.

To probe further into the broad perspectives under which the "cold war" might be seen by the U.S. public, five ways of looking at the U.S.-U.S.S.R. problem situation were posed. These five are by no means exhaustive of perspectives but they do range over the scale of viewpoints and they provide a check on the more spontaneously expressed opinions already reported and encountered early in the interview. The five in the order of their acceptance are as follows:

"The cold war with Russia is a fight between two very different ways of life with different values and ideas."   89% agree

"Our problems with Russia are just like having trouble with a 'bad guy' or a delinquent who won't behave."   63% agree

"We have a cold war with Russia because the United States and Russia are each trying to do what they want and their interests interfere with each other."   55% agree

"Our troubles with Russia are just a question of which country is going to survive as a powerful nation."   49% agree

"We have a cold war with Russia because the United States and Russia don't really try to work together and understand one another."   29% agree

These findings would not seem to conflict with what has already been reported. No group of significant size disagreed with the first proposition and this perspective would tend to substantiate the conclusion that much of the cold war is seen as an ideological conflict.

Most of the disagreement with Proposition 2 centered around the idea that things were worse than that. Most "disagreers" regarded the proposition as almost too simple and perhaps flippant. . . . the situation they saw was much more complex.

Disagreement with Proposition 3 focused on the idea that U.S. interests were reasonable (primarily peaceful) and not in conflict with foreign interests, whereas Russian interests were overbearing, belligerent and "beyond reason."

The modal or most common ground for disagreement with Proposition 4 was that coexistence and mutual survival are possible. The word "powerful" in the proposition seems to be more overlooked than stressed by those who disagreed, though it appeared to be emphasized by those who agree with the power-struggle perspective.

Proposition 5, with which only a minority agreed, was objected to primarily on the basis that almost half of the population saw the U.S. as having at least started the second mile whereas Russia was seen as uncooperative.

Our problems with the U.S.S.R. are thus very much seen as a black-and-white affair, especially in terms of U.S. sincerity, rightness, and focal interest on peace. Our problems are seen as loaded with danger but not necessarily explosive. The major immediate goal would seem to be peace, not victory; and the conflict, though seen in physical terms, is heavily loaded with the recognition of ideological dispute. However, there is also a recognition that the problems are complex and that policies aimed at improving the situation should be a mixture of strategies, a portfolio of policy investments, a recipe in which ingredients can be changed as desired, and a package plan with both coherence and latitude. Although there are large groups of people who agree on a perspective on the nature of the problem, the groups are considerably smaller who agree on what policies to adopt.

Lest there be some misunderstanding, it should be stressed that the public dissension and differences of opinion regarding policy, already reported, were mostly in response to queries about what policies would reduce the chances of war. In such a context, deterrence, arms control, tough stances, disarmament, etc. were mentioned. However, when the questioning shifted to what should be stressed in U.S. foreign policy in other international relations than those directly *vis à vis* Russia, there was strong and majority support for technical and economic aid to foreign countries and international cooperation. These measures are seriously opposed by less than one person in ten. However, there are criticisms of the programs and recommendations for improvements even from supporters. About one adult in three refuses to make recommendations as to what the U.S. should be focusing on in its foreign relations.

It would appear that foreign aid programs are seen less as a measure to reduce the chances of war than they are seen as measures to "hold" the advance of Russian or communist influence *and* as a necessary ingredient of what we should offer to the neighborhood of nations. Most of the criticisms by supporters focused on the caliber of persons sent abroad, the misuse of funds as opposed to the good use of supplies and technical aid, and the type of image of the U.S. that we put into our foreign relations including the image created by some of our domestic problems.

NUCLEAR EXCHANGE

The expansion or extension of Russian or Communist influence is regarded as the continuing threat that keeps the "cold war" going. There is no *majority* agreement on how to handle this threat except through "aid" programs, though compromise solutions might well be able to solicit majority support if they permitted certain combinations of policies that tended both to maintain security *and* show promise of reducing tensions. Interview answers hinted at this but no direct questions were raised on this matter. However, since only a tiny majority say that they think the U.S. will do badly in the cold war, and although problems on how to handle long- and short-term problems will continue to be grounds for differences of opinion, the real threat lies in the possibility that things will get out of hand and involve nuclear war. Crises create flurries of anxiety and apprehension and domestic actions provide cues to the public on the seriousness of what is reported in the mass media.

President Kennedy's remarks on civil defense, the Berlin crisis, and the course of developments in Laos, the Congo and Cuba provided a crisis stimulus to the American public by the fall of 1961. The fact that the public began to relax its apprehensions is reflected in the shift in estimates of war expectancy between October and November of 1961.

Within a period of just four to six weeks the number regarding the likelihood of war as better than 50:50 dropped from 34 to 31 per cent and the proportion regarding the chances as less than even rose from 31 to 37 per cent. These are small shifts but they represent millions of people. The change is more dramatic if one looks at estimates of timing. In October, 31 per cent thought that war might come within two years. By November only 23 per cent thought so. The number who cared to give a time estimate at all dropped from 51 to 42 per cent.

There is more fear that we might get into a small, local war than there is the fear that we will get into a world war. Fifty-eight per cent thought the chances were better than even that we might get into some local war within the next two or three years. Seventeen per cent regarded such a possibility as unlikely or very improbable.

Given the occurrence of such an involvement, 42 per cent thought it was likely that things might get out of hand and lead to a big world war. Twenty-nine per cent regarded such a development as unlikely even if we did get involved in local hostilities.

If the U.S. were to get into some armed conflict directly with Russia, even if the involvement was highly localized, relatively few—only 15 per cent—thought it likely that nuclear bombs could be kept out of it. In other words, people thought the chance of escalation to nuclear war was high if the U.S. and Russia ever became involved in direct rather than proxy armed conflict. This is undoubtedly the reason why the Berlin crisis was seen as particularly alarming.

Questions were not asked on the strategy of attack if a nuclear war were precipitated, i.e., military versus population targets, etc., but respondents were asked whether they thought that the area where they lived would be better, about the same, or worse off than major target areas elsewhere in the United States. One adult in five expects to be in an area hit worse than other areas of the country. Forty per cent expect their condition to be about the same as most of the United States or about average, with some places worse and some better off. Only one in four say that they think they will be better off than most of the country.

On the other hand, few people indeed expect to be virtually immune from attack hazards. About 44 per cent of the adult population of the U.S. expect annihilation. Another 15 per cent give themselves about as much of a chance as the residents of Hiroshima. A further 11 per cent see heavy damage, fire and fallout dangers but the possibility of survival.

Only about 21 per cent can be categorized as foreseeing conditions of slight hazard. About one in ten expect no danger at all though most of them predict confusion, fear and "hard times." Thus, there is no doubt that the majority of the U.S. public regard a nuclear exchange as catastrophic for the nation.

Information about fallout or information about international affairs seems to make very little difference to one's estimates about the seriousness of attack when possible "local" conditions are described. Looking at just the top 20–25 per cent of the population, who are most informed about international affairs, 58 per cent of them expect an attack locally which would be as bad as or worse than World War II atomic attacks; 59 per cent of the general public fall into the same category.

WHO THINKS WAR IS LIKELY?

Although notions about the seriousness of attack do not seem to be very predictable from such factors as extent of information about world affairs, education, income, sex, etc., the judged likelihood of an attack (or of war) appears to be more related.

Women are more likely than men to think that war is likely. (If one omits from the calculation those who have no opinion, and twice as many women as men refuse to make a judgment.)

Those with high incomes tend to see war as less likely than those with lower incomes.

Those with higher education tend to see war as less likely than those with less education.

Those with more information about world affairs such as Berlin, the Congo, the Peace Corps, Troika, etc. tend to regard war as less likely than those with less information.

Thus one might conclude that those with low income, low education, low information (and similar somewhat correlated factors) tend to be more apprehensive and more pessimistic than those who fall higher on the distribution of these characteristics. However, this less privileged group also is heavily loaded with people who claim to have *no* opinion or expectation about the likelihood or imminence of war, a piece of ignorance or a lack of attention or consideration that considerably facilitates a lessening of tensions about such matters.

Some further insight into what is going on psychologically is gained if one, in a very complex analysis, relates likelihood of attack *and* projected relative severity of attack to some of the variables just mentioned. It is difficult to talk about several variables at one and the same time so recourse will be made here to the use of tabular material even though most of the tables on which this text is based are relegated to the end of this report.

For clarity of display purposes, the varied permutations between expectation of war and imminence or timing of such likelihoods were simplified into three "classical type" categories: those who thought war was likely and might well occur within two years; those who thought war was possible, but not likely, but might occur within two years; and those who regarded war as unlikely, but if it did occur would most probably not happen for at least five years. The first group should feel very threatened. The second group should have some serious apprehensions. The third group should not be too tense or worried or apprehensive. (Other points of view are discarded from this presentation of findings to simplify the tables.)

Now, if one adds to this grouping a further division of those who think they will be *as badly off as most people* in the U.S. and those who think they will be *better off,* under attack conditions, than most people in the U.S., some large differences appear.

Those with high incomes see war as less likely than those with lower incomes but they are much more likely to hold this perspective *if they see themselves as seriously exposed to attack hazards.*

Those with some college education are not much influenced by estimates of relative local hazard, but those with high-school education or less are more likely to see war as likely and imminent *if they see themselves as relatively safer from attack hazards.*

Somewhat similarly, those with "high information" on world affairs are not so influenced in their estimates of war likelihood and imminence as are those with "low information."

Men are much more likely to think that war is unlikely *if they see themselves as living in areas exposed to relatively severe attack.* For women this is not true. Women are more prone than men to see war as likely, and even more prone to do so *if they regard themselves as living in relatively safer areas.*

As a word of caution, it should be noted that most respondents do not fit these types listed in the tables. There are numbers of people who do not guess at the likelihood or imminence of war; there are others who do not guess at the severity of attack; some see war as likely but far away; some regard war as improbable but as imminent if it should occur; and so forth. . . . all of these mixed types were excluded. The tables include all those in the national sample that satisfied the six types of categories and provided the additional information necessary for inclusion in the tables. Thus the percentages are not strictly to be taken at face value. They are unreliable, but the differences are so large that they reflect the psychological forces that are at play in these "textbook" or "classic" examples of the perspectives involved. A complex analysis involving these additional mixed-types does not destroy the findings of the analysis presented here but their presentation is extremely confusing and complex.

Attack worse "here" than most of the U.S.		INCOME			EDUCATION		
		Under $4,000	$4,000– $7,500	$7,500 or more	8th grade or less	Grades 9–12	College
War very likely in 2 years or less		64%	25%	11%	45%	28%	21%
War possible in 2 years or less		36	25	17	33	24	21
War unlikely; 5 yrs. away if it happens		*	50	72	22	48	58
	N	100% (22)	100% (48)	100% (36)	100% (16)	100% (32)	100% (46)
Attack worse "else-where" in the U.S.							
War very likely in 2 years or less		71%	48%	28%	60%	60%	27%
War possible in 2 years or less		24	13	29	7	16	17
War unlikely; 5 yrs. away if it happens		5	39	43	33	24	56
	N	100% (34)	100% (46)	100% (28)	100% (30)	100% (50)	100% (32)

* Less than 0.5 per cent

Attack worse "here" than most of the U.S.		INFORMATION**			SEX		Mentions "shelters" spontaneously as saving lives after an attack
		Low	Medium	High	Male	Female	
War very likely in 2 years or less		38%	37%	17%	18%	45%	30%
War possible in 2 years or less		24	19	26	18	35	30
War unlikely; 5 yrs. away if it happens		38	44	57	64	20	40
	N	100% (16)	100% (32)	100% (46)	100% (66)	100% (40)	100% (40)
Attack worse "else-where" in the U.S.							
War very likely in 2 years or less		67%	38%	33%	37%	71%	71%
War possible in 2 years or less		22	8	14	17	10	18
War unlikely; 5 yrs. away if it happens		11	54	53	46	19	11
	N	100% (36)	100% (26)	100% (30)	100% (70)	100% (42)	100% (54)

** Low   — 1–2 items on Information Scale (See Tables)
  Medium — 3–4 "   "   "   "
  High   — 5–6 "   "   "   "

Attack worse "here" than most of the U.S.		ATTITUDE TOWARD ARMS CONTROL MEASURES			Have or Plan to Have a Shelter
		Supportive	Mixed	Opposed	
War very likely in 2 years or less		14%	30%	42%	7%
War possible in 2 years or less		19	30	26	15
War unlikely; 5 yrs. away if it happens		67	40	32	—
	N	100% (42)	100% (26)	100% (38)	
Attack worse "elsewhere" in the U.S.					
War very likely in 2 years or less		21%	55%	61%	7%
War possible in 2 years or less		8	18	16	25
War unlikely; 5 yrs. away if it happens		71	27	23	5
	N	100% (28)	100% (22)	100% (61)	

Thus it appears that the likelihood of attack, its imminence if it occurs, and the estimate of local consequences—*all taken in combination*—are predictable patterns of perspective when allied with such factors as sex, education, information, income, etc.

These three parameters for defining the threat are also fairly predictive of attitudes toward the *seemingly* contradictory policies of shelter and disarmament.

"POLICY" REACTIONS TO "ESTIMATE-OF-THE-SITUATION" REACTIONS

"Shelter policy" (a rather vague term at the time of this study) is *most strongly supported by those who see nuclear attack as likely and very imminent and hitting other areas more severely than that in which the respondent lives.* The supporters tend to be women more than men, the less informed more than the well informed, those with lower incomes more than with higher incomes, and those with less than college education.

"Arms control, test bans, disarmament steps in one form or another, and similar measures" seem to be *most strongly advocated by those who see nuclear attack as unlikely and not very imminent, if it were to occur, but the severity of local hazards is not so relevant.* Many think such policies should be tried but hesitate to recommend them because of the hazards involved.

*   *   *

DEFENSE SPENDING:

KEY TO CALIFORNIA'S GROWTH[1]

James L. Clayton

THE MAGNITUDE of federal defense spending during the past ten years has become so overwhelming that it is difficult for even the interested layman to comprehend its economic significance. From 1950 to 1959, procurement actions[2] by the Department of Defense (DOD) reached the staggering figure of $228 billion. This was an increase in volume of defense expenditures of 246 per cent, whereas during the same period the nation's business as a whole expanded 76 per cent.[3] The United States is currently spending $25 billion annually for defense procurement—now the nation's largest business —which includes aircraft, guided missiles, electronics equipment, ships, tanks, ammunition, etc., and over $5 billion for experimentation and research in order to develop and perfect these weapons. So important has defense spending become that in order to secure a greater share of this huge annual expenditure for their home state, several United States senators have "declared war" on each other, charged one another with "piracy," introduced bills into Congress for the avowed purpose of "getting more contracts," or pugnaciously "stood up on [their] hind legs and roared" disapproval of their minute share of the defense pie.[4]

Such senatorial exuberance becomes understandable immediately if one examines the enormous economic impact that federal defense spending has had on the nation's leading recipient of defense expenditures—California. In the Golden State defense spending has served as a monolithic catalyst, vastly accelerating California's industrial expansion and population explosion during the past decade. This study will undertake to describe in detail how

[1] Appreciation is expressed to the Volker Foundation's Graduate Seminar in Economic History for a grant which made the preparation of this paper possible.

[2] A procurement action is a contract let by the Department of Defense for the purchase of supplies and services, including construction. For a detailed breakdown see U.S. Congress, Senate, Procurement Subcommittee of the Committee on Armed Services, *Procurement Study*, 86th Cong., 2d Sess., 1960.

[3] See U.S. Congress, Joint Economic Committee, *Background Material on Economic Aspects of Military Procurement and Supply*, 86th Cong., 2d Sess., 1960, p. 3.

[4] See 105 *Congressional Record*, 86th Cong., 1st Sess., pp. 6828, 6829, 9020, 10522, and A2281; *New York Times*, March 8, 1959, p. 1; and *Congressional Quarterly*, March 24, 1961, pp. 463–78.

this occurred, for California is the classic instance of the impact of defense spending on the economy of a single state.

WHAT CALIFORNIA RECEIVES

In 1953, California toppled New York from her position as the nation's leading state per net value of military prime contract awards[5] for supplies, services, and construction. Since that time, awards to the Golden State have more than doubled the annual amount any other state has received. California's share of production awards now accounts for 23.7 per cent of the total awards to all of the states in the nation, totaling $5.2 billion in fiscal 1959 and $4.8 billion in fiscal 1960.[6] If defense expenditures are increased in the 1960's (and the international and domestic political situation seems to indicate that they will be), it is very probable that California will increase the lead she already holds.[7] There is a good reason for this assertion because California receives 40.1 per cent of all awards for experimental, developmental, testing and research contracts.[8] Research contracts are in many respects the production contracts of tomorrow. These awards amounted to $2.1 billion for California's industrial and educational institutions during fiscal 1959.[9] There are more active-duty military and civilian DOD personnel stationed in California than in any other state; hence a greater percentage of the Defense Department's payroll accrues to and is probably spent there.[10] This is a major windfall, for the DOD civilian and military payroll is equal to the payroll of California's largest manufacturing industry (aircraft and parts). The mere maintenance of such a large establishment will require large expenditures on a continuing basis. The importance of this windfall at the present time is best illustrated by the fact that military payrolls alone add over one million dollars daily to San Diego's growing economy.[11]

Another fact to be noted is that California's share of government contracts has been rising while her rivals' share has been falling or remaining constant.

---

[5] A military prime contract is a procurement award of $10,000 or more.

[6] See U.S. Office of the Secretary of Defense, "Military Prime Contract Awards by State," annual reports.

[7] For a contrary view see the editorial entitled "Yield not to Political Temptation," *Missiles and Rockets,* April 17, 1961, p. 54. The editor suggests the Kennedy Administration might be tempted to penalize California for producing Kennedy's opponent and for voting Republican in the 1960 presidential election. This writer has found no evidence for such an assumption, nor is any presented in the editorial. The reader may draw his own conclusions as to the likelihood of a president elected on a razor-thin margin alienating a pivotal state because of an alleged pique.

[8] Letter to the writer from the Office of the Secretary of Defense, dated July 1, 1960.

[9] *Ibid.*

[10] See *Background Material . . . , op. cit.,* p. 24; *Congressional Quarterly, loc. cit.* There were 207,875 active duty military personnel and 140,445 DOD civilians stationed in California on June 30, 1960, with a combined annual payroll of $1.5 billion.

[11] See *San Diego Business,* January 1960, p. 1.

Beginning at only 13.2 per cent of the net value of prime contract awards in 1951, California's awards soared to a high of 26 per cent by 1954, fell momentarily to 18.6 per cent in 1957 due to the cut-back in defense spending for aircraft, then recovered and rose to 24 per cent by 1959.[12]

In contrast to California's rising share of the defense budget during the past decade, the Golden State's major competitors lost defense business during the 1950's. Illinois and Michigan, for example, lost over 50 per cent of their 1950 share in the military procurement program by 1956. Other important industrial states which declined in relative standing during the same period were Pennsylvania (37 per cent), New York (34 per cent), and Ohio (28 per cent).[13] New York has been most concerned and since early 1960 has been exerting every effort to recapture first place but without success.

TABLE I

Net Value of Military Prime Contract Awards of $10,000 or More for Supplies, Services and Construction: California Compared to Total for all States

Fiscal Year	Amount (in thousands)	Per cent of Total
1951	$3,897,915	13.2
1952	4,907,845	12.8
1953	4,161,835	15.4
1954	2,761,574	26.0
1955	2,813,676	20.1
1956	3,311,203	20.1
1957	3,381,927	18.6
1958	4,457,666	21.2
1959	5,282,659	24.0
1960	4,839,252	23.7

Source: Office of the Secretary of Defense.

Finally, California's commanding position in the defense business in comparison with other important states may be quickly determined by glancing at Table II.

WHAT CALIFORNIA RETAINS

A large proportion of defense money initially let to prime contractors is subcontracted to other firms. For every dollar given to a prime contractor,

---

[12] Although state breakdowns for research and experimental contracts are available only since 1958, it appears that this upward trend may have been even more pronounced with respect to this type of contract since California's share of research is so high.

[13] See U.S. Congress, Senate, Subcommittee of the Committee on Armed Services, *Military Procurement,* 86th Cong., 1st Sess., 1959, p. 310; and *New York Times,* May 17, 1959, p. 80.

TABLE II

States Receiving the Largest Percentage of Important Defense Expenditures Fiscal 1959*

	Rank of State		
	First	Second	Third
Military Prime Contracts for Services, Supplies, and Construction†	California	New York	Texas
Military Prime Contracts for research and development	California	New York‡	Maryland‡
Number of active-duty military personnel with the state	California	Texas	Virginia
Number of civilian personnel working for the DOD within the state	California	Virginia	Pennsylvania
Amount of defense spending per capita	Alaska	California	Washington

* Breakdown includes all major expenditures except for maintenance, operations, and miscellaneous expenditures.
† Does not generally include military owned and operated establishments, and is based upon the initial awards to firms where the product is finally processed and assembled.
‡ Estimated position.
Source: Compiled from DOD reports for fiscal 1959 and U.S. Cong., Joint Economic Committee, *Military Procurement Hearings*, 86th Cong., 2d Sess., 1960, *passim*.

about fifty cents goes to a major subcontractor. However, according to one study, about 17 per cent of the California prime defense dollar goes to California subcontractors.[14] This means that approximately 64 per cent of the initial amount let to California prime contractors either remains with that firm or is subcontracted to another California firm. On this basis about $40 billion has been awarded California since 1950 in the form of initial contracts.[15]

---

[14] See "The Defense Industries of California," an eye-catching pamphlet prepared and published by several California local Chambers of Commerce (Los Angeles: 1959), p. 35.

[15] There are no precise data on the amount of subcontracts either entering or leaving California. When one considers that over 20,000 firms are expected eventually to take part in the production of the B-70 Bomber, which is only one of several military prime contracts held by the North American Aviation Corporation, it is clear why this is so. In many cases the dollar volume of subcontracted components even exceeds the value of the components manufactured by the initial contractor. This figure does not seem excessive, however, for an examination of over $1.4 billion worth of prime military contracts let in California during 1958 and 1959 revealed that over half of the first-tier subcontractors represented California firms. Moreover, the extraordinary growth of California's defense industries (see below), including the large number of new factories and expansions, is convincing evidence that a large percentage of the initial contract remains in the Golden State.

Since the amount of subcontracting which takes place in California lies at the heart of any study of this nature the reader is referred to *Background Material . . . , op. cit.*, pp. 109–21; U.S. Office of the Secretary of Defense, "Report of the One Hundred Larger Prime Contractors," December 1959, appendix; U.S. Congress, House, Subcommittee for Special Investigations of the Committee on Armed Services, *Weapons System Management and Team System Concepts in Government Contracting*, 86th Cong., 1st Sess., 1960, pp. 45–80; and U.S. Congress, Senate, Select Committee on

There are no reliable figures on the number of subcontracts coming to California firms from other states, but this figure must be quite sizable because of the large concentration of subsidiary defense industries located in California. For example, in 1958 the Martin Company of Denver, Colorado, received a prime contract for the Titan Missile amounting to $385 million. Forty-seven million dollars of that initial contract was subcontracted to major firms in California—a larger amount than was placed in any other state. Possibly some of this Titan money was subsequently re-subcontracted elsewhere, but the point is that hundreds of millions of dollars in the form of out-of-state subcontracts have also found their way into California during the past decade.

Unfortunately, there are also no reliable data on the extent of the subcontracting of research contracts. It is reasonable to assume, however, that an even higher percentage of this money remains with the initial contractor since many research contracts are placed with colleges, universities, and other non-profit organizations and usually involve only one location.[16] Several billion dollars have been retained by the Golden State in this manner.

In summary, California retains a very high percentage of its initial defense grants; undoubtedly, receives in addition a considerable number of contracts initially granted to other states; and unquestionably, retains most of its research and developmental awards. A conservative estimate of these awards plus the annual military and civilian payroll of the Department of Defense in California shows that over $50 billion[17] defense dollars have been funneled into California's economy during the past ten years. This is more than twice the amount received by any other state.

WHY CALIFORNIA RECEIVES THE LION'S SHARE OF THE MILITARY DEFENSE BUDGET

According to Thomas C. Werbe, Jr., Deputy Assistant Secretary of Defense (Supply and Logistics), this unprecedented and expanding volume of prime contract awards to California is "primarily a product of the upward trend in military procurement of aircraft, missiles, associated electronics, and

---

Small Business, *Case Study in Subcontracting by Weapons-System Contractor,* 86th Cong., 1st Sess., 1960.

[16] Of 103 government agencies and non-profit institutions which received prime research contracts of over $200,000 during fiscal 1959, only 24 involved more than one location.

[17] This estimate is determined in the following manner: Assuming the accuracy of the California State Chamber of Commerce's figure that 64 per cent of the initial grants are retained in California, $40 billion has gone to and remained in California since 1950. Since California has always emphasized research contracts (see below) and because most of these contracts are not subcontracted, it is not unreasonable to assume that $5 billion has accrued to California in this manner since 1950, based on the 1959 figure of $2.1 billion. Add to this several hundred million dollars in out-of-state subcontracts and between $8 and $10 billion in military and civilian DOD payrolls for the same period and $50 billion does not appear to be an exaggeration.

related research and development work, and the existence in California of substantial research, development and production facilities that are able to compete successfully for this work." [18] Aircraft, guided missile systems, electronics and communications equipment now account for 63 per cent of the total net value of all military procurement actions; whereas during the Korean War procurement actions were much more diversified. Since California was the nation's leading manufacturer of aircraft and parts at the beginning of the decade, it was only natural that the bulk of this expanding defense business should accrue to that state.[19]

Another important factor in bringing defense industry to California is the emphasis that state placed on scientific and technological education and research during the 1950's. The University of California, Stanford University, and the California Institute of Technology are among the nation's best engineering schools. Generally speaking, graduates from these schools tend to remain in California which already has a high percentage of the competent scientists and technicians in the aircraft, missile, and electronic fields.[20] These excellent universities and the outstanding scientists associated with them, along with more than two dozen other important scientific facilities located throughout the state, largely explain why California received 40 per cent of all research contracts in fiscal 1959.[21] Obviously, this emphasis on research has been a paramount factor in winning a correspondingly high percentage of production awards. In fact, there is good evidence that the willingness of California firms to take research as well as high-profit contracts during the Korean War boom accounts for the fact that California replaced New York as the leading defense contractor during the decade of the fifties.[22] New York short-sightedly emphasized the immediate returns of the production contracts. Congressman John Taber (R, N.Y.) claims that the lack of initiative on the part of New York businessmen and city administrators may also be a factor.[23]

---

[18] Letter to Congressman David King (D, Utah) from Thomas C. Werbe, Jr., Deputy Assistant Secretary of Defense (Supply and Logistics), dated July 15, 1960.

[19] One-third of the nation's aircraft workers were employed in California in 1947. During the three years following the Korean War about 4,000 employees per month were added to the aircraft industry. See *Employment in California,* California Department of Industrial Relations, 1953.

[20] More than one-fifth of the members of the National Academy of Science were California residents in 1958, including eleven winners of the Nobel Prize. See California Senate, Joint Resolution No. 1, First Extraordinary Session of the California Legislature, 1958.

[21] The DOD awards research contracts to those organizations with the "highest competence . . . required for successful conduct of the work involved." In determining this competence the DOD emphasizes the availability of experienced personnel, test facilities, and willingness to devote resources to the proposed contract. See *Procurement Study, op. cit.,* p. 94.

[22] Speaking before the Senate, Senator Jacob K. Javits (R, N.Y.) stated that during the industrial expansion of the Korean War, New York firms accepted preponderantly high-profit production contracts and declined research contracts, whereas California took research contracts as well. *Congressional Record,* June 23, 1959, p. 10522.

[23] *New York Times,* April 18, 1960, p. 1.

The Defense Department's policy of assigning the responsibility for the overall development of a weapons system[24] to a single prime contractor also tends to funnel defense money to California. Under this system the Defense Department, after negotiation of the contracts, assigns the whole project, such as the B-70 Bomber, to a single concern. About 50 per cent of the net value of military procurement actions are negotiated in this manner. The rest are advertised or negotiated competitively. Such a policy, by its very nature, favors the larger aircraft firms, many of which are in California, since they are usually the most capable of handling such gigantic projects. As a result defense business has tended to concentrate into fewer firms,[25] and all weapons system subcontracting is controlled by the prime contractor with the approval of the Department of Defense. By winning large weapons system awards and letting out only those contracts which they do not want themselves, some firms have enlarged their operations by as much as 300 per cent. For example, Convair at San Diego retained rather than sublet a contract for air conditioning carts for the B-58 tactical program when it would have been more efficient to have other more specialized companies perform this work.[26] Another result of the weapons system process is that the initial contractor gains from subcontractors and bidders information and ideas which it is then able to use to strengthen its own competitive position even further.[27]

Another significant factor in awarding contracts to California has been the practice by certain defense contractors of hiring recently retired high-ranking military personnel with contacts in the Pentagon as company representatives. Although this practice is widespread throughout all defense industries, it is interesting to note that several California firms are among those corporations which hired the largest number of ex-officers.[28] Even though no specific case of "influence peddling" was proved by the House subcommittee investigating this situation, the House of Representatives felt that this practice was despicable enough to outlaw it and passed a bill requiring a two-year

---

[24] A "weapons system" is usually defined as "an instrument of combat, such as an aircraft or missile, together with all related equipment and supporting facilities required to bring the instrument on its target or place of function."

[25] Small business has been getting increasingly fewer defense awards, dropping from 25 per cent of the total awards by value assigned in 1954 to 16 per cent of the total value assigned in 1960. Small business now receives only 4.1 per cent of aircraft and missile contracts which account for almost half of all procurements. Defense Department bulletins also show that the number of principal subcontractors has been dropping since 1958. See *Background Materials . . . , op. cit.,* p. 70; U.S. Congress, Senate, Select Committee on Small Business, *Lack of Competition in Military Procurement and its Impact on Small Business,* 87th Cong., 1st Sess., 1961.

[26] See *Case Study in Subcontracting by Weapons-System Contractors, op. cit., passim.*

[27] See Sterling Livingston, "Weapons System Contracting," *Harvard Business Review,* July-August, 1959.

[28] For a list of these companies see U.S. Congress, House, Subcommittee for Special Investigations of the Committee on Armed Services, *Employment of Retired Commissioned Officers by Defense Department Contractors,* 86th Cong., 1st Sess., 1960, p. 9.

"cooling off" period before any high-ranking officer may accept a position with a firm doing business with the Department of Defense.[29]

WHERE THIS DEFENSE MONEY IS GOING
WITHIN CALIFORNIA

This massive defense outlay has been concentrated in a relatively small area of California. Consequently, its impact on the state's economy is not difficult to observe. Although precise contract figures for every county and city are not available for each year during the last decade, a tabulation of more than 1,500 defense contracts let in California for fiscal 1959 and 1960,[30] a close reading of the California State Chamber of Commerce Economic Surveys of 1954 and 1958, and an examination of the yearly statistical data for the in-between years, indicate that Los Angeles County receives the majority of these awards and that as few as three counties do about 90 per cent of the California defense business.

The reason for the concentration of awards in the Los Angeles area is obvious since most of California's defense industries have their primary facilities located there. Four Los Angeles aerospace companies alone accounted for over $3.1 billion in production and research contracts during

TABLE III

Military Prime Contract Awards of $500,000 or More for the Top Ten California Counties per Value of the Awards for Fiscal 1959

County	Amount awarded firms within that county (in millions)	Per cent of total
Los Angeles	$2,591	61
San Diego	615	14
Santa Clara	570	13
Sacramento	157	04
Orange	70	02
Contra Costa	70	02
Marin	20	—
Kings	17	—
San Bernardino	17	—
San Mateo	8	—

Note: Military bases not included.
Source: Compiled from DOD listings of contracts let in California during fiscal 1959 supplied to the writer by that office.

---

[29] See *Congressional Quarterly Almanac,* 1959, p. 727; 1960, p. 279.

[30] These contracts provided the bulk of the research materials for this study and include all research awards over $10,000 for fiscal 1959 and for the first nine months of fiscal 1960; all production awards of $500,000 or more for fiscal 1959 and fiscal 1960; or about 80 per cent of all California awards over $10,000 for the past two years. Source: Office of the Secretary of Defense.

fiscal 1959. Moreover, most of the research now being done for the defense industries occurs there. Seventy-one per cent of California's research awards were garnered by Los Angeles County in fiscal 1959. San Diego ranked second in that year with 15 per cent of the prime contract awards and 13 per cent of the research and development contracts. Most of this money went for the development of the F-106 weapons system and missile research. Santa Clara County was third with 14 per cent of the production contracts and 9 percent of the research awards. The Lockheed Aircraft Company, located at Sunnyvale and Palo Alto, secured the biggest awards for missile research and development. Finally, Sacramento County should be mentioned, since 4 per cent of the procurement actions and 5 per cent of the research awards were placed there chiefly with Aerojet-General.

The cities which received the largest net value of defense awards in fiscal 1959 are for the most part located in Los Angeles County. There the City of Los Angeles received the lion's share. Other important recipients were Santa Monica, El Segundo, Downey, Culver City, Canoga Park, and Burbank. Outside Los Angeles County some major centers were San Diego, Sunnyvale, and Sacramento. If one included Palo Alto, Azuza, and Pasadena, this list would also include the top cities which received research contracts during fiscal 1959. Moreover, reports for fiscal 1960 clearly show that the pattern of defense spending by city and by county was very similar to what it was during fiscal 1959.

THE IMPACT OF DEFENSE SPENDING ON CALIFORNIA'S INDUSTRIAL GROWTH

The defense industry is now California's most important manufacturing industry. It accounts for almost one-fourth of all those persons employed in manufacturing in the state, and for over one-half of the average increase in employment between 1947 and 1956, if aircraft and parts, electronics, and some of the expansion in the metal industries are included.[31] About 400,000 persons out of the 6 million labor force are employed in defense industries, or about one out of every 15 employed. Most of these workers are concentrated within a small area, however, as 90 per cent of all those employed in the aircraft and parts industry and 65 per cent of those employed in the communications equipment industry work in Los Angeles County.[32]

The defense industry is the major determining factor in the phenomenal growth of California's fastest growing industries. Between 1947 and 1957

---

[31] See *Economic Survey of California and Its Counties: 1958,* prepared by the Research Department of the California State Chamber of Commerce, (Sacramento: 1958), pp. 837–38. Hereafter referred to as *1958 Survey.*

[32] U.S., Bureau of the Census, *Annual Survey of Manufacturers for 1957,* pp. 58, 70, 71; and *1958 Survey,* p. 940.

those industries showing the greatest growth per number of employees added were: communications equipment (1,851 per cent), electrical machinery (830 per cent), aircraft and parts (592 per cent), scientific instruments (550 per cent), to say nothing of the ordnance industry which soared 150-fold.[33] Defense spending is the major source of income for all of these industries. For example, defense contracts account for over 90 per cent of the aircraft business, and since the aircraft and parts industry is largely located in the Los Angeles area, over 80 per cent of the value added in the transportation industry since 1947 accrued there.[34] The expansion in the electrical machinery industry is primarily due to electronics and guided missile contracts placed after the outbreak of the Korean War. The same is true, but to a lesser extent, in the non-electrical machine industry.[35]

This concentrated defense spending, including its indirect effects on other industries, is one of the main reasons why 44 per cent of the estimated total for new plants and expansion took place in Los Angeles County from 1947 to 1956. Under the stimulus of certificates of rapid amortization (which permit that portion of the cost of a facility contributing to the defense program to be written off for tax purposes within five years), announced capital investment expansions were highest in the transportation industry during 1953 (over twice that of any other industry) and in the electrical machinery industry during 1955 and 1956.[36] During 1957 the transportation industry fell to fifth place in capital investment owing to a cut-back in defense spending but was back in third place by 1958. The electrical machinery industry held steady in second place during these years.

The large expenditures California received for defense purposes during the 1950's also assisted that state in weathering recessions in the national economy. According to Dr. George S. Roche,[37] unemployment was lower than the national average in California during the 1954 recession because of the continued expansion of the aircraft industry during that year. Moreover, defense outlays speeded California's recovery following the 1958 recession, and materially assisted the boom of 1959.

The most spectacular impact on the industrial growth of a geographic area is to be found in San Diego County, where over three-fourths of the 75,000 workers in manufacturing are employed in defense industries.[38] From 1950 to 1957 the number of wage and salary workers increased from 12,000 to 55,000, the latter figure being only slightly less than the World War II

---

[33] See *Economic Survey Series,* Research Department, California State Chamber of Commerce, Series of 1958 and 1959. See also "California: State of the Future," *Economist* (London), July 9, 1960, p. 151.

[34] *Economic Survey of California and Its Counties: 1954,* California State Chamber of Commerce, (Sacramento: 1954), *passim.* Hereafter referred to as *1954 Survey.*

[35] *Ibid.,* p. 609.

[36] *Economic Survey Series, loc. cit.,* No. 36.

[37] See "California Department of Employment News Letter," Vol. 13, No. 2, December, 1959.

[38] "The Defense Industries of California," *op. cit.,* p. 40.

peak. Moreover. defense outlays from 1947 to 1954 made San Diego County the fastest growing industrial county in California in number of production workers and value added. It is not an exaggeration to say that the whole economy of the county is dependent on defense industries and military installations which, if materially restricted, would cause a severe depression in that area. As a result, San Diego business leaders have embarked on a five-year industrial diversification program,[39] and the state of California has set up the Economic Development Agency for the purpose of placing many unemployed defense workers with non-defense firms. Paradoxically, however, 40,000 of the 60,000 persons who were laid off because of the recent contraction in the aircraft industry resulting from the shift to missile work have found jobs in other defense-oriented concerns.[40]

The industrial growth of Los Angeles County, although not as spectacular or as completely oriented to defense spending as that of San Diego County, has also been affected materially by government spending. About 20 per cent of the working force of the county is engaged in defense industries, mostly aircraft and parts, which is the county's largest industry. The aircraft industry as a whole increased by just under 200 per cent from 1947 to 1956.[41] The electrical equipment industry is the county's second largest industry, growing 60 per cent since 1947 and employing 66,500 persons in 1956.[42] Both of these industries are very highly dependent on national defense expenditures.

Defense spending, although not as heavy as in San Diego and Los Angeles counties, has also measurably assisted industrial growth in parts of Santa Clara and Sacramento counties in Central California. In Santa Clara County the most important industry is the processing of food; but electrical machinery is the fastest growing industry, and much of this activity has been stimulated by defense contracts granted to several research laboratories and production plants located in San Jose, Mountain View, Sunnyvale, and Palo Alto. In Sacramento County the expansion of employment in the manufacture of jet and rocket engines and propellants has made the transportation industry its fastest growing one.[43]

THE EFFECT OF DEFENSE SPENDING ON POPULATION GROWTH

It has long been established that expanding industries mean expanding population and vice versa.[44] This fact was recently re-emphasized for the Golden State by Professor James Gillies, who showed that the three fastest

[39] See 1959 and 1960 issues of *San Diego Business* (bi-monthly).
[40] "California: State of the Future," *Economist, loc. cit.*, pp. 151–52.
[41] *1958 Survey,* pp. 940–41.
[42] *Ibid.*
[43] See *1954 and 1958 Surveys* under the appropriate county headings.
[44] For an excellent recent study see Donald J. Bogue, *The Population of the United States,* (Glencoe: Free Press, 1959).

growing California cities in manufacturing employment, Los Angeles, San Diego, and San Jose, were also the top three cities in population growth.[45] Professor Gillies concluded that "a condition for population expansion of major proportions is the expansion of major base industries."

Obviously, most of California's population increase since 1950 has been due to in-migration, since natural birth and death rates can account for but a part of the phenomonal addition of 5,130,981 persons in ten years. Why did all these people come to California? The strongest and most universal motive behind population migration has been shown to be economic opportunity;[46] hence, it is submitted that the mushrooming industries of those California counties where population growth was fastest is the key to understanding why that growth took place.[47] Let us now examine this hypothesis in relation to defense spending.

The state of California showed the largest population growth of all states in the nation from 1950 to 1960, adding almost three times more people than Florida, the state with the next largest addition.[48] Most of this increase took place in Los Angeles County, followed by Orange, San Diego, Santa Clara, and Sacramento counties. One is struck by the fact that except for Orange County, the counties in which the number of persons added is greatest are the same counties in which defense spending has been distributed during the past decade! Table IV illustrates this point.

TABLE IV

Comparison of Counties in Which Defense Spending Was Concentrated and Counties in Which Population Growth Was Greatest 1950 to 1960

Top four counties receiving the most defense money*	Top five counties which showed the largest population increase†	
Los Angeles	Los Angeles	(1,887,084)
San Diego	Orange	(487,701)
Santa Clara	San Diego	(476,203)
Sacramento	Santa Clara	(351,768)
	Sacramento	(225,638)

* Based on DOD awards for fiscal 1959 and 1960, annual economic reports of California Chamber of Commerce, and *1954 and 1958 Surveys*. These data are insufficient to give a further breakdown of counties in order of defense spending.
† Bureau of the Census, Advanced Reports for the 1960 Census for California.

---

[45] James Gillies, "Industry's Role in Metropolitan Growth: A Public Management Problem," *California Management Review*, Winter 1960, pp. 38–40.

[46] See Bogue, *op. cit.*, p. 416.

[47] Californians are prone to attribute this influx to an admittedly delightful climate, but a recent survey by the San Diego Economic Research Bureau of 1,000 immigrants to San Diego County—allegedly the most enticing of all California watering places—revealed that 40 per cent of these newcomers were motivated by economic opportunity or military assignments, whereas 35 per cent were enticed by the salubrious climate.

[48] See U.S. Bureau of the Census, *1960 Census of Population*, Advanced Reports, "Final Population Counts for California," pp. 1–3.

In Los Angeles County the most spectacular population growth has been in the Antelope Valley, which extends into Kern County, where some communities have grown as much as 800 per cent in seven years![49] One of the main reasons for this growth has been the concentration and expansion of several aircraft companies producing and testing jets, the location of an Air Force plant, and the expansion of a major Air Force Base. Recently, however, this area has been undergoing a severe readjustment due to the decline in aircraft construction.

Less spectacular but even more important is the San Fernando area surrounding the city of San Fernando but lying within the city limits of Los Angeles. This area has more than tripled its population since 1950. There are several aircraft factories and the important new missile center of Van Nuys located here, but defense spending is not the only reason for this expanded growth. Generally speaking, however, those Los Angeles County industrial communities which are primarily dependent on defense industries or at least have a large share of their manufacturing economy based on such spending grew faster on the average from 1950 to 1958 than did similar communities in the same county which have a more diversified industrial base. To illustrate, of the 28 or so important industrial communities lying within Los Angeles County, the defense-industry oriented centers grew on the average from 12 to 15 per cent faster than did their more diversified sister communities. Some of the more notable examples are: Culver City (63 per cent), Downey (152), El Segundo (78), Hawthorne (103), to say nothing of Palmdale (700 per cent).[50]

The fastest growing communities in Orange County are located in its northern part close to the industrial centers of Los Angeles County. Anaheim grew the most with an almost unbelievable increase of 616 per cent for the decade! Next was Fullerton with 303 per cent. These two communities are also the most important defense contract centers of the county, but defense spending is only one of several factors working here.

In Santa Clara County, Sunnyvale registered the greatest increase in population (438 per cent) between 1950 and 1960. It is among other things the home of Lockheed Aircraft's Missile System Division, which received a single contract of over $400 million for missile research and development in fiscal 1959. Although not the only factor, defense spending could be said to be the major factor in this community's growth. The second fastest growing community was Santa Clara with 403 per cent. This growth is due to reasons other than defense spending; but Mountain View, the site of a major jet airbase and several aeronautical and electronics laboratories, was third with 307 per cent. Defense spending was the main reason for this growth.

---

[49] *1958 Survey*, p. 957.

[50] See *1958 Survey*, pp. 947–58; and *1960 Census of Population, loc. cit.*, Los Angeles County communities, *passim.*

Other communities in California, but outside Santa Clara County, in which defense spending played a major role in population growth are Ontario (104), Livermore (268), Belmont (187), and Folsom (132 per cent).

In summary, a majority of the fastest growing areas of the four California counties which added the most population are those communities which are primarily or to a great extent dependent upon defense industries. As these industries were given increasingly larger defense contracts which necessitated enlarging operations and expanding production, it was natural that they should draw more and more people into their vortex. Because this occurred, others were attracted to the same area to supply the growing market for goods and services. In short, the cold war of the fifties has had the same effect on the population growth of California's defense-oriented counties as did the hot war of the forties.

NEW PROBLEMS ON THE HORIZON

California's phenomenal rise to this new position as the nation's fastest growing industrial state has not been one of unmixed blessings. Some grave problems also face the state as a direct result of this massive concentration of defense money. Southern California is now more vulnerable to attack in the event of war. Nearly one-fifth of the transportation equipment industry of the United States—which includes aircraft and missiles production—is now located in California and concentrated chiefly in Los Angeles County.[51] Moreover, nearly one-fifth of our total defense procurement program is centered in two counties, Los Angeles and San Diego. To illustrate, a nuclear bomb with a destruction radius of 15 miles dropped by a hostile power in the neighborhood of Huntington Park would knock out more defense industry than in any other area of similar size in the United States.

To be first in defense production also means to be the first destroyed in the event of war. If the residents of Los Angeles and San Diego are aware of this there is little evidence that it makes any difference. Perhaps recent forecasts that 80 million casualties would result from a nuclear attack on the United States leads them to believe they are in no worse position than other target cities with a lower bombing priority.

A problem that does interest Californians, however, is the likelihood of a serious cut-back in defense expenditures. If these expenditures were stopped completely, one out of every four persons employed in manufacturing would be laid off immediately with three out of four in San Diego County. A total cut-back at this time seems unrealistic, however, in spite of much disarmament sentiment. But if California's share of the procurement program were

---

[51] See *California Manufacturer's Annual Register,* 1961, (Los Angeles: Times-Mirror Press: 1961), p. xxviii.

reduced to what it was during the Korean War—as the New York Congressional Delegation and others are advocating[52]—the amount of California's procurement contracts would be cut nearly in half. Consequently, a large but indeterminable number of Californians would be forced to find work in other pursuits. This happened recently on a smaller scale when aircraft procurement was cut back in favor of missile development and 60,000 defense workers were thrown out of work.

Whether such a cut-back would cause a severe depression in the Golden State is still an open question. New York's share of the defense procurement program was exactly halved by fiscal 1959 from what it was during the Korean War but manufacturing activity continued to grow.[53] Individual manufacturers were hard hit, particularly in the Buffalo area.[54] California's defense industries are far more concentrated than New York's are, however, and this might be a sufficient factor to bring about a recession in the areas of concentration.

Following World War II the consequences of the cut-back in defense procurement were not disastrous despite many predictions to that effect. The reason usually given for this good fortune is that the wartime increase in California's population created a sufficient demand for goods and services to prevent a serious cut-back in employment.[55] But by 1949 California did have a serious recession with 178,000 out of work in Los Angeles County alone. This recession has also been variously interpreted, but the reason given in Los Angeles was that there was an over-supply of laborers.[56] Why this was not also true of 1945 has never been explained adequately as far as this writer is aware. For these reasons few economists are willing to predict what would happen if defense funds were seriously restricted.

To meet this problem California set up the Economic Development Agency to find ways of diversifying her defense industry. This agency feels the answer to possible cut-backs lies in transferring defense workers into "import industries" [57] such as cotton goods. California now imports about $5 billion in goods and services, about the same amount she is currently receiving in procurement contracts. Whether skilled defense technicians can be transferred successfully into textile workers, etc., remains to be seen.

---

[52] See fn. 4.

[53] New York lost $2.4 billion and California would lose $1.9 billion.

[54] Letter to the writer from Mrs. Vera R. Russell, Acting Director, Bureau of Business Research, New York State Department of Commerce, dated March 15, 1960.

[55] For an interesting analysis of California's continued growth after 1945, see Carey McWilliams, *California: the Great Exception,* (New York: Current Books: 1949), Chapter entitled "The Fabulous Boom."

[56] See Robert R. Dockson, "Our Employment Problem," *Proceedings of the Los Angeles County Conference on Unemployment* (Los Angeles: n. p.: [1950?]), p. 16.

[57] See "California: State of the Future," *Economist, loc. cit.*

CONCLUSIONS

With the close of the decade of the fifties, California has furnished another impressive chapter in a story which began with the forties, a story of what happens to a state when billions of defense dollars are poured into its economy. Expenditures for defense served as a geometrically expanding catalyst, pushing ahead California's rate of industrial growth at a pace unequalled by any other state, and drawing an unprecedented number of people into its industrial vortex. As a result the economy of the whole state was given new impetus and a surging vitality only slightly less spectacular than the wartime boom of the early 1940's. The underlying cause of this economic boom was the Defense Department's acceleration of aircraft production at a time when California's industrial base was best prepared to accept this increased emphasis. Credit must also be given to California's alert and progressive management, research, and technical personnel engaged in defense production for their efforts in meeting this new and vitally important management challenge. Finally, it was neither "politics" nor "piracy" but an inevitable process of expansion reinforced by competent leadership which has made California the defense industry colossus of the nation.

Whether this new and lofty status will be permanent in light of the furious jealousy it has generated among rival states, such as New York, only time will tell. But unless sectional politics intervene in the defense contract process (which is unlikely), California's position of leadership is guaranteed for the foreseeable future. Whether such a concentration of defense spending is really "good" for California or "good" for the nation is likely to be debated hotly in the coming years.

PART THREE:

Strategic Alternatives

THE NATURE AND FEASIBILITY OF WAR AND DETERRENCE

Herman Kahn

* * *

THE THREE KINDS OF DETERRENCE

It is important to distinguish between three types of deterrence: *Type 1 Deterrence* (which the British call "passive deterrence" on the plausible, but possibly incorrect, assumption that it requires no act of will to respond to a violation) is the deterrence of a direct attack. It is widely believed that if the United States were directly attacked, its response would be automatic and unthinking. *Type 2 Deterrence* (which the British have called "active deterrence" because it clearly takes an act of will to initiate) is defined as using strategic threats to deter an enemy from engaging in very provocative acts other than a direct attack on the United States itself. *Type 3 Deterrence* might be called "*tit-for-tat* deterrence." It refers to those acts that are deterred because the potential aggressor is afraid that the defender or others will then take limited actions, military or nonmilitary, that will make the aggression unprofitable. These three types of deterrence will be discussed in turn at length.

Type 1 Deterrence (Deterrence against a Direct Attack)

Most experts today argue that we must make this particular type of deterrence work, that we simply cannot face the possibility of a failure. Never have the stakes on success or failure of prevention been so high. Although the extreme view that deterrence is everything and that alleviation is hopeless is questionable, clearly Type 1 Deterrence must have first priority.

In spite of the many words lavished on Type 1 Deterrence, most discussions of the conditions needed for such deterrence tend to be unrealistic. Typically, discussions of the capability of the United States to deter a direct attack compare the preattack inventory of our forces with the preattack inventory of the Russian forces—that is, the number of planes, missiles, army divisions, and submarines of the two countries are directly compared. This is a World War I and World War II approach.

The really essential numbers, however, are estimates of the damage that the retaliatory forces can inflict after being hit. Evaluation must take into account that the Russians could strike *at a time and with tactics of their choosing*. We strike back with a *damaged* and perhaps *uncoordinated* force, which must conduct its operations in the *postattack environment*. The Soviets may use *blackmail* threats to intimidate our response. The Russian defense is completely *alerted*. If the strike has been preceded by a tense period, their active defense forces have been *augmented* and their cities have been at least partially *evacuated*. Any of the emphasized words can be very important, but almost all of them are ignored in most discussions of Type 1 Deterrence.

The first step in this calculation—analysis of the effects of the Russian strike on U.S. retaliatory ability—depends critically on the enemy's tactics and capabilities. The question of warning is generally uppermost. Analyses of the effect of the enemy's first strike often neglect the most important part of the problem by assuming that warning will be effective and that our forces get off the ground and are sent on their way to their targets. Actually, without effective warning, attrition on the ground can be much more important than attrition in the air. The enemy may not only use tactics that limit our warning, but he may do other things to counter our defensive measures, such as interfering with command and control arrangements. Thus it is important in evaluating enemy capabilities to look not only at the tactics that past history and standard assumptions lead us to expect, but also at any other tactics that a clever enemy might use. We should not always assume what Albert Wohlstetter has called "U.S. preferred attacks" in estimating the performance of our system. We should also look at "S.U. preferred attacks"—a sensible Soviet planner may prefer them!

The enemy, by choosing the timing of an attack, has several factors in his favor. He can select a *time* calculated to force our manned-bomber force to retaliate in the daytime, when his day fighters and his air-defense systems will be much more effective. In addition, he can choose the *season* so that his postwar agricultural problems and fallout-protection problems will be less difficult.

The second part of the calculation—consequences of the lack of coordination of the surviving U.S. forces—depends greatly on our tactics and the flexibility of our plans. If, for example, our offensive force is assigned a large target system so that it is spread thinly, and if because of a large or successful Russian attack the Russians have succeeded in destroying much of our force, many important Russian targets would go unattacked. If, on the other hand, to avoid this we double or triple the assignment to important targets, we might over-destroy many targets, especially if the Soviets had not struck us successfully. For this and other reasons, it would be wise to evaluate the damage and then retarget the surviving forces. Whether this can be done depends critically on the timing of the attack, the nature of the targeting process, and our postattack capability for evaluation, command, and control.

Our attack may also be degraded because of problems of grouping, timing, and refueling; in some instances our manned bombers might be forced to infiltrate in small groups into Soviet air territory and lose the advantage of saturation of the Soviet defenses. Whether or not this would be disastrous depends a great deal on the quality of the Russian air-defense system, especially on whether it has any holes we can exploit, and the kind and number of penetration aids we use. This aspect is complicated and classified.

Another point that may be of great importance is that modern nuclear weapons are so powerful that even if they don't destroy their target, they may change the environment so as to cause the retaliating weapon system to be inoperable. The various effects of nuclear weapons include blast, thermal radiation, ground shock, debris, dust, and ionizing radiation—any of which may affect people, equipment, propagation of electromagnetic signals, etc. One might say that the problem of operating in a postattack environment after training in the peacetime environment is similar to training at the equator and then moving a major but incomplete part (that is, a damaged system) to the arctic and expecting this incomplete system to work efficiently the first time it is tried. This is particularly implausible if, as is often true, the intact system is barely operable at the equator (that is, in peacetime).

In addition to attacking the system, the enemy may attempt to attack our resolve. Imagine, for example, that we had a pure Polaris system invulnerable to an all-out simultaneous enemy attack (invulnerable by assumption and not by analysis) and the enemy started to destroy our submarines one at a time at sea. Suppose an American President were told that if we started an all-out war in retaliation, the Soviets could and would destroy every American because of limitations in our offense and our active and passive defenses. Now if the President has a chance to think about the problem, he simply cannot initiate this kind of war even with such provocation. Against even stronger strategic postures there will still be opportunities for using postattack coercion. In some cases it will cost the Soviets nothing to use tactics combined with threats which, if they work, will greatly alleviate their military problems; if they do not work, the situation will be almost unchanged anyway. I do not have the space here to discuss the timing, control, communication, and persuasion problems involved in making different kinds of postattack coercion feasible, but they do not look insurmountable.

One of the most important and yet the most neglected elements of the retaliatory calculation is the effect of the Russian civil-defense measures. The Russians are seldom credited with even modest preparedness in civil defense. Analysts sometimes go so far as to assume that peacetime civilian activities will continue on a business-as-usual basis hours after Russian missiles or planes have been dispatched. The analysts may then proceed to worry about conventional day-night variations in population. This is not only ridiculous, it is also symptomatic of the lack of realism and the prevalent tendency toward underestimating the enemy.

A much more reasonable alternative that would apply in many situations —that the Russians might at some point evacuate their city population to places affording existing or improvisable fallout protection—is almost never realistically examined. If the Russians should take steps to evacuate their cities, the vulnerability of their population would be dramatically reduced.

The Soviets also know that they can take an enormous amount of economic damage and be set back only a few years in their development. Not only did they do something like this after World War II, but what is even more impressive, they fought a war *after* the Germans had destroyed most of their existing military power and occupied an area that contained about 40 per cent of the prewar Soviet population—the most industrialized 40 per cent. According to Soviet estimates, by the time the war ended they had lost about one-third of their wealth—almost the proportion we would lose if we lost all of the A country. The Soviets rebuilt the destroyed wealth in about six years. Moreover, since 1931 they have had a vigorous program to disperse their industry, a program that seems to have been stepped up since World War II. It is quite likely that their B country is at least as capable of restoring society as ours. Much more important, they probably *know* the capabilities of their B country.

The difficulties of Type 1 Deterrence arise mainly from the fact that the deterring nation must strike second. These difficulties are compounded by the rapidity with which the technology of war changes and the special difficulty the defender has in reacting quickly and adequately to changes in the offense. The so-called missile gap illustrates the problem. The Russians announced in August, 1957, that they had tested an ICBM. Evidence of their technical ability to do this was furnished by Sputnik I, sent aloft in October of that year. Early in 1959 Khrushchev boasted that the Soviet Union had intercontinental rockets in serial production. We have little reason to believe that they won't have appreciable numbers of operational ICBM's about three years after their successful test—which would be in August, 1960.

Suppose that in 1957 and 1958 we had refused to react to this "hypothetical" threat, so that when the autumn of 1960 appeared we had not completed the needed modifications to our defenses to accommodate this development. What kind of risk would we have run?

I will assume (on the basis of newspaper reports and Congressional testimony) that we had approximately 25 *unalert* SAC *home* bases in 1957. In accordance with the proposed hypothesis of doing nothing, I will (incorrectly) assume that we still have 25 bases in 1960. The number of missiles that the Russians would need in order, hypothetically, to destroy these 25 SAC bases depends on their technology. Assume that their missile has a probability of one in two of successfully completing its countdown and destroying the SAC base at which it is launched. What would we have risked? Simple calculation indicates that our risk would have been substantial. For example, if the Russians had 125 missiles, then even if their firing time were spread out over an hour or so, it would still be possible for Mr. Khrushchev's aides to push 125 buttons and expect that there would be a better than even chance that they would destroy all of the aircraft on the ground at SAC home bases, about one chance in three that only one such base would survive, and a very small probability that two or more bases would survive. The Soviets could well believe that their air defense would easily handle any attacks launched by aircraft from one or two bases. If they are prepared to accept the risk involved in facing an attack from, say, four or five bases, then they need only about 75 missiles, each with a single-shot probability of one-half; if they had 150 missiles, the single-shot probability could be as low as one-third and still be satisfactory to a Soviet planner willing to accept retaliation from four or five surviving bases.

This kind of missile attack is much more calculable than almost any other kind of attack. It is so calculable that many people believe that the results of such an attack can be predicted just by applying well-known principles of engineering and physics. It looks so calculable that even a cautious Soviet planner might believe that he could rely on the correctness of his estimates; thus he might find it the path of caution to attack while the opportunity was still available.

Actually, even with tested missiles, results of attacks are not really mathematically predictable. The probability of extreme variations in performance, the upper and lower limits, cannot be calculated accurately. But laymen or narrow professionals persist in regarding the matter as a simple problem in engineering and physics. Therefore, unless sophisticated objections on the possibilities of intelligence leaks, firing discipline, reliability of the basic data, field degradation, etc., are raised, even an inarticulate Russian general could probably force the following conclusions on a group of hostile, skeptical, and busy civilians, whether they wanted to believe them or not: that in this hypothetical case (where the Russians had 125 missiles, each with a single-shot probability of one-half), if they were to push these 125 buttons and also launch a supplementary coordinated attack with IRBM's and tactical bombers on U.S. and allied overseas bases, there would be a reasonable chance that the Soviet Union would get away scot free; that there would be a good chance that they would suffer very little damage; and that there would be no chance at all that they would suffer as much damage as they suffered in World War II.

Let us consider some of the caveats that this Russian general would have to concede if somebody raised them, and try to judge how serious Khrushchev or the Presidium would find them.

The first is that there be no intelligence leak. Given the small number of missiles involved and the tight security in the Russian empire, this might look like a reasonably safe assumption. But whether the Russians would be willing to rely on our lack of intelligence is very hard to say. The Russians might think it possible for us to have a very senior spy or, even more worrisome, for them to have a defector—possibly in the Presidium itself.

The second caveat concerns firing discipline, that is, that nobody fires either prematurely or too late. If we work on our original assumption that the U.S. posture remains unchanged since 1957, when alerts were measured in hours or so, this is not a rigid requirement. However, if we give ourselves credit for a 15-minute alert, this would mean that the Russian missile is so reliable that when they press the buttons the majority of the missiles are actually ready to be fired. If the Russian missiles have a "hold" capability— that is, if they can be ready some minutes or hours early and then maintain this ready position, this may not be a difficult requirement, although it could decrease the effective reliability. (We are defining a missile's *reliability* here as including the probability that it takes off within a few minutes of the assigned firing time. Given that the Soviet missiles have a "hold" capability, this may not be a much smaller number than if we define reliability as the probability that the missile takes off within a few hours of the assigned firing time.) A small reduction in reliability would simply mean that the Russians would need a few more ICBM's. A large reduction would most likely put the Soviets out of business.

There is an interesting interaction between firing discipline and measures designed to reduce the possibility of intelligence leaks. If the Soviets trained with very realistic exercises so that even the people involved in the exercises could not distinguish until the last minute the exercise from the real thing, then such exercises could be used to disguise preparations for attack. But there would be a tendency for somebody to fire prematurely, perhaps causing an accidental war. If, on the contrary, the Soviets try to prevent this breach of firing discipline by the use of severe threats and indoctrination so that nobody will fire prematurely, then they run the opposite risk that people will refuse to believe the order when it comes, unless alerted ahead of time.

The third caveat is that they must have accurate intelligence about the U.S. military posture. Given U.S. security practices currently in vogue about the position and use of our SAC bases and the ease with which information could be obtained about last minute changes, this also could look feasible. Probably the only requirement is to try to get the information.

Much more important, they need accurate data about themselves—the yield, accuracy, and reliability of their ICBM's, for example. While it is surprisingly hard to get reliable estimates of these quantities, only very sophisticated people will know this. If the Soviets have some extra margin of performance for insurance—that is, if they have a much better technological capability than they need—then they do not require extremely accurate estimates of this capability. On the other hand, if their equipment is just marginally satisfactory, then even though they have an adequate capability they are unlikely to know this.

Last and most important is the question of field degradation. Let us go back to our Russian general's persuasion problem. It is perfectly possible, for example, for this general to take the members of the Presidium out to the range and show them, say, 5 or 10 ICBM's lined up, and ask them to select one and make a cross on a map. The range personnel could proceed to fire that ICBM and hit near enough to the cross to make the general's point. Or even more convincingly, they might fire all 5 or 10 ICBM's at once.

This would be an impressive demonstration, but a question arises. What happens when the missiles are operated in the field by regular military personnel? While the Russians have a tradition of at least initial incompetency (for example, in the Crimean, Japanese, and Finnish wars, as well as in World Wars I and II), they have, since World War II, emphasized reliability of equipment, sometimes at the cost of other performance. One would assume that if they could obtain accuracy and yield at all, they could obtain it reliably. Nevertheless the worry might remain, How far off from range performance will we be?

It should also be noted that so long as our strategic bases are soft, missile attacks present the Russians with possibilities for the use of a postattack blackmail strategy almost as extreme as the one mentioned previously. If the Russians concentrate their attack solely against strategic bases and airburst their weapons (which is the most efficient way to use a weapon against a soft target), there will be no local fallout effects. Then unless one of the weapons goes astray and hits a major city, deaths would be limited to a few million Americans as the result of blast and thermal effects. The Soviets could then point out (unless we had appreciable levels of air offense, air defense, and civil defense surviving) that they could totally *destroy* our country (while we could only *hurt* them), and did we really want to pick this moment to initiate the use of nuclear weapons against open cities?

While it would take a moderately reckless Soviet decisionmaker to press the 125 ICBM buttons even if the assumptions were as favorable as originally hypothesized, it would be even more reckless for the United States to rely on extreme Soviet caution and responsibility as a defense. In any case, our Type 1 Deterrence can be strained, and in some moderately plausible situations even a cautious Soviet government might prefer pressing buttons if the odds were so much in its favor. The mere recognition by U.S. and European decisionmakers of the possibility of such an attack could dominate or distort all international relations.

The actual situation differs from this hypothetical one. As our newspapers report, we have taken many measures to alleviate this problem. It would not be appropriate to discuss here how adequate these measures are and the risks we may or may not be running. The measures we have adopted may or may not give us an adequate factor of safety. In any case it is necessary to react rapidly to changes in the enemy's posture.

The need for quick reaction to even "hypothetical" changes in the enemy's posture is likely to be true for the indefinite future, in spite of the popularity of the theory that once we get over our current difficulties we will have a so-called minimum nuclear deterrent force that will solve the Type 1 Deterrence problem. Some even maintain that it will solve all strategic problems.

A last point will be made about Type 1 Deterrence. When people evaluate the quality of our Type 1 Deterrence they usually ask if it is sufficiently strong to prevent the Soviets from attacking us in cold blood. This is probably misleading. As I tried to point out when discussing the possible consequences of our intervening in Hungary, Type 1 Deterrence can be strained. Thus it is probably best to evaluate the quality of one's Type 1 Deterrence by asking how much strain it could accept and still be depended on. The next topic will indicate that plausible circumstances may arise in which we may wish to indulge in acts that would strain our Type 1 Deterrence.

Type 2 Deterrence (Deterrence of Extreme Provocations)

A quite different calculation is relevant to U.S. Type 2 Deterrence, although it is still a Soviet calculation (but this time a Soviet calculation of an American calculation). The Soviet planner asks himself, If I make this very provocative move, will the Americans strike us? Whether the Soviets then proceed with the contemplated provocation will be influenced by their estimate of the American calculation as to what happens if the tables are reversed. That is, what happens if the Americans strike and damage the Russian strategic air force, and the Russians strike back uncoordinated in the teeth of an alerted U.S. air defense and possibly against an evacuated U.S. population? If this possibility is to be credible to the Soviets, it must be because they recognize that their own Type 1 Deterrence can fail. If Khrushchev is a convinced adherent of the balance-of-terror theory and does not believe that his Type 1 Deterrence can fail, then he may just go ahead with the provocative action.

It is important to realize that the operation of Type 2 Deterrence will involve the possibility that the United States will obtain the first strategic strike or some temporizing move, such as evacuation. Many people talk about the importance of having adequate civil and air defense to back our foreign policy. However, calculations made in evaluating the performance of a proposed civil- and air-defense program invariably assume a Russian surprise attack and—to make the problem even harder—a surprise attack directed mostly against civilians. This is unnecessarily pessimistic, for the calculation in which one looks at a U.S. first strike in retaliation for a Russian provocation is probably more relevant in trying to evaluate the role that the offense and defense play in affecting some important aspects of foreign policy.

Under this assumption, if we have even a moderate nonmilitary defense program, its performance is likely to look impressive to the Russians and probably to most Europeans. For example, the crucial problem of obtaining adequate warning will have been greatly lessened, at least in the eyes of the Soviets. They are also likely to think that we have more freedom than we will have. The Soviets may believe that we are not worried by the possibility that they will get strategic or premature tactical warning. This could be true in spite of the fact that in actual practice such an attack would probably involve a considerable risk that the Soviets would get some warning. Any planning would have to be tempered by the sobering realization that a disclosure or mistake could bring a pre-emptive Russian attack.

The possibility of augmenting our active and passive defense is very important. That is, rather than striking the Russians if they do something very provocative, we might prefer to evacuate our city population to fallout protection, "beef up" our air defense and air offense, and then tell the Russians that we had put ourselves into a much stronger position to initiate hostilities. After we had put ourselves in a position in which the Russian retaliatory strike would inflict much less than a total catastrophe, the Russians would have just three broad classes of alternatives:

1. To initiate some kind of strike.
2. To prolong the crisis, even though it would then be very credible that we would strike if they continued to provoke us.
3. To back down or compromise the crisis satisfactorily.

Hopefully the Soviets would end up preferring the third alternative, because our Type 1 Deterrence would make the first choice sufficiently unattractive and our Type 2 Deterrence would do the same for the second.

Type 3 Deterrence (Deterrence of Moderate Provocation)

The most obvious threat that we could muster under Type 3 Deterrence would be the capability to fight a limited war of some sort. Because this subject is complicated and space is limited, I will not discuss this particular Type 3 Deterrence capability—although it is important and necessary. Instead, I shall consider some of the nonmilitary gambits open to us.

Insofar as day-to-day activities are concerned, the things that seemingly regulate the other man's behavior are nonmilitary. For example, among other things, a potential provocation may be deterred by any of the following effects or reactions:

1. Internal reactions or costs
2. Loss of friends or antagonizing of neutrals
3. Creation or strengthening of hostile coalitions
4. Lowering of the reaction threshold of potential opponents
5. Diplomatic or economic retaliation
6. Moral or ethical inhibitions
7. An increase in the military capability of the potential opponent

Space permits discussion of only the last subject, which is both very important and badly neglected. It has become fashionable among the more sober military experts to regard mobilization capabilities as examples of wishful thinking. And indeed, in the few *hours* or few *days* of a modern war, large-scale production of military goods will not be possible.

PROVOCATION A SPUR TO MILITARY CAPABILITY

What deters the Russians from a series of Koreas and Indo-Chinas? It is probably less the fear of a direct U.S. attack with its current forces than the probability that the United States and her allies would greatly increase both their military strength and their resolve in response to such crises. The deterrent effect of this possibility can be increased by making explicit preparations so that we can increase our strength very rapidly whenever the other side provokes us. For example, in June, 1950, the United States was engaged in a great debate on whether the defense budget should be 14, 15, or 16 billion dollars. Along came Korea. Congress quickly authorized 60 billion dollars, an increase by a factor of four!

No matter what successes the Communist cause had in Korea, that authorization represents an enormous military defeat for the Soviets. However, it was almost three years before that authorization was fully translated into increased expenditures and corresponding military power. It is very valuable to be able to increase our defense expenditures, but this ability becomes many times more valuable if authorizations can be translated into military strength in a year or so. If the Russians know that deterioration in international relations will push us into a crash program, they may be much less willing to let international relations deteriorate. The problem is, Would we have time to put in a useful program? After all, the basic military posture (including installations) must be of the proper sort if it is to be possible to expand it within a year or so to the point where it is prepared to fight a war in addition to being able to deter one. Our current posture (1960) is probably far from optimal for doing this.

If preparations like these were at least moderately expensive and very explicit, the Russians might find it credible that the United States would initiate and carry through such a program if they were provocative even, say, on the scale of Korea or less. The Russians would then be presented with the following three alternatives:

1. They could strike the United States before the buildup got very far. This might look very unattractive, especially since the buildup would almost certainly be accompanied by an increased alert and other measures to reduce the vulnerability of SAC.
2. They could try to match the U.S. program. This would be very expensive.
3. They could accept a position of inferiority. Such an acceptance would be serious, since the United States would now have a "fight the war" capability as well as a "deter the war" capability.

In each case the costs and risks of their provocation would have been increased, and it is likely that the Soviets would take these extra costs and risks into account before attempting any provocation. If they were not deterred, we could launch the crash program. Then we would be in a position to correct the results of their past provocation or at least to deter them in the future from exploiting these results.

It might be particularly valuable to have credible and explicit plans to institute crash programs for civil defense[1] and limited-war capabilities. It seems to be particularly feasible to maintain inexpensive and effective mobilization bases in these two fields, and the institution of a crash program would make it very credible to the Russians, our allies, and neutrals that we would go to war at an appropriate level if we were provoked again.

It is important to understand that we have this asset: the ability to spend large sums of money rapidly. Let us, for example, assume a new Berlin crisis in two or three years. Assume also that the United States has done nothing to improve its Type 2 Deterrence capability, and very little to improve its limited-war capability, but it does have a first-rate Type 1 Deterrence (one that could punish the Soviets if they attacked us, but one that could not protect the United States). Under these circumstances it would be most improbable that we would initiate either a thermonuclear or limited war if the Russians gradually put the squeeze on Berlin. Nevertheless, State Department negotiators would try in all likelihood to get the Soviets to back down by threatening that we would do something very violent—that we would use our military forces. But our negotiators would be afraid to spell out our threat, for nothing that they could present would be both credible and effective.

Even today the Russians have told us that any talk of our maintaining our position in Berlin by force is "bluff." If we send soldiers, they say they will kill them; if we send tanks, they will burn them; if we send bombers, they will destroy our cities. The Soviets are saying that at any level of violence we care to use they can either meet that level on the spot or promise such a severe punishment that we will be deterred. The Russians also point out that Berlin is a chess game, not a poker game, and that everybody can see what our capabilities are.

If the Soviets are right—that our only alternatives are violence or defeat —where defeat would be an acceptance of some new and unsatisfactory status of Berlin, then the Soviets could probably succeed in talking us into adopting a face-saving method of losing Berlin rather than one that would make it clear to all that we had suffered a serious defeat.

In actual fact we do have some very strong cards to play, but if we do not know what these cards are, we may be tricked out of playing them. If we

---

[1] For a discussion of the possibilities, see Herman Kahn, *Some Specific Suggestions for Achieving Early Non-Military Defense Capabilities and Initiating Long-range Programs,* The RAND Corporation, Research Memorandum RM-2206-RC, January 2, 1958, rev. July 1, 1958.

refused to accept a face-saving defeat and the Russians persisted in rubbing our noses in the dirt, then it would be clear to all in NATO that unless we did something spectacular to recover the situation, these nations could no longer rely on us for any kind of protection. Under such circumstances the United States might order an attack. It is much more likely that it would authorize enormous defense budgets, probably at least at the 100-billion-dollars-a-year level. These funds would be designed not only to improve our current posture but also to buy large limited-war forces and such things as civil defense and the corresponding military forces that would give us a credible capability for initiating a war at some appropriate level of violence if a humiliating crisis should be repeated. There would also be enormous pressure under these circumstances on the NATO nations to combine into an even tighter alliance and to mobilize their resources for their defense. This would mean that as in Korea, even if we lost Berlin in the military sense, the Russians would have lost this particular campaign. While Berlin is important ethically and politically, its loss would not compare to the greatly increased power and resolve on the side of the West.

This is one of the major threats we can bring to bear on the Russians. If we are not aware that we have this threat, if we believe that doubling the budget would really mean immediate bankruptcy or other financial catastrophe, then the Russians can present us with alternatives that may in the end result in their winning the diplomatic, political, and foreign-policy victory. It is important that we understand our own strengths as well as our possible weaknesses.

CONCLUSIONS

Even if we have acquired the highest-quality Type 1 Deterrence capability, we must still be able to fight and survive wars as long as it is possible to have such a capability. This is true not only because it is prudent to take out insurance against a war's occurring unintentionally, but also because we must be able both to stand up to the threat of fighting a war and to credibly threaten to initiate one. We must make it risky for the enemy to force us into situations in which we must choose between fighting and appeasing. We must have an "alternative to peace," so long as there is no world government and it is technologically and economically possible to have such an alternative. It is most likely that this "alternative to peace" must include a general-war capability as well as a limited-war capability.

Under current programs the United States may in a few years find itself unwilling to accept a Soviet retaliatory blow, no matter what the provocation. To get into such a situation would be equivalent to disowning our alliance obligations by signing a non-aggression treaty with the Soviets—a non-aggression treaty with almost 200 million American hostages to guarantee performance. Before drifting into such an "alliance," we should ask ourselves, What does it mean to live with this non-aggression treaty? Can we prevent it from being "signed"? Can we delay its "ratification"? Those who would rely on limited means to control possible Soviet provocations must ask themselves the question, What keeps the enemy's counteraction to acceptable limits if there are no credible Type 2 Deterrence capabilities? Those who think of very limited capabilities or mutual-homicide threats either separately or in combination as being sufficient to meet our Type 2 Deterrence problems are ignoring the dynamics of bargaining and conflict situations. When two men or two nations are arguing over something that both feel to be of moderate importance, it is common for things to get out of control, for prestige to become committed, and for threats and counter-threats and actions and counteractions to increase in almost limitless intensity—that is, unless there are internal or external sanctions to set and enforce limits.

These remarks will distress all who, very properly, view the thought of fighting a war with so much horror that they feel uneasy at having even a high-quality deterrent force, much less a credible capability for initiating, fighting, and terminating all kinds of wars. While one can sympathize with this attitude, it is, I believe, close to being irresponsible.

The threat of force has long been an important regulatory factor in international affairs; one cannot remove or greatly weaken this threat without expecting all kinds of unforeseen changes—not all of them necessarily for the better. True, many of the measures that preserve our ability to fight and survive wars may turn out to be temporary expedients that will not solve our long-run security problems, but this does not mean they are not important. You cannot reach 1970 or 1975 if you do not successfully pass through 1960 and 1965. If we neglect our short-term problems, we are bound to run serious risks of a disastrous deterioration in the international situation or in our own posture. This, in turn, may make it impossible to arrive at a reasonable, stable state.

In fact, insofar as the balance-of-terror theory is correct, if any nation actually is militarily provocative, then, no matter what our previous threats have been, we must meet that behavior by using limited means or simply allow that nation to get away with whatever it is trying to do. The aggressor. will realize this too and gain confidence from the realization. For this reason any attempt to use threats of mutual homicide to control an aggressor's behavior (short of trying to deter him from an attack on one's own country) is ill advised. Even if one means that threat seriously, it will still not be credible to the enemy or ally—particularly if the challenge is in any way ambiguous.

Since it now seems most unlikely that the Soviet menace will go away of itself and since we have eschewed preventive war as a possibility, we must seek the solution to our problems along the path of some degree of coexistence or collaboration. To do this effectively we must appear extremely competent to the Soviet leaders. They must feel that we are putting adequate attention and resources into meeting our military, political, and economic problems. This is not a question of attempting to bargain from strength, but one of looking so invulnerable to blackmail and aggressive tactics that Soviet leaders will feel it is worth while to make agreements and foolish not to. We must look much more dangerous as an opponent than as a collaborator, even an uneasy collaborator.

I have the impression that up to about 1956–57 the average senior Russian had an enormous respect for U.S. planners and decisionmakers—which they now (in 1960) have begun to lose. Many of their comments on remarks made by some of our military and political leaders are contemptuous. In the precarious present and the even more precarious future it would be well to go to some trouble not only *to be* competent as an antagonist to the Russians, but *to look* competent.

Ideally, winning the cold war would mean the establishment of peaceful, democratic, and prosperous nations everywhere and the complete elimination of all international conflicts of greater significance than those that, for example, occasionally plague U.S.-British relations. No sober student of the international scene visualizes anything of this sort occurring! Even a more limited objective—the attainment of a physical security that is independent of Soviet rationality and responsibility—is probably unattainable. There is no acceptable way to protect ourselves from a psychotic Soviet decisionmaker who launches a surprise attack without making rational calculations.

But the situation is worse than this. It is most unlikely that the world can live with an uncontrolled arms race lasting for several decades. It is not that we could not match Soviet expenditures; it is simply that as technology advances and as weapons become more powerful and more diverse, it is most likely that there will have to be at least implicit agreements on their use, distribution, and character if we are not to run unacceptably high risks of unauthorized or irresponsible behavior. No matter how antagonistic the Soviets feel toward us, they have common interests with us in this field. This does not mean that they will not try to exploit the common danger to obtain unilateral advantages; it simply means that there is an important area for bargaining here, one that we must fully exploit.

As a prerequisite to exploiting it we must do our homework. We must know what we are trying to achieve, the kinds of concessions that we can afford to give, and the kinds of concessions that we insist on getting from the Soviets. All of this will require, among other things, much-higher-quality preparations for negotiations than have been customary.

The intellectual quality of discussion could probably be improved if criticism were both more discerning and more savage. We should learn to distinguish between first-strike and second-strike forces, between Type 1 and Type 2 Deterrence, between the use of credible and silly threats of retaliation, between "bankruptcy" and a reduction in standards of living, between sober and reliable measures and desperate gambles or "calculated risks," between deterrence by assumption and deterrence by objectively capable systems, etc.

Aside from the ideological differences and the problem of security itself, there do not seem to be any other objective quarrels between the United States and Russia that justify the risks and costs to which we subject each other. The big thing that the Soviet Union and the United States have to fear from each other is fear itself. (I am making some very optimistic assumptions. One is that the Soviets would really be willing to give up any hope of world domination to be achieved by the use of military force. Another is that they would give up their curious notion that the only satisfactory *status quo* is a situation in which the Soviet World increases every year and the Free World decreases, and that all kinds of subversive and violent activities are part of this peacetime *status quo*. On the other hand, our understandable hope that one day the satellite nations will be liberated does not look to the Soviets like a reasonable acceptance of *status quo*.)

Aside from the caveats given above about Soviet and United States expectations and hopes, and the problem of security itself, both the Soviet Union and the United States are *status quo* powers. In this respect, the situation is quite different from what it was in World War I when all the great powers competed in trying to carve out empires for themselves, both inside and outside Europe. Today a normal increase of two or three years in the gross national product of either Soviet Russia or the United States is of much greater significance both militarily and economically than quite sizable additions or subtractions of territory. This means that we can both afford to be relaxed about changes in our respective "spheres of influence." But even if it were conceded that all we have to fear is fear, this would not imply that the problem is simple, or even that it can be eliminated by any kind of arrangements that are practical for the next decade or so. It is only to say that there do not seem to be any fundamental blocks to making things more manageable and safer than the current arrangement, which is an almost uncontrolled arms race ameliorated by some implicit (and vague) agreements and some unilateral actions.

Even if we arrive at some arms-control agreements that eliminate the most dangerous aspects of the competition, we may still need the threat of force to regulate the minor clashes that occur. While many people are suggesting various versions of a "rule by law" to prevent minor clashes from becoming major ones, I am not very hopeful that we can succeed totally. Such efforts are to be encouraged—in fact they are indispensable—but they can alleviate the problem only to the point where inevitable conflicts of interest can be handled, not eliminated. We will still need a balance of terror or other military sanctions to persuade those who would be tempted to use violence to use other machinery instead. If the balance is to be stable and not subject to being overturned by minor changes in tactics, posture, technological innovation, or cheating on arms-control agreements, then initially it will have to be based on a massive program.

However, we must also take seriously the problem of alleviating the conflict by arms control and international agreement. We do not have unlimited time. Our problems are being increased rapidly by many things, including the mounting rate of technological progress, the "revolution of rising expectations," increasing nationalism, and an increasing diffusion of the newer military technologies. It is possible that there may be some invention, discovery, or crisis that simply cannot be handled even momentarily in our present international society. Progress is so fast, the problems are so unprecedented, and the lead-times for cultural assimilation are so long that it is difficult to believe that muddling through will work. We will need much better mechanisms than we have had for forward thinking, imaginative research into problems of strategy and foreign policy, and anticipating future developments and planning to meet them.

These mechanisms can be made available. The tools actually or potentially available to the analyst, planner, and decisionmaker, both organizational and technical, are many times better than anything we have had before. It is just barely possible that with determined efforts by large numbers of responsible people we can achieve enough to make a significant difference. The survival of our civilization may depend on this effort's being made. Let us hope that it can be.

DETERRENCE BY

DENIAL AND PUNISHMENT

Glenn H. Snyder

I. INTRODUCTION

The prominence given to "deterrence" as a central objective of United States national security policy is traceable directly to the development of nuclear weapons and long-range airpower. Identification of the concept with air-nuclear technology has fostered the notion that deterrence is accomplished primarily, if not exclusively, by threatening the enemy with overwhelming punishment for his aggression, or at least with costs greater than the value he attaches to his strategic objective. This focus on the cost factor has tended to divert attention away from the deterrent qualities of military forces whose function is chiefly to contest the control of territory and population rather than simply to inflict costs. I refer, of course, to ground forces, tactical air forces, and naval forces. An absolutely sharp distinction between the punishment and denial functions cannot be made, nor can either function be attributed exclusively to any particular kind of military force. Strategic airpower can assist in denying territory to the enemy by striking at the sources of supply of the enemy's ground forces. Land power obviously punishes in the process of attempting to block the enemy's ground assault.[1] The difference lies in the dominant function: the primary function of strategic air-nuclear power is to reduce the enemy's will either to start a war or to continue one once started, by posing the prospect of unacceptable costs; compared to this function, the effect of strategic air action on the enemy's capability to fight on the ground is incidental. Similarly, the dominant utility of surface forces lies in their capacity to deny the enemy his territorial objective; the costs they inflict in so doing are instrumental and subsidiary to this primary function.

Prior to the air-nuclear age, the functions of punishment and denial were more or less inseparable in that they were both performed by the same set of weapons.[2] Long range airpower partially separated the function of

---

[1] Other forms of military power which have deterrent significance, such as air defense, civil defense, and war potential, are deliberately excluded from this analysis in the interest of brevity and simplicity.

[2] This statement is subject to some qualification. By such measures as naval blockade, long-range shelling of cities and the taking of hostages, the non-combatant population

punishment from the function of contesting the control of territory, by making possible the assault of targets far to the rear, the relation of which to the land battle might be quite tenuous. Nuclear weapons vastly increased the degree of punishment which could be inflicted by airpower. The joining of these two streams of technological development greatly increased the relative importance of prospective *cost* as a deterring factor and reduced the importance of possible failure in the aggressive enterprise. Moreover, it forced nuclear powers to make a conscious choice between punishment capacity and denial capacity in the allocation of resources for military purposes. At one level of analysis this choice can be posed as one between a capability to deter and a capability to defend territory at minimum cost if deterrence should fail. With this choice, however, this paper is not concerned. It deals only with the choice between deterrents, that is, with the effects of different kinds of military force upon the probability of enemy aggression. Although the deterrent utility of denial forces stems primarily from their utility in defense of territory, the two kinds of utility are theoretically separable. In sum, the paper will attempt to explore the deterrent effects of denial forces, compare the essential natures of punishment deterrence and denial deterrence, and show how the two forms of deterrence interact in either mutual support or competition. It is hoped the discussion will suggest some criteria for making optimum choices between the two types of deterrence in different situations and contingencies. The term "punishment deterrence," incidentally, does not refer only to deterrence by the threat of "massive retaliation"; it encompasses all threats of nuclear reprisal whatever their degree of severity.

The paper is not concerned with the deterrence of a direct Soviet assault on the United States. Deterrence of this contingency is almost exclusively an airpower job (with assists from civil defense, continental air defense, and naval strategic capabilities—the last-named destined, no doubt, to play an increasing role in the future). The analysis deals entirely with those contingencies which a denial capability can play a significant role in deterring— namely Soviet aggressive moves around the periphery of its empire in Europe and Asia.

II. PUNISHMENT AND DENIAL DETERRENCE COMPARED

The deterrent value of any particular kind in military power rests upon its effects on four essential factors in the enemy's cost-gain calculus. In considering any aggressive move, the Soviets must assess (1) the probability of a

---

of an opponent could be directly subjected to punishment or threats of punishment which bore little or no relation to the land battle. And of course the practice of reprisals to punish infractions of the rules of international law has a long history.

military response,[3] (2) the costs they can expect to suffer as a result of the response, (3) their valuation of the territorial prize, and (4) the probability of success in their territorial aim. The differential effect of punishment and denial deterrents on each of these factors is shown in the following table. The effects are stated with excessive absoluteness in the interest of highlighting them; it is to be understood that the effects listed in each category are merely shorthand references to differences in *tendency*, as compared to the other category.

Punishment	*Denial*
(1) Generally low	(1) High
(2) High	(2) Relatively low
(3) Constant	(3) Constant
(4) High	(4) Low

Certain qualifications should be made immediately. The differences with respect to factors 1 and 2 are greatest when the punishment envisaged is "massive" in degree and when the denial strategy contemplates the use of conventional forces only. If the punishment threat is one of limited or "selective" reprisals, the Soviets must expect a higher probability of its being carried out as well as lower costs. Similarly, if the denial strategy includes the use of nuclear weapons tactically, the values assigned to factors 1 and 2 tend to move closer to those obtaining in a punishment strategy. While the table states that the Soviets' valuation of the prize is "constant"—that is, the same whether they expect a punishment or a denial response—in reality their valuation may be affected by their expectation regarding the probable response. For example, either type of response is likely to involve some damage to the assets located on the territorial objective, but to a different degree, and the Soviets' valuation will be affected by their estimate of the probable damage. Although the enemy can expect relatively low costs (factor 2) if the defenders' response is limited to an attempt to deny him conquest, he must recognize that any violent conflict, however limited its beginning, may eventually become a full-scale one. Therefore, even the prospect of a response initially limited to denial must raise a specter of costs for the enemy well beyond those which the surface forces themselves are capable of inflicting. Despite such qualifications (to which several others might be added) the table does illustrate an important point: that denial deterrents, i.e., surface forces, tend to have moderate effects on three factors in the calculus (1, 2, and 4), whereas a punishment deterrent has an extreme effect on only

---

[3] I.e., the "credibility" of a threat to respond. The best discussion of the credibility function in deterrence is W. W. Kaufmann, "The Requirements of Deterrence," in W. W. Kaufmann (ed.), *Military Policy and National Security*, Princeton, 1956, pp. 12–39.

one (2—possible costs). If a denial capacity tends to pose relatively low costs for the enemy, he has nevertheless to consider the near-certainty of some violent response and the chances that he will be frustrated in his objective. The probability of some response to the aggression is higher for denial deterrence than for punishment deterrence because the cost of the response to us is likely to be much lower and because there is some chance of our being able to frustrate the aggression. With punishment deterrence, on the other hand, especially when the punishment threatened is "massive," the cost to us of carrying out our threat is certain to be high (as a result of the enemy's counter-retaliation), and to contribute nothing or very little directly to the prevention of conquest. While the making of a nuclear punishment threat may be rational if we think it will considerably reduce the probability of enemy attack, its actual fulfillment is likely to seem irrational after the enemy becomes committed to the enjoined act, since the enemy will probably obtain his objective in any case, and is likely to inflict retaliatory costs upon us for which we will be able to show no corresponding gain.[4] Therefore, we will have a strong incentive to go back on our commitment to the reprisal, and the enemy can be expected to anticipate this.

To have an adequate denial capability, preferably one situated near or in a threatened area, is the surest sign we can make to the enemy that the area is valued highly by us. For if we want to hold some place badly, we will want to have some rational means for dealing with the situation in case the punishment deterrent fails. Although there are some reasons (to be explored later) why a denial capability may detract from the credibility of the punishment deterrent, this obvious indication of high valuation provided by a ready denial capability can only support the entire deterrent posture, including the threat of punishment. There are several reasons why a strong denial force may enhance the will to carry out a punishment strategy—not the least of which is that it would mitigate or eliminate an important factor eroding that will: the low likelihood that loss of the territorial prize can be prevented by punishment action alone. Even if our denial force were incapable of holding, the enemy would have to reckon that the stronger it is, the more likely we are to believe that the application of strategic airpower would be the marginal factor that would clinch victory.

Denial deterrence presents the enemy with a threat which is more easily calculable than punishment deterrence. The essential calculation in denial deterrence is a comparison of relative capabilities, the intent to use the available capabilities for defense purposes being fairly certain, for reasons noted earlier. While there are some aspects of military capability, such as

---

[4] Conceivably, a gain might be counted in terms of strengthening the credibility of our retaliatory threat with respect to other contingencies. However, the exchange of reprisals would have to be very limited indeed to find justification on this ground. An adequate civil defense system of course would make the decision to carry out the reprisals much less agonizing, and the threat to carry them out more credible.

morale, which can hardly be appraised with any reliability short of the ultimate test of battle, military capabilities in general are composed of rather concrete elements which an efficient intelligence system can assess with some confidence. For the Russians, a comparison of capabilities is made easier by the liberal release of public information about them in Western countries. The Soviets' calculation of the punishment deterrent threat, on the other hand, is more difficult since it depends largely on their estimate of our intentions. The assessment of intentions is a highly uncertain business, involving such intangible and unknowable factors as value preferences, the degree and direction of possible irrationality, emotional behavior in a crisis, etc. If we can face the Communists with ground and tactical forces obviously capable of blocking territorial conquest, deterrence is assured with far greater certainty than can ever be the case with punishment deterrence. For the usual object of aggression is some territorial prize and if attainment of the prize is foreclosed, attack is obviously foolish; if conquest is possible, there is always the chance that aggression will be risked, even in the face of possibly very high costs.[5]

There is a certain disadvantage to the defending side in the relative certainty of the denial calculus, however, which is worth pointing out. If our denial capability is not strong enough to defend successfully, the Russians probably will know this and it will have very little deterrent value, even though such value will rise steeply once our denial forces become large enough to be effective. The uncertainty connected with punishment deterrence, on the other hand, will enjoin prudence upon the enemy; even though he thinks there is little chance of our punishment threat being carried out, he can never be sure. The grievous deprivations which he might well suffer if the punishment were actually imposed make it all the more important that he make substantial allowance for his own possible miscalculation. Therefore, a punishment deterrent threat will have some deterrent utility even though its general credibility may be very low.

It should also be noted that a deterrence policy emphasizing denial capability is likely to be considerably more expensive in preparation than a policy based primarily on threats of punishment. The forces for punishment deterrence are necessary in any case to deter the Soviets from using their own strategic nuclear power, i.e., for "basic deterrence." If threats of nuclear punishment are used to deter other Soviet moves as well, they are not likely to require much additional expenditure beyond that necessary for basic deterrence. But deterrence by a strategy of denial imposes additional costs, and substantial ones, over and above those necessary for basic deterrence. In considering these additional costs, however, it must be remembered that

---

[5] It is assumed that the enemy will not be able to dissuade us from using an effective denial capability by accompanying his act of aggression with a threat of nuclear obliteration should we respond at all. This is a possibility, but we will have reason to believe that our own nuclear threat will deter him from carrying out his.

forces for denial deterrence have additional utility beyond their utility for deterrence—namely their utility for "defense" in case deterrence should fail.

When both kinds of deterrence are in use, the deterrent effects of each may be divided into *direct* and *indirect* effects. Direct effects may be subdivided further into *denial* effects (impact on the enemy's perception of his chances of successfully completing the particular territorial conquest) and *cost* effects (influence on the enemy's estimate of the cost of an aggressive move). The indirect effects are the influence of one deterrent upon the effectiveness of another. *Complementary* effects tend to support other deterrents; *depreciatory* effects tend to undermine them.[6] It is convenient to discuss these various effects first in the context of the deterrence of major aggression, and then in connection with deterrence of minor enemy moves. Deterrence in NATO strategy—in particular, the deterrent interaction of the "sword" and the "shield"—forms a useful starting point.

III. DETERRENCE OF MAJOR AGGRESSION IN WESTERN EUROPE

It has been officially stated that the primary objective of NATO military strategy is to deter Soviet aggression in the Western European area.[7] The chief instrument of deterrence is the "sword," composed of the U.S. Strategic Air Command, the Bomber Command of the Royal Air Force and such British and U.S. naval forces as are able to contribute to a long-range bombing offensive on the territory of the Soviet Union. However, NATO strategists, notably General Lauris Norstad, Supreme Commander of NATO's military forces, also ascribe a significant deterrent role to the "shield," the forward line of ground, sea and tactical air forces guarding the East-West frontier.[8] It is appropriate, therefore, to examine the deterrent functions of the shield in terms of the categories outlined above.

Clearly, the existing central shield ground force of some 14 or 15 divisions (less than 10 of which are effective divisions), or even the proposed force of 30 divisions, is, by itself, incapable of denying any territory to the Soviets

---

[6] To speak of both complementary and depreciatory effects resulting from a given policy is not to be contradictory; these terms refer to opposing sets of considerations which should be weighed and compared in appraising the deterrent effectiveness of the policy.

[7] See testimony of General Lauris Norstad in U.S. Congress, House Committee on Appropriations, *Mutual Security Appropriations for 1959,* Hearings, 85th Congress, 2nd Session, p. 560.

[8] By far the most significant portion of the shield is that consisting of the American, British and other allied forces deployed on the "central front" in West Germany, and it is this portion to which the word "shield" refers in the present discussion unless otherwise specified. Technically, the shield also includes active local forces on the northern and southern fronts (Scandinavia, Greece, Turkey and Italy). In addition, various NATO countries have some active forces not deployed in the forward line which could be brought up to support the shield, and also reserves which are mobilizable in varying periods of time.

that they wish to take with full force. It could inflict costs on an attacker, and if nuclear weapons were used, these costs would be high. But they probably would not be high enough, by themselves, to dissuade the Soviets from attacking, since the Soviets would be sure of gaining the valuable prize of a substantial part of Western Europe. Neither would these costs be significant as a supplement to the costs which might be inflicted by activation of the "sword": If "massive retaliation" were to be carried out, the costs from this source would be so high that the Soviets would hardly be concerned about the direct military costs suffered at the hands of NATO ground forces. The utility of the shield in deterring major aggression must be looked for not in its direct denial capability, but rather in its indirect *complementary* effects —that is, in the extent to which it strengthens the probable or evident willingness of the West to activate the strategic airpower deterrent.

Complementary Effects of the NATO "Shield"

One complementary function is that of the "trip-wire": the placement of even small contingents of U.S. and British ground forces on the East-West border will put the Soviets on notice that any attack on Western Europe will immediately involve the United States and Britain, and will increase the chances that strategic air retaliation will take place. This effect depends not on the physical size of the shield, but on its composition—the fact that it contains forces belonging to the countries which will take the ultimate decision on strategic retaliation. Such forces commit the national honor and prestige of their countries, to a greater degree than if this commitment rested only on a treaty containing a somewhat equivocal promise to defend continental allies.

A force considerably smaller than the existing one, and involving only American and British forces, would be sufficient for a trip-wire. It is sometimes argued that a part of the present NATO shield is therefore redundant, since it contributes nothing to the trip-wire and cannot hope to cope with a serious Russian ground attack. But forces beyond those necessary for the trip-wire and yet too weak to defend against full-scale attack nevertheless do contribute to the deterrence of such an attack. Facing only a thin barrier, the Soviets might feel that they could breach it and overrun continental Europe before NATO could reach a decision to retaliate. The Western powers would then be faced with a *fait accompli;* their problem would then be one of undoing a conquest rather than preventing one. Strategic nuclear retaliation in such circumstances would seem quite futile. Retaliation against the Soviet Union itself could hardly be expected to get the Red Army out of Western Europe after it had seized complete control; on the other hand, if retaliation could be undertaken before the completion of conquest, Western leaders might retain some hope that retaliation could stop the Red Army's advance, either by drying up its sources of supply, or by withering the Soviets' will to continue the fighting. Any attempt to force their with-

drawal by strategic nuclear action after the Soviets had overrun Western
Europe would probably require the nuclear bombing of targets in Western
Europe, including major cities, a move which the British and American
leadership would find extremely repugnant. It follows from this reasoning
that any delay in the Soviet advance which a substantial "shield" might
enforce would increase the likelihood of strategic nuclear retaliation.

A delay of the Soviet advance enforced by a heroic delaying action by
American and European ground forces would provide a maximum of
emotional fuel, as well as the time, for the American and British publics to
experience a "slow burn," an emotional mobilization that might well be the
marginal factor which would persuade an indecisive leadership to take
retaliatory action.

Even though the leadership did shrink from "massive" retaliation, it would
experience severe moral, as well as popular and military pressure to do
something to help the forces resisting the Soviet advance. This might well
take the form of less-than-massive strategic nuclear action, designed either
to support threats of heavier strikes should the Soviets continue their aggression, or to contribute something to the land battle. Besides increasing the
chances that such a decision would be taken, a stubborn delaying action
would also provide time for a series of reprisals to be effective—that is, to
convince the Soviets that further fighting would cause them to suffer costs
beyond the value of their prospective gain. Our will to continue the reprisals
presumably would become more evident with the passage of time; in addition, the less territory given up to the Red Army before and during the
reprisals, the less gain the Soviets would have to give up in heeding the
ultimatum which no doubt would accompany the reprisals. Indeed, a substantial surface capability probably is essential to the success of a strategy of
limited nuclear reprisals. If the aggressor can foresee successful conquest
with near-certainty, with negligible costs in surface action, he will break off
his attack and retire to the *status quo* only if he anticipates costs from the
nuclear reprisals greater than the value of the objective. Or, if the defender
threatens reprisal costs approximately equal to the value of the objective,
the aggressor will desist only if he foresees with certainty that the threatened
reprisals will actually be carried out. But if the aggressor must also consider
a prospect of substantial costs in the ground warfare, he may well be deterred even if he is somewhat less than certain that the reprisals will take
place, or if the threatened reprisals promise costs to him less than the value
of his objective. And of course the less the severity of the reprisals which
the defender thinks it necessary to threaten in order to deter, the greater
the credibility of the threat. In sum, when punishment deterrence rests on
the prospect of reprisals of considerably less than massive proportions (and
this is the prospect which the enemy, if he is realistic, must consider most
probable, however much our massive threat is reiterated), then the direct

costs which the enemy must expect in the surface battle provide an important complement to the punishment deterrent, by increasing the credibility of the latter, and by reducing its required credibility and/or severity.

The enemy is most apt to think we are serious about carrying out massive retaliation if we clearly reserve this extreme response for contingencies which seem to threaten our very survival. If, in other words, we make provision for a limited response to relatively minor Soviet encroachments—at substantial cost in preparedness—we make it easier for the Soviets to believe that we really mean to retaliate with strategic nuclear airpower in the event of a major attack. Such obvious qualification and limitation of the all-out threat will show that we are not relying entirely on bluff, that we are creating, at considerable expense, a capability for rational response to a variety of challenges. Perceiving this, the Soviets are likely to think that we regard massive retaliation as being also a rational response in those contingencies for which we have created no effective alternative means of action. Too much reliance on strategic nuclear power and "massive" threats, on the other hand, will generate a certain amount of "threat inflation"—a depreciation of the value of all such threats even when applied to the most serious transgressions.

The enemy may well doubt that we will set off all-out war until it is clear to us that the Soviet objective is conquest of Western Europe, and until we are sure that this intention cannot be moderated by negotiation. If we have a shield force which can provide the time for the enemy's intent to become clear, and for negotiations to dissuade him from this intent, massive retaliation can be reserved for circumstances in which we are sure the enemy's objective is both far-reaching and unshakeable; having been so reserved, this threat must seem more believable.

A strong shield, even though insufficient to hold against a large-scale assault, would nevertheless force the Soviets to undertake a considerable build-up near the point of attack, thus providing advance warning which would serve to alert NATO's air and civil defense systems and perhaps allow some reinforcement of the shield in the danger area. In addition, the enemy would know that such a concentration of his forces would make them an inviting target for tactical atomic weapons.

The complementary effects mentioned so far have been those which have to do with enhancing the Soviet expectation of *deliberate* nuclear retaliation. Other effects flow from a raising of the chances that an attack will generate conditions favorable to an *accidental* spiraling of the war to all-out proportions. In general, the Soviets must consider that the longer the ground battle is prolonged, the more time and the more occasions there will be for such accidents to occur. One of the more likely "accidents" might be the provocative use of nuclear weapons by some battlefield commander acting under the extreme stress of battle, or deliberately disobeying orders in order to save his unit. As Bernard Brodie has pointed out, the distinguishing feature of the limitation of modern war is that it involves the deliberate withholding from action of weapons of great military effectiveness.[9] The more effective the delaying action of the ground forces, the more military commanders are likely to chafe under such "unnatural" restrictions which, if lifted or ignored, would (it might seem to them) make all the difference between winning or losing the territorial prize.

Not only the increase in available time, but also the rise in the intensity of battle which would result from any strengthening of the "shield" would be conducive to the inadvertent initiation of full-scale war. If tactical nuclear weapons were used under some tacit or explicit limitation on permissible targets, there would always be the chance of some accidental violation of the limitations being interpreted by the other side as intentional, which might lead to a fairly rapid raising of the limitations to the point where one side or the other began to fear an imminent all-out attack, causing it to unleash a full-scale thermonuclear assault to gain the advantage of the first strike. Some tolerance of infractions could be counted on, since both sides would wish to avoid all-out war, but there is no assurance that any particular accident or mistake would be within the limits of tolerance.

Depreciatory Effects of the NATO "Shield"

Against the "complementary" deterrent utility of surface forces must be set their "depreciatory" effects—that is, the considerations which would support a tendency for them to *reduce* the chances of all-out war, or reduce the credibility of the threat of nuclear punishment. In the preceding discussion a number of reasons were advanced why the "cushion of time" provided by denial capacity may support threats of nuclear punishment in Europe. It is possible to argue on other counts, however, that the longer the time between the initiation and the completion of conquest, the less the chances that strategic nuclear retaliation would take place. A strong delaying action on the ground would provide more time for intra- and inter-governmental consultation about a retaliatory response. But nuclear retaliation as the result of a carefully considered decision might seem less likely than retaliation as a more or less automatic response, especially when the retaliation being considered is of massive dimensions. The terrible consequences of all-out nuclear war would no doubt be imagined very vividly by leaders when they had time for serious deliberation—more vividly, perhaps, than if the decision had to be a quick one, in which case it would be more likely that prior plans and policy declarations would be carried out more or less automatically. Since most of these plans and declarations have been oriented around the principle of deterrence by massive punishment, it may well be doubted whether they are grounded on full and adequate consideration of the costs

---

[9] Bernard Brodie, "More About Limited War," *World Politics,* Vol. X, No. 1 (October, 1957), pp. 114–115.

involved in carrying them out if deterrence should fail—costs which no doubt would be visualized with greater clarity in the process of making a deliberate decision whether or not to accept them. If a quick decision is needed, the civilian leadership of the United States and Britain are likely to rely heavily on the counsel of their military advisers whose thinking will be heavily conditioned by the existing plans and who can be expected to favor the quick application of all the available power. If some time is available, however, the voices of caution are more likely to make themselves heard and with greater effect. In addition, time would give the Soviets opportunity to inhibit a retaliatory response by suggesting negotiations, threatening counter-retaliation, or promising "peaceful co-existence" with Britain and the United States.

A thesis more often heard is that surface and tactical forces tend to erode the credibility of the retaliatory threat by providing the means for an alternative, less costly, response. It does seem plausible that if the Western powers were to create enough surface capability to block successfully a full-scale Soviet intrusion into Western Europe, the credibility of our threat to retaliate massively in that event would decline. Such a capability would indicate two things: (1) a *desire* to avoid the consequences of all-out nuclear war, and (2) an *opportunity* to respond effectively to a major Soviet challenge by means which would not necessarily precipitate a thermonuclear holocaust. The Soviets would still have to recognize some chance of all-out war as a consequence of aggression by them, if only because strategic nuclear warfare might still be set off by accident or by mutual fears of pre-emptive strategic attack, but they could count on its probability being rather low. Similar statements could be made with respect to less-than-major aggressions: if we have sufficient surface forces to deal with them effectively, the Russians will hardly expect us to deliberately and unnecessarily compound our own costs by even limited strategic nuclear action. But presumably the Soviets would be deterred anyway by the unlikelihood of their making any territorial gains.

Of course the direct deterrent effect of surface and tactical forces depends on the *Soviet* appraisal of their strength, not our own estimate of their capability relative to the enemy's. But some depreciation of the strategic nuclear deterrent may occur even when the Soviets give the defending force little or no chance of holding. If the Western powers were to give the impression that *they* think the shield can hold (whatever the Russian appraisal) and obviously base their plans primarily on a strategy of denial, the credibility of their massive retaliation threats would also be weakened, for they would then be seen to have created what *they* regard as an effective alternative response. Against this, however, the Russians would have to weigh all the factors mentioned earlier as "complementary effects," including the point that the presence of substantial denial forces in an area provides solid evidence of a high valuation of the area, which would indicate at least a strong possibility that we would be willing to invoke strategic retaliation should the denial forces prove incapable of holding when put to the test. It might be argued that the greatest depreciatory effects on the punishment threat occur with either a very large or a very small denial force in or near an area—the former because it would provide a viable alternative; the latter because it would betray a low valuation.

The credibility of the Big Deterrent may be affected not only by the physical existence of the shield, but also by declaratory statements about the role of this force in western strategy. The leading spokesman on NATO strategy is General Lauris Norstad, the Supreme Commander, Allied Powers in Europe. General Norstad ascribes three primary functions to the shield, as follows:

1. To hold or delay a Soviet attack "until the total weight of the retaliatory power could be brought to bear."

2. To deter wars "arising from miscalculation, border incident or probing operation invited by weakness on the NATO periphery."

3. To provide "essential military and political flexibility."

On this third point, General Norstad has stated:

> If we concentrate only on weapons and forces for general war, we deny to ourselves the capacity to dispose of lesser situations, and could suggest an opportunity for limited aggressions, which ultimately could bring us disaster. In other words, we must be able to respond to less than ultimate incidents with decisive, but less than ultimate means. By this I am not suggesting that limited wars are possible along this sensitive frontier of NATO. It would be very unlikely, I feel, that a serious incident could remain limited.[10]

These statements are notable, first, because they do not claim for the shield any function or capability of blocking a full-scale Soviet advance on the ground, as an alternative to invoking massive nuclear punishment. Rather, primary reliance for preventing conquest of the area is to be placed on strategic airpower, and the defensive function of the shield is only to "hold until the total weight of the retaliatory power could be brought to bear." [11] In other words, airpower and nuclear weapons are given a major

---

[10] U.S. Congress, Senate Committee on Foreign Relations, *Mutual Security Act of 1958*, Hearings, 85th Congress, 2nd Session, p. 187.

[11] The precise reason why time is necessary to allow retaliatory power to be "brought to bear" is not stated by General Norstad. The words quoted suggest that he has in mind the time necessary to make the decision to retaliate and perhaps to allow for repeated strikes by retaliatory forces. Conceivably, he may contemplate a strategy of successive limited nuclear reprisals against the Soviet Union, spaced in time to allow the Soviet leaders maximum opportunity to change their minds before suffering the ultimate costs. Other statements by General Norstad and other spokesmen indicate that the shield must hold until enough time has elapsed for the retaliation to "take effect." This seems to connote something rather different: that time is necessary to allow for sufficient attrition of the Red Army's sources and means of supply to bring its advance to a halt, and perhaps also to bring about a sufficient degree of suffering,

denial capacity and role, with the surface forces of the shield playing only a supporting role. Whatever the validity of the implicit thesis—that strategic air-nuclear power can prevent or undo the conquest of territory—to describe the shield as a necessary component in a "winning" strategy of nuclear retaliation, rather than as an alternative to such a strategy, tends to minimize its depreciatory effect on the nuclear deterrent. In fact, it gives positive support to the Big Deterrent by providing additional evidence to the Russians that we have a motive other than punishment for invoking strategic nuclear retaliation in case of war in Europe.

The contrary must be said of point 3,[12] for here General Norstad is indicating the desirability and possibility of a less-than-massive response. He is saying, in effect, that "lesser situations" and "limited aggressions" will not or may not be answered with massive retaliation, that an alternative response, to be provided by the shield, is necessary. That General Norstad recognized the depreciatory effect of such statements on the credibility of the Big Deterrent is indicated by the last two sentences that have been quoted, denying any implication that a limited war in Europe is possible. This obviously creates a contradiction, for if there are going to be "less than ultimate" incidents requiring "less than ultimate" means, surely any war resulting from the use of such means could only be described as a "limited war." The contradiction perhaps can be explained as indicating General Norstad's desire to avoid any undercutting of the Big Deterrent by his remarks about "less than ultimate" incidents and means, and perhaps also a desire to avoid contradicting the official dogma—that any major aggression in Europe will set off a general nuclear war.

Other statements by General Norstad on this point carry somewhat richer overtones. Take, for example, the following:

> I think it is essential that the West have the means of dealing with less than ultimate incidents, with something other than massive retaliation. We must have some intermediate means. We must have some choice, some option, between all or nothing. The shield, we feel, is the minimum force which is necessary to give us that capability. I am not

destruction, and consequent loss of morale in the Soviet Union to make its leadership willing to capitulate. Apparently, General Norstad did not intend to refer to any of the other benefits of time which were discussed above under the rubric of "complementary effects." For him to have mentioned these benefits, which have to do with increasing the likelihood of a massive response rather than supporting its effectiveness after it is initiated, might have weakened the retaliatory threat, since it would have implied that a massive response was something less than certain in the absence of a strong shield.

[12] Point 2 on General Norstad's list, in which he refers to the deterrence of "border incidents" and "probing operations" will be discussed later in this paper under the heading of "Deterrence of Minor Aggression in Western Europe." General Norstad apparently had in mind somewhat more serious contingencies in his Point 3, i.e., aggressions more serious than "border incidents" but not serious enough to warrant an all-out response.

suggesting that we can have a limited war, because I do not think that is possible in the NATO area. It is much too critical an area, regardless of what the Russians may decide. They may decide they want to keep a war limited, but it is my judgment that in a very short time it could not be kept limited. However, if we have the means of dealing with these less-than-ultimate incidents, with less-than-ultimate means, I think we will prevent those incidents from occurring, unless of course there is a decision to go to World War III.[13]

One notable aspect of this statement is that it injects a sort of fatalistic pessimism which, whether intended for that purpose or not, tends to mitigate the depreciatory effect of the suggestion of a limited response. General Norstad's remarks might be translated as follows: Although both sides may wish to keep the conflict limited, and although we intend to defend our interests on the lowest feasible level of destruction, there are factors in the situation, some of them almost beyond human control, which inevitably will push the war toward the ultimate level of intensity. Such pessimism of course is well grounded in the technological and psychological factors touched upon earlier, as well as in the "critical" nature of the European area, mentioned by General Norstad. To allude to such factors, or in general to the impossibility of limiting war, is to reduce the depreciatory effect by substituting more or less automatic "forces of nature" for the threat of deliberate retaliation.

The last sentence quoted above suggests another important point. It says, in effect, that although "less-than-ultimate incidents" will not remain so for long, a capacity to deal with them on less than an ultimate basis will prevent them from occurring—that is, deter the Soviets from attempting them. This preserves the threat of all-out war while at the same time suggesting the need for a limited *deterrent* to backstop the Big Deterrent, as distinct from a limited response to substitute for a massive response in case of *failure* of the deterrent. General Norstad may have wished to suggest, in other words, that although we were certain that a less-than-ultimate incident would set off a full-scale war, the Russians might not be sure and might be tempted to try some sort of limited conquest. If this were the case, they would be effectively deterred only by a ground force strong enough to deny them their objective, or to throw some doubt on their chances of gaining it. Obviously, if we are convinced that the Big Deterrent has lost its potency, it makes sense to create lesser ones which seem more credible. But even if we are not so convinced, we can hedge against the possibility and still minimize the degree to which the smaller deterrent erodes the massive threat by making clear to the enemy that the reason for the creation of the smaller one is not that we have lost our will to retaliate massively, but because we think the enemy thinks we have.

---

[13] *Mutual Security Appropriations for 1959*, Hearings, *op. cit.*, pp. 564–65.

It is worth repeating that although the direct, complementary and depreciatory effects are mutually offsetting, they are not mutually exclusive. They are opposing considerations which the enemy will have to weigh and compare in calculating the probable costs and gains from his aggression. Furthermore, their relative impact is not likely to remain constant through changes in the size of the denial force. To take a hypothetical example, the Soviets' expectation of the probability of massive retaliation following their attack on Western Europe might rise with additions to the shield up to the level of 40 divisions. This would be occasioned by an excess of "complementary" effect over "depreciatory" effect up to this level. At 40 divisions the depreciatory effect might begin to dominate because above this strength the Russians would note that the West was extremely serious about providing the means for some response to major aggression other than massive retaliation. If at this point, the Russians were still confident, however, that the NATO ground shield could not block their conquest of Europe, they might become increasingly likely to try it, since they would perceive a declining probability of their suffering massive destruction as a consequence. This increase in the likelihood of attack (i.e., weakening in the overall deterrent) might continue until the shield reached a strength of, say, 55 divisions, at which point the Soviets might begin to recognize a substantial probability, say .50, that their assault would be blocked on the ground. With further increments to the shield, the chances of Soviet aggression would fall—i.e., the *direct* deterrent effect of the shield itself would more than offset its depreciatory effect on the West's threat of strategic nuclear retaliation. According to this hypothesis, there would be a weakening of the overall deterrent between 40 and 55 divisions as a result of the lack of symmetry between the direct and depreciatory effects.

IV. DETERRENCE OF MINOR AGGRESSION IN WESTERN EUROPE

As with most analytical distinctions in the field of foreign and military affairs, the dichotomy between "major" and "minor" aggression is not clear-cut.[14] There may be major aggressions in Asia and minor ones in Europe, although generally we tend to think of Asia as the natural theater of "limited war" and Europe as the central arena for "general war." Conceivably, the enemy could undertake a minor aggression using substantial force, although the obverse is difficult to imagine. The essential criterion for making this important but difficult distinction is the *evident operational objective* of the enemy. We do not deter "big wars" or "little wars"; we deter

---

[14] The terms "major" and "minor" are used rather than "all-out" and "limited" because the latter have come to connote chiefly the intensity of war, or the nature of the means used to fight a war, rather than the aim of the act which precipitates the war.

enemy acts, some of which would indicate a purpose that challenges our vital interests or survival, and others of which would not. Whether or not the act sets off a "big war" or a "little war" depends upon our response, the nature of which depends upon our assessment of the enemy's objective, and the value we place on denying him the objective. But the trouble with attempting to appraise the enemy's objective is, first, that objectives tend to grow with initial success, and secondly, that the enemy has the option of breaking up his large objectives into pieces, none of which seems "worth" a costly war. The appraisal must consider not only the immediate aim, but also what changes are likely to take place in both immediate and long-term aims if the initial move is not frustrated. And it must consider whether the immediate purpose is but a stage in a larger purpose which the enemy hopes to attain *seriatim*. It must recognize that the enemy always will be interested in making his aims appear limited, whatever the geographical arena.

A major Soviet aggression in Europe, launched with full force at the outset, must be considered unlikely at present in view of the West's retaliatory power. It would, of course, become more likely if the Soviets were to achieve such a marked advantage in offensive and/or defensive air-nuclear strength as to be able to neutralize our retaliatory power or to bring it down to dimensions which they could accept. But short of this, the more likely challenge would seem to be the "creeping" aggression, the series of nibbles no one of which would seem serious enough to warrant nuclear retaliation.

The second of the three functions of the NATO shield, as described by General Norstad (but the most important function, according to him), is to deter wars "arising from miscalculation, border incident or probing operations invited by weakness on the NATO periphery." General Norstad also speaks of "accidents" and of the possibility of the Soviets "trumping up a pretext" to cross the line. He is clearly thinking of the danger of minor aggression—that is, Soviet moves which would not clearly indicate an intention to occupy Western Europe or a substantial part of it. He apparently thinks of such moves in two categories. One would be deliberate military intrusions designed to grab a limited piece of territory, in the interest either of marginally expanding the Soviet orbit for its own sake, or of testing the willingness of the West to precipitate war. The other category is "incidents" or "accidents" which might occur without the volition of the high command of either side. Such an incident might result from a clash between East and West German frontier forces, or from an East German revolt which some West German forces crossed the border to support, thereby involving themselves in a skirmish with Soviet forces. General Norstad elaborates on this function of the shield as follows:

> . . . if this forward line of the NATO countries were undefended, or were held by only a token force, which would be practically the same

thing, it would be quite a simple matter for the Russians, or their satellites supported by the Russians, to move across that line. It could be either as a result of a border incident or more likely as a result of a deliberate probing operation to put us in a position of political disadvantage. Against an undefended line, this would be easy to do, and no substantial force would be required on their part; they would get something for nothing, and I don't have to point out to you that this would put us in an extremely difficult situation. . . . We, together with the other NATO members, would have the responsibility of doing something about it. Should we fail to do something, it is perfectly obvious what would happen to the NATO alliance.

* * *

If we did not respond . . . we would destroy something of tremendous value. However, if we decide to carry out our obligations under the treaty, we would be confronted with the necessity of using substantial force ourselves, and I am talking now about heavy retaliatory forces. I believe that this country and the alliance would take the proper action in a case of this kind, but I do not have to suggest that this would be an extremely difficult decision to make.

On the other hand, if the forward line were defended, and defended with reasonable strength, a border incident of the kind I have described could be held in check. If there were a decision to set off a probing operation, then there would be force to stop it—not to hold an all-out attack, but to hold it for a short period of time. During that time, the Russians would have to give consideration, not only to the forces of the shield, which are relatively light, but also to the fact that this action on their part would compel them to use some significant force, involved in which would be consideration of the full consequences of the retaliatory forces as well. As a consequence, we feel the most important function of the shield forces is really not to fight, not even to defend, but to complete the deterrent.[15]

Here General Norstad brings out an important point: that the side which is able to commit its military forces first has the advantage in competitive deterrence. Then the other side must bear the responsibility for precipitating the mutual costs of war—costs which may be well beyond the value of the immediate strategic objective for either side. To illustrate General Norstad's apparent reasoning: if the Soviets were to occupy Schleswig-Holstein quickly (which they could easily do if they faced only a flimsy shield), they would then be committed to defend Schleswig-Holstein against a counter attack by NATO forces. The West would then have to bear the psychological burden of initiating substantial conflict, a heavy burden indeed if the only available response were strategic nuclear war, but heavy enough even in a local response. An attempt to eject the invaders might well eventuate in all-out war,

---

[15] *Mutual Security Appropriations for 1959,* Hearings, *op. cit.,* pp. 563–64.

since it would require the application of substantial force. If the expected costs were greater than the value of Schleswig-Holstein to the West, the imperatives of honor might not be sufficient to generate a response. The Soviets could be expected to do everything possible to inhibit a response; presumably they would occupy the conquered area in considerable force so as to raise as high as possible the costs of repelling them. They would no doubt proclaim that they had no more territorial ambitions. They would offer to negotiate and perhaps hint that their occupation would only be temporary. They might threaten to increase their commitment of forces and take more territory if NATO attempted to push them back to the original border; such threats might well include a little judicious "nuclear black-mail." In such circumstances, as General Norstad says, the decision to respond at all would certainly be "difficult."

But if the West maintained a strong shield force on the border it would be committed in advance to a determined and costly defense of the territory, and the responsibility for deciding to set off a substantial conflict would rest with the enemy. To put the matter another way: when deterrence depends on the projection of a willingness to precipitate a mutually undesirable out-come if the enemy makes the move to be deterred, there is a high premium on "automating" the response, for if the response is a matter of free choice, the enemy is likely to suspect that it will not be carried out. Perhaps the best way to automate a threatened response is to deploy the forces which will make the response in such a way that the enemy cannot avoid coming into conflict with them, thus precipitating the response. This type of automation is more feasible in denial deterrence than in punishment deterrence, in which the instruments of the response are located far to the rear and their activation depends upon some centralized decision rather than upon the actions of individual soldiers and units under orders to defend a frontier. However, some of the automating effect of a strong shield rubs off on the punishment deterrent because the enemy knows that any aggressive move by him will trigger off war at a level of intensity which would very well spiral to higher levels.

A strong shield would tend to foreclose an enemy attempt to make a sub-stantial gain by a series of small grabs of territory, or contrived "incidents," since it would enable NATO to deal directly with such limited and ambig-uous moves, at relatively small cost, without having to predict the enemy's ultimate intent. Should the enemy decide to undertake deliberate aggression, the shield would force him to betray large objectives with his first move, since a serious attempt to breach the shield would require large forces and would indicate a willingness to accept high costs. Thus a strong forward wall not only directly deters those enemy moves with which it can itself cope, but also tends to complement the punishment deterrent by ensuring that the stakes in any conflict which the enemy stands to win will appear high enough to implicate the Big Deterrent with some degree of credibility. In this latter function, which is distinct from the other complementary effects mentioned earlier, the shield tends to integrate its own denial deterrent qualities with the punishment deterrent function of the strategic retaliatory forces.

V. DETERRENT IMPLICATIONS OF TACTICAL NUCLEAR WEAPONS

The NATO shield now has a "dual capability." It is capable of tactical nuclear warfare by virtue of the provision of nuclear weapons and warheads to the U.S. forces in the shield and the gradual equipping of the other forces with missiles capable of carrying a nuclear warhead, while yet retaining its capacity to fight by conventional means. The "nuclearizing" of the shield enhances its "integrating" effect on the overall deterrent posture. If the shield forces were only conventionally equipped, the thesis expounded by General Norstad (as interpreted above by the present writer)—that a strong shield tends to implicate the Big Deterrent in the deterrence of even minor aggression by forcing the Russians to commit large forces and signal a willingness to suffer substantial costs, thus in turn signalling a major objective— might seem somewhat dubious. Even assuming a shield considerably stronger than the existing one, the Soviets might feel that an assault with forces sufficient to breach the shield on a limited sector of the front would not trigger a strategic nuclear response since the ensuing war still might not be intense enough to indicate unambiguously a serious intent to overrun the whole of Western Europe or a considerable portion of it. But, facing such a shield which is also equipped with tactical nuclear weapons, the Russians must recognize a strong chance that this nuclear capability will be used if they commit enough forces to penetrate the shield conventionally. The Western allies would then recognize a Russian aim which they probably would consider sufficient at least to justify the initiation of low-level nuclear warfare. The cost expectation produced by this probability might alone be sufficient to deter an aggression of limited objective. The "automating" effect mentioned earlier thus comes into play at the tactical nuclear level: upon the enemy falls the burden of having to initiate nuclear war in order to obtain an objective.[16]

---

[16] Secretary of State Dulles showed that he recognized this "passing the buck" function of tactical nuclear weapons when he said in a magazine article in October, 1957: ". . . it may be that by the 1960 decade the nations which are around the Sino-Soviet perimeter can possess an effective defense against full-scale conventional attack and thus confront any aggressor with the choice between failing or himself initiating nuclear war against the defending country. Thus the tables may be turned, in the sense that instead of those who are non-aggressive having to rely upon all-out nuclear retaliatory power for their protection, would-be aggressors will be unable to count on a successful conventional aggression, but must themselves weigh the consequences of invoking nuclear war." John Foster Dulles, "Challenge and Response in Foreign Policy," *Foreign Affairs*, Vol. 36, No. 1 (October, 1957), p. 31.

Suppose, however, that the enemy did decide to attack. He would then indicate a willingness to accept the costs of tactical nuclear warfare, from which it might well be presumed that his aim was expansive enough to warrant the strategic use of nuclear weapons by the West. Thus a strong conventional shield, reinforced by a tactical nuclear capability, tends to strengthen a Soviet expectation that any serious move will be answered rather promptly with strategic nuclear retaliation. It "builds a bridge," as it were, between the minor aggression and the major response, by ensuring, or at least increasing the chances, that any aggression will be interpreted, at its outset or soon after, as having a major objective.[17]

The degree of automation could be increased by giving the military commanders advance authority to use tactical nuclear weapons if necessary to hold the line. There is no evidence that such authorization has been given, but Secretary Dulles hinted at the possibility when he said on November 20, 1957, that if an attack were made on NATO forces "like that on Pearl Harbor," the decision to shoot back would be made by the commanders on the spot.[18]

Should the bridge still appear shaky, it could be further strengthened by providing tactical and strategic nuclear weapons to the continental allies, under their control. It is perhaps a moot point whether the European allies or the United States would be the more willing to initiate tactical nuclear warfare—the United States certainly seems prepared to do so to prevent large or middle-sized Soviet gains in Europe; on the other hand, important groups in the European countries often talk as if they would prefer Soviet occupation to any kind of nuclear warfare. However, tactical weapons in the hands of the forces of countries like West Germany and France would add a significant additional probability that Soviet aggression would meet some form of nuclear response. Perhaps the greatest weakness would be at the hinge between the tactical and strategic nuclear levels. Even if the Soviets stood to win at the tactical nuclear level, the United States and Britain might prefer to see Europe occupied rather than suffer the costs of strategic nuclear war; moreover, they might well doubt that warfare at this level could prevent occupation. However, if the continental allies possessed a strategic capability, there would be a strong chance that at least one of them would consider its use to be its last chance for avoiding political extinction, and would prefer to act on this chance rather than acquiesce in political extinction as a result of defeat in a tactical nuclear war. They

---

[17] Admittedly, this effect depends on some asymmetry in valuations: for the West to be willing to respond at a level of intensity higher than that at which the enemy initiates the conflict requires that the West value a given objective somewhat higher than does the enemy. It may be presumed, however, that such asymmetry does exist, if only because an area or political entity is usually valued much higher by the side which already possesses or controls it than by the side which merely covets it.

[18] *New York Times,* Nov. 21, 1957, p. 1.

would already be suffering severely as a result of the tactical nuclear warfare; they might view the additional costs from strategic warfare as only marginal and they could believe with some assurance that the initiation of such warfare would activate the strategic capabilities of the United States and Britain, or, alternatively, that the imminence of such activation would persuade the Soviet Union to call off the war. If there were a significant advantage to be gained by a first massive strike, the peripheral powers would feel a very strong pressure to follow the lead of their continental allies. This pressure would follow from their knowledge that the Soviets would also be contemplating the advantage to be gained by a first strike against the United States and Britain and might interpret the initial blow by the continental ally as indicating the imminence of a U.S.-British strike against them, which they would wish to blunt with a forestalling attack.

Of course, it is the Soviet advance contemplation of this logic and the Soviet expectations deriving therefrom which are important for deterrence. Presumably, the Soviets will be deterred from even minor aggression if they can be made to see that whatever their real or stated aims, and whatever the level of intensity at which they initiate the fighting, the Western allies are substantially committed, by the logic of their own interlocking interests, to an eventual all-out response before accepting limited defeat. If this is their expectation, they will see that limited aggression with limited means is a bad bargain for them, and they will be left with the alternative of prefacing any aggressive move on the ground with a massive strike at the West's retaliatory forces. If they are not able to eliminate enough of these forces to bring their own probable costs in all-out war down to a level commensurate with their expected gains, presumably they will be deterred from this move.

Significantly, the bridging of this gap in the spectrum of deterrence—the gap which lies between a weak shield and the massive retaliatory capability of the peripheral powers—does not crucially depend on the creation of a capability to fight and win a limited war. It depends only on the creation and appropriate deployment of forces with sufficient defending and striking power to force the enemy to indicate objectives serious enough to justify a response at a destructive level just higher than the level at which the enemy initiates the conflict, and just higher than subsequent levels at which he seems willing to continue the war. Indeed, there is an inherent contradiction between this logic and the logic of limited war. Limited war logic requires that we be prepared to restrict our response to dimensions which involve costs which we are willing to accept, and that this intention be unequivocally communicated to the enemy, in the hope that he will observe similar limitations. Limited defeat is assumed to be preferable to warfare at higher levels of intensity. Maximum deterrence of limited aggression requires implantation of the opposite expectation in the enemy's mind—that we will always try to avoid even limited defeat by stepping up the intensity of the war—and deterrence is greatly enhanced if this expectation depends not merely on our verbal declarations but also on the existence of forces and capabilities, so deployed, committed and controlled that they ensure that a response at ever higher levels of intensity will seem rational by the logic of the interests involved—the interests, at least, of some members of the defending coalition who have the capacity to implicate the interests of the others.[19]

We have been speaking of tactical nuclear weapons as a means of "linking up" the denial deterrent function of the ground force shield and the punishment deterrent function of SAC and the RAF Bomber Command. In this role, they act chiefly as a "complementary" deterrent; they increase the likelihood that Soviet aggression in Europe will set off a massive response, but they do so primarily because of the punishment they are capable of exacting. They inflict costs, which, if the Soviets show a willingness to accept them, tend to show an intent serious enough to justify application of the Big Deterrent. Tactical nuclear weapons may also complement the Big Deterrent as a result of their denial effect; they increase the holding capability of the shield and thus provide the complementary benefits of time and "seriousness" which were outlined earlier.[20] In addition, tactical nuclear warfare is much more likely than conventional warfare to give rise to "accidents" leading to the inadvertent explosion of full-scale war. And, aside from accidents, tactical nuclear war can easily shade into a "spiraling" situation born of deliberate decisions to step up the intensity of the war just a bit to convince the enemy of the high costs that will follow his continued rejection of terms of settlement. The enemy will have to recognize that the line between tactical nuclear warfare and limited strategic reprisals (and between limited reprisals and not-so-limited reprisals) is a blurry one and that we are more likely to carry out our threat of massive retaliation if we can approach its fulfillment gradually than if it requires a decision to up the intensity of the war from the conventional to the strategic nuclear level in a single move. As against these considerations, if the enemy does not follow the "linking" logic expounded above, and if the creation of NATO's tactical nuclear force is clearly tied to a limited war strategy, the tactical capability may depreciate the credibility of the massive retaliatory threat.

Besides such indirect effects, a tactical nuclear capability obviously has a direct deterrent impact, by virtue of the costs it can itself inflict and what it adds to the defending forces' chances of blocking territorial conquest. Such

---

[19] These comments on the difference between the logic of a limited war strategy and that of a deterrent strategy are not intended to indicate a preference for one or the other. The latter is emphasized here because this is a paper primarily about deterrence, not limited war.

[20] We are assuming what seems to be the generally, though not unanimously, accepted opinion: that tactical nuclear weapons work to the advantage of the defense—that is, that they improve the denial capability of ground forces of given size even against an aggressor who also has such weapons. This would seem to be at least partly contradicted by the Army's thesis that tactical nuclear war will require more manpower than conventional war.

weapons allow the initiation of nuclear war at a relatively low level of intensity, thus minimizing the psychological strain of having to make the decision to start nuclear warfare and lowering the size of the stakes which are likely to set off nuclear action. Thus, the enemy must expect a much higher probability of some response in nuclear form than if strategic nuclear warfare were our only alternative to a conventional response.

It can be argued that the possibility of tactical warfare spiraling to the ultimate level of destruction might deter the West from initiating such warfare. In considering this possibility, however, the enemy must take note of the strong United States and NATO commitment to use tactical nuclear weapons in the event of a serious Russian attack in Europe—a commitment which presumably will become more and more "automatic" as the shield's nuclear capability is perfected.

VI. PUNISHMENT AND DENIAL DETERRENCE IN NON-VITAL AREAS

What can be said about the choice between punishment and denial deterrents in less vital areas? How does the valuation of the strategic prize affect their relative merit and their reciprocal effects?

It is often stated that the threat of massive retaliation is absolutely worthless with respect to minor objectives because its credibility is nil. The basis for this statement is that the enemy will know we place only slight value on the area and will therefore consider any massive threat as pure bluff. But suppose, as is fairly likely, that the objective carries a low value for the enemy as well as for us.[21] Then, although the enemy will place little credibility on our massive threat, a little may be enough. He may not want to take even small risks with respect to non-vital areas, especially since it is generally in these areas that his non-military means of expansion are likely to be most fruitful. Conversely, the enemy may be willing to take large risks in major areas, a consideration which may raise the value of keeping a denial deterrent in these areas. In fact, it is precisely such reasoning which forms one of the present administration's arguments for maintaining substantial ground forces in Europe. To quote Secretary Dulles again:

> Some areas are so vital that a special guard should and can be put around them. Western Europe is such an area. Its industrial plant

---

[21] There may be some geographical objectives, of course, which are valued fairly highly by the enemy but are marginal for us, and vice versa. It is worth noting, in further qualification, that the "value" of a place may be much greater to either side than its strategic value in terms of resources and location; for example, considerable value may reside in the *act* of defending or retaliating, quite apart from intrinsic strategic value. This latter form of value, which could perhaps be called a combination of deterrent value and political value, is well illustrated in the United States attitude toward the Chinese offshore islands.

represents so nearly the balance of industrial power in the world that an aggressor might feel that it was a good gamble to seize it—even at the risk of considerable hurt to himself. In this respect, Western Europe is exceptional.[22]

One does not usually risk much to obtain little, even when the mathematical expectation is one of gain rather than loss. It is more common for individuals to risk much to gain much, sometimes even when the mathematical expectation is against them, and presumably the same could be said of nations. Moreover, when the gamble is non-repeatable and the possible loss absolute or near-absolute, there will be profound reluctance to take any risks at all for the prospect of only modest gains. Thus logical considerations seem to point to the conclusion that if the credibility of our punishment threats tend to be proportionate to the value which the enemy thinks we ascribe to an area, and if the enemy's valuations are roughly symmetrical with those he imputes to us, such threats will be at least as effective for deterring aggression in non-vital areas as in a major theater such as Europe.

The wide divergence of this hypothesis from the common sense conclusion stimulates a search for qualifying factors. It might well be that below a certain probability of retaliation, the probability becomes insignificant in the Communist calculus—for practical purposes equal to zero. The obvious willingness of the Communists to engage the West on various secondary and tertiary fronts since World War II—despite the U.S. monopoly of atomic weapons—seems to bear this out. Another plausible qualifier is that the Communist leaders may think the probability of retaliation varies over a much wider range than do our valuations, or that they believe the U.S. valuation of secondary prizes is much less than their own.

The enemy is likely to consider massive retaliation by the United States irrational in any contingency except direct nuclear attack on the United States. Nevertheless, the "gap" between the costs (for us) of this response and the probable costs of the severest response which the enemy might consider rational for us is likely to seem much smaller in the case of a full-scale assault on Western Europe than in the case of an attack anywhere in Asia or the Middle East. Considering the degree of our emotional and prestige involvement in Europe, the Soviets may feel that an attack there would generate enough irrationality to take us "over the threshold"—enough, that is, to set off a massive response—whereas they might feel that the much greater gap between the cost of such a response and our valuations in Asia could never be bridged by any degree of irrationality that might be stimulated by an attack there.

The effectiveness of punishment deterrence in Asia and the Middle East is vitiated by the many and varied opportunities available to the enemy for

---

[22] John Foster Dulles, "Policy for Security and Peace," *Foreign Affairs,* Vol. XXXII, No. 3 (April, 1954), p. 358.

presenting his challenges there in ambiguous form. A nuclear punishment response will be inhibited if the aggressive act can be made to seem accidental, if provocation can plausibly be claimed, if the forces involved can be pictured as "volunteers" not controlled by their government, or—perhaps the most likely case—if the aggression takes the form of covert assistance to an indigenous rebellion. In general, deterrence by the threat of punishment requires the positive assignment of responsibility for the aggression, that this responsibility be seen to rest with a responsible government in clear control of the forces involved, that the intent of the aggressive forces be viewed as serious enough to warrant the application of punishment, and that the act to be punished be clearly identifiable as falling within the class of acts covered by a previous threat. If these conditions are not met, not only is the moral justification for punishment weakened, but we will find it easy to renege on our commitment to punish, with minimum loss to our prestige and to the credibility of future punishment threats. A capacity to deny territory to the aggressor by conventional means will be more effective than threats of punishment in deterring such forms of aggression. In addition to the lesser risk involved, the activation of conventional surface forces does not require a determination of the responsibility for, and ultimate intent of, the initial aggression, nor does it require a clear-cut enemy act. Their function is simply to prevent losses as a result of the aggression; the circumstances surrounding the initiation of the conflict are not nearly as controlling as in deterrence by punishment.

When we consider only clear-cut aggressions and reprisals of less than massive dimensions, the case for punishment deterrence in Asia improves. The Communists must attach a significant probability to a less-than-massive nuclear response to aggression in such places as the Taiwan Strait and Korea. Limited nuclear reprisals in these areas are less likely to eventuate in general nuclear war than they are in Europe, first, because the Soviet Union itself (or its armed forces) will not be the recipient of the reprisals, and secondly, because the actual recipient (most probably Communist China) does not yet have the capacity for a nuclear response against the United States. Whatever the political liabilities incurred by the use of nuclear weapons in Asia (which would be great),[23] their use is not as likely to result in unacceptable damage to the United States itself as in the case of war in Europe. The probabilities would change markedly, of course, if the Communist Chinese were to obtain control of nuclear weapons with long-range delivery systems.

The rationale of a limited reprisal strategy is not so much to "win" the immediate battle in the sense of physically repelling the enemy's ground

---

[23] Political implications—i.e., the differential effects of denial and punishment strategies on political attitudes of allies and uncommitted countries—have been deliberately excluded from this analysis. Such effects might be decisive in striking an optimum balance between the two strategies.

attack, as it is to teach the enemy about the costs he can expect to suffer if he continues his aggressive ways. The object might be either to persuade him to give up the immediate objective and agree to a settlement, or to dissuade him from future aggressions. The opportunities for such "teaching" are considerably greater in Asia than they are in Europe. In Europe, once the Soviet Union commits itself to a major offensive, it is not likely to stop as a result of limited nuclear reprisals. But in Asia it would seem more likely, if the Soviet Union retains any control over the situation, that it would attempt to persuade its aggressive satellite or ally to desist. Its own prestige would not be involved to the same extent as if its own forces were engaged, and it would presumably fear the extension of the war. Also, in Asia the teaching effects would be greater with regard to subsequent situations, for if the United States shows a willingness to use nuclear weapons there, considerable support is added to threats to use them in other contingencies. The use of nuclear weapons in a major area such as Europe would not necessarily indicate a willingness to use them elsewhere.

The obverse of this point is that if we threaten retaliation in a minor contingency and then do not retaliate, the cost of being caught bluffing is smaller than it would be if the threat applied to a major contingency. Not to carry out a threat when the object of contention is low in value does not necessarily indicate a reluctance to carry out similar threats when a vital interest is involved. But if we should fail to carry out our threat of punishment in Europe, the result would be practically to wipe out the effectiveness of punishment threats in other areas.

The deterrent effect of denial forces is a function chiefly of their *size, location,* and the degree of *mobility.* Presumably, the greater the size of U.S. ground and naval forces, wherever they are located, the greater their deterrent influence upon possible aggression anywhere; the enemy must consider that even if his aggression meets with initial success, the United States may try to reverse it if it has the capability to do so.[24] But forces located near trouble spots, and/or with mobility sufficient to get them to attacked areas in time to affect the outcome, have a significantly greater restraining effect with respect to aggression in those areas, than do forces elsewhere. The Communists will expect a greater likelihood of United States intervention if intervention can prevent the consolidation of the fruits of the aggression. This is, or at least should be, part of the rationale for maintaining U.S. ground contingents in Okinawa and Hawaii, and the Marine complement with the Sixth Fleet in the Mediterranean. Even U.S. forces which are committed to the defense of specific areas may nevertheless be used for intervention in nearby areas; demonstration of this possibility by the movement

---

[24] This reasoning would apply even to unmobilized forces; war potential can have a deterring effect if it is coupled with an evident willingness to repel limited aggressions even after their objective has been consolidated.

of troops from Germany in the recent Lebanon crisis no doubt strengthened our general deterrent posture in the Middle East.

Deterrence by denial is maximized, however, if the forces are physically present on the threatened territory, and particularly if they are deployed on the boundary. Such deployments make clear a U.S. determination to fight. They pass to the enemy the responsibility for initiating war with the United States. In the absence of such deployments, the enemy might try to deter our response by initially committing forces of such size that they raise the cost of our response higher than our valuation of the objective; the enemy must recognize that as a result of the commitment of our prestige in the form of American combat forces, we will be willing to suffer considerably higher costs than would be warranted by the intrinsic value we attach to the territorial objective. The two divisions we maintain in Korea and the patrolling of the Taiwan Strait by the Seventh Fleet are good examples of forces deployed in relatively minor areas which exert this "trip-wire" or "automating" effect. Determined attacks by ground and naval forces in those areas would immediately involve the United States and would probably cause the projection of considerable additional U.S. power to these theaters as well as raising the strong possibility of a nuclear response. Although the forward deployment of given denial capabilities tends to enhance the deterrence of attacks on the objectives where they are stationed, it might be argued that such deployment weakens the overall deterrent posture by reducing flexibility. Forces located at the armistice line in Korea, for example, may not be as readily movable to Southeast Asia, say, as troops on Okinawa or Hawaii which are perhaps closer to central transportation facilities and not committed to the defense of a specific sensitive front. The choice between concentration in a strategic reserve and on-the-spot readiness must be made in the light of existing circumstances—available transportation, degree of threat facing the area from which the forces would be moved, ability of indigenous forces to hold a line temporarily, etc.

Local indigenous forces will of course exercise some deterrent effect if they are strong enough to defend successfully or to hold until outside assistance can arrive. In some minor areas, especially if the enemy can be fairly confident of achieving his ends there by political and economic penetration, simply the costs which a local defending force can inflict (apart from its capacity to defend) may be sufficient to deter. Our military aid programs and the work of our military missions and advisory groups should be mentioned in this connection as instruments of deterrence. However, military missions do not exert any significant "trip-wire" deterrent effect. In the symbolism of international military life, they are technicians; they do not invoke the national presence and prestige as do fighting troops. They do, of course, indicate a U.S. interest in the continued independence of the host country, but they do not ensure with certainty or near-certainty a U.S. military reaction if the country is attacked. A question worth asking is whether our deterrence of minor aggression would not be considerably enhanced if our military missions in Asia were made to double as combat forces. Their assignment to the defense of a sector of the host country's frontier in case of war need not interfere unduly with their peacetime training activities. Or, as an alternative, the individual members of the missions might be assigned positions of subordinate command in the host country's armed forces, provided of course that this was politically acceptable to the host country.[25] Either of these alternatives might significantly increase the commitment of our prestige to the successful defense of the country. Such deliberate involvement of the national prestige is the obverse of the attempted disinvolvement of prestige which has been practiced by both the Soviets and the Communist Chinese in their use and threatened use of "volunteers."

The interaction between punishment deterrence and denial deterrence in Asia can be discussed in terms of the categories used earlier. The "shield" in Korea, for example, exercises not only direct deterrence as a result of its considerable capacity to hold and its ability to inflict costs on the aggressor, but also both complementary and depreciatory effects with respect to the credibility of the threat to impose nuclear punishment. However, the depreciatory effect on the threat to invoke massive punishment is much less than in Europe because the credibility of this threat is already very low. Moreover, the depreciatory effect on the threat to exact lesser nuclear reprisals is probably low because such reprisals, and defense on the ground, are not so clearly alternatives to each other as are "massive retaliation" and a denial strategy. In Korea, the extant threat seems to postulate that the nuclear response will be an integral part of the denial strategy, whether it takes the form of tactical nuclear warfare within Korea or strikes against the sources of Communist military capability in China.

In the deterrence of minor aggression, the complementary effect actually works both ways. Not only can a denial capability support a threat of nuclear punishment; the punishment threat may add significantly to the deterrent qualities of the denial forces. It may do this by restraining the enemy from committing overwhelming surface forces to his attack, thus keeping his force commitment down to a level with which our own denial forces can deal successfully. No doubt an important factor deterring a new outbreak of war in Korea is the high probability that if forces other than North Korean ones were to participate in the attack, the source of these additional forces (presumably Communist China) would be subjected to some form of bombardment, very likely nuclear. Even if the additional forces came from the country already involved in the fighting, the commitment of these forces might be deterred by nuclear threats; in any case the country concerned

---

[25] In the early days of the Korean War, some members of the U.S. military mission assumed *de facto* command of the South Korean units to which they were assigned.

would have to consider that its commitment of ground forces sufficient to defeat the defenders would increase the chances of its suffering some form of nuclear retaliation.

VII. SUMMARY

In general, deterrence by denial and deterrence by punishment have significantly different effects on the enemy's cost-gain calculus. Denial deterrents are characterized by a higher probability of being applied and by much greater effectiveness in blocking enemy gains, although the costs they pose for the enemy are relatively low. Punishment deterrents raise a prospect for the enemy of very high costs, but our will to use them is uncertain and they are ineffective in denying the enemy territorial gains. The deterrent utility of a denial force is distinct from, and to be added to, its defense utility—its utility in blocking the enemy's assault and preserving territorial values for the defender should deterrence fail. In addition to its direct deterrent effect, a denial capability both complements and depreciates the deterrent effect of threats of punishment, but in different degree and proportion, depending on the value of the objective, the size of the denial force, and the degree of punishment threatened. The depreciatory effect tends to be greater the higher the value of the objective to the defender. It is less with respect to threats of the limited use of nuclear weapons than with respect to threats of "massive retaliation."

A denial capability is more useful than the threat of punishment in deterring and dealing with ambiguous forms of aggression. In Europe, a strong ground force shield deters "probes" and minor "incidents," not only by its own capability to deal with them, but also by forcing the enemy to indicate a major intent with his initial move, thus raising the probability that we will respond with the strategic as well as the tactical elements of our nuclear deterrent.

The choice between punishment and denial deterrents is likely to be most agonizing with respect to areas which we value most highly, such as Western Europe. These are the areas where we will want to maintain a substantial denial capability, both as an extra deterrent to supplement and complement the threat of nuclear punishment and as a means of holding the area if it is attacked. But these are also the places where the retaliatory threat is most credible in the absence of a denial capability and where the maintenance of such a capability is likely to have the most serious consequences in undermining the credibility of the punishment threat. In less vital areas, the credibility of the massive threat is low in any case, so the maintenance of a denial capability in or near these areas will not have a significant depreciatory effect on this threat. The enemy is likely to consider seriously only limited punishment threats in such areas, and this type of threat is likely to be supported rather than weakened by the existence of a denial capability.

THE LIMITING PROCESS
IN THE KOREAN WAR[1]

Morton H. Halperin

THE PROBLEMS of limiting local war in the nuclear-missile age have been analyzed by a number of military strategists;[2] particular local wars have been examined by historians and political scientists. This essay represents an attempt to fuse the two approaches and to test the logically derived hypotheses of the strategist against a historical event. Korea was the catalyst which forced policy-makers and strategists to take limited war seriously. An understanding of why and how the war remained limited, in addition to contributing to an evaluation of an important event in the cold war, should be of value in analyzing other local wars, past and future.

THE LIMITS OBSERVED

Before exploring the pressures for restraint, I will briefly outline the limits which were observed by both sides in terms of geography, kinds of weapons, targets and the participation of particular countries.

Geography

Both sides limited ground fighting during the war to the Korean peninsula. The war began with the North Korean invasion of South Korea, and Communist ground troops fought both north and south of the thirty-eighth parallel.

The United Nations forces also restricted their ground and air attacks to the Korean peninsula.[3] One of the major expansions of the war (in terms

---

[1] This is part of a study of the theory of limited war. For a general theoretical discussion of the limiting process, see Morton H. Halperin, *Limited War in the Nuclear Age* [New York, 1963]. Among the many people who commented on my discussion of the Korean War in the context of my larger study, I would like to thank Allen S. Whiting and Ellen Moot whose comments on this essay were especially valuable. Mrs. Moot also did research for the paper and made extensive editorial improvements.

[2] This literature is listed in the bibliography of Halperin, *Limited War in the Nuclear Age*.

[3] There is some evidence that on at least one occasion United Nations planes strayed over the Yalu and bombed and strafed Chinese villages. See Allen S. Whiting,

of the geographical limit) was the crossing of the thirty-eighth parallel by United Nations ground forces and the march up to the Yalu River, the northern border of North Korea. Nevertheless, the war remained restricted to the Korean peninsula.

Kinds of Weapons

Perhaps the most dramatic and the most frequently discussed limit in the Korean War was the abstention by both sides from the use of atomic capabilities. It should be recalled that these capabilities were substantially smaller than they are now. Both sides had only fission weapons (and no fusion bombs), and both (but particularly the Soviets) had very small stockpiles. Nevertheless, these weapons were potentially decisive, particularly if they had been used in a geographical area more extensive than the Korean peninsula. They would also have had significant impact on the battle had they been used just in Korea. The failure to use nuclear weapons was the only major weapons limit observed by the United Nations forces.[4] On the other hand, the Communist troops not only failed to use nuclear weapons, but also did not employ submarines.[5]

Participation of States

Only the North Koreans and South Koreans participated in the war with all their available forces. The Communist Chinese sent in a large number of troops, but, as Peiping continually stressed, all of them entered the war as "volunteers," for Peiping never declared war. Although there is some evidence that some Russian pilots flew planes for the Chinese Communists,[6] Russia did not overtly intervene with military forces, either air, sea, or ground. Nor did any other Communist state send troops to fight in the war. The Russians supplied large quantities of materiel to both Chinese and North Korean troops and gave them extensive diplomatic support.[7]

On the other side, while a large number of states participated in the defense of South Korea, none of them officially declared war, not even the United States. All contributed troops to a United Nations Command in what was termed by the United States a "police action." But the United Nations did exercise one important restraint on the states involved in the war. It refused the offer of Chiang Kai-shek to send Chinese Nationalist troops into

---

China Crosses the Yalu: The Decision to Enter the Korean War (New York, 1960), 97–100.

[4] Except for biological and chemical weapons.

[5] U. S. Congress. Senate Committee on Armed Services and Committee on Foreign Relations, *Military Strategy in the Far East,* 86th Congress, 1st Session, 1951, p. 1719. Hereafter cited as "MacArthur Hearings."

[6] Robert Frank Futrell, *The United States Air Force in Korea 1950–1953* (New York, 1961), 370.

[7] Whiting, 68–99.

battle.[8] Even after the Chinese Communists came in, the renewed offer of Chinese National troops was rejected.

Targets

Even within the confines of North and South Korea, both sides refrained from attacking important military targets within the area of combat. The Communists did not attack any targets in South Korea.[9] As a result, Pusan and Inchon, the two major ports through which the United Nations supplied its forces, and therefore highly important military targets, remained free from air harassment, although attacks on them probably would have seriously hampered the United Nations military effort. Pusan, which frequently operated at night, was well-lit and a virtually perfect military target. Yet neither port was attacked either from the air or with mines. Nor were there air attacks on convoys of trucks or trains carrying supplies or on troops in the field in South Korean territory.[10]

Thus, except for North Korean guerrilla operations behind the lines, there was no interdiction of American logistical lines in United Nations territory or international waters. The United Nations confined its interference with Communist supply movements to North Korea except for bombing the Yalu bridges at the middle.

Moreover, the Communists never challenged America's air supremacy or sought to use air operations for anything but dog fights at a low level against the United Nations planes. In addition, the Communists refrained from attacking American planes on the ground or American airfields in South Korea, Japan and Okinawa. Finally, American naval vessels off the Korean coast, including the carriers basing aircraft that were operating in the combat zone, were not attacked either by Communist submarines or aircraft, but were fired on from the shore when in range.

In limiting its operations, it is important to note that the United Nations command did not impose comparable restraints on its forces. For example, attacks were made on armies in the field. Convoys were bombed, and the bridges across the Yalu, the key supply points of the Chinese Communists, were attacked. Nevertheless, the United Nations did impose restrictions on targets within the zone of battle. These will be discussed below.

FOREIGN POLICY OBJECTIVES

Prior to the outbreak of the Korean War, the United States believed that a major objective of the Soviet Union was to expand the area under the control of international Communism as far as possible. Thus, in responding

---

[8] Harry S. Truman, *Memoirs, Vol. II: Years of Trial and Hope* (Garden City, N. Y., 1956), 343.
[9] "MacArthur Hearings," 751.
[10] "MacArthur Hearings," 5.

to the North Korean attack—which had not been anticipated—American objectives were developed in the framework of the belief that the attack was part of a general plan for expansion and perhaps a prelude to general war.[11] The United States sought to prevent the success of this Communist attempt to expand by the use of force in the belief that allowing the Soviets to succeed in Korea would encourage aggression elsewhere. General Bradley expressed this purpose at the MacArthur hearings in describing Korea as "a preventive limited war aimed at avoiding World War III." [12] President Truman later described his objectives in intervening in the Korean War in similar terms:

> Communism was acting in Korea just as Hitler, Mussolini, and the Japanese had acted ten, fifteen, and twenty years earlier. I felt certain that if South Korea was allowed to fall Communist leaders would be emboldened to override nations closer to our own shores. If the Communists were permitted to force their way into the Republic of Korea without opposition from the free world, no small nation would have the courage to resist threats and aggression by stronger Communist neighbors. If this was allowed to go unchallenged it would mean a third world war, just as similar incidents had brought on the second world war.[13]

The defense of Korea was partly motivated by the feeling that the action was necessary to convince the West Europeans that the United States would come to their aid. The Administration was wary of exposing itself to Soviet aggression in Europe by committing its military power in Korea. During the Korean War, in fact, the major American build-up occurred in Europe and not in the Far East. The Administration was also aware of the danger of splitting the North Atlantic Treaty Organization alliance in a dispute over Far Eastern policy. A major objective throughout the war was to prevent adverse repercussions in Europe while using the episode to strengthen NATO and build up its military capability.[14] America's NATO allies, particularly the British, applied constant pressure on the United States to prevent expansion of the war and to bring it to a swift conclusion. Following an almost inadvertent reference by President Truman at a press conference to the possibility of using atomic weapons, British Prime Minister Clement Attlee flew to the United States to confer with Truman and to propose the seeking of a cease-fire in Korea to be followed by the admission of Communist China to the United Nations.[15] Partly because the defense effort in Korea was carried on under UN auspices, the United States felt obliged to consult constantly with its allies on policy and was influenced by their con-

---

[11] "MacArthur Hearings," 942, 954, 971, 2585, 2630.
[12] "MacArthur Hearings," 154.
[13] Truman, 333.
[14] Truman, 387.
[15] Truman, 396–413.

tinuous efforts to halt the expansion of the war and to bring about its conclusion.

Soviet objectives were more closely related to the situation in the Far East. The Soviets were interested in the capture of South Korea for its own sake and probably expected a relatively quick and easy North Korean victory.[16] In addition, the Soviets probably hoped to prevent Japan's alignment with the Western powers. Whiting has suggested the nature of the Soviet Far Eastern objective:

> In view of the multiple pressures directed at Japanese foreign policy, the Communist leaders may have conceived the Korean War as serving ends beyond the immediate control of the peninsula. Military victories in Taiwan and Korea could be heralded as ushering in the Communist era in Asia, that is demonstrating the impotence of America's "puppets," Chiang Kai-shek and Syngman Rhee. The resultant effect upon Japan might swing opportunistic groups behind existing neutralist opposition to Yoshida and prevent his supporting American policy.[17]

The Chinese objectives in entering the Korean War were also based on general political considerations, but of a defensive nature. According to Whiting, the Chinese also hoped to influence the course of United States–Japanese relations.[18] Moreover, they were worried about the loss of prestige they would suffer if they allowed the Western "imperialists" to march unhindered to their borders. And they were perhaps most concerned with the beneficial effects of United Nations success in Korea on the many opponents of the Communist regime still active in China and on Taiwan. Whiting concluded:

> In sum, it was not the particular problems of safeguarding electric power supplies in North Korea or the industrial base in Manchuria that aroused Peking to military action. Instead, the final step seems to have been prompted in part by general concern over the range of opportunities within Korea that might be exploited by a determined, powerful enemy on China's doorstep. At the least, a military response might deter the enemy from further adventures. At the most, it might succeed in inflicting sufficient damage to force the enemy to compromise his objectives and to accede to some of Peking's demands. Contrary to some belief, the Chinese Communist leadership did not enter

---

[16] Whiting, 40.

[17] Whiting, 37. This interpretation of Soviet strategy in the Korean War was offered by John Foster Dulles right after the North Korean attack. Dulles, who was at the time the State Department planner for the Japanese Peace Treaty, suggested that the Korean attack may have been motivated in part by a desire to block American efforts to make Japan a full member of the free world. He conjectured also that the attack may have been ordered because the Communists could not tolerate the "hopeful, attractive Asiatic experiment in democracy" that was under way in South Korea (*The New York Times*, July 2, 1950).

[18] Whiting, 156–62.

the Korean War either full of self-assertive confidence or for primarily expansionist goals.[19]

The Chinese apparently entered the war with the aim of saving at least some of North Korea. Their minimal objective was to preserve the identity of Communist North Korea rather than its total territorial integrity.[20]

In an effort to secure the political effects discussed above, American battlefield objectives and war termination conditions underwent considerable fluctuation during the course of the war. When the United States first intervened, its objective was simply to restore peace and the South Korean border.[21] Very early in the war and after the Chinese intervention, the United States considered a total withdrawal from Korea.[22] Later its battlefield objective expanded to include the unification of Korea. But in the end, the United States accepted a truce line which closely approximated the *status quo ante.* As Neustadt has pointed out, Truman's original decision to seek the unification of Korea failed to take into account the political objectives that the United States was pursuing, and in the end, according to Neustadt, the recognition of this forced the abandonment of the unification effort:

> Had the unification of Korea been Truman's dearest objective, its announcement as a war aim would have been another matter. But it was among the least of the objectives on his mind. In July and August 1950, in December after Chinese intervention, in his struggles with MacArthur, and thereafter through his last two years of office, his behavior leaves no doubt about the many things he wanted more than that. He wanted to affirm that the UN was not a League of Nations, that aggression would be met with counter-force, that "police actions" were well worth their cost, that the "lesson of the 1930's" had been learned. He wanted to avoid "the wrong war, in the wrong place, at the wrong time" as General Bradley put it—and any "war," if possible. He wanted NATO strengthened fast, both militarily and psychologically. He wanted the United States rearmed without inflation, and prepared, thereafter, to sustain a level of expenditure for military forces and for foreign aid far higher than had seemed achievable before Korea.[23]

Once the Soviets recognized that they could not easily secure their objective of demonstrating American weakness and unwillingness to use force, they seemed to have abandoned the battlefield objective of capturing all of

---

[19] Whiting, 159.

[20] Whiting, 155.

[21] Truman, 341.

[22] Courtney Whitney, *MacArthur: His Rendezvous with History* (New York, 1956), 429–31, 438.

[23] Richard E. Neustadt, *Presidential Power: The Politics of Leadership* (New York, 1960), 126.

Korea. They may have been willing to accept an end to the war with part or perhaps even all of North Korea in Western hands, and ultimately settled for a virtual restoration of the *status quo ante*.

DOCTRINE

The North Korean attack on South Korea suggested the willingness of the Communists to seek a limited objective by a limited use of force. The Soviets probably intended to seize South Korea with the use of North Korean forces and then to halt their military operations. When the United States intervened, they recognized their miscalculation of American intentions, while proceeding on the assumption that American intervention need not lead to world war. The attack upon South Korea, moreover, seems to have been motivated by the Soviet compulsion to fill power vacuums. In view of the specific United States declaration that South Korea was outside its defense perimeter, the Soviets could have reasonably counted on a quick and easy victory by the North Koreans.[24] But, while Communist conduct during the war reflected a doctrine that included the limited use of military force, and limited objectives, neither the Chinese nor the Russians seemed to have any idea of the optimum methods of communicating intentions and capabilities to the other side in the course of such a war.

American doctrine, on the other hand, seems to have been much less hospitable to the limitation of warfare. It would appear that the United States had not foreseen the possibility of Soviet military action in South Korea or any other local area unconnected with a general Soviet military offensive. The result was the American decision not to prepare for the defense of South Korea in view of the low estimate of its value in a general war. Thus, the decision of June of 1950 to defend South Korea was not based on a re-estimate of South Korea's military importance, but on a recognition that something had occurred for which American military doctrine had not been prepared.[25] It is important to note that, in its policy decisions throughout the war, the United States was operating without any general theoretical notions of the nature of limited war in the atomic age, and its decisions were probably affected by the lack of such theory.[26]

Each side's image of the other's doctrines and intentions influenced its decisions. The Soviets clearly underestimated the likelihood of American intervention. In the Soviet view, the American declaration that it would defend South Korea only as part of its United Nations obligations had

---

[24] Whiting, 40.

[25] "MacArthur Hearings," 1110.

[26] For a discussion of the development of the theory of limited war, see Halperin, *Limited War: An Essay on the Development of the Theory and an Annotated Bibliography,* Harvard Center for International Affairs (Cambridge, Mass., 1962), Occasional Paper No. 3, 1–14.

meant that the United States would not in fact defend South Korea. The Soviets failed to anticipate the partly moral and partly political American reaction to aggression. They were insensitive to the importance that the United States would attach to repelling "illegal" aggression, as opposed to less clear-cut violations of international law.

The American decision to intervene in Korea and the subsequent decisions were also based on and influenced by estimates of Soviet doctrine and intentions.[27] In assessing the motives and operating doctrine of the North Korean attack, American policy-makers gave consideration and, to some extent, credence to five different interpretations, as follows:

(1) The "diversionary move" interpretation. In view of the number of other areas, particularly Western Europe, that appeared more militarily significant than South Korea, the South Korean attack was seen as a diversionary move, aimed to draw American resources away from the areas where they were most important. Truman reports that he shared this view in part and was determined not to leave Europe vulnerable to Soviet aggression.[28]

(2) The "soft-spot probing" interpretation. By this image of Soviet doctrine, the Soviet compulsion to fill power vacuums had led to the attack on South Korea which had been abandoned by the United States and which was clearly incapable of defending itself.

(3) The "testing" interpretation. This was the view that seemed most to influence Truman's image of the North Korean attack.[29] It recalled the progress of Hitler's aggressive moves and asserted that the North Korean attack should be seen as a prelude to attacks in other areas if that aggression were allowed to succeed. This view differed from the "soft-spot probing" interpretation in its assumption that the Communists' success in Korea would encourage them to attempt aggression in the other areas where Western defense capabilities were far stronger. In short, the purpose of the Korean attack was to probe the firmness of Western intentions, and not simply to fill a power vacuum.

(4) The "demonstration" interpretation. By this interpretation, the Soviets were mainly concerned with demonstrating their own strength and American weakness in order to promote, on a long term basis, important shifts in political allegiance throughout the world.

(5) The "Soviet-Far-East-strategy" interpretation. This interpretation put emphasis on the idea, discussed above, that the Soviets hoped to prevent the entrance of Japan into the Western camp and to pave the way for further Communist expansion in the Far East.

As George has pointed out, the inclination of American policy-makers

---

[27] This discussion of the American image of Soviet doctrine is based on Alexander L. George, "American Policymaking and the North Korean Aggression," *World Politics,* VII (January 1955), 209–32.

[28] Truman, 437.

[29] Truman, 333.

toward the "testing" interpretation of Soviet doctrine—in which the Korean attack was equated with Hitler's early expansionist moves—may have reinforced the likelihood that the United States would intervene in Korea.[30] If the "soft-spot probing" interpretation of Soviet conduct had been accepted instead, the United States might have been more prone to cede South Korea while taking steps to prevent the existence of power vacuums elsewhere. It was the belief that successful aggression would embolden the Soviets that made the defense of South Korea seem so crucial.

THE FEAR OF GENERAL WAR

In an analysis of the limiting process, it is important to say again that the Korean War was fought before the era of intercontinental ballistic missiles and fusion weapons. Thus, while both sides could have expanded the war quickly and decisively, there was not the danger that now exists of a sudden unleashing of nuclear missiles which within an hour could destroy a large part of both the United States and the Soviet Union.

Even without this threat of a mutually devastating strategic exchange, the danger of a world war was nevertheless present, and it is significant that both sides seem to have been determined to avoid its occurrence. Truman has reported that the major American aim in Korea was to prevent a third world war; the United States was determined not to give the Soviets any "excuse" to initiate global war.[31] The Russian decision to remain out of the war seemed to be partly motivated by a fear of igniting a global war. In this situation where neither side could gain a decisive advantage by going first, both sides seemed to recognize that, no matter who started the global war, both would suffer major losses. While the United States could have attacked the Soviet Union with its relatively limited stockpile of atomic weapons, it could probably not have prevented a Soviet ground attack in Western Europe which might result in Communist domination of the European continent. The Soviets had no capacity to attack the United States and could not have prevented an American attack on the Soviet Union. While both sides avoided forcing the other into starting a global war, neither was preoccupied with the possibility of "pre-emption" by its adversary.

The United States was, however, concerned that the Korean War should not lead it to expend those military capabilities which were considered an important deterrent to general war. Whereas today there is a somewhat clearer distinction between the main forces to deter and fight a general war and forces primarily designed for local war, in Korea the United States was, in fact, using the troops and the material which it felt were necessary to deter general war. At the MacArthur hearings, Air Force General Vanden-

---

[30] George, 220.
[31] Truman, 345.

berg rejected a Senator's suggestion that the United States should commit a major part of the American Air Force to the Korean War effort. He argued instead that the United States must get a cease-fire

> without endangering that one potential that we have which has kept the peace so far, which is the United States Air Force; which, if utilized in a manner to do what you are suggesting, would [sic.], because of attrition and because the size of the Air Force is such and the size of the air force industry is such that we could not still be that deterrent to [general] war which we are today.[32]

DOMESTIC POLITICAL PRESSURES

During the Korean War, the Truman Administration continued to pursue its domestic political goals. Despite the war, it was "politics as usual" on both sides of the political fence. The President was busily engaged in promoting his Fair Deal program, consolidating the position of the Democratic Party, strengthening his Northern and Western liberal support in Congress, and calming the political crises raised by such men as Senator McCarthy. Nor was the Administration immune to criticism from the Republican Party which felt it possible, necessary, and desirable to attack the Administration's conduct, as well as to question the basic concept of limited war.

After the MacArthur hearings, a Republican minority report declared: "We believe that a policy of victory must be announced to the American people in order to restore unity and confidence. It is too much to expect that our people will accept a limited war. Our policy must be to win. Our strategy must be devised to bring about decisive victory." [33]

These few sentences suggest a number of important assumptions about the nature of wartime politics. The first is the notion that the unity of the American people can be achieved only with a declaration that victory is the goal. A further implication is that, after such a declaration, the method of achieving a battlefield victory becomes a "military" problem, that is, beyond the realm of partisan domestic politics. On the other hand, once the government admits that there are other political considerations that affect and moderate the goal of a strictly military victory, then, according to this Republican statement, it is legitimate to criticize the particular policy adopted. Unity will come only when the country is asked to back an absolute goal. If there is no such goal, then it is the duty of the opposition to examine and critically appraise the war effort.

Congress, as a whole, also felt itself free to criticize. The inquiries into the

---

[32] "MacArthur Hearings," 1385.
[33] "MacArthur Hearings," 3590. The Senators signing the report were Styles Bridges, Alexander Wiley, H. Alexander Smith, Bourke B. Hickenlooper, William F. Knowland, Harry P. Cain, Owen Brewster and Ralph E. Flanders.

firing of General MacArthur were striking in that they required the Administration, *during the war,* to justify its conduct and to explain publicly what it hoped to accomplish in the war and how it was conducting the war, as well as to explicate a host of particulars which must have been of as much interest to the Communists as they were to the Senators across the table.[34]

The quotation from the Republican Senators also reflects the then still strong American opposition to limited war.[35] The Senators stated flatly that the American people would not accept the strategy of limited war, and indicated their rejection of the strategy as well. The implication is that during a limited war the American government will be subjected to attacks from the political opposition, from Congress, and from public citizens on two grounds: on the legitimacy of fighting a limited war, and on the particular tactics employed in the war.

The general public seems to have shared the Republican Senators' dissatisfaction with the course of the Korean War, at least in its later stages. On the other hand, the public apparently approved the decision of the Eisenhower Administration to end the war short of victory. The public's disapproval of the Korean campaign probably added to the margin of Eisenhower's victory in 1952; his ending the war enhanced the Republican image as the party of peace and increased the Eisenhower plurality in 1956. On the other hand, at least according to the results of the Michigan Survey Research Center voting studies, the Korean War did not have a major or lasting impact on popular political attitudes.[36]

American political leaders seem to have over-estimated the effect of the war on the voting public. Korea is taken as demonstrating—as to some extent it did—that local wars are not popular with the American public. Leading the United States into one or expanding it is likely to be perceived as a political liability; ending one on almost any terms may be a political asset.

---

[34] This is not to say that hearings did not provide a unique and invaluable opportunity for the Administration to communicate what it wanted to communicate to the Chinese and the Russians. But it does not seem likely that the Senators' questions at this hearing had that motivation. The point made here is that Congress forced the Administration to give this testimony during the war without any apparent consideration of the effect it would have on the American war effort. While the hearings were reviewed on security grounds before their release, the pressure to approve publication was great and leaks were inevitable.

[35] This view is an extreme form was expressed by one of MacArthur's biographers as follows:

> MacArthur understood what Truman did not, that the admixture of military strategy with political expediency can produce national disasters . . . . He felt, as experience has long taught, that once the diplomats have failed to preserve the peace, it becomes a responsibility of military leadership to devise the strategy which will win the war. (Whitney, 509.)

[36] Angus Campbell *et al., The American Voter* (New York, 1960), 49, 50, 527, 546, 555.

All these domestic pressures undoubtedly influenced the manner in which the Truman Administration conducted its Korean operations, both by hampering its freedom of action and by increasing the costs of various actions.

THE GREAT DECISIONS

The remainder of this essay will explore several of the major decisions to limit or expand the Korean War and the general nature of the Korean War limiting process.

Atomic Weapons

As was noted above, the most dramatic limit on the Korean War was the failure of either side to use its atomic weapons. According to Brodie,[37] there were four reasons why nuclear weapons were not used by the United States:

(1) The Joint Chiefs of Staff and civilian policy-makers continued to feel that the war in Korea was basically a Soviet feint. There was, therefore, a strong case for conserving the then relatively limited stockpile of atomic weapons for the principal war which, they thought, would come in Europe. Their fear was not that the employment of nuclear weapons would lead to an expansion of the war and a Soviet attack on Europe, but rather that Korea was deliberately designed as a decoy to get us to exhaust our nuclear stockpile and our conventional military resources, so that the Soviets could later attack with impunity in Europe. It was the desire, then, to save resources and not the fear of provoking the enemy that was one of the main causes of the American decision not to use nuclear weapons in Korea.

(2) American policy was also affected by the reports of local commanders that there were no suitable targets for nuclear weapons in Korea. While the impact of this view was considerable, it apparently reflected an uninformed attitude about the possible uses of nuclear weapons. Commanders in the field came to think, for example, that atomic bombs were of little use against bridges, a belief which Brodie explained as follows:

> This odd idea probably resulted from a misreading of the results at Hiroshima and Nagasaki. Some bridges were indeed badly damaged at those places and some were not, but for the latter it was generally forgotten that a bridge only 270 feet from ground zero at Hiroshima was actually 2,100 feet from the point of explosion, and also that it received its blast effect from above rather than from the side.[38]

Nuclear weapons were still relatively new and had not been extensively

---

[37] Bernard Brodie, *Strategy in the Missile Age* (Princeton, 1959), 319–21.
[38] Brodie, 319n.

tested, and it is probable that commanders in the field were too busy to search out potential targets for nuclear weapons.

(3) Our allies, particularly the British, were strongly and emotionally opposed to the use of nuclear weapons in the Korean War.[39] This pressure from our allies strengthened our own anxieties and moral doubts about again using these terrible new weapons.

(4) A subsidiary reason for the failure to use nuclear weapons in the Korean War was the fear of the retaliatory employment by the Soviets of the few atomic weapons in their possession against Pusan or Japan, despite the American near-monopoly over these weapons. Brodie doubts, however, if this fear played a conscious part in the relevant decisions.[40]

The United States, then, was concerned with the vulnerability of Europe and with co-ordinating policy with her allies. It was also determined not to be drawn in by a Soviet feint in Korea. But it is important to note that the first and second factors will not obtain in the future. The American stockpile of tactical nuclear weapons is now so great that military commanders may urge their use precisely because they are a non-scarce military resource, and certainly no argument can be made that they should not be used because they are scarce. Military officers now have a much better understanding of the capabilities of nuclear weapons, which, moreover, now come in much smaller sizes. Thus, it will be clear to military commanders that there would be suitable targets for their use in any conceivable future major limited war. While we can expect continued pressure from our allies against the use of nuclear weapons, it is possible that certain allies might advocate their use in some situations. There will, however, be other international political pressures—for example from the uncommitted or neutral states—against nuclear weapons, and the possibility of a Soviet nuclear response will be a much more important determinant of the decision.[41]

We know much less about the details of the Russian decision not to use atomic weapons in Korea. The Russians seemed determined not to supply any materiel to the forces fighting in Korea which could clearly be labeled as having been supplied by them after the war began. This would certainly be the case with atomic weapons.[42] In addition, the Soviet stockpile of such weapons was so small that its use in a localized military encounter might have seemed wasteful.

Here again, the limit observed by both sides seems not to have resulted

---

[39] See, for example, Truman's report of his conversation with Attlee about the use of atomic weapons. (Truman, 410–11.)

[40] Brodie, 320.

[41] For a discussion of the factors which should influence American policy on the use of nuclear weapons, see Halperin, "Nuclear Weapons and Limited War," *The Journal of Conflict Resolution*, V (June 1961), 146–66.

[42] It was also true of the MIGs along with which the Soviets probably supplied Russian pilots.

from an attempt—or even an awareness of the need—to bargain with the enemy. However, the Soviets were probably more restrained than the United States by the fear that the initiation of nuclear attacks would be met by a response in kind.[43]

The Chinese Communists seem genuinely to have feared the possibility of the American use of nuclear weapons when they intervened in the Korean War. According to Whiting, the Chinese felt that a nuclear response was a real possibility; intervention was considered risky; and every effort was made to delay it and to minimize its consequences.[44] The extent of this Chinese concern was reflected both in its shelter-building program and in domestic Chinese Communist propaganda. But Peiping was reassured by the three-week testing period of relatively small Chinese intervention which revealed that United States aircraft, although authorized to bomb the Korean ends of the Yalu bridges, were forbidden to venture into Chinese territory.

The background of the limit on the use of atomic weapons in the Korean War, then, suggests a failure of both sides to understand what the other side was likely to do and what the other side's fears and goals were. It also suggests that, to a large extent, the determination of limits is based on considerations other than those that result from the battlefield interaction. Some of the other limiting points established in the war reveal the same pattern.

Chinese Intervention

One of the major expansions of the Korean War was the decision of the United Nations Command to cross the thirty-eighth parallel. This decision was based partly on the military consideration that one could not stand by and allow the enemy forces to regroup for renewed attack just beyond the border. It was also made on political grounds. When the battlefield conditions changed in its favor, the United States decided to pursue the unification of Korea by military means. In crossing the parallel the United Nations Command was aware of the risk that it might trigger Chinese Communist intervention, and tried by reassuring statements to prevent it. But, it apparently underestimated the Chinese reaction, and, at the same time, it failed to develop a concurrent strategy which, by retaliatory threats or other sanctions, could succeed in preventing Chinese intervention. As Whiting has suggested,[45] the threat to use atomic weapons on the Chinese mainland, if the Chinese intervened, might have been a much more effective deterrent than the attempt to reassure them that a march to the border did

---

[43] However, if the use of atomic weapons had been confined to the Korean theatre—that is, if the decision to use the weapons was not coupled with a decision to expand the war in some other way—it is not clear who would have gained from an atomic exchange.

[44] Whiting, *passim*.

[45] Whiting, 162.

not presage an attack on mainland China.[46] The threat to use atomic weapons would have involved major political costs for the United States, and it is not clear that the American government would have warned of a possible atomic attack, even if it recognized its likely effect. Had it been aware that the fear of greater expansion might have deterred Chinese intervention, an alternative course might have been to threaten to expand the war to China with conventional weapons. But even this was not done. In fact a decision was made that Chinese intervention would not lead to conventional bombing beyond the Yalu. MacArthur reportedly believed that this decision had been leaked to the Chinese.[47]

In choosing, instead, to inform the Chinese of its limited objectives, the United States also considered it important to reassure the Chinese that their hydroelectric plants would not be jeopardized by a march up to the Yalu. But, as Whiting has pointed out:

> It was widely believed in Western circles that a determining factor in Chinese Communist concern over North Korea was the reliance of Manchurian industry upon power supplies across the border as well as along the Yalu River. This belief prompted explicit reassurances from Western spokesmen, both in Washington and at Lake Success, concerning "China's legitimate interests" near the frontier. Yet we have seen that Peking ignored this issue completely in its domestic as well as its foreign communications. The absence of propaganda about the protection of the hydroelectric installations, despite the need to maximize popular response to mobilization of "volunteers," suggests that this consideration played little if any role in motivating Chinese Communist intervention.[48]

In its advance through North Korea, then, the United Nations Command was attempting to communicate two points to the Chinese Communists: first, that it was prepared to go up to but not beyond the Yalu, and second, that it was prepared to respect China's legitimate interests in the northern regions of North Korea. It sought, therefore, to establish its limited objectives: that United Nations forces would take all North Korea, that the North Korean government would cease to exist, but that China's legitimate industrial interests would be protected. And it sought to assure the Chinese that the capture of North Korea would not be used as a springboard for an attack into China. It assumed that these were the limits in which the Chinese were interested, and that these would serve to keep the Chinese out of the war. But Chinese interests were different and could only be satisfied by different boundary conditions to the war.

---

[46] Panikkar, the Indian Ambassador in Peiping, reported that the Chinese expected an atomic attack, but were nonetheless prepared to intervene. See K. M. Panikkar, *In Two Chinas* (London, 1955), 108.

[47] Whitney, 455–56.

[48] Whiting, 151–52.

Neustadt argues that the Chinese were not in any way affected by the announcement of the United Nations aim to destroy the North Korean government:

> To judge from what the Chinese said, and later did, Peking's concern was with MacArthur's military progress, never mind its foreign policy objective. Chinese concern was not confined to anything so simple as a buffer zone along the border; an entity called North Korea, not the border, was at stake (perhaps in roughly the same sense that South Korea, under reverse circumstances, was for Washington). Even had the United Nations promised restoration of an independent North once all resistance ceased—which, naturally, no one proposed—I know of nothing to suggest that Peking would have withheld intervention. The Communist world does not take kindly, it appears, to the dismantling of the member state's facilities for government: the party and the army. MacArthur's military progress threatened both, no matter what came after. In short, the military risks and the diplomatic dangers usually associated with MacArthur's march across the parallel existed independent of the words used in the UN resolution. MacArthur's march was authorized before the words were seen, much less approved, at Lake Success.[49]

Even if we assume that Neustadt was attempting to justify the policy of an Administration with which he was connected, it seems clear that Washington was convinced in retrospect that its declarations did not influence the Chinese decision to enter the war and that no other declaratory policy could have altered the Chinese decision. American policy-makers have concluded that once the decision was made to cross the thirty-eighth parallel, nothing could be done to affect the Chinese decision. In fact, the State Department reportedly argued in December of 1950 that the Chinese decision to intervene was made prior to the crossing of the thirty-eighth parallel. In one sense, at least, this conclusion may be wrong: the Chinese position might have been altered by threats to expand the war with the use of atomic weapons against China. Moreover, it is by no means certain that the Chinese were interested in preserving the total territorial integrity of North Korea. It is possible, as Whiting suggests, that an American commitment to advance only part way up the peninsula—that is, to permit the maintenance of the North Korean government in some part of its territory—might have been sufficient to deter the Chinese entrance into the war:

> Neither before [n]or during the first three months of war [Whiting wrote] did the degree of interest in Pyongyang evinced by Peking warrant acceptance at face value of its concern for a "just" peace, based upon the status quo ante.
> This is not to say that the Chinese Communist leadership was pre-

---

[49] Neustadt, 125; see also 123–24.

pared to accept with equanimity the total defeat of North Korea. As a minimal goal, intervention must have been attempted to preserve an entity identifiable as the DPRK, and to prevent unification of all Korea under U.N. supervision. The late date of Chinese Communist entry into the war suggests that it was the political importance of the North Korean government, rather than its territorial integrity, that was at stake. Although intervention was officially predicated upon U.N. crossing of the thirty-eighth parallel, no Chinese People's Volunteers and Democratic People's Republic of Korea defense lines were established during the August–October period, not even to protect Pyongyang. To Peking, a "just" Korean peace was not an end in itself but rather a means towards fulfilling other related goals of policy.[50]

Thus, even after the crossing of the thirty-eighth parallel, Chinese intervention might have been prevented, had the United States acted differently. Although it tried to impose limits on expansion, the United States failed to grasp adequately either the reasons that the Chinese felt intervention was necessary or the threats that might have deterred their intervention. Both sides expanded the war, the United Nations by crossing the thirty-eighth parallel and the Chinese by entering the war. Both sides failed to convey to each other the kind of counteraction to be expected which might have deterred expansion. China attempted to prevent the crossing of the thirty-eighth parallel by declaring her intention to intervene, but this intention, relayed by the Indian Ambassador,[51] was not taken seriously by the United Nations Command. The United Nations sought to prevent the Chinese entrance, not by threatening a further expansion, but by attempting to satisfy the Chinese security interests that, it was assumed, might lead her to enter the war.

Despite these two major acts of expansion which followed closely on each other, the war remained limited, and this fact suggests the fallacy of the proposition that the limitation of a war depends on neither side drastically expanding the war at any point. These were major expansions, but neither seems to have brought the sides close to decisions to initiate global war or to expand very substantially the area or intensity of the local war.

Ports and Troops

Despite the fact that United States planes taking off from airfields in South Korea and Japan, and from aircraft carriers, consistently bombed targets in North Korea, the Communists engaged in almost no bombing south of the thirty-eighth parallel. This was one of the major asymmetries of the war both from a legalistic point of view and in terms of interfering with the military operations of the enemy. Both sides apparently devoted considerable attention to the question of what targets to attack, and a variety of motives affected the relevant decisions.

---

[50] Whiting, 155–56.
[51] Panikkar, 111.

The American decision to bomb targets in North Korea was made prior to the commitment of American ground troops in June 1950. A month later permission was given to bomb industrial targets in North Korea, but the use of incendiary bombs was not permitted because of the civil damage that would have resulted. The Air Force was not allowed to bomb the areas close to the Soviet and Chinese borders. Rashin was the single industrial center within the forbidden area and it was the only industrial target in North Korea which was not destroyed by mid-September when an end to industrial bombing was ordered by the Joint Chiefs.[52] With this task completed, the bombing of the North Korean halves of the Yalu bridges was authorized. Because of the restrictions imposed, the operation was only partly successful and came to a halt with the freezing of the Yalu in late November. It was not until June 1952 that attacks on the hydroelectric plants in North Korea were authorized; within two weeks almost ninety per cent of the North Korean power capacity was destroyed.[53]

American attacks on targets in North Korea steadily expanded. The attacks were aimed at affecting the immediate military situation. The restraints observed had several motives: (1) to avoid extensive civilian destruction considered undesirable on both humanitarian and propaganda grounds; (2) to avoid a spill-over of the war into China or the Soviet Union—the spill-over into China prior to her entry into the war probably did not have a major impact on Chinese policy, but it did create propaganda and political difficulties; (3) to avoid damaging, in the case of the hydroelectric plants, targets considered vital to the Chinese, so as to avoid their entrance into the war, presumably in retaliation.

The Communists exercised far greater restraint on their air forces. Except for a few night "heckling" attacks from small biplanes in the spring of 1951, no air attacks were made on any targets in South Korea. The Communist restraint was not the result of the absence of inviting military targets. The port of Pusan was an extremely inviting target for bombardment and mining. It was the key to the American logistic effort and frequently was lighted up all night. American logistic convoys and troops in the field also could have been hampered by air attacks. A number of factors seem to have influenced the Communist decision not to respond in kind to United Nations air attacks on North Korea:

(1) The Communists may have believed that it would have been very difficult, if not impossible, for the United Nations to continue its operations in Korea if Pusan came under heavy attack. It might also have been obvious that, once the United Nations committed itself to the defense of South Korea, it was no longer in a position where it could afford to accept complete withdrawal. Therefore, if attacks on its logistic lines made impossible its continued conflict of an effective ground war in Korea, the United States

---

[52] Futrell, 174–86.
[53] Futrell, 449–52.

might have been forced to engage in strategic strikes against the Chinese, if not the Russian, homeland.[54] If the Communists found this supposition credible, they may have concluded that, once their initial grab for South Korea failed, they could not afford to do anything that would lead to their complete control over South Korea.[55] They may have recognized that American confinement of the war to the Korean peninsula was dependent on her ability to fight there effectively.

(2) In order to avoid attacks on Chinese air bases just north of the Yalu, Red airmen were not allowed to attack United Nations positions from these bases. Although the Communists were permitting the United States the sanctuary of bases in Japan and on aircraft carriers, they apparently were afraid that they would not be granted a similar sanctuary for bombing operations. United States planes managed to keep the North Korean airfields out of commission throughout the war. Thus, given that the Chinese limited the use of their fields to staging operations and to fighter planes, they were incapable of bombing operations.[56]

(3) There is some evidence to suggest that Soviet pilots constituted a significant part of the "Chinese" air force during the Korean War.[57] If this is true, the explanation for target restraint may have been the desire to avoid the capture of Soviet airmen. This proof of direct Soviet involvement in the war would at the least have been politically damaging and, from a Soviet point of view, might have created an intolerable risk of American retaliation.

By the end of the war the United States was exercising almost no target restraint in North Korea and the Communists were doing no bombing in South Korea. Each side was guided by a complex series of motives and incentives. However, despite the asymmetry of the actions there is nothing to suggest that either side treated its decisions on targets as being closely related to, affected by, or likely to affect, the opponent's decisions on these questions.

CONCLUSIONS

The development of the limiting process in the Korean War seems to have been the work, on the whole, of the civilian decision-makers, at least on the American side, in rejecting or approving requests by the military to

---

[54] The United States had secured British concurrence to bomb bases in China in the event of heavy air attacks from Chinese bases on United Nations troops (*House of Commons Debates*, 5th Series, CDXCVI, 970, Feb. 26, 1952) and this was probably communicated to the Chinese. However, Truman reported that he was convinced that Russia would intervene if Manchurian bases were bombed. (Truman, 382–83.) It is not clear that the American threat was considered credible by the Chinese.

[55] This thesis implies that the Chinese would not have driven the United Nations forces off the Korean peninsula by ground action even if they had the capability. There is no evidence to substantiate or invalidate this point.

[56] Futrell, 266, 637–38.

[57] Futrell, 370, 651–52.

engage in military operation which would have the effect of expanding the war. In some cases, particularly on the question of using atomic weapons, the military never made the request, and so, in some sense, no decision was made. On three occasions, General MacArthur was refused his requests: to employ Chinese Nationalist troops, to impose a naval blockade on China and to bomb bases and supply lines in China.[58] But a number of MacArthur's requests for permission to expand the war were approved. These included the commitment of American ground forces, the Inchon offensive, and the crossing of the thirty-eighth parallel.

In deciding whether to go on the offensive in the war, Truman reports that the National Security Council recommended the consideration of three factors: action by the Soviet Union and the Chinese Communists, the views of friendly members of the United Nations and the risk of general war. It is clear that this and other decisions were also influenced by American objectives and doctrine, as well as by domestic political pressures.[59] The balancing of the factors varied from decision to decision, but all played a role in the major decisions to limit or expand the war.

Much less is known about the Communist decision-making process or the factors which influenced their decisions to limit or expand the war. The initial decision to keep the Chinese out of the war seems to have been based largely on domestic conditions in China, particularly the desire of the Chinese to implement their program of economic growth and development, and their desire to avoid military entanglements at a time when they had not yet consolidated their hold over their own country.[60] The reasons for the Russians' abstention from open intervention in the war are less clear. It is apparent that Russia was determined not to do anything that directly labeled her as a participant. She did not publicize the participation of any Russian "volunteers" in the war, nor provide any atomic capability, although she did supply large amounts of conventional military equipment. One likely explanation is the Russian fear that her intervention would lead to total war, and, it should be remembered, the strategic balance at this stage was one that drastically favored the West. The United States had the capability of inflicting great destruction on the Soviet homeland with its stock of atomic weapons, while the Soviets had no capability of directly attacking the United States, although they might have been able to take a large part of Western Europe with ground forces. Thus, the Soviets, aware of their inferior strategic position, were probably determined to keep out of the war and to provide no excuse for a direct American attack on the Soviet Union.

It should be noted that both sides apparently arrived at their decisions to

---

[58] "MacArthur Hearings," 13.

[59] Truman, 359.

[60] It was probably based also on the belief that the United States would not intervene and that the North Korean army would capture all of South Korea. (See Whiting, 40, 45–46.) The reasons for their entrance into the war were discussed above.

limit the war for different reasons and with minimal attention to the battle-field interaction. In addition, they observed very different limits: that is, both did not abstain from the same actions. What we did in North Korea was quite different from what the Communists did in South Korea, but the Chinese used a much greater percentage of their gross national product than we did. Nevertheless, while we used naval vessels and airplanes to bomb troops and airfields beyond Korea, they did not. The United States engaged in logistical interdiction, the Communists did not. Each side, then, observed its own series of limits and restraints only in some general way related to, and dependent on, the limits of the other side.

At least a few of the limits were symmetrical. Both sides restricted their military operations almost entirely to Korea, and neither used nuclear weapons. There was lack of symmetry in that all the military targets in North Korea were attacked but some in South Korea were not. The United States attacked the Chinese points of entry—the Yalu bridges—but the Chinese did not attack ours—the ports. Both sides observed a number of what Schelling has called "legalistic" limitations.[61] The United Nations carefully observed both the Chinese and Russian borders and tried to avoid crossing them inadvertently. There was symmetry in the absence of official declarations of war. The United Nations troops participated in the war in a "police action" capacity, and none of the countries involved, including the United States, declared war. The Chinese used "volunteers," and the Russians supplied equipment and, presumably, technicians but little manpower for the battle.

In some cases, the limits represented a recognition of the battlefield inter-action—if one side did something the other was likely to reciprocate—which would result in expansions of the war benefiting neither side. But the origin of many of the limits observed, and part of the explanation for others, lay not within the dynamics of the war itself, but within the domestic and international context in which the war was fought.

---

[61] Thomas Schelling, "Nuclear Weapons and Limited War," *The Strategy of Conflict* (Cambridge, Mass., 1960), 257–66.

GUERRILLA WARFARE AND
U.S. MILITARY POLICY:
A STUDY

Peter Paret
John W. Shy

THE 1960's, a Marine Corps officer recently said, may be "the decade of the guerrilla." Events in Southeast Asia, in Africa, and in the Caribbean do indeed seem to bear out his prediction. No longer is the irregular warrior a military orphan. The Administration has proposed a rapid expansion of "unconventional warfare capabilities," a call to which Congressmen and journalists have responded with enthusiasm. Even *The New York Times* has printed a primer on the subject culled from Mao Tse-tung.[1]

Most of us will agree that this swing in attitude is overdue. For too long, nuclear weapons have monopolized the nation's intellectual energies and material resources. Even the growing interest in the possibility of limited war has largely accepted the traditional definition of "war." Only now, when guerrillas in Laos, Cuba, the Congo, and Algeria have directly touched our national interest, do we seem to be awakening to the full range of military possibilities. More reflection on earlier events in Greece, Palestine, Indochina, Indonesia, the Philippines, Malaya, Cyprus, and even Kashmir and Kenya might have shortened this unfortunate time lag in our thinking.

But just as many people have tended in the past to regard a certain weapon or doctrine, whether "massive retaliation" or "limited war," as the single solution to our military problems, there is now a danger that such tendencies will shift toward the guerrilla and subversion. This kind of attitude, to which few of us are immune, reflects a weakness for gadgets and fashions that has no place in our thinking on defense. The enthusiasts of guerrilla warfare have made their case after a long, dry season of neglect. The time has come, however, to balance the discussion. We need to analyze what we have learned about guerrilla operations, and to clarify our thinking about the relation of guerrilla warfare to American foreign and military policy.

---

[1] See [the *Marine Corps Gazette*, Vol. 46 (January, 1962),] pp. 5–10 for this text.

The first question to ask is a simple one but perhaps for that reason is usually ignored: What are the functions of guerrilla warfare?

Historically—both before and after Spanish peasants fighting against Napoleon put "guerrilla" into the dictionary—the irregular has usually been defending his country against foreign invasion. The twentieth century, however, has brought two other functions more clearly into view: The guerrilla may be a weapon of insurrection, aiming at the capture of political power; and he may be the instrument of foreign aggression. Today the second and third functions are our primary concern, although guerrilla operations against conventional attack or in the aftermath of a nuclear strike remain conceivable.

The insurrectionary and aggressive functions of guerrilla warfare are not new in themselves. People discontented with their governments and agents of foreign powers have often been involved in violent uprisings that used unorthodox military tactics. What *is* comparatively new is the development of a body of theory that has systematized the technique of using guerrilla warfare for the seizure of national or international power and has placed the irregular fighting among the weapons systems of modern war.

Colonel T. E. Lawrence, leader of the Arab guerrilla campaign against Turkish communications in World War I, was the first of the new partisan "leader-theorists" to have appeared in the twentieth century. These men, in their actions as well as in their writings, have extended Clausewitz' analysis of the armed populace as a military instrument, to include the use of irregulars for political purposes. While Mao Tse-tung is deservedly the best known among them, Mikhail Frunze, Leon Trotsky, and, most recently, Che Guevara, are others of importance.

What can these men teach us? They have described the conditions under which guerrilla warfare can be initiated and sustained. They have analyzed both the techniques and the objectives of guerrilla warfare. Finally, perhaps surprisingly, they have revealed the inherent limitations of this form of combat.

An Algerian rebel leader recently explained the necessary conditions for guerrilla warfare in terms of "terrain." He was using the word both in an unconventional and in its conventional, geographical, sense. Strategically, irregulars need considerable space in which to pursue hit-and-run operations successfully. Mao, for example, has doubted whether extensive guerrilla warfare could ever occur in a country as small as Belgium. Tactically, irregulars require rough country, with few people and poor roads difficult of access to their opponents.

But the Algerian leader was also using "terrain" in the extended sense of "political terrain." Internationally, diplomatic support for the guerrillas can weaken their opponent, provide moral and material assistance, and even furnish military sanctuary that may compensate for inadequate space in the area of active operations. Internally, guerrillas must have the active support of some, and the acquiescence of most, of the civilian population.

Internal popular support is the indispensible condition for successful guerrilla action. This fact makes the relationship between the military and civilian realms more intimate than in any other type of warfare. Although this point is often stated, its rationale is too little understood. Why must the guerrilla have a firm psychological base among the people?

First, the irregular fighter is recruited by some ideological commitment—however crude it might be—and not primarily by administrative machinery. Only such commitment can sustain the self-control and unit discipline demanded by this most punishing kind of combat. Agents, infiltrated from abroad, may play an important role, but perhaps the greatest advantage of the guerrilla is that he is a native, fighting among people and over ground he has known since birth.

Second, civilian support helps to solve the critical problems of logistics and intelligence. The local populace provides food, shelter, medical care, and money. More important, it furnishes the information the guerrilla must have in order to enjoy both surprise when he attacks and security from attack by his opponent. Even when the mass of the people seem no more than apathetic, afraid, and unhappy at being caught in the midst of an internal war, they are not truly neutral. If the guerrillas are succeeding, then the people are giving them vital intelligence and denying it to their opponents. As Guevara has written: "One of the most important characteristics of a guerrilla war is the notable difference that exists between the information the rebel forces possess and the information the enemies possess."

Popular support is indispensable to the guerrilla because he is militarily weak, a fact easily forgotten. After all, the guerrilla fights as he does because he lacks the weapons, equipment, supplies, technical skills, and often numbers needed to fight in any other way. Seldom if ever has anyone deliberately chosen a guerrilla strategy when other choices existed. If sufficient military strength is available, conventional organization and tactics produce a decision more quickly; if the goal is political, strength makes possible a *coup d'état* instead of a costly, protracted civil war.

Even the American revolutionaries, whose armed populace gave them enormous guerrilla potential, used partisan warfare only as a last resort. This traditional reluctance to employ guerrillas unless forced to do so is understandable. Guerrillas do great damage to the very society they are trying to defend or control because their weakness keeps them from protecting people or property. Their strength derives not so much from weapons and organization as from changeable popular attitudes. In short, guerrilla warfare as a military means to a political end is both costly and risky. Civil War historians who are fond of praising the partisan exploits of Mosby in northern Virginia should remember the sequel: Sheridan devastated the

Shenandoah Valley, and Mosby, deprived of his guerrilla base, ultimately failed.

True, guerrilla warfare has one major advantage in this nuclear age. If employed as an instrument of foreign aggression, it constitutes an "ambiguous threat" by confusing the legal, political, and even military bases for an effective international response. But most of the native guerrillas and their civilian supporters must have a stronger motive for fighting than serving the convenience of a foreign power. The internal conditions for irregular warfare must be right before the guerrilla becomes available as a means of aggression.

The weakness of the guerrilla himself and his consequent need to gain and maintain strength among the civilian population largely determine his techniques and objectives. Unable to destroy his opponent physically by direct, military action, he fights psychologically by indirect, political means. Never attacking unless overwhelmingly superior, and never fighting long enough to be caught by a counterattack, the guerrilla leader uses combat itself as a psychological weapon. With an unbroken string of victories, however insignificant many of them may be, he creates confidence in ultimate success among his supporters. At the same time, he fosters a growing despair among his opponents.

The guerrilla converts his reliance on the civilian population into an advantage. Because he cannot hold ground or even do large-scale damage to enemy forces, his objective becomes control of the population. He pursues this objective not only by politically organizing and indoctrinating the people, but also by educating his own men in their role of winning civilian support. The "Three Disciplinary Rules" and "Eight Points of Attention," which Mao formulated as early as 1928, make it plain to all irregular soldiers that they are expected to behave not as conquerors or bandits, but as disciplined representatives of a new social and economic order.

This new order, Mao also declares, is at the heart of the struggle. "Without a political goal," he writes, "guerrilla warfare must fail, as it must if its political objectives do not coincide with the aspirations of the people." Land reform, nationalism, corruption, poverty—these are the issues exploited by modern guerrillas to win people over. Once it is organized, and convinced of both the certainty and the justice of a guerrilla victory, the civilian population replaces the traditional tools of war with a less tangible form of strength.

The required integration of military and political action goes beyond formulating a popular program and then letting the partisans themselves act as its salesmen. Even the smallest tactical operation may have political implications. For example, an attack on an enemy strong point seems necessary, but may alienate the local inhabitants or expose them to reprisals against which they cannot be protected. The political consequences may well outweigh the possible military gain and the raid is not carried out. The Algerians have adopted perhaps the most extreme solution to this problem of politico-military coordination by introducing a political officer, who himself has had previous experience as a military commander, at every echelon down to the section.

It is useful, with our new concern over guerrilla warfare, to imagine ourselves in the position of the guerrilla leader. We then see that he is face to face with some serious difficulties and certain inherent limitations. In *La Guerra de Guerrillas*, Che Guevara, like Mao, understandably stresses the positive side of irregular warfare. But a close reading of his book reveals a series of dilemmas for the guerrilla leader.

Above all, the guerrilla leader must be continually active—harassing enemy communications, ambushing isolated posts and detachments, creating by acts of violence a general climate of insecurity. His movement thrives and grows on continual, small successes. At the same time, he must never risk a defeat. Defeat not only hurts his small, poorly equipped forces, but it also weakens partisan morale and civilian confidence. The psychological damage may be greater than the military. This was probably true of the July, 1961, battle in South Vietnam, where the Viet Cong lost fewer than 200 of their 5,000–10,000 fighters. The guerrilla leader attempts to walk a fine line between rashness and necessary boldness.

Second, there is a dilemma posed by terrain on the one hand, targets on the other. The rougher the terrain, the more secure is the guerrilla force. But the rougher the terrain, the more difficult is it for guerrillas to find local supplies and to hit the most important military and political targets. Guevara admits that the cities and the suburbs are the sensitive areas that must be attacked and indoctrinated, but that precisely those areas are most dangerous for guerrilla operations. Even the flatter, more fertile, and heavily populated farmlands constitute "unfavorable terrain."

There is also the matter of guerrilla discipline. Guevara notes that individual conviction drives most guerrillas to fight but they must submit to a discipline that is extremely severe by regular standards. Only under such discipline can they meet the extraordinary physical and emotional demands placed upon them by irregular warfare (similar demands nearly destroyed the combat effectiveness of Allied long-range penetration groups in Burma in 1944). In Cuba, one method of solving this conflict between individual motivation and extreme regimentation was to let unit committees, rather than combat commanders, perform certain judicial functions. Nevertheless, even such self-imposed discipline cannot afford any doubts about the cause or the leadership. For this reason, guerrillas themselves seem to be especially vulnerable to psychological attack.

The guerrilla leader faces still another dilemma in dealing with the civilian population. Although many of the people may be discontented, their discontent must be translated into willingness to commit or support illegal, violent acts. Generally they are brought to do this by a combination of political persuasion and military success. But rarely if ever has a guerrilla movement been able to avoid more coercive techniques, including the use of terror. The crucial question then becomes whether coercion, and especially terror, will alienate people more than it intimidates them.

Some American officials and journalists have recently argued that terror alone, used by guerrillas infiltrated into an area, can maintain the popular base needed for guerrilla warfare. But Che Guevara, in his field manual for Latin American revolutionaries, does not seem to agree. He returns to the question of coercion repeatedly, never quite clarifying the answer, but clearly revealing the complexity of the problem. "Treason," he admits on the one hand, must always be "justly punished." Guerrillas display "absolute implacability" toward "contemptible persons." And especially in "unfavorable terrain"—cities or farmland—where propaganda is most important but military operations are most hazardous, the guerrillas eliminate "recalcitrant enemies . . . without leniency. . . . There can be no enemies in dangerous places."

On the other hand, Guevara rejects terrorism as a general policy because it "is a negative weapon that produces in no way the desired effects, that can turn a people against a given revolutionary movement, and that brings with it a loss of lives among those taking part that is much greater than the return."

There is some historical evidence supporting his point. The Greek Communists, although successful for a time in using coercive methods, eventually drove over a half-million of what should have been their strongest supporters off the land and into the cities. The Malayan Communists, once committed to a policy of terror, found that it undermined their campaign of political indoctrination and they abandoned it within a year. In southwestern Korea, North Korean guerrillas successfully terrorized the peasants until threats ceased to be certain of execution. Then terror began to boomerang. Even the Algerians claim to have given up the large-scale use of terror, as a means of keeping Moslems in line, after finding its disadvantages too great.

Terrorism, of course, can have other important uses besides maintaining popular support. A government too weak to provide a popular rallying point, a government without the administrative machinery or military strength to perform its minimum functions, may find that terrorism so completely disrupts life that peace on any terms seems preferable. Employed against a colonial regime weakened by political difficulties at home and abroad, terrorism alone may achieve the objective of the guerrillas. This happened in Palestine and Cyprus. In Cyprus, EOKA never engaged in large-scale irregular combat although its operations had all the other characteristics of guerrilla warfare—a popular cause, civilian protection of the partisans, and governmental difficulties in obtaining information and maintaining order without further alienating the population. In the end, the British decided that a political settlement in Cyprus was preferable to all-out war against the insurgents.

But the use of violence by the partisans against civilians remains an ambiguous, not an invincible, weapon for the guerrilla leader. Indiscriminate or selective terror, less extreme forms of coercion, even sabotage if it disrupts civilian life too greatly, may have a backlash that repels rather than attracts popular support. At times, however, guerrilla forces must resort to these techniques, and the guerrilla leader must deal with the difficult problems of just when and how to use them, and how to keep them under control.

Unfortunately, Guevara barely touches on the last and greatest dilemma of the guerrilla leader (the rottenness of the Batista regime largely solved it for the Cuban revolutionaries). As we shall see, the big problem lies in the difficult choices involved in pushing the war to a victorious conclusion.

The belief that irregular operations must be regularized if partisans are to win has become one of the dogmas of guerrilla theory. Before Mao, both experience and doctrine had primarily concerned the defensive function of guerrilla warfare, which takes for granted a friendly regular army that eventually invades the country and operates in conjunction with the partisans. Mao was the first to see clearly that such an army might be created from the guerrilla force itself. Having consolidated their position through irregular warfare by the early 1930's, the Chinese Communists began to engage in more conventional operations. They reverted to a guerrilla strategy against the Japanese invasion in 1937, but after 1945, drawing upon his pool of combat-trained manpower, Mao used primarily regular forces in expelling Chiang from the mainland.

When there is no chance of large-scale foreign intervention, and when the enemy is politically and militarily strong, with both the will and the intelligence to use his strength, the dogma of regularization undoubtedly holds true. The psychological character of guerrilla warfare then becomes only the means of creating and consolidating the popular base, which in turn must eventually provide enough soldiers sufficiently well trained to defeat the enemy in open battle. But there are a number of pitfalls on the road to regular operations—regularization may be not just a dilemma, but a complex of dilemmas.

The first of these is proper timing of the transition. Premature regularization invites military disaster but overlong attachment to irregular operations may exhaust the population. The Chinese Communists worried most about the latter danger, the vice of "guerrillaism"; the Algerian rebels had to resist the opposite temptation, of seeking the domestic and diplomatic prestige of conventional operations before being militarily ready. One reason for the ultimate defeat of the Greek Communists appears to have been that before they could afford to do so they were fighting as regular forces, with heavy weapons and territorial bases.

Territorial bases are mentioned by Guevara as being of great value even before any attempt is made to regularize operations. They make it possible to have training and rest areas, supply dumps, and hospital facilities. Of course, he adds, they must be "secure," but how to make them secure against first-class regulars is not answered. Bases, it would seem, offer the sort of fixed target that counterguerrilla forces always seek and rarely find.

In China and Indochina, guerrilla groups turned into regular armies capable of defeating large enemy forces. In both cases, this was achieved with foreign assistance, and there is little evidence that victory can ever be gained without such help. To be sure, guerrillas will supply themselves with arms and ammunition by raids, and the civilian population will provide other essentials. But the FLN required the sanctuary of Tunisian territory and even Castro needed outside support, including the crucial U.S. arms embargo against Batista in 1958. Yet foreign aid can be a two-edged sword for the guerrilla leader. The aims of the guerrilla movement and its foreign ally will never coincide exactly, and the differences may be important, especially if exploited by their mutual enemy. This need to acquire foreign aid makes possible the third function of guerrilla warfare—its use as an instrument of aggression. But even Communists, with their talent for linking local grievances and Russian or Chinese foreign policy in a single ideological framework, do not always find it easy to dominate a guerrilla movement. At the same time, the guerrilla leader may find it difficult to bargain for outside help without undermining or compromising his own objectives.

In all of these dilemmas, the guerrilla leader must display exceptional judgment. Guerrillas, unlike more conventional forces, lack the strength to make up for faulty decisions. Moreover, a shrewd opponent who understands the nature of irregular warfare can considerably narrow the area in which sound decisions by the guerrilla leader are possible.

We have outlined the nature of guerrilla warfare—its setting, objectives, techniques, and limitations. What do these factors mean for the United States? We are not here urging specific solutions to specific problems, but our analysis may offer some guidelines for thinking about the general problem of the relationship of guerrilla warfare to American policy.

Guerrilla warfare concerns the United States in three different ways:

1. In planning to employ guerrillas defensively, thus strengthening the ability of non-Communist states to resist regular attack.

2. In employing guerrillas as offensive weapons.

3. In bolstering the defenses of a friendly nation fighting guerrillas, or threatened by them.

Too often these areas are confused, or lumped together under the phrase "unconventional warfare capabilities." Since they deal with different problems, they should be kept distinct.

The first area—planning to use guerrillas as a defensive weapon—needs little discussion. It appears most applicable to NATO, as a means of making

Western European peoples indigestible for a conventionally armed invader, or able to conduct the broken-back war that may follow thermonuclear strikes. Any such plan must, however, meet several important considerations. One is the fact that guerrillas, because of their weakness, must rely for protection on a nearly impenetrable counterintelligence screen. Would not peacetime reserve guerrilla units be subject to infiltration, or even to the capture of so many personnel in the initial shock of invasion, that the entire organization would be fatally compromised? The resistance movements of World War II were recruited under wartime conditions, certainly disadvantageous in some ways, but perhaps essential if a guerrilla force is to survive.

If the problem of security seems solvable, there is a geographical difficulty to consider. Western Europe is a fairly constricted area, with a high density of people and communications and with few natural bastions. Most of it is very "unfavorable terrain." Undoubtedly guerrilla warfare is possible in Western Europe for a short time, especially if the Communist invaders are heavily engaged against Western regular forces. But it seems a dubious NATO strategy to rely on guerrillas as a major deterrent or as a means of prolonged resistance. Everything will depend, of course, on the willingness of the civilian population to fight back. In short, it may prove difficult if not impossible to stockpile effectively the components of guerrilla warfare.

Using guerrillas as an offensive weapon, either to put pressure on the Communists or to overthrow a government obnoxious to the United States, has recently received considerable attention. In case of major war, it would clearly be a way to exploit discontent in the Communist rear—in Hungary, for example. But its employment as a weapon in the Cold War, or as a new instrument of American diplomacy, is another matter.

All would agree that it is in the satellite area that the launching of guerrilla movements seems most profitable. Yet is it not precisely this area where such ventures are most risky? Communist regimes are past masters of this kind of warfare and could be expected to fight back with ruthless efficiency rather than become less militantly Communist. If a guerrilla movement *should* achieve some success, despite or perhaps because of Communist repression, there would be real danger of escalation to a higher level of violence. The United States, through some miscalculation of this almost incalculable kind of warfare, might find itself with the unhappy choice of abandoning friends or raising the stakes. Some analysts of nuclear strategy have seen Western-backed satellite revolt as the most likely occasion for a Russian surprise attack on the United States.

Aside from the direct danger to ourselves, our potential allies in these countries would undergo great and prolonged suffering. It is doubtful if they could ever win without American armed support, and except in an all-out war that would seem out of the question. In other words, we would be asking these people to act as pawns in our global strategy. Besides, if somehow it should free itself from Communist control, could a society terribly damaged by internal war be stable without resort to totalitarian techniques? Is the United States interested in such an outcome, and is it willing to bear the responsibility for liberating people by these means?

Finally, does the United States have the capacity to conduct covert military operations on an extensive scale? The Cuban venture was not a fair test because its concept largely rejected guerrillas in favor of a more conventional strategy. Nevertheless, there is a reason to suspect that our ability to conceal from others and from our own population what we are doing is not very great. It has been argued that the adoption of guerrilla subversion as American policy would lead to fundamental changes in both our internal structure and our international objectives. To many Americans, such changes are unacceptable in that they seem to erode the very basis of our national existence.

Not only may objections be raised on grounds of principle, there are practical reasons for treating with caution any proposed employment of guerrillas to overthrow governments. If such a break with what we like to think of as traditional policy also ruptures the general American consensus on national purpose, then we may have weakened ourselves internally more than any international gain might be worth. Although the Cold War is certainly not a popularity contest, we may also make it more difficult for actual and potential allies to conclude that it lies in their interest to work with us.

For example, a government under guerrilla attack might find it impossible to accept help from an aggressive United States without discrediting itself in the eyes of its own population as a tool of imperialism. In such an eventuality, the United States would have suffered, not just a drop in nebulous international prestige, but a tangible military reverse. W. W. Rostow, in one of the most complete statements yet made by the Administration on guerrilla warfare,[2] has argued this point persuasively: "Despite all the Communist talk of aiding movements of national independence, they are driven in the end, by the nature of their system, to violate the independence of nations. Despite all the Communist talk of American imperialism, we are committed, by the nature of our system, to support the cause of national independence. And the truth will out."

Public interest in the employment of guerrillas by the United States has tended to dilute discussion of what is in fact our most pressing problem: how to fight against guerrillas. Such discussion as has occurred has generally taken the form of debate between the exponents of military aid and the exponents of economic aid to underdeveloped areas. It should be clear from the character of guerrilla warfare, however, that neither military measures nor political measures by themselves will solve the problem of defense against guerrillas.

For purposes of analysis, counterguerrilla action may be separated into

---

[2] See [*op. cit.*,] pp. 54–61 for his text.

three tasks, but they are so intimately related that success in one task often depends on progress in the others. The tasks are to defeat the guerrilla militarily, to break his connection with the civilian population, and to re-establish governmental authority and social order.

Professional soldiers are familiar with the tactical problems of fighting irregulars but a few points can be profitably made here. Successful counter-guerrilla operations, as in the Philippines, have always combined a grid system of territorial control with mobile striking forces. The mobile striking forces cannot normally be made up of friendly civilians, organized and trained to fight as guerrillas. Instead, they are composed of the best regulars, able to exploit all the technological and administrative advantages of modern military organization, and to employ them in unconventional fashion as well. Since the territorial forces are mainly police or home-defense units, the role for friendly guerrillas in counterguerrilla action seems very limited.

The French attempted to use such guerrillas in Indochina but without much success, mainly because they did not have the popular base from which to operate. Similarly, the United States should not expect to base its military action against guerrillas on local popular support, especially in the early stages of a conflict. French regular troops, on the other hand, never seem to have been able to operate unconventionally. The British forces in Malaya, with a smaller war on their hands, succeeded to a remarkable extent in using irregular tactics against Communist guerrillas. It is important for the United States to understand this distinction between guerrilla tactics available to both sides, and guerrilla organization, which is naturally opposed to the government.

In Indochina, the French also failed to break the line between the guerrillas and the civilian population. Their failure was due not to a lack of understanding but to a lack of firm decisions on countermeasures. Troops in the field, frustrated by the sullen uncommunicativeness of the population, were allowed to commit occasional excesses and often to be simply rough in their handling of civilians. In the same way, until it was stopped, police brutality in South Korea and the Philippines actually helped the Communist partisans.

It is not simply a question of being kind to the natives but of keeping some legal framework intact. Counterguerrilla forces represent the government to most of the people caught in the midst of a guerrilla war. If these forces act more irresponsibly than the guerrillas themselves, the government can hardly hope to appeal to people as their protector and benefactor. Admittedly, the government will often have to employ some unusually harsh coercive measures in breaking the guerrilla-civilian link, but such measures must above all be legally formulated and applied. No government, unless it plans to resort to truly totalitarian techniques, can use terrorism or indiscriminate brutality against its own people without undermining its position.

Though the conduct of troops in the field can ruin any governmental plan for severing the guerrilla from his popular base, there is much more to accomplishing this task than having well-behaved soldiers. One obvious requirement is a psychological-warfare program. On the basis of past experience, this program must be highly sophisticated if it is to succeed. It does not tell lies, because the civilian target of the program knows more about the guerrillas than the government does. It does not confuse people potentially sympathetic to the guerrillas with the guerrillas themselves, because it seeks to break, not reinforce, the links between them. It will sometimes spread information that would normally be classified, because immediate and convincing reports of successful military operations are the best means of persuading people that support of the guerrillas is unwise.

Another standard method of denying the guerrilla his popular base is the resettlement of populations. Resettlement has been successful with the Chinese squatters in Malaya, and partially so with the Arabs in Algeria. But when calculating the military advantages of resettlement and planning the details of the program, full weight must be given to its political, economic, and social effects, which are often extremely harmful.

The ultimate technique in isolating guerrillas from the people is to persuade the people to defend themselves. Militia-type local defense units help in the military defeat of the guerrillas. Gradually they may replace the territorial garrison forces and free regulars for mobile operations. They protect their communities, ambush raiders, and furnish intelligence and security to mobile forces in the vicinity. But at least as important is their political function: Once a substantial number of members of a community commit violence on behalf of the government, they have gone far toward permanently breaking the tie between that community and the guerrillas.

The third task in the conduct of counterguerrilla operations consists in assisting the threatened government to re-establish social order and its own authority. Although this task seems wholly nonmilitary, it in fact attacks the underlying discontent that sustains violence. Neither economic aid from the United States nor domestic authoritarianism is an adequate answer to this problem. The government in question must administer reform effectively and honestly but without seeming to be simply responding to the program of the guerrillas. Moreover, despite certain obvious short-run disadvantages, the government will probably gain in the long run if it permits more rather than less political activity—including criticism of the government. Such activity gives discontented persons a choice other than supporting either the government or the guerrillas, and it keeps discontent above ground, where the government can measure and alleviate it.

Perhaps such a reform program sounds impossibly idealistic, but its planks are based on the British accomplishment in Malaya. For those who still doubt that basic reform and guerrilla warfare are connected, there is the example of the late Ramón Magsaysay, who crushed the Huk rebellion as much with reform as with weapons. The United States must of course decide whether it is ready to interfere in the political affairs and even in the administration of weak and often irrational friends, and help them—force them if necessary—to carry out the needed program. At the same time, the United States itself must be clear on what kinds of reform it will support, and what kinds are too radical to be compatible with its own objectives and political situation.

There is little hope that, in place of reform, the United States can simply persuade the people of a guerrilla-infested state to change their minds. For years French army officers, who have become the leading theorists of "revolutionary warfare," persisted in ignoring the simple fact that most Algerian Moslems were not interested in becoming part of a greater French nation. The idea that the minds of illiterate, economically backward people can be manipulated over a wide range of desires is probably wrong. In any case, we do not have the time to try it. Instead, the United States must accept the fact that real grievances, producing real demands, provide most of the impetus for guerrilla war, and we must prepare to meet or at least undercut those demands.

It would be false to conclude this discussion of guerrilla warfare on an optimistic note. Guerrillas present a difficult and an expensive problem for American military policy. But the first step in solving the problem is to understand it. The second step is to base action on that understanding, even when momentary pressures argue otherwise. The greatest danger in dealing with guerrillas is oversimplification; the second greatest is impatience. Approaches to the problem that unduly stress either military or nonmilitary action are the worst kinds of oversimplification, though each may seem tempting when one has lost patience with a more complex approach. Only by constantly recalling the fundamental structure of guerrilla movements, and by continuously putting what may seem like fine theoretical distinctions into practice, can the intricate but essential coordination of political and military action be maintained toward ultimate success.

THE CIVIC ROLE OF THE MILITARY:
SOME CRITICAL HYPOTHESES

Davis B. Bobrow

THE CIVIC ROLE of the military has become a principal American instrument to cope with Communist revolution, political instability, and economic backwardness. Expressed in the doctrine of civic action, the civic role refers to "the use of military forces on projects useful to the local population at all levels in such fields as education, training, public works, agriculture, transportation, communications, health, sanitation, and others contributing to economic and social development, which would also serve to improve the standing of the military forces with the population." [1]

This article attempts to stimulate systematic work on the civic sector of military behavior in order to understand it as a social process and to evaluate it as an instrument of American foreign policy. Against the background of the problems which have produced the civic role concept, the article presents two sets of hypotheses. The first set hypothesizes that particular factors which tend to operate in predictable ways determine the acceptance, conduct, and consequences of civic action. Based on these statements, the second set hypothesizes the value of the civic role concept to United States foreign policy in different situations.

We make the assumption that, in the absence of validated statements about the civic action process, fruitful hypotheses can be derived from knowledge of other social processes and actors. This assumption applies to the selection of determinants and to inferences about their operation. As an example of the latter, we hypothesize that, *ceteris paribus,* a greedy general manifests behavior similar to that of a greedy mayor or bureaucrat. Unless our assumption is accepted, social scientists cannot at this time clarify the value of the civic role activities emphasized in our military assistance programs.

I. THE BACKGROUND

What we can call a "passive" civic role, i.e., respect for the sensibilities of friendly and neutral civilians, has long been part of official United States military doctrine. However, the "active" civic role concept defined in the

---

[1] Major Robert L. Burke, "Military Civic Action," *Military Review,* Vol. XLIV, No. 10 (Oct. 1964), p. 63.

first paragraph has emerged recently in response to a number of foreign policy frustrations. The advocates of civic action assume that these actions will ameliorate problems in counterinsurgency, in the domestic economic and political policies of underdeveloped states, and in their regional and cold-war foreign policies by modifying the behavior of Communist insurgents, indigenous armies, and indigenous governments.

We can begin this summary of the assumptions which the advocates make about the civic action process with the effects on Communist insurgents. If friendly counterinsurgent armies play an active civic role, they will reap the same benefits as the insurgents have from similar activities. Accordingly, the rebels will first lose their popular base and, with the flow of men, supplies, and information diminished, experience military defeat. [2] This rationale has been most fully developed by the French theorists of psychological warfare. [3]

For indigenous armies, the advocates assume that an extensive civic role will diminish three patterns of behavior which are disadvantageous for the United States. First, civic action involvement will motivate the military to assist rather than veto political and economic reform. Accordingly, if South American armies are given extensive civic roles, they will expedite reform programs rather than staging *coups d'état* against their authors. Second, civic action involvement will motivate the military to give priority to domestic development rather than to external ventures. Accordingly, if the Egyptian and Indonesian military become heavily involved in, for example, village-level development tasks, the probabilities of regional military conflict will decline. Third, civic action involvement will motivate the military to acquire economic and managerial skills and multiply their commitment to mass modernization. Accordingly, if the Pakistani army emphasizes its civic role, the Ayub Khan regime will be both more competent in and more dedicated to modernization.

The advocates also assume that military civic action will improve the domestic and foreign policies of indigenous governments. These effects are based on assumptions about the characteristics of a military establishment with an extensive civic role. If a government is hostile to political and economic development, inefficient, unskilled, or corrupt, it will either accommodate itself to or be replaced by military leaders who, by definition, will be partisans of development, efficient, skilled, and honest. If a government pursues policies of regional aggrandizement or Communist-inclined nonalignment, the military will, at least, not support these policies and, at best, oppose them. The reasoning here is that extensive military civic duties reduce military demands for regional adventures and Communist hardware and

---

[2] Lt. Col. Harry F. Walterhouse, "Civic Action—A Counter and Cure for Insurgency," *Military Review*, Vol. XLII, No. 8 (Aug. 1962), pp. 47–54.

[3] Perhaps the most informative analysis of the French experience is that of Peter Paret, *French Revolutionary Warfare* (New York: Frederick A. Praeger, 1964).

improve the government's domestic popularity, therefore reducing the need for political diversion in the form of a foreign "victory." Some, but not all, advocates also reason that the officer corps is more firmly nationalistic and anti-Communist than civilian politicians. Accordingly, since civic action will increase military leverage on the politicians, it will minimize civilian tendencies to cooperate with and be absorbed into Communist spheres of influence.

Obviously, these assumptions all produce the conclusion that civic action is thoroughly in the American interest. To explore the validity of that conclusion, we must explore the validity of the assumptions on which it rests. These assumptions are really one-half of a number of function statements. The other side of these statements contains four factors and their relationships: the aspirations of the indigenous population; the strategy and capability of the local Communist movement; the indigenous military; and the indigenous government. The acceptance and conduct of civic action primarily depend on the two institutions responsible for internal order and popular satisfaction: the local military and the local government. The consequences of a military civic role primarily depend on the extent to which it satisfies popular demands and copes with Communist maneuvers. For the preliminary purposes of this article, we can treat popular demands and Communist maneuvers as parameters within which the different traits of armies and governments affect military civic action. Accordingly, the statement of these parameters in the following paragraphs amounts to a series of qualifications on the assumptions of civic action advocates. For civic action programs to produce the effects which their advocates assume, it is necessary but not sufficient for their immediate effects to lie within the following parameters.

The aspirations of the populations of the developing areas can be crudely summarized: physical security, a stable or predictable environment, material improvement, and membership in a national community, i.e., a new political identity. Obviously, if in its civic role the military coerces civilians, confiscates their resources, and provides few local benefits, these parameters are crossed. Although unrecognized by the French psychological warfare staff in Algeria, it is equally obvious that a civic action program dominated by foreigners conflicts with aspirations for a new political identity.

We cannot say that complete satisfaction of these aspirations is a necessary condition for the assumptions sketched earlier. However, we can say that prevention of any widening of the gap between aspirations and expectations is such a condition. Accordingly, civic action programs cross the popular aspirations parameters when they generate levels of aspiration in excess of their rewards. An example would be a road from a village to an urban center which exposes civilians to information which escalates their economic and political demands without any economic or political increment.

The failure to meet the conditions imposed by popular aspirations has a multiplier effect because of the strategy of local Communist movements in the underdeveloped states. Three principles of Communist strategy and one axiom about public opinion are important for our discussion. First, Communist propaganda attempts to increase popular conviction of the legitimacy and importance of the aspirations listed above. Second, Communist activities are designed to widen the felt gap between aspirations and expected rewards. Third, Communist organizations seek to appear to be the most promising organizations to fulfill popular aspirations. The implications for the civic role of non-Communist armies are also three: the aspirations can probably not be altered by substitution; rewards from civic action must race against rapidly rising aspirations; and the popular evaluation of official civic action performance rests on a comparison with Communist behavior. The final implication leads us to a public opinion axiom we can label "incumbent handicap." Simply, a unit of incumbent performance counts for less than a similar unit of insurgent performance. This means, for example, that if the civic role of the insurgent military matches that of the official army, the insurgents tend to gain in popular support. The rebels can argue effectively that their civic action programs are only a small sample of what they intend to do for the people once they achieve power, while incumbent civic action programs reveal the full extent of the benefits which the counter-revolutionary regime intends to give to the people. In sum, for a civic action program to have the counterinsurgency effects which the assumptions of its advocates require, it must out-compete Communist programs to meet rapidly inflating popular aspirations.

The crude parameters of popular aspirations and Communist strategy provide a set of measurements to evaluate the usefulness of American attempts to export the civic action concept. The paragraphs below contain hypotheses about the "buyers" of this export: indigenous armies and governments. These hypotheses are testable statements of the tendency of different characteristics of armies and governments to produce different values on the measuring rods summarized above. In applying a small number of variables to the behavior of indigenous armies and governments, we have been able to avoid confining ourselves to the consequences of an assumed level of civic action by the military. Instead, these variables also generate hypotheses about the acceptance and implementation of civic action by the military. Consequently, we can infer problems and choices for United States foreign policy at all three stages in the export of the civic action concept.

Of course, these statements are hypotheses and are not empirically validated; they also contain in every instance a clause to the effect that all other things remain equal. These limitations do not deprive the exercise of value if we keep the intellectual goal in mind: to make progress toward a set of reliable, generalized statements to predict the content of the civic sector of military behavior and its effects on the state in which it occurs. Because our hypotheses derive from knowledge of other social processes, they present a logical starting point which rests on past work. It seems inefficient to start to build new instruments if those in being can do the job. Of course, the critic who remarks that all other things are never equal is correct. However, we know from the history of economic theory that the *ceteris paribus* assumption has enabled economists to develop powerful theories which have real world applications. Accordingly, we have empirical confirmation of the usefulness of this procedural ground rule.

II. THE INDIGENOUS MILITARY

Five variables of the local armed forces appear to warrant attention for reasons indicated below. These are: social composition, skill level, public image, relation to civilian authority, and standard of self-evaluation. These variables, and alternative positions on each, affect in different ways what the military wants to do in its civic role, what it has the capacity to do, and what reception its actions encounter.

1. Social Composition

We hypothesize that the willingness of military personnel to undertake civic action tasks and civilian support for these tasks correlate with the extent to which the social composition of the military and civilian populations are similar. Accordingly, the highest probability for military acceptance of a civic role which benefits the nation as a whole, and of civilian support for such a mission, occurs when all major population groups are represented at all rank levels in the military. Conversely, military personnel tend to reject, and civilians to suspect, nationally oriented civic roles when major population groups are significantly underrepresented in the armed forces. These hypotheses follow from common notions in the study of political behavior. When we apply them to the attitudes of the military, they can be summed up in the proposition that common identification produces empathy; when applied to civilian perceptions, that common identification insures that officials feel obligated to their constituents. The "ethnic ticket" famed in Massachusetts attempts to capitalize on the latter proposition.

If these hypotheses are valid, an American policy which stresses civic action should also stress the need for indigenous armies to manifest balanced social composition. The fact that the armed forces of underdeveloped states, and particularly the officer corps, often are monopolized by one or two social groups confronts United States officials with a choice. Washington can either impel indigenous armies to diversify their social base or accept a diminution in the gains expected from civic action. The choice becomes complicated when we recognize that diversification may degrade the combat effectiveness of these armies in the short run as it lessens their unity.

2. Skill Level

We hypothesize, first, that the ability of the military to conduct civic action correlates with its skill level and, second, that military personnel seek authority and tasks commensurate with their skills. Accordingly, to fulfill the tasks mentioned by civic action advocates, military personnel should be literate and command basic mechanical and administrative skills. However, the probability that they will accept the grubby tasks of village-level modernization and refrain from demands for significant authority in development programs declines when they acquire complex mechanical and administrative skills. The latter hypothesis rests on the accepted notion that people tend to seek opportunities to use their abilities and become frustrated if opportunities are denied.

These hypotheses suggest that an American priority on civic action should be accompanied by efforts to insure that indigenous armies have sufficient but not excessive skills. Again, we know that indigenous armies often diverge from the ideal position on our variable. If skills are inadequate, Washington should support a pervasive educational program in the local armed forces. If skills are excessive, Washington should encourage steps to separate indigenous specialists from the military and place them in civilian life. Looking ahead, the United States should refrain from military assistance which generates excessive skills. Parenthetically, we can observe that indigenous resistance to a pervasive education program in the armed forces can stem from two fears which have strongly negative implications for American programs to export the civic action concept. These are fears of United States influence in the local military and of political unreliability consequent on the involvement of military personnel in political and economic change.

3. Public Image

This variable refers to the picture which the public holds of the military and the military image of that picture, and assumes that these pictures are identical. We hypothesize that civilians perceive the intentions and effects of civic action through the prism of their perception of the military. Accordingly, the greatest probability of civilian support for an extensive civic role occurs when they already regard the military as a valued friend; the least probability, when they regard the military as an exploitative, coercive institution. To formulate these hypotheses, we have applied the principle that an individual's evaluation of the actions of another tends to be biased in the direction of previously held images of the other actor. A second hypothesis becomes relevant if we confine ourselves to large-scale civic action programs which represent an innovation in the mission of the military. The willingness of military personnel to accept civic action as a major mission is inversely correlated with the extent to which the military perceives itself to be popular. Accordingly, the military units most popular with civilians are the least likely to perceive the advantages of an innovative civic role; the least popular, the most likely to perceive its benefits. The reader probably recognizes the roots of these statements in the notion that the disapproval of others tends to motivate changes in behavior while the approval of others has a stabilizing effect.

Because we have assumed congruity of two images, that which civilians hold of the military and that which the military perceives civilians to hold, our hypotheses suggest a paradox for civic action. Simply, the optimal conditions which follow from the hypotheses do not occur simultaneously. For example, an army which civilians respect and trust can lend a halo to social change through civic action, but it has relatively little incentive to undertake a new mission or, for that matter, to modify the existing order. In contrast, an army which civilians mistrust diminishes the popularity of social change programs through civic action, but has greater incentive to accept a new assignment.

If the United States places a priority on the export of civic action, each of these paradoxical cases entails other decisions in Washington. To increase the appeal of civic action to a popular army, the United States should work for the domestic situation which persuades the officer corps that civic action is necessary for continued popularity. (Of course, the officer corps may respond to this American design with charges of foreign interference.) If Washington advocates civic action by an unpopular military establishment, American officials should reconcile themselves to an initial popular response which will be, at best, apathetic.

4. Relation to Civilian Authority

This variable refers to the rights and obligations which military personnel assign to themselves *vis-à-vis* civilian office-holders. We offer two hypotheses relevant to this variable and the behavior of the military and one about the relationship of positions on this variable to civilian contributions to national development.

First, military civic action duties increase the ability of the armed forces to behave autonomously, i.e., they weaken civilian authority. The basic reasoning responsible for this hypothesis would surprise no political man. When an organization expands its area of responsibility and becomes an intermediary between a constituency and another organization, it gains in power relative to the other organization. Obviously, the preceding hypothesis and supporting proposition refer to the ability of the military to translate civic action into autonomy. Our second hypothesis deals with its willingness to do so. Military personnel use increased opportunities to act independently of civilian authorization to the extent that they have not internalized a generalized obligation to obey civilians. Accordingly, the least probability for autonomous military behavior as a result of civic action occurs when obedience to the civilian regime is deeply engrained in a generalized form, i.e., the military personnel tend to view civic action assignments merely as another set of orders issued by its masters. On the other hand, in the absence of internalized controls, military personnel are most likely to use civic action assignment to implement their political and economic preferences and to build popular loyalties. We predict an intermediate result if the controls internalized by military personnel have not been generalized to apply to the expanded civic role envisioned by civic action advocates.

If these hypotheses are valid, United States advocates of civic action by armies without generalized internal controls must choose between two unpleasant alternatives. These are the decay of civilian authority, a result contrary to the claims summarized at the beginning of this article, and institutional control mechanisms familiar from the armies of totalitarian states. There is reason to believe that the latter alternative can enhance civilian control, but not the political democracy claimed as a fruit of civic action. The political control apparatus of totalitarian states, probably the only means which can be quickly installed in unreliable armies, appears suited to insure obedience to one political group but not to civilian authority in general.

The third hypothesis involving this variable states that the contribution of civilian specialists to the national development process correlates inversely with the autonomy of the military. Accordingly, when civic action by the military decreases its obedience to civilian authority, the value of an extensive civic role becomes modified by the decrease in the input of civilian specialists. These statements follow from the common observation that when one group rejects the authority of another group, two effects result. The first group tends to dismiss the associates of the second. Also, individuals who associate themselves more with the rejected than with the rejectors tend to feel rejected as well. When applied to civic action, these observations suggest that the programs of an autonomous military establishment tend to disregard the feelings and abilities of civilian experts. In turn, this disregard reduces both the incentive and the opportunity for these experts to contribute to national development. [4]

If the chain of reasoning just developed has validity, it appears that the objectives of civic action advocates may be better served if some armies are induced not to participate in civic action. Obvious means include the bribery of glamor weapons, high salaries, and foreign training junkets.

5. Standard of Self-Evaluation

This variable refers to the ends which military personnel use to evaluate their achievements and allocate their energies. We hypothesize that the standard of self-evaluation affects the extent to which the military accepts the civic role position by civic action advocates, and implements that role

---

[4] The Turkey of Ataturk and the Egypt of Nasser are sometimes offered as examples of the opposite effect. However, a closer examination of these two cases leads to a different conclusion. Ataturk imposed stringent controls on the military and minimized its civic role; Nasser has worked hard to divest himself of the image of a military officer, e.g., his care to appear in civilian clothes. Instead of discrediting our hypotheses, the Turkish and Egyptian cases point out the absence of logical entailment between leadership by a man whose profession has been that of a military officer and the autonomy of the military establishment.

to produce the consequences which the advocates expect. Accordingly, the highest probability for the realization of the fruits of civic action occurs when military personnel measure themselves in terms of their contribution to domestic policy and general well-being. Probabilities are significantly lower when the measurement is made either in terms of the welfare of military personnel or contribution to foreign policy. We derive these hypotheses from the principle that men prefer actions which they expect to be subjectively most worth while.

In the paragraph above, we have indicated the relationship between grossly different standards of self-evaluation and civic action performance. Three types of standards which are less than ideal have somewhat different implications and, because they often characterize military personnel and the mythology of military institutions, merit brief discussion. When the standard of personal material welfare predominates, members of the military tend to reject the hard work of village-level civic action and to exploit civic role duties. When the standard of combat excellence predominates, they tend to reject civic action as irrelevant to their mission and sometimes as a deliberate attempt by civilian officials or American advisors to demean the indigenous armed forces. Any civic action duties which an army with this standard implements exhibit disinterest and may generate hostility toward civilian authorities. Finally, when the standard of national grandeur predominates (i.e., external prestige as a function of domestic development, regional significance, and international autonomy), military personnel accept a civic action mission in principle but attempt to divert significant resources to the quest for regional and world stature.

If the United States government emphasizes civic action, the disfunctional products attributed to three common standards of self-evaluation above suggest corollary American policies. In case of the standard of personal material welfare, the United States should attempt to bribe the military into somnolence while encouraging domestic pressures which will change the standard. In case of the standard of combat excellence, Washington should apply an appropriate mix of two techniques. The first would discredit the feasibility of achieving combat excellence. An example would be to deny indigenous armies the hardware held by great-power forces. Of course, this tactic works only if hardware is not readily available from another source, e.g., the U.S.S.R. The second technique would define civic action excellence as a prime measure of combat excellence. For example, the United States would try to persuade indigenous officers that the Pentagon attaches high prestige to civic action missions, that American officers do not regard civic action as a minor chore. Of course, this may require United States commanders to assign significant numbers of American military personnel to civic action duties for prolonged periods of time. In case of the national grandeur standard, American officials would take steps to convince indigenous military personnel that domestic development was, at least, a neces-

sary condition and, in large part, a sufficient condition for regional significance and international autonomy. If this conviction were instilled, military
personnel would be more motivated to allocate resources to domestic uses.

Obviously, when a particular indigenous army manifests disfunctional
positions on several of our variables, the feasibility and usefulness of a civic
action program decrease and the corollary requirements of such a program
for United States policy increase.

III. THE INDIGENOUS GOVERNMENT

Of course, the feasibility and usefulness of American efforts to export civic
action also depend on the behavior of indigenous governments. Three variables have particularly direct relevance to the manner in which these governments accept, implement, and are affected by an extensive civic action
program. These are the government's base of support, development and
welfare program, and foreign policy.

1. Base of Support

This variable refers to the extent to which the population is committed
and organized to support the government and to the extent of popular support perceived by government officials. The reality and the perception are
assumed to be congruent. We hypothesize: first, the willingness of governments to support civic action correlates with the adequacy of popular support to control the military; and, second, the attainment of the political
results posited by advocates of civic action tends to correlate with the adequacy of the government's base of support. Accordingly, the governments
most willing to accept civic action and most likely to participate in a program which achieves optimal results rest on the established and organized
support of the bulk of the population. Our acceptance hypothesis follows
from the principle that the willingness of an organization to expand the
responsibilities of another is, at least in part, a function of its perceived base
of support. The effects hypothesis rests on the historical observation that
significant military autonomy does not seem conducive to democratic political development.

It seems useful to apply our hypotheses to two types of support bases
which occur frequently in developing areas and are less than optimal for
civic action. When the government rests on the support of a small oligarchy,
it tends to fear that the military, a coercive substitute for popularity, will
become hostile if ordered to undertake civic action. Also, such governments
tend to fear that civic action will disturb the apathy of the general population and lead to new demands for governmental services. When the support
for the government simply consists of the personal following responsive to a
charismatic leader, civic action by the military tends to be either rejected
or subordinated to other interests. Like a Sukarno, the charismatic leader

opposes civic action when he expects it to intrude the military between himself and his popular following. However, he will at times sanction civic action to block significant intrusion by another threat to his base of support, e.g., the Indonesian Communist Party.

If our hypotheses are valid, United States officials must recognize repercussions of the export of civic action to countries whose government's support resembles our oligarchic or charismatic types. In the oligarchic cases, an extensive civic role generates high probabilities for displacement of the government by newly involved civilians or by a disgruntled officer corps. When a charismatic leader rules, United States advocacy for civic action represents an invitation to political suicide unless we also assist the leader to organize his support and to match the benefits which the people receive from the military. As an alternative, the United States can accept an increased probability of military takeover.

2. Development and Welfare Program

Obviously, support for the development and welfare programs inherent in civic action correlates with a government's existing commitments to use civilian resources for similar purposes. This leads us to the banal, but sometimes overlooked, conclusion that United States advocacy of civic action for nations whose governments oppose its development and welfare purposes has no operational value without an implicit commitment to assist favorably disposed civilians or officers to take power.

3. Foreign Policy

We hypothesize that the willingness of governments to allocate military resources to civic action correlates inversely with (a) their fear of external attack; and (b) their desire for external military ventures. Accordingly, those governments which perceive no need for defensive or offensive forces most welcome civic action, largely as a device to lessen the resource drain of existing military units. The basic principle used here is that organizations evaluate the alternative functions of subordinate institutions in the light of perceived future needs.

These hypotheses suggest that if the United States wishes to enhance the exportability of the civic action concept, Washington officials will take steps to induce developing countries to de-emphasize the military component in their foreign policy. When indigenous governments perceive significant defensive needs, America should attempt to modify the threat which other states pose and the perceived need to rely on indigenous military establishments for defense. For example, the United States would persuade neighboring states to employ their military in civic action, withhold from these states the equipment necessary to support offensive action, and provide a credible military umbrella. When the plans of indigenous governments reflect perceived offensive military needs, the United States should make civic action more acceptable by measures to modify the perception of either the probability of successful offense or the need for expansionist victories.

What have we gained from this exercise in disciplined speculation? Hopefully, we have become alert to the implications of different characteristics of armies and governments for civic action—its acceptance, its implementation, and its consequences. Until we have engaged in an exercise such as this which formulates testable statements with significant policy implications, we are unlikely to make progress toward reliable predictions about the feasibility and value of American efforts to export the civic action concept.

To the extent that the reader finds our hypotheses tenable, he will question the expectations of civic action advocates which underlie much of our current military assistance planning. Indeed, the general implication of our hypotheses is that the local armies and governments best suited to the official American image of civic action are those already best qualified to meet popular aspirations and frustrate Communist maneuvers. Those indigenous armies and governments whose unsatisfactory behavior gave rise to the American adoption of the civic action doctrine are the least willing and able to use this strategy effectively. The irony of this situation points to the unremoved need for American efforts in many cases to modify either the local military or government or to reconcile ourselves to a curtailed set of objectives for the future of the developing nations.

THE POSSIBLE AND
THE NECESSARY[1]

Herman Kahn

I WOULD LIKE to discuss . . . the many different reasons people have for objecting to civil defense and also some of the reasons people have for being in favor.

I think it is worth doing this in order both to expose and to clarify the controversy.

In civil defense one is entering a field which is, in some sense, new; in which there is no one with adequate experience; nobody has fought and survived a thermonuclear war. One must therefore substitute for experience. We must think about the problem, using both paper and pencil. In most paper studies it is somehow crucially important, at least I found it so in the studies I have done for the military services, to be clear on why and what.

* * *

FIGURE K-1

Some Common Reactions to Civil Defense

1 Completely ineffective.
2 Too effective—will touch off a United States-Soviet Union arms race or even a United States or Soviet Union strike.
3 Both 1 and 2 above.
4 Neither 1 nor 2 above.

I have on this chart the three major reasons why people object to civil defense and one reason for being for it. Each of these first three positions is argued with great intensity and force, and often rather persuasively by their respective adherents.

EFFECTIVENESS OF CIVIL DEFENSE

The first position is that civil defense is completely ineffective, that it is not worth buying, that money, energy, or thought spent on such preparations is wasted.

---

[1] The title is mine [Ed.].

This position is held by many different kinds of people.

For example, some relatively conservative people (misusing the word "conservative" a little bit) argue against civil defense because it is defensive. They argue that one cannot win a war by digging holes in the ground, that civil defense is like the maginot line, that history has shown that defense is a mistake.

I believe that much of this antagonism to defense is a result of the kind of training we have in our Western military academies. It turns out that in this training we emphasize the so-called offensive spirit. We try to train people to be daring, to be courageous, to be almost reckless. We do this because we know that in an actual operation in the field, where a man may have to send his comrades, himself, or his friends to their death, it is likely to be disastrous to his morale if he worries too much about what the enemy can do to him. There are many historical examples of military disasters being caused by commanders being too cautious or afraid and, by and large, we emphasize these kinds of situations.

I have found from our own studies, however, that it simply is misleading to argue by the slogan "offense versus defense," that whether one wants to be on the offensive or the defensive side cannot be determined solely by such slogans or even by the question of the morale of the participants.

It is probably correct that as far as an individual is concerned, he feels better when he is on the offensive. He feels as if he is doing something to the other side.

When he is on the defensive, he may not feel as good. The other side is doing something to him. For this very simple reason it is, from the morale point of view, much better to be on the offense than on the defense. The offense also usually has the advantages of the initiative. However, these advantages of the offense may not dominate; they may not determine whether you win or lose the war; whether you survive or die. By and large, in our studies we do not worry about the charge of being defensive. The charge is simply irrelevant, if we have done our study properly.

There is a much more serious reason why some people worry about civil defense being ineffective. This is that it will not do the thing it is supposed to do, that civil defense will not actually defend or otherwise perform as promised.

DEFENSE OF WAR MOBILIZATION BASE

Some of the early work in this field tried to evaluate civil defense by its ability to contribute to the postattack war mobilization base. That is, if one goes back to World War II, he finds this the classical reason for civil defense. Civilians represented a second line of defense. They supplied men, materials, and morale to the fighting forces. It is historically true that the United States found its ability to mobilize men and materials after the war had started crucial to its success in the Civil War, World War I, and World War II. Postattack mobilization has also been the main purpose of civil defense in European countries.

However, today almost all strategists believe—there are some exceptions, so I should emphasize that I said almost all—that it is not possible to defend a war mobilization base against a determined attack by an enemy who is trying to prevent war mobilization, even by heroic efforts in the civil defense area.

I am not saying that one could not support a very small military effort after a thermonuclear war has started. I am saying that the size of the military effort that could be supported by a postattack mobilization is so small compared to the effort that has been carried out by the forces that were in being before the war started, that in most situations it is not very inaccurate to ignore the military resources that can be mobilized postattack.

If you believe this remark, then the classical reason for civil defense—to aid the war effort directly—has disappeared. This opinion is certainly documented, correctly or incorrectly, in the studies I have done. When I ask myself, for example, what is it about the Soviets that frightens me, I do not ask about their war production capabilities after the war has started. When we study campaigns, or at least when I study campaigns, against the Soviets, I myself do not think of their cities, as being legitimate military targets.

I feel that, if we bomb their cities, then, with a few possible exceptions, we will be bombing them because we are trying to punish the Soviets; we will be bombing them for malevolent or reprisal reasons and not because they are military targets. It is also my belief that to some extent the Soviet planners either now think the same way or soon will think this way. However, the Soviets, I believe, would put greater stress on, say, lengthy wars of attrition than we would in this country.

In the RAND Corp. I was known as a long-war man because I studied wars that lasted 2 to 30 days. That was long as compared with the wars which last 30 minutes or 2 hours or 8 hours. However, even my long wars are not long enough for the operation of a postattack mobilization base.

Nonetheless, I would not be at all surprised to learn that some top Soviet planners study wars lasting 1, 2, or 3 years. I would also believe it to be a reasonable conjecture that either now or in the immediate future, Soviet planners would also think of thermonuclear wars as being short and, therefore, they would not be impressed by civil defense preparations as deterring them from direct attack on the United States.

The fact that we can give some protection to a factory worker or a machine tool or a mine or even a city would not, by and large, make them fear the United States any more than if we could not protect these particular things.

If you believe this, and I do, then one must say that civil defense does not contribute much to deterring a Soviet attack on United States. I will have more to say about this subject in a few minutes. However, I would like to make clear that from this point of view, I agree with those who believe civil defense is ineffective.

CIVIL DEFENSE TO INSURE SURVIVAL

However, it is not the purpose of civilians to protect the military. People are ends not means. We protect people because we are people. Without people there are no values and, therefore, one can ask a different question: Can we go into civil defense or should we go into civil defense not because it helps us fight a war more effectively but simply because war can happen and it is better to have a country after the war is over than not.

It is better to have more people than less people; it is better to have more property than less property; it is better to recuperate rapidly than slowly.

In other words, we may want civil defense simply as insurance. In fact, insurance is a very good analogy here. If one buys fire insurance on his house, this does not mean that he is reckless with matches. He does not buy insurance because he plans to risk a fire, but simply because a fire can occur. If one buys a safety belt for his car, he generally does not drive more recklessly. The buyer may simply feel that an accident can happen, and that the safety belt will give him some added and worthwhile but still insufficient protection.

Therefore the next question which comes up is, Can civil defense be used to protect lives, protect property, or to facilitate recuperation after a war is over?

Rather surprisingly, I think most people have the impression that the answer to this question is also "No." Let me show you a chart that indicates some reasons for this point of view. (See fig. K-2.)

FIGURE K-2

Tragic But Distinguishable Postwar States

Dead:	Recuperation (Years)
2,000,000	1
5,000,000	2
10,000,000	5
20,000,000	10
40,000,000	20
80,000,000	50
160,000,000	100
Will the survivors envy the dead?	

This chart, which I took from a book I recently published, is entitled "Tragic But Distinguishable Postwar States." I mean by this title that it should be possible for any person to distinguish between wars which result, say, in 20 million dead Americans and wars which result in 40 million dead Americans. I mean further that if this American has to choose between a war with 20 million dead Americans and one which results in 40 million dead Americans, other things being equal, he prefers a war in which there would be 20 million dead Americans.

It is practically impossible for people to make such a remark, to actually say, "I prefer a war which results in 20 million dead rather than one which results in 40 million dead." They want to say, "Why should I have a war at all?" They want to know, "Why do you tell me to choose between a war in which there will be 20 million dead Americans and a war in which there will be 40 million dead Americans? I do not want to choose." Because they do not want to choose, they choose by default. They ignore the problem.

I have actually been severely criticized by colleagues and others for emphasizing this notion that 20 million dead is better than 40 million dead.

Almost everybody is willing to make the remark, that 40 million dead is worse than 20 million dead. That appears to be a reasonable remark.

The reason why I turn it around is that I am trying to get certain programs started. When one is trying to get a program done, it can only be done by giving people a reasonable goal.

We spend in this country or were spending about $5 billion a year for air defense. It is no particular secret that this system has serious inadequacies. Historically, if you trace down why these inadequacies occurred, many of them occurred because some of the air defense enthusiasts were trying to do too much. They were trying to get a system which would work close to 100 percent, and in the attempt failed to get a system which would work well at much lower levels.

I am not criticizing air defense. There are many complicated reasons why what was done was done. In any case, it is a valuable system. However, I am pointing out that even if there are billions of dollars authorized for a system, the designers, by aiming too high, can get too little. One must aim for realistic goals.

REALISTIC GOALS FOR CIVIL DEFENSE

The above remark applies with particular force to civil defense programs. I think we are going into civil defense in a very realistic fashion. One reason I believe it is realistic is because we are explicitly saying that we are not trying to save everybody in every circumstance. Instead we are saying, "Let us save those that can be saved."

This does not mean that we do not care about those who cannot be saved. It simply means that, if deterrence fails, we cannot do anything about those we cannot save.

If you believe this, if you believe that it is better to have only 40 million dead as opposed to 80 million, or better to have 80 million than 160 million, then I think you can show that civil defense is effective.

It can almost without question, under many plausible circumstances, move the results of a war from the bottom part of this chart to somewhere near the top.

Whether or not you think this is worth doing seems to be mainly correlated with how willing you are to face the fact that war may occur, that our programs to avoid war may fail.

Let me add one comment to indicate why I think it is important explicitly to have limited goals. Let us assume that we have a system such that if a war occurred we would expect to have 60 million Americans killed, and that by dint of great efforts, by working very hard, by being very clever, very intelligent, and very dedicated, we developed a system such that if a war occurred 20 million were killed, instead of 60 million. Assume also that we then had a war and 20 million people were in fact killed and not 60 million. That is, the system worked perfectly.

Can you imagine the designers, builders, and operators then saying, "We had a success. The system has indeed worked well." And then going around congratulating themselves? They could not do it. There would be 20 million dead Americans, men, women, and children, and few would claim that the result was even a qualified success. Most would say it was a failure.

Actually, I would claim it was a success, in some very relevant sense. Unless we recognize that it is a success, we cannot expect people to build such systems. Few if any people will work hard for goals which are defined as being failures right from the beginning. I believe this is the main reason why people actually think of civil defense as ineffective. They think it is ineffective because even a success is not very successful in their eyes. It still looks like a failure. It is only a success in comparison with what could have happened. Unless you keep your sights clearly on that fact, you simply won't be able to say the system is effective.

THE POSTATTACK ENVIRONMENT

There is one important question which is raised by the effects of modern weapons today, the question of survivors envying the dead. This is an important point; the most frightening possible point. This question is raised mainly because modern weapons have long-lasting effects.

This committee and the Joint Committee have been the two principal sources of information on these effects, so I will not surprise you when I say, perfectly soberly and reasonably, that if there is a war today the environment will be more hostile to human life for say, 10,000 years.

Now, one can argue this statement; it might be wrong. However, the best scientific evidence indicates that it is correct, that the environment will be more hostile to human life for 10,000 years or so. I am thinking now of the longer lived, radioactivity due to carbon 14.

To many people this statement carries the implication that it is not worth living in that hostile environment. That is, of course, much too quick and shallow an opinion. As testimony before this committee and before the Joint Committee at the 1959 hearings has brought out, while the environment would be more hostile, it would not be so hostile as to preclude normal and happy lives for the survivors.

In other words, the survivors can rebuild, they can reconstruct and, in many cases, they would not notice the greater hostility of the environment. It would be a statistical effect which would be discernible in the mortality tables, but not by the average individual's personal observation.

The average individual would go through life running somewhat greater risks of various types of diseases and greater risks of having genetically deformed children, but when these risks are compared to the risks normally run today, they are not startlingly larger. The quality of life would not necessarily have been changed dramatically.

When trying to explain this point, when trying to explain that civil defense is not ineffective because of these long-lived, long-term effects, one can get into very serious trouble.

Let me go over some of the phrases which I have just used to indicate what happens.

NORMAL POSTWAR LIFE

I made the comment, both here and in my book, that objective studies indicate that the postwar environment would not be so hostile as to preclude normal and happy lives.

I would conjecture that I have gotten about 50 letters, mostly from psychiatrists taking me to task for that remark. Partly, I think, they object to the term "normal and happy"; I suppose they would argue that people are not normal and happy today, so why do I think the war would make a difference?

I am not, of course, claiming that the war would make people happier or more normal, but what I claim to say, and as far as I know it has not been contradicted by any evidence, is that insofar as one can lead a normal and happy life today, the long-term physical conditions after most wars would not be such as to preclude living a normal and happy life then.

I think the reason why I received such a hostile reaction to this remark has to do with some very natural human reactions. Let me give a sort of homely example which illustrates one of the problems one must surmount if one wishes to explain what we might face postwar.

Imagine for a moment that you have a friend, who is a mother and who has just lost her only child, and that she is grieving over her loss. Life looks totally black. She may literally not be able to envisage ever recovering from her grief. The world may seem permanently out of kilter. This is the end.

You might walk up to this woman and say: "In 5 years you will in some sense have recovered from your grief; you will be laughing at jokes. You won't forget your child. You may even be reminded of him very intensely every now and then. But nevertheless you will be leading a normal and happy life."

That is, by and large, an accurate prediction. But she won't thank you for making it. She will be very angry at you, and so will all of her friends. They will say it was not appropriate to bring this analysis up; the mother's grief deserves respect. One should not ignore it, and by making this comment you seem to be ignoring it.

However, in the kind of things this committee is considering, one must be this hardheaded, this callous, if you will, in order to understand the problems involved.

One must be able to recognize that for most people deep grief is transitory, that most people recover, that life does go on—even if many, including trained psychoanalysts, reject the idea.

COMPLETE RANGE OF
CIVIL DEFENSE PROBLEMS MUST BE FACED

There is another reason why people think civil defense is ineffective. This is more technical than the ones I have discussed. This reason is illustrated by the next chart. . . . (See fig. K-3.)

FIGURE K-3

A Complete Description of a Thermonuclear War
Includes the Analysis of

1 The prewar time-phased program.
2 Performance during different attacks.
3 Postattack fallout problems.
4 Postwar survival, patch up, and restart.
5 Interim production, inventories, and imports.
6 Long-term recuperation.
7 Postwar medical problems.
8 Genetic problems.

There are good sound technical reasons for worrying about the effectiveness of civil defense. Any man today who says that we, as a Nation, can survive a war is saying something very complicated. He is saying that we can handle all of the problems that are lumped together in each of the eight phases of a thermonuclear war which are mentioned on this chart. If we fail on any one of these phases in a crucial way then we may have failed completely. In a sense, one gets no credit at all for a grade of 90 per cent, even if it deserves an A for effort.

He is saying, first of all, that we will have the program in place the day the war occurs.

Now, I read last week's testimony before this committee, and I noticed that several times members of the committee were concerned as to the rate at which the program would be put in. Skepticism was expressed as to whether or not the program will move fast enough.

Such skepticism can be justified by historical examples. By and large, defense programs in this country have lagged, and unless an urgent effort is made they will continue to lag. So one must worry that the program will be in place at the time it is needed.

This worry about phasing also includes worries about possible enemy reactions. One must worry that the enemy does not go faster than we do, so that by the time we have procured programs adequate for 1960, it is 1965 and we are facing a new threat which has obsoleted our 1960-type preparations.

There is one important factor which helps alleviate the problem of obsolescence. There are many different kinds of wars which can occur, and there are many different prewar circumstances which can change the character of the war. I will have a lot to say about this in a few moments. But I would just like to mention that even though the program may be obsolete for some wars and some circumstances, it is likely to retain much value for other wars or circumstances. However, it is difficult for even professional analysts to keep these many cases in mind.

We have again a psychological reaction which is very hard to fight. Most people, including professional analysts, want to worry about the worst case that can happen.

SURPRISE ATTACK—THE WORST CASE

Now, it is literally true, as far as I can see, that if the enemy is determined to kill Americans with a surprise attack out of the blue that is directed against population, then no program that is currently being suggested is going to cut the loss of lives much below half the population.

Therefore, if he is trying to kill Americans with a surprise attack out of the blue, that is a problem which is very difficult, if not impossible, except even here one can argue that he prefers 90 million dead to 180 million dead.

But our weakness in the worst case does not settle the problem. Most wars that are actually likely to occur would have a quite different character and programs which are designed to meet less ferocious wars or less difficult wars can be very valuable.

We do not refuse to go to a doctor when we have pneumonia because he cannot cure cancer. His ability to cure pneumonia is valuable to us precisely because we may catch pneumonia when we do not have cancer.

The same principle is applicable to programs which are designed for special situations, programs which will not work under all situations, but may still be valuable in the special situation. In some ways this is the character of the program we are discussing here today.

Actually you have already had some testimony as to the effects of different kinds of wars, and Norman Hanunian will discuss some effects on casualties in more detail later. I will therefore leave this question of the different kinds of wars, except for a sort of typology discussion at the end of my testimony.

The next problem is protection against the effects of fallout. This committee has heard much testimony already with regard to this important problem and, in addition, the witness who follows me, Norman Hanunian, will discuss the performance of different degrees of fallout protection. The witness following him, Jerry Strope, will discuss some recent developments in the more adequate forms of fallout protection, so I will not discuss the problem of fallout protection today. In fact, I would like to emphasize that important as fallout protection is, it may have been overemphasized recently to the neglect of other very important aspects of civil defense.

REORGANIZATION AFTER ATTACK

The next problem, the problem of getting things started again, is a very difficult one to analyze. In fact, it is quite clear that nobody can do a study which will prove rigorously that if you give the social organism the kind of shock that a large thermonuclear war would give, that the social organism would not in some sense die. Nobody can demonstrate rigorously how things can be put together after the disorganization of an attack.

This inability to demonstrate viability is not a shocking or a new thing. If you lose a leg, no doctor can demonstrate that if he gets you to the hospital he can get the blood stopped and that you will survive even with the best medical treatment. He cannot do this rigorously because no one knows enough about the bodily process involved to demonstrate the details of the healing process.

One has to depend on faith and previous experience. Other people have lost a leg and have survived, and, therefore, one believes that you can also under those circumstances.

Even if you only cut your finger, neither I nor anyone else can prove that it will heal, because, again, nobody understands the full details of the mechanism of clotting and healing. But we know you do get healing, and we also know if you put sulfa or iodine on the cut, it increases the probability of healing and decreases the probability of infection.

Civil defense has the same character, except that we lack a relevant experience. In order to argue that the social mechanism will restart, one must have faith in the ability of people to improvise, to meet emergencies reasonably intelligently, and then one can give them facilities and make other preparations to help them meet these emergencies, to improve their capability to improvise and organize.

But even after elaborate preparation, one will still be depending upon the survivors' ability to rise to the occasion. If the survivors were robots, that could only rigidly obey preset instructions, one would indeed have serious doubts about the possibility of restarting things.

Insofar as we have historical examples, and some of them are close to thermonuclear wars in intensity, people do seem to rise to the occasion. Faith that they will do so is not an unreasonable or desperate hope. It is the expected thing. It is what a gambler would be willing to bet will happen, even though one cannot prove it will happen. Therefore, while whatever studies that are done will have an important gap in them, I do not believe that our inability to demonstrate feasibility rigorously is an annihilating weakness. On the other hand, it is clear that much fruitful work can be done in analyzing feasibility and looking for difficulties and ways to circumvent them.

RESTARTING PRODUCTION

The next problem is the maintenance of economic momentum. This is also a tricky problem and one which Sidney Winter will discuss at some length. The problem of the maintenance of economic momentum at an adequate level reflects the fact that it is not only necessary to be able to recuperate eventually, but one must recuperate before one runs out of supplies to such an extent that major additional hardships are inflicted on the survivors.

To go back to the patient analogy, it may be perfectly correct to estimate that if one gets the patient to the hospital he will recover, but if one fails to get him to the hospital he may still die.

While the patient has an intrinsic capability to recover, he still needs such things as warmth, sustenance, care, food, and medicine while recovering. In our case these things can only be supplied out of stocks on hand, postattack production, and imports from other countries. The sum of these must be at a high enough level to do the job.

One thing which makes me optimistic about U.S. recovery is the fact that for the highest priority items, food, shelter, water, and clothing, we need not have any shortages, at least nationally. In other words, all of the attacks we have analyzed, at least for the early 1960's, leave enormous stocks of these items; therefore, one does not have the problem of split-second timing in postattack recuperation. For example, we will not face starvation even if we do not get agriculture going for a year or two.

Of course, preparations must be made for utilizing these resources, particularly food. As I understand, these preparations will be made. There are plans being drawn up to predistribute the food before the attack, so that we will not have to depend on the national transportation system after the attack to distribute it. These preparations are not necessary because studies indicate that the national transportation system would work adequately. Most of us think it will work, but we cannot rely on these studies. We prefer to insure against it not working, against our studies being wrong.

LONG-TERM RECUPERATION

The next problem is the long-term recuperation problem. Recuperation here has many facets: economic, social, political, psychological, and, in a subtle way, moral.

The only one which has been studied with any care is the economic. Here I think we can say with some confidence that if we can handle phases 4 and 5 adequately, the economy will come back with amazing resilience; in other words, countries like the United States are extremely competent, once they get started, at producing capital and consumer goods. Sidney Winter will have more to say about this subject later, but, depending upon the war, one would conjecture that we could rebuild the destroyed wealth in less than a generation, in all likelihood, in say, 10 years after the kind of war that is usually envisaged.

I am not going to say much at the present time on the social, psychological, political, and moral problems of recuperation. Some discussion may come out of the later testimony and, if there is time, I would like to make some additional comments at the end of the hearings. I cannot speak as an expert in any of these fields, but, if there is time, I would still like to make some additional comments.

But I would like to say now that in terms of studies which have to be done and in terms of the most serious questions which remain unanswered, these social, psychological, political, and moral questions are currently the hard questions. Many feel they are the dominating questions.

However, it is my personal belief, speaking less as an expert than as a man who has read widely, that these problems have been grossly exaggerated.

Most people will not be psychologically deranged. One is not, for example, going to break up family relationships by a war. The family relationship is a very stable one.

One is not even going to obliterate the basic fact that people are Americans. By and large, they will be about as honest, hard-working, reliable, and responsible as they are today. While everybody's lives and thoughts will be affected by the war, the character structure of the survivors is unlikely to be changed in any startling fashion.

The political questions are more difficult. We live today in a very stable country. It is one of the few countries in the world in which the government does not worry about revolution and subversion as major problems, because we do not expect the Government to be subverted or overturned. However, such an event could occur as a result of a war. Even if we won the war, it is conceivable that we might no longer live in a democracy.

However, even though a war is a cataclysmic event, it seems to me a reasonable conjecture, particularly if preparations have been made, that our political democracy could survive most wars. But this statement has more faith in it than analysis. It is not a statement which I would try to maintain before a hostile and skeptical audience. I hope, however, that this and similar statements will soon be subjected to a more careful and deeper examination than I am capable of giving them.

MEDICAL AND GENETIC PROBLEMS

I will not discuss the postwar medical problems and the genetic problems, the next two items on the chart. This committee and the Joint Committee have had more than enough testimony on this subject. It is all in the record. There is no point in bringing it up today except to make the point that in the middle and late fifties there was a widespread belief among scientists, among people who should know, that one could not survive these problems. In other words, the belief in the "end of history" was an expert's belief, rather than a layman's belief.

In fact, if the layman had been told fully and frankly what the experts believed, he would have been horrified. Seemingly reasonable, knowledgeable, and responsible people held the most extreme and extravagant views. The picture and book, "On the Beach," reflected these views.

I would say that today, by and large, these extreme views are no longer held—at least for the kind of war that seems plausible in the early and mid-sixties. The end of the world, end of history, doomsday, and so on, are not appropriate descriptions.

DOOMSDAY MACHINES

I am not denying, by the way, that it is not technologically possible for us, if we wish, to build doomsday machines. I believe that we have the knowledge today to build such devices. I mention in my book that it might take less than 10 years and less than $10 billion to build devices which could actually destroy all unprotected human life.

All I am saying today is that such devices have not been built, and there are good reasons to believe that they will not be built in the near future.

The fact that they can be built is, correctly, the source of the gravest apprehension. This fact is one of the main things which gives urgency to our attempts to negotiate arms control.

Many people believe, and I am among them, that unless we have adequate arms control such devices will be built, say, before the year 2000, and that is a very serious problem indeed. But I do not expect them to be built within the next 5 or 10 years.

THE COMPLEX PROBLEM OF SURVIVAL

This summarizes, in rather rough form, the complexity of the notion that a nation can survive a war. I would like to emphasize again this complexity. The man who believes we can survive a war believes we can handle every one of the problems on this chart, each one of which is incredibly complex.

The man who believes he cannot survive a war simply has to believe that we fail on one of these problems.

To use a standard phrase, there are no prizes given for handling seven of these problems. We have to handle all eight.

So, to believe that a nation can survive a war is a complicated belief. To believe that one cannot survive a war is a simple belief. And by and large, it is easier for most people to believe simple things than complicated ones.

I believe that a persuasive case can be made for national survival but it is a difficult one to make in a give-and-take debate.

Let me now return to my first chart. (See fig. K-1.)

To summarize my reaction to the first point on this chart, the common belief that civil defense is completely ineffective, I would simply state that for a very large range of programs, particularly including the current suggested program, one can make a case which will stand up before the most skeptical and most hostile audience, that these programs are effective enough to more than justify the money that is to be spent on them, so long as the criteria of effectiveness includes the questions: "If a war occurs, how many lives are likely to be saved, how much property is likely to be saved, how much is recuperation facilitated?" In other words, I believe that the argument of total ineffectiveness is completely wrong and can be dismissed by serious people.

CIVIL DEFENSE AS TRIGGER FOR ARMS RACE OR WAR

The second attitude is more complicated and controversial and is exactly the opposite of the first attitude. Many antagonists of civil defense argue it is too effective, that it will touch off an arms race or even a Soviet Union or United States strike.

I will discuss the arms race first. To the extent that one feels that civilians are a target, then an attempt to protect civilians may touch off a greater effort by the Soviets to be able to destroy them. If we build an adequate shelter system, they may then build larger missiles and procure more of them.

Or equally important, if the Soviets fear that because we have civil defense preparations we are more likely to strike them in a crisis or in an emergency, then they may have to keep their forces more alert. This could make them more accident prone, or trigger happy. We might then have the problem of what is known as false pre-emption or anticipatory retaliation. That is, they may strike us because they think that we are going to strike them. This is sometimes called striking second, first.

All of these problems could be raised by certain kinds of civil defense programs.

THE "SELF-FULFILLING PROPHECY"

I do not believe that, by and large, either the program being recommended today or even much larger programs would raise such problems in a serious fashion. I think that most of the people who worry about this are worrying about the so-called self-fulfilling prophecy, not as an analytical proposition but as sort of a magical proposition. Let me describe what I mean.

The term self-fulfilling prophecy comes from psychology or psychoanalysis. It refers to the fact that if you are hostile and suspicious toward a person, you will often act in a manner that reflects your hostility and suspicions.

Even if the other person is innocent, he will notice your hostility. This will arouse in him reactions of hostility and suspicion. You will then observe at his reactions and say, "See I was right." And since he will indeed have confirmed your hostility and suspicion, you will become more hostile and suspicious; in time this will make him more hostile and suspicious. The mutual action and counteraction will build up to such a point that it can either lead to violence or stabilize at such a high level of hostility and suspicion that the possibility of violence is ever present.

It is quite clear that this self-fulfilling prophecy does occur both between individuals and nations.

If one is hostile and suspicious, it will arouse hostility and suspicion, which will in turn increase and intensify the original feelings.

However, this admission of mine does not settle the problem.

In 1959 and 1960, I gave a series of public and semipublic lectures. At almost everyone of these lectures, someone brought up the self-fulfilling prophecy. The first time they brought it up, I had been through a very relevant experience. In answer to the question, I related this experience and I have used that same story ever since. With the permission of the committee, I would like to use it again today.

I started by telling about a friend of mine who is an embezzler. He actually exists. This chap has been in jail twice, and at the time I had been asked this question he was under indictment for the third time and out on bail.

After he had been indicted I asked him, "Why do you do it? You have been caught twice, actually three times. Why do you keep repeating this pattern of behavior? Aside from being immoral, it obviously isn't successful. Why do you do it?"

He looked me right in the eye and said, "I can't help it. People trust me."

He put the blame exactly where it belonged, on the excessive trust of the other individuals. He is an outgoing fellow; he does not have much character and he just cannot help it if he is excessively tempted.

In discussing the self-fulfilling prophecy, I sometimes refer to the "self-defeating prophecy." This is a prophecy which defeats itself. For example, it can happen that if one prepares for war, he deters the war. This can happen. It has happened in the past.

Or to go back to the story, if one worries about embezzlement, one may take precautions and not be embezzled. I would conjecture that the self-defeating prophecy plays as big a role in international and other human affairs as the self-fulfilling prophecy.

For this reason we simply cannot reject programs just because they reflect some hostility and suspicion of the Soviet Union. Some hostility and suspicion is justified. There are reasons why we have it. This hostility and suspicion was not created overnight by our own imaginations working overtime.

THE PACE OF THE ARMS RACE

I would believe that as long as one is careful with his programs, then the problem of stimulating the arms race has been grossly exaggerated. This is not to mean that one could not stimulate the arms race. While we are in a dangerous arms race today we are not running anywhere near as fast or as hard as we could; we could make it more dangerous.

It seems to be true, for the current programs of both sides, that both sides are being careful. Neither side seems to be doing the kinds of things which they might do if their only concern were to beat the enemy.

Both sides are acting with a great deal of restraint, both budgetary and technologically, and one would like to keep these restraints operative and even increase them.

One would not like frivolously or carelessly to increase the pressures toward an accelerated arms race except, perhaps, in response to a changed situation.

The Berlin crisis may well result in an increased arms race, but this is mostly not our fault. It is the result of a crisis that has mainly been manufactured by the Soviets and one may have to react to it. In fact, it is exactly the threat that we may accelerate the arms race that might lead the Soviets to be cautious.

PREVENTIVE WAR RISK

As to the next point on the chart—the belief that civil defense by the United States might lead to a preventive war by the Soviet Union, because they were afraid that we intended to be aggressive, or even a preventive war by the United States because of our belief that we might hold casualties to less than 50 million, I find this almost beyond belief. The notion that some people have, that unless one can guarantee total annihilation, the other side will not be deterred, or conversely, unless we can promise the Soviets that every single citizen we have will be killed, he will worry about our striking him in a surprise attack out of the blue seems to be a gross overestimate of both sides' desires to strike each other.

It is my personal belief that one could protect every citizen of this country and every citizen of Russia from being a casualty with 100 percent reliability, and one would still have both sides deterred under most circumstances. After all, the empty cities are still hostages. This property, which has been so laboriously created and which has such immense historical and cultural significance, is a very precious and valued hostage.

In addition, a country is not going to war lightly just because it could reduce fatalities from 60 million to, say, 20 million. Twenty million dead is a very impressive number of dead and the property, in addition, is a very impressive hostage all by itself.

There are circumstances, particularly in a very tense crisis, in which certain kinds of civil defense programs might tend to convert the crisis into a war. But these are the very circumstances when these programs are most needed.

I will come back to this later in my discussion of the different kinds of wars, but I just want to make the point now that hard situations can occur. In these situations, a total unwillingness to face any immediate risk of war may simply mean that one must choose surrender or appeasement and perhaps war eventually.

Let me repeat it, because it could be so important. Harsh choices can occur. We may have to choose between risk of immediate war or be willing to appease or surrender. Under these circumstances civil defense can make a difference in our choice and thus increase the risk of immediate war.

Let me now discuss the third reaction on the chart—the belief that civil defense is simultaneously both completely ineffective and too effective. At first sight this sounds like and often is a contradiction, a lapse in logic, by a critic who is not thinking very hard. (See fig. K-1.)

CIVIL DEFENSE BAD ENOUGH TO FAIL, GOOD ENOUGH TO FOOL

However, sometimes the point is made in a sophisticated fashion. The critic could say, for example, that the civil defense program does not work; it is ineffective, but it will fool the Government, to the point where it is more reckless or the civil defense program will fool the people, and then the people will themselves be more reckless or allow the Government to be.

Now, I happen to think that this last view is almost completely wrong. I have position No. 4 on the chart. I think the suggested civil defense program does work but that it does not work so well that it triggers off an accelerated arms race. I do not think any of the testimony this committee has heard about the performance of this program could make this committee feel reckless.

AVOIDANCE OF THINKING ABOUT WAR

I think the common reaction of both one and two is simply a visceral reaction to dismiss the whole subject. The critics do not want to think about a thermonuclear war actually being fought. Civil defense forces them to think about this possibility so they use any argument which comes to mind to dismiss the possibility.

As this committee well knows, most people—and I am including many professional analysts in this category—do not want to face the reality of potential thermonuclear war as something which might be fought. They prefer deterring it, abolishing it, wishing it away, thinking it away, ignoring it, or in some other way denying its existence as a problem worthy of consideration together with other programs.

*   *   *

THE IMPOSSIBLE AND
THE EVIL[1]

SANE

As an organization dedicated to the achievement of comprehensive, inspected disarmament, a strengthened United Nations, and world economic development, the National Committee for a Sane Nuclear Policy submits the following statement to contribute to the important discussion of the implications of civil defense planning.

Regretfully, we feel obligated to oppose any stepped-up civil defense program—regretfully because one cannot lightly oppose a program which offers possible protection to some of our fellow citizens. We do so after careful deliberation. We do not take a position on which agency should administer the program.

Our position is based on the following considerations:

1. The administration's requested new measures are clearly tied to the Berlin crisis, yet even if the funds are voted the projected program would do little except to create false hopes of protection.

2. Civil defense in general is a basically unrealistic concept in the thermonuclear age, if our standard is the preservation of our society and most of our people.

3. The kind of civil-defense program which could save the most lives would require the establishment of a garrison state in America.

It was in his major policy speech on Berlin, July 25, that President Kennedy spelled out his civil defense proposals. He told the American people that in the event of an attack upon this country "the lives of those families which are not hit in a nuclear blast and fire can still be saved—if they can be warned to take shelter and if that shelter is available." Such shelter will not be available for most of our population between now and the expected climax of the Berlin crisis this fall, no matter what this committee of Congress does, no matter what the Defense Department does.

We cannot buy a civil defense program before the Berlin crisis runs its course. First, Mr. Kennedy's proposals are limited largely to the study of available public shelters. Second, Mr. Kennedy's speech tacitly admits that only families which are some distance from nuclear blast and fire can be saved from that other component of modern war, radioactive fallout. In

---

[1] The title is mine [Ed.].

other words, they must be in shelters miles from where the bombs drop if they are to have a hope of survival.

This program will not build shelters where bombs will fail to fall. It will merely designate public buildings and other facilities which were not constructed for shelter purposes as protection against possible H-bomb attack. Yet even if the Government succeeds in supplementing these designated shelters with a warning system which can get people into them in less than 15 minutes—a highly unlikely situation in metropolitan areas where the average working person spends more than half an hour going from home to his work—the problem is hardly solved. People must stay in shelters at least 2 weeks after an attack. They must have food, a sanitary system, an oxygen supply, and other facilities in order to sustain life. Where are these other facilities in the proposed program?

Obviously, they are not included. We are confronted with a paper program. The public may not be aware of this, feeling instead that something has been done to assure its safety in case of war. That is why we say the projected program would do little except to create false hopes of protection.

There is, however, another possibility which is more dangerous. It is that the Russians will interpret an increased civil defense program as preparation for war over Berlin. The logic of voting money for civil defense preparations which can save hardly any lives in case of war before the year's end may escape the Kremlin leaders. We all know that they often fail to understand the subtleties of American life; this time they may react only to the fact of increased appropriations. Will they interpret this as a sign of American preparations for a first strike? Will they decide to build more powerful weapons in order to penetrate deep shelters?

To date, the evidence is overwhelming that the Russians have taken their civil defense program no more seriously than we have our own. On June 5, 1951, *Newsweek* reported:

"Moscow.—It sounds odd, but Washington's clamor for bigger and better civil defense has no counterpart here. The sharpest observers see no signs of stepped-up contruction of air-raid shelters (although the new subways could double in that role). Air-raid drills are held in factories but rarely for the general public. Moscow's sirens, in fact, haven't sounded since World War II."

Osgood Caruthers, reporting from Moscow in the July 18 issue of the *New York Times,* confirms this impression. He indicates that there are no practice alerts in Moscow, no outward sign of even the most rudimentary preparations against nuclear blast and fallout, and no evidence of construction of shelters visible to foreign military experts who have traveled through the Soviet Union.

This lack of current preparation is consistent with reports coming from the Soviet Union for the past several years. Dr. A. Allan Bates, vice president of the Portland Cement Association of Chicago, visited construction projects throughout that country in 1960 as a member of an exchange delegation from the cement and concrete industry. Dr. Bates has informed us that there were no signs of shelters being built into the thousands of apartment houses which he saw in the process of construction.

The report of the House Military Operations Subcommittee on "Civil Defense in Western Europe and the Soviet Union," issued April 27, 1959, shows that the Russians gave civil defense manuals which are incongruously old-fashioned in the thermonuclear age. But the report fails to show any substantial civil defense activities in being.

In recent efforts to justify its expenditures, the Office of Civil and Defense Mobilization has cited claims to the contrary. These claims are based largely, we submit, on Soviet manuals and not on eye-witness observations. If the Russians were to judge American efforts in the civil defense field from viewing CDM manuals, film strips, and other propaganda media, they would no doubt come to the conclusion that every American family has a fallout shelter resembling the average Soviet apartment, complete with attractively packaged canned goods, toilet paper, and recreational materials.

Regardless of what the Russians do, one must still ask the question of whether civil defense is realistic in view of the fantastic destructive power of thermonuclear weapons and the speed of delivery systems. While there seems to be no question that shelters can protect people from short-lived radioactive fallout, that happens to be the only effect of an H-bomb explosion against which there is any possible precaution. Even then, we are told by Dr. Ralph Lapp, radiation levels inside a shelter must be 100 times lower than outside following an attack.

Let us turn to those other twin offshoots of the H-bomb: blast and fire storm. According to Harrison Brown and James Real, writing in "Community of Fear," a single 10-megaton H-bomb "would exterminate virtually all but the most deeply sheltered things within a radius of 5 miles." Scorching winds could injure unprotected people on the outer fringes of a 2,000 square-mile area. The same weapon would produce a fire storm which would burn until there was nothing left to consume, drawing in all available oxygen for miles around.

There have been fire storms before, in Hamburg, Tokyo, and Hiroshima. The first two were set by a rain of incendiary bombs during World War II, the one in Hiroshima by an atomic bomb equal to 20,000 tons of TNT. But the H-bomb in question here would be equal to 10 million tons of TNT. It would set everything ablaze within a radius of at least 25 miles. Gas storage tanks, oil wells, automobile service stations, scrub brush, all wood and paper, and many things not flammable at ordinary temperatures would burst into flame from bomb temperatures higher than those on the surface of the sun.

The average underground shelter would become a crematorium in a nuclear fire storm. The ventilation system, drawing in air from the outside, would heat temperatures to as high as 1,000 degrees. Shelters would have to be sealed off from the world above ground and would require manufactured oxygen. But the entire supply of oxygen manufactured in the United States in 1960 would not meet the needs of a city of 100,000 population in an underground shelter for more than 2 weeks. This estimate was made by Norman Cousins on the basis of research for his recent book, *In Place of Folly*.

Faced with a fire storm, what could fire departments do if, somehow, they survived with all their equipment intact? It is likely that only natural barriers such as mountains and waterways would prevent one fire storm from merging with the next. This kind of conflagration surpasses the imagination.

Assuming human beings were sheltered far from an H-bomb blast and remained protected until short-lived radioactive debris no longer presented a hazard, there would still be danger from such long-life radioactive elements as strontium 90, cesium 137, carbon 14, yttrium 90, and others. Not only would these more persistent radioactive materials represent a continuing hazard from direct contact, but could also contaminate food and water supplies. The use of chemical and bacteriological weapons in an attack would further complicate continued human existence.

The list of additional practical problems in the wake of a thermonuclear attack is imposing. Some of these problems have barely been discussed by those who pretend that survival and recovery can be treated within a conventional frame of reference. Chief John N. Wolfe of the Environmental Sciences Branch of the AEC's Division of Biology and Medicine, testified at the Joint Committee on Atomic Energy's 1959 hearings that fire storms would burn the dryer forests of the Rockies, the Northwest, and the Pacific coast; wipe out the dry oak and pine forests from New England to Virginia, and the pine on the Atlantic and Gulf Coastal Plains. In the farmland of the Mississippi Valley, with the crops harvested, Dr. Wolfe said, fire is likely to be more local, less severe, but widespread.

Erosion and floods would follow. New dust bowls would appear. It would require 1,000 years to replace forests now dominated by species of trees 400 and 500 years old. "Along with fire, flood, and erosion," Dr. Wolfe testified, "which would also decrease productivity of the landscape or render it inaccessible to people in uncontaminated refugia, would come intensification of disease, plant and animal, including man."

Another problem which has received no attention is mass blindness. Philip Wylie, the noted writer who was named an expert consultant on civil defense by President Truman, described in the September 1960 issue of the *Rotarian* magazine why he no longer considers civil defense a feasible program. Among other reasons he cited this:

"Granting clear weather, the explosion of a medium-sized H-weapon, day or night, would cause all persons indoors or out within view of the fireball to look at it, by uncontrollable reflex. And such people, seeing the fireball bloom into glaring reality—whether in an air or ground burst—would be made blind instantly, even at distances of 40 miles from the explosion. Sudden light, thousands of times brighter than the sun, would make them turn around to see the source. They would have several seconds to do that, before they felt heat or blast and even if they were too distant to feel either. And that instinctive glance would burn their retinas so that they would be sightless.

"These unguessable scores of thousands in and around cities, walking, driving cars and buses and trucks, piloting commercial planes, driving locomotives, farming, shopping, whatever, would, after one glance, be helpless. Their cars, trucks, trains, and planes would smash. People in the countryside would be unable even to find their way home. And even cloudy weather would merely lessen the area where an H-bomb would blind (even if it did not otherwise harm) the people able to see the fireball—an area, in clear weather, on the order of 5,000 square miles per 'shot'."

No doubt the advocates of an increased civil defense program will tell us that there is a warning system that will permit 180 million Americans to take cover—within 15 minutes—and thus avoid exposure to the blinding flash. Those of us who recall that a few inches of snow almost paralyzed Washington on the eve of Inauguration Day, 1961, with some motorists requiring 5 hours to reach Dupont Circle from Capitol Hill, will remain somewhat skeptical.

Yet another aftereffect of thermonuclear attack has received little attention. That is the psychological shock to the survivors. An article, "The Survivors of Hiroshima," which appeared in the August 1961 issue of *Redbook* magazine, describes the dazed and apathetic condition of those who lived through the first atomic bomb exploded over a city. In following weeks, many of these people turned into savage and hardened criminals in the struggle to survive. What will be the nature of the scars left on the survivors of an H-bomb attack which can wipe out in a few hours several times the number of people exterminated by Eichmann and his associates in 4 years?

It is difficult for us, in view of the facts we have outlined here, to understand exactly what Herman Kahn means when he writes that "the amount of human tragedy" would "not preclude normal and happy lives for the majority of survivors and their descendants."

But let us ignore for a moment whether the survivors would be normal and happy or subhuman and wretched, and ask ourselves whether thermonuclear war will leave behind anything resembling the society we are now trying to protect.

The effects of a heavy thermonuclear attack, taking into account only deaths from fallout occurring up to 60 days, were studied for the Joint Committee in 1959 by Hugh Everett III and George E. Pugh of the Institute for Defense Analysis. Their graph of an attack proportional to population density, appearing on page 876 of the 1959 hearings, shows that total casualties in an untrained population—with emergency instructions to remain under shelter after attack—range from 60 to 98 per cent. This theoretical situation is close to the one prevailing today, except that our untrained population has few shelters. The total casualties in a trained population with 6 months to build shelters range from 38 to 89 per cent for the same yield of weapons, 2,000 to 20,000 megatons. By adding deaths from blast and fire storm to those from fallout, even in the relatively lighter attack, the number of deaths would be staggering.

As the noted physicist, J. Robert Oppenheimer, has observed: "What some of us know and some of our governments have recognized, all people should know and every government understand: If this next great war occurs none of us can count on having enough living to bury our dead."

Hanson Baldwin, military affairs editor of the *New York Times,* has reported that "studies show that if about 30 per cent of the population of any country is killed, wounded, or put out of action, that country will no longer function as a rational and coherent social organization" (January 14, 1961).

Therefore we can only conclude that in even the smallest "heavy" thermonuclear attack projected for the Joint Committee, this country will cease functioning as a rational and coherent social organization. For even with a well-trained and sheltered population, 38 per cent of our people—over 68 million men, women, and children—would become casualties from fallout alone.

In this highly interdependent society of ours, can we imagine let alone cope with 68 million dead, amidst radioactive debris and disrupted medical, sanitary, transportation, and communication facilities? If the trained personnel of the AEC required 6 days to remove the radioactive bodies of the three employees who died in a recent nuclear reactor accident in Idaho, what would the survivors of an H-bomb attack do with millions of radioactive corpses? What would happen to industrial production without workers or power supply? Or with workers but without power? What would happen if autos, trucks, and trains were "hot" and rail centers and roads were vaporized? Would there be farmers to harvest the radioactive crops, or to plant untouched seed in scorched earth? Would the United States, which has been so slow to share its farm surpluses with the undernourished of the world in peacetime, distribute this bounty to the survivors of the horrors of wartime? Will there be a United States worthy of the name? A government? A country—or just a graveyard?

We submit that it would be as useless to expect a coherent society after a thermonuclear war as to count upon the exercise of personal freedoms. It may be that in time the survivors could resurrect something approaching civilization. But again one is forced to wonder whether the dazed and perhaps genetically damaged remnants could even hope to restore the losses, when our present presumably healthy society has not solved such relatively minor problems as unemployment, depressed areas, and agricultural surpluses.

Herman Kahn, in his major work *On Thermonuclear War,* tells us that recovery, or at least economic recovery, is quite possible. However, in his review of the book in *Science,* Donald N. Michael, then of the Brookings Institution, points out that "Kahn does not apply the same careful analysis he used on hardware to the human condition in the postattack period. The considerable data available from history and the laboratory about the behavior of groups, individuals, and leaders under extreme threat, in the face of sudden disaster, or in ambiguous situations is ignored. Also ignored are the profound problems of establishing adequate, integrated leadership and command and control in a postattack society, for such a society may well be bereft of many layers of responsible, trained, civilian leaders."

Despite the inability of civil defense to defend our society and perhaps a majority of our people, there are those who would say that if it saves anyone it is a worthwhile program. Although we are convinced that the only defense is peace, let us examine what a substantial civil defense program would entail.

First, people in target areas, and probably in the nearby cities, would have to be written off and fallout shelters constructed for the remainder, preferably far out in the countryside. It is said that the Soviet first strike is aimed at our missile and airbases rather than at cities. However, there is no reason to expect that any H-bomb war would be limited to a single volley. Moreover, to expect the Russians to refrain from bombing cities is to show more trust under the acute tensions of a devastating war than we do under the pressures of a tense peace.

Second, shelters would have to be stocked with food, which would have to be replaced periodically because of shelf spoilage, and with other facilities to permit large numbers of people to live in close proximity under ground for at least 2 weeks.

Third, some authority would have to be designated to decide which citizens are to occupy which shelter, and enforce this decision. Some people are already thinking of this problem. According to a UPI dispatch from Las Vegas on July 28, J. Carlton Adair, plans and programs officer for the local civil defense organization, has called for the establishment of a 5,000-man militia to keep out Californians in case California is hit in a nuclear war, but Nevada is not. "They could come in like a swarm of human locusts," Mr. Adair said of the surviving Californians, "and pick the valley clean of food, medical supplies, and other goods. Our law enforcement agencies are not numerically equipped to handle such an influx of humanity, so we have drawn up plans for a militia."

In connection with the problem of occupation of shelters, we are compelled to ask, most respectfully because the question is a legitimate one, whether public fallout shelters in Southern States will be segregated or desegregated.

Fourth, shelter-management cadres would have to be trained in the techniques of operating mass shelters, and the citizens who are designated to use them would also have to be trained in their roles.

Fifth, evacuation routes from homes and places of work to the shelters would have to be planned and kept open in time of attack.

Sixth, postattack leaders would have to be carefully chosen and trained in advance. There will be no place for town meetings afterward.

If such a system is to operate reasonably well, the people must be disciplined. They would have to respond to evacuation drills on extremely short notice in the middle of the night. They would have to accept the decisions of others on questions involving life and death. They would have to forgo the democratic process. In short, they would have to accept a garrison state. Thus, in preparing to survive war the United States would lose the values it was girding to defend.

Even if this were not the case, the financial costs of a substantial civil defense program would be enormous. While estimates have varied widely, an idea of the dimensions of the problem may be obtained from an estimate made just for Los Angeles County. There, Mackintosh & Mackintosh, consulting engineers, estimated at $6 billion the cost of shelters with oxygen supplies and other minimal facilities. Yet this would still be inadequate to save the inhabitants of the county from blast and firestorm.

At its present level, the civil defense program raises some questions which no one apparently cares to think through. We wonder whether the advocates of a larger program are ready to answer them. When the Chicago School Board rejected an offer by the Office of Civil Defense to build a demonstration bomb shelter in one of the schools a few years ago, Mrs. John B. Allen, the only mother on the board, observed: "I am not sure we would want to add the use of bomb shelters to our children's education. Children would be certain to ask for an explanation of the shelter and to ponder its meaning. They are very practical. They don't think adults build something they don't plan to use. I am not certain our teachers are prepared to answer questions they would ask about who is going to drop a bomb, and how soon."

It is time we became as practical as children. It is time we realized that fallout shelters will not save us. It is time we prepared to walk erect like men instead of burrowing like moles.

If we had put just a fraction of the billion dollars spent on civil defense since 1951 into preparation for disarmament negotiations and the strengthening of international institutions, perhaps we would not today be discussing this problem with such intensity.

To take civil defense seriously in the age of thermonuclear-tipped missiles is to prepare for the end of our society. This frame of mind is difficult to couple with the initiatives needed in order to reverse the momentum of the arms race and wage a battle for the minds of men. It seems to assume that

American leadership is powerless, and that the Communists should be allowed to set the rules for international conduct. We reject this defeatist vision of America, and prefer to invest equal and greater amounts of money and energy in seeking the alternatives to the war against which there is no defense.

DISARMAMENT AS
A STRATEGY

Clark C. Abt

TYPES AND CHARACTERISTICS OF DISARMAMENT

Disarmament has been considered both as a panacea for the problems of international conflict and as a dangerous distraction from the hard problems of assuring national military security. It is the intention of this essay to argue that while disarmament is no panacea, neither does it necessarily reduce national security. Some forms of disarmament may enhance military security for all, other forms may enhance the security of one nation at the expense of others, and yet other forms may threaten the security of all. It is necessary to distinguish among forms and strategic contexts of disarmament to achieve a rational appraisal of the favorable possibilities, dangers, and uncertainties.

Disarmament embodies the unfortunate ambiguity of both a process and a state to which that process is intended to lead. The zealots of disarmament have often confused the two, assuming that the *state* of disarmament could somehow be born full-grown into the world, without a long and complex *process* of disarmament. Some opponents of disarmament have realistically, but narrowly, focused on the difficulties of achieving a *process* of disarmament, tending to neglect the intended *state* of disarmament, as if that goal were too nebulous to be taken seriously. But to define an efficient process for achieving a specific state of disarmament, it is necessary to consider the desired characteristics of that state. And to achieve that desired state, it is necessary to consider the process of achieving it.

The objective state of disarmament has too often been assumed to consist wholly of pacification—an objective rarely achieved for long, in spite of strong economic and humanitarian motivations. Historically, disarmament has been negotiated most frequently for the purpose of stabilizing a current equality or superiority of military power.

More recently, a major objective of disarmament policy has been to reduce the danger of accidental war. Since, from the military-technical viewpoint, improved security, integrity, and reliability of command and control are safer ways of reducing the danger of accidental war, this objective has not been decisive in influencing national policy. However, now that better understanding of command and control problems has developed awareness

TABLE Ia
Local Disarmament and Some Associated Gains, Costs, and Risks

	Partial Disarmament			Qualitative and Quantitative		Complete Disarmament
	Qualitative by types	*Quantitative by percentage*	*by absolute number*	*by percentage*	*by absolute number*	
Payoff	Some capabilities, e.g., large missiles or major defense systems, are easy to detect with assurance	Makes possible an across-the-board, checked thinout		Probably most practical for thinout		Simply inspected local pacification of potential escalation source—can reduce cost of local statements to both sides
Gains		Reflects balanced force ratios	Easily counted	Achieves balanced disarmament, maintaining agreed ratios	Eliminates conflict over critical inventories; readily confirmed	
Costs	Tactical disadvantage and/or disruption of area defenses—difficult to agree on intermilitary utility	Requires declaration of initial inventories, which may weaken deterrence and influence of weaker party	Requires knowledge of opponent's initial inventory for balanced numbers	Requires declaration of initial inventories, which may weaken deterrence and influence of weaker party	Requires knowledge of opponent's initial inventory for balanced numbers	Local disarmed area defenseless, must rely on collective security or U.N. peace force; may also be loss of vital link in a chain of defenses
Risks	May induce modernization of forces	Arms may be resupplied from adjacent armed areas; difficult to enforce. If declaration is correct, may risk attack; if exaggerated, too much disarmament	May not be balanced disarmament if initial inventory intelligence is inaccurate	If declaration is correct, may risk attack; if exaggerated, excessive disarmament required	Subject to rapid rearmament; may not be balanced disarmament if initial inventory intelligence is inaccurate	May leave disarmed area defenseless against low end of war spectrum, i.e., invasion by police forces, before allied still-armed forces or U.N. could intervene—sealing problem

that controlled and deliberate military response requires survivability and increased time for decisions and diplomatic bargaining, disarmament may be reconsidered, in a different way than previously, as a means for reducing the danger of war.

It has been suggested that absence of arms could prevent war, on the assumption that arms themselves were the major source of conflict. However, only universal amnesia could remove the knowledge of how to construct weapons. A more sophisticated view might consider disarmament as a means of reducing the danger of war, for the different reason that it can provide increased warning time for defense preparations and negotiations for limiting or peacefully resolving the conflict. This is the culmination of a historical sequence of *objectives* of the state of disarmament:

1. Pacification (1815–present).
2. Reduction of economic costs of military security (1850–present).
3. Stabilization of the balance of military power (1815–present).
4. Equalization of military power vs. stabilization of superiority of power (1930–55).
5. Reduced danger of accidental war (1950–60).
6. Reduced danger of war by provision of increased warning time (1960–?).

One or more of these six objectives of the state of disarmament may or may not be achieved by one or more of five different *types of disarmament states:*

1. Local disarmament.
2. General disarmament.
3. Complete disarmament.
4. Qualitative partial disarmament (some specific types of armament).
5. Quantitative partial disarmament (some percentage or absolute number of a given armament).

Tables Ia and Ib list some of the more obvious strategic gains, costs, and risks in each of the combinations. The net resultant, or payoff, of balanced risks, costs, and gains depends on the weight attributed to each factor. These weights change with national outlook and strategic political context.

The basic variables of disarmament are: participants, areas, functions or capabilities, and time schedules. The different general types of disarmament states—variously combining participation, areas, forces, force ratios, and times—may be achieved by one or more of twelve general *types of disarmament processes:*

1. Progressive zonal—(areas)
2. Progressive functional—(forces)
3. Reciprocal
4. Simultaneous $>$ (ratio)
5. Balanced
6. Unbalanced $>$ (ratio)

TABLE Ib

General Disarmament and Some Associated Gains, Costs, and Risks

	Partial Disarmament					Complete Disarmament
	Qualitative by types	*Quantitative*		*Qualitative and Quantitative*		
		by percentage	*by absolute number*	*by percentage*	*by absolute number*	
Payoff	Eases inspection of major weapons, increasing confidence in detection of violation; may eliminate particularly con-stable and mutually stalemated weapons	Residual forces render small, undetectable violations indecisive	Easily counted	Probably most all-around practical for large, mixed modern forms	Eliminates conflict over initial inventories; readily confirmed	Achieves much longer strategic warning time because of time required for decisive rearmament, increasing possibilities for negotiation and compensatory retaliatory buildup; possible increase in confidence of detecting violations due to simplified inspection
Gains		Reflects balanced force ratios		Achieves balanced disarmament maintaining agreed ratios		
Costs	Tactical disadvantages may ensue resulting from different military utilities of same weapon types to two antagonists	May not be practical for concentrated activities, e.g., fissionable materials refining plants; Requires initial inventory declaration which may be an embarrassment	Requires knowledge of opponent's initial inventory for balanced numbers	Requires declaration of initial inventories, which may weaken deterrence of abrogation of other parties	Requires knowledge of all nations' initial inventories for balanced numbers	Military superiority and its attendant deterrent and bargaining advantages

TABLE 1b (Continued)
General Disarmament and Some Associated Gains, Costs, and Risks

	Qualitative by types	Partial Disarmament				Complete Disarmament
		Quantitative		Qualitative and Quantitative		
		by percentage	by absolute number	by percentage	by absolute number	
Payoff						
Risks	May shift tactics to other, less predictable weapons and forces	Difficult to get agreement on equal capability of asymmetrical forces and nonuniform weapons		If declaration correct or too low, may tempt attack; if too high, requires excessive disarmament	May not be balanced disarmament if initial inventory intelligence is inaccurate	May merely postpone arms race to beginning of hostilities; increased significance and instability of small violations at zero inventory

7. Multilateral
8. Unilateral $\Big\}$ > (participation)

9. Graduated
10. "Instantaneous" $\Big\}$ > (time)

11. Controlled
12. Uncontrolled $\Big\}$ > (verification)

Any one of these processes may be carried out according to negotiated agreement, or the required disarmament may be voluntarily exceeded, or it may be violated. Whether a nation chooses to comply, exceed, or violate a disarmament agreement, it may communicate these actions in ways that are truthful, exaggerated, or omit the truth. The three types of disarmament actions and the three means of communicating them form nine possible combinations, as shown in Table II with some reasons for each.

TABLE II

Nine Ways of Executing a Disarmament Agreement

	Communications of Actions		
Actions	*Truthful* *Action = Appearance*	*Exaggeration* *Action < Appearance*	*Omission* *Action > Appearance*
Comply with the Terms	Ideal behavior, minimizing uncertainty and maximizing confidence	Propaganda exploitation, leading to discounting of declarations	Suggestion of violation while actually complying may be used to provoke abrogation or cheating by an opponent
Exceed the Terms	Attempt to accelerate disarmament for economic, propaganda, or tactical decoy purposes	Further propaganda exploitation	May achieve earlier resource savings while preserving appearance of greater strength for deterrence and political bargaining
Violate — *Do Less than Comply*	Open abrogation to discredit agreement, terminate it	Flaunted abrogation to show contempt, threaten, bully opponent	Evasion, for secret advantage, as insurance against opponent's evasions or for nonmilitary political reasons

STRATEGIC USES OF DISARMAMENT

Military strategies are continuations of more political concepts for achieving national policy objectives. Disarmament may be used as a military strategy, as well as the engagement, maneuver, modification, or increase of armaments. We may consider disarmament as a strategy because it is a sequence of moves calculated to achieve specific objectives in a given environment. The dynamics of multilateral disarmament are just as significant for the balance of power as are the dynamics of multilateral arms races. Processes of multilateral disarmament may abort, become stabilized, accelerate, lead to open military conflict, or lead to peaceful cooperation. Historically, arms races have often led to a military clash followed by diplomatically negotiated peace. Certain situations of disarmament may also lead to negotiated peace followed by preventive, pre-emptive, or retaliatory rearmament and military conflict.

Disarmament as a strategy is incomplete unless it is coupled with concern for the capacity to rearm. In its very essence, a strategy is a sequence of hypothetical acts attempting to achieve a solution to a conflict of power, which disarmament also is. For example, while unilateral disarmament might remove one's own threat to an opponent, and hence permit or even induce him to disarm if his military costs are very high and the gains from aggression are very low, if the opponent judges that the gains from unopposed aggression outweigh the costs, then unilateral disarmament provides no military deterrent or defense against such attack. On the other hand, bilateral disarmament, if effectively inspected, can provide assurance that sufficient strategic warning and time are available to the complying parties to respond to violations of disarmament by rearming. The threat of rearmament may either deter rearmament by making it profitless as a means of changing the balance of power or defend against it if it is not deterred.

Let us examine some of the major strategic purposes to which disarmament states may be put for defensive purposes:

1. Reduction of the danger of war resulting from an uncontrolled arms race.
2. Reduction of the danger of war from accidental initiation of existing military capabilities.
3. Reduction of an opponent's relative military advantage to military parity by mutual complete disarmament.
4. Reduction of international tensions interfering with national policy objectives.
5. Reduction of the absolute economic burden of armaments.
6. Reduction of a relatively unfavorable economic burden of armaments that erodes an economic balance of power, by reducing both sides' economic expenditures on military capability.

All of these measures are essentially defensive and attempt to reduce a foreign military threat by paying the price of a tacitly- or explicitly-negotiated reduction of one's own capability. A nation choosing any one of these means to reduce a foreign military threat must abandon growth and expansion by military coercion, prepare for it in secrecy and strike by treachery, or shift to nonmilitary forms of increasing its national power, i.e., economic and political persuasion.

The following are some offensive employments of disarmament as a means for national aggrandizement:

1. Reduction of an unfavorable balance of military power to zero, with the purpose of then reinitiating an arms race from a more favorable position

—at worst, beginning at equal capability and, at best (as a result of secrecy), with a rearmament time advantage.

2. Evasion of the disarmament agreement during the process of disarmament, with the specific purpose of exploiting increasing relative power for aggression or other military-political objectives.

3. Changing the nature of international conflict from the military sphere, where possibly little may be gained because of mutually deterring stalemates, to another sphere of activity, such as the economic, where one believes one's self to enjoy superiority.

4. Disintegration of the opposing bloc's system of alliances, if they are based primarily on a common military defense against a common military threat. Intensive propaganda for disarmament of the most impractical kind can also, through public opinion, play on members of an opposing coalition and act as a substantial divisive force in domestic politics.

5. Making the world safe for guerrilla warfare, by disarming mobile modern forces capable of decisively supporting local counterinsurgency efforts.

DISARMAMENT PROCESS

We should avoid both the experimentally- and analytically-unwarranted faith that international conflict will be automatically eliminated, or even necessarily reduced, by disarmament. On the other hand, we should look beyond the clichés and oversimplifications suggesting that the only feasible basis for disarmament is an unjustified mutual trust.

The essential question for national policy planners is not so much whether disarmament of a given scope, intensity, and reliability yields *any* advantage to a potential enemy, but rather whether it yields *relative* and absolute advantages to one's own nation. One may imagine situations in which a given disarmament may yield one's potential opponent a relative advantage, but either the absolute advantages to one's self are sufficient to justify participation or the alternatives of an uncontrolled arms race appear even more dangerous. There may be cases in which a relative, but not decisive, disadvantage during the process of disarmament is traded for an anticipated advantage during the eventual state of disarmament.

Seen functionally, the disarmament process is the reallocation of national resources from external to internal applications, together with the dismantling of extant military forces. Nations usually disarm after eliminating or reducing a major military threat, and turn their energies to internal development. We must broaden our temporal viewpoint to consider whole cycles of disarmament and rearmament to determine what advantages for mutual security may occur.

It has often been argued that the concept of general and complete disarmament implies world government enforced by a world police force, and that such a police force must be capable of overpowering any remaining national force. This would appear to be a rather premature conclusion, in view of the ability of highly industrialized nations to rearm rapidly (within a year) and the great difficulty of pre-emptively destroying that rearmament capability by a force small enough to remain clandestine in an inspected and disarmed world. Thus, while a United Nations police force may be a useful means of settling secondary clashes, e.g., those in the Middle East and Congo, it is not likely to have a viable capability against the superpowers without growing large enough to threaten world military dictatorship. It is at least conceivable that general and complete disarmament might be enforced without benefit of an all-powerful world police force, but rather by the threat of rapid compensatory, and even retaliatory, rearmament.

After disarmament, would the West or the Communist powers respond more effectively in modernization of potentially military technology? The answer to this question depends on estimates of the relative imaginativeness of planning, flexibility, and technological-resource-concentrating ability of nations, as well as their relative industrial capacity and natural wealth.

The problem is to change the nature of the military world so that, in crises, the balance of decision lies with nontotalitarian states. Current postures of time scarcity may be more favorable to centralized totalitarian control than would be those of a disarmed world having enough inspection and surveillance to provide warning of, and for, rearmament. In a disarmed world, rearmament capacity will depend largely on industrialization—in which the West dominates—and effective decision-making—which, given enough time by warning of rearmament, is roughly equal.

How can one evaluate the effectiveness of disarmament as a strategy? Effectiveness depends on national objectives, the nature of the disarmament process, and the actions of the principal adversaries. If the national objective is aggressive expansion of power, this will not necessarily lead to the election of a disarmament system whose verification procedure is so poor as to permit cheating. It is quite possible that surprise rearmament (what might be called a surprise attack by military procurement) or political-economic measures may be considered the most effective instrument for national expansion. On the other hand, a nation having as its national goal the preservation of the current balance of power, by as peaceful means as possible, will tend to have an inherent interest in an effectively verified disarmament system, as much to remove its own otherwise rationally justified motivations for military preparedness as to assure the impossibility of military exploitation by an opponent.

Form and Content

The particular form and content of the disarmament process are of significance to the absolute and relative capacities of the participant nations to carry out certain foreign and domestic policy measures. Thus, if only intercontinental weapons are disarmed, for example, the Soviet Union can

achieve a firepower superiority over Western Europe undeterred by the disarmed intercontinental firepower of the United States. If all conventional
forces, including police forces, are disarmed, the Soviet Union may lose its
capability to maintain Communist regimes loyal to the Kremlin in the Eastern European nations, while Western regimes would not be endangerd. If
disarmament affects only overseas military bases, then Western capacity for
limited war and political deterrence is greatly reduced, without any substantial compensating reduction of Communist military capability. If, on the
other hand, all land-based military installations are to be dismantled, the
Communist forces may suffer a slight disadvantage because of the large
surface naval forces of the Western alliance. Again, if all missile forces over
1500-nautical-mile-range capability are disarmed, the West suffers a disadvantage, while if all missile forces of, say, over 100-nautical-miles capability
are disarmed, the Soviet Union probably suffers a relative disadvantage.
Thus the content of a disarmament agreement can critically affect the
balance of power and the relative military strategic capabilities of the participants (see Table III).

TABLE III

Estimated Effect of Disarmament of Selected Military Forces on the East-West Balance of Power

Disarmament Favors East	Disarmament Favors West	Uncertain Whom Disarmament Favors
ICBM's	IRBM's (land based)	Anti-Ballistic Missile Defenses
Missile-firing Submarines	All Submarines	Space Weapons
All Surface Ships	Armored Divisions	Nuclear Weapons*
Aircraft Carriers	Infantry Divisions	
Foreign Bases	Guerrilla Forces	
Long-range Bombers	Medium Bombers	
Biological Weapons	Fighter Aircraft	

* Disarmament of only tactical, compact, low-yield nuclear weapons might favor the East, but it
is difficult to see how these could be disarmed separately from strategic nuclear weapons,
whose disarmament would not clearly favor East or West.

Pace

The pace of the disarmament process is also extremely significant for the
strategic military capabilities of the participants. If general disarmament is
carried out at a very rapid rate, as desired by the Russians (in less than five
years), the instabilities of alliance adjustments and economic readjustments
suffered in the West may be temporarily greater than those in the more
centrally coordinated Communist bloc. If disarmament is carried out very
slowly, on the other hand, and accompanied by substantial international
inspection, the West maintains its considerable firepower superiority while at
the same time greatly reducing the secrecy advantage of the Communist
bloc, to the latter's great strategic and political disadvantage.

Geographic Area

The geographic area where the disarmament process is begun, when it is begun, and its geographic scope, are very significant for regional strategic and political developments. Consider the effect of the initiation of a Rapacki-type Central European disarmament in the course of a German constitutional and succession crisis. The political anxieties and civil disorders accompanying such a move might well result in a Communist coup d'état. And what are the chances for Soviet complete disarmament if only the United States participates, but not West Germany or Communist China?

Effectiveness

The principal adversaries' responses to disarmament measures must be considered in order to estimate the effectiveness of disarmament as a strategy. Disarmament may lead to either a decrease or an increase in international tensions, in the energy with which a nation pursues its competitive foreign policy goals, and in the militant and subversive nature of those pursuits. For example, intensive paramilitary activity by the Communists, in a process of otherwise uneventful disarmament, could stimulate Western rearmament—at least of forces useful in counterinsurgency operations.

A conservative security strategy attempts to achieve national security from all foreign aggressions by means of deterrence and, if that fails, military action against the aggressors' forces and their industrial base. The psychological mechanism of deterrence attempts to persuade an opponent that his costs will exceed his gains if he resorts to aggression. The physical mechanism of military action executes this threat when deterrence fails, attempts to destroy enemy war-making capacity, and thus also attempts to minimize the losses resulting from enemy action. A mechanism of deterrence may act against not only the decision to execute a threat but also an adversary's decision to create a threat capacity.

Defense against a threat may render it ineffectual; minimize its effectiveness; or, by the assurance of the presence of a defense, deter it. Thus, a capacity for effective military action functionally merges with what we have called deterrence. Military action and military deterrence differ in that some kinds of deterrent forces are not effective in the actual fighting of a war or in active defense, while all significant military forces have some deterrent value.

How does the generalized process and state of disarmament compare with more militant strategies in the effectiveness of deterrence and military action?

Table IV shows three major military doctrinal alternatives open to the United States and the Soviet Union, with their consequent force and information requirements. The inspection requirements for disarmament follow from the information requirements minus the information available from open sources and intelligence. The maximum allowable evasion level,

TABLE IV

Force and Information Requirements for Military Alternatives

National Goals	Survival Plus Defeat of Adversary	Survival—Competitive Draw	Survival—Cooperative Draw
Strategic Doctrine	Counterforce capability plus insurance (current) —fight the threat	Minimum or finite deterrent plus partial disarmament —deter the threat	General and complete disarmament —reduce the threat
Force Requirement	Great superiority of military force	Rough equality of military force	Rough equality of military rearmament potential, or dominant U.N. peace force
Payoff	Minimizes damage from nonrational attack; weakens nuclear blackmail by inferior power	Dampens the quantitative arms race; resource savings; permits "safe" internal wars	Savings; reduced risk of war through increased warning and negotiation time
Cost	Risks provoking arms race by appearing to make credible counter-force-disarming first strike	If deterrence fails, cannot reduce damage from nonrational attack by "blunting" pre-emptive strike; may be destabilized by technological innovation	Secret and decisive rearmament, or unstable rearmament race; danger of world dictatorship, world civil war from U.N. peace force
Strategic Context — General War	Prevail with heavy losses	Annihilation or capitulation	Possibly long, primitive and vicious
Strategic Context — Limited War	Constraint on escalation for inferior power; temptation for superior power	Maximum danger of excessive escalation—deterrence gap between local defense and nuclear holocaust	Loses to, or beats, U.N. peace force
Strategic Context — Cold War	Controlled or uncontrolled arms race plus low-level conflict	Armed stability plus low-level conflict	Allowable nonmilitary conflicts

TABLE IV (Continued)

Force and Information Requirements for Military Alternatives

Estimated Obsolescence Date	1965–70 (Due to mobile and hard survivable forces and ineffective defenses)	1970–75 (N countries with nuclear weapons plus mobile launch platforms result in inability to identify aggressor and hence noncredibility of deterrence)	Whenever massive violation requires compensatory rearmament
Maximum Allowable Evasion of Negotiated Disarmament	~ 50 ICBM's(?)—very small (as large as one is willing to suffer retaliation—Sino-Soviet and Anglo-American differences)	Modest (as large as acceptable uncertainty of ability to retaliate)—about twice nation's absolute inventory	Depends on size and control of U.N. peace force
Information Requirements	Targeting of enemy forces; technical intelligence for penetration and kill effectiveness	Only enough data to indicate that opponent does not possess counterforce capability plus enough technical intelligence to assure effectiveness of countervalue strike	Same(?) plus political assurance; open world(?); intentions of potential violation-capable groups
Inspection Requirements for Verifying Disarmament	Maximum inspection to assure continued counterforce targeting	Modest inspection or national intelligence	Considerable, since small force may now be decisive
Acceptable Uncertainty of Inspection System Performance	Very low	Modest	Varies with size and control of U.N. peace force—larger force permits more uncertainty

TABLE IV (Continued)

Force and Information Requirements for Military Alternatives

National Goals		Survival Plus Defeat of Adversary	Survival—Competitive Draw	Survival—Cooperative Draw
Military Acceptability of Required Degree of Inspection	*To U.S.*	Modest	Modest	High
	To U.S.S.R.	Extremely low	Low	Modest
Political Acceptability	*To U.S.*	High	High	Modest
	To U.S.S.R.	Low	High	Low
Operability = Performance Over Economic Cost for Both U.S. and U.S.S.R.		Low	High	Unknown

from the military point of view, is given in the form of a rough estimate based on the requirements of the basic strategic doctrines. Note how the different strategic doctrines require very different degrees of security information and inspection. It may be seen that the type of inspection system chosen to verify disarmament depends strongly on the nature of the strategic military doctrine that is being implemented.

Although the choice of the minimum or "finite" deterrence doctrine greatly eases requirements for inspection, it is an unappealing doctrine for a nation that already possesses the "safer" and more impressive unilateral counterforce capability. (It *is* safer if we cannot rely on the rationality of our adversary or if we cannot rely on the assumption that our idea of rationality is the same as his.)

The "fight the threat" counterforce strategy may become obsolete with an expected lag in AICBM defense effectiveness behind offensive ICBM capabilities, and the proliferation and increased survivability by mobility of ICBM's, making counterforce attacks ineffective. Beyond 1975, the survivable deterrent forces now being built also become obsolete as a means of assuring military security, because multiple national nuclear threats from mobile launch platforms make it impossible to identify an aggressor, and thus make deterrence by retaliation incredible.

MEASUREMENT AND MOTIVATION

The criteria of military security, logistic operability, and political acceptability may be reduced to a common dollar base. This is clearly the case with military security, where, for example, vulnerability to counterforce strike resulting from loss of secrecy of deployment following inspection requires compensating expenditures for restoring survivable firepower by means of hardening, mobility, or proliferation. Logistic costs are obviously expressible in dollar units. It is with political acceptability costs that there is some difficulty. As an approximation, it might be assumed that political costs may be decomposed into component military and economic costs, which are then accessible to combination with the other costs. The component of "ideological" cost and its dollar equivalent is beyond estimation at this time.

Neither balanced limitation of the quantity of comparable forces nor maintenance of comparable technological quality can assure mutual security, so long as the yet unmeasurable factors of leadership, tactical doctrine, and morale remain potentially decisive. Germany defeated France and the British Expeditionary Force in 1940 using technologically comparable, but quantitatively inferior, forces, chiefly because of superior tactical doctrine.

Perhaps one of the best ways to achieve a stable balance of power is to have it consist of opposed elements that cannot be changed quickly enough to escape detection and compensatory actions. The balance-restoring forces must respond more rapidly than the balance-disturbing, or revolutionary, forces. This requires a power system in which destabilizing actions are highly visible and rather slow. Such a system is an open, or inspected, disarmed world.

In an open, disarmed world, the critical parameter in the stability of national security is thus not the absolute military power available, nor even the power relative to adversaries, but rather the ratio of the rates of one's own and one's opponents' arming capacities. The United States may enjoy superiority in this critical parameter.

Undercurrent conditions of force asymmetries and uncertainties concerning the military utility of various forces and weapons obstruct a mutually acceptable balanced disarmament process. How many Soviet divisions equal an American division? Once estimated (possibly by analysis of a small number of special cases), how does this conversion factor vary with leadership, doctrine, morale, geography, weather, and strategic context? In a reciprocating sequence of purely counterforce missile strikes, how many Soviet ICBM's are the effective equivalent of a United States ICBM? What happens to the conversion factor if one or both sides employ mixed strategies and if they bargain differently? In a limited war far from both United States and Soviet heartlands, how many Soviet trawlers, submarines, and guerrilla battalions equal how many aircraft carriers, rangers, and friendly neutrals?

Tacit or negotiated arms control agreements or unilateral acts might reduce some force asymmetries, increasing the chances for rationally balanced disarmament. Convergence of opposed military technologies and organizations could be consciously pursued, as a means of achieving the commensurability of opposed forces required for rationally calculable balanced disarmament.

A politically very implausible but illustratively appealing way of achieving such commensurable forces rapidly would be to limit all military forces to qualitatively identical, interbloc-standardized equipments, organizational units, and employment doctrines. Initially no limits would be placed on the quantities of forces, since these could subsequently be reduced in a balanced way relatively easily once they were rendered commensurate. Inspection for verifying balanced disarmament would now no longer present a technical intelligence threat, since no secrets could be learned from identical types of equipment in the enemy's hands. With weapons no longer depending on secrecy of land deployment for survivability, substantial inventory inferiority could be tolerated by the Soviets without risk of decisive counterforce attack. Geographically unlimited access for verification of inventories and qualitative weapon uniformity would no longer present a decisive counterforce targeting threat. If access for inspection were considered politically unacceptable due to subversion and propaganda threats, the uniform opposed forces could even be deployed to nonnational areas, e.g., oceans or neutral desert areas. All of this is politically farfetched, indeed, but illustrates the problem.

In a disarmament negotiator's ideal world, uniformity of equipment could be assured by joint development and manufacture or, perhaps, by neutral third parties under joint United States-Soviet contract and control if joint manufacture is politically unfeasible. Uniformity of organizational units and employment doctrines could be achieved by joint administration and training or by thoroughgoing automation if the former is too unpalatable to competing ideologies and cultures.

The realization of this disarmament negotiator's nirvana would be an open, thoroughly inspected world in which the major powers would all have identical weapons, military units, and tactical doctrines of a form and deployment rendering them mutually invulnerable over large variations of force ratio. Competition over weapons inventories, within such arms controls, would be permitted. For a few years, the more aggressive nations might continue to strive for force ratio superiority. Probably it would not take them too long to realize that such superiority no longer constituted an effective instrument of national policy, while yet being quite expensive. The time would then be ripe for roughly-balanced reductions to a level where other, possibly less violent, means of national competition might become dominant.

But how could negotiated or tacit agreement by our adversaries to this other means toward balanced disarmament be achieved? To motivate our adversaries to cooperate with us in arms control measures making a balanced disarmament process rationally realizable, we need to make it unprofitable for them to do otherwise. One possibility is to accelerate the arms race, "raise the ante" of committed resources, to a degree making unbearable the economic burden to their less affluent society. If it were politically feasible substantially to increase income taxes and economically feasible to maintain private capital investment for growth or, in turn, politically feasible to supplant private with public investment, this approach could be taken more seriously. Given the current nature of United States domestic politics, it probably cannot be taken seriously now.

A less expensive and more effective means of making noncooperation in arms control unprofitable is to employ partial and local disarmament measures to achieve major savings, which are then applied to directly, but nonviolently, threaten other policy objectives of our adversaries. For example, savings from partial disarmament might be invested in scientific and industrial growth, providing an even more potent base for increased armaments should they be required, or the basis of aid to contested underdeveloped areas, or both. United States military aid to South America might be replaced by further economic and technical assistance, creating social improvements likely to prove a more effective bulwark against Communism than local military establishments (and incidentally maintaining a United States monopoly on hemispheric military power). Savings from partial and/or local disarmaments could be invested in improved intelligence collection and processing, capable of unilaterally reducing the secrecy advantage of the Communist areas.

Professor Hans Morgenthau has said, "A mutually satisfactory settlement of the power contest is a precondition for disarmament." Perhaps this is not the only precondition, or even the most achievable one. Perhaps a shift in the nature of the power contest, unilaterally initiated, can make it intolerably expensive for an adversary to refuse at least partial and/or local disarmament. Perhaps in some areas and strategic contexts our resources are more effectively employed on means other than arms, and a demonstration of this could lead to Communist imitation or stubborn defeat. In such ways, disarmament might excel military means as a strategic instrument of national policy. Verified disarmament may be the most effective military strategy in the future. Our problem now is to identify the characteristics of processes capable of achieving such a state while preserving the security of all nations.

DISARMAMENT PAYOFFS TO EAST AND WEST

The strategic payoffs of disarmament for a given nation or bloc consist of the degree to which strategic gains exceed losses. Strategic gains are the achievement of national policy goals or degrees of them, provided these are in the rational self-interest of the nation or bloc concerned. (Nazi Germany's policy goal of world conquest was not in the national self-interest of Germany, but only in its self-perceived self-interest.) Perceived strategic gains may be toward the achievement of national goals perceived as self-interest but actually detrimental to national interests. Strategic losses are the immediate, opportunity costs of contradicted or postponed national goals, together with the immediate and opportunity costs of national material, intellectual, and socio-cultural resources. Again, perceived costs may differ greatly from actual costs. The actual strategic payoff differs from the perceived payoff to the degree that actual gains and losses differ from those perceived.

In what terms may strategic gains and losses be estimated? It is first necessary to define national or shared bloc goals. This is at best an uncertain affair, as the many visionary and yet hackneyed and diffuse essays on this topic attest. Yet the effort must be made, however inexact the current results, with the hope that political science will eventually improve in precision. Below are listed some of the major general policy goals of the Western bloc:

1. Reduce the risk of war or its destructiveness if it cannot be avoided.
2. Make possible a world order consistent with Western goals of political liberty, economic enterprise and wealth, and social justice.

3. Maintain military deterrent and defensive power, either in Western national forces or in some United Nations force that is nonpartisan, to deal with potential aggressors.
4. Create a favorable image of Western nations abroad.
5. Obtain friendly trade and military defense relations with as many nations as possible.

Communist bloc policy goals compare as follows:

1. Same as for the West.
2. Make possible the world domination of communism, with its versions of liberty, enterprise, and justice.
3. Maintain military deterrent, defensive, and offensive power, either in the Communist bloc or in a bloc-controlled international organization (probably *not* the U.N.), to deal with Western intervention in revolutionary wars of liberation and Western counterrevolutions and possibly to aggressively exploit power vacuums and weak Western states.
4. Same as for the West (for Communist nations).
5. Same as for the West.

Some of the relations between the above bloc policy goals and specific disarmament questions reveal some of the immediate strategic payoffs that are held in common or in conflict between the two blocs.

The first payoff is reduction of the risk of war through improved command and positive control of weapons, by permissive links and other technological innovation in the West and by extremely rigid and formal political control in the Communist bloc.

Second, reduction of the destructiveness of war, if it cannot be avoided, through attempts to limit the total number of weapons, the types of weapons employed, and the manner of their employment. In the West this has led to a doctrine of arms management of aggression; in the Communist bloc it has been expressed by periodic attempts to ban the use of certain weapons, and in particular the first use of such weapons. In the West the counterforce doctrine has also been developed to limit the amount of damage that would be imposed on civil targets by a retaliating enemy.

A third payoff is the enhancement of world order consistent with bloc goals. A very different style in disarmament proposals indicates the different strategic objectives of the West and the East. The West prefers to have as much inspection as possible with slow disarmament, giving an equal, or even increased, assurance of effective deterrence and defense against Communist attack in the process of disarmament. The East, also from its own rational self-interest, prefers to have maximum speed of disarmament with the minimum of inspection, and preferably a differential rate of disarmament such that strategic parity is achieved as soon as possible, improving its relative power position vis-à-vis the West. Furthermore, the East defines certain "just wars of liberation" as essentially excluded from disarmament coverage. The centralist (Soviet) position in Communist doctrine today (also accused of being right-wing revisionist by the so-called left-wing adventurists, e.g., the Chinese Communists and Albanians) is that military conflict is no longer inevitable with the capitalist West. Khrushchev apparently is willing to gamble on a doctrine of military noninterference in local revolution, on the assumption that more often than not these revolutions will develop into Communist states.

The gains in Western bloc policy goals might be (in decreasing order of importance): (1) stabilization of power superiority, (2) reduced danger of accidental war, (3) pacification of international conflict, and (4) reduced economic burden. A comparable rank ordering in Communist bloc policy goals might be: (1) reduced economic burden, (2) equalization of military power, (3) reduced danger of accidental war, and (4) pacification of international conflict.

Economic motives predominate in Soviet writings extolling the virtues of disarmament, while in the West disarmament is at best defended against the charge of inducing depression and disruptive unemployment. The West primarily wants effective disarmament to achieve a more stable form of military security from aggression, and hence ranks highly its potential gains in the stabilization of its current power superiority and reduced danger of accidental war. The Communists undoubtedly would consider it a strategic gain to achieve military equality with the West. Pacification of the ideological conflict is probably considered a fond hope by leaders and elites in both blocs, but has had more manifest appeal for the liberal Western tradition.

The Soviet Union's ordering of strategic gains to be achieved by disarmament might be: (1) reduced economic burden, (2) reduced danger of accidental war, (3) equalization of military power, and (4) pacification of international conflict. On the other hand, the Chinese People's Republic (C.P.R.) might rank strategic gains as follows: (1) equalization of military power, (2) reduced economic burden, (3) reduced danger of accidental war, and (4) pacification of international conflict.

The utility distances between these estimated strategic gains are not uniform. In fact, the Chinese People's Republic may not consider "pacification of international conflict" a gain. A significant strategic gain not listed, that may appeal to the U.S.S.R. but not to the C.P.R., is the reduction of Western capacity to intervene in what Khrushchev has called "just wars of liberation." The latest "democratic centralist" line from Moscow suggests that revolutionary internal wars will result in Communist victories if only the Western powers can be kept from intervening, while the "left dogmatists adventurist" line of Peiping suggests that such wars must be actively supported by Communist states to be assured of success—a condition not to be achieved in a state of disarmament.

The likely persistence of internal or revolutionary armed conflict—whether Communist sponsored, as in Vietnam, or merely Communist exploited, as in Cuba—may suggest a payoff to the Communists independent of whether or not they actively aid, or just confidently observe, the process. Guerrilla warfare, one of the principal techniques for effecting revolutionary political change in the underdeveloped transitional societies, can probably be employed within any enforceable definition of general and complete disarmament. Guerrilla warfare requires chiefly dedicated men and small arms and explosives. Guerrilla warfare has great cost effectiveness and has been known to gain victories over established regimes ten times the strength of the guerrilla armies and incomparably better equipped with heavy weapons and logistics. One can readily imagine how much more effective guerrilla warfare would be in a disarmed world against governments lacking even the limited advantages of modern military technology. But what, then, are the potential payoffs of disarmament for the Western bloc, and the United States in particular? We know that the world situation is not purely competitive, or zero sum, as the game theorists say. Just because there are disarmament payoffs to the Communists, and the West is in conflict with the Communist bloc, does not mean that there cannot exist at the same time disarmament payoffs for the Western powers too.

The disarmament payoffs which the West could enjoy in common with the Communist bloc are certainly the reduced economic burden of national security, possibly the reduced danger of war (if it is really reduced), and somewhat less possibly the reduced damage of wars that cannot be avoided. We have already discussed how protracted paramilitary conflict is likely to be even less inhibited in a disarmed world and suggested that this might favor the Communists. This is not *necessarily* the case, if the West were capable of initiating or retaliating with some guerrilla warfare of its own—say, in Eastern Europe.

The economic benefits of disarmament, while favoring all participants, would undoubtedly favor the Communists *relatively,* and this relative gain might even outweigh the absolute loss to the West of economic resources if there were no disarmament. On the other hand, provided the inspection procedures were effective, the West probably has the industrial capacity to beat the Communist bloc in a rearmament race. The danger lies in the West's relatively slow strategic decision-making when domestic economic interests must be disturbed—as they would have to be for massive and urgent rearmament.

The disarmament payoff for the United States would probably be greater than for its European and other allies located on land masses contiguous with the Sino-Soviet bloc. There are three primary reasons: First, the United States carries the principal economic burden for military defense against Communist aggression. Second, the United States is still protected from direct ground forces invasion by distance and oceans. Third, and least potent, is that the greater area of the United States makes it less vulnerable to a decisive surprise attack from a modest clandestine store of nuclear weapons. Everything considered, the nearby neighbors of the Sino-Soviet bloc risk much more by disarmament than does the United States. One can even conceive of a Soviet invasion of Western Europe carried out within the terms of a disarmament agreement by nothing more than millions of security police armed with small arms travelling by automobile, truck, and commercial aircraft.

In summary, the disarmament payoffs unique to the Communist bloc are chiefly the reduction of the economic burden that it is relatively less capable of carrying than the West, the equalization of immediately operational military power, and possibly the less risky pursuit of "just wars of liberation" unfettered by Western military intervention. The disarmament payoffs unique to the Western bloc are much less clear, although there are important payoffs which it shares with the Communist bloc, e.g., reduced economic burden and possibly reduced risk of accidental war. Possibly the reduced isolation of the Communist bloc nations from the West (a possible consequence of disarmament) would gradually draw them into neutralism, or at least away from direct bloc control. The United States has more to gain and less to risk from disarmament than its European and Asian allies. The Soviet Union risks more than the Eastern European nations and, ironically, the Chinese People's Republic, while at the same time its economic gains from disarmament may also be greater than that of its allies. In a state of general and complete disarmament, Eastern Europe would have little to fear from Western Europe, but the Soviet Union might have reason to be concerned about the Chinese, in addition to having to find new ways to assure the political loyalty of Eastern Europe. The discrepancies of national and bloc interest in disarmament suggest why it has not previously been possible to achieve a global disarmament agreement.

THE ROLE OF DETERRENCE

IN TOTAL DISARMAMENT

Thomas C. Schelling

A SHARP DISTINCTION is often drawn between arms control and disarmament. The former seeks to reshape military incentives and capabilities; the latter, it is alleged, eliminates them. But the success of either depends on mutual deterrence. Short of universal brain surgery, nothing can erase the memory of weapons and how to build them. If "total disarmament" is to make war unlikely, it must reduce the incentives. It cannot eliminate the potential for destruction; the most primitive war can be modernized by rearmament as it goes along.

To determine whether and how disarmament might make war less likely we have to look at what the military opportunities, risks, dangers, fears and potential capabilities would be in a disarmed world. If nations now suspect each other of contemplating war, we have to suppose that they might suspect each other of contemplating rearmament. If nations are willing to risk war, or to threaten it, they certainly might risk rearming or threatening to rearm. Nations thought capable now of being panicked into war might be panicked into rearmament. To suppose the contrary is to assume away the problem that disarmament is intended to help solve.

An international military authority is commonly proposed as a part of plans for total disarmament. It does make a difference whether or not we assume the existence of such an authority to police the otherwise disarmed world. But for the visible future it is a little extreme to suppose that an international force could contain or deter the United States and the Soviet Union; more than that, the concept poses problems of deterrence not wholly unlike those that would confront the major powers in a fully disarmed world. So we shall first consider universal disarmament without any international security force. And we shall assume a world disarmed to the levels proposed by those who favor the most drastic "total disarmament."

There are good reasons why this phrase should be set off in quotation marks. An obvious one is that there can be no absolute assurance that some nuclear weapons have not been kept. But, cheating aside, war can be waged with even the most primitive weapons, especially with the help of commercial aircraft, ships, trucks, radios and the other paraphernalia of industrial

Reprinted from *Foreign Affairs*, April, 1962.

society. More important, if war breaks out a nation can rearm unless its capacity is destroyed at the outset and kept destroyed. By the standards of 1944, the United States was fairly near to total disarmament when World War II broke out. Virtually all munitions later expended by United States forces were nonexistent in September 1939. "Disarmament" did not preclude U.S. participation; it just slowed it down.

As we eliminate weapons, warning systems, vehicles and bases, we change the criteria of military effectiveness. Airplanes are more important if missiles are banned; complex airplanes are needed less if complex defenses are banned. Since weapons themselves are the most urgent targets in war, to eliminate a weapon eliminates a target and changes the requirements for attack. At some stage in disarmament a donkey becomes a means of delivery, though we assume that " total" disarmament stops short of that.

The difficulty cannot be avoided by banning weapons of attack and keeping those of defense. If nations were large, self-sufficient islands, coast artillery might seem useless for aggression and valuable safeguards against war and the fear of war. But they are not; and in the present era, "defensive" weapons often embody equipment or technology that is superbly useful in attack and invasion. Moreover, a prerequisite of successful attack is some ability to defend against retaliation or counterattack. In a disarmed world, whatever lessens the scale of retaliation reduces the risk a nation runs in starting war. Defenses against retaliation thus are close substitutes for offensive power.

II. GENERAL WAR IN A DISARMED WORLD

Disarmament would not preclude the eruption of a crisis; war and rearmament could seem imminent. Even without possessing complex weapons, a nation might consider initiating war with whatever resources it had, on grounds that delay would allow an enemy to strike or mobilize first. If a nation believed its opponent might rush to rearm to achieve military preponderance, it might consider "preventive war" to forestall its opponent's dominance. Or, if confidence in the maintenance of disarmament were low and if war later under worse conditions seemed at all likely, there could be motives for "preventive ultimatums," or for winning a short war through coercion with illicitly retained nuclear weapons, or for using force to impose a more durable disarmament arrangement.

The decision to attack might be made reluctantly, motivated not by the prospective gains of victory but by the disadvantages of not seizing the initiative. Motives to undertake preventive or preëmptive war might be as powerful under disarmament as with today's weapons—perhaps more powerful.

In a disarmed world, as now, the objective would probably be to destroy the enemy's ability to bring war into one's homeland, and to "win" sufficiently to prevent his subsequent build-up as a military menace. The urgent targets would be the enemy's available weapons of mass destruction (if any), his means of delivery, his equipment that could be quickly converted for strategic use, and the components, stand-by facilities and cadres from which he could assemble a capability for strategic warfare.

Suppose both sides have violated the agreement and possess nuclear bombs at least in the scores or hundreds (or suppose the attacker has, and must anticipate that his opponent has). The attacker's first objective is to forestall the delivery of bombs in return. Compared with the present, the disarmed world would offer the attacker both advantages and disadvantages.

An advantage is that the time scale of attack may be more lenient. The victim may have a secret nuclear stockpile; but if he is unprepared it will take time to bring together, say, commercial aircraft, crews and the hidden nuclear weapons, and to improvise fueling arrangements and target plans. To do this in the hostile environment of even small-scale nuclear attack might be difficult. But the attacker would be coördinated rather than surprised and could make effective use of evacuation procedures or of any air defenses he could improvise.

If, instead, each side has plans for the contingency and maintains a "reserve force"—some part, say, of its commercial air fleet and crews—the victim of attack may react quickly. The attacker's own air defenses have been banned by agreement (and air defenses may be hard to conceal) ; in these conditions a retaliatory force of even low efficiency may be effective if it is large and dispersed.

If the aggressor has nuclear weapons and the victim does not, the latter's response will depend on how rapidly production can be resumed. Standby capacity may be available, or there may be nuclear facilities that can be converted to produce weapons. If these facilities have not been destroyed, the lag may be short, but a matter of days at least. Critically important would be the defenses, the dispersal or the secrecy of the facilities for producing nuclear materials or for assembling nuclear weapons. If the sites are few in number, of known location, above ground and without air defense, they would be destroyed before operations could be resumed. If the production facilities are in secret locations, we may as well assume that nuclear weapons also exist.

III. A WAR OF NUCLEAR MOBILIZATION

In the event that neither side had nuclear weapons, asymmetrical lead-times in nuclear rearmament could be decisive. Whether it took days or months, the side that believed it could be first to acquire a few dozen megatons through a crash rearmament program would expect to dominate its opponent. This advantage would be greatest if nuclear facilities themselves were vulnerable to nuclear bombardment: the first few weapons produced would be used to spoil the opponent's nuclear rearmament. Even if facilities

are deep under the ground, well disguised or highly dispersed, a small difference in the time needed to acquire a few score megatons might make the
war unendurable for the side that is behind. If one side appears likely to
gain the decisive advantage, it might find "preventive rearmament" coupled
with a surrender ultimatum an irresistibly attractive move.

It would not necessarily be essential to possess nuclear weapons in order
to destroy nuclear facilities. High explosives, commandos or saboteurs could
be effective. "Strategic warfare" might reach a purity not known in this
century: like the king in chess, nuclear facilities would be the overriding
objective. Their protection would have absolute claim on defense.

In such a war the object would be to preserve one's mobilization base and
to destroy the enemy's. To win a war would not require overcoming the
enemy's defenses—just winning the rearmament race. If commandos can
bypass home defenses, and paralyze the adversary's nuclear mobilization base,
the jig is up—unless all participants can do this to each other. If they can,
the prospect is for a bizarre kind of "broken-backed" war, bizarre because
no back is broken, and the struggle to acquire nuclear weapons goes on—
hopefully not too fast and too furiously to allow parallel negotiations for an
agreed stalemate or a second try at "disarmament."

Another kind of warfare may emerge—"nuclear coercion." If an attacker
possesses illicit nuclear weapons that can be dropped on a country that is
unable to retaliate promptly, it might force a surrender through the destruction of cities and the threat of destroying more. Or the coercive campaign
could combine preclusive destruction of the mobilization base with the
demoralizing effects of concurrent civil damage. The expectation would be
that, if significant rearmament could be retarded, capitulation would be
forthcoming.

Such a war might be less destructive than war under present conditions,
not primarily because disarmament had reduced the attacker's capability but
because, with the victim unable to respond, the attacker could adopt a more
measured pace that allowed time to negotiate a cease-fire before he had
reduced his victim to rubble. Victory, of course, might be achieved without
violence. If one side appears to have an advantage so convincingly decisive
as to make the outcome of the war seem inevitable, it could then deliver
an ultimatum instead of weapons.[1]

Disarmament might also cause nuclear weapons to be a greater equalizer
among nations than they are now. A future Castro might be in a better
position to plague or coerce the great powers by secreting nuclear weapons
on his territory. In a world in which such forms of nuclear mischief have

---

[1] Deterrence being largely a matter of credibility, it might not always be an advantage to have it believed that one is complying with the prohibition on nuclear weapons.
At the slightest suspicion that others might be initiating preparations, a government
might prefer to hint that it was already prepared. A small nuclear capability might be
used to demonstrate a larger professed capability.

replaced the space-age machinery of war and in which the push-button has given way to improvised aerial ferries, the military environment may become less predictable and possibly more unstable.

To sum up: a stable military environment will not result automatically from a ban on weapons and the facilities to make them. The timing of war and rearmament, and the role of speed and initiative, will remain critically important in a world in which the pace of war is initially slowed. War may become more calculable and less fearsome. And there would remain, even in the design of "total disarmament," the difficult choice between minimizing war's destructiveness and minimizing its likelihood. If disarmament is to discourage the initiation of war and to remove the incentives toward preëmptive and preventive war, it has to be *designed* to do that. Disarmament does not eliminate military potential; it changes it.

IV. LIMITED WAR IN A DISARMED WORLD

While disarmament would eliminate the guns, it would not eliminate the trucks, aircraft, ships, communication equipment and canned food that are required for limited military campaigns. Nations could be expected to have plans for limited-war mobilization, including limited departures from the arms agreement itself.[2]

As important as the direct consequences that disarmament would have for limited war would be the indirect consequences. If disarmament reduces fears of general war—if explosion or escalation into general war seems a less likely prospect, or less disastrous if it should occur—the result may be fewer inhibitions on limited war. There could also be new restraints. If it is perceived that the outbreak of local wars may destroy the agreement itself —either through a sudden breakdown or steady erosion—this may create a determination to preserve what has been achieved and a recognition that to abandon restraints would signal "open season" on military competition. Of course, the more all parties value the climate of disarmament, the more can be gained by threatening to disturb it.

As "limited war" is possible, so is "limited violation" of disarmament. Since limits on hostilities can evidently be observed during war itself, limits on rearmament might be arrived at in similar fashion, even in the course of limited hostilities. The responses of countries not participating in the war would be important—perhaps an important brake, possibly a stimulus, on the resumed armament.

In limited war as in general war under conditions of "total disarmament," timing would be important. Offensive strategy in a limited war is often designed to achieve a *fait accompli*. Defense against this strategy in a dis-

---

[2] The Chinese civil war of 1948–49 may illustrate how extensive a war can be fought with poor weaponry and primitive logistical support. Or the American Civil War.

armed world would depend on the ability of the defender (or protector) to rearm in time to repel or to stalemate the aggression. If we reflect on the critical timing of the North Korean invasion and the shortage of ammunition that plagued us throughout the whole Korean campaign, or the problems of the preëmptive landing of Marines in Lebanon or the progress of the Suez campaign, it is evident that logistical considerations can be decisive. The likelihood that limited aggression will be deterred by the threat of limited rearmament may therefore depend on the mobilization speed that can be achieved from a standing start.

V. THE DETERRENCE OF REARMAMENT IN A DISARMED WORLD

Many concepts that apply to the deterrence of war apply to deterrence of rearmament: "preventive" rearmament, "preëmptive" rearmament, "escalation" of rearmament, "catalytic" rearmament, and rearmament stimulated by misinformation, misinterpretation, accident, false alarm, unauthorized conspiracy and other processes analogous to those that might trigger "inadvertent war" in an armed world. In addition, there are the possibilities of rearmament bubbling up out of a crisis, occurring in the course of a limited war or being undertaken by cool premeditation.

But despite the parallel, rearmament is not war. The fears, motives and moral attitudes that make initiation of war an opprobrious act do not apply with the same force to rearmament. The question whether to remain disarmed or to initiate limited rearmament could become a legitimate political issue. If the disarmament is so delicately balanced that there is great advantage in being the first to rearm, the mere existence of a political party pledged to abandon the disarmament treaty might disturb the arrangement. And to the extent that the treaty explicitly allows certain weapons or a mobilization base, continuing developments in technology will make armament, as well as disarmament, a proper topic of discussion and continuing negotiation.

The essential requirement is for some stable situation of "rearmament parity." If disarmament is to be durable, it must be apparent that the disadvantages of being behind in case an arms race should resume are not too great and that, in the face of ambiguous evidence of clandestine rearmament or overt evidence of imminent rearmament, nations can react without haste. The straightforward elimination of so-called "military production facilities" might, by sheer coincidence, provide the stability; but stability is more likely if there is a deliberately designed system of "stable equal readiness for rearmament." It is impossible to eliminate the ability to rearm; one can only hope to stretch the time required to reach, from the word "go," any specified level of rearmament. The problem is not *whether* to leave a mobilization base for rearmament, but what kind.

It is not certain that maximizing the time required to rearm is a way to deter it. Lengthening the racecourse does not necessarily lessen the incentive to be first under the wire. But it may reduce the advantage of a small head-start; it may allow time to renegotiate before the race has too much momentum; and it may reduce the confidence of a fast starter that he could win if he called for a race.

If rearmament is undertaken to improve mutual deterrence, not to achieve offensive superiority, it may not matter whether some nations fall behind. The leader will not necessarily race as fast as he can; for if he does, other nations may have to regard his behavior as a declaration of war and to respond accordingly. If a low-grade war of nuclear reprisal is within the capability of some laggard in the rearmament race, he may feel obliged to initiate such a war to disrupt another's rearmament; thus rearmament could lead to preëmptive action and trigger a war. On the other hand, this prospect may help deter rearmament itself.

The likelihood of war, then, depends on the character of the disarmament. If mobilization potentials are such that a head-start is not decisive and the racecourse is long, preëmptive action may be delayed until motives are clear. This, however, presents a dilemma analogous to that of deterring limited war today: the smaller the fear that rearmament will precipitate general war, the smaller the inhibition on rearmament.

Important elements for stability in a disarmed world would be the dispersal and duplication of standby facilities for rearmament and of reserve personnel or cadres around which rearmament can be mobilized. Dispersal is important because of the interaction between rearmament and war itself. If a nation can achieve just enough production of weapons to disrupt its opponent's rearmament, it may gain a decisive advantage. Once the race is on, a few easily-located facilities for producing nuclear weapons might invite a "preventive" and very limited war. If instead there were, say, scores or hundreds of laboratories able to produce unconventional weapons and if their destruction would require substantial military capabilities, there might be less incentive on one side to acquire and exploit a small advantage and less fear on the other of falling a little behind and being taken advantage of.

Nations are now willing to threaten war; in a disarmed world they certainly might threaten rearmament. The agreement itself would certainly have to be renegotiated from time to time, or continuously; and, just as a threat of "no sale" hangs over the head of commercial traders, so will the threat of rearmament hang over the heads of negotiators. The main sanction on the negotiations will be that, in the absence of a satisfactory agreement, nations may take unilateral steps for their own security or take steps to put pressure on others.

VI. ATTITUDES TOWARD REARMAMENT

The terms of an agreement must take into account what the attitude toward rearmament would be in the disarmed world. One approach would be that any overt rearmament would be a mortal sin, a total failure of the disarmament process, a contingency that can neither be planned for nor discussed coolly within countries or between governments. Alternatively, rearmament might be viewed as we view war now—as a tragedy and a failure of policy, but a tragedy that can occur, that can even occur from motives of self-defense, that can perhaps be limited and contained, and that need not signal the termination of all efforts at settlement and reconciliation.

The first attitude, which would try to insulate rearmament from the cold war and deprecate any planning for the contingency of rearmament, might be preferable if it could promise to create sufficiently strong inhibitions. If, instead, we have to expect—as surely we do—lapses under even the most ideal disarmament scheme, it is better to plan for such contingencies and to create the expectation that occasional lapses need not trigger a real arms race or the full fury of war itself. We cannot have it both ways. For if we recognize "limited rearmament" as a possibility and prepare for "limited responses" against it, we take some of the curse off rearmament, just as plans for limited war seem to legitimize war. This is a genuine dilemma.

Rearmament has other dimensions than speed and volume. We should distinguish between rearmament aimed at stable deterrence and rearmament aimed at brinkmanship or war. In this country we would certainly want to have careful rearmament plans so that, in the event we found ourselves unavoidably drawn into a renewed arms race, our actions would be consistent with deterrence of war and with an effort to slow down the pace of rearmament. The further rearmament goes and the more unstable the environment which it creates, the harder it will be to get back to the business of disarmament if we wish to.

It will also make a difference whether military and strategic planning is permitted and expected or frowned on. The dilemma is that stability will require careful planning of a kind inconsistent with the philosophy that military planning is illegal, immoral and a sign of evil intent. If nations suddenly awoke to rearmament dangers of which they had not been aware, their response might be more undisciplined and more unstable in the absence of military planning than if vigilance had been deliberately maintained.

It should not be expected that reduced tensions will be the natural consequence of a disarmament agreement. Not everyone will be confident that disarmament provides a viable military environment or promises the political atmosphere most conducive to peace and good relations. It is hard to believe that any sober person under any conceivable world arrangement could come to believe with confidence that war had at last been banished from human affairs until there had been at the very least some decades of experience. There will be surprises, rumors and sharp misunderstandings. Even if something that looks like "general and complete disarmament" is achieved, it is not out of the question that responsible governments might decide that international apprehensions would be reduced if they possessed more secure, more diversified and more professionally organized mobilization bases or weapon systems, with more freedom to improve them, drill them and discuss the strategy of their use.

It is even conceivable that a "rearmament agreement" would be negotiated in the interest of reducing tensions, the likelihood of war, the scope for "rearmament blackmail," the Nth-country problem, and perhaps even the economic costs of preparedness. It might be that moderate though expensive modern weapon systems, professionally organized and segregated from the main population centers, would provide less—not more—military interference in everyday life than a "total" disarmament agreement under which every commercial pilot carried emergency mobilization instructions in his briefcase. In any event, a decision on total disarmament, taken jointly by the major powers, would not bring an end to arguments about arms control.

VII. AN INTERNATIONAL MILITARY AUTHORITY

Some kind of international authority is generally proposed as part of an agreement on total disarmament. If militarily superior to any combination of national forces, an international force implies (or is) some form of world government. To call such an arrangement "disarmament" is about as oblique as to call the Constitution of the United States "a Treaty for Uniform Currency and Interstate Commerce." The authors of the Federalist Papers were under no illusion as to the far-reaching character of the institution they were discussing, and we should not be either. Here, however, we can focus only on those aspects of an International Force that directly affect the military environment.

One concept deserves mention in passing: that the projected police force should aim to control persons rather than nations. Its weapons would be squad cars, tear gas and pistols; its intelligence system would be phone taps, lie detectors and detectives; its mission would be to arrest people, not to threaten war on governments. Here, however, we shall concentrate on the concept of an International Force to police nations—and all nations, not just small ones. The most intriguing questions are those that relate to the Force's technique or strategy for deterring and containing the former nuclear powers.

The mission of the Force would be to police the world against war and rearmament. It might be authorized only to stop war; but some kinds of rearmament would be clear signals of war, obliging the Force to take action. There might be, explicitly or implicitly, a distinction between the kinds of rearmament that call for intervention and the kinds that are not hostile.

The operations of the Force raise a number of questions. Should it try to contain aggression locally, or to invade the aggressor countries (or all parties to the conflict) and to disable them militarily? Should it use long-range strategic weapons to disable the country militarily? Should it rely on the threat of massive punitive retaliation? Should it use the threat or, if necessary, the practice of limited nuclear reprisal as a coercive technique? In the case of rearmament, the choices would include invasion or threats of invasion, strategic warfare, reprisal or the threat of reprisal; "containment" could not forestall rearmament unless the country were vulnerable to blockade.

Is the Force intended to do the job itself or to head a world-wide alliance against transgressors? In case of aggression, is the victim to participate in his own defense? If the Indians take Tibet, or the Chinese encourage armed homesteading in Siberia, the Force would have to possess great manpower unless it was prepared to rely on nuclear weapons. A Force could not be maintained on a scale sufficient to "contain" such excursions by a nation with a large population unless it relied on the sudden mobilization of the rest of the world or on superior weaponry—nuclear weapons if the defense is to be confined to the area of incursion. But the use of such weapons to defend, for example, South Viet Nam against Chinese infiltrators, Western Europe against the Soviet bloc, East Germany against West Germany or Cuba against the United States, would be subject to the ordinary difficulties of employing nuclear weapons in populated areas. A country threatened by invasion might rather capitulate than be defended in that fashion. Moreover, the Force might require logistical facilities, infrastructure and occasional large-scale manoeuvres in areas where it expects to be called upon. Keeping large forces stationed permanently along the Iron Curtain is a possibility, but not one that brings with it all the psychological benefits hoped for from disarmament.

A sizeable intervention of the Force between major powers is not, of course, something to be expected often in a disarmed world. Nevertheless, if the Force is conceived of as superseding Soviet and American reliance on their own nuclear capabilities, it needs to have some plausible capability to meet large-scale aggression; if it hasn't, the major powers may still be deterred, but it is not the Force that deters them.

A capability for massive or measured nuclear punishment is probably the easiest attribute with which to equip the Force. But it is not evident that the Force could solve the problems of "credibility" or of collective decision any better than can the United States alone or NATO collectively at the present time. This does not mean that it could not solve them—just that they are not automatically solved when a treaty is signed. If the Force is itself stateless, it may have no "homeland" against which counter-reprisal could be threatened by a transgressor nation; but if it is at all civilized, it will not be wholly immune to the counter-deterrent threats of a transgressor to create civil damage in other countries. These could be either explicit threats of reprisal or implicit threats of civil destruction collateral to the bombardment of the Force's own mobilization base. (The Force presumably produces or procures its weaponry in the industrial nations, and cannot be entirely housed in Antarctica, on the high seas or in outer space.)

If it should appear technically impossible to police the complete elimination of nuclear weapons, then we should have to assume that at least minimal stockpiles had been retained by the major powers. In that case, the Force might not be a great deal more than one additional deterrent force; it would not enjoy the military monopoly generally envisaged.

One concept needs to be disposed of—that the Force should be strong enough to defeat a coalition of aggressors but not so strong as to impose its will against universal opposition. Even if the world had only the weapons of Napoleon, the attempt to calculate such a delicate power balance would seem impossible. With concepts like preëmption, retaliation and nuclear blackmail, any arithmetical solution is out of the question.

The knottiest strategic problem for an International Force would be to halt the unilateral rearmament of a major country. The credibility of its threat to employ nuclear weapons whenever some country renounces the agreement and begins to rearm itself would seem to be very low indeed.

The kind of rearmament would make a difference. If a major country openly arrived at a political decision to abandon the agreement and to recover the security it felt it had lost by starting to build a merely retaliatory capability and sizeable home-defense forces, it is hard to envisage a civilized International Force using weapons of mass destruction on a large scale to stop it. Limited nuclear reprisals might be undertaken in an effort to discourage the transgressor from his purpose. But unless the rearmament program is accompanied by some overt aggressive moves, perhaps in limited war, the cool and restrained introduction of nuclear or other unconventional weapons into the country's population centers does not seem plausible, unless non-lethal chemical or biological weapons could be used.

Invasion might offer a more plausible sanction, perhaps with paratroops armed with small nuclear weapons for their own defense; their objective would be to paralyze the transgressor's government and mobilization. But if this should be considered the most feasible technique for preventing rearmament, we have to consider two implications. We have provided the Force a bloodless way of taking over national governments. And a preëmptive invasion of this kind might require the Force to act with a speed and secrecy inconsistent with political safeguards.

There is also the question of what kinds of rearmament or political activity leading to rearmament should precipitate occupation by the Force. In our country, could the Republicans or Democrats campaign on a rearmament platform, go to the polls and win, wait to be inaugurated, denounce the agreement, and begin orderly rearmament? If the Force intervenes, should it do so after rearmament is begun, or after a party has introduced a rearmament resolution in Congress? The illustration suggests that one function of the Force, or the political body behind it, would be to attempt first to negotiate with a potential rearming country rather than to intervene abruptly at some point in these developments.

Again, the character of rearmament would make a difference. Suppose the President presented a well-designed plan to build an obviously second-strike retaliatory force of poor preëmptive capability against either the International Force or other countries, but relatively secure from attack. If he justified it on the grounds that the current military environment was susceptible to sudden overturn by technological developments, political upheavals, irrepressible international antagonisms, the impotence of the Force for decisive intervention, the corruption or subversion of the Force, or other such reasons, then the authorization of a drastic intervention by the Force in the United States would be less likely than if the President ordered a crash program to assemble nuclear weapons, trained crews and long-range aircraft. It would make a considerable difference, too, whether rearmament occurred at a time of crisis, perhaps with a war going on, or in calmer times.

The point of all this is simply that even an International Military Authority with an acknowledged sole right in the possession of major weapons will have strategic problems that are not easy. This is, of course, aside from the even more severe problems of political control of the "executive branch" and "military establishment" of the world governing body. If we hope to turn all our international disputes over to a formal procedure of adjudication and to rely on an international military bureaucracy to enforce decisions, we are simply longing for government without politics. We are hoping for the luxury, which most of us enjoy municipally, of turning over our dirtiest jobs—especially those that require strong nerves—to some specialized employees. That works fairly well for burglary, but not so well for school integration, general strikes or Algerian independence. We may achieve it if we create a sufficiently potent and despotic ruling force; but then some of us would have to turn around and start plotting civil war, and the Force's strategic problems would be only beginning.

VIII. CONCLUSION

This is not an essay against disarmament, even "total disarmament." It is simply a warning against the notion that there is any once-for-all solution to the problems of world peace and government. It is against the notion that if only disarmament is "total" enough, we can forget about deterrence and all that. It is against the notion that under "total" disarmament there is no military potential to be controlled, balanced or stabilized.

There should be no divorce between deterrence and disarmament. If disarmament is to work, it has got to improve deterrence and to stabilize deterrence. Until a much greater community of interest exists in the world than is likely in this generation, war will have to be made unprofitable. It cannot be made impossible.

It is sometimes argued that to perpetuate military deterrence is to settle for a peace based on fear. But the implied contrast between arms control and total disarmament is not persuasive. What would deter rearmament in a disarmed world, or small wars that may escalate into large ones, must be the apprehension of a resumed arms race and war. The extent of the "fear" involved in any arrangement—total disarmament, negotiated mutual deterrence, or anything else—is a function of confidence. If the consequences of transgression are plainly bad—bad for all parties, and little dependent on who transgresses first—we can take the consequences for granted and call it a "balance of prudence." What keeps us from stepping off a train before it stops is not "fear"; we just know better.

PART FOUR:

Quality Control

INTELLIGENCE AND POLICY-MAKING

IN FOREIGN AFFAIRS

Roger Hilsman, Jr.

WHEN HE set out to form a secret intelligence agency for President Roosevelt in 1941, "Wild Bill" Donovan made little effort to curb his own characteristic receptivity to the new, the different, and even the unorthodox. Completely in character, he took up with quick enthusiasm the novel idea that scholars—those dreamy inhabitants of ivory towers—would be ideal for the job. He believed that by searching through the Library of Congress and through the files of the many government agencies these men could uncover much of the information for which secret agents risked their lives. In a sense, he dedicated the Research and Analysis Branch of the wartime Office of Strategic Services to the task of making the romantic secret agent obsolete. Since then, more and more people have come to believe that research—and the social sciences—have at last found a home within the formal structure of government.[1] This belief alone is a good reason to examine the new intelligence, but there is still another: since the war, the Central Intelligence Agency, the Office of Intelligence Research in the State Department, and even the intelligence units in the three service departments have elbowed their way into the business of foreign affairs and there they intend to stay.

A look at these new organizations is thus in order. The first task here will be to identify the doctrines which govern their role in foreign affairs and to deduce something of why these particular doctrines, of all the possible ones, came to reign. The second task will be to set up a working model of the intelligence function and, lastly, we shall attempt to evaluate American doctrine in the light of that model.

AMERICAN DOCTRINES OF INTELLIGENCE

Most people believe that the primary function of intelligence is to give warning of the hostile plans, military or political, of other nations. They also assume that this kind of information will come from espionage. However, government officials and the better-informed laymen do not entirely agree—

---

[1] See Sherman Kent, *Strategic Intelligence for American World Policy*, Princeton, N.J., 1949; and George S. Pettee, *The Future of American Secret Intelligence*, Washington, D.C., 1946.

they have some faith in those intelligence units devoted to research and analysis. Apparently, this faith is a secondary result of the Congressional investigation of the attack on Pearl Harbor. Since the United States supposedly had so much information that might have revealed the Japanese plans, it was difficult at first for the onlooker to see how American officials could have failed to realize that Pearl Harbor would be attacked. As the investigation proceeded, however, one explanation came to be widely accepted. In essence, the argument is that all the information necessary to recognize that the Japanese were planning an attack was available in Washington. But the information had come across the desks of top officials in disordered fragments, and these hard-pressed and overworked people, responsible for so many things besides divining the intentions of the Japanese, never had the time to correlate the odds and ends of information and thus see their obvious significance. If there had been a research and analysis unit studying, correlating, and assembling these odds and ends, the argument concludes, Pearl Harbor would never have been surprised.[2]

In addition to giving warning, intelligence must also supply the information on which policy can be based. General Donovan, for example, says that the justification for intelligence is to be found in the nature of any decision for action: before you can make a decision, you must get information. "Then," he writes, "you've got to evaluate and interpret that information. When you do this, then you have a decision that you feel confident is an informed decision. Government is no different. Government policy, too, must be based upon a tested knowledge of the facts. What facts? The capabilities, the intentions, and the policies of other nations. . . . [Intelligence is] just the careful gathering and analysis and interpretation of many bits of evidence." [3]

But this information, it is believed, must not go out from intelligence in haphazard driblets. For example, General Vandenberg, one of the first heads of the Central Intelligence Agency, sees intelligence work as a process of building up, piece by piece, a "picture" of what is happening in the world.[4] The intelligence units of the service departments will in this way furnish the military, naval, and air "pictures," and the State Department unit the political and sociological "picture." The Central Intelligence Agency, like a central assembly line, will then put these and its own original work to-

[2] See Pettee, *op.cit.*, p. 7; Seth W. Richardson, General Counsel for the Joint Investigating Committee on Pearl Harbor, "Why Were We Caught Napping at Pearl Harbor?" *Saturday Evening Post*, May 24, 1947; Kent, *op.cit.*, p. 160; and William J. Donovan, "A Central Intelligence Agency: Foreign Policy Must Be Based on Facts," *Vital Speeches*, May 1, 1946.

[3] *Ibid.*, p. 446.

[4] Testimony of General Hoyt S. Vandenberg, *Hearings Before the Committee on Armed Services, United States Senate, Eightieth Congress, First Session, on S. 758,* Part 3 (U.S. Govt. Printing Office), p. 491.

gether, and present an "over-all picture in a balanced, national intelligence estimate, including all pertinent data." [5]

Admiral Hillenkoetter, for three years director of CIA, is even more explicit on this point. Today's intelligence operator, he writes, is more likely than not "a researcher, engaged in hard, painstaking work, poring over foreign newspapers and magazines, reference works and similar materials, endlessly putting fact upon fact, until the whole outline appears and the details begin to fill in." [6] His job is "to winnow the extraneous data from the vital facts and to set these facts in proper perspective, thereby providing the factual basis for high-level policy decisions affecting our national security." [7] The role of intelligence thus becomes, according to the Admiral, one of working a "gigantic jigsaw puzzle" which finally emerges as a "picture" containing all the relevant facts arranged in their proper relationship to each other.

This picture-puzzle analogy, which recurs endlessly, also serves to explain other aspects of the intelligence process. It provides, for example, one of the most important tests for new information. The credibility of new information, intelligence people say, is partly established by the ease with which the information finds its place in the emerging "picture." And this "picture" also shows what new information is needed. In his testimony before Congress, for instance, General Vandenberg argues that as the "mosaic" is built up by the work of the different departmental intelligence units, a number of "gaps" will become visible. He pleads that a "centralized intelligence agency, intent on completing the national intelligence picture, must have the power to send out collection directives and request further material to fill these gaps." [8] Apparently he believes that what information is relevant and necessary is determined only by the facts themselves. The implication of this—in fact, of the whole picture-puzzle analogy—is that the process of analysis is a question merely of assembling facts in much the same common-sense way that one puts together a broken vase: by looking at the pieces and seeing how they fit.

People concerned with intelligence also insist that although policy is "based" on the "picture" supplied by intelligence, an intelligence organization should never suggest or recommend policy. General Donovan, for example, wants an intelligence agency that is central mainly because "intelligence must be independent of the people it serves so that the material it obtains will not be slanted or distorted by the views of the people directing operations." [9] Thus the danger is bias, and the cure is an intelligence orga-

---

[5] *Ibid.*, p. 499.

[6] Rear Admiral Roscoe H. Hillenkoetter, "Using the World's Information Sources," *Army Information Digest*, III, No. 11 (November 1948).

[7] *Ibid.*, p. 4.

[8] Testimony of General Vandenberg, *Hearings on S. 758*, p. 498.

[9] Donovan, *op.cit.*, p. 446.

nization which is independent and which never suggests, or even thinks of, policy.[10]

The role of intelligence, then, is to give warning of future events and to furnish the information, analyzed and arranged in a pattern, on which policy should be based. And there is great emphasis on the importance of independence for intelligence and on the dangers of bias and slanted information if intelligence becomes involved in policy.

One would assume that the people who adopted this division of labor had considered how it would increase or lessen their personal power. The policy and operating official may have supported it as a solution that protected his own domain, and the intelligence officer as a compromise that cut out at least one area in which he might have primacy. It would be a mistake, however, to assume that these are cynical men who think only of their narrow personal interest; the impression received by an outsider is that they are conscientious and sometimes almost naively sincere. It appears reasonable to suppose, in fact, that the high degree of similarity in the reasoning of both the policy officials and the intelligence men is due not to compatible power interests alone, but to a combination of factors. As a tentative hypothesis, it is submitted that one of these is a set of shared assumptions and attitudes which influences the thinking of these officials on the specific problem of a role for intelligence.[11] Much evidence tending to support this hypothesis can be found in material of the kind cited above—

---

[10] It is, in fact, difficult to overemphasize the insistence on this idea. For example, Allen W. Dulles, now serving as a special advisor to the Director of CIA, says: "But for the proper judging of the situation in any foreign country it is important that information should be processed by an agency whose duty it is to weigh facts, and to draw conclusions from those facts, without having either the facts or the conclusions warped by the inevitable and even proper prejudices of the men whose duty it is to determine policy and who, having once determined a policy, are too likely to be blind to any facts which might tend to prove the policy to be faulty. The Central Intelligence Agency should have nothing to do with policy. . . . All we can do is to see that we have created the best possible mechanism to get the unvarnished facts before the policy makers, and to get it there in time." (Allen W. Dulles, Memo Respecting Section 202 [CIA] of the Bill to Provide for a National Defense Establishment, dated April 25, 1947, as published in *Hearings on S. 758*, p. 525.)

[11] The concept that individuals of the same cultural group share a way of looking at things by means of which they interpret events and in terms of which they choose courses of action is, of course, well established in the field of cultural anthropology. See, for example, Ruth Benedict, *Patterns of Culture*, Penguin Books, 1949, and *The Chrysanthemum and the Sword*, Boston, 1946; Abram Kardiner, Ralph Linton, Cora Du Bois, and James West, *The Psychological Frontiers of Society*, New York, 1945; Clyde Kluckhohn, *Mirror for Man*, New York, 1949; Ralph Linton, *The Cultural Background of Personality*, New York, 1945. The literature on peculiarly American attitudes includes: Margaret Mead, *And Keep Your Powder Dry*, New York, 1942; Geoffrey Gorer, *The American People: A Study in National Character*, New York, 1948; Ralph Barton Perry, *Characteristically American*, New York, 1949; and Gabriel A. Almond, *The American People and Foreign Policy*, New York, 1950. Professor Almond systematizes observations made about the American character since the time of De Tocqueville in 1834 and uses these and a number of his own observations in analyzing American opinion on foreign affairs.

books, magazine articles, newspaper stories, Congressional hearings, and government documents. This material, however, may lag behind current thinking. Hence sixty-five government officials, a selected sample of both producers and consumers of intelligence, were actually interviewed.

The Attitudes of the Operating Officials

Let us begin with the consumers of intelligence, the policy and operating officials. Their reaction to the various kinds of intelligence product was, if anything, calm. Some felt that the periodic intelligence summary and comment—the daily, weekly, or monthly "newspaper" reporting and commenting upon "significant" events—was useful as a check to see if they were getting full information through their own channels or as an aid in keeping up with events in countries outside their own area of responsibility. The encyclopedic country survey[12] was not so widely known among the operators as the "daily," but one official was most pleased with the survey made on a country in his area. He said that it had brought together widely scattered information, and gave one a background with which to handle day-to-day problems. The so-called long-range research project, on the other hand, had few defenders. The feeling seemed to be that such projects turned out to be academic tomes which had little in common with real problems.

In general, the operators seemed most pleased with the kind of report that intelligence people call "backstopping." By this term the intelligence man means either a chronological history of events leading up to a problem, or a mechanical search for facts tending to support a policy decision that has already been made. The word implies that one is protecting the operator by supplying him with facts to defend his position. Thus one official cited the case of an old quarrel which had recently come before the United Nations. As the policy people were not intimately familiar with the case, intelligence was asked for an historical study, and turned up some useful background information. The official being interviewed said this paper had helped him get a clear picture of what he was judging. He added that this was an ideal example of the function of intelligence. Since policy people did not have time for such things, and since they were generalists—experts in political relations rather than in a particular area—they needed background, history, and a description of the general situation to help them in making policy. The function of intelligence was to fill this need by preparing factual statements without prejudice.

Another official remembered that some time ago they had discovered that title to the Coronados Islands, a very small group off the coast of California, was in doubt. His office needed something to support a recommendation, which they wanted very much to make for political reasons, that the United

---

[12] This is a continuously revised report containing "background" information on each country in the world. See Pearl Harbor *Hearings* (U.S. Govt. Printing Office), p. 783.

States should renounce any claims. By going over old deeds, maps, diaries, and so on, the intelligence units were able to show that American officials had always assumed that these islands were not possessions of the United States. The policy people were thus able to recommend the official renunciation of American rights with the historical background as support.

Opinion among the operators on the warning function, although it differs only slightly, falls roughly into two groups. A typical official of one group said he thought the purpose of intelligence was to pick up odd facts. Suppose, he said, that every blue spruce in a certain country was being cut down. What did you use blue spruce for? The antenna of the intelligence man should catch this fact, but seeing the meaning of it was not the province of intelligence. For one thing, the intelligence man did not have the practical experience the policy man did. He hadn't been around and consequently didn't know as much about the area, and the people, and the high officials of the country. Intelligence should pore over the figures and find the freak statistic. This kind of warning would be very useful; it would give the policy people a valuable breathing spell.

However, other policy officials did not agree. Intelligence should be encouraged, one official said, to sound a warning when it felt, after going over the information, that something unpleasant was going to happen or that some new problem was coming up. He added that nevertheless he still felt the major function of intelligence was to see that the policy people had all the facts—those that supported the policy, and especially those that didn't. After all, policy people were human, too. Like everyone else, they tended to overlook facts that were inconvenient. You had a better chance of getting the whole picture if intelligence was separate so it could get *all* the facts.

It is already clear that the operators support the information-furnishing role. However, let us take as a further example the testimony of one of the most influential of the officials interviewed. He said the theory behind the present division of labor was that only an independent intelligence organization could be objective. The intelligence man had no aim in life except to report facts as he saw them. In practice everyone probably had ideas on policy. But he felt that the theory—that there would be more objectivity if the person collecting facts was divorced from policy—was pretty sound. If intelligence people attuned their minds to policy questions, they couldn't be objective.

He said that on the policy side, experience was most important. Any good student or scholar had been trained in analysis, but there was a great difference between analyzing the Versailles Treaty and evaluating things today as they were actually happening. In analyzing diplomatic facts that called for action, there was no training except experience. George Kennan, the head of the Policy Planning Staff, was better than the research people at seeing implications. What was the difference? It was the difference between a lifetime habit of dealing with realities and a lifetime habit of dealing with libraries. The official said that he would rather have a country doctor perform a lobotomy on him than one of those brilliant medical students who had done nothing but study. More professionals were needed and less experts and students. This was what the Foreign Service did: it produced professionals; it gave experience and proper training. Take a man who knew everything in history, and another who was a professional, a man who had operated; the operator was much better. So when all the facts were laid out on the table, the official went on, the operator came up with sensitivity. The operator had an antenna, the official said, illustrating his words by putting the backs of his hands on his forehead and wriggling his fingers—the operator had an antenna which quivered when the right fact came up. This ability came from experience. To have it, you had to get wet—to get in and swim around a bit. The interviewer then interrupted to ask why, if the operator was the only one who could tell which facts were pertinent, it was necessary to have a man collect facts who was not concerned with policy. The official said that the point was that the policy man was also vulnerable to bias, even though he was usually better at interpretation than the research people. Therefore you still needed someone to line up the facts so the operator would have them *all* staring him in the face. Then the operator could say, "This is a fact, but we don't have to pay any attention to it. This one, however, is the key." But, the official continued, the operator shouldn't have to line up the facts because he might overlook or not want to face an important one.

When the interviewer had already said good-bye, gathered up his notes, and started out the door, the official called him back to say that there was one more thing which would illustrate the point. He said he had once written a memo that intelligence should not be defined as *evaluated information,* but simply as *information.* The point was that if you used the former definition you could not be completely objective because you were already two steps up from your base—the unvarnished facts.

Here is the same reasoning that we found in the testimony of the other officials quoted, but at greater length and with more clarity. These officials, first, put an extreme emphasis on the importance of having *all* the facts. They also fear that the person who is attempting to solve a problem, who is thinking of policy, will become the unreasoning advocate of some pet solution. And they distrust the research man—they see the researcher as a long-haired academic, poring over musty books in dusty libraries far from the realities of practical life. On the other hand, they think that "practical" experience is the true—in fact, the only—path to knowledge and judgment. They seem to believe that out of practical experience there develops, in some automatic though mysterious way, a sort of sixth sense. They are convinced that only the man with practical experience—armed as he is with this almost magical capacity for accurate hunch, with this *feel* for things—can sweep away the tangle of doubts and complexity and seize the one effective course of action.

Most of the operators interviewed, then, supported a role for intelligence which was merely one or another modification of the two functions of giving warning and furnishing information. Significantly, furthermore, the reasoning behind their position was based on identical premises. Even if two officials differed widely—as widely, that is, as the narrow range of opinion would permit—even then, they seemed to share the same set of basic assumptions and attitudes.[13] In other words, two men usually did not reach varying conclusions (always within the general framework) because they began with different premises, but because they applied a slightly different weighting in the latter stages of their reasoning.[14]

Thus the evidence available seems to support our contention that the operators share a set of assumptions and attitudes which channels their thinking about the role of intelligence. Although generalizations about the nature of these assumptions and attitudes can be little more than tentative, we are perhaps justified in offering a few.

Activism. In general, we can say that the operators tend to be conscientious and serious about their work. Contrary to popular opinion, there are few time-servers in at least this part of the governmental bureaucracy. Indeed, most of these men are extremely ambitious; they tend to drive themselves hard, to work late and arrive early. Besides being highly motivated, they are also oriented toward action, toward getting something done. The continuing, long-range problems of our time, problems of values and of survival, do not have as much urgency for them as the immediate problems which come in daily with the cables. The fact that these immediate problems are subsidiary, mere facets of the larger problems, does not seem to make these men act differently. Time and time again they have ostensibly solved these subsidiary problems and buried them in the out-box only to find them reborn and appearing again in the in-box. But the feeling remains that one must be "timely" and act at once on every paper. The operators seem to feel a pressure to get things done that is no less enormous because it is self-generated. Accordingly, they have no patience with a lengthy analysis of involved alternatives; they tend to develop solutions to their problems by doing, by taking action.

---

[13] The common set of basic assumptions explains, of course, the narrowness of the range of opinion.

[14] Another official, for example, said that since intelligence people had not had the right kind of experience, it would be a mistake if intelligence started to make policy. But the official thought that intelligence should make a few policy suggestions even though some people might say it was completely out of bounds. When playing around with the data, an intelligence man might sense something. An experienced policeman walking down the street might not see a thing, but he would *sense* a riot in the offing. The official said that he, himself, often had these feelings. Maybe while he was reading a telegram from some embassy overseas he would get a hunch. Of course, it was just a hunch, but it was a very, very useful thing to have. The major role of intelligence should be to get the facts, but if the intelligence man got an inference from the facts, it should be all right for him to pass it along.

Simplism. There is also a certain distrust of complex solutions. The operators speak of "selling" a policy, and they prefer it to be neatly packaged, with dramatic, persuasive argument and telling legal logic.[15] On the whole, they reject the complex reasoning, numerous qualifications, and generally experimental and searching attitude of a more or less scientific approach. Although there is evidence that he respects the involved thought of the engineer or physical scientist, the operator apparently feels that social problems are best met by practical "common sense." [16] He seems to feel that social problems, and their solutions, are essentially straightforward. Thus many of the higher officials expect to be briefed or "filled in" on a subject quickly and simply. They do not like long papers both because they feel they cannot spare the time to read them, and because they tend to feel that most problems are not so subtle or complex as to require extended treatment—the one-page, one-side-only brief must suffice.

Organizational tinkering. Many operators also seem to have a peculiar and remarkably resilient faith in reorganization as a means for improving foreign policy and the conduct of foreign affairs. Whatever opportunity reorganizations give to the power-seeker, there is little doubt that officials who urge a change are sincere. Each has a pet scheme for reorganization which he implies—and sometimes fairly shouts—will result in a marked improvement. And this faith in organizational tinkering has not faltered in the face of a lack of improvement attributable to any of the upheavals of the past.

All these assumptions, traits, and attitudes probably shape the thinking of policy people in some degree. The kind of activism and simplism discussed above creates a state of mind which tends to reject any organization devoted to the lengthy process of analytical research, and even to question the need for the more or less subtle analysis of the complex which such an organization tries to make. And a faith in organizational tinkering—by providing an outlet for feelings of doubt when events careen past leaving policies in their wake—seems to make a basic self-searching unnecessary.

Attitudes toward facts. Other assumptions and attitudes, however, seem to have a more direct influence. Of these the most important is the complex of assumptions about the role of facts. The implied assumption in the many expressed attitudes toward facts is that truth is obvious once all the facts are known. Coupled with this feeling is the fear, as we have seen, that the man who is concerned with policy will inevitably become the advo-

---

[15] See also Alexander H. Leighton, *Human Relations in a Changing World,* New York, 1949, pp. 152–54.

[16] See also Almond, *op. cit.,* p. 51. There is probably some relation between distrust of complex and subtle reasoning on social problems on the one hand, and the tendency to look down on the research man and university professor-expert on the other. The relation between this latter form of anti-intellectualism and the attitude toward experience, however, is probably much closer. See the section on experience below.

cate of a pet scheme. If he collects facts, as well as thinks of policy, he will tend to select facts which support his policy rather than find the true answer by collecting all the facts. By having one man collect facts without thinking of policy and another use the facts to make policy, one at least guarantees that the policy man will have to face the unpleasant facts that do not support his policy. This reasoning implies not only that a set of facts contains a self-evident answer (and that every problem does, in fact, have an answer), but also that it contains only one true answer. It also implies that facts admit of only one interpretation and that any reasonable man cannot help seeing this single meaning if he is forced to look at *all* the facts. Thus the policy man who has become wedded to an incorrect policy can be faced with the unpleasant facts which he has ignored and be made to see the one right solution.

One might comment here that it is, to say the least, strange that these assumptions are accepted with so little question. Certainly anyone would agree that an investigator could spend his lifetime collecting facts about even the simplest problem in international relations and not make a dent in the infinite number available. If a man wishes to solve a problem, whether in everyday living or in foreign affairs, he obviously needs a certain number of facts. But he cannot begin, willy-nilly, to collect *all* the facts, for he would soon be buried in a mountainous pile of them—and most would be irrelevant. Inescapably, he must find some means to select the facts he needs.

It seems obvious that all thinking involves notions of how and why things happen. Even the "practical" man who despises theory has a number of assumptions and expectations which lead him to believe that when certain things are done, certain results follow. A decision, otherwise, would never be made, an action never taken. And these assumptions and expectations, even when they are only implicit, are just as much "theory" as the hypotheses of science, social or physical. It is this "theory" that helps a problem-solver select from the mass of facts surrounding him those which he hopes are relevant. Suppose, for example, that I have missed my way and decide to go up to the nearest house to ask for directions. The yard of this house is fenced, and in the yard is a dog. If I open the gate, will the dog bite me? To make a decision, I need some facts. But which of the thousands available will be useful? If I were an expert on dogs, I would be familiar with generalizations about which breeds tend to be friendly. Such a "theory" would be most suitable for my purpose, and I could collect facts about the hair, body, tail, ears, feet, and eyes—the facts indicated by other "theories" which describe the features categorizing a certain breed of dog. However, without the necessary "theory" I would end up with a jumble of facts that had no meaning *to me,* and from which I could draw no conclusions. But I do have another "theory"—that friendly dogs wag their tails, and that vicious ones growl. Watching it carefully, I observe that this dog neither wags its tail nor growls. Since I cannot get the facts necessary for this theory it is useless to me, and I still cannot make a decision. I have, however, one other theory—that most dogs bite when a stranger comes into their fenced-in yard. And I have already collected the facts and reached the primary conclusions necessary for this theory: my more basic theory about what characteristics determine whether or not a living creature falls into the category I call *dog* has directed me to certain facts; these I have noted by looking at the animal before me and reached the conclusion that it is a dog. I therefore decide to go to another house, the yard of which is free of any animals whatsoever.

In the above example, I was equipped with theories that told me not only what to expect if the facts were of one kind or another, but also what kind of facts to look for and where to look for them. Suppose, however, that the problem I face is new and that I simply cannot find a suitable theory. When the first man met the first dog, the man probably chose his course of action in terms of a set of assumptions appropriate to other animals but unsatisfactory for predicting the reactions of the new creature. The dog probably behaved in unexpected ways, and before the man met another dog, he undoubtedly thought about the problem and tried to work out a set of assumptions that would include the new facts.

The scientific observer presumably works in similar fashion. His interest in a problem may be roused because some facts have come to his attention which do not fit into the then current theories. Or it may be roused because some new concept from an apparently unrelated field may point to a body of facts previously ignored. He begins his investigation by making his assumptions and tentative hypotheses explicit. By logical thought he seeks to be able to say that if his hypothesis is correct, he should find a certain kind of fact in a certain place under certain conditions; and that if his hypothesis is false, he should find another kind of fact in another place under other conditions. He then makes a careful search for facts of both kinds. If he finds only facts that fit into his hypothesis he assumes it to be correct; if he finds only facts that do not he assumes it to be incorrect. If, as frequently happens, he finds some of both kinds, his next task again calls for thought: he must modify his hypothesis to include the two kinds of facts, or find a new hypothesis. He then proceeds once more to look for evidence.

Facts cannot in themselves contain self-evident or obvious answers. If they did, anyone could follow the above procedure and human knowledge would have grown at a much, much faster rate than it has. There seems to be a difference not only in the quality of the conceptual tools which different men bring to a problem, but in the quality of mind they bring as well. Certainly many of the great discoverers had no more facts available to them than were readily at hand to anyone. Although some facts may have been hidden from mankind until the development of tools such as the microscope, most have been in plain view but unnoticed until some able mind forged the tools of thought which revealed their importance.[17] Any reader of the New

---

[17] And, more often than not it was a conceptual tool that pointed out the need for a mechanical one such as the microscope.

York or London *Times,* for instance, had in front of him the facts which Keynes used to foresee the economic consequences of Versailles. Yet of all the readers, many of whom read carefully and were thoroughly familiar with the facts, only Lord Keynes gave meaning and significance to those facts.

Although facts do not contain self-evident answers, in some circumstances they do, of course, convince. If two men have essentially identical expectations and assumptions, but disagree on the evidence, a new fact will settle the question. If we both agree that dogs that wag their tails do not bite, but disagree as to whether or not a particular dog will bite, then a fact—the dog suddenly wags its tail so that we both see the act—will settle the question so far as we two are concerned. But since many facts will fit rather nicely into two or more "theories," such happy circumstances do not occur as often as one might wish. We have all had the experience of thinking that some new fact will certainly have convinced the opponent in yesterday's argument of the error of his ways, only to find that the opponent has attached a quite different meaning to the same fact and is dismayed to find that it does not convince us of the error of our ways. Although it is widely felt that truth lies in the unvarnished facts, in a sense the contrary seems to be the case. The meaning, so to speak, is not in the facts themselves, but in the varnish!

Attitudes toward experience; anti-intellectualism. The operator's complex of attitudes toward experience seems to have as great an influence on his thinking about a role for intelligence as that toward facts. He looks down on the thinker, and says that only the man with practical experience can make policy successfully. But what does the operator mean by "experience"? Reading the pages of a book on, say, the Soviet Union is experience, but it is obvious that this is not the kind that is meant. When pressed, the operator gives as examples the experience in consular and diplomatic posts abroad and also that of being a policy man in Washington. The word "experience" thus seems to mean some special kind of first-hand participation as one of the actors in the specific kind of event under discussion.

Again, one might remark that little of what any man knows comes from this kind of experience. None of us know first-hand that Columbus discovered America or anything else that happened before our birth. We must also admit that few of the events of even our own time are known to us except through newspapers and the radio. And there are still other categories of knowledge that do not come primarily from experience. Scientists, for example, know much of the nature of both atoms and stars, but no man has experienced an atom, or known the stars from personal experience as anything but twinkling points of light in a telescope or as blobs on a photographic plate. The knowledge has come not so much from experience—even if "experience" is defined as gathering observable data—as from the analytical and creative processes of thought. All of us, in sum, speak with confidence about a thousand things we have never done, and know a great deal about things we have never seen, touched, smelled, tasted, nor heard. Of all we know, only a minimum comes from first-hand experience. And few would have it otherwise. A man does not wish his child to learn to stay away from high-voltage wires by being electrocuted or even by seeing some-one else electrocuted, but rather by assimilating the knowledge created by other men.

This is not, of course, to say that first-hand experience is valueless. It is valuable in many ways. Teachers, for example, have long known that the knowledge that water is composed of hydrogen and oxygen is more vividly demonstrated and easier to remember if the student actually performs an experiment in electrolysis. Secondly, a man who has absorbed everything available on a given subject with a minimum of first-hand experience may still have much to learn. In first-hand experience he gets the necessary practice in applying his knowledge to a specific problem. He perfects, in short, all the skills of application—a facility in a practical situation for pick-ing out from a welter of extraneous detail the factors indicated by his knowledge; a sense of timing; an ability to attach weights to different factors which in the real world never occur in the isolation possible in the labora-tory.

As a rule of thumb, it is also reasonable to expect a man with first-hand experience in a field to know more of that field than men who have had absolutely no experience in it, whether first-hand or second-hand. But notice that this is not because the man has absorbed the essence of the subject matter by some mysterious process similar to osmosis, but because he has from interest and necessity devoted more thought to the subject. If he has brains and ability he will thus have mastered the existing knowledge of the field and may, perhaps, have added to that knowledge as well. The same thing, however, can be said of the student. The "first-hand" experience of the student in studying, analyzing, and writing about a problem is usually as great an incentive for thought as the first-hand experience of the actual doer. Also, we might add that since the student often starts with better con-ceptual tools, he, as a type, probably has a slightly better chance of arriving at some valid conclusions. His greatest disadvantage is probably the limited opportunity for testing.

First-hand experience, finally, may give an opportunity to observe some kinds of facts which are not communicable to others and which are there-fore available only to a principal actor in a certain type of event—say, war. It is equally true, however, that the student of war may have the opportunity to seek out many facts about war denied to the participant in any given war, and acquire a broader and deeper knowledge of military affairs—excluding always the skills of application—than the most battle-scarred of veterans. Clausewitz never commanded an army, nor Mahan a fleet, and Stephen Crane, who exactly captured the emotional impact of war in *The Red Badge of Courage,* never saw a battle nor heard a shot fired in anger.

Attitudes toward experience: "know-how." The operators, however, seem to feel that the benefits of first-hand experience are of even greater significance than those received from second-hand participation. The implication of their expressed attitudes is that knowledge itself is the natural, automatic, and unsought by-product of a certain number of years of "practical" experience. Thus they attach very little importance to the role of thought in developing new knowledge. They feel that if a man wishes to add to the fund of knowledge needed to deal with problems in foreign affairs, he must get out and do. By actual doing he also acquires, they believe, an intuitive antenna of sensitivity to the significant fact, an instinctive feeling for the correct solution.[18] The man with long experience can thus "play by ear." He has acquired "know-how"—the talent in industrial and business America (where the term originated) for operating by feel in a complex but familiar and intimately known situation, the ability to overcome obstacles by improvisation on the basis of an informed hunch.[19]

The Attitudes of the Intelligence Men

One would expect that, if only from a desire for power, the position of intelligence people would differ greatly from that of the operators. In fact, however, neither the position nor the reasoning behind it differs significantly. Take, for example, two typical interviews. The first official was asked if intelligence had done anything to explore the possible courses of action open to the United States in any of the projects he had described. He said that they had not; their charter did not call for that sort of work. He felt, however, that this was not unwise. A line could be drawn between intelligence and policy, and if it could, there should be specialization. A good place to draw a line was between furnishing information on the one hand, and formulating and executing policy on the other. Of course, the line shouldn't be firm and fast, and policy people were now too sensitive to what was policy. But if one gave an intelligence organization an inch, it would take a mile; there would be very little information and lots of policy from intelligence if it did policy work of any sort. The job of intelligence should be to get the facts. An ideal intelligence organization should assemble the facts on a problem, and stay out of policy. Someone had to collect the facts. Even now, the official said, too many policy decisions were made without them.

The second official said that the need in the United States was for a level at which the facts could be collected and evaluated objectively. Policymakers should be given the unvarnished facts so they would have a suffi-

---

[18] It is difficult to reconcile the inconsistency between the assumption that facts contain self-evident answers and the assumption that only the man with "practical" experience can choose an effective course of action. However, since attitudes and assumptions of this kind are partly subconscious, there is no necessity that they be consistent. Indeed, it would be cause for suspicion if they were.

[19] See also Almond, *op.cit.*, p. 51.

ciently large background and basis for decisions and would be aware of all the implications of what they were doing. The official said to take, for instance, the Soviet satellites. If conditions in the satellites were much better than we imagined, intelligence should say so. Even if the information was unfavorable to our policy, intelligence should pass it along. Intelligence should tell the whole story, but once the information had left the intelligence organization, its job was done. It was up to the geographic desk people to decide how to use the facts and information, and what to do about the problem. The idea was that in this way intelligence could be objective and avoid slanting information to fit policy. And in his opinion the idea was very sound.

Clearly, then, there is little difference of opinion between the intelligence man and the operator on the broad role of furnishing information and on the assumptions about facts which seem to lie directly behind that role. Most intelligence officers also implied an equal faith in the power of first-hand experience and the value of "know-how," the ability to *sense* the situation abroad. Accordingly, they tend to prefer the man with "area" experience or experience in wartime intelligence to the man with special training. They also find themselves unable to question the operator's assertion that only the man with operating experience is able to foresee the effects of alternative courses of action and to formulate policy recommendations.

Most intelligence officials also shared the other attitudes of the operator. These attitudes were operative in several fields, but one—the subject of "current" intelligence—will serve as an illustration. One official said that a big problem was reconciling research and intelligence (he added parenthetically that he defined intelligence in this case as dealing with *very* current events, as analyzing and commenting and making predictions about the future possibilities of current world developments). The problem was personnel. The man who liked to do research was not ready or qualified to do the "current" intelligence job. The "current" type of person was essentially a more lively person, although he was, perhaps, not so deep-thinking. People who were equally good at both jobs were rare indeed. Some research men were needed, but getting a true research man to comment on the "daily" was like yanking a tooth. The official personally welcomed the emphasis on "current" intelligence; he thought it was fun. He also thought it had to be emphasized in order to gear the intelligence unit in with the rest of the government. He did feel, however, that intelligence should not be expected to do the same amount of research as before.

A second official felt that the periodic report was the key to the whole intelligence operation. He said that the object of these reports—daily, weekly, and monthly—was to present a picture of the area as a whole in terms of American security. Intelligence should call attention to emerging events so the policy people could do something about them. Intelligence should always be "current." He said that the country survey called for research, but that estimating the situation in a country and what was going to happen in the future belonged to the estimates field. The job in current, reportorial intelligence, on the other hand, was evaluating information. In this, they took information and considered its source and probable validity and decided whether it meant anything—no research was required. The estimative type of intelligence, the most important type, was based on a number of reports and sometimes a little research came in, too. They decided on the capabilities of the enemy and his most probable line of action. This kind of work required ability. Although it was hard to generalize about personnel, one could say that most university people were of little use because they had spent all their lives on something like five minutes of the Battle of Gettysburg. In his office they didn't like the adulation of the printed word that was found in most university people. The official felt that as a general rule newspaper people were the best.

This emphasis on "current" intelligence testifies to the intense desire of most intelligence people to participate in the momentous goings-on of government. The cables leading into Washington are continually hot with exciting daily problems; by a hurly-burly process decisions are reached, policy made, action taken, operations carried out. And most intelligence people want to be in on it all. It seems likely that in part this desire is personal ambition. But it also seems likely that both this desire and an emphasis on things "current" occur as a syndrome with an action orientation similar to that which is characteristic of the operator. Certainly we can say that neither the desire to take part in daily decisions nor an emphasis on the "current" is consistent with an orientation that could be called contemplative.

It is also clear that these men share the anti-intellectualism of the operator and do not think of themselves as intellectuals or even researchers. And this attitude is not necessarily the result of a quarrel between the officials who have higher academic degrees and those who do not; the second official— the one who preferred newspapermen to scholars—was himself a doctor of philosophy.[20]

---

[20] Although they were in the minority, some officials had a markedly different set of attitudes. One of these said that he was against the emphasis on "current" intelligence. The whole State Department was organized for quick news; what was lacking was an outfit to think and look deep. Intelligence was always being called on for the answers to spot questions, and was never given time for research. The official said that one of their best men had just resigned—simply because the atmosphere was getting to be such that a person with that kind of academic background and intellectual ability couldn't work. The real scholars were being driven out. This "current" intelligence was a curse. Take a country like Indonesia. Who was going to do the basic studies about its economics, politics, and commerce? Even if everyone worked on these studies, it would still not be enough—and the big contribution lay here. The U.P. and A.P. could do the "current" stuff; the big job should be done by intelligence. The official said that he wanted to underline again and again the problem of personnel. They must set the organization up in such a way that the right kind of people would find it a favorable environment. They had already lost too many of their good people. The vehement, emotionally charged reaction of this man to the pressure for "current" in-

The Area of Disharmony

Thus there seems to be the same complex of attitudes among the intelligence people as there is among the operators. But this does not mean that the two groups are in perfect accord. There is, for example, the old quarrel about the warning role. The operators, as the reader will recall, fell into two groups—those who were willing to let intelligence "interpret" information for warning, but not for policy, and those who refused to let them interpret anything at all. The intelligence men, on the other hand, were virtually unanimous in believing that warning is one of their primary and most important roles. They felt that if anyone is to interpret information to give warning, it should be intelligence.

However, as one might expect, intelligence officers are much more detailed in their ideas on the nature of warning. As they see it, warning is a much bigger job than merely the kind of analysis which would have revealed the Japanese decision to attack Pearl Harbor. Warning to them also implies predicting the trend of international events—foreseeing future problems of every sort. Their job is to gather information on developments abroad, to assemble that information into a "picture" of the existing situation, and then to "project" that "picture" into the future. Intelligence, they feel, should be the organization responsible for recognizing that a problem exists; it should be the one to call attention to the need for policy wherever need appears.

There are also other sources of bickering and bitterness. The loose definition of the word "policy" provides a spacious theater for battles of any size. The equally loose definition of the word "fact" is also troublesome. A statement, for example, that a proposed ally is undemocratic is often regarded as an unvarnished fact by the man who makes the statement, and not as a conclusion. To the operator, on the other hand, it is likely to appear as neither a fact nor a conclusion, but an implied recommendation for policy.

And there are other differences. For one thing, there seem to be more atypical intelligence men than there are atypical operators. For what it is worth, there also seem to be more men with the higher academic degrees in intelligence than there are in policy. But there is one further difference that is probably more significant than any of the others: intelligence men, unlike the operators, are not very happy. One official, for example, said that in his opinion intelligence was isolated; there was not even a forum at which it could be heard. On one problem, about which the intelligence people had felt strongly, they had submitted their predictions in a special paper. But the paper was not even challenged—it was just ignored.

---

telligence seems, at least in part, to be a personal withdrawal from the competitive, high-pressure environment of daily operations and decisions. He is obviously not anti-intellectual nor does he seem to feel any compulsion to come to a conclusion or make a decision. He seems more than willing to let any number of immediate problems lapse in order to delve into the particular kind of basic problem he thinks most important. There is little doubt that this official not only reaches different conclusions from most of his colleagues, but begins the mental journey from a different starting place.

It is, of course, a humiliating experience to feel useless and unimportant. But when one believes, as most intelligence people apparently do, that correct policy—like Pallas Athene from the head of Zeus—springs full-blown from the facts, he is not only frustrated when he decides that policy is made without benefit of the information supplied by intelligence, but bewildered and indignant as well. One official, for example, said that "the whole damned thing" was wrong. Before they did anything else, policy people should call on intelligence for the information and an estimate. Then they should make their policy. In reality, however, policy was made without intelligence or was only supplemented by intelligence. Intelligence people always had to analyze what had already happened, or merely to give support for policy decisions that were already made. Intelligence did nothing but hack work and research. In practice, the thing was all backwards.

It may well be true that the practice is all backwards—at least in terms of what most officials think is the proper division of labor. If so, the unhappiness of the intelligence officer is understandable; it comes from the daily violence done to his beliefs by the routine behavior of the operator. And yet there is something more than this. So many intelligence officers put such great stress on their objectivity and freedom from the bias which they feel involvement in policy brings that the observer begins to think that they protest too much. There is no question of deliberate hypocrisy, yet one cannot help suspecting that although it is upsetting to feel that the logical sequence of events is disregarded and incorrect decisions therefore made, it is to the usual intelligence official even worse to feel that he himself is ineffective on *policy*. The special poignancy of his unhappiness seems to be precisely this—that it is double. The intelligence officer is hit with a kind of emotional one-two; he feels that the world is upside down, and that he and his work are, inexplicably and unjustly, impotent.

The Present Solution

Thus the present solution of the intelligence problem has been hammered out by the alternating blows of both the situational and the cultural. One of these influences, as we have said, is the simple one of power and prestige. Another, of a different kind, is the setting in which the intelligence problem must be solved. Bureaucracy, whether public or private, has certain characteristics, and these provide a framework into which any solution, if it is to be workable, must fit.

But it seems clear that other forces have also been at work. The hypothesis offered here, to repeat, is that one of these has been a shared set of basic attitudes and assumptions. The word "intelligence" apparently conjures up in the minds of American officials a complex of assumptions about the role of facts, fears of bias in the use of facts, attitudes toward experience and "know-how," and feelings of anti-intellectualism—all of which occur in a milieu that is normally characterized by activism, simplism, and a faith in organizational tinkering.[21] The evidence available seems to support the supposition that much of the thinking of these officials on the problem of intelligence is done in terms of these assumptions, expectations, traits, and attitudes; that these are, in fact, the conceptual tools with which the problem is solved, the intelligence organizations are assigned a role, the doctrines on the operation of that role are built up, and the peculiar kind of receptivity, or lack of it, to the products of an intelligence unit is created.

*　　*　　*

[21] There are undoubtedly other assumptions and attitudes which have also influenced thinking on the intelligence problem. However, since the human mind does not seem to be capable of using more than a limited number of thought-tools during a specific and relatively short space of time, it is not likely that the final number will be large.

ASSUMPTIONS OF RATIONALITY
AND NON-RATIONALITY
IN MODELS OF THE
INTERNATIONAL SYSTEM

Sidney Verba

I

It is a truism that all action within the international system can be reduced to the action of individuals. It is also true, however, that international relations cannot be adequately understood in terms of individual attitudes and behaviors. Models of the international system usually deal with larger units, nation-states, as prime actors. To what extent can such models give us adequate explanations of international relations without some built-in variables to deal with individual decision-making?

It may be that some processes in international relations can be adequately explained on the level of social structure without explicit consideration of the personality, predispositions, attitudes, and behavior of the individual decision-maker. In that case, the introduction of variables dealing with individual behavior would complicate the model without commensurate pay-off in terms of increased understanding and prediction. This would be true if the impact of individual decision-making on the behavior of nations in their relations with other nations were slight, or if the impact varied randomly (because, for instance, of idiosyncratic factors) among the population of international events that one was trying to explain. If, on the other hand, models of the international system that either ignore or make grossly simplifying assumptions about individual decision-making can explain international relations only very imperfectly, it may well be worth the additional effort to build variables about individual decision-making into them.[1]

This paper will deal with the place of assumptions and theories about

---

[1] We ask that a model give adequate explanation and prediction of international events, not perfect explanation and prediction. There are, however, no hard and fast rules as to what is adequate explanation. In a sense, the test is a psychological one: an explanation is adequate when the "mind comes to rest." And this will depend upon the nature of the problem, its importance, complexity, and the interests of the people working on it.

individual decision-making in models of the international system. The individuals in whose behavior we are interested are all those whose activities either alone or with others have some perceptible impact upon the international system. This then includes masses and elites, governmental and non-governmental figures. Behaviors that will be considered as affecting the international system range from the minimal one of holding an opinion about an international situation as a member of the public to the authoritative decision made by some major government official. If one conceives of the international system as consisting of activities involving interaction among two or more nation-states, and the act of any single state is considered an input into that system, it is clear that the main impact of the activities of individuals upon the international system takes place on the level of the internal decision-making process that determines what input a nation will make into the international system. This is the case because with rare exceptions the roles of individuals within their own nations and the norms associated with these roles outweigh in importance their roles within the international system. We shall therefore concentrate on the individual as a role-holder in the foreign policy-formulating structure of his own nation.

Theories that attempt to explain and understand the course of international relations make varying assumptions about the actions and motivations of individual actors. Two approaches can be called the rational and the non-rational. Each makes a simplifying assumption about the way in which individuals act in international situations. Non-rational models assume that when an individual is faced with a choice situation in relation to an international event (a governmental decision-maker faced with a threat from an adversary nation, an ordinary citizen hearing about an insult to his head of state), he responds in terms of what we shall call non-logical pressures or influences. These are pressures or influences unconnected with the event in question. A gross case occurs when an individual responds aggressively to an international event because of internal psychological pressures toward aggression having their root in childhood experiences. A non-logical influence is any influence acting upon the decision-maker of which he is unaware and which he would not consider a legitimate influence upon his decision if he were aware of it. The latter criterion is difficult to make operational, but inferences can be drawn from the individual's value system. In any case, the former criterion will serve as an adequate indicator of the existence of such non-logical influences.[2]

---

[2] An attitude or behavior rooted in such non-logical influences may be considered to be a "symptom," in the Freudian sense of the word; that is, ". . . an overt tension-reducing response whose relationship to an unconscious motive is not perceived by the individual." See Irving Sarnoff, "Psychoanalytic Theory and Social Attitudes," *Public Opinion Quarterly*, XXIV (Summer 1960), pp. 251–79.

It may be useful to distinguish between motives that are non-logical and motives that are inappropriate. If, for instance, an individual responds to an international decision-making situation in terms of his desire for organizational promotion rather

Rational models of individual decision-making are those in which the individual responding to an international event bases his response upon a cool and clearheaded means-ends calculation. He uses the best information available and chooses from the universe of possible responses that alternative most likely to maximize his goals. The rational decision-maker may, for instance, respond aggressively to an international event, but the aggressive response will have its source in calculations based upon the nature of the international situation. It will be directed against the real enemy—the nation threatening or inflicting damage to one's interests—and the decision-maker will have some reasonable expectation of achieving his ends through the aggressive response. Furthermore, the decision will either have no psychological side-effects on the decision-maker (he will not experience tension release or guilt because of it), or, if there are psychological side-effects, they will be irrelevant as far as the nature of the decision is concerned.[3]

In most cases, neither of these models of individual behavior represents a complete description of actual behavior. They are presented rather as simplifying assumptions about individual behavior. But the choice of assumption has serious consequences for the adequacy and usefulness of the theory of which it is a part. For even if we are interested in the behavior of nation-states, the implicit or explicit assumptions we make about individual behavior will affect our understanding of state behavior. Let us consider the non-rational models first.

*   *   *

III

An alternative simplifying assumption about the processes by which individuals make decisions relevant to international affairs is an assumption of rationality. Essentially, this assumption is that the decision-maker will follow a specified set of rules in making his decisions. The particular set differs in various models of rationality, but the crucial point is that the rules can be specified. These rules indicate what information the decision-maker will use and how much further information he will seek. They specify the way in

---

than the welfare of his nation, his motives may be considered inappropriate even in terms of his own value structure (he may feel guilty), but they are not non-logical as long as they are conscious motives.

[3] An individual may respond to an international event in terms of the event itself and still not behave "rationally," as the term is ordinarily used. (We shall consider the concept of rationality more fully below.) He may respond foolishly because of inadequate information. Or he may respond in anger and haste—not in the cool manner of the rational decision-maker—but the anger may be due to the acts of the adversary nation rather than to the previous existence of latent aggression in the individual. This type of behavior, while not rational, fits easily into the model of rational behavior, for its deviation from rationality is along the dimensions considered significant in the model of rationality.

which calculations will be made, and, given the set of values that the decision-maker holds, they also specify the decision that will be arrived at, or at least the parameters within which it will fall. In this way, the varied decisional situations within the international system can be reduced to more manageable proportions. No model and no theorist, no matter how committed to holistic principles, can encompass the totality of a situation. The rationality model simplifies by specifying which variables are to be considered by decision-makers. Furthermore, by specifying the rules to be used by a decision-maker, it defines his behavior by these rules. All other behaviors— other information he seeks or receives, other modes of calculation, his personality, his preconceptions, his roles external to the international system— are irrelevant to the model. This eliminates an entire set of variables that are particularly hard to deal with in a systematic manner. Furthermore it allows one to consider all decision-makers to be alike. If they follow the rules, we need know nothing more about them. In essence, if the decision-maker behaves rationally, the observer, knowing the rules of rationality, can rehearse the decisional process in his own mind and, if he knows the decision-maker's goals, can both predict the decision and understand why that particular decision was made. Knowing, then, the process by which decision-makers respond to various turns in international affairs, the observer can concentrate on the events in the international system and greatly simplify his task of observation.

But to assess the usefulness and limitations of the rationality model in the understanding of international relations it is necessary to deal with three questions: What are the rules of rationality that are used to define the decision-making process? To what extent do individuals live up to the rationality model? And insofar as they do not live up to it—that is, insofar as the actual behavior of states in concrete situations cannot be predicted and/or explained by the model—to what extent is it still a useful tool of analysis? The answer to the last question will depend upon such factors as the extent to which deviations from the model are significant in terms of their effects on the behaviors of individuals and states and, if some of the deviations are significant, the extent to which corrections for them can be built into the model, perhaps at some later stage of analysis.

There are numerous definitions of rational behavior. These range from complete sets of rules to be followed in making decisions to more limited definitions centering around the state of psychic tension of the decision-maker (a rational decision is a cool and clearheaded decision) or specifying one aspect of the decision-making process (a rational decision-maker calculates the effects of his decisions). We will examine some of the characteristics attributed to rational decision-making and then consider the way in which such rationality models fit into models of the international system.

The most usual concept of rationality is that it is a process of means-ends analysis. The simplest case of means-ends analysis involves a single goal sought by the decision-maker. In this case, insofar as the goal is empirical (i.e., insofar as it is possible to tell if it has been attained), rational choice is the selection, among alternatives, of the action that maximizes the goal. If more than one value is relevant in the situation, it is necessary to add several steps to the model. The various values have to be listed in order of importance, and alternatives have to be compared not in terms of which maximizes one value, but in terms of which provides the best value-mix.

The means-ends model, especially insofar as it specifies that one chooses the alternative that best attains one's ends, implies several other decision-making characteristics. Ideally all possible alternatives must be considered— or, if that is impossible, certainly a great number or at least all the obvious ones. Furthermore, the alternatives must be considered on their merits—that is, in terms of their contribution to the values of the decision-maker. This latter point presents some serious difficulties: if the decision-maker has a variety of goals, the alternative that would maximize the goal most relevant to the decision at hand—e.g., in a market decision, the alternative that would maximize the monetary gain—may at the same time involve great costs in terms of some other value (say, prestige or leisure) that would make it rational to reject the alternative. Since all values that may be affected by a decision are relevant to that decision, we must specify more carefully what is meant by considering an alternative on its merits. Doing so implies: (1) considering only those values that will in fact be affected by the alternative —i.e., having accurate information and making correct assessments of the outcomes—and (2) making such calculations consciously. If the individual chooses an alternative that does not maximize the goals he consciously considers to be pertinent in the situation, the decision cannot be called rational even though it maximizes others of his values which he did not consider. On the other hand—in a market situation, for instance—if an individual does not choose the alternative that maximizes monetary gain, the decision will still be rational so long as the other values relevant to the situation are consciously considered. If he refuses to drop some unprofitable activity of the family business because he believes such action would be disloyal to the memory of his father, and if the goal of loyalty is consciously invoked in the situation, the decision is rational, given his set of values. But if the relationship with family tradition is not consciously invoked and if it has effects in a situation in which it would be considered irrelevant by the decision-maker if he were aware of it, the decision will have been made on other than rational grounds. The criterion of consciousness has been added to avoid the problem of having to accept all acts as rational for which the observer or participant could, with hindsight, think of a goal that it maximized.

Thus the notion of means-ends calculations introduces the need for accurate information, correct evaluation, and consciousness of calculation. Another usual characteristic attached to this set of rational characteristics is that decisions be made coolly, with a clear head. Essentially this derives from the requirement of accurate calculations. It does not specify that the individual must avoid emotional involvement in the outcome or experience no emotion during the process of deliberation. Whether or not he does so is irrelevant as long as his calculations are not affected by his emotion. (This problem is more complex than can be gone into here, for an emotional state may change an individual's value hierarchy and thus affect his calculations. Though one can argue that emotion ought not to affect the means selected, it is more difficult to dismiss as irrational the effect of emotion on one's goals.)

The means-ends rationality model is a simplification. Individuals do not in fact make decisions in this way. However, this in itself does not make the model useless as a tool, since all theories and models involve simplification. What is necessary is to look at the nature and extent of the simplification. A growing body of theoretical and empirical work on decision-making suggests that though individuals do calculate advantages when making decisions, the method of calculation is quite different from that postulated in the means-ends rationality model.[11]

One set of reasons why the rationality model is not an adequate description of decision-making lies in human frailty. The type of calculation required by the model for anything but the simplest choices is beyond the powers of any individual, group, or presently designed individual-computer system. There may be too many significant variables, inadequate information, variables that are not easily quantifiable, or decisional methods that are not advanced enough. This raises serious problems for the use of rationality models, for to make the concept of means-ends rationality operational, some rules must be specified for judging whether or not such a decision-making technique has been used. Since the rules of means-ends rationality specify that one selects from the universe of alternatives the alternative that maximizes one's values, the objective observer, trying to decide if this approach to decision-making has been followed, would have to be able to make the same calculations that the method demands from the actual decision-maker. He would have to know the "right" decision, even if the actual decision-maker did not. If there are grossly different alternatives, one of which clearly maximizes the values believed by the decision-maker to be relevant to the situation while the others do not, the invocation of the

---

[11] The following discussion draws upon a variety of works dealing with rationality, including the work of Herbert Simon and James G. March and their associates on organizational decision-making (see, in particular, March and Simon, *Organizations,* New York, 1958, and Cyert and March, "A Behavioral Theory of Organizational Objectives," in Mason Haire, ed., *Modern Organization Theory,* New York, 1959); Thomas C. Schelling, "Toward a Strategy of International Conflict," The RAND Corporation, P-1648, 1959; Harold Garfinkel, "The Rational Properties of Scientific and Commonsense Activities," *Behavioral Science,* V (January 1960), p. 72; Charles E. Lindblom, "Policy Analysis," *American Economic Review,* XLVIII (June 1958), pp. 298–313; and Lindblom, "The Science of Muddling Through," *Public Administration Review,* XIX (Winter 1959), pp. 79–88.

"objective scientific observer" test of rationality is meaningful. But such situations are rare. They occur most frequently when one is dealing with a group that is, from the point of view of modern Western scientific thought, "foolish"—that is, a group that makes no serious attempt to approximate the rationality model in its decision-making because of lack of commitment to such an approach. Even in these situations it is often difficult to tell if the rules of rationality are being followed, for the calculations that the objective observer must make will founder on the question of the values that are operative in the situation. Usually the assumption will have to be made that there is a single overriding goal, such as increased economic production, whereas in reality a variety of other goals may be involved. But when faced with a decision made by an individual or group as highly trained and sophisticated as he is, the outside observer is probably no more able to judge whether the resulting decision meets the criteria of rationality than are the actual decision-makers. Their frailty is his frailty too. And . . . the foreign policy elites will usually have high levels of information, be committed to rationality values, and so forth. Therefore, either one needs an objective observer whose wisdom and omniscience are much greater than those of the policy-maker or one has to assume that what the policy-maker selects is the best (most rational) alternative—a definition of rationality that is circular and gets us nowhere.[12]

But human frailty is perhaps the least important reason why the rationality model is inadequate to explain decision-making. Individuals fail to make decisions according to the criteria of the model not merely because they are foolish, or not well enough trained, or because they just do not try hard enough. Deviations from the model of rationality may take several other significant forms.

The first such deviation involves the value structure required for the rationality model. In order for a decision-maker to maximize a particular value or a set of values, he must be aware of his own values and be able to order them in terms of their significance to him. Such clear self-awareness is rare. This is true not merely because values conflict—because peace may conflict with prosperity or defense may conflict with deterrence—but because individuals do not have a clear set of value preferences that exist independently of the situation and can be matched against a variety of alternatives to see which gives the best value outcome. Instead, one's values depend in part upon the situation one is facing and what is attainable in that situation. One's preferences may change during a decision process. In actual policy decisions, as Lindblom points out, means and ends are not isolated from each

---

[12] In terms of training, skills, values, and information, there is no reason to expect higher levels of rationality among detached observers than among decision-makers. There are, however, certain important structural characteristics of the situations in which decision-makers and detached observers operate that make it likely that the detached observer will more closely approximate the rationality model. This will be discussed below.

other and handled independently. A policy choice is usually a choice of a set of means as well as a set of ends.[13]

Means-ends calculations are made more difficult by the fact that policy decisions—especially in international relations—represent collective decisions. As numerous authors have shown, if arriving at a value ordering for an individual is difficult, arriving at a joint preference ordering for a group is even more difficult, if not logically impossible. Different members will prefer different goals, and policy will often be formulated by bargaining among the members of a foreign-policy coalition. Furthermore, for any member of the foreign policy-making coalition, a particular policy decision affects both his goals in regard to the external system (i.e., what sort of foreign policy he prefers) as well as his goals in regard to the internal policy-making system (i.e., what position he wants to attain or maintain within the organization). Any policy alternative will therefore be considered in relation to a variety of goal systems that may not be consistent. It is not only that deterrence may conflict with defense, but that some members of the coalition may prefer deterrence to defense, others may prefer defense to deterrence, and others may prefer both though they conflict. And in each case the preference will be based upon both the type of foreign policy that the individual would like to see his nation follow and the effects of choosing one alternative over the other on the position he would like to attain within the foreign policy-making organization. This situation is most obvious when one considers the process of foreign policy-making in the United States, where bargaining among the various branches of the government, between government and non-governmental groups, and within the various branches of the Executive has become the normal means of reaching policy decisions.[14] But it is probable that in all decision-making systems within a bureaucratic structure (and this then applies to all modern states, demo-

---

[13] Lindblom, "Policy Analysis" and "The Science of Muddling Through," *loc.cit.* This suggests why the rational model of economic man, though also inadequate, is not as inadequate as the rational model of political men. Though it oversimplifies economic choice situations to say that there is a single goal which is easily quantifiable and under which various alternatives can be rated one against another, nevertheless this is more closely approached in economic calculation, where the sphere of activity is essentially defined by its concentration around a set of values having to do with maximizing economic gain, than it is in political affairs, where the sphere is not defined by a set of values relevant to it but by the employment of certain means for the maximization of any or all values held by the individual or the group. This may also explain why rationality models have been used in international relations largely in connection with military problems—more specifically, in connection with the problems of nuclear deterrence. The reason may be that the relevant goals within this limited sphere are less ambiguous (deterring an attack, avoiding nuclear destruction) and easier to place in a hierarchy.

[14] On bargaining as a process of making foreign policy, see Samuel P. Huntington, "Strategy and the Political Process," *Foreign Affairs,* XXXVIII (January 1960), pp. 285–99; and Roger Hilsman, "The Foreign-Policy Consensus: An Interim Research Report," *Journal of Conflict Resolution,* III (December 1959), pp. 361–82. On the general subject of bargaining as a characteristic of the American political process, see Robert A. Dahl, *A Preface to Democratic Theory,* Chicago, 1956, ch. 5.

cratic or non-democratic) such coalition formation is a standard part of decision-making.

One of the requirements of means-ends rationality is that a set of goals be mutually consistent. This requirement is violated both when members of the coalition have goals inconsistent with those of other members (and insofar as various members each have some influence over organization policy, the organization will have conflicting goals), and when individuals themselves have goals that are inconsistent. Under the means-ends rationality model, the only way to handle such a goal conflict is to adjust the goal structure so that it is consistent. One goal must be dropped or downgraded. In such situations, however, rearranging goals to form a consistent set is not the only mechanism of adjustment; the relationship between the conflicting goals can, for instance, be denied. This can be done by separating the goals in one's mind either in terms of time (maximize X today and Y tomorrow) or in terms of spheres of activity (maximize X in relation to foreign policy, and Y in relation to domestic policy).[15] When decisions are made within a group bargaining situation, it becomes easier for a variety of conflicting values to coexist and form the basis of policy. Different goals can be pursued by different sub-groups of the organization and in this way the conflict among them obscured. Since the rationality model cannot deal with inconsistent goal structures and since such structures are not uncommon, the model is limited in explaining much organizational decision-making.

Another weakness in the rationality model is that it makes unrealistic assumptions about the way in which information, and in particular information about alternatives, is acquired. Policy alternatives are not simply presented to the decision-maker for his selection. He must seek them, a process that is difficult and time-consuming. Studies of decision-making suggest that individuals do not consider all possible alternatives and, what is more important, make no attempt to do so. Rather they scan alternatives with persistence and simplicity biases. They seek alternatives that are as similar as possible to past choices so that experience can be used as a guide. Few alternatives are considered. In fact, the process is not one of narrowing down the range of choice by eliminating possible alternatives as time goes on. Fewer alternatives are considered at the beginning of a decision than toward the end. It is only when a particular alternative is close to being accepted as policy and its implications become clear that other alternatives will be brought up by coalition members who fear injury from the proposed decision.[16]

---

[15] See, in this connection, Robert Abelson and M. Rosenberg, "Symbolic Psychologic: A Model of Attitudinal Cognition," *Behavioral Science,* III (January 1958), pp. 1–13.

[16] See R. M. Cyert, W. R. Dill, and J. G. March, "The Role of Expectations in Business Decision-Making," *Administrative Science Quarterly,* III (December 1958), pp. 307–40; Richard C. Snyder and Glenn D. Paige, "The United States Decision to Resist Aggression in Korea," *ibid.,* pp. 341–78; and John W. Gyr, "The Formal Nature of a Problem-Solving Process," *Behavioral Science,* V (January 1960), p. 39.

Lastly, the model of means-ends rationality treats each decision as if it were a separate entity. But a decision-maker cannot do so. He operates within a structure in which there has been previous commitment to policy and organizational vested interests in policy. A new policy will therefore tend to be not the best of all possible policies, but a relatively small variation on a present policy; it will be, to use Lindblom's word, an "incremental" policy. The choice will often be between two alternatives—the status quo or some limited modification of the status quo. And the criterion of choice will not be: "Is it the best possible action?" but: "Is it better or, at least, no worse than the present policy?" [17]

It is clear that when the decision-maker begins to search for an adequate choice rather than for the best choice—when decision-makers stop maximizing and begin "satisficing," to use Simon's term—it becomes very difficult to use the rationality model. When the operating rule was to find the best alternative, the observer, as we saw, could both predict and explain the decision that was made. There is only one best alternative. There may, however, be many adequate alternatives, and the rules of rationality do not specify how one chooses among them.

*   *   *

---

[17] Lindblom, "The Science of Muddling Through."

THE BELIEF SYSTEM AND
NATIONAL IMAGES:
A CASE STUDY[1]

Ole R. Holsti

I. THE BELIEF SYSTEM AND NATIONAL IMAGES

Even a cursory survey of the relevant literature reveals that in recent years —particularly in the decade and a half since the end of World War II— students of international politics have taken a growing interest in psycho-attitudinal approaches to the study of the international system. It has been proposed, in fact, that psychology belongs at the "core" of the discipline (Wright, 1955, p. 506). Two related problems within this area have become particular foci of attention.

1. A number of studies have shown that the relationship between "belief system," perceptions, and decision-making is a vital one (Rokeach, 1960; Smith *et al.*, 1956; Snyder *et al.*, 1954).[2] A decision-maker acts upon his "image" of the situation rather than upon "objective" reality, and it has been demonstrated that the belief system—its structure as well as its content—plays an integral role in the cognitive process (Boulding, 1956; Festinger, 1957; Ray, 1961).

2. Within the broader scope of the belief-system-perception-decision-making relationship there has been a heightened concern for the problem of stereotyped national images as a significant factor in the dynamics of the international system (Bauer, 1961; Boulding, 1959; Osgood, 1959b; Wheeler, 1960; Wright, 1957). Kenneth Boulding, for example, has written that, "The national image, however, is the last great stronghold of unsophistication. . . . Nations are divided into 'good' and 'bad'—the enemy is all bad, one's own nation is of spotless virtue" (Boulding, 1959, p. 130).

---

[1] The author wishes to express his deep gratitude to Professors Robert C. North, James T. Watkins, IV, and Thomas A. Bailey for their advice and encouragement on the larger study from which this paper is derived; to Charles A. McClelland and Richard Fagen for their useful comments on this paper; and to Mrs. Helen Grace for preparing the figures.

[2] Although in the literature the terms "belief system" (Rokeach, 1960, pp. 18–19), "image" (Boulding, 1956, pp. 5–6), and "frame of reference" (Snyder *et al.*, 1954, p. 101) have frequently been used synonymously, in this paper "belief system" will denote the complete world view, whereas "image" will denote some subpart of the belief system.

The relationship of national images to international conflict is clear: decision-makers act upon their definition of the situation and their images of states—others as well as their own. These images are in turn dependent upon the decision-maker's belief system, and these may or may not be accurate representations of "reality." Thus it has been suggested that international conflict frequently is not between states, but rather between distorted images of states (Wright, 1957, p. 266).

The purpose of this paper is to report the findings of a case study dealing with the relationship between the belief system, national images, and decision-making. The study centers upon one decision-maker of unquestioned influence, John Foster Dulles, and the connection between his belief system and his perceptions of the Soviet Union.

The analytical framework for this study can be stated briefly. The belief system, composed of a number of "images" of the past, present, and future, includes "all the accumulated, organized knowledge that the organism has about itself and the world" (Miller *et al.,* 1960, p. 16). It may be thought of as the set of lenses through which information concerning the physical and social environment is received. It orients the individual to his environment, defining it for him and identifying for him its salient characteristics. National images may be denoted as subparts of the belief system. Like the belief system itself, these are "models" which order for the observer what will otherwise be an unmanageable amount of information (Bauer, 1961).

In addition to organizing perceptions into a meaningful guide for behavior, the belief system has the function of the establishment of goals and the ordering of preferences. Thus it actually has a dual connection with decision-making. The direct relationship is found in that aspect of the belief system which tells us "what ought to be," acting as a direct guide in the establishment of goals. The indirect link—the role that the belief system plays in the process of "scanning, selecting, filtering, linking, reordering, organizing, and reporting" (McClelland, 1962, p. 456)—arises from the tendency of the individual to assimilate new perceptions to familiar ones, and to distort what is seen in such a way as to minimize the clash with previous expectations (Bronfenbrenner, 1961; Ray, 1961; Rokeach, 1960). Like the blind men, each describing the elephant on the basis of the part he touches, different individuals may describe the same object or situation in terms of what they have been conditioned to see. This may be particularly true in a crisis situation: "Controversial issues tend to be polarized not only because commitments have been made but also because certain perceptions are actively excluded from consciousness if they do not fit the chosen world image" (Rapoport, 1960, p. 258). These relationships are presented in the following figure.

The belief system and its component images are, however, dynamic rather than static; they are in continual interaction with new information. The impact of this information depends upon the degree to which the

Input   Output

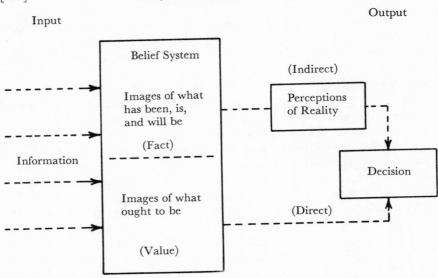

Fig. 1. The dual relationship between belief system and decision-making.

structure of the belief system is "open" or "closed." According to Rokeach,

> At the closed extreme, it is new information that must be tampered
> with—by narrowing it out, altering it, or constraining it within isolated
> bounds. In this way, the belief-disbelief system is left intact. At the
> open extreme, it is the other way around: New information is assimi-
> lated *as is* . . . thereby producing "genuine" (as contrasted with
> "party-line") changes in the whole belief-disbelief system [Rokeach,
> 1960, p. 50].

Thus while national images perform an important function in the cognitive process, they may also become dysfunctional. Unless they coincide in
some way with commonly-perceived reality, decisions based on these images
are not likely to fulfill expectations. Erroneous images may also prove to
have a distorting effect by encouraging the reinterpretation of information
that does not fit the image; this is most probable with rigid "models" such
as "totalitarian communism" or "monopolistic capitalism" which exclude the
very types of information that might lead to a modification of the models
themselves (Bauer, 1961; Wheeler, 1960).

II. JOHN FOSTER DULLES AND THE SOVIET UNION

The selection of John Foster Dulles as the central figure for my study
fulfilled a number of historical and research requirements for the testing of
hypotheses concerning the relationship between the belief system and perceptions of other nations. He was acknowledged as a decision-maker of first-
rate importance, and he held office during a period of dramatic changes in
Soviet elites, capabilities, and tactics. In addition, he left voluminous public

pronouncements and writings on both the Soviet Union and on the theoretical aspects of international politics, thus facilitating a reconstruction of salient aspects of both his belief system and his perceptions of the Soviet Union.

The sources used in this study included all of Dulles' publicly available statements concerning the Soviet Union during the 1953–1959 period, derived from a content analysis of 434 documents, including Congressional testimony, press conferences, and addresses.[3] These statements were transcribed, masked, and quantified according to the "evaluative assertion analysis" technique devised by Charles E. Osgood and his associates (Osgood *et al.*, 1956; Osgood, 1959a).[4]

All of Dulles' statements concerning the Soviet Union were translated into 3,584 "evaluative assertions" and placed into one of four categories:

1. *Soviet Policy:* assessed on a friendship-hostility continuum (2,246 statements).

2. *Soviet Capabilities:* assessed on a strength-weakness continuum (732 statements).

3. *Soviet Success:* assessed on a satisfaction-frustration continuum (290 statements).

4. *General Evaluation of the Soviet Union:* assessed on a good-bad continuum (316 statements).

The resulting figures, when aggregated into time periods, provide a record of the way in which Dulles' perceptions of each dimension varied. From this record inferences can be made of the perceived relationship between the dimensions.

Dulles' image of the Soviet Union was built on the trinity of atheism, totalitarianism, and communism, capped by a deep belief that no enduring social order could be erected upon such foundations.[5] He had written in 1950, for example, that: "Soviet Communism starts with an atheistic,

---

[3] The author has corresponded with a number of Dulles' close associates. They almost unanimously stated that Dulles' public assessments of various characteristics of the Soviet regime were identical with his private beliefs.

[4] The method involves the translation of all statements into one of two common sentence structures.

1. Attitude Object$_1$ (AO$_1$)/Verbal Connector (c)/Common-meaning Evaluator (cm)

2. Attitude Object$_1$ (AO$_1$)/Verbal Connector (c)/Attitude Object$_2$ (AO$_2$)

For example, the sentence, "The Soviet Union is hostile, opposing American national interests," is translated to read:

1. The Soviet Union/is/hostile (form 1).

2. The Soviet Union/opposes/American national interests (form 2).

The value of AO$_1$'s are computed on the basis of values assigned to the cm's, c's, and AO$_2$'s. These range from $+3$ to -3, depending upon their direction and intensity.

[5] "Dulles was an American Puritan very difficult for me [Albrecht von Kessel], a Lutheran, to understand. This partly led him to the conviction that Bolshevism was a product of the devil and that God would wear out the Bolsheviks in the long run, whereas many consider it a perversion of Russian qualities" (Drummond and Colbentz, 1960, p. 15).

Godless premise. Everything else flows from that premise" (Dulles, 1950, p. 8). Upon these characteristics—the negation of values at or near the core of his belief system—he superimposed three dichotomies.

1. The "good" Russian people versus the "bad" Soviet leaders.[6]
2. The "good" Russian national interest versus "bad" international communism.[7]
3. The "good" Russian state versus the "bad" Communist Party.[8]

That image of the Soviet Union—which has been called the "inherent bad faith of the Communists" model (Kissinger, 1962, p. 201)—was sustained in large part by his heavy reliance on the study of classical Marxist writings, particularly those of Lenin, to find the keys to all Soviet policies (Dulles, 1958b).

In order to test the general hypothesis that information concerning the Soviet Union tended to be perceived and interpreted in a manner consistent with the belief system, the analysis was focused upon the relationship Dulles perceived between Soviet hostility and Soviet success, capabilities, and general evaluation of the Soviet Union. Specifically, it was hypothesized that Dulles' image of the Soviet Union would be preserved by associating decreases in perceived hostility with:

1. Increasing Soviet frustration in the conduct of its foreign policy.
2. Decreasing Soviet capabilities.
3. No significant change in the general evaluation of the Soviet Union.

Similarly, it was hypothesized that increasing Soviet hostility would be correlated with success and strength.

The results derived through the content analysis of Dulles' statements bear out the validity of the hypotheses. These strongly suggest that he attributed decreasing Soviet hostility to the necessity of adversity rather than to any genuine change of character.

In a short paper it is impossible to include all of the evidence and illustrative material found in the full-length study from which this paper is derived. A few examples may, however, illuminate the perceived relationship presented in Table 1.

---

[6] "There is no dispute at all between the United States and the peoples of Russia. If only the Government of Russia was interested in looking out for the welfare of Russia, the people of Russia, we would have a state of non-tension right away" (Dulles, 1958a, p. 734).

[7] "The time may come—I believe it will come—when Russians of stature will patriotically put first their national security and the welfare of their people. They will be unwilling to have that security and that welfare subordinated to the worldwide ambitions of international communism" (Dulles, 1955b, p. 329).

[8] "The ultimate fact in the Soviet Union is the supreme authority of the Soviet Communist Party. . . . That fact has very important consequences, for the State and the Party have distinctive goals and they have different instruments for getting those goals. . . . Most of Russia's historic goals have been achieved. . . . But the big, unattained goals are those of the Soviet Communist Party" (Dulles, 1948, pp. 271–2).

TABLE 1

Period		Hostility	Success	Capabilities	General Evaluation
1953:	Jan–Jun	+2.01	−1.06	+0.33	−2.81
	Jul–Dec	+1.82	−0.40	−0.30	−2.92
1954:	Jan–Jun	+2.45	+0.46	+2.00	−2.69
	Jul–Dec	+1.85	−0.25	+1.93	−3.00
1955:	Jan–Jun	+0.74	−1.81	−0.80	−2.83
	Jul–Dec	+0.96	−1.91	−0.20	−2.33
1956:	Jan–Jun	+1.05	−1.68	+0.37	−2.91
	Jul–Dec	+1.72	−2.11	−0.22	−3.00
1957:	Jan–Jun	+1.71	−2.10	−0.28	−2.79
	Jul–Dec	+2.09	−1.01	+0.60	−2.93
1958–1959	Jan–Jun	+2.03	+0.02	+1.47	−2.86
	Jul–Feb	+2.10	−1.20	+1.71	−2.90

Correlations[9]

	N	r	P
Hostility–Success (Friendship–Failure):			
6 Month Periods (Table Above)	12	+0.71	0.01
12 Month Periods	6	+0.94	0.01
3 Month Periods	25	+0.58	0.01
Hostility–Strength (Friendship–Weakness):			
6 Month Periods (Table Above)	12	+0.76	0.01
12 Month Periods	6	+0.94	0.01
3 Month Periods	25	+0.55	0.01
Hostility–Bad (Friendship–Good):			
6 Month Periods (Table Above)	12	+0.03	n.s.
12 Month Periods	6	+0.10	n.s.
3 Month Periods	25	+0.10	n.s.

The 1955–1956 period, beginning with the signing of the Austrian State Treaty and ending with the dual crises in Egypt and Hungary, is of particular interest. As shown in Figure 2, Dulles clearly perceived Soviet hostility to be declining. At the same time, he regarded that decline to be symptomatic of a regime whose foreign policy had been an abysmal failure and whose declining strength was forcing Soviet decision-makers to seek a respite in the Cold War. That he felt there was a causal connection between these factors can be suggested by numerous statements made during the period.[10]

---

[9] Correlations, based in rank ordering of variables, were computed using Spearman's formula: $r = 1 - \dfrac{6\Sigma D^2}{N(N^2 - 1)}$ (McNemar, 1955, p. 208).

[10] "It is that [United States] policy, and the failure of the Soviet Union to disrupt it, and the strains to which the Soviet Union has itself been subjected which undoubtedly require a radical change of tactics on the part of the Soviet Union" (Dulles, 1955a, p. 914).

"Today the necessity for [Soviet] virtue has been created by a stalwart thwarting of efforts to subvert our character. If we want to see that virtue continue, I suggest that it may be prudent to continue what produced it" (Dulles, 1955c, p. 8).

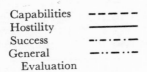

Capabilities   – – – – –
Hostility   ————
Success   –·–·–·–
General   –··–··–··–
    Evaluation

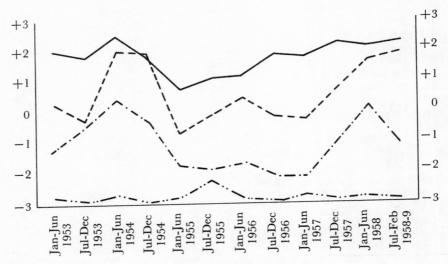

Fig. 2. Dulles' perceptions of the Soviet Union, 1953–1959.

The process of how Soviet actions were reinterpreted so as to preserve the model of "the inherent bad faith of the Communists" can also be illustrated by specific examples. Dulles clearly attributed Soviet actions which led up to the Geneva "Summit" Conference—notably the signing of the Austrian State Treaty—to factors other than good faith. He proclaimed that a thaw in the Cold War had come about because, "the policy of the Soviet Union with reference to Western Europe has failed" (U.S. Senate, 1955, p. 15), subsequently adding that "it has been their [Soviet] system that is on the point of collapsing" (U.S. House of Representatives, 1955, p. 10).

A year later, when questioned about the Soviet plan to reduce their armed forces by 1,200,000 men, he quickly invoked the theme of the bad faith of the Soviet leadership. After several rounds of questions, in which each reply increasingly deprecated the value of the Soviet move in lowering world tensions, he was asked, "Isn't it a fair conclusion from what you have said this morning that you would prefer to have the Soviet Union keep these men in their armed forces?" He replied, "Well, it's a fair conclusion that I

"The fact is, [the Soviets] have failed, and they have got to devise new policies. . . . Those policies have gradually ceased to produce any results for them. . . . The result is, they have got to review their whole creed, from A to Z" (U.S. Senate, 1956, p. 19).

would rather have them standing around doing guard duty than making atomic bombs." In any case, he claimed, the reduction was forced by industrial and agricultural weakness: "I think, however, that what is happening can be explained primarily by economic factors rather than by a shift in foreign policy intentions" (Dulles, 1956, pp. 884–5).

There is strong evidence, then, that Dulles "interpreted the very data which would lead one to change one's model in such a way as to preserve that model" (Bauer, 1961, p. 227). Contrary information (a general decrease in Soviet hostility, specific non-hostile acts) were reinterpreted in a manner which did not do violence to the original image. In the case of the Soviet manpower cuts, these were attributed to necessity (particularly economic weakness), and bad faith (the assumption that the released men would be put to work on more lethal weapons). In the case of the Austrian State Treaty, he explained the Soviet agreement in terms of frustration (the failure of its policy in Europe), and weakness (the system was on the point of collapse).

The extent to which Dulles' image of the Soviet Union affected American decision-making during the period cannot be stated with certainty. There is considerable evidence, however, that he was the primary, if not the sole architect of American policy *vis à vis* the Soviet bloc (Adams, 1961; Morgenthau, 1961; Davis, 1961). Moreover, as Sidney Verba has pointed out, the more ambiguous the cognitive and evaluative aspects of a decision-making situation, and the less a group context is used in decision-making, the more likely are personality variables to assert themselves (Verba, 1961, pp. 102–3). Both the ambiguity of information concerning Soviet intentions and Dulles' *modus operandi* appear to have increased the importance of his image of the Soviet Union.[11]

III. CONCLUSION

These findings have somewhat sobering implications for the general problem of resolving international conflict. They suggest the fallacy of thinking that peaceful settlement of outstanding international issues is simply a problem of devising "good plans." Clearly as long as decision-makers on

---

[11] "Nor was the Secretary of State, in either his thinking or his decisions, much affected by what the Department of State knew and did. Dulles devised the foreign policies of the United States by drawing upon his own knowledge, experience and insight, and the Department of State merely implemented these policies" (Morgenthau, 1961, p. 305).

"He was a man of supreme confidence within himself. . . . He simply did not pay any attention to staff or to experts or anything else. Maybe in a very subconscious way he did catalogue some of the information given him but he did not, as was characteristic of Acheson and several others of the Secretaries of State with whom I have worked, take the very best he could get out of his staff" (Anon., 1961).

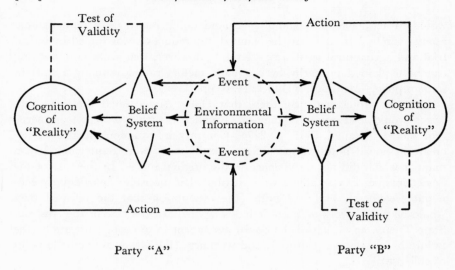

Source: (Ray, 1961, p. 21)

Fig. 3.   The indirect relationship between belief system and action.

either side of the Cold War adhere to rigid images of the other party, there
is little likelihood that even genuine "bids" (North *et al.*, 1960, p. 357) to
decrease tensions will have the desired effect. Like Dulles, the Soviet decision-makers possess a relatively all-encompassing set of lenses through which
they perceive their environment. Owing to their image of "monopoly capitalism," they are also pre-conditioned to view the actions of the West within
a framework of "inherent bad faith."

To the extent that each side undeviatingly interprets new information,
even friendly bids, in a manner calculated to preserve the original image, the
two-nation system is a closed one with small prospect for achieving even a
desired reduction of tensions. If decreasing hostility is assumed to arise from
weakness and frustration, and the other party is defined as inherently evil,
there is little cause to reciprocate. Rather, there is every reason to press
further, believing that added pressure will at least insure the continued good
conduct of the adversary, and perhaps even cause its collapse. As a result,
perceptions of low hostility are self-liquidating and perceptions of high
hostility are self-fulfilling. The former, being associated with weakness and
frustration, do not invite reciprocation; the latter, assumed to derive from
strength and success, are likely to result in reactions which will increase
rather than decrease tensions.

There is also another danger: to assume that the decreasing hostility of
an adversary is caused by weakness (rather than, for example, the sense of
confidence that often attends growing strength), may be to invite a wholly
unrealistic sense of complacency about the other state's capabilities.

In such a closed system—dominated by what has been called the "mirror image"—misperceptions and erroneous interpretations of the other party's intentions feed back into the system, confirming the original error (Ray, 1961).[12]

If this accurately represents the interaction between two hostile states, it appears that the probability of making effective bids to break the cycle would depend upon at least two variables:

1. The degree to which the decision-makers on both sides approach the "open" end of Rokeach's scale of personality types (Rokeach, 1960).
2. The degree to which the social systems approach the "pluralistic" end of the pluralistic-monolithic continuum. The closer the systems come to the monolithic end, the more they appear to require the institutionalization of an "external enemy" in order to maintain internal cohesion (North, 1962, p. 41; Wheeler, 1960).

The testing of these and other hypotheses concerning the function of belief systems in international politics must, however, await further research. Certainly this looms as a high priority task given the current state of the international system. As Charles E. Osgood has so cogently said,

> Surely, it would be a tragedy, a cause for cosmic irony, if two of the most civilized nations on this earth were to drive each other to their mutual destruction because of their mutually threatening conceptions of each other—without ever testing the validity of those conceptions [Osgood, 1959b, p. 318].

This is no idle warning. It has been shown empirically in this paper that the characteristics of the reciprocal mirror image operated between the two most powerful nations in the international system during a crucial decade of world history.

REFERENCES

ADAMS, SHERMAN. *Firsthand Report*. New York: Harper & Bros., 1961.

ANON. "Letter to Author by an Associate of Mr. Dulles." August 25, 1961.

BAUER, RAYMOND A. "Problems of Perception and the Relations Between the United States and the Soviet Union," *The Journal of Conflict Resolution*, 5 (1961), 223–9.

BOULDING, KENNETH E. *The Image*. Ann Arbor: University of Michigan Press, 1956.

---

[12] "Herein lies the terrible danger of the distorted mirror image, for *it is characteristic of such images* that they are self-confirming; that is, each party, often against its own wishes, is increasingly driven to behave in a manner which fulfills the expectations of the other. . . . Seen from this perspective, the primary danger of the Soviet-American mirror image is that it impels each nation to act in a manner which confirms and enhances the fear of the other to the point that even deliberate efforts to reverse the process are reinterpreted as evidence of confirmation" (Bronfenbrenner, 1961, p. 51).

————. "National Images and International Systems," *The Journal of Conflict Resolution,* 3 (1959), 120–31.

BRONFENBRENNER, URIE. "The Mirror Image in Soviet-American Relations: A Social Psychologist's Report," *The Journal of Social Issues,* 17 (1961), 45–56.

DAVIS, S. R. "Recent Policy Making in the United States Government." In D. G. BRENNAN (ed.). *Arms Control, Disarmament, and National Security.* New York: George Braziller, 1961.

DRUMMOND, R. and COBLENTZ, G. *Duel at the Brink.* Garden City, N.Y.: Doubleday, 1960.

DULLES, JOHN F. "Interview," *Department of State Bulletin,* 39 (1958a), 733–9.

————. "Not War, Not Peace," *Vital Speeches,* 14 (1948), 270–3.

————. "Our Foreign Policies in Asia," *Department of State Bulletin,* 32 (1955b), 327–32.

————. "Reply to Bertrand Russell," *Department of State Bulletin,* 38 (1958b), 290–3.

————. "Tenth Anniversary of the U.N.," *Department of State Bulletin,* 33 (1955c), 6–10.

————. "Transcript of News Conference, May 24, 1955," *Department of State Bulletin,* 32 (1955a), 914.

————. "Transcript of News Conference, May 15, 1956," *Department of State Bulletin,* 34 (1956), 880–6.

————. *War or Peace.* New York: Macmillan, 1950.

FESTINGER, LEON. *A Theory of Cognitive Dissonance.* Evanston, Ill.: Row, Peterson & Co., 1957.

KISSINGER, H. *The Necessity of Choice.* Garden City, N.Y.: Doubleday, 1962.

McCLELLAND, CHARLES A. "General Systems and the Social Sciences," *Etc.: A Review of General Semantics,* 18 (1962), 449–68.

McNEMAR, Q. *Psychological Statistics.* New York: John Wiley & Sons, Inc., 1955.

MILLER, G. A., GALANTER, E., and PRIBRAM, K. H. *Plans and the Structure of Behavior.* New York: Holt, 1960.

MORGENTHAU, HANS J. "John Foster Dulles," In N. A. GRAEBNER (ed.). *An Uncertain Tradition.* New York: McGraw-Hill, 1961.

NORTH, ROBERT C., KOCH, HOWARD, and ZINNES, DINA. "The Integrative Functions of Conflict," *The Journal of Conflict Resolution,* 4 (1960), 353–74.

NORTH, ROBERT C. "Some Informal Notes on Conflict and Integration." Unpublished manuscript, 1962.

OSGOOD, C. E., SAPORTA, S., and NUNNALLY, J. C. "Evaluative Assertion Analysis," *Litera,* 3 (1956), 47–102.

OSGOOD, C. E. "The Representational Model," In I. POOL (ed.). *Trends in Content Analysis*. Urbana, Ill.: University of Illinois Press, 1959a.

———. "Suggestions for Winning the Real War with Communism," *The Journal of Conflict Resolution*, 3 (1959b), 311–25.

RAPOPORT, A. *Fights, Games, and Debates*. Ann Arbor: University of Michigan Press, 1960.

RAY, J. C. "The Indirect Relationship Between Belief System and Action in Soviet-American Interaction." Unpublished M.A. Thesis: Stanford University, 1961.

ROKEACH, M. *The Open and Closed Mind*. New York: Basic Books, Inc., 1960.

SMITH, M. B., BRUNER, J. S., and WHITE, R. W. *Opinions and Personality*. New York: John Wiley & Sons, Inc., 1956.

SNYDER, R. C., BRUCK, H. W., and SAPIN, B. *Decision-making as an Approach to the Study of International Politics*. Princeton, N.J.: Princeton University Press, 1954.

U.S. HOUSE OF REPRESENTATIVES. Committee on Appropriations. *Hearings*. (June 10, 1955), Washington, 1955.

U.S. SENATE. Committee on Foreign Relations. *Hearings*. (May 5, 1955), Washington, 1955.

———. *Hearings*. (Feb. 24, 1956), Washington, 1956.

VERBA, SIDNEY. "Assumptions of Rationality and Non-Rationality in Models of the International System," *World Politics*, 14 (1961), 93–117.

WHEELER, H. "The Role of Myth System in American-Soviet Relations," *The Journal of Conflict Resolution*, 4 (1960), 179–84.

WRIGHT, QUINCY. "Design for a Research Project on International Conflict and the Factors Causing Their Aggravation or Amelioration," *Western Political Quarterly*, 10 (1957), 263–75.

———. *The Study of International Relations*. New York: Appleton-Century-Crofts, Inc., 1955.

THE H-BOMB DECISION:

HOW TO DECIDE

WITHOUT ACTUALLY CHOOSING[1]

Warner R. Schilling

PRESIDENT TRUMAN made his first H-bomb decision on January 31, 1950. He ordered the Atomic Energy Commission to continue its efforts to determine the technical feasibility of a thermonuclear weapon. The rate and scale of the effort were to be fixed jointly by the AEC and the Department of Defense. He also ordered the Department of State and the Department of Defense to re-examine the nation's strategic objectives and plans, both diplomatic and military, in light of the forthcoming developments to be expected in Soviet nuclear weapons capabilities. Both directives had been recommended to the President in a report submitted the same day by a special committee of the National Security Council, composed of the Secretaries of State and Defense and the Chairman of the Atomic Energy Commission.[2]

The report of the special committee and the President's subsequent decision marked the first resolution of a policy discussion that had begun in September, 1949, with the discovery that the Russians had exploded a fission bomb. This discussion had been broadly concerned with the implications of the Soviet explosion for American security and with the question of what actions the United States should undertake as a result of it. The first purpose of this article will be to contrast the content and form of the President's decision with that of the policy discussion that had preceded it. The point of this contrast will be to illustrate the "minimal" character of the decision made on January 31st. Of all the courses of action considered and debated during the preceding five months, that chosen by the President represented one which seemed to close off the least number of future alternatives, one

---

[1] This article is based on part of the research conducted on the H-bomb decision by the present writer in connection with the Civilian-Military Perspectives Project of the Institute of War and Peace Studies, Columbia University. Research and article have both benefited greatly from the guidance and criticism of the Institute's Director, William T. R. Fox. Earlier versions of the article were prepared for discussion at the Arms Control and National Policy Seminar, California Institute of Technology, and the December 1960 meeting of the American Historical Association.

[2] See Harry S. Truman, *Memoirs* (New York, 1956, 2 vols.), vol. 2, p. 309.

that left the most issues still undecided. The second and third purposes of this article will be to advance an explanation for the minimal character of the decision and to indicate some of the policy consequences that followed from its having been made in this manner.

THE POLICY BACKGROUND

The explosion by the Russians of a fission bomb on August 26, 1949, was an event which took American policy-makers by surprise and one for which they had prepared neither specific plans nor a general strategy. The Joint Chiefs of Staff, taking what many believed to be a pessimistic view, had not expected the Soviet Union to detonate a fission weapon until 1952. Although steps had been taken prior to August, 1949, to provide for the detection of such an explosion, nowhere in the government had any formal attention been given to the question of what actions might be appropriately taken once the evidence of an explosion had been detected. The absence of forward planning can be attributed in part to the absence of any formal deadlines or pressures compelling planning groups in State, Defense, or the Commission to undertake it. It can also be attributed to the absence of any generally agreed-on body of strategic thought regarding the foreign policy implications of nuclear weapons which could have served as a point of departure and frame of reference for more specific plans.

Since the end of the Civil War, the continental security of the United States had been doubly insured. First, by virtue of its superior military potential which completely overshadowed that of the other Great Powers, the United States had no need to fear any nation. The weapons of World Wars I and II and the distribution of the people, skills, and resources necessary to make and use these weapons were such that no single foreign nation could conceivably mobilize enough military power from inside its own frontiers to assault successfully the American continent. Secondly, by virtue of the balance of power abroad, the United States could afford to leave its potential largely unmobilized. The interests and arms of the other Great Powers were so committed one against the other that none was free to direct its strength against the United States. In time of peace these Powers did not dare turn their backs on more immediate enemies, and in time of war their hands were full fighting them. The American continent was subject to only one serious military threat: the possibility that through conquest and alliance the people, skills, and resources of the Old World might be gathered together into one hostile combination. Only in this event could the United States be confronted with a military potential roughly equivalent to its own. The result, if not in all instances the intent, of American intervention in World Wars I and II had been to remove this contingency from the realm of reality.

Following World War II two revolutionary changes occurred in this security position. The first was the inability of the European Powers to re-establish a balance of power on the European continent. The nations of Western Europe were in no position to prevent the Russians from achieving at their ease what had just been so painfully wrested from the hands of the Germans: an empire from the Urals to the Atlantic embracing all the peoples, skills, and resources of the Old World. The United States moved resolutely to meet this situation, both through policies designed to substitute American power for European (the Truman Doctrine, the North Atlantic Treaty) and through policies designed to restore to the Western Europeans themselves the capacity to balance the Russians (the Marshall Plan, the Mutual Defense Assistance Program).

These policies, which constituted the main burden of American security policy between 1945 and 1949, were addressed to a real and immediate problem. They were, however, essentially pre-nuclear in their rationale. The advent of nuclear weapons had not influenced the American determination to restore the European balance of power. It was, in fact, an objective which the United States would have had an even greater incentive to undertake if the fission bomb had not been developed. Nor were nuclear weapons believed to have qualitatively altered the military problem of achieving that objective. The American monopoly of the atomic bomb was seen as greatly facilitating the task of defeating the Red Army (and hence in deterring an attack by it), but in the judgment of at least two of the three services it would still be necessary to maintain sufficient ground strength on the con-tinent to permit the mounting of the large-scale land offensive which they believed would be required in order to terminate the war.[3]

In the summer of 1949 the second revolutionary change in the American security position, that occasioned by the advent of Soviet nuclear weapons-systems, had yet to occur. This was a development destined to change com-pletely the strategic significance of the traditional components of American security. The new weapons were so cheap and so destructive, relative to the old, that the Soviet Union would have the ability to mobilize from inside its own frontiers enough military power to accomplish what had heretofore been beyond the means of any single foreign nation: the capacity to strike a mortal blow at the American continent. The consequences were two-fold: the industrial superiority that had guaranteed victory in two World Wars was no longer the equivalent of overwhelming military potential, and the United States could no longer afford to leave its potential largely unmo-bilized during time of peace. Unlike the case of the Kaiser's or Hitler's Germany, the conquest of the people, skills, and resources of the Old World

---

[3] For the rationale of the American interest in restoring the European balance of power, see Walter Millis and E. S. Duffield, editors, *The Forrestal Diaries* (New York, 1951), pp. 341, 349–351. For military doctrine regarding a war in Europe, see e.g. General Omar Bradley, "This Way Lies Peace," *Saturday Evening Post*, vol. 220, October 15, 1949, and Walter Millis, Harvey C. Mansfield, and Harold Stein, *Arms and the State* (New York, 1958), pp. 237–245, 247–249.

would not be a necessary first step in a Soviet attack on the United States. As a result, the United States would no longer be able to count on the unfolding of such conquest (1) to provide time for Americans to alert themselves to danger and to arm to meet it, and (2) to provide allies to preoccupy the enemy until they were ready. In fact, the import of the second revolution was to diminish that of the first. The more developed Russian transcontinental nuclear striking power, the less important would be the addition of Western Europe's people, skills, and resources for a Soviet attack on the United States and, perforce, the less significant the distribution of power on that continent for the security of the United States.

The implications of the advent of nuclear weapons for American security were stark. American policy between 1945 and 1949 had by no means been blind to these possibilities, and two major policies had been formulated to meet them. The first was the proposal made for international control of atomic energy, which by the fall of 1947 appeared to have little prospect of being accepted by the Soviet Union. The second was the development of a military doctrine to cope with the contingency of two-way nuclear war. The character of this doctrine can be seen in the report released in January, 1948, by the President's Air Policy Commission. Bluntly entitled "Survival in the Air Age," the Finletter Report called for a "new strategy" to provide victory in an atomic war if it came and, hopefully, by confronting the enemy with the "prospect of a counterattack of the utmost violence," to persuade him not to attack in the first place.

According to the Report, this strategy would require an Air Force capable of smashing the Russian cities and factories. The prospect of such a "devastating price" would make the Soviets hesitate to attack. The Air Force would also need the capability of launching a counteroffensive against the Russian air forces "at the earliest possible moment" in order "to silence the attack on the United States mainland and give us the time again to build up our industrial machine and our manpower to go on to win the war." The Soviet objective, on the other hand, would be to smash American industrial power "at the outset" and to destroy the American air defense and counterattack forces. Basically, however, what was outlined in the Finletter Report was not so much a "new strategy" as the problems and choices over which the discussion of strategy was to ponder for years thereafter. The Report took no note of the possible conflicts between a strategy designed to deter atomic attack and a strategy designed to win an atomic war. Neither did the Report confront the question of why, if the United States could achieve a counteroffensive blow of the magnitude described against Russian cities and delivery forces, the Russians could not do the same or better with their attacking blow, and, in this event, against what and with what would the United States launch its counterattack?[4]

These, then, were the three major postwar security policies that the

---

[4] See *Survival in the Air Age*, A Report by the President's Air Policy Commission (Washington, 1948), pp. 6, 10, 12, 14, 20, 23–25.

United States had evolved by the eve of the Russian explosion: the effort to restore the European balance of power; the effort to secure international control of nuclear weapons; and the effort to evolve a force for two-way atomic war and a strategy to guide it. The three objectives were by no means carefully interrelated. Just as the strategy to restore the European balance of power made no provision for the time when American security would cease to turn on the stability of that balance, so the strategic doctrine outlined in the Finletter Report, while correctly anticipating that the future pivot would be the stability of the Soviet-American balance of terror, made no provision for the possibility that the United States would continue to have a political and military stake in the independence of Western Europe. As for the proposal for international control, this, if accepted, would require a substantial revision of the forces required to implement both of the other objectives. It should also be noted that each of these three policies had the potential of pointing the American response to the Russian explosion in a different direction. With the passing of the American monopoly on the atomic bomb, the defense of Western Europe might now require a larger commitment of ground forces than had heretofore been necessary. The need to prepare for two-way atomic war, on the other hand, would seem to call for the allocation of additional resources to the weapons for air attack and defense and an expansion in the size of the nuclear stockpile. Finally, the development by the Russians of their own nuclear weapons could be seen as the proper occasion to reopen and redouble the effort to secure their control by an international agency.

It was against this background of policy that discussion began in September, 1949, on the question of what should be done now that the Soviet Union had exploded an A-bomb. The major participants in this discussion came from five government institutions: the Departments of State and Defense; the Atomic Energy Commission (including a number of scientists employed in full or in part by the Commission or its subcontractors); the Office of the President; and the Joint Committee on Atomic Energy of Congress. By far the bulk of the policy discussion among these participants took place informally, and the degree and effect of the initiative exercised through these informal contacts fully support the insight of the observer who commented that the Federal Government is the last stronghold of private enterprise in the United States. Although a number of the participants had begun by December, 1949, to leak some of the subject matter of the discussion to the press, the policy discussion was for the most part closed to the general public.

The formal development of the policy discussion was tied to the bureaucratic history of a particular issue, that of whether to undertake an intensive effort to make a thermonuclear weapon. This matter was placed on the agenda of the Atomic Energy Commission on October 5th for reference to the Commission's main scientific advisory body, the General Advisory Committee. Both the report of the GAC, submitted on October 30th, and that submitted by the five Commissioners to the President on November 9th made it clear that the issue was hardly one that could be decided without reference to political and military as well as technical considerations. For this reason, and because he was well aware of the differences that were developing both between and within the major governmental bodies involved in the issue, the President referred the issue on November 10th to the previously noted special committee of the National Security Council. Under the auspices of this committee a working group was set up, composed of representatives from each of the three Executive agencies concerned: State, Defense, and the AEC. In addition to the work done jointly by this group, each agency also conducted a variety of independent studies into aspects of the problem, and the ultimate products of this activity were the recommendations submitted by the special committee to the President on January 31, 1950. It should be noted that throughout this period the Joint Committee on Atomic Energy was active in exploring the issue and voicing its views, through letters and personal visits by the Chairman to the President.

It will be the purpose of the following section to present a summary description of the issues and alternatives that were developed during the course of these proceedings. Although there will be occasional references to individual or institutional views, the purpose of the section is not to describe in any detail the positions held by particular individuals or government bodies with regard to the issues and alternatives discussed. The views of most of the individuals concerned were quite complex, and individual views within the same government bodies were by no means uniform. Many individuals and agencies took similar policy positions but for quite different reasons, and the views of some individuals and agencies changed over the time period involved. The summary is meant to delineate not individual or institutional positions but rather the range and content of the major policy proposals and considerations that were produced as a result of these five months of debate and deliberation.[5]

ISSUES AND ALTERNATIVES

The discovery that the Soviet Union had exploded an A-bomb several years before it had been expected to do so suggested to many that one

---

[5] The information in the preceding paragraphs and the sections that follow can largely be found in two published sources: Truman, *op. cit.*, vol. 2, ch. 20, and United States Atomic Energy Commission, *In the Matter of J. Robert Oppenheimer*, Transcript of Hearing before Personnel Security Board (Washington, 1954). The article also draws upon extended personal interviews during 1956–1958 with sixty-six of the participants in the events discussed. Given the character of interview data and the particular focus of this article, it is the present writer's conclusion that the best way to meet scholarly obligations to both readers and participants is by omitting citation for the points that follow. The same considerations are responsible for the fact that these pages omit reference to individuals except where stylistically infeasible. Detailed description and citation will, of course, be later available with the publication of the whole study of the H-bomb decision.

response should be to step up the pace of America's own nuclear weapons program. Since plans had just been completed to provide for a major expansion in the facilities for producing fissionable material and to undertake the development of fission weapons of much larger power and varied size than those heretofore fabricated, the focus of attention turned to the prospects for making a fusion weapon. The possibility of such a weapon had first received detailed study in 1942, and it had been a continuing concern of the atomic energy program ever since. It had proved, however, a recalcitrant technical problem and, both during the war and after, work on it had been given a much lower priority than work on the development and improvement of fission weapons.

The idea, in the fall of 1949, that a greater effort to make a fusion weapon was now in order received some stimulus from what were believed at the time to be some promising new technical approaches to the problem, but the major motive for reconsidering the state of the program was provided by the Russian explosion. Those who advocated a greater effort were moved by two considerations. One was the idea that if the United States could develop a bomb with thousands of times the energy release of the Hiroshima bomb, it would be able to maintain its qualitative lead over the Soviet program and thereby minimize the political and military disadvantages of the loss of its fission monopoly. Even more compelling, in the minds of most advocates, was the possibility that if the United States did not move more energetically to explore this possibility, the Soviet Union might be the first to achieve such a capability.

This reasoning seemed so persuasive to its advocates that many did not bother to think through in much detail, especially in September and October, exactly what advantages the United States could get from such a weapon that it could not secure through its superior stockpile of fission bombs or, for that matter, just what it was that the Russians might do if they secured an H-bomb first. It seemed sufficient and obvious that in the first instance American interests would be advanced, and that in the second they could only be hurt. Nor were the advocates of a greater effort very definite during September and October with regard to the rate and scale of the effort they had in mind. The analogy of the effort made during the war to develop the A-bomb came naturally to mind, and it was in these terms that the proposal was formally placed on the agenda of the Commission.

The issue of the rate and scale of the program could not be left in such ambiguous terms. The particular thermonuclear design which most of the participants had in mind, the so-called "Super," required as one of its major components a large amount of tritium. The most feasible method of making tritium was to bombard lithium with neutrons, and neutrons which were used to make tritium would not be available to make plutonium. Accordingly, the manufacture of tritium for the Super would mean foregoing the manufacture of fission bombs. Moreover, the scientific talent of the nation,

as well as its supply of neutrons, was limited. Scientists put to work on the
Super would be scientists not available to work on the new fission weapons.
A more intensive effort to make an H-bomb would, in short, involve costs to
the nation's A-bomb program.

The discussion that developed among the participants about the costs that
an expanded H-bomb program would entail for the A-bomb program proved
to be one of monumental confusion and misunderstanding. The least of the
difficulties was that no one knew just how much tritium the Super would
require. The major difficulty was that (a) the participants were reasoning
from diverse premises about the kind of effort to be made and about the
value of the weapons involved, and (b) the divergent character of these
premises were by no means always made clear in the arguments that were
then joined.

Thus, the development of any consensus with regard to the plutonium
costs involved was handicapped by the fact that some participants were
thinking in terms of making only enough tritium in the Hanford reactors to
support a test program, others contemplated a larger diversion of those piles
in order to have a stockpile of tritium immediately on hand with which to
fabricate a number of usable weapons in case the Super proved feasible, and
still others were thinking in terms of building a number of new reactors for
the production of the tritium stockpile, and it was not always clear whether
they expected those reactors to be in operation before or after a demonstration of feasibility. The discussion of the talent costs was similarly complex.
Some scientists did not see how additional talent could be put to work
profitably on the problem even if it was made available. In their view the
Los Alamos Laboratory was already doing about all that could be done.
Others were convinced that the problem had been starved for talent all
along. The development of a consensus on this point was further complicated by the fact that some thought the additional talent could be secured
by bringing in scientists not then working on fission weapons, and others
believed that if more people were put to work on the Super they would have
to come mainly from those already engaged in fission work.

Difficult as it was for the participants to reach any common conception of
what kind of expanded H-bomb program they were talking about and what
kind of cost it would bring to the A-bomb program, this was only half the
problem in reaching a conclusion about the rate and scale of the effort to be
made. A judgment about the desirability of foregoing any given number of
plutonium bombs or incurring the delay or loss of any given number of
improvements in the development of fission weapons would depend on the
application of some criteria for comparing the relative military utility of
A-bombs and H-bombs. One of the major reservations expressed by the
scientists on the GAC about the idea of embarking on a large-scale H-bomb
program was the result of the application of such criteria. They were by no
means confident that the Super could be delivered by air, and they thought

there would be few targets for which a bomb of such large yield would be suited. They concluded that the military purposes of the United States would be much better served by the A-bombs and A-bomb developments which would otherwise have to be foregone or postponed.

Illustrative of how different participants were talking about different things is the fact that the GAC judgment cannot be directly compared to that of the Joint Chiefs of Staff. At the time of the GAC report, the Chiefs were on record before the Joint Committee as desiring an accelerated effort to develop the Super, but they had not been specific about the rate and scale of the effort they had in mind and, hence, the A-costs they were willing to incur. When the Commissioners submitted their report, guidance on this point had yet to be produced by the military, and this was one of the questions to which they urged the President to secure an answer before making his decision.

The issue of the rate and scale of the effort to be made on the H-bomb thus turned, in part, on the issue of the relative military utility of H- and A-bombs. The discussion of this issue was conditioned, in turn, by the issue of what strategic doctrine should guide American military policy. It was here, at the level of general strategy, that some of the most significant differences existed among the participants. The three issues were so interrelated, however, that the participants were not always able to distinguish against what (and even for what) they were arguing.

The GAC report is a case in point. Many of its members were by no means persuaded that the doctrine of strategic bombing was a desirable military policy. Their views were not far removed from those of the Admiral (who was also a member of the Military Liaison Committee to the AEC) who had argued before the House Armed Services Committee in October, 1949, that strategic bombing was militarily unsound, morally wrong, and not suited for achieving the kind of political conditions the United States would want to obtain at the conclusion of a war. The GAC's recommendation against the development of the H-bomb was grounded, in part, on the belief that its only utility would be for the bombing of large cities and the objection to a military doctrine which would lead to the mass slaughter of Russian men, women, and children. The point was blurred, however, by their failure to carry through and make clear that they had equivalently strong objections to the use for this purpose of the products of the expanded fission program which they did support.

Another issue of doctrine interjected into the debate related to the conditions under which the United States would use nuclear weapons. It was argued by some that a decision with regard to the H-bomb program could not be rationally made until it was first decided for what purpose the United States was accumulating nuclear weapons: for the purpose of deterrence and retaliation only, or with the intent of so incorporating them into military plans and structure that the United States would initiate their use regardless of whether they had been employed by the enemy. The point to the argument was the idea that if weapons were being accumulated for the first purpose only, given the great value which the Russians attached to their industrial plant, a limited number of fission bombs would be sufficient to serve it.

The preference for a strategy based on last-resort use and for a clear-cut rejection of the principle of first use was strong among those who had major reservations about the desirability of strategic bombing and those who doubted the capacity of the American public to conduct itself rationally in a world in which conflict with the Soviet Union would continue to be deep and basic but in which a resort to violence would become increasingly suicidal. Among the participants in the Department of Defense, however, these arguments received a different reception. There was no great interest in adopting a strategy which seemed to bind the United States to fight only on terms of the enemy's choosing, and there was determined opposition to the idea that the need for an H-bomb program turned on the making of such a choice. It was the judgment of these and other participants that for an effective performance of the task of deterrence as well as that of fighting a victorious war the armed services would need the most powerful weapons they could secure.

The idea that an over-all review of national policy and a decision with regard to these strategic issues should precede the further development of the H-bomb was energetically pressed at the NSC level by the Chairman of the AEC, David Lilienthal. One reason why he did so relates to still another issue: that of the relative utility of conventional as compared to nuclear weapons. During the NSC discussions, Lilienthal was shocked to learn just how dependent the military were on nuclear weapons, and he became convinced that what the United States needed far more than the H-bomb was a large-scale increase in conventional armaments. This conclusion was influenced in part by the prevailing military judgment that nuclear weapons alone could not win World War III, but it also reflected Lilienthal's own conviction that the foreign policy purposes of the nation would be better served by a military posture that was not so dependent on the use of large bombs against urban targets.

It was Lilienthal's contention that the decision on the Super should be delayed until an effort had first been made to review the nation's strategic doctrine and to consider the desirability of reducing the nation's dependence on large-yield nuclear weapons by increasing the size of its conventional forces. He believed that if the decision to press for the Super was made first it would prejudice the chances for a later review of that choice and greatly lessen the opportunity to secure conventional rearmament. There would be little prospect of persuading Congress and the public to support an expensive conventional rearmament program, he argued, once the Super program was announced, for most would conclude from the announcement that the security of the United States was in good shape and that the answer to the Russian A-bomb had been found.

One other major issue was raised in connection with the H-bomb debate and that was the question of its relationship to the effort to secure international control of atomic energy. The feeling was strong among many, especially the GAC and members of the Commission, that with the development of the Russian A-bomb the world had reached a crossroads in history. From this point it stood fair to continue into the mounting tensions of a nuclear arms race and perhaps, in time, into the horrors of nuclear war. The most appropriate thing to do at this time, so it seemed, was not to rush to try to make even bigger bombs but rather to make a last determined effort to reverse the direction that international politics had been taking since 1945. To those who thought in these terms the urgency of those who advocated a more intensive H-bomb program seemed both intemperate and short-sighted. To those who thought negotiation with the Russians fruitless, the insistence on delay seemed quixotic and dangerous.

The specific ideas advanced by the GAC and some of the Commissioners as to what might be done to reopen the international control negotiations or to otherwise try to move the world away from a nuclear arms race were, however, most indefinite and not very clearly stated. Some suggested that the United States increase the scale of its research on the H-bomb but not go all-out on the H-program without first reopening the international control negotiations with the Russians. Others recommended not pushing ahead at all on the H-bomb until it and the control of nuclear weapons in general had been first discussed with the Russians. (The minority annex of the GAC report suggested, in this connection, that the two Powers might agree not to make the H-bomb. Since its successful development was believed to require a test, violation of the agreement could be easily detected.) The most extreme position was that taken by the majority of the GAC, which recommended that the United States unilaterally announce that it was not going to make the weapon.

This last recommendation illustrates the interconnection among all the issues involved in the discussion. The judgment of those who made it was that the United States would not be losing much: a weapon that looked as if it would be very hard to make; one which would cost more in A-bombs than its military utility was worth; and one which if used would be employed in a manner highly repugnant to the values for which American culture was supposed to stand. It was believed that the Russians would not try very hard to make it themselves, given the cost of the weapon, the uncertainty that it could even be made, and the American example. Renunciation, so it was thought, was an opportunity for America to gain considerable moral prestige at very little cost and to make some contribution to the possible limitation of warfare in the future.

THE DECISION EXAMINED AND EXPLAINED

It is appropriate at this point to recall the content of the President's decision on January 31st: that an effort be made to determine the technical feasibility of a thermonuclear weapon; that the rate and scale of the effort be fixed jointly by the AEC and the Department of Defense; and that the State and Defense Departments undertake concurrently to review the nation's foreign and military policies in light of the prospective nuclear capabilities of the Soviet Union.

This decision stands in some contrast to the issues and alternatives just described. Had the President decided the issue of the rate and scale of the H-bomb program? Had he decided that the military utility of the Super would be worth the A-costs involved? Had he made a decision about the military and political desirability of strategic bombing? Had he decided whether military doctrine with regard to nuclear weapons was to be governed by the principle of first use or that of last resort? Had he decided that the nation needed bigger nuclear weapons more than it needed large-scale conventional rearmament? Had he decided not to renew negotiations with the Soviet Union on the subject of international control?

The President had decided none of these things. This is not, of course, to say that he had decided nothing at all. He had quite definitely decided that the United States would not unilaterally renounce the effort to make an H-bomb. Although a literal reading of his directive with regard to the determination of feasibility would indicate that he had ordered the AEC and Defense only to continue what they had already been doing, there was certainly an implication that they should approach the task with a greater sense of urgency than had heretofore been the case. The directive also made it evident that the President had not endorsed an intensive H-bomb program. The directive said nothing about production facilities for the Super, nor did it even specify that the determination of feasibility was to include a test program.

The President had also decided to order the re-examination of the nation's strategic plans that so many had urged. He further decided not to wait until the completion of that review before making his H-bomb choice. He had similarly decided against two other alternatives which involved a delay in his making that choice: the alternative of first exploring the possibility of international control, and the alternative of first endeavoring to secure a large increase in conventional arms.

The President did make choices, but a comparison of the choices that he made with those that he did not make reveals clearly the minimal character of his decision. It bears all the aspects of a conscious search for that course of action which would close off the least number of future alternatives, one which would avoid the most choice. Thus the President had affirmed his interest in exploring the feasibility of an H-bomb, but he had said nothing about testing a device if one were fabricated, nothing about producing a weapon if the device were ever tested, nothing about how many weapons would be produced if any were made, nothing about whether such weapons would ever be used if produced, and nothing about the purposes for which such weapons would be employed if ever used.

An explanation for the minimal character of this decision is to be found partly in the views and power of those who shaped the recommendations of the special committee of the NSC, partly in the character of the American governmental process, and partly in the perspectives with which the participants approached the problem of choice. With regard to the first factor, the decisive influence on the outcome of the H-bomb discussion proved to be that of the State Department. It was the Secretary of State who spoke with authority, so far as the President was concerned, with regard to the various foreign policy hopes and fears that had conditioned the views of many of the other participants. It was also the Secretary of State who held the balance of persuasion, so far as the President was concerned, on those issues on which the representatives of the Department of Defense and the Atomic Energy Commission were divided.

The State Department was responsible for rejecting the various alternatives which involved some approach to the Russians with regard to international control before undertaking to accelerate the American H-bomb program. It was, in the opinion of Secretary of State Dean Acheson and those who assisted him on the NSC committee, simply not a time period in which the Russians were interested in serious negotiations. All that could be expected from approaching them would be stalling tactics which might embarrass or perhaps even completely inhibit the American program while leaving the Russians free to push ahead on their own.

The State Department sided with the Secretary of Defense, Louis Johnson, in stressing the importance of not delaying in the effort to discover whether the Super could be made, although the reasoning in the two Departments was somewhat different. A number of planning groups within the Department of Defense had given careful study to the military utility of the Super, and the suggestions that it was in all probability not worth making struck them all as unsound, to say the least. (One member of the GAC was later to observe that the GAC report had the unprecedented effect of unifying the services.) If the judgments of some of the scientists were grounded on a concern for what the world would look like after an H-bomb war, and those of the military on a concern for what it would be like to have to fight an enemy who had a monopoly on such a powerful weapon, those of the State Department representatives reflected a concern for the diplomatic opportunities the Russians would gain from such a monopoly for political blackmail around the Soviet periphery. Most of Acheson's advisers took this possibility very seriously, as did the Secretary himself.

The State Department's strong interest in avoiding the possible consequences of the Russians getting the H-bomb first also led Acheson to side with Defense with regard to the alternatives of reviewing the nation's strategic plans and of securing an increase in conventional weapons before making a choice about the H-bomb program. Acheson was quite willing to undertake such a review concurrently (as was Defense), and, as the Department's work on this review in the spring of 1950 was to show, he was prepared to push hard for an increase in conventional weapons. But he wanted no delay on the H-bomb research.

Lilienthal's arguments for the priority of a conventional weapons program might plausibly have been expected to win him some allies in the Pentagon, especially in the Army. They did not, largely because they were suspect. The fact that they associated Lilienthal with many of the GAC views led most of the military representatives to discount his argument as a device to delay the H-bomb for what were, really, other reasons. There was, moreover, a history of AEC-Defense disputes over the rôle of the AEC in determination of military requirements that made the defense representatives especially unresponsive to what was considered AEC meddling. President Truman, who had the greatest stake in not dissipating the persuasive lever that the Russian A-bomb gave him if he was later to press for a large-scale rearmament program, was not in the habit of examining the decision immediately before him for its implications for his future choices, and he, too, proved unresponsive to the argument.[6]

The character of the President's decision owes much to the coincidence of State and Defense views. It must also be attributed, however, to one of the major necessities of the American political process: the need to avert conflict by avoiding choice. The distribution of power and responsibility among government élites is normally so dispersed that a rather widespread agreement among them is necessary if any given policy is to be adopted and later implemented. Among the quasi-sovereign bodies that make up the Executive the opportunities to compel this agreement are limited. Agreement must be given, and it will not long be given for nothing. This condition of mutual dependence, the need, as it were, to "build a consensus" that includes one's enemies as well as one's friends, produces a strain toward agreement in the political process that is as fully characteristic of that process as the conflicts in which the participants are continually engaged.

There are many occasions when the necessary amount of coöperation can be achieved only by the device of avoiding disagreement, that is, by postponing the consideration of issues over which long and determined conflicts

---

[6] For Truman's decision-making style in this respect, see Richard E. Neustadt, *Presidential Power* (New York, 1960), pp. 172–173.

are certain to be waged. The H-bomb decision is a case in point. The issues which the President did *not* decide were all matters which, if he had endeavored to resolve them, would have pushed one group or another of his subordinates into passionate opposition. The President's position in the political process, however unique, is one which finds him, too, dependent upon the coöperation of others for the success of his policies, and Truman, in this instance, saw no reason to go out of his way to stir up a momentous struggle within his administration. Although he carefully read all the documents involved, from the GAC report through the NSC studies, Truman's own position on the H-bomb issue was the same in January as it had been in October when he first had heard of it. If the bomb could be made, he did not see how the nation could afford to let the Russians get it first, and he was therefore prepared to back whatever program made sense to the Departments concerned.[7]

If the President had no interest in maximizing conflict, neither had the members of the special committee. Acheson was quite aware of the gulf between Lilienthal's views and those of Johnson. Indeed, he was obliged to meet each separately, since Lilienthal's and Johnson's personal relationship had deteriorated to the point where they could not profitably meet together. He was therefore consciously searching for the common ground between them. The military representatives on the NSC working group, for their part, proved not only willing but eager to follow the lead of the State Department and back a recommendation that called for only a determination of the feasibility of the Super. The responsible officials in the Department of Defense had never been among those demanding an H-bomb program on the scale of the Manhattan District. They were determined primarily in their opposition to the views and recommendations that had been advanced by the GAC and some of the Commissioners.

The final factor conditioning the character of the decision was the nature of the perspectives with which the participants approached the problem of choice. The influence of Truman's "one decision at a time" approach has already been noted. The perspective that the military members of the NSC working group brought to the decision was: "what needs to be decided *now?*" What needed to be decided now, in their view, was whether the government would make an urgent effort to determine the feasibility of the weapon. This would settle the immediate problem of defeating those who argued for delaying the program, for one reason or another, and those who argued that the weapon was of insufficient value to justify diverting any

---

[7] The analysis in these two paragraphs owes much to the stimulation of Gabriel Almond, *The American People and Foreign Policy* (New York, 1950), pp. 143–145; Neustadt, *op. cit.,* esp. ch. 3; Roger Hilsman, "The Foreign-Policy Consensus: An Interim Report," *Conflict Resolution,* December 1959; and Samuel P. Huntington, "Strategic Planning and the Political Process," *Foreign Affairs,* January 1960.

more neutrons and talent to pursue it. What need at this point, they reasoned, to stir up discussion regarding the production or use of the weapon. By avoiding these issues, Defense would avoid certain conflict with the AEC and possible conflict with State. Avoiding these issues would also permit the Department to present a unified front to its enemies. The Army and Navy were as persuaded as the Air Force that the nation had to have this weapon, if it was to be had, and that it should be secured before the Russians got it. But there was real potential for disagreement among the services once the issues of production and use became operational. If very large amounts of tritium were to be manufactured, the plutonium foregone might well cut into that which the Army and Navy hoped would soon be available for their use, and at this point the doctrinal issues that divided the services with regard to the relative importance of strategic bombing as compared to other approaches to victory would be certain to arise.

The perspective with which the State Department representatives approached the decision was one that worked, in this instance, to the same end as that of the military but was significantly different in its rationale. Instead of asking "what has to be decided *now*," they asked: "what is the *least* possible that can be decided." The purpose was not so much to avoid conflict as it was to keep as many alternatives open for the future as possible, in order to be in a position to take maximum advantage of new information or changed conditions. It was with this perspective in mind that State drafted the recommendations that the special NSC committee later submitted to the President.

Of the three agencies, the perspective of the Commission representatives came closest to that of "what is the *most* that has to be decided." In fact, both State and Defense representatives had the feeling that the Commission was deliberately holding up the H-bomb program as a means of trying to force them to confront some of the major choices involved. The end result of the tactics of State and Defense, however, was to leave Lilienthal with very little to argue against or to argue for. Rate and scale? No one was urging an all-out program that would entail extremely large fission costs. Military utility? All that was being advocated was an effort to determine whether and at what expense the Super could be made; what better way to treat the question of its military value. Issues of strategic doctrine? State and Defense were to start immediately to review them, and an H-program so modest as not even to specify the conducting of a test could hardly be said to prejudice the results of such a review in advance. International control and the need for conventional weapons? Both of these matters would be given intensive study by the State-Defense review. Lilienthal could not shake the feeling that even in its minimal form the decision would prejudice the opportunity to depart from a big bomb strategy and he so argued to the end, but he had by now the feeling that there was no one at the NSC level with whom to argue.

CONSEQUENCES OF THE DECISION

One consequence of the minimal character of the President's decision was that all the issues on which he had avoided making any choice came back at him again. Thus, by the winter of 1951-1952 the disputes and dissatisfactions regarding the rate and scale of the program had reached such proportions that Air Force officials were considering setting up a weapons laboratory of their own. Similarly, in 1950 new investigations indicated that the tritium required for the Super would be much greater than that estimated at the time of the President's decision. This information, together with the concern that the Korean War might soon develop into all-out war with Russia, served in December, 1950, to reopen the discussion of the military utility of H- as compared to A-bombs and the desirability of incurring significant costs to the fission program in the effort to make it.

The State-Defense review, which became NSC-68, addressed itself boldly to the need to increase America's conventional weapon strength, but it did not really come to grips with the issues of nuclear strategy that had been raised during the H-bomb debate. Thus in December, 1951, when a group of scientists were active in urging the development and production of a large number of A-bombs for tactical use in the ground defense of Western Europe, the rationale for the proposal was in part the search for a strategy that would serve American security without requiring the bombing of cities. Their hope was that if the Red Army could be defeated through the battlefield use of A-bombs, the Strategic Air Command would be relieved of the burden of deterring a Soviet ground attack and free to exercise an option as to whether it struck the Soviet cities and initiated, thereby, an exchange that would bring bombs down on European and American cities as well. The issue of strategic bombing remains partly unsettled even today, as does the issue of last-resort use versus the principle of first use, although the terms are now "city-busting" versus "counter-force" and "second-strike" versus "first-strike" strategies. Similarly, the issue of conventional weapons versus nuclear weapons constituted a major source of debate during the whole of the Eisenhower administration.

The H-bomb decision is hardly the only occasion on which the policy process has produced a minimal decision. The continuous winnowing and worrying of the same old issues is an inevitable consequence of a political process that depends on the voluntary coöperation of independent and competing élites for the formulation and conduct of policy. Major policy changes can, for the most part, be effected only through slow and incremental change. However, as the same issues come around for the second, third, and nth time, they do so in a context slightly altered by the previous minimal choices to which they have been subjected.

The unilateral renunciation idea, for example, could hardly be advanced, after the President's decision, in the same form that the GAC had recommended it in October, 1949. It had to reappear in the form advanced by some other scientists in February, 1950: that the United States pledge itself not to be the first to initiate the use of H-bombs. Similarly, when the international control issue reappeared in November, 1952, with the proposal that the United States not set off its hydrogen device until it had first tried to negotiate an agreement with Russia not to test H-bombs, the conditions of the problem were not quite those that had prevailed when the same proposal was made in the minority annex of the GAC report. In place of an agreement on a device which no one even knew how to make, agreement would now have to be made with regard to a device which one side knew how to make and the other, presumably, did not.

The question might well be asked if there is not a possibility that through a sequence of minor "tactical" or minimal decisions the Government might some day find itself occupying a new "strategic" position without ever having made the major choice to get there. The answer, in a word, is yes, and again the H-bomb decision provides an illustration. On February 24, 1950, scarcely three weeks after the President's decision, the Joint Chiefs of Staff submitted a memorandum to the President requesting "an all-out development of hydrogen bombs and means for their production and delivery." The Chiefs, Johnson reported, wanted to undertake quantity production of the H-bomb as soon as possible.

Once again, Truman summoned the special committee of the NSC with Sumner Pike now serving in place of Lilienthal, who had submitted his resignation in November, 1949, but had stayed on to see the H-bomb decision through. On March 1st, this committee recommended that, without prejudice to the State Defense review which was still under way, the research program should proceed to a test stage as soon as possible and that preparations be made for the quantity production of the H-bomb without waiting for the results of the test. The President so ordered on March 10th, and construction began shortly thereafter on the Savannah River reactors.

So far as those who in the fall of 1949 had advocated an intensive H-bomb effort were concerned, the program instituted in the spring of 1950 represented all that they had ever had in mind. The AEC and the Department of Defense had no basic policy disagreements in the design of this program. Although initially skeptical of the military need for an all-out H-bomb program, Pike believed that if a determined effort was going to be made to make an H-bomb a parallel production program should accompany it. Having alerted the Russians to the fact that the United States was urgently trying to make the bomb, it was to be expected that the Russians would move fast themselves and the United States had therefore better do the same.

So far as the Department of Defense was concerned, the memorandum of February 24th was designed to "button down" the decision of January 31st. What had to be decided *now* was the issue of production. Defense had no more interest than Pike in ending up in 1951 or 1952 with a handful of successful test devices and no plant with which to make the weapon. Neither did it want weapons without carriers, although in this respect the February memorandum was somewhat redundant since the January decision had also authorized the Air Force to undertake a carrier program. Unlike the Department of State, Defense had no interest in keeping the issues of production and use open. The orderly development of military plans and programs required a clear and early decision, not the flexibility and freedom sought by State. The February memorandum was, then, an invitation to State and the AEC to dispute now, if they wished, the decision to produce the H-bomb in quantity and to develop a capability to use it.

For the reasons noted, there was no dispute from the AEC. What of the Department of State and the idea that the decision to determine feasibility left open the decisions to test, to produce, and to use? There was no dispute from the Department of State either, despite the fact that the State-Defense review of strategic plans was not completed. Some of the State Department representatives have advanced the argument that a decision to produce the means for production was not yet a decision to produce the weapon, but this is to stretch words further than reality. A more accurate reading of the reasoning in the State Department would be that, while their responsibilities did not dispose them to push for quantity production, they saw no good reason for opposing it. In retrospect, it would seem that Lilienthal's sense of what was afoot on the 31st of January was not mistaken. The minimal decision permitted the Department of Defense to achieve its objectives in two bites and to take its possible opponents one at a time, and while the January decision might not have prejudiced the chances for an unfettered look at the H-bomb program, the March decision certainly did.

One cannot draw a straight line from January-March, 1950, to the present. The decisions here discussed are but two of the points from which one would have to plot the course of American policy from then to now. Whether the subsequent choices with regard to nuclear weapons policy were of the same order as those just described is, so far as the present writer is concerned, an unknown matter. Given, however, the propensity of the political process for minimal decisions, it would be plausible to expect that they were.

The H-bomb decision is essentially a tragic story. The GAC was "right" in sensing that the development of the H-bomb would drive twentieth century man deeper into the box that he has been building for himself with his military technology, doctrine, foreign policy, and cultural ethos. The GAC was also "right" in asserting that it was a time to stop, look, and think. But the GAC was not alone in seeing the dimensions of the box. It was every bit as apparent to most of the advocates of the Super program. The trouble was that no one had any good ideas of how to get out of the box. Nor are they apparent today.

Basically, the H-bomb decision is a story of international rather than domestic politics. It affords a classic example of the traditional security dilemma. Both the Soviet Union and the United States would no doubt have preferred a world in which neither had the H-bomb. Each, however, wished to avoid a world in which the other had the H-bomb and it did not. Both rushed to make it, and they ended in a worse position than that in which they had begun.

THE POLICYMAKER AND
THE INTELLECTUAL

Henry A. Kissinger

ANY OBSERVER of the American scene must be struck by the tentative quality of our policy both foreign and domestic. Major parts of the world are undergoing revolutionary upheaval; but we seem hardly aware that peoples abroad find increasingly little in America with which to identify themselves. Beyond any disagreement or dissatisfaction over specific policies there exists an ever-growing distrust or at least incomprehension of America's purposes.

It would be comforting to believe that this state of affairs is due to particular mistakes of policy that can be reversed more or less easily. Unfortunately the problem is more deep-seated. Our policymakers' lack of vigor is matched by that of many of their critics. It has been a long time since there has been a real debate on policy issues beyond a bland competition for slogans such as co-existence or flexibility.

This stagnation is often ascribed to the fact that the best people are not attracted into government service. But it may be pertinent to inquire how qualified our eminent men are for the task of policymaking in a revolutionary period. Others trace the cause of our difficulties to the lack of respect shown the intellectual by our society. However, a case could be made for the proposition that in some respects the intellectual has never been more in demand; that he makes such a relatively small contribution not because he is rejected but because his function is misunderstood. He is sought after enthusiastically but for the wrong reasons and in pursuit of the wrong purposes.

ADMINISTRATIVE STAGNATION

One of the paradoxes of an increasingly specialized, bureaucratized society is that the qualities rewarded in the rise to eminence are less and less the qualities required once eminence is reached. Specialization encourages administrative and technical skills, which are not necessarily related to the vision and creativity needed for leadership. The essence of good administration is co-ordination among the specialized functions of a bureaucracy. The task of the executive is to infuse and occasionally to transcend routine with purpose.

Yet while the head of an organization requires a different outlook from that of his administrative subordinates, he must generally be recruited from their ranks. Eminence thus is often reached for reasons and according to criteria which are irrelevant to the tasks which must be performed in the highest positions. Despite all personnel procedures and perhaps because of them, superior performance at the apex of an organization is frequently in the deepest sense accidental.

This problem, serious enough in the private sector, is even more complicated in government. In a society that has prided itself on its free-enterprise character, it is inevitable that the qualities which are most esteemed in civilian pursuits should also be generally rewarded by high public office. But very little in the experience that forms American leadership groups produces the combination of political acumen, conceptual skill, persuasive power, and administrative ability required for the highest positions of government.

Our executives are shaped by a style of life that inhibits reflectiveness. For one of the characteristics of a society based on specialization is the enormous work load of its top personnel. The smooth functioning of the administrative apparatus absorbs more energies than the definition of criteria on which decision is to be based. Issues are reduced to their simplest terms. Decision making is increasingly turned into a group effort. The executive's task is conceived as choosing among administrative proposals in the formulation of which he has no part and with the substance of which he is often unfamiliar. A premium is placed on "presentations" which take the least effort to grasp and which in practice usually mean oral "briefing." (This accounts for the emergence of the specialist in "briefings" who prepares charts, one-page summaries, etc.) In our society the policymaker is dependent to an increasing extent on his subordinates' conception of the essential elements of a problem.

The bureaucratization of our society reflects not only its inevitable specialization but also certain deep-seated philosophical attitudes all the more pervasive for rarely being made explicit. Two generations of Americans have been shaped by the pragmatic conviction that inadequate performance is somehow the result of a failure to properly understand an "objective" environment and that group effort is valuable in itself. The interaction of several minds is supposed to broaden the range of "experience," and "experience" is believed to be the ultimate source of knowledge.

Pragmatism, at least in its generally accepted forms, produces a tendency to identify a policy issue with the search for empirical data. It sees in consensus a test of validity; it distrusts individual effort or at least individual certitude and it tends to suppress personal judgment as "subjective."

The low valuation of personal views produces a greater concern with the collection of facts than with an interpretation of their significance; therefore the myth in our government that intelligence does not advise, it only reports. It leads to a multiplication of advisory staffs and a great reliance on study groups of all types. Each difficulty calls into being new panels which frequently act as if nothing had ever been done before, partly, at least, because

the very existence of a problem is taken as an indication of the inadequacy
of the previous advice.

The situation is compounded by the personal humility that is one of the
most attractive American traits. Most Americans are convinced that no one
is ever entirely "right," or, as the saying goes, that if there is disagreement
each party is probably a little in error. The fear of dogmatism pervades the
American scene. But the corollary of the tentativeness of most views is an
incurable inward insecurity. Even very eminent people are reluctant to stand
alone, and they see in concurrence one of their chief tests of validity.

Philosophical conviction and psychological bias thus combine to produce
in and out of government a penchant for policymaking by committee. The
obvious insurance against the possibility of error is to obtain as many
opinions as possible. And unanimity is important, in that its absence is a
standing reminder of the tentativeness of the course adopted. The committee
approach to decision making is often less an organizational device than a
spiritual necessity.

In this manner, policy is fragmented into a series of *ad hoc* decisions
which make it difficult to achieve a sense of direction or even to profit from
experience. Substantive problems are transformed into administrative ones.
Innovation is subjected to "objective" tests which deprive it of spontaneity.
"Policy planning" becomes the projection of familiar problems into the
future. Momentum is confused with purpose. There is greater concern with
how things are than with which things matter. The illusion is created that
we can avoid recourse to personal judgment and responsibility as the final
determinant of policy.

The debilitating tendency of this approach is often obscured in the private
sector of our society because the goals of our economic effort are relatively
limited. They involve less the creation of a policy framework than successfully operating within one—itself a conciliatory procedure. But when the
same method is applied to national policy, its limitations become dramatically apparent. Many of our policymakers begin their government careers
with only superficial acquaintance with the problems of their office. This is
partly because the rise to eminence has often absorbed most of their energies,
partly because civic consciousness, where it exists, most often finds its outlet
on the local level. Whatever the reason, few of our executives (or lawyers
with a business background) can benefit in government from the strong will
which is often their outstanding trait and which gained them success. Consciously or not, our top policy-makers often lack the assurance and the conceptual framework to impose a pattern on events or to impart a sense of
direction to their administrative staffs. Their unfamiliarity with their subject
matter reinforces their already strong tendency to identify a policy breakdown and a policy solution with an aggregate of administrative proposals.

The impact on national policy is pernicious. Even our highest policy
bodies, such as the National Security Council, are less concerned with

developing over-all measures in terms of a well-understood national purpose than with adjusting the varying approaches of semi-autonomous departments. The elaborateness of the process is compounded by the tendency of advisers to advise; for silence may be taken to mean not that the idea under discussion is good but that the adviser is inadequate. The committee system is more concerned with co-ordination and adjustment than with purpose.

A policy dilemma is produced because the advantages and disadvantages of alternative measures appear fairly evenly balanced; otherwise there would be no need for discussion. (This leaves aside the question to what extent the committee procedure encourages a neutral personality to which the pros and cons of almost any course of action always seem fairly even and which therefore creates artificial dilemmas.) But in assessing these alternatives the risks always seem more certain than the opportunities. No one can ever prove that an opportunity existed, but failure to foresee a danger involves swift retribution. As a result, much of the committee procedure is designed to permit each participant or agency to register objections, and the system stresses avoidance of risk rather than boldness of conception.

Our method of arriving at decisions and the attitudes of our officials distort the essence of policy. Effective policy depends not only on the skill of individual moves but even more importantly on their relationship to each other. It requires a sense of proportion; a sense of style provides it with inner discipline. All these intangibles are negated where problems become isolated cases each of which is disposed of on its merits by experts in the special difficulties it involves. It is as if in commissioning a painting, a patron would ask one artist to draw the face, another the body, another the hands, and still another the feet, simply because each artist is particularly good in one category. Such a procedure in stressing the components would lose the meaning of the whole.

The result is a paradox: the more intense the search for certainty by means of administrative devices, the greater is the inward insecurity of the participants. The more they seek "objectivity," the more diffuse their efforts become. The insecurity of many of our policymakers sometimes leads to almost compulsive traits. Officials—and other executives as well—tend to work to the point of exhaustion as one indication that they have done all that could be asked. The insecurity of many of our policymakers sometimes is also shown by the fact that almost in direct proportion as advisory staffs multiply they are distrusted by those at the top. Officials increasingly feel the need for "outside"—and therefore unbiased—advice. Memoranda that are produced within the bureaucracy are taken less seriously than similar papers that are available to the general public. Crucial policy advice is increasingly requested from *ad hoc* committees of outside experts. (See, e.g., the Gaither Committee on national defense or the Draper Committee on economic assistance.)

These committees are often extraordinarily useful. They provide a fresh point of view. They can focus public discussion. They make possible the tapping of talent that would otherwise be unavailable, particularly in the scientific field. (A good case in point is James Killian's method of operation as science adviser to the President.) They may even galvanize the bureaucracy. Nevertheless they suffer from serious drawbacks. Whatever the previous experience of the members, they require extensive "briefing." This places an additional strain on the bureaucracy, while the members of the committee are frequently ready to make their best contribution at the point when the group is disbanded. Then again, the committee is inevitably drawn from the same segment of society as the top officials. Its members have therefore also been victims of the prevailing administrative pace. And the committee process, with its trend toward the fragmentation of policy and its bias toward simplified approaches, is almost as pervasive in *ad hoc* groups as in regular governmental committees.

In some respects *ad hoc* groups can even be said to represent an important diversion of talent. The number of outstanding individuals with experience in a given field is severely limited. As a result the same group is called again and again on related tasks. Its discussions soon become predictable and sometimes even stereotyped. The ideal situation would be a "leap-frogging" process in which the current high officials expend their intellectual capital while others, usually outside government, develop new concepts and approaches. But constant membership on committees causes many of their members to stagnate and freezes them at the level of the experience or effort that gained them their reputation.

Moreover, outside groups are handicapped by the fact that unless they constitute themselves into a pressure group seeking to mold public opinion— a function beyond their scope and usually contrary to their purpose—they can be effective only if they convince the bureaucracy. If they are too far in advance of existing thinking, they are ignored. If they only confirm what has already been considered within the government, they are unnecessary. *Ad hoc* committees generally can be effective only in a narrowly circumscribed area which may be somewhat ahead of official views but which rarely touches the essence of the problem: to challenge the existing assumptions or to define a new sense of direction.

The committee system not only has a tendency to ask the wrong questions, it also puts a premium on the wrong qualities. The committee process is geared to the pace of conversation. Even where the agenda is composed of memoranda, these are prepared primarily as a background for discussion, and they stand and fall on the skill with which they are presented. Hence quickness of comprehension is more important than reflectiveness, fluency more useful than creativeness. The ideal "committee man" does not make his associates uncomfortable; he does not operate with ideas too far outside of what is generally accepted. Thus the thrust of committees is toward a standard of average performance. Since a complicated idea cannot be easily absorbed by ear—particularly when it is new—committees lean toward what fits in with the most familiar experience of their members. They therefore produce great pressure in favor of the *status quo*. Committees are consumers and sometimes sterilizers of ideas, rarely creators of them.

For all their cumbersome procedure and their striving for "objectivity," there is something approaching frivolity about many committees. Ideas are accepted because no one can think of an objection fast enough; or they are rejected because they cannot readily be grasped. Unfortunately, not everything that sounds plausible is important and many important ideas do not seem plausible—at least at first glance, the only glance permitted by most committees. Rapidity of comprehension is not always equivalent to responsible assessment; it may even be contrary to it. The result is a vicious circle: in the absence of well-understood goals each problem becomes a special case. But the more fragmented our approach to policy, the more difficult it becomes to act consistently and purposefully. The typical pattern of our governmental process is therefore endless debate about whether a given set of circumstances is in fact a problem, until a crisis removes all doubts but also the possibility of effective action. The committee system, which is an attempt to reduce the inward insecurity of our top personnel, leads to the paradoxical consequence of institutionalizing it.

The result is that American policy displays a combination of abstractness and rigidity. Our method of arriving at decisions and the qualities it reflects and rewards place a greater premium on form than on substance. Thus on any given issue some paper will be produced for almost any eventuality. But because policy results from what are in effect adversary proceedings, proposals by the various departments or agencies are often overstated to permit compromise, or phrased vaguely to allow freedom of interpretation. In any case, what is considered policy is usually the embodiment of a consensus in a paper. The very qualities which make the consensus possible tend to inhibit sustained and subtle effort: for the statement is frequently so general that it must be renegotiated when the situation to which it applies arises.

The rigidity of American policy is therefore a symptom of the psychological burden placed on our policy-makers. Policies developed with great inward doubt become almost sacrosanct as soon as they are finally officially adopted. The reason is psychological. The *status quo* has at least the advantage of familiarity. An attempt to change course involves the prospect that the whole searing process of arriving at a decision will have to be repeated. By the same token, most of our initiatives tend to occur during crisis periods. When frustration becomes too great or a crisis brooks no further evasion, there arises the demand for innovation almost for its own sake. Yet innovation cannot be achieved by fiat. Crisis conditions do not encourage calm consideration; they rarely permit anything except defensive moves.

The combination of unreflectiveness produced by the style of life of our most eminent people in and out of government, faith in administrative processes, and the conversational approach to policy accounts for much of the uncertainty of our policy. It leads to an enormous waste of intellectual resources. The price we pay for the absence of a sense of direction is that we appear to the rest of the world as vacillating, confused, and, what is most worrisome, increasingly irrelevant.

THE DEMAND FOR INTELLECTUALS

In a revolutionary period, then, it is precisely the practical man who is most apt to become a prisoner of events. It is most frequently the administrator who is unable to transcend the requirements of the moment. Are there any groups in our society who can overcome this impasse? How about those who are not engaged in administrative tasks nor part of large organizations; the individuals who devote themselves to furthering or disseminating knowledge—the intellectuals?

Any survey of the contemporary American scene reveals, however, that the problem is more complicated than our refusal or inability to utilize this source of talent. Many organizations, governmental or private, rely on panels of experts. Political leaders have intellectuals as advisers. Throughout our society, policy-planning bodies proliferate. Research organizations multiply. The need for talent is a theme of countless reports. What then is the difficulty?

One problem is the demand for expertise itself. Every problem which our society becomes concerned about—leaving aside the question whether these are always the most significant—calls into being panels, committees, or study groups supported by either private or governmental funds. Many organizations constantly call on intellectuals. As a result, intellectuals with a reputation soon find themselves so burdened that their pace of life hardly differs from that of the executives whom they advise. They cannot supply perspective because they are as harassed as the policy-makers. In his desire to be helpful, the intellectual is too frequently compelled to sacrifice what should be his greatest contribution to society: his creativity.

Moreover, the pressure is not only produced by the organizations that ask for advice: some of it is generated by the self-image of the intellectual. In a pragmatic society, it is almost inevitable not only that the pursuit of knowledge for its own sake should be lightly regarded by the community but also that it should engender feelings of insecurity or even guilt among some of those who have dedicated themselves to it. There are many who believe that their ultimate contribution as intellectuals depends on the degree of their participation in what is considered the active life. It is not a long step from the willingness to give advice to having one's self-esteem gratified by a consulting relationship with a large organization. And since individuals who challenge the presuppositions of the bureaucracy, governmental or private, rarely can keep their positions as advisers, great pressures are created to elaborate on familiar themes rather than risk new departures that may both fail and prove unacceptable.

The great valuation our society places on expertise may be even more inimical to innovation than indifference. Since the American intellectual is so strongly committed to the same pragmatic values as the rest of society, it produces a tremendous overspecialization. This in turn makes it difficult for the intellectual to introduce a general perspective even from the vantage point of his own calling. Panels of experts are deliberately assembled to contain representatives of particular approaches: a committee on military policy will have spokesmen for the "all-out war" as well as for the "limited war" concept. A committee on foreign policy will have proponents for the "uncommitted areas" as well as specialists for Europe. These are then expected to adjust their differences by analogy with the committee procedure of the bureaucracy. Not surprisingly, the result is more often a common denominator than a well-rounded point of view.

This tendency is compounded by the conception of the intellectual held by the officials or organizations that call on him. The specialization of functions of a bureaucratized society delimits tasks and establishes categories of expectations. A person is considered suitable for assignments within certain classifications. But the classification of the intellectual is determined by the premium our society places on administrative skill. The intellectual is rarely found at the level where decisions are made; his role is commonly advisory. He is called in as a "specialist" in ideas whose advice is compounded with that of others from different fields of endeavor on the assumption that the policymaker is able to choose the correct amalgam between "theoretical" and "practical" advice. And even in this capacity the intellectual is not a free agent. It is the executive who determines in the first place whether he needs advice. He and the bureaucracy frame the question to be answered. The policymaker determines the standard of relevance. He decides who is consulted and thereby the definition of "expertness."

The fact that the need for excellence is constantly invoked is no guarantee that its nature will be understood. Excellence is more often thought to consist in the ability to perform the familiar as well as possible than in pushing back the frontiers of knowledge or insight. The search for talent consists more frequently in seeking personnel for well-understood tasks than in an effort to bring about an environment that constantly produces new and not yet imagined types of performance. The "expert" not uncommonly is the person who elaborates the existing framework most ably, rather than the individual charting new paths.

The contribution of the intellectual to policy is therefore in terms of criteria that he has played a minor role in establishing. He is rarely given the opportunity to point out that a query delimits a range of possible solutions or that an issue is posed in irrelevant terms. He is asked to solve problems, not to contribute to the definition of goals. Where decisions are arrived at by negotiation, the intellectual—particularly if he is not himself part of the bureaucracy—is a useful weight in the scale. He can serve as a means to filter ideas to the top outside of organization channels or as a legitimizer for the viewpoint of contending factions within and among departments. This is why many organizations build up batteries of outside experts or create semi-independent research groups, and why articles or books become tools in the bureaucratic struggle. In short, all too often what the policymaker wants from the intellectual is not ideas but endorsement.

This is not to say that the motivation of the policymaker toward the intellectual is cynical. The policymaker sincerely wants help. His problem is that he does not know the nature of the help he requires. And he generally does not become aware of a need until the problem is already critical. He is subject to the misconception that he can make an effective choice among conflicting advisers on the basis of administrative rules of thumb and without being fully familiar with the subject matter. Of necessity the bureaucracy gears the intellectual effort to its own requirements and its own pace: the deadlines are inevitably those of the policymaker, and all too often they demand a premature disclosure of ideas which are then dissected before they are fully developed. The administrative approach to intellectual effort tends to destroy the environment from which innovation grows. Its insistence on "results" discourages the intellectual climate that might produce important ideas whether or not the bureaucracy feels it needs them.

For these reasons, research institutes set up by governmental agencies have sometimes reflected the views of their sponsor even when they were financially independent. As long as the sponsoring agency retains the right to define the tasks of its research agency—or even the majority of these tasks—it will also determine the point of view of the product. The uniformity of the administrative approach is after all primarily the result less of fiscal control than of all the intangibles of fellowship and concern produced by association with a particular group and constant concentration on the same range of issues. It is not overcome if the "outside" research institute has no greater possibility for applying a wider perspective than its sponsoring agency has.

Thus though the intellectual participates in policymaking to an almost unprecedented degree, the result has not necessarily been salutary for him or of full benefit for the organization using him. In fact, the two have sometimes compounded each other's weaknesses. Nor has the present manner of utilizing outside experts and research institutes done more than reduce somewhat the dilemmas of the policymakers. The production of so much research often simply adds another burden to already overworked officials. It tends to divert attention from the act of judgment on which policy ultimately depends to the assembly of facts—which is relatively the easiest step in policy formation. Few if any of the recent crises of U.S. policy have been caused by the unavailability of data. Our policymakers do not lack advice; they are in many respects overwhelmed by it. They do lack criteria on which to base judgments. In the absence of commonly understood and meaningful standards, all advice tends to become equivalent. In seeking to help the bureaucracy out of this maze, the intellectual too frequently becomes an extension of the administrative machine, accepting its criteria and elaborating its problems. While this too is a necessary task and sometimes even an important one, it does not touch the heart of the problem: that purpose must dominate the mechanism if we are to avoid disaster. The dilemma of our policy is not so much that it cannot act on what it has defined as useful— though this too happens occasionally—but that the standards of utility are in need of redefinition. Neither the intellectual nor the policymaker performs his full responsibility if he shies away from this essential task. . . .

INNOVATION: II

MILITARY SYSTEMS ANALYSIS

E. S. Quade

THE ANALYSIS OF weapons and strategies for future wars presents a new kind of problem, different in a practical sense from any treated by operations analysts in World War II, or even in the Korean War. The aim in planning may now be how to deter war or even how to disarm with security, as well as how to wage war. A broad context, a rapid rate of technological change, and a resourceful enemy clothed in secrecy make extremely hazardous any prediction of the environment--usually five, ten, or more years in the future—in which the weapons and strategies are to be used, and the effect of their introduction into that environment. In this area of long-range military planning, as opposed to the operational use of given military units or weapons, piecemeal component optimizations and cost-effectiveness comparisons of competing postures and strategies must be replaced by an over-all treatment in which emphasis is placed on an integrated simultaneous consideration of all the major relevant factors.

Systems analysis, that is, analysis to suggest a course of action by systematically examining the costs, effectiveness and risks of alternative policies or strategies—and *designing additional ones if those examined are found wanting*—represents an approach to, or way of looking at, complex problems of choice under uncertainty. It was developed originally to deal with long-range military problems but is now used extensively by managers and engineers of large industrial enterprises, such as telephone companies and producers and distributers of electric power. It offers a means of discovering how to design or to make effective use of a technologically complex structure in which the different components may have apparently conflicting objectives; that is, an approach to finding the best balance among risks, objectives, and cost. Its purpose is to place each element in its proper context so that in the end the system as a whole may attain its objectives with a minimal expenditure of resources.

It was not the systematic approach but the subject matter which originally suggested the name. The first post-World War II military studies were primarily concerned with weapon systems. Evaluations undertaken to enable a decision-maker to choose among systems, to discover whether a given system could accomplish the desired objectives, or to set up a framework within which tests of the system could be prepared were naturally called "systems analysis." With slightly different emphasis, the terms "systems research," "systems design," "systems engineering," and, lately, "operations research" [1] are also used.

As an example of a relatively narrow problem in which a systems approach might be helpful, let us examine one which might arise in choosing a next-generation air defense missile from among several possible configurations. Consider, for example, guidance and control. Without taking a "system" point of view, it might seem obvious that if the accuracy of our missile can be improved, the result will be more enemy missiles or planes shot down. It does not follow at all, however, that the missile with the highest accuracy will necessarily maximize the effectiveness of the over-all defense system or, for that matter, will even give the missile component of the system its highest potential for killing enemy vehicles. Any numerical values which measure the kill capability of a missile-defense system must depend on at least four factors: first, the number of missile emplacements within whose range the invaders must fly; second, the number of missiles that can be launched during the time the enemy is within range; third, the probability that a given missile will be operative; and fourth, the probability that an operative missile kills its target. An increase in the accuracy of the missile would probably increase this fourth factor. But this would result in an over-all increase of kills only if the values of the other factors were not materially lowered by whatever change was necessary to bring about the increase in accuracy.

If, for example, additional guidance and control equipment were added to the missile to improve its accuracy, the resulting increase in weight might reduce the range or the speed of the missile. This in turn could reduce the number of missiles that might be launched in an engagement. Also, the greater complexity of more accurate guidance equipment might degrade the reliability. Consequently, in spite of the increased accuracy, the over-all effectiveness might be reduced. Moreover, there is the very likely possibility that the more accurate missile might cost more and, since the total expenditure is certainly a constraint, the purchase of missiles which are individually more accurate might lead to fewer launching sites and fewer missiles.

Indeed, in these days of deterrent weapons, certain less obvious factors—for example, the state of readiness, the vulnerability, and the susceptibility to countermeasures—may contribute equally to deterrence and be the items

---

[1] There is no clear line of demarcation between operations research and what we are calling systems analysis; the difference is a matter of degree. Until recently operations research has tended to emphasize mathematical models and optimization techniques. The operations-research analyst is usually trying to use mathematics, or logical analysis, to help a client improve his efficiency in a situation in which everyone has a fairly good idea of what "more efficient" means. The systems analyst, on the other hand, is likely to be forced to deal with problems in which the difficulty lies in deciding what ought to be done, not simply in how to do it. In such a situation, far more attention must be devoted to establishing objectives, criteria, and alternatives. The total analysis is thus a more complex and less neat and tidy procedure which is seldom suitable for a quantitative optimization over the whole problem.

which dominate the costs of the system. The certainty with which a weapon can be fired after an attack may be more essential than its accuracy. Operational and logistic factors such as mobility, data requirements, communications, supplies, maintenance, personnel, and training must all be considered in a systems approach. For example, before deciding to use an unusual substance as a fuel, on the grounds that it would enhance the range of the missile, the logistical implications in the decision must be investigated. The fuel may be so toxic that it will require inordinately complex handling for supply, transport, and storage. If so, the over-all performance of the system may be degraded, or the costs raised, in spite of any increased range or speed that might develop.

Thus, in this problem of choosing an air-defense missile, a systems approach is indicated. The context must be broad enough to embrace everything pertinent to all the alternative systems. The analysis would ordinarily take one or the other of two equivalent forms. For a given desired level of military effectiveness, the systems analyst might attempt to determine which alternative, or combination of alternatives, will imply the least cost. Or, for a specified budget level, he might try to find out which alternative, or combination of alternatives, will maximize effectiveness. In either case, the total systems analysis would require numerous substudies—for example, operations research to investigate problems of deployment or logistics, cost analysis to estimate the dollar costs of the several alternatives, and possibly even war gaming to suggest enemy penetration tactics.

The simplest category of systems analysis involves a choice from within a class of essentially similar alternatives. The problem of choosing the next-generation air-defense missile belongs to this category. The possible alternative missile systems may differ widely with respect to accuracy, range, payload, and certain other characteristics, such as alert status. But they are likely to be similar in certain fundamental aspects in which the uncertainties are the greatest—for example, in the estimates associated with how far their performance in combat will fall below that of the proving ground, in enemy reactions to their development and use, and in their logistics and support problems. Since they are essentially similar means for accomplishing the same objectives, and are associated with the same time period, many uncertainties are likely to affect all designs in the same direction and approximately to the same extent. In analysis in which the alternatives are relatively similar, it is easier to take uncertainty into account and to apply measures to alleviate its consequences; also, one feels that the failure to handle this factor adequately is not so likely to invalidate the analysis.

On the other hand, a broader problem for systems analysis might involve the design of an entire air-defense system to protect the United States from damage. This would be difficult, but not merely because of the wider context involved. The value of an air-defense system is measured by more than its ability to prevent damage in event of a surprise attack which begins all-out war; for example, in peacetime it polices our borders and prevents intrusions. Better protection, however, results from preventing war, or, if war comes, from keeping it away from our country. Doing this depends on offensive power and national policy for using it—and on air defense. Thus the problem of finding agreement on a working basis for objectives and criteria is not likely to be an easy one.

Even after criteria and objectives have been tentatively set, considerable practical difficulties remain. Here, alternative subsystems with complementary but essentially different tasks, such as radar and antimissile missiles, would compete for resources. Moreover, even with weapons which have essentially the same objectives, say air-defense missiles for point defense and those designed for area coverage, new difficulties arise because such factors as the warning times required for their employment, their differing utilities under different enemy tactics, and even the support structure may be entirely different. The level of knowledge about the various ingredients will be different. Of course, for weapons such as aircraft there is much past experience to guide the investigator with respect to such things as maintenance requirements, reliability, and the like. For missiles, this backlog of experience does not exist. But even more serious are the effects of uncertainties about alternatives which contribute to damage reduction in entirely different ways —say, shelters and alert missiles. Further, since (as we mentioned earlier) a better way to prevent damage is not to have a war, the analysis has to consider also how these elements affect the likelihood of war, as well as the chances of survival if war comes.

It is not easy to tell someone how to carry out systems analysis. We lack adequate theory to guide us. The attention of the practitioners, when it has turned to methods, has been focused mainly on the development of mathematical techniques. This attention has met with great success. Models have now become easier to manipulate, even with many more variables represented. Computational obstacles cause comparatively little difficulty. It is the philosophical problems, such as occur in providing assurance that the model is meaningful, in devising schemes to compensate for uncertainty, or in choosing appropriate criteria, that are troublesome. This lack of a guiding theory must be expected, for systems analysis is a relatively new discipline.

Systems analysis, particularly of the type required for military decisions, is still largely a form of art and not of science. An art can be taught in part, but not by means of definite fixed rules which need only be followed with exactness. Thus, in systems analysis we have to do some things that we think are right but that are not verifiable, that we cannot really justify, and that are never checked in the output of the work. Also, we must accept as inputs many relatively intangible factors derived from human judgment, and we must present answers to be used as a basis for other judgments. Whenever possible, this judgment is supplemented by inductive and numerical reasoning, but it is only judgment nonetheless.

One hope for guidance is to turn to science. The objective of systems analysis and operations research, in contrast to that of pure science, is primarily to recommend—or at least to suggest—policy, rather than merely to understand and predict. Thus systems analysis seems to be more nearly engineering than science. For purposes of distinction, one might say that science seeks to find things out while engineering uses the results of science to do things well and cheaply. Systems analysis has this latter objective; while every possible use of science and scientific methods is made, additional guidance is required, for it is necessary to decide what is well and what is cheap in each given situation.

Thus, systems analysis is sometimes described as the application of the "scientific method" to problems of economic choice. Even though it is by no means clear that there is any unique method which can be termed scientific, the analysis advances through something like the following stages:

FORMULATION — clarifying, defining, and limiting the problem;
SEARCH — determining the relevant data;
EXPLANATION — building a model and exploring its consequences;
INTERPRETATION — deriving the conclusions;
VERIFICATION — testing the conclusions by experiment.

A systems analysis always involves the first four of these stages but frequently omits the last. In military systems analyses, experiment is ordinarily not available; if we are lucky, our weapon system will be obsolete before there is a war, and we will never find out whether it was really satisfactory or not. The analysis, however, advances by iteration, passing through these stages more than once.

The discussion of method is divided into four sections, corresponding to the first four stages listed above.

FORMULATION

Formulation implies an attempt to isolate the questions involved, to define the meaning of the variables or factors that are operative, and to state relationships among these factors. The relationships may be extremely hypothetical, since empirical knowledge may be in short supply, but they will help to make the logical structure of the analysis clear. In a sense, this is the most important stage, for the time spent restating the problem in different ways, redefining it, or expressing its limits, brings to light whether it is spurious or trivial and points the way to its solution. The tendency all too frequently is to accept the original statement of what is wanted exactly as proposed, and then to set about building a model and gathering information, scarcely giving a thought to how the answer will contribute to the decisions which it is trying to assist. In fact, because the concern is with the future, the major job may be to decide what the policy maker should want to do. Since systems studies have resulted in rather important changes not only in how the policy maker carries out his activity but in the objectives themselves, it would be self-defeating to accept the customer's view of what the problem is.

An analogy with medical practice may be drawn. No doctor ignores a patient's description of his symptoms, but he cannot allow the patient's self-diagnosis to override his own professional judgment. The medical analogy is not entirely applicable, however—the businessman or military commander ordinarily knows more than anyone else about his operations and what, if anything, might be wrong with them. Even so, he may not be so sound in his knowledge of how these operations affect, and [are] affected by the context in which they occur.

How is the analyst to know his formulation of the problem is superior? *His one advantage lies in analysis.* That is, the process of problem formulation itself should be the subject of analysis. The systems analyst always has some idea as to the possible solutions of the problem; otherwise, he probably should not be working on it, for his analysis will prove to be too formal and abstract. At this early stage the analyst essentially makes an attempt to solve the problem before the facts are known. It is this attempt which gives him a basis for better formulation.

The problem itself does not remain static. Interplay between a growing understanding of the problem and of possible developments will redefine the problem itself. Primarily, as the result of discussion, the original effort to state the problem should suggest one or more possible solutions or hypotheses. As the study progresses, these original ideas are enriched and elaborated upon. Each hypothesis serves as a guide to later results—it tells us what we are looking for while we are looking. The final statement of the conclusions and recommendations usually rests on a knowledge of facts about the problem which are not known to the analyst at the start. Frequently, a hypothesis must be abandoned and an entirely new one considered.

Analysis must be an *iterative procedure;* that is, a process of successive approximation. The various stages in analysis—problem formulation, data collection, model building, and computation—may follow each other in that order only within a single iteration; the tentative solution we obtain at the end of the first approximation helps us to better prepare a second formulation of the problem. Figure 1 attempts to indicate this iterative character of analysis. In a certain sense it is impossible to formulate a problem completely before it is solved, or, in other words, the final problem statement may have to be written simultaneously with the final answer. It is not a mistake to hold an idea in the early stages as to the solution; the pitfall is to refuse to abandon such an idea in the face of mounting evidence.

Even for small-scale individual problems, the number and complexity of factors under consideration at any one time must be reduced until what is left is manageable. In systems analysis, the complexity of the "full" problem frequently far outruns analytic competence. To consider anything like the

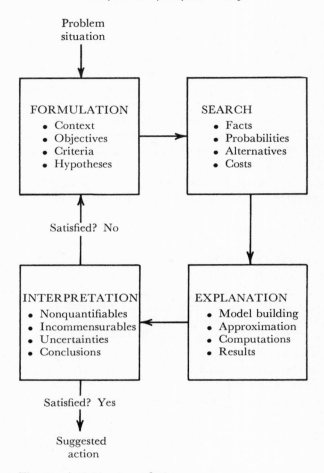

Fig. 1. Activities in analysis.

complete range of possible alternative solutions may be impossible. The vast majority of alternatives will be obviously inferior; there is no harm in leaving these out. The danger is that some solution which is better than that un-covered by the analysis will also have been left out. The number of alter-natives available in completely unrestrained situations are too numerous to be examined. Constraints must be imposed, but by preliminary analysis, not arbitrary fiat. Such constraints must be regarded as flexible so that they may be weakened or removed if it appears in later approximations that their presence is a controlling factor.

Something must always be left out, otherwise problems are too big. For example, the decision to use a particular air-speed indicator in a new fighter should fundamentally rest on the military worth of the available indicators. It is futile to try to make this choice by considering all possible wars in which this equipment might be used. Yet, even though it may be beyond his capability to do a complete job, the analyst can at least do some thinking about the larger problem. The dangerous path is to reduce the problem by fixing factors which would have been allowed to vary, if sufficient thought had been given to the larger problem.

Certain elements are common to systems analysis as well as to every problem of economic choice, although they may not always be explicitly identified:

1. *The objective* (or objectives). Systems analysis is undertaken primarily to suggest or recommend a course of action. This action has an aim or objective. Policies or strategies, forces or equipment are examined and compared on the basis of how well and cheaply they can accomplish this aim or objective.

2. *The alternatives.* The alternatives are the means by which objectives can be attained. They need not be obvious substitutes or perform the same specific function.²

3. *The costs.* Each alternative means of accomplishing the objectives involves certain dollar costs or specific resources used up.

4. *A model* (or models). This is a set of relationships, mathematical or logical, relevant to the problem at hand, by means of which the costs incurred and the extent to which the objectives are attained are associated with each alternative.

5. *A criterion.* This is the rule or test needed to tell how to choose one alternative in preference to another. For each alternative, it attempts to measure the extent to which the objectives are attained as compared with the costs or resources used up.

A characteristic of systems analysis is that the solutions are often found in a set of compromises which seek to balance and, where possible, to reconcile conflicting objectives and questions of value. It is more important to choose the "right" objective than it is to make the "right" choice between alternatives. The wrong objective means that the wrong problem is being solved. The choice of the wrong alternative may merely mean that something less than the "best" system is being chosen. Frequently we must be satisfied with merely a demonstration that a suggested action is "in the right direction," anyway. This may be all that is possible.

In the choice of objectives, the iterative character of systems analysis stands out. It is impossible to select satisfactory objectives without some idea of the difficulty and cost of attaining them. Such information can only come as part of the analysis itself.

The problems in the selection of suitable objectives and criteria are the most difficult in systems analysis. . . .

---

² Thus, to protect civilians from air attack, warning shelters, "shooting" defense, counterforce, and retaliatory striking power are all alternatives.

The costs to be considered in choosing among alternatives, moreover, should be the "new" costs, that is, the net additional resource drain or "incremental cost" that would be incurred because of the choice of a particular alternative. Because a certain system may inherit facilities, personnel, or equipment from previous systems, its incremental costs may be much lower than what it would cost if it were to exist "in isolation." Also in comparing military capabilities, costs have sometimes been computed on the basis of what the various systems would cost independent of the existence of other systems or other capabilities. In this light consider, for example, a Navy supercarrier. In a paper comparison to estimate its value in a limited-war role, if no credit were assigned to its central war capabilities, then on a cost-effectiveness basis it would be handicapped unfairly in comparison with a weapon system that had only a single role.

Great attention must be paid to initial conditions; that is, to the assumptions which limit the problem and set the background against which the initial attempt at a solution is to be made. The situation is not like that of an empirical science, which starts with observed facts, but more like that of mathematics, where the results take any "validity" they might have in the real world from the initial assumptions. The difference is that for the systems analysis to give correct guidance, it is important that the assumptions be the "right" assumptions.

Once the problem has been broken down into its components—which is what analyzing the problem means—some of the components can be further analyzed, using various techniques; but others may defy analytic techniques. In that case, because the problem has been broken into smaller pieces, the systems analyst may be able to find individuals who have direct, sound experience and on whose "considered" judgment he can rely.

Considered judgment differs from intuitive judgment in that the logic behind the opinion is made explicit. Both are based on an individual's experience and background, but when the reasoning is explicit, an observer can form his own opinion from the information presented. Judgment permeates systems analysis—judgments as to which hypothesis is better than another, or which approach is more fruitful, or what facts are relevant. The ideal is to keep all judgments in plain view.

Uncertainty in long-range military planning problems being as great as it is, it is well—particularly early in the study—not to attach much significance to small differences in cost and effectiveness of alternative systems. Specifically, it is important to look for differences of the sort that have a chance of surviving *any* likely resolution of the uncertainties. The question to address is which alternatives have a clear advantage rather than the question as to precisely *how much* better one alternative is than another or even, initially, which ones move us toward the attainment of the objectives.

SEARCH

This phase is concerned with finding the facts, or evidence, on which the analysis is based. It is necessary to look for ideas (and evidence to support them), including the invention of new alternatives, as well as to look for facts. Unless we have alternatives, and ideas about them, there is nothing to analyze or to choose between. If in the end we are to designate a preferred course of action, we must have discovered earlier that such a course exists. In long-range problems, the total number of alternatives may be endless, and we must use judgment to eliminate the unreasonable.

Many facts are hard to come by. The actual operational performance of future weapons in combat cannot be predicted with any degree of certainty. Purely theoretical studies or operations research of weapon characteristics must be depended upon. In systems analysis as contrasted with most other forms of engineering, a great many more inputs are a matter of judgment rather than a result of measurement or engineering analysis.

When should an inquiry stop? It is important to remember that in this sort of a problem, inquiry is rarely exhaustive. Inquiries are partial, and the decision-maker must get along without the full advantage of all the potentiality of operations research and the scientific approach. Inquiries cost money and time; they cost in whatever values one is dealing in. They can cost lives; they can cost national security. It might be interesting to know what the Russians could do if we succeed in dropping an armed Atlas on Moscow. It might be an easy observation to make, but some of the costs seem to prohibit this type of investigation. One should never fall into the error of feeling that inquiry is free of cost. There are many contexts in which we can ignore the cost of inquiry; but paradoxes arise if we allow ourselves to forget that almost all inquiries must stop far, far short of completeness, either for lack of funds, of time, or of justification for spending further funds or time on them. It is out of the question to collect all the information that is required for exhaustive analysis, and it is out of the question to process it.

As an analogy, consider the example of a physician who uses a clinical laboratory to help him decide whether or not his patient has one of several obscure ailments which have many similar symptoms. Even when all the reports are in, the doctor's inquiry may not be complete. He could probably do a lot more laboratory analysis. If the problem is simply one of diagnosis, one of the very best procedures would be to slaughter the patient and perform a thorough autopsy. The cost here is prohibitive, not only prohibitive by the standards of modern society but prohibitive simply by the fact that the physician's goal is to help the patient live a longer and fuller life. He would only frustrate himself if he bought knowledge at the price of the life he is trying to guard.[3]

_____
[3] This is not to say he might not risk life in trying to guard it; he might order such

EXPLANATION

After obtaining some idea of what the facts and alternatives are, it is necessary to build up some way to explain them and to determine their implications.

In order to make much progress with real-world problems, we must ignore a great many of the actual features of a question under study and abstract from the real situation certain aspects, hopefully, the relevant ones, which together make up an idealized version of the real situation. This idealization we call a "model."

In the general process of formulating a problem and gathering data about it, the analyst will have developed some ideas of what the major influencing factors are, that is, the factors which provide discrimination with respect to the possible courses of action. To produce quantitative results, it is necessary to assign a scale of measurement to each factor and to show its dependence on certain parameters. Next, the interaction of the factors must be described. Then we have a model. That is, the result of isolating those factors pertinent to the problem or the decision at hand, abstracting them, assigning a scale of measurement, and then describing their interactions builds the model.

For most phenomena, there are many possible representations; the appropriate model depends as much *on the question being asked* as on the phenomena about which it is asked. There are thus no "universal" models—that is [to] say, no one model that can handle all questions about a given activity.

Sometimes representation by the model is mathematical, by means of a series of equations or a computer program. At other times, particularly where detailed specification of the relationships between factors is extremely difficult—for example, in studying the behavior of human organization—the representation may be by a simulation or by a war game. A gaming model cannot be expected to tell us what an optimal response to an uncertain state of affairs might be, but it can do much to make the players aware of such uncertainties and of the necessity of formulating their plans in such a way as to cope with all foreseeable contingencies. Indeed, an important asset to all systems analysis is the spirit of gaming. This consists in explicitly looking at possible moves and countermoves, in examining and designing a wide range of alternatives, and in looking for substitution possibilities—all against a hostile opponent.

It should be emphasized that, in many important systems analyses, no need arises to build formal models explicitly. When such cases occur, the analysis may be extraordinarily effective since it may be completely understood by the policy maker. The essence of systems analysis is not mathematical techniques or procedures. A computing machine or a technique like linear programming may or may not be useful, depending on the problem

---

tests as a spinal puncture or a liver puncture, or other inherently dangerous procedures. Many diagnostic procedures are dangerous and are used when the danger is justified, but a doctor will not make a complete sacrifice of what he is trying to protect.

and the extent of our information. The essential thing is a listing of the alternatives and an examination of their implications and costs in order that they may be compared.

The widely useful operations-research techniques for optimization, when they are used at all in systems analysis, are used much more extensively in component studies than they are at the heart of the over-all problem. Before any mathematical technique can be applied to a real-world problem, we must construct a quantitative model of the processes involved. This model expresses the effectiveness of the alternatives under examination as a function of a set of variables some of which are under control. Once this is done, a solution can be determined mathematically, since formal statements of relationships between the variables exist. The solution obtained from such a model will be a usable solution to the real-world problem if and only if the model is a reasonably accurate representation of the real-world situation with respect to the question at issue. In situations of great complexity, such as those associated with major military decisions, only pieces of the problem can be represented with confidence. The submodels for these pieces or components can frequently be put in a form in which they can be handled by techniques like dynamic programming or queueing theory. But even here, the new and more advanced techniques, while they are useful and promise to become more so, are seldom necessary since—except in relatively few instances—more elementary tools are usually adequate.

The design of models to assist in the decision process is in large measure an art, for it requires selection or composition, plus instinct and a sense of form, to achieve a desired effect. Wide experience and the collaboration of many people are helpful; but in cases in which we are modeling a complex future situation, modeling must be accepted as an art.

All of the assumptions of the model must be made explicit. If they are not, this is a defect. A mark of a good systems analyst (or any wise person communicating with others) is that he state the basis on which he operates. This does not imply necessarily that he makes better assumptions but only that his errors will be more evident.

The contrast between the relative amount of time usually spent on designing a model and that spent in computing its consequences can give bias in judging what is important. It is the design of the model and the faithfulness with which it represents those aspects of the phenomena being modeled which are significant for the question under consideration, not how far or how extensively we push the computation.

The validity of conceptual or mathematical models cannot, in the type of analysis we have been talking about, be tested by the methods of controlled experiment. The best that can be done is to test them by their workability. For example, we try to determine answers to the following questions:

(1) Can the model describe correctly and clearly known facts and situations?

(2) When the principal parameters involved are varied, do the results remain consistent and plausible?

(3) Can it handle special cases in which we have some indication as to what the outcome should be?

(4) Can it assign causes to known effects?

Whether or not one model is better than another does not depend on its complexity, realism, or computability, but solely on whether it gives better predictions.

"Working" the model, trying out various strategies and concepts of operation, is the nearest thing systems analysis has to scientific experimentation. Deductions based on operating the model frequently suggest new directions of effort. That is to say, starting with the relatively few parameters which characterize the systems in terms of the model, it is important first to show what changes in these would improve the performance of a system as measured by the model, and then to consider whether corresponding changes could also be made in the real system which would lead to improved performance in the real world. In this way, working the model contributes to system design.

Two aspects of model building are particularly troublesome: quantification and the treatment of uncertainty.

Some variables are difficult to quantify, either because they are not calculable, like the probability of war, or because no scale of measurement has been set up, like the effect on NATO solidarity of some unilateral United States action. This leads either to their neglect, for they tend to be ignored, or to their entry only through a qualitative modification of a solution achieved through the manipulation of variables which have been quantified. Thus the effect of the quantitative variables is built in, while the nonquantitative ones are subject to forgetfulness and may be easily lost in the welter of qualitative considerations that must be weighed, when the problem of what action to recommend on the basis of the solution from the model arises.

One argument for the omission of a particular variable is that the solution of the problem is virtually insensitive to it. The fact that many variables fall into this category makes analysis possible. If the results were not insensitive to all but a relatively small number of variables, analysis would have to yield completely to guesses and intuition. Insensitivity can occur either because a factor is irrelevant or trivial in its quantitative effects or because it has roughly the same effect on all of the alternatives under consideration. *The point is that this insensitivity must be discovered.* Sometimes logical reconnoitering is sufficient, but usually analysis is required, with arbitrary values assigned to factors we are unable to calculate.

If nonquantitative variables are not to be neglected without mention or dismissed with some spurious argument, such as the one that they act in opposite directions and hence cancel out,[4] then how are they to be treated?

---

[4] It is not enough to know that two variables act in opposite directions; their quantitative impact must also be estimated.

The usual method is to attempt to take them into account through modification of the solution rather than to incorporate them into the model. But this in itself represents a particular method of quantification, for, by altering the solution to take account of the previously omitted variables, the analyst is implicitly valuing them. Since we always have some insight into the range of values that a factor might take, we can, even in the worst cases, assign the factors an arbitrary value and observe the effect on the solution. It seems to be an empirical fact that results seldom come out of optimization problems until they are quantitative; consequently, every effort should be made to quantify.

Systems analysis is concerned with problems in which the essence is uncertainty about the future. Such analysis, as well as any other attempt to answer the same questions, must necessarily face this uncertainty squarely, treat it as an important element in the problem, and take it into account in formulating recommendations. The treatment of uncertainty is not merely a difficulty in principle, but is a considerable practical problem.

Statistical uncertainty—that is to say, uncertainties having more or less objective or calculable probability of occurrence—can be handled in the model by Monte Carlo or other methods. Such uncertainties, like those in cost or missile accuracy, can be annoying, but not devastating, like the "real" uncertainties associated with the prediction of what the environment may turn out to be during the lifetime of the systems under consideration.

These latter uncertainties about the future behavior of things that are beyond the practical ability of analysts to predict belong to the class of real uncertainties. Under real uncertainty, we consider events to which individuals may attach subjective probabilities, like the probability of war, but which we cannot calculate. With regard to air defense, for example, real uncertainty involves such questions as, "Will we have warning? If we get it, will we believe it? What surprises does the enemy have?" For such uncertainties, there is frequently widespread disagreement about the pertinent probabilities and even confusion and vagueness within any one person.

The best way to compensate for uncertainty is to "invent" a better system or policy which provides insurance against the whole range of possible catastrophes; the difficulty is to discover how to do this.

Sensitivity and contingency analyses help us to select or design the alternatives so that their performance will not be sensitive functions of unknown parameters.

In "sensitivity analysis" several levels are used for values of key parameters —not just the expected or most probable values—in an attempt to see how sensitive the results are to variations in these parameters. The hope is to obtain a dominant solution in which the ranking of the preferred alternative is essentially insensitive to reasonable variations in values of the parameters in question. "Contingency analysis" investigates how a system chosen with one assumption about the environment would measure up to the performance of its alternatives, if radical changes in the environment were to occur.

Thus, sensitivity analysis might test the alternatives for a wide range of enemy capabilities or for the consequences of having planned for one level of capability when another is experienced. Contingency analysis might test the alternatives under a change in criteria or compare them in an environment in which France, say, had become part of the Communist Bloc.

Since a system analysis is a study which attempts to influence policy, it must make a convincing comparison of the relevant alternatives. It must demonstrate that some course of action A is better than alternative possible courses of action B, C, D. . . . To do this, the analysis may have to be done in two stages: First, find out what to recommend, and second, make these recommendations convincing.

After we are convinced to our own satisfaction what the preferred system or policy is, how can we show that under any reasonable assumption the system or policy designed or selected by the analyst is indeed to be preferred? One way to do this is to use either an *a fortiori* or a break-even analysis. To make an analysis *a fortiori,* we bend over backwards in making the comparisons to "hurt" the system we think is best and "help" the alternative systems. If it then turns out that after we have done this we can still say we prefer the handicapped system, we are in a strengthened position to make recommendations. Sometimes we cannot do this—say, if we concede the exaggerated performance claims for rival systems and the pessimistic estimates about the systems we like. In this case, we might try a *break-even* analysis: We find what assumptions we have to make about important values in order to make the performance of the two systems come out to be essentially the same. Then we can simply ask people to judge whether these assumptions are optimistic or pessimistic.

INTERPRETATION

After a solution has been obtained from a model, this solution must be interpreted in the light of considerations which may not have been adequately treated by the model, since the model was but a single representation of the real world chosen by the analyst. The solution of a problem which has been simplified and reduced to mathematical form by drastic idealization and aggregation of the real world factors is not necessarily a good solution of the original problem.

In the attempt to interpret the results of analysis, there are special problems associated with military questions. Many factors used in the computations are not and cannot be measured. Sometimes this is because of time limitations; other times it is because factors such as the enemy defense strength, or degradation in combat of complicated man-machine combinations, are not accessible to measurement but have to be assessed on the basis of experience or pooled judgment. The results of computations must be examined to see if they depend critically upon estimations such as these.

It is important for the man who is to use analysis to distinguish between what the analysis shows and the recommendations for action the analyst makes on the basis of what he thinks the study implies. Frequently, when new minds—management, for example—review the problem, they bring new information. Even though the solution obtained from the model is not changed, recommendations for action based on it may be.

Practices such as that suggested by the following statement can lead to serious error: "If several alternatives have similar cost and effectiveness, and these results are quite sensitive to the values assigned to the input, some other basis for decision must be found." This may amount to saying that if, after honest analysis, it must be concluded that we are fundamentally uncertain which of several alternatives is best, the issue should then be resolved on the basis of some specious side criterion not originally judged adequate to discriminate. On the contrary, the point to stress, if such results are found, is that the decisions must be made on the basis of forthright recognition of the fundamental uncertainty. The implication is that in this case unique optimization results are not to be trusted, and therefore they should not be trusted.

If, in the judgment of the analyst and those who are to use his analysis, the alternative ranked highest is good enough, the process is over; if not, more and better alternatives must be designed or the objectives must be lowered. Analysis is sufficient to reach a policy conclusion only when the objectives are agreed upon by the policy makers. In defense policy in particular, and in many others as well, objectives are not, in fact, agreed upon. In these cases, the choice, while ostensibly between alternatives, is really between objectives or ends. Hence, nonanalytical methods must be used for a final reconciliation of views. The consequences computed from the model may provide guidance in deciding which objectives to compromise. It is not obvious how to do this, however, and judgment must again be applied.

By definition, no judgment is known to be correct. Because systems analysis ordinarily goes beyond objective analysis, it relies heavily on considered judgment. No matter what may be the hopes of professional analysts, the judgment applied by the decision maker in the last phase of a study limits the influence of the previous analyses. At its best, analysis can embrace only a part of a broad-scope problem, it gets no foothold at all on some objective elements, and before it organizes an understanding of all objective elements it becomes too complex to handle.

*   *   *